AMERICAN HISTORY UNBOUND

AMERICAN HISTORY UNBOUND

Asians and Pacific Islanders

Gary Y. Okihiro

 UNIVERSITY OF CALIFORNIA PRESS

University of California Press, one of the most distinguished university presses in the United States, enriches lives around the world by advancing scholarship in the humanities, social sciences, and natural sciences. Its activities are supported by the UC Press Foundation and by philanthropic contributions from individuals and institutions. For more information, visit www.ucpress.edu.

University of California Press
Oakland, California

Library of Congress Cataloging-in-Publication Data

Okihiro, Gary Y., author–.
   American history unbound : Asians and Pacific Islanders / Gary Y. Okihiro.
     p. cm.
   Includes bibliographical references and index.
   ISBN 978–0-520–27435–8 (pbk, alk. paper) —
   ISBN 978–0-520–96030–5 (electronic)
    1. Asian Americans—History.   2. Pacific Islander Americans—
History. 3. United States—History I. Title.
E184.A75O378 2015
973—dc23   2014041933

Manufactured in the United States of America

24 23 22 21 20 19 18 17 16 15
10 9 8 7 6 5 4 3 2 1

In keeping with a commitment to support environmentally responsible and sustainable printing practices, UC Press has printed this book on Natures Natural, a fiber that contains 30% post-consumer waste and meets the minimum requirements of ANSI/NISO Z39.48–1992 (R 1997) (*Permanence of Paper*).

CONTENTS

ILLUSTRATIONS

ACKNOWLEDGMENTS

I was dragged kicking and screaming into writing this textbook. An editor at a commercial house invited me, on the recommendation of a colleague, to write "a more up-to-date alternative to the most commonly adopted books" for courses in Asian American history. It was January 2010, and her invitation reminded me of a Cornell colleague's advice never to write a textbook except for the money. Historians, she pointed out, receive scant scholarly notice for derivative works like textbooks, and publishers make constant and insistent demands to write and revise the work in response to readers' reactions in order to increase classroom adoptions and sales. I have yet to appreciate fully my colleague's sage warning.

I submitted a book proposal in March 2010, and by the following month the editor had secured five anonymous reviews of the proposal. The speed was amazing, familiar as I was with academic presses that customarily moved at a snail's pace. There was strong agreement on the need for an up-to-date book despite a "lingering fondness" for the standard texts by Ronald Takaki and Sucheng Chan, she reported, and in May 2010, I received a book contract. By July 2011, I had completed ten chapters, about three-fourths of the manuscript, when the editor relayed to me the "shocking news" about the sale of her company and cancellation of all history book contracts, including mine.

Bereft of a publishing home, I wrote Niels Hooper, my editor at the University of California Press. Niels had already published two parts of my trilogy on space/time, *Island World* (2008) and *Pineapple Culture* (2009), and he encouraged me to submit the textbook to UC Press. The timing was perfect, he reassured me. I am truly grateful to Niels and UC Press for providing a welcoming and congenial home for this work.

I am also extremely grateful to the anonymous reviewers from the commercial publisher and UC Press who encouraged me and provided helpful criticisms and suggestions. I am proud to acknowledge my former student, Moon-Ho Jung, who provided his usual meticulous, well-considered reading of one of the many iterations of my ponderous manuscript. For a similar act of collegial generosity, I also stand in awe of the faculty reviewer on the advisory board of UC Press who provided thoughtful advice that could only have come from a careful reading of some seven hundred manuscript pages.

Generations of students have played central roles in the writing of this textbook. When first I taught U.S. history, primarily white students challenged my presumption to teach their nation's history; their racism enraged me but kept me on my toes. Now, nearly forty years later, I offer no apologies for having written *American History Unbound*. Asian and Pacific Islander students have provided me with other challenges. Most insisted on their inclusion in my accounts as Chamorros, Chinese, Filipinos, Hawaiians, Japanese, Koreans, South Asians, Vietnamese, and so forth. A few declared interest only in their groups of birth and blood: they had, they said, no affiliations with other Asians or Pacific Islanders, much less other peoples of color in the United States or the third world. All of those students have influenced the writing of this historical narrative, and I gratefully acknowledge my debt to them.

I hold in great admiration the work of my colleagues Ronald Takaki and Sucheng Chan, both renowned scholars who have been hugely influential in the field of Asian American studies and U.S. history more broadly. Their textbooks, published in 1989 and 1991, not only legitimated the emerging field of Asian American studies and helped to define it but also are foundational to the claim that Asians have histories in the United States and are indispensable subjects of the nation-state.

Numerous archivists and colleagues have helped me secure images and obtain rights to reproduce the illustrations in this textbook. Deserving of special mention are Jenn Delgado and Terrie Albano, People's World; Layce Johnson, Idaho State Historical Society; Marcia Kemble and Brian Niiya, Japanese Cultural Center of Hawai'i; Kenneth Klein, Korean American Digital Archive, University of Southern California Libraries; Sang-Hyop Lee and Michael E. Macmillan, Center for Korean Studies, University of Hawai'i at Mānoa; Karen Leonard, University of California, Irvine; Samip Mallick, South Asian American Digital Archive; Jessica Miller, Archives of Michigan; Catherine Powell, Labor Archives and Research Center, San Francisco State University; Barbra Ramos, UCLA Asian American Studies Center; Melissa Shimonishi, Hawai'i State Archives; Vanessa Tait and Adnan Malik, Doe Library, University of California, Berkeley; Woody Vaspra, World Council of Elders; Priscilla Wegars, Asian American Comparative Collection, University of Idaho; Tami Winston, Photo Resource of Hawai'i; and Nicola Woods, Royal Ontario Museum, Toronto, Canada. I am grateful for their efficient attention and, above all, their kind courtesy.

Carolyn Bond, my developmental editor, has been my steadfast companion on the excruciatingly long journey from draft to book. We did not always agree, but her keen eye and candid appraisal have sharpened my thinking and clarified my writing. I owe her a great debt of gratitude for foregrounding the concept of *ocean worlds,* which is now the basis of a key chapter in this work. Erika Bűky has been more than a copyeditor; she has saved me from numerous errors of fact and instances of careless writing.

On a personal note, for as long as we have known each other, my wife, Marina A. Henríquez, has been my partner and comrade in my life's work, and that solidarity has strengthened my purpose and resolve.

Like all survey texts, this history relies on the work of scores of scholars, activists, and collectors who left behind writings, oral histories, photographs, tapestries, stones, and documents of all sorts. Secondary studies of virtually all aspects of the lives of Asians and Pacific Islanders, despite gaps, have filled rows upon rows of sagging bookshelves. Taken together, those guides enable us to apprehend our condition and decipher the thoughts and deeds of our forebears. We should remember their gifts with gratitude, and, when possible, commemorate their names. We find ourselves in those articles of our constitution as individuals and as members of collective communities. Such histories liberate and shake foundations from generation to generation.

INTRODUCTION

American History Unbound is a work of history and anti-history, a representation and a counter-representation. While history purports to be the past, history as written is the historian's depiction of that past—a representation. While scripting this history of the peoples called Asians and Pacific Islanders in the United States, I write with and against existing historical representations. That body of writing is referred to as historiography, or history as written.

HISTORIOGRAPHY

The principal historiographical context for this textbook is the vast literature called American history, which essentially chronicles the formation of the white nation. I critique the narratives that make up that literature as negligent in their discounting of nonwhite peoples of the United States and skewed in their depiction of the nation's past. Inclusion of nonwhites presents a vastly different perspective on the white nation.

A second body of writings that informs this history is the national histories of racialized minorities or peoples of color. In this context, I use *national* to refer to the practice of separating and distinguishing peoples of color in the United States, sometimes known as cultural nationalism. This historiography distinguishes one group from others, and many works in this genre acknowledge few connections among the pasts of African Americans, Asian Americans, Latinos, and Native Americans (a term I use as encompassing both American Indians and Pacific Islanders). In fact, many of these works see a group's history as unique and resistant to comparative treatment. I appreciate the differences, but I also stress the aspects that unite peoples of color.

A third historiography or context within which I write, and from which this work emerges, is the standard histories of Asians and Pacific Islanders. These by and large stress the United States in isolation from Asia and foreground Chinese and Japanese while neglecting Koreans, Filipinos and other Southeast Asians, South Asians, and West Asians. They also separate Hawai'i from the U.S. mainland, often on the mistaken assumption that race relations in the islands differed significantly from those on the continent. As a consequence, Asian American histories often ignore Pacific Islanders. In addition, some Pacific Islanders, as Native Americans, claim greater solidarity with American Indians because of similarities arising from indigenous worldviews and movements for political sovereignty. In this history, I consider Asians and Pacific Islanders together.

WHITE NATION

I claim the title *American History* as a critique of the convention and conceit, common in the United States, that misappropriate the continent and its original peoples. This book, *American History Unbound,* is a history of the United States, its lands and peoples, and not a history of America, that is, the continent and the peoples called *American.* Named after a human trafficker, Amerigo Vespucci, the continent was arbitrarily divided between north and south. Viewed from space, the continent has no such line or border. America extends undivided from its northern reaches in what we now know as Alaska and Canada to its southern fringes in Chile and Argentina, and Americans are the continent's indigenous peoples.

The United States consists of land, over which the state exercises sovereignty, and people, its citizens. The land, including the American continent and Pacific and Caribbean islands, was acquired through conquest and purchase. Peoples native to and settled in those territories thereby became Americans, though not completely. American Indians and Mexicans, treated as spoils of conquest, were not given the full rights of citizenship. Puerto Ricans and Filipinos, considered natives of "unincorporated" territories, followed divergent paths: Puerto Ricans became U.S. citizens in 1917, while Filipinos lost their status as U.S. "nationals" and became Asian "aliens" in 1934. Hawaiians and Alaska's indigenous peoples, natives of "incorporated" territories, became U.S. citizens. Contrarily, the people of the "unincorporated" territory of Guam, where "America's day begins," are U.S. citizens, while the people in American Samoa, also an "unincorporated" territory, are "nationals."

The rest of the republic's peoples, including those at its center—whites—and at its margins—Africans and Asians—are migrants to the land. The British and Europeans, through the artifices of whiteness and birth, installed themselves as the nation's people, its citizens. Their efforts to keep the U.S. nation-state white and to maintain white supremacy as globally triumphant constituted the color line and the systems of oppression against which peoples of color have struggled to achieve self-determination.

I deploy the title *American History* in another way also: as a commentary on U.S. histories that claim that title. Like all national histories, these texts aspire to shape a national consciousness among a nation's citizenry. Designers of nations believe that its constituent peoples are a "race" that shares a common ancestry, past, and culture, and that elements foreign to that citizen race create disunity and conflict. In that light, John Jay, a founding father and a leading architect of the U.S. nation-state, declared in an essay titled "Concerning the Dangers from Foreign Force and Influence" that Americans were one people with common ancestors, language, religion, and culture.

Jay's "one people" were Europeans who called themselves "free persons" and "whites" in the constitution of the nation. Those not included in that category, with all its attributes of race, class, sex, gender, and nation, represented Jay's "foreign dangers." These assumptions are replicated in standard narratives of American history, revealing the ideology and politics at work in those discourses. Only around the mid-twentieth century did U.S. history textbooks begin to reflect the nation's breadth, highlighting especially the presence of African Americans. Yet the architecture of U.S. history remains white at its core. American Indians constitute the environment for initial white settlement and expansion, and then they vanish; African Americans, Asians, and Latinos appear as minor notes in a multicultural anthem. The absence of peoples of color in the normative narratives of the white nation is treated as merely an oversight and aberration, and now their inclusion affirms that chronicle's claims to progress and democracy.

This book offers a counter to that national history. It contends that since the English invasion and colonization of America, peoples of color, instead of participating in a multicultural nation, have been systematically excluded from the privileges and protections of the "citizen race." In his majority opinion in the *Dred Scott v. Sandford* case of 1857, the U.S. Supreme Court Chief Justice Roger Taney found peoples of color to be "another and different class of persons." The phrase "We, the people" in the U.S. Constitution was never intended to embrace peoples of color: that is the premise on which the white nation was conceived. Insofar as whites named and treated nonwhites as an undifferentiated group, this history of Asians and Pacific Islanders shares a common ground with all persons of color.

To the invaders, American Indians were impediments to the freedoms of whites, a view especially inscribed in whites' acquisitive belief that they had the right to occupy land without regard for those already living there. English foreigners became natives on their sovereign estates through conquest and expulsion, and American Indians became aliens. The process began when the first English settlers claimed the land on which they settled as their private property. In 1763 the British Parliament drew an artificial line roughly along the Allegheny Mountains, establishing lands to the east as British territory. Despite the border's porous nature, that segregation between "citizens" and "aliens" demarcated the nation and its people.

After the War of Independence, the new nation acknowledged that convention with the Treaty of Greenville in 1795, which recognized Indian sovereignty in territories not claimed by whites. In 1832, the U.S. Supreme Court, in *Worcester v. Georgia*, held that the Cherokee nation constituted a "foreign state." This status was affirmed three decades later by Chief Justice Taney in the *Dred Scott* case, in which he wrote that the U.S. signed treaties with American Indian nations "under subjection to the white race"; accordingly, in the United States, whites constituted the "citizen race," and American Indians were classified as "aliens."

That alienation shifted with the white flood, which by the late nineteenth century engulfed the entire continent from sea to shining sea. The 1890 U.S. Census, taken in the year of the Wounded Knee massacre, following the final bloody wars of conquest waged mainly against Indians of the Great Plains, announced that the entire continent had been filled (by whites). Manly conquest of "virgin land" was what President Theodore Roosevelt narrated as U.S. history: "Of course our whole national history has been one of expansion. . . . That the barbarians recede or are conquered, with the attendant fact that peace follows their retrogression or conquest, is due solely to the power of the mighty civilized races which have not lost the fighting instinct, and which by their expansion are gradually bringing peace into the red wastes where the barbarian peoples of the world hold sway."[1]

Once conquest was achieved, American Indians were absorbed into the nation. Although the United States signed treaties with American Indian peoples, the Supreme Court ruled, in a series of decisions known as the Marshall trilogy (of 1823, 1831, and 1832), that American Indians constituted "domestic dependent nations" and "wards" of the federal government: they were not independent, sovereign nations because they were "incapable in law." The Dawes Act (1887) sought to dissolve Indian nations and assimilate American Indians as individuals, and in *Lone Wolf v. Hitchcock* (1903), the U.S. Supreme Court affirmed the plenary powers of Congress over its wards. In 1924 Congress bestowed U.S. citizenship on American Indians born after that year, and in 1940 it made all American Indians U.S. citizens. The attempt to assimilate American Indians as political and cultural subjects continued (following a brief pause during the New Deal) when Dillon Myer, as chief of the Bureau of Indian Affairs, pursued the policy appropriately called *termination* during the 1950s. Under termination, the federal government treated American Indians as individuals and citizens, and not as members of sovereign Indian nations. (Myer had experience with the displacement and erasure of people of color, having administered the concentration camps for Japanese as the director of the War Relocation Authority during World War II.) Thus, over the centuries, American Indians were at first excluded as "foreign" nations and peoples and later assimilated and rendered domestic dependents, wards, and colonized subjects of the imperial republic.

Like American Indians, Africans were considered "aliens" during the colonial period and, as such, were denied full community membership. In 1669, a Virginia Colony jury determined that Anthony Johnson was "a Negroe and by consequence an alien," and therefore his son could not inherit his land. Race determined citizenship. The U.S. Constitution of 1787 specified that Africans were not "free Persons" but "three fifths of all other Persons" and therefore did not merit full representation in Congress. Chief Justice Taney confirmed this view in the *Dred Scott* case: "Negroes of the African race" and their descendants "are not included, and were not intended to be included, under the word 'citizens' in the Constitution," he wrote, "and can therefore claim none of the rights and privileges which that instrument provides for and secures to citizens of the United States." Moreover, he pointed out, the 1790 Naturalization Act, whose purpose was to define the nation's people, limited citizenship to "free white persons," making clear the separation between the "citizen race," or whites, and "persons of color." The latter category included Africans.

That distinction changed with three pivotal amendments to the U.S. Constitution: the Thirteenth Amendment (1865), which ended slavery; the Fourteenth Amendment (1868), which granted citizenship to those born in the United States and promised "to any person within its jurisdiction the equal protection of the laws"; and the Fifteenth Amendment (1870), which extended the vote to men regardless of "race, color, or previous condition of servitude." In 1870, Congress extended naturalization to African Americans. The African American citizen, although without equal rights, modified the complexion of the "citizen race" and thus of the nation. The change marked a radical break with the past: it was, in fact, revolutionary.

Still, as in the colonial era, African Americans were kept in a position of political and economic dependency through racial segregation. In *Plessy v. Ferguson* (1896), the Supreme Court held that racial segregation in private businesses did not violate the Fourteenth Amendment's equal-protection clause. Separate was equal. That interpretation was overturned in the Supreme Court's *Brown v. Board of Education* decision in 1954, but the court's principle of equal application persists today in bans against same-sex marriage. Nevertheless, states routinely denied African Americans access to the ballot through property and literacy requirements from the end of Reconstruction until the Voting Rights Act of 1965, and racism persists in housing, employment, education, the justice and penal system, and interpersonal relations.

Mexican Americans were a people made through conquest, akin to American Indians. In 1845, after an Anglo revolt, the imperial republic admitted Texas, which was Mexican territory, into the union. The United States secured that annexation following war with Mexico and the Treaty of Guadalupe Hidalgo (1848). The treaty granted U.S. citizenship to Mexican residents of the ceded lands, including California and New Mexico and territory north of the Rio Grande River. Mexicans were thus rendered white by treaty. Yet many Mexicans, like Indians, lost their farmlands and were widely denied equality in employment, housing, and education on the bases of race, class, and culture.

The contradiction between Mexicans as white, as defined by treaty, and Mexicans as a "mongrel" race, as defined by popular opinion, was widely mirrored in judicial decisions. Courts decided, in accordance with the one-drop rule as applied to African

Americans, that children of unions between whites and nonwhites were "colored"—as in the cases *In re Camille* (1880), involving a white father and an American Indian mother, and *In re Young* (1912), involving a white father and a Japanese mother. Still, courts were compelled to conclude, as in the case *In re Rodriguez* (1897), that Mexicans were white and thus citizens. At the same time, being considered white in theory disallowed Mexicans' claims of racial discrimination in practice, such as all-Anglo juries deciding the fate of Mexicans because such juries legally constituted trial by their peers.

The state segregated Mexican children in inferior schools on the basis of language and "migrant farming patterns," a practice affirmed by a Texas court in *Independent School District v. Salvatierra* (1930). Also in 1930, the category *Mexicans* was distinguished from the white race in the U.S. Census. This creation of a separate racialized category facilitated the expulsion of about half a million Mexicans and Mexican Americans from the United States during the Great Depression, when their labor was no longer required. That expulsion complemented the 1935 Filipino Repatriation Act, by which the state provided free transportation back to the Philippines for Filipinos. These removals underscored the status of both Mexicans and Filipinos as migrant laborers.

NATIONAL HISTORIES

Paralleling white national histories of the United States are national histories of peoples of color: African Americans, American Indians, Asian Americans, Latinos, and Pacific Islanders. In their drive for self-determination, peoples of color both in the United States and in the third world turned to strategies of national liberation. After World War II, the decolonization movements in Africa and Asia strove for the creation of independent nation-states. Within the United States, peoples of color saw their condition as that of colonized subjects and similarly sought self-determination.

Although effective, these strategies were also divisive. Anticolonial struggles created new nations in Africa and Asia, and in the United States they created distinct identities for African Americans, American Indians, Asian Americans, Latinos, and Pacific Islanders—each with their own history and culture, each paramount, unique, and paradigmatic. The establishment of the academic fields of African American and Native American studies illustrates the point.

Derivative of U.S. national history and the white/black racial binary is the notion of African American exceptionalism, the view that African Americans hold a unique place in the nation's history. Proponents point to the numbers of African Americans, the length and intensity of the relations between whites and blacks, the importance of slavery and the conflict over slavery, and the African American freedom struggles. In fact, some maintain that the histories of nonblack peoples of color are distant, at times unrelated, variations on the theme of African American history. Such views often subscribe to a hierarchy of color and of degrees of oppression.

Some scholars in Native American studies stress the unique position of indigenous peoples in relation to the settlers of the colonial nation-state. In contrast to its treatment of other peoples of color, they note, the United States signed treaties with Native Americans, the U.S. Supreme Court confirmed that American Indians constituted foreign peoples and, on incorporation, "domestic dependent nations." Although considered U.S. citizens since 1924, American Indians still retain tribal memberships and loyalties. Self-determination and sovereignty, accordingly, are key aspects of the anticolonial struggles of indigenous peoples, and these qualities contrast with the drive for civil rights within the U.S. nation-state that characterizes the histories of African Americans, Asian Americans, and Latinos.

This book writes against these nationalist interpretations of U.S. history. While not denying the signal importance of African Americans to the nation's past, the unique situation of American Indians as "domestic dependent nations," or the different histories and experiences of all nonwhites, I stress the connections among peoples of color in the United States and the world. Not only African Americans and American Indians but also Pacific Islanders and Asians were excluded by the 1790 Naturalization Act and its restriction of citizenship to "free white persons." California's Supreme Court Chief Judge Hugh Murray affirmed in *People v. Hall* (1854) that there was an unbridgeable gulf between "a free white citizen of this State" and American Indians, Africans, Pacific Islanders, and Asians—those "not of white blood." However, unlike American Indians and Pacific Islanders, whose utility to the state lay mainly in their land, Asians, like African Americans and Latinos, were deemed useful primarily as laborers.

The essentialized classification *nonwhite* led to instances of assimilation among peoples of color, through alliances, marriage, and community membership. Pacific Islander and Asian men served as slaves and servants to whites; appealed to whites and antislavery societies for manumission; married American Indian, African, and Mexican American women; were counted in the U.S. census as colored and mulatto; fought in African American units in the Civil War; and were buried in colored cemeteries. They served employers as migrant laborers, mainly in agriculture but also in the mines and on railroads; formed unions irrespective of race; and married and produced bicultural children.

Unlike other U.S. peoples of color, Asians and Pacific Islanders continued to be seen as "aliens ineligible to citizenship" until the twentieth century. Through treaty provisions and legal cases, Mexicans, African Americans, American Indians, and Puerto Ricans acquired U.S. citizenship, albeit absent its full rights and properties. Hawaiians became U.S. citizens through the Organic Act (1900), which formalized Hawai'i's annexation to the union. Although the Fourteenth Amendment allowed Asians to gain U.S. citizenship by birth, even that right was contested, as when the state denied California-born Wong Kim Ark his rights as a U.S. citizen in 1894. When Wong Kim Ark returned to California after visiting China, immigration officials denied him entry on the basis of the Chinese Exclusion Act of 1882. He contested that denial, and in 1898 the U.S. Supreme Court ruled in his favor. Only in the mid-twentieth century did the United States grant naturalization rights to Asians: they were extended to Chinese in 1943 and to South Asians and Filipinos in 1946. Japanese and Koreans had to wait until 1952.

Like the postbellum extension of citizenship to African Americans and American Indians, granting Asians naturalization rights and citizenship was revolutionary. It represented a break with the founding social contract of the United States, which had limited membership to "free white persons," and thereby transformed the nation.

ASIANS AND PACIFIC ISLANDERS

The term *Asian American* was invented in the late 1960s, for the purposes of political solidarity and mobilization. Asians living in America determined that a shared history of Orientalism and oppression united them and that by organizing as a group named by Europeans, they could counter white supremacy more effectively. Following the Italian Marxist Antonio Gramsci, the literary critic Gayatri Spivak has named that argument *strategic essentialism*, or a temporary strategy pursued in a war of positions. Readers should think of categories such as *Asian Americans* and *Pacific Islanders* as temporary contrivances in the struggle against oppression—as contextual, relational, and impermanent.

Asian American is an elastic term. When first used, it referred principally, if not exclusively, to Chinese and Japanese. Some of the founding figures in the emerging field of Asian American studies insisted that it applied only to those born in the United States and not to the migrant generation born in Asia. Gradually, through the initiatives of the neglected ethnicities, it grew to embrace Koreans, Filipinos, and other Southeast Asians, along with South Asians and, most recently, West Asians, such as those from Iran, Iraq, Saudi Arabia, and Turkey.

Despite that immense diversity and geographic spread, Asian American studies still tilts toward the Chinese and Japanese. Although this textbook rejects that bias, it draws on a secondary literature that is weighted more heavily toward East Asians, to the neglect of Southeast, South, and especially West Asians. Likewise, among Pacific Islanders, by which I mean the indigenous peoples of Hawai'i and of the U.S. territories of Samoa, and Guam, the histories of Hawaiians and Hawai'i are foregrounded. Those deficits I acknowledge as a consequence of my ignorance and the state of the field.

I recognize Chamorros, Hawaiians, and Samoans as indigenous peoples—as Native Americans. I also see them as once-sovereign peoples, like American Indians; as colonized subjects, like American Indians, Latinos, and Filipinos and other Asians; and as migrant laborers and dependent peoples, like all peoples of color. Unlike some Pacific Islander scholars, I include Pacific Islanders in this history in solidarity with those who link their past and present with Oceania and its unimpeded flows and continuities with the Indian Ocean and Asia.

The standard narrative of Asian American history begins with Asians, mainly Chinese, immigrating to California to escape poverty and political repression and in search of new opportunities, not unlike Europeans in the transatlantic circuit of uprooting and transplantation. Writing against this version of Asian American history, I maintain that Asians did not go to America; Americans went to Asia. I thus situate this telling within the expansion of European imperialism. The presence of Asians in America and Pacific Islanders within the U.S. orbit is a consequence of that expansion. Further, Pacific Islanders and Asians did not migrate for the same reasons as many Europeans, who were pushed by necessity and pulled by opportunities. Rather, Europe and the United States recruited Pacific Islanders and Asians as migrant laborers in the global traffic of goods and labor. Pacific Islanders, additionally, lost their lands, waters, and sovereignty to the imperial order.

Thus I propose that migrant labor forms the first phase of Asian American history, and dependency, as I will explain, the second phase. Because both migrant labor and dependency were means by which to exploit and oppress Asians, I see them as parts of the anti-Asian movement. This formulation differs from the established views. Moreover, I contend that Pacific Islander and Asian migrant labor follows a long tradition of relations between whites and nonwhites in U.S. history, principally the relations in which Native American lands supplied the abundance that supported white freedoms, and African Americans, Asian Americans, and Latinos provided the labor that helped to build and sustain the white nation.

The standard narrative of Asian American history also says that the Chinese, and the anti-Chinese movement, set the pattern for all other Asian migrant groups. According to the historian Ronald Takaki, "As the first Asian group to enter America, the Chinese merit our close attention. What happened to them in the nineteenth century represented the beginning of a pattern for the ways Asians would be viewed and treated here."[2] In fact, the Chinese were not the first Asians to arrive in America, and, each Asian group faced different historical conditions and acted in distinctive ways.

In addition, despite criticisms and modifications of the "California thesis," as it was advanced by the sociologist Mary Roberts Coolidge in her foundational *Chinese Immigration* (1909), her account of the anti-Chinese movement remains the standard interpretation. Broadly, Coolidge argues that the responses of whites to Chinese migrants arose from the particular conditions of nineteenth-century California. By contrast, this book depicts the anti-Chinese and anti-Asian movements as aspects of national and global patterns of migrant labor and dependency.

Standard versions of Asian American history exemplify a focus on California that represents places east of that golden state as derivative, sometimes inauthentic locations of Asian America. I write against that convention. Asians and Pacific Islanders visited and resided in Mexico and its northern territories, the South and Northwest, and the East Coast long before the mid-nineteenth-century migration of Chinese to California.

Another form of exceptionalism in Asian American history is the view that Hawai'i inverts the rule of majority-minority relations: in the islands, Asians constitute a majority and whites a minority, and because of demography and the "aloha spirit" of Hawaiian culture, there is no "race problem." I write against this view also. Colonized Hawai'i, because of the oligarchy and plantation economy, in many ways anticipated events in the continental United States in articulating racism and enacting land alienation and labor exploitation. Moreover, and importantly, the inclusion of Chamorros, Hawaiians, and Samoans in this history speaks to ideas of indigeneity and sovereignty—matters largely unaddressed by Asian American history but of signal importance to Native Americans, who are allied peoples of color.

THEORY

Theory is central to this version of American history: theory helps to explain and assign significance to past human experience, which I understand as both discourse and material condition. By *discourse* I mean conversations among scholars enabled by a shared ideology and language. As a network of interests, a discourse exemplifies the power to know, define, and assign meaning. Race, gender, sexuality, class, and nation, for example, constitute discourses: they arise from the power to name, classify, and rank peoples in binaries and hierarchies of white and nonwhite, men and women, heterosexual and homosexual, owners and workers, citizens and aliens. To engage in those discourses requires entry into their language and ideology, together with an understanding of their assumptions and rules.

By *material condition* I mean the world of substance, starting with life forms, their physical environments, and their properties and states. To my mind, material conditions for humans are the means and relations of production. That is, humans meet their perceived needs by exerting labor, physical and intellectual, on the land and natural resources around them. They thereby produce food and shelter; clothe themselves; and conceive of art, religion, and culture, and explanations for their existence and social relations. Discourses accompany and advance material conditions. What follows is a brief discussion of the theories that inform this textbook's explanation of society and history.

SOCIETY

My understanding of the human condition is based on a concept I call *social formation*, which holds that society and its changes over time are produced by the locations and articulations of power around the discourses and material conditions of race, gender, sexuality, class, and nation. Power is thus the central feature and subject of the social formation.

Discourses of vertical relations, or hierarchies, arise from and inhabit the economy, the polity, and the society. Those discourses and material conditions are mutually constituted and constituting: they are relational. Poverty produces privilege, political power is realized in the absence of power, and the other defines the self. While discourses and material conditions can operate singly, for instance, as race or as nation, they can also intersect to form gendered races, sexualized genders, and so forth. Likewise, the economy can produce the citizen worker, and the polity can create the racialized alien.

The theory of social formation helps to explain structures and functions of human design, both discourses and material relations, such as *imperialism, world-system, migrant labor,* and *dependency,* which are key concepts in this book. These constitute discourses and material conditions designed by those who possess the power to establish and populate them. And operating within them all are the categories and hierarchies of race, gender, sexuality, class, and nation—the social formation.

Imperialism describes a phase of capitalism and the expansion of nations, as extensions of the idea of sovereignty, outside their territorial boundaries. It produces empires and colonies. There is disagreement over the exact phase of capitalism during which imperialism occurs. Some hold that it takes place only during the stage of monopoly capitalism, which is generally seen as the coming together of industrial and financial (banking) capitalism to form monopolies. Others believe that imperialism is a product of industrial capitalism, driven by a search for resources and new markets. Still others use the term *imperialism* to describe capitalism's expansion during the period of mercantile (trade) capitalism, which preceded industrial capitalism. As I use it in this text, *imperialism* refers to capitalism's expansion more broadly, beginning in the fifteenth century with Europe's search for Asia.

World-systems theory purports to explain the career of capitalism and its appropriation of land and labor from the fifteenth century onward. Although the term is usually rendered as plural because of the variables of place and time, systems are singular in that each consists of a core, a periphery, and the relations between the two. The core (sometimes also referred to as the *metropole*) is a place of high capital concentration, while the periphery is one of low capital concentration. Capital flows from the periphery to the core, resulting in the core's development and the periphery's underdevelopment. Conquest and colonization structure those processes, relations, and movements, making them systematic and dynamic. From the fifteenth through the nineteenth century, Europe was the core of the world-system, and Africa, America, and Asia were its peripheries. However, resistance to incorporation and anticolonial struggles have challenged and altered that world-system.

Migrant labor is a product of the world-system. Places of underdevelopment supply pools of cheap labor, which colonizers transport to plantations and factories wherever it is needed. From the fifteenth century onward, enslaved American Indian and African workers and indentured Asian laborers in the periphery cultivated the sugar, cotton, tobacco, and tropical fruits that enriched the core. The laborers were selected by race, ethnicity, gender, and age to maximize efficiency and minimize cost. For most manual labor, young men were preferred over children and the aged; and for sailing, whaling, mining, construction, and agricultural tasks, men were preferred over women. Conversely, women and children provided cheap labor for plantations, and women were recruited for and labored in industries like canneries and garment factories and to produce the next generation of workers. Those preferences of migrant labor governed the migration of Asians. The expulsion of migrants through "repatriation" drives signaled the end of their utility to their employers.

Dependency is a condition of economic, political, and social subservience, at first produced through segregation and later by assimilation. The social formation of race, gender, sexuality, class, and nation justifies hierarchies of work grades and wages; eligibility for citizenship and the vote; and segregation, followed by cultural assimilation or Anglo-conformity. Separation ensures the purity and vigor of the superior stock and culture, as the discourse of race claims, and white supremacy is justified by the gradual uplift and eventual absorption of subordinate peoples. Even if segregation is not enforced by law, other instruments, such as schools, churches, and prisons, along with ideologies and traditions, can perpetuate dependency through a process of coercion called *hegemony*. Under hegemony, as Antonio Gramsci describes, dependent subjects consent to their subordination and reliance on the ruling class.

Humans, however, possess *agency*, or the power to move, and movement is history and a matter of perspective. I agree with the French philosopher Michel Foucault that power can circulate throughout the social formation. At the same time, power is located in the discourses and material conditions created by the ruling order. That exercise of power I call *oppression*, which is expressed in multiple and complex ways in the social formation. The rulers, however, are not omnipotent. In fact, I believe, like the U.S. historian Herbert Aptheker, that oppression inspires *resistance*. Subjects possess agency, as demonstrated by their resistance. The struggle between oppression and resistance is the movement that animates and makes history.

HISTORY

While historians routinely deny the theoretical and political attributes of their narrations of the past, I readily admit that theory and politics inform this version of history. Throughout this book, I represent history as the expressions of ordinary people, frequently considered to be "without history" because of their alleged insignificance and lack of merit and worth. Insofar as the masses are not historical figures in the usual sense, writing them into history is a work of anti-history. As if to underscore their historical erasure, common people left few records in the nation's archives, which prominently chronicle the words and deeds of great men and their instruments and expressions of power. As a part of the new social history that gave voice to those judged marginal to U.S. history—nonwhites, women, queers, workers, and immigrants—the inclusion of Asian and Pacific Islander pasts democratizes national histories of the elites.

Pertinent here is a distinction between *identity* and *subjectivity*. I understand identity as a notion of self that is largely a matter of biology. Developmental psychologists frequently see identity as evolving in stages from infancy to adolescence to adulthood, following biological patterns of growth. By contrast, subjectivity is an understanding of the self as a representation and, for some, a discourse and performance. The subject is a creation of language and ideology and of those depictions and enactments of the self. While identities appear fixed depending on life cycles, subjectivities are in process, being made and changing. One's subject position, accordingly, is situational and contingent.

Where possible, I have included the perspectives of Asians and Pacific Islanders in their own words, which often take the form of published and edited oral documents or conversations. Inevitably, these texts bear the imprint of the tellers and historians who solicited, edited, and narrated them. Thus, as the historian Joan Scott has pointed out, experience, like other forms of historical evidence, must be interrogated and critiqued despite the claims of that experience to be subjective and unmediated. Subject positions, we know, are historical creations and are hence rooted in and variable over time and place. These must be figured into the calculus.

While respectful of time and place because of the particularities of those dimensions, this version of American history violates a strictly chronological and regional accounting. It takes a thematic and comparative approach that I call *historical formation*. I thus examine subject matters comparatively to ascertain continuities and ruptures, and I understand geographical distinctions like oceans and lands, continents and islands as places of crossings as well as separations.

TAXONOMIES

There were no "Asian" or "Pacific Islander" peoples before they were so named by others. They, along with most humans, called themselves by their own designations, according to family and kinship groupings, place and village names, and larger-scale affiliations such as nations and empires. The power to ignore those self-representations and to impose new names onto other peoples was largely a prerogative and project of Europeans. In this undertaking, imperialism enabled Europeans to impose their mappings as globally accepted conventions. Their taxonomies frequently assign many different peoples and cultures to single, undifferentiated groups, a process called *essentializing*, and they remain fictions only made real by humans.

There are at least two key ideas in the essentialization of peoples into groupings called *races*. The first is the notion of *geographical determinism* proposed by the ancient Greeks, which held that the properties of plants, animals, and peoples were determined by the geographies or environments in which they lived. Accordingly, by dividing the Earth into continents—Europe, Asia, and Africa, each with its own distinctive environments and life forms—the ancient Greeks categorized peoples into Europeans, Asians, and Africans.

The second, related idea is the notion of *biological determinism*, which again originated with the ancient Greeks. This concept derives from the idea that physical, mental, and even behavioral traits, or natures, are passed from parent to child in the blood, that is, by inheritance. Peoples of superior intelligence and physical conformation, the ancient

Greeks held, reproduced superior offspring. According to the early biological determinists, these traits were transmitted through bodily fluids, called the *humors*. Europeans would much later attribute the transmission of such traits to genetics. Generalizing from the individual to the group, biological determinists identified separate races with distinctive physical, mental, and behavioral characteristics.

RACIAL GEOGRAPHIES

Among the Greek philosophers, Hippocrates (ca. 460–377 B.C.), often called the father of medicine, was perhaps the most influential proponent of geographical and biological determinism. In *Airs, Waters, Places,* he asserted that the physical environment shapes the forms and characters of people. He also discussed the idea of "seed," a gesture toward the role of men in reproduction, as the mechanism that transmits physical and behavioral traits.

Hippocrates gave "Asians" and "Europeans" as examples of how climate holds sway over human bodies and natures. His taxonomies were racialized and sexualized. The hot and wet Asian climate, Hippocrates claimed, produced soft, fleshy bodies. Breathing that moist, stale air gave the skin a yellow tinge like that of jaundice. The mild and uniform seasons made for mellow natures and a disinclination for hard work: thus Asians were lazy, gentle, and easily led. They were a race of women—weak, pleasure seeking, and group oriented. By contrast, the harsh and dry European climate shaped hard, lean bodies, and its sharp seasonal changes induced variety and diversity, energy, and an independent spirit. Europeans were a race of men—strong, mentally acute, and individualistic.

Aristotle (384–322 B.C.), in his *Politics,* refined the idea of Europeans while distinguishing Greeks from Asians, whom he considered slaves by nature. The Greek race, Aristotle held, differed from its northern European neighbors, who were full of spirit but wanting in intelligence, and from Asians, who were intelligent but cowardly. The Greeks, situated between those extremes, were both high-spirited and intelligent and were thus fit to rule the world.

Even though we now recognize geographical determinism as false, the idea is still highly influential. Natural history museums, for instance, commonly organize their presentations of the world and its life forms on the basis of geography. Accordingly, we might visit the "Africa Hall," with its displays of flora, fauna, and peoples presented as typifying the continent, along with adjoining halls representing Asia, Europe, and America. Those distinctions support the false proposition that peoples, plants, and animals form discrete categories. In fact, their borders blur, and they move frequently and in large numbers across those geographic demarcations, which themselves are human inventions.

RACIAL BIOLOGIES

In addition to ascribing human traits to geographical determinism, Hippocrates suggested that they could be transmitted to subsequent generations through the "seed." In the fourth century B.C., Plato suggested that the best men should mate with the best women to produce ideal citizens for his republic. Biological determinism would supplement and ultimately replace the notion of geographical determinism in natural history, although both ideas persist in the popular imagination.

Following centuries of thinking dominated by the Catholic Church, a new philosophy arose in the eighteenth century, the period called the Enlightenment or the Age of Reason, according to which reason, not faith, was believed to be the sole reliable authority for explaining the human condition. Like the ancient Greeks, intellectuals of the Enlightenment were imperialists in their assumed mastery over nature, along with their assertion of the power to name and classify natural phenomena and to describe and predict outcomes.

The science of taxonomy flourished in this period, beginning with the work of the Swedish naturalist Carl Linnaeus (1707–78), whose *Systema naturae* established a new method of grouping plants and animals that became the standard system of classification. In addition, Linnaeus organized humans, *Homo sapiens,* into four varieties by color, posture, and temperament. In turn, temperament arose from the four bodily humors that allegedly shaped a person's disposition. Choler, or yellow bile, made one prone to anger; blood made one cheerful; melancholy, or black bile, produced a sad person; and phlegm created a sluggish or phlegmatic person. The American or Indian, ruled by yellow bile, was red, stood upright, and was prone to anger; the European, ruled by blood, was white, muscular, and cheerful; the Asian, ruled by black bile, was yellow, stiff, and melancholic; and the African, ruled by phlegm, was black, relaxed, and phlegmatic. Those caricatures are familiar to us today as commonplace stereotypes of race.

Linnaeus's student Johann Friedrich Blumenbach (1752–1840) followed his teacher in naming four human "varieties" or races, and he cited the ancient Greeks for his claim that their characteristics were determined by climate. In his work *On the Natural Varieties of Mankind,* Blumenbach designated the Caucasian (European) and its "degenerations"—Mongolians (Asians), Ethiopians (Africans), and Americans (Indians)—on the basis of color, hair texture, stature, and skull shape. In a subsequent edition of the book, he added a fifth category, the Malay or Pacific Islanders. His resultant racial geometry placed Caucasians at the apex of a triangle, with Mongolian and Ethiopian as the two base points, and American and Malay as intermediary varieties linking the points of the triangle.

Linnaeus and Blumenbach, like the ancient Greeks, held that variations in human behavioral and physiological attributes were determined by geography. But they also believed that those traits were transmitted to subsequent generations through the blood. Some of the flaws in this reasoning were pointed out by the anthropologist Franz Boas in the early twentieth century. Human physical types, or "races," are not tied to behaviors or cultures. Thus, for instance, an Asian could learn to speak English, a European tongue, and subscribe to Enlightenment ideas of humanism and freedom.

European taxonomies produced the designations we now know as Asians and Pacific Islanders, corresponding to Blumenbach's Mongolians and Malays. It is imperative to

Caucasian

American   Malay

Mongolian   Ethiopian

FIGURE 1
Blumenbach's racial geometry. After Stephen Jay Gould, *The Mismeasure of Man* (New York: W. W. Norton, 1996), 409.

understand that those racialized, gendered, and sexualized categories, which may appear to be natural and self-evident, are European inventions and that they arose in specific historical circumstances. The power to name and classify came during a period of European expansion into America, Africa, and Asia. Those hierarchies of race—positing whites as normative and superior to degenerate, deviant nonwhites —served to justify and maintain European imperial conquests and colonization. Aristotle's assertion that Asians, by nature, could not govern themselves, whereas the Greeks were fit to rule the world illustrates the way that discourses produce and in turn are produced by material conditions.

ORIENTALISM

Like the ancient Greeks who named Asians as other, in opposition to themselves, Europeans deployed the discourse of Orientalism to assist them in naming and ruling over Asians.

The literary scholar Edward W. Said declared in his book *Orientalism* that, since antiquity, the Orient has been almost an invention of Europeans. He argued that Orientalism was a style of thought and a whole network of interests used to describe, structure, and dominate its subject. Although those representations constitute an imagined topography, they attain reality through institutions, laws, and practices, especially those determining the relationship of the colonizer and the colonized. In Said's view, Orientalists, or intellectuals engaged in the discourse of Orientalism, maintain that Orientals are incapable of representing themselves, and Europeans accordingly must represent them. As a discourse and discipline, then, Orientalism conveys the power to exert authority and mastery over ostensibly unruly places and peoples.

Said's discussion of Orientalism focuses on eighteenth- and nineteenth-century French and British schools of thought that created European subjects and Oriental objects through discourses of difference involving race, gender, and sexuality. Yet similar representations and relations arose centuries earlier with the ancient Greeks, and they emerged not only from theorizing but also from extensive and durable relations with Asia. The lands and peoples east of Greece—the Orient—remained a mix of fact and fantasy, a projection of what the self, or Europe, was not.

We find that mix of fact and fantasy in the account of Scylax of Caryanda, a Greek officer in service to the Persian king Darius. Scylax sailed the western coast of India around 515 B.C. He claimed that the land was exceedingly bountiful and rich and the people varied, with settled agriculturalists and wandering nomads in the north, black people in the south, and cannibals farther south yet. Some of the people, he wrote, had feet so large they used them as umbrellas to shield themselves. Many of the plants and animals were exotic and strange, but some were also familiar. Above all, Scylax wrote invitingly, there was gold in profusion, extracted from giant anthills in the northern deserts. About two hundred years later, Megasthenes' firsthand account, *Indika*, described gold-digging ants, people with feet turned backward, and dog-headed people whose speech was limited to barking.

Indians, Arabs, Greeks, and Romans sailed between Africa and Asia carrying goods that percolated into the Mediterranean world, especially during the Roman Empire. The best description of that commerce, the *Periplus of the Erythrean Sea* (i.e., the circuit of the Indian Ocean), written in Greek around A.D. 50, describes the trade as centering on India but also involving Chinese products. From Asia came animal furs and hides, live animals and plants, ivory, pearls, tortoiseshell, silks, spices, aromatics, and female slaves in exchange for Rome's precious metals. Some in Rome lamented that these luxury items drained the empire's treasury.

Since the era of ancient Greece and Rome, Asia has remained Europe's most implacable opponent, and wars have been a primary feature of the engagement down to the twenty-first century. The ancient Greeks fought against Persia a century and a half before Alexander's thrust into India in the fourth century B.C. Warfare continued with the seven crusades of the eleventh through the thirteenth century, which aimed to drive the "infidel" Muslims from the Holy Land. During the Fourth Crusade of 1202–4, the Venetians reduced Constantinople (Istanbul, Turkey) to rubble, thereby eliminating Venice's biggest economic rival and giving it a near monopoly on trade in the Mediterranean, religious motives notwithstanding. Trade, in fact, was perhaps the greatest contribution of the crusades, and commerce led to the rise of port cities like Venice, Florence, Genoa, Antwerp, and Amsterdam and a merchant class. Particularly attractive to European traders was the eastern Mediterranean, which was the western terminus of the commerce with India and China.

Central and West Asians blocked direct European contact with South and East Asia until the Mongols of Genghis Khan and his successors swept across Central Asia into Eastern Europe in 1240, plundering Poland and Hungary. Some two decades later, the Polo brothers, Niccolo and Matteo, from Venice apparently reached China, where they served Kublai Khan, and returned to Venice in 1269. They set out again, joined by Niccolo's son, Marco, whose account of China, *Book of the Marvels of the World* (ca. 1300), was Europe's most comprehensive travel narrative of Asia before the sixteenth century. His representations of Cathay, or China, astonished readers with their depictions of cities, canals, ports, roads, architecture, printed books, and wealth that far outstripped

European achievements. From this account Europeans for the first time learned of Cipangu, or Japan, the islands beyond China where gold and pearls could be found in great abundance.

In reality, Asia did not possess inexhaustible wealth, and Asians were not so easily vanquished as the early, disparaging categorizations of Asian peoples suggested. Asians built immense civilizations, rich and highly stratified, but they also lived in small-scale social and kin groups. Yet such was the power of Orientalism that Europeans who reached America, beginning with Christopher Columbus, projected what they had heard or read about Asia onto America and its "Indians." On landing in the Bahamas, Columbus was certain he would find people with tails on islands just beyond, and on Hispaniola he forced Indians to search and dig for gold and silver, which he was sure Asia possessed in abundance.

Orientalism derived its force from the power to create and impose discourses and material relations. European discourses, especially taxonomies, disciplined and ordered what they saw as wild and primitive subjects, justifying the subjection of peoples, the expropriation of their land, and the exploitation of their labor. In the process, Europeans advanced an imperial world-system, with its flows of capital and labor. Colonized subjects resisted those impositions in their movements for self-determination, and that agency and the changes it wrought made history.

AMERICAN HISTORY

American History Unbound emerges from but also rewrites the standard narratives of nation. Through their struggles for sovereignty and the full rights of citizenship and membership, Asians, Pacific Islanders, and indeed all peoples of color in the United States, despite their discursive and material "minority" status, have transformed, and revolutionized, the nation. In that sense, American history from the fringes of the national consciousness reveals and clarifies the nation's past and promise of equality in their fullness and entirety.

I conceive of *American History Unbound* spatially as a national and transnational work, and temporally as "deep history," or the study of origins.[3] Viewed this way, the United States materializes from the European Enlightenment and the modern world-system. The Enlightenment, drawing from the ancient Greeks, gave rise to sciences that named, classified, and attributed characteristics to lands, continents, and peoples (called varieties or races), along with the flora and fauna of each region and climate. Dominion was based on the rule of sovereignty, the idea and exercise of self-determination that eventuated into the idea of the nation and its peoples or "races." That principle of power over lands and peoples extended beyond the nation to its empires and colonies as natural, sovereign rights.

Capitalism built the modern world-system to supply its needs for resources, labor, and markets—the wealth of nations—beginning with the search for the Orient, or Asia.

MAP 1

World ocean. From this perspective, the earth has a single ocean, and all of its lands are islands.

America was an accidental outcome of that project. The United States started as New Spain and Jamestown, peripheral settlements intended to enrich investors in Spain and England. Moreover, on independence from Britain, the United States, like other European settler colonies, relinquished its position on the periphery and became a part of the core.

American exceptionalism to the contrary, *American History Unbound* situates the United States as a nation among nations, as a continental core and an island periphery, and as a social formation in process, both within its borders and beyond.[4] From the outside looking in, we might see the United States as a foreign and strange place. Consider the nineteenth-century Chinese account, astonishing in our time, that depicted the United States as "an isolated island in the ocean" with unnamed birds and animals.

American History Unbound also offers a corrective to the myth of continents that denies historical significance to oceans and islands.[5] The myth bestows continents with importance because of their size, diversity, and agency (attributions associated with whites and men), while dismissing islands for their smallness, homogeneity, and passivity (traits associated with nonwhites and women). In that scheme, continents act upon and move islands. But the Tongan scholar and writer Epeli Hau'ofa offers a conception of Oceania to counter what he calls the "mental reservations" imposed by continental men: he represents it as a "sea of islands," an immense spread of islands connected, not separated, by waters.

In this work, I celebrate oceans and Oceania, which are decolonizing discourses and material conditions. In fact, I begin with those fluid worlds, untethered from the seemingly fixed, immobile continents.

PART 1

WORLD HISTORY

Pacific Islanders and Asians produced the material conditions to sustain life, formed diverse societies, and conceived of religious beliefs and systems of knowing long before the arrival of Europeans in their oceans. In Asia, great rivers and agriculture enabled complex, large-scale social organizations, and Asian and African sailors navigated and mastered the ocean's winds and currents to transport goods, languages, and cultures. Pacific Islanders spread from their Southeast Asian homeland as far west as Africa, east to America, south to New Zealand, and north to the Hawaiian Islands. Those movements produced hybrid peoples, languages, and cultures even as indigenous forms survived and evolved.

When Europeans set sail from Italian cities to the eastern shore of the Mediterranean, and from Portugal and Spain south to Africa and west to America, they were seeking their vision of Asia. Their discourses of Asian decadence and European superiority accompanied the material conditions of mercantile capitalism, stimulating trade and justifying colonization. European expansions into the Mediterranean, Atlantic, Indian, and Pacific eventuated into world-systems, with flows of goods and labor extracted from Europe's periphery to enrich the core. Within the Atlantic system, the American colonies served their European masters; and after independence, the United States became part of the core.

1

OCEAN WORLDS

Many of us believe that the place of human habitation is land, and that the oceans form vast, uninhabited barriers between lands and peoples. Perhaps that belief arises from the longstanding human practice of turning to the interiors of the landmasses called continents to seek opportunities, possibilities, and even renewals. Related to this idea is U.S. history's "frontier hypothesis," whereby the inland frontier levels class distinctions and summons self-reliance, an independent spirit, rugged individualism, ingenuity in the face of adversity, and a democratic spirit. The frontier offers rebirth and the realization of the American dream.

Many of us, in addition, see continents as lands rich in resources, favoring the rise of great civilizations, whereas islands represent tiny, isolated, insignificant specks of land. Scientists apprehend enormous diversity on continents, from geological formations to plant and animal life forms, which move, interact, and change. They understand islands, in opposition, as places of isolation, like laboratories, in which geologies and organic communities are simpler and not inclined to change as much as on continents. Charles Darwin, accordingly, studied the processes of natural selection and evolution on Pacific islands unconcerned with complicating external factors, while Margaret Mead described Samoan life cycles and sexualities unperturbed by interactions with other peoples.

Islanders might offer a contrasting vision, in which the oceans are extensions of lived, worked, and imagined spaces. Land and water form continuities, not separations. Coastal peoples on larger landmasses can easily agree with that point of view. Oceans can inspire the imagination and beckon with the prospect of innovation and transformation. Pacific

Islanders, as we will see, covered immense distances by island hopping, but they also saw their Oceania as encompassing places of production for sustenance, sacred spaces, homes for ancestors and divinities, and places for living and social relations.

Those representations of continents and islands involve intersecting concepts of race, gender, sexuality, class, and nation—the social formation. As inferior peoples, islanders are racialized as nonwhites; as small, confined spaces, islands signify women; as places where nature's abundance prevails, tropical islands exude unbridled, if not deviant sexualities; and as childlike peoples, islanders constitute a dependent class and conjure improbable nations. Those distinctions reveal the discursive power of continents over islands even as they exemplify how geographies, like the other elements of the social formation, are social constructs.

Continents, really, are also islands, surrounded as they are by water. The earth has but one ocean, which flows freely around the globe. Africa, Asia, and Europe form a single landmass, which the ancient Greeks called the "world island," and in the geologic past, America was a part of Africa. Islands and continents rise from the same tectonic plates. From the world's ocean emerged the Mediterranean, Atlantic, Indian, and Pacific worlds, whose waters formed conduits, not impediments, and sustained creativity, production, and systems of belief. Together, the earth's waters and lands make up a shared space on which humans map and materialize their diverse and dynamic worlds.

In this chapter, we steer a course away from land to examine the connections between land and water. Those affiliations produced ocean worlds. We consider islands as significant places and island peoples as active creators of those ocean worlds. Finally, we come to understand Asians and Pacific Islanders as historical agents working their waters and lands long before the advent of Europeans and their engulfing world-system. Pacific Islanders and Asians devised technologies that allowed them to sail the oceans; they created far-flung, long-distance trade networks and flows of goods and labor; and they spread and modified languages, religions, and cultures, producing ideological and material changes. Asian and Pacific Islander lives were never static; they were always in motion, like the waters.

ASIA

Asia is immense, diverse, and mobile. In Asia and Africa—notably Persia, Egypt, India, and China—people built societies around vast and complex systems of agriculture. Those civilizations arose in Mesopotamia (present-day Iraq) and Egypt around 4000 B.C., in India around 3000 B.C., and in China around 2000 B.C. Their dominions expanded and contracted over time, and their peoples were a varied and mutable mix of indigenous folk and invaders. Their great rivers—Mesopotamia's Tigris and Euphrates, Egypt's Nile, India's Indus, and China's Yellow and Yangtze—and fertile valleys enabled the production of agricultural surpluses sufficient to feed the rise of cities and large-scale, complex social organizations.

FIGURE 2

An example of Islamic architecture, the Taj Mahal in Agra, India, built 1630–33. *National Geographic* magazine, 1888.

Families were the basis of society, and social hierarchies were based on criteria such as class, gender, age, occupation, and education, which shifted from time to time. In most years, agricultural production provided sufficient food to sustain the population, though natural disasters such as floods, droughts, and plagues of locusts led to famines in which millions died. Grains like wheat (in the drier areas), rice, sorghum, and millet, along with buckwheat, beans, cabbage, eggplant, lentils, peas, peppers, squash, and taro, milk and milk products, fish, and chicken (native to Southeast Asia), supplied excellent nutrition. Spices, pickled vegetables, seaweeds, and fish sauces provided seasoning for otherwise bland staple starches, and specialists refined cuisines and devised distinctive food cultures.

Buddhism, which emerged in India at about the time of ancient Greece, linked India with Southeast Asia. Trade between the two regions also carried with it Hinduism and other aspects of Indian civilization. Conversion to Islam, which arose in modern-day Saudi Arabia in the seventh century A.D., connected diverse peoples, including Arabs, Africans, Persians, and Turks. It transformed philosophy, politics, jurisprudence, commerce, and art, which had been dominated by Jews, Christians, and Zoroastrians until at least A.D. 1000. Muslim military states emerged and occupied key areas, such as the Mamluks in Egypt and Syria; the Safavids in Persia and Iraq; the Timurids in Central Asia, who later became the Mughals of India; and the Ottoman Empire in Turkey and the Balkans. Those states struggled over religious, commercial, and political power, but they also built empires, established public order, and promoted economic prosperity.

Islam was the vehicle for commerce between Muslim Arab and Indian traders and merchants, and the new religion made inroads as far east as the coast of China. Islam was especially appealing to peoples in Southeast Asia, including Indonesia and the Philippines, and many Islamic sultanates arose in that vast region of islands and seas. The people of Southeast Asia in turn influenced Islam, changing it into a religion that affirmed many of their pre-Islamic beliefs and cultures, such as greater gender equity; stressing Islam's tenet that all persons are equal before God; and modifying rules and observances governing diet, fasting, and prayer.

Centuries before the advent of Europeans, thus, Asians and Pacific Islanders created and inhabited ocean worlds in the waters later named by Europeans as the Indian and Pacific oceans. Their peoples, called "races" by Europeans, interacted and mixed without those distinctions.

THE INDIAN OCEAN WORLD

The Indian Ocean world, spanning the globe from eastern Africa to Asia, consisted of numerous coastal lands and peoples, who thrived on farming both land and sea. Because of the vagaries of the weather and agricultural production, the waters and their bounties may have provided a more reliable source of sustenance than the land.

On the western edge of the Indian Ocean world, maritime communities lined the East African coast, where a large portion of the population engaged in fishing and in trade for foods, raw materials, and articles not readily available locally. Exploitation of land and sea along those shores began between two thousand and three thousand years ago, and human activity there was noted in the *Periplus of the Erythraean Sea*.

The Red Sea and Persian Gulf carved inroads from the Indian Ocean toward the Fertile Crescent, which stretched from Egypt through Syria to Mesopotamia. The waters of the Red Sea and Persian Gulf thereby connected the civilizations of the Indus River, the Tigris and Euphrates, and the Nile. Grains, cloth, pottery, ivory, resins, beads, and metal objects were among the commodities exchanged in maritime trade. These stimulated the growth of crafts and manufacturing, along with the development of specialists, merchants, and elites who handled and profited from the trade between Asia and Africa.

Refining their shipbuilding and navigational techniques over time, South Asian sailors navigated eastward to the sprawling network of islands in Southeast Asia and to Burma and Vietnam, introducing not only trade goods but also cultural and religious forms. In turn, Southeast Asian mariners in large outriggers journeyed westward, carrying Chinese and Southeast Asian commodities to entrepôts in southern India and the small islands of Sri Lanka. From those ports, Arabian and Persian ships took the goods to destinations in the Persian Gulf, Arabia, and the Mediterranean.

That long-distance maritime traffic helped to structure Asian and African social formations. Those material and cultural exchanges passed through port cities to reach far inland. Traders and then immigrants from Southeast Asia sailed to Madagascar, off the

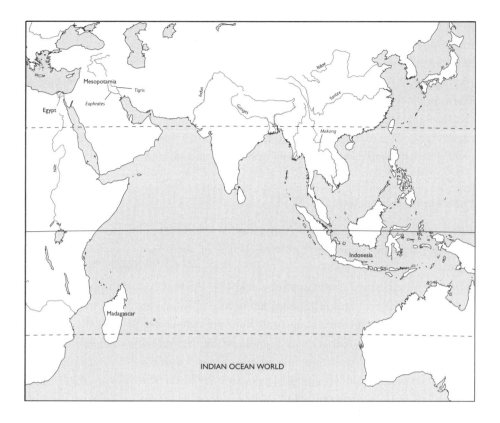

MAP 2

Indian Ocean world. Afro-Asia—Africa and Asia—and its inland sea.

[handwritten: These things introduced from Southeast Asia to Africa,]

southeast coast of Africa, bringing important crops like yams, bananas, taro, and sugar-cane, along with the chicken, while Arab and African sailors and traders settled in port cities on India's west coast. Cultures and languages remained distinct, but they also conducted transactions in a common language. Swahili, for instance, a language of the East African coast, is essentially of the African Bantu family but includes many loan words and structures from Arabic and Gujarati, a language of India.

[handwritten margin: Swahili: common trade language]

While ancient Greece and Rome spun myths about a distant, desirable, exotic, and antagonistic Orient, for Asians Europe was not a destination of much interest. More important were the Indian Ocean and its circuits of goods, labor, and culture. The Mediterranean world, in fact, reached toward Asia as a supplicant: the Red Sea was a door to the Indian Ocean world.

By 1405, when the Ming Dynasty admiral Zhenghe left China for India, Arabia, and East Africa, the Indian Ocean trade was more than a thousand years old. Zhenghe's seven expeditions were notable for their scale and technological achievements and were probably the first systematic contacts between China and East Africa. For twenty-eight years, some sixty vessels, including the biggest ships ever built up to that time—four hundred feet long, with four decks, double hulls, and watertight compartments, and equipped with compasses and detailed sailing directions—plied the seas. They carried up to five hundred soldiers and cargoes of silk, porcelains, and other export goods, and they returned to China laden with spices, tropical hardwoods, giraffes, zebras, and ostriches. The voyages ended in 1433, perhaps because of their great expense, but they are a reminder that the Indian Ocean was alive with commerce long before the Portuguese finally rounded the Horn of Africa and entered the Indian Ocean, and then, with the help of African and Asian pilots, managed a landing in India in 1498.

THE PACIFIC OCEAN WORLD

Before the advent of humans, the Pacific was like the planet's other waters, unmarked and mingling indiscriminately with other bodies of water that were later named the Atlantic, Indian, Arctic, and Southern Oceans. In reality, Pacific waters are unbounded, flowing freely among other oceans and mixing with seas now named the Celebes, Coral, Japan, South China, Sulu, and Tasman, among others. Its major currents move in opposite directions north and south of the equator and are complicated by vertical convections. The Pacific can be mapped variously by its shrinking size—about an inch each year, due to plate tectonics—its fluctuating surface temperatures, its swirling winds, and its variant salinities, as well as its widely divergent topography of immense mountain ranges, called "chains," seamounts, and precipitously deep trenches. Its life forms, the most varied of all the planet's waters, offer another way of conceiving of the Pacific. Although plants and animals throughout the Pacific are related through recurrent migrations, they are also particular to specific habitats, such as the rich coral reefs in the ocean's tropical zone and the equally prolific kelp forests of its temperate zone.

Perhaps as long as one hundred thousand years ago, hunter-gatherers crossed the shallow seas from Southeast Asia to Indonesia, New Guinea, and Australia. As sea levels rose with the end of last glacial period, those peoples, speaking languages of the Austronesian family, developed maritime skills to travel among their island homes. (An alternative theory places the origin of Austronesian peoples on China's southern coast, associated with Hemudu culture some seven thousand years ago.)

One of those groups of Austronesian speakers, the Malayo-Polynesians, was particularly successful in migrating; some of them sailed westward about two thousand years ago to populate Madagascar and thereby people the Indian Ocean world. Others voyaged eastward into the Pacific and Oceania, which reaches from Southeast Asia to America. In that way, Austronesian speakers spanned over half the planet, bridged the worlds of the Indian and Pacific oceans, and gave rise to remarkably divergent cultures, from Malagasy in the far west to Hawaiian in the northeast.

The racial category *Malay* was created by the European taxonomer Blumenbach in 1795. In the 1830s, a French traveler, Jules Dumont d'Urville, created the arbitrary divisions and groupings of Pacific Islanders as Melanesians, Micronesians, and Polynesians,

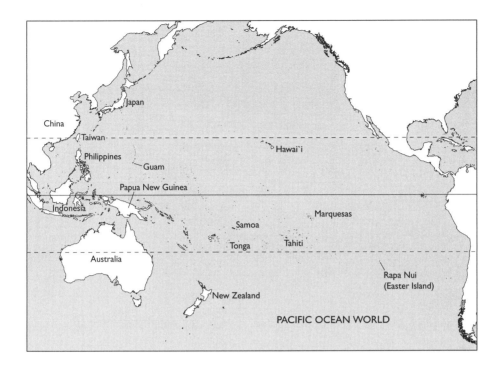

MAP 3

Pacific Ocean world. Oceania and its sea of islands.

based on alleged skin color (Melanesians) and the size and numbers of islands (Micronesians and Polynesians). Although we retain these categories, the truth about those islanders, like that of the waters they inhabit, is far more complex, varied, and nuanced than those externally imposed classifications.

By 2000 B.C., Malayo-Polynesian single- and double-hulled sailing canoes, fitted with outriggers, were crossing the waters of Southeast Asia for trade and long-distance migration. Island hopping toward the rising sun, these Malayo-Polynesians settled in New Guinea around 1500 B.C. From there they spread into Melanesia and Micronesia, and around 1000 B.C. they arrived in western Polynesia. Throughout the Pacific, the people who came to inhabit a certain island or archipelago were not a single group of migrants but the result of multiple voyages from different directions. *— Voyges led to inhabiting new land*

long distance migration with outriggers.

Like the maritime peoples of the Indian Ocean world, the Polynesians built and improved on canoe technology and accumulated immense navigational knowledge of the sea, its currents, and the celestial bodies to steer their vessels to destinations known and unknown. From Tonga and Samoa in western Polynesia—the Polynesian homeland and center of further dispersion—they sailed eastward to the Marquesas and to Rapa Nui (Easter Island). As early as A.D. 300 they headed north to Hawai'i, crossing the equator to the Northern Hemisphere, where the location and arrangement of heavenly bodies appeared different from their familiar setting.

FIGURE 3
Corals, fishes, and myriad life forms populate the ocean worlds. U.S. Fish and Wildlife Service.

not only did learn new cultures/tradition, but even old abandoned old ones.

As they moved from island to island, they took with them linguistic, social, and religious ideas and practices, while also abandoning some and developing others. Cultures diffused but also interacted and modified in the engagement with other peoples and with different lands and seascapes.

The technologies required for this immense, global dispersal illustrate the complicated routes created and traveled by Pacific Islanders. For instance, many features of their canoes indicate an Indonesian origin, but they also exhibit local modifications and improvements. The initial groups of migrants from Indonesia, who settled in the western South Pacific, perhaps journeyed in square-sailed, double-outrigger canoes, whereas subsequent mariners, traveling in larger double canoes rigged with sails of a different design, settled in the islands of the eastern South Pacific.

The canoes of Oceania carried migrants and their food supplies over vast distances. Canoe making involves a host of variables, including the choice of wood and its carving and sealing, the dimensions and curve of the hull, ropes for bindings and lashings, booms to lash two parallel canoes, platforms to support passengers and their belongings, the designs and rigging of sails, and the size, length, and shape of the paddles. These material assemblages, through their distribution and spread, reveal clusters of common derivation and retention, invention and divergence through space and time. Canoe making also involved cultural and religious sanctions and requirements.

making boats for voyage required knowledge of other cultures.

Much as the ocean's corals, seaweeds, and fishes dispersed across the ocean over time, evolving and adapting, migrant people adapted to particular places, evolved in isolation, and experienced recurrent migrations and interactions. Motion is a matter of perspective. For instance, Polynesian voyagers navigated by thinking of their vessels as stationary while islands, seen and unseen, moved past them.

The sweet potato, developed by American Indians, was distributed throughout the islands of the eastern South Pacific before the arrival of Europeans, suggesting long-distance contact between American Indians and Polynesians. Similarly, the coconut, probably of Southeast Asian origin, was established along the Pacific coasts of Panama and Colombia before the Spaniards arrived, indicating travel and contact in the opposite direction, from islands to continent. Both plants are unlikely long-distance ocean travelers, so their transplantation almost certainly involved human activity. The distribution of those essential food crops, along with the sailing technologies required to move them such long distances, suggest mobility and human agency on the part of Pacific Islanders, contradicting the histories of isolation, seclusion, and paralysis ascribed to dreamy island worlds by Europeans.

On their vessels, the islanders of Oceania traversed immense distances, and for many voyaging was a preferred way of life. In this sense, the people were of both the land and the sea, which was a "sea of islands," as poetically phrased by Epeli Hauʻofa. The peoples of Oceania formed affiliations with and drew resources from both the land and the sea and all their material abundance and spiritual manifestations.

PACIFIC ISLANDERS

Here we consider the islands of Guam, Hawaiʻi, and Samoa because these became a part of the United States. They and their peoples, accordingly, form aspects—some would argue central figures—of American history.

GUAM

Over five thousand years ago, skilled proto-Austronesian-speaking mariners, perhaps from the Philippines, steered their outrigger canoes northward, following the ocean's currents to the Mariana Archipelago and the island of Guam in the western South Pacific. These same currents had earlier carried algae, corals, fishes, and seeds from Southeast Asia to the islands, and migratory birds and windborne insects found and made homes there. Life forms on those islands thus carry features of the distant biotic communities whence they originated.

The proto-Austronesian speakers who first settled the archipelago named it "land from the sea," accurately describing islands that literally emerged from the ocean's depths some sixty million years ago through the collision of tectonic plates that produced a mountain range, the tips of which form the island chain. The proto-Austronesians adapted and changed through innovation and frequent encounters with continental and other island peoples to become the Chamorros.

Accomplished navigators and canoe designers and makers, the Chamorros traveled widely to fish and trade, and they engaged in both peaceful and hostile contact with foreigners who visited their islands. The sophisticated Chamorro canoes were light, swift, and graceful, seeming to skim the water's surface. The plant foods the original migrants from Southeast Asia had brought with them, such as bananas, taro, rice, breadfruit, yams, and coconuts, were cultivated in the islands' interiors, where the soil was relatively rich and freshwater was available for irrigation.

In their creation story, which solidifies their claim to these lands, Chamorros hold that the first people, two men, emerged from a rock, the Lalas Rock at Fouha Bay on Guam Island. One of the men turned into a woman to enable reproduction and the start of the Chamorro lineage (the Chamorros trace their ancestry through the mother's line). Forming kin groups, or clans, Chamorros lived in settlements along Guam's coast and in the interior. As the population increased and lineages branched out to establish their own villages, social stratification and conflict both within and among kin groups developed. Higher classes tended to live along the ocean's shores to control and profit from interisland commerce, while commoners worked the island's fertile interiors. Unique to Guam, noble families lived in structures built on posts or *lattes* from three to sixteen feet tall: the higher the house, the more powerful its owner.

Patriarchies ruled the clans and lineages, and ancestor veneration helped to link and solidify kinship associations that were otherwise divergent and increasingly distant. Labor was divided by gender. Women generally collected wild fruits, shellfish, and seaweeds; wove mats and sails from tree fibers; and tended the vegetable gardens. Men helped in plant cultivation, and they were the fishermen and seagoing traders. Rice growing is distinctive to Guam, and Marianas red-ware pottery has features characteristic of local Marianas ceramic traditions while also resembling Lapita ware, which is associated with the earliest spread of proto-Polynesians from Southeast Asia.

Chamorro society produced specialists such as priests, designers and builders of canoes and houses, and men engaged in interisland trade and warfare. Chamorros remembered histories to secure their claims to the land and waters, and they accumulated and conveyed navigational knowledge and skills from centuries of seafaring and observations of celestial bodies, ocean currents, and winds. Through an ideology of reciprocity and obligation, Chamorros spun a web of social cohesion and affiliation that continued through the sixteenth century and the first European contact.

SAMOA

As was the case with the people of the rest of the Pacific Islands, Samoa's peoples descended from proto-Austronesian speakers who sailed from Southeast Asia to other islands, and they formed an eastern branch, grouped later by Europeans as Polynesians.

About 1000 B.C., the Polynesians developed languages and cultures distinctive to the eastern South Pacific, centering on the islands of Tonga and Samoa.

By A.D. 300, the people of Samoa had moved inland away from the initial coastal settlements. They cleared the forests to build their villages, and eventually ceased making Lapita-style pottery and switched to wooden containers. Those changes had profound social consequences because ceramic technologies held material and spiritual meanings, and their manufacture required craft and religious specialists. Permanent settlements, population increases, and structures such as houses, stone walls, and roads suggest evolving social hierarchies and specializations, and oral histories confirm wars and raids among islands and peoples.

Samoans, along with other Polynesians, were superb horticulturalists, as shown by their inland villages located on fertile, arable soil. Their pottery and wooden vessels suggest the permanent settlements that farming required. Although agriculturalists, Samoans were equally at home on the sea, as demonstrated by the frequency and astonishing distances of their travel to other islands.

It was from Tonga and Samoa that Polynesians mariners sailed to find and settle the Marquesas Islands, and their voyages ranged as far as Rapa Nui. From the Marquesas, they achieved their northernmost reach, Hawai'i. Their highest achievement in farming and navigation was perhaps the Polynesian settlement of Hawai'i.

[handwritten margin note: led to the discovery of Hawaii]

HAWAI'I

For over a thousand years before the advent of Europeans, successive waves of Polynesian voyagers and settlers arrived in the Hawaiian Islands. Over thirty million years earlier, like Guam and other Pacific islands, the Hawaiian Islands had emerged as the tips of a mountain range that grew from the ocean floor not from tectonic plate collisions but as volcanic formations that reached skyward. The *Kumulipo*, the Hawaiian song of creation, describes that mating of sea, land, and sky and their biotic communities.

Amidst the abundance of the islands, the voyaging Polynesians gave rise to the Hawaiian people. By the late eighteenth century, the Hawaiian Islands supported the largest, most densely populated society of all the Polynesian islands, supported by the productivity of its lands and waters. Horticulture was the mainstay of the economy. The primary unit of land *was the ahupua'a,* a narrow, wedge-shaped area, marked off by an *ahu* (altar), that started from an apex in the highlands and widened out toward the coastline. With this design, producers had access to all of the land's resources, from the tall trees and colorful birds of the higher elevations to the lowland fields for crops and the bounty of the ocean's shores, reefs, and deeps.

The windward, better-watered side of the islands allowed intensive cultivation of taro, the staple, in terraced fields and wetlands. On the leeward side farmers grew dry-land crops such as sweet potatoes. Like other seafaring Polynesians, migrants to Hawai'i brought in their canoes taro, yams, sweet potatoes, gourds, bananas, sugarcane, coconuts, and breadfruit along with small animals like dogs, pigs, and chickens. Family groupings, connected to ancestors and deities, were the basis of the society, and lineages shared and cared for the resources of the land and sea.

Over time, and with new migrations arriving from Tahiti roughly between 1100 and 1400, occupational specializations and social hierarchies developed. A chiefly class, the *ali'i*, ruled over commoners, *maka'ainana*. The priests, or *kahuna*, tended to spiritual and ceremonial matters. With the installation of the *kapu* system, or rules of conduct, which specified privileges for the elite and restrictions for the masses, the social hierarchy gained legitimacy and power. The chiefs levied a tax on the labor of commoners and therewith built extensive taro terraces, irrigation networks, fishponds, and temples. Still, people shared the bounties of land and sea, both of which were considered sacred, and there was no concept of private property. *The ali'i* might hold the land, but the masses made it productive. As Hawaiians note, "The land remains the land because of the chiefs, and prosperity comes to the land because of the common people."[1]

THE ATLANTIC AND PACIFIC WORLDS

The Atlantic world intruded into the Pacific with the making of the Spanish empire. In 1513, Spain's Vasco Nuñez de Balboa traversed Panama's isthmus, waded into the Gulf of San Miguel (after having waited for hours for the tide to come in for a choice moment), gazed across the Mar del Sur (the South Sea), and issued the grandiose claim of "real and corporeal and actual possession of these seas and lands and coasts and ports and islands of the south, and all their annexures and kingdoms and provinces to them pertaining . . . in the name of the Kings of Castile present or to come . . . both now and in all times, as long as the world endures until the final day of judgement of mortal man."[2] The South Sea was renamed the Pacific (peaceful) Ocean in 1520, when another of Spain's taxonomists, Ferdinand Magellan, emerged from the turbulent straits at the southern tip of the American continent that to this day bear his name.

Despite Balboa's claim, the Pacific remains Oceania, a Pacific Islander world. Before arriving in the islands he called the Philippines in honor of his patron, Philip II of Spain, Magellan first landed on the island of Guam in 1520. The islanders boarded his ships and took what they wanted; in retribution, Magellan dispatched forty armed soldiers to burn and sack the islanders' homes and killed seven of them. Three days later, he set off for the Philippines, where in 1565 the Spaniards built a trade colony as a terminus for their Manila galleons.

Originally, the Spaniards had named the string of islands that included Guam the Islas de los Ladrones, meaning, in contempt for their native peoples, "islands of thieves." Later, as they colonized the islands, the Spaniards renamed them the Marianas, after the seventeenth-century Spanish queen, Mariana. This reference to a ruler half a world away stood in sharp contrast to the islanders' own name for their home, "land from the sea."

Largely because of its strategic location as an approach to Manila, Guam became an outpost of the Spanish Empire centuries before Europeans conquered other Pacific islands. Guam remained free despite being claimed by Spain, and from 1565 it was ruled by Mexico's viceroy. Guam's Chamorro islanders traded with visiting Spanish galleons and with English and Dutch vessels throughout the sixteenth and seventeenth centuries. In 1668, the arrival of Jesuits tightened the Spanish colonizers' hold, and in 1676, a Spanish administrator took up residence on the island.

The invaders tried to systematically dismantle and replace the islanders' web of social cohesion and affiliation. They induced conflicts between the Chamorro nobility and commoners, tempting the elites to form and exploit alliances with the crown and Church, while the islanders as a body resisted conversion to Catholicism, at times through the force of arms. A brutal "pacification" campaign began in the 1670s, in which a common strategy was the forced breakup and relocation of Chamorro and other recalcitrant island communities. By 1695, when the wars ended, only five thousand Chamorros survived of the estimated fifty thousand original inhabitants, as a result of both Spanish killings and a devastating smallpox epidemic. Following the Spanish-American War, the United States obtained Guam, along with the Philippines, from Spain in the Treaty of Paris of 1898.

European oceanic empires featured profitable commerce, extractive colonies, and naval bases to enforce their claims. Interest in establishing military bases in the Pacific to protect the shipping lanes with Asia drew the United States, Germany, and Britain to Samoa, in the eastern Pacific, for its fine harbor at Pago Pago. In 1878, the U.S. secured a treaty with Samoan chiefs for a naval station at Pago Pago and for a hand in Samoa's foreign relations. For about a decade, the foreign powers competed for dominance in the islands. In 1899 they agreed to divide the islands between the United States and Germany and to compensate Britain with other Pacific islands, all without the consent of the governed.

Hawaiians discovered Europeans when they spotted the ships of British Captain James Cook off the island of Kaua'i on the morning of January 18, 1778. Unlike the Polynesian navigators who sailed to find land and settle Hawai'i, Cook made landfall by accident on his way to search America's West Coast for a Northwest Passage that connected the Atlantic with the Pacific. Cook placed the Hawaiian Islands on European maps marked by grids of longitude and latitude and named them the Sandwich Islands in honor of the Earl of Sandwich, the first lord of the Admiralty. Although he failed to find a Northwest Passage , Cook's cartography led to European and American landings in Hawai'i, resulting in enormous changes to the waters, lands, and peoples wrought principally by American missionaries, traders, and whalers from New England's Atlantic seaboard. The Atlantic, indeed, inundated the Pacific.

SUGGESTED READINGS

Johnson, Rubellite Kawena. *Kumulipo: The Hawaiian Hymn of Creation,* vol. 1. Honolulu: Topgallant Publishing, 1981.

Malo, Davida. *Hawaiian Antiquities.* Translated by Nathaniel B. Emerson. Honolulu: Bishop Museum Press, 1951.

Matsuda, Matt K. *Pacific Worlds: A History of Seas, Peoples, and Cultures.* Cambridge: Cambridge University Press, 2012.

PRIMARY DOCUMENTS
DOCUMENT 1

From Davida Malo, *Hawaiian Antiquities,* trans. Nathaniel B. Emerson (Honolulu: Bishop Museum Press, 1951), 4–5.

Born in 1795 on the Big Island of Hawai'i, Davida Malo trained early in Hawaiian history, literature, and dance. He learned from noted specialists like Auwai, a chief under the first king, Kamehameha, and a genealogist, an authority on law and religion, and Hawaiian culture. Malo also received instruction from Christian missionaries; he converted to Christianity and was ordained as a minister. Despite general contempt for Hawaiian culture among missionaries, Malo was an avid collector of materials on precontact Hawai'i, and he coauthored the first "Moolelo Hawaii" (Hawaiian history) in about 1835 or 1836. He also completed a biography of King Kamehameha, which is now lost, and wrote *Mo'olelo Hawaii,* which was published as *Hawaiian Antiquities* in 1903. Written in Hawaiian by a Hawaiian scholar, the work is one of the few sources on precontact Hawai'i.

In Hawaiian ancestral genealogies it is said that the earliest inhabitants of these islands were the progenitors of all the Hawaiian people.

In the genealogy called Kumu-lipo it is said that the first human being was a woman called Lailai and that her ancestors and parents were of the night (*he po wale no*), that she was the progenitor of the (Hawaiian) race.

The husband of this Lailai was named Ke-alii-wahi-lani (the king who opens heaven); but it is not stated who were the parents of Ke-alii-wahi-lani, only that he was from the heavens; that he looked down and beheld a beautiful woman, Lailai, dwelling in Lalawaia; that he came down and took her to wife, and from the union of these two was begotten one of the ancestors of this race.

And after Lailai and her company it is again stated in the genealogy called Lolo that the first native Hawaiian (*kanaka*) was a man named Kahiko. His ancestry and parentage are given, but without defining their character; it is only said he was a human being (*kanaka*).

Kupulanakehau was the name of Kahiko's wife; they begot Lehauula and Wakea. Wakea had a wife named Haumea, who was the same as Papa. In the genealogy called Pali-ku it is said that the parents and ancestors of Haumea the wife of Wakea were *pali,* i.e., precipices. With her the race of men was definitely established.

These are the only people spoken of in the Hawaiian genealogies; they are therefore presumably the earliest progenitors of the Hawaiian race. It is not stated that they were born here in Hawaii. Probably all of these persons named were born in foreign lands, while their genealogies were preserved here in Hawaii.

DOCUMENT 2

An Account of the Creation of the World According to Hawaiian Tradition, trans. Queen Liliuokalani (Boston: Lee & Shepard, 1897).

Lili'uokalani, the last monarch of the Hawaiian kingdom, translated the *Kumulipo* while being held captive by usurpers in Iolani Palace and had it published in 1897. The queen cited in her introduction several reasons for the *Kumulipo*'s importance. The translation, she wrote, "will be to my friends a souvenir of that part of my life," and is of "inestimable value" because language changes, "and there are terms and allusions herein to the natural history of Hawaii, which might be forgotten in future years without some such history as this to preserve them to posterity. Further, it is the special property of the latest ruling family of the Hawaiian Islands, being nothing less than the genealogy in remote times of the late King Kalakaua,—who had it printed in the original Hawaiian language,—and myself." In this sense, the *Kumulipo* validates the kingdom's rightful claim to sovereignty set against the illegal, forcible takeover by white conspirators and their U.S. ally.

One verse in the *Kumulipo* describes the creation of the Hawaiian islands from the sea:

Filling, filling full
Filling, filling out
Filling, filling up
Until the earth is a brace holding firm the sky
When space lifts through time in the night of Kumulipo.

In subsequent verses, correspondences emerge: the "seaweed living in the sea" and "fern living on land," the "fragrant red seaweed living in the sea" and the "succulent mint living on land," and the "manauea seaweed living in the sea" and the "manauea taro living on land." The people too, the *Kumulipo* tells, are of the sea and the land.

Another, separate document, a praise song, presents another cosmogony for the islands. It describes how the famed fisherman Kapuhe'euanu'u (the large-headed octopus), snagged and pulled up the islands of Hawai'i from the sea:

A land found in the ocean,
Thrown up out of the sea,
From the very depths of Kanaloa,
The white coral in the watery caves
That caught on the hook of the fisherman,
The great fisherman of Kapaahu,
The great fisherman, Kapuhe'euanu'u..

The following excerpts are from the *Kumulipo:*

THE FIRST ERA, OR AGE FIRST VERSE

At the time that turned the heat of the earth,
At the time when the heavens turned and changed,

At the time when the light of the sun was subdued
To cause light to break forth,
At the time of the night of Makalii (winter)
Then began the slime which established the earth,
The source of deepest darkness.
Of the depth of darkness, of the depth of darkness,
Of the darkness of the sun, in the depth of night,
> It is night,
> So was the night born.

SECOND VERSE

Kumulipo was born in the night, a male.
Poele was born in the night, a female.
A coral insect was born, from which was born perforated coral.
The earth worm was born, which gathered earth into mounds,
From it were born worms full of holes.
The starfish was born, whose children were born starry.
The phosphorous was born, whose children were born phosphorescent.
The Ina was born Ina (sea egg).
The Halula was born Halula (sea urchin).
> *Shell-fish.*

The Hawae was born, the Wana-ku was its offspring.
The Haukeuke was born, the Uhalula was its offspring.
The Pioe was born, the Pipi was its offspring (clam oyster).
The Papaua was born, the Olepe was its offspring (pearl and oyster).
The Nahawele was born, the Unauna was its offspring (mussel and crab in a shell).
The Makaiaulu was born, the Opihi was its offspring.
The Leho was born, the Puleholeho was its offspring (cowry).

The Naka was born, its offspring was Kupekala (rock oysters).
The Makaloa was born, the Pupuawa was its offspring.
The Ole was born, the Oleole was its offspring (conch).
The Pipipi was born, the Kupee was its offspring (limpets).

Kane was born to Waiololi, a female to Waiolola.
The Wi was born, the Kiki was its offspring.
The Akaha's home was the sea;
Guarded by the Ekahakaha that grew in the forest.
A night of flight by noises
Through a channel; water is life to trees;
So the gods may enter, but not man.

THIRD VERSE

> *Seaweed and grasses*
Man by Waiololi, woman by Waiolola,
The Akiaki was born and lived in the sea;

Guarded by the Manienie Akiaki that grew in the forest.
A night of flight by noises
Through a channel; water is life to trees;
So the gods may enter, but not man.

FIFTEENTH VERSE

A husband of gourd, and yet a god,
A tendril strengthened by water and grew
A being, produced by earth and spread,
Made deafening by the swiftness of Time
Of the Hee that lengthened through the night,
That filled and kept on filling
Of filling, until, filled
To filling, it is full,
And supported the earth, which held the heaven
On the wing of Time, the night is for Kumulipo (creation),
    It is night.

SIGNIFICANT EVENTS

5000 B.C.	Hemudu culture
3000 B.C.	proto-Austronesian speakers settle Guam
1000 B.C.	Malayo-Polynesians settle Samoa
A.D. 10	Austronesians settle Madagascar
50	*Periplus of the Erythraean Sea*
300	Polynesians settle Hawai'i
11th–15th centuries	Italian city-states and Mediterranean world
1100	Polynesians from Tahiti arrive in Hawai'i
1405	Admiral Zhenghe leads Chinese expedition to Africa
1498	Vasco da Gama reaches India
1513	Vasco Nuñez de Balboa gazes on the Mar del Sur
1520	Ferdinand Magellan lands on Guam
1521	Magellan names the Philippines in honor of Philip II of Spain
1565	Manila galleon trade begins
1778	Hawai'i mapped by James Cook
1878	U.S. treaty with Samoa for Pago Pago
1898	United States acquires Samoa

2

THE WORLD-SYSTEM

The modern world-system is a product of ocean worlds. Like the Indian and Pacific worlds, European ocean worlds linked land with water on which commerce flowed, resulting in complex material and ideological exchanges and coercions as well as hybrid peoples, languages, and subjectivities. Europeans, Asians, and Africans converged on the Mediterranean world, while the Atlantic world involved Europeans, Africans, and indigenous peoples of America. Because European expansion and commerce were predicated on securing the goods of Asia, Asians were prominent participants in European ocean worlds and the modern world-system. In that sense, Asia was the object of European imperialism.

Europe, Asia, and Africa are connected by the Mediterranean Sea, which has long carried commercial traffic and linguistic, religious, and cultural exchanges and impositions. Some scholars place the origins of the modern world-system in the onset of the trade between the Mediterranean world and Asia. Around 1500 B.C. the Phoenicians, preeminent maritime traders, spread from modern-day Lebanon to Africa's Mediterranean coast. Trading in wood, slaves, glass, and dye, their culture lasted for over a thousand years. About 500 B.C., Greek traders established colonies along Africa's Mediterranean coast eastward. As early as the first century B.C., products from India reached the Roman Empire at the Red Sea. Long after Rome's fall, from the eleventh to fifteenth centuries A.D., Italian city-states like Venice, Genoa, Florence, and Milan emerged to control Asian commerce in the Mediterranean, marking what many consider to be the beginnings of mercantile or trade-based capitalism and the modern world-system.

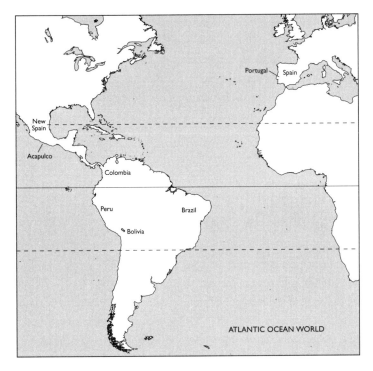

MAP 4
Atlantic Ocean world. In this world, Europe is a creation of Africa and America.

In the fifteenth century, the rise of the Iberian states eclipsed the Italian city-states and shifted trade from the Mediterranean to the Atlantic. Sugar had entered the Mediterranean from Asia; now Spain transplanted sugarcane to islands off the West African coast. Sugarcane was probably domesticated in New Guinea and around 8000 B.C. spread to China and India, where sugar production was highly developed. By the eighth century A.D., sugar plantations appeared on the eastern shores of the Mediterranean, and crops like sugarcane, rice, sorghum, cotton, citrus fruits, and plantains accompanied the spread of Islam into the Mediterranean world.

Merchants from Venice and Genoa built sugar plantations on Mediterranean islands like Crete and Cyprus. Plantations involved large tracts of land, foreign conquerors and landowners, imported laborers, and production of a single crop for export. Spain, Portugal, and other European nations carried that model of production into the Atlantic world. Atlantic commerce was triangular: Europe, at the apex, sent its manufactures to Africa to purchase enslaved laborers; European ships transported their human chattels to America and the Caribbean islands; and they returned to Europe laden with tropical goods such as sugar, rum, and cotton, produced by American Indian and African laborers. The Atlantic world, accordingly, was built on extractive, exploitative relationships, not on a trade-based system of exchanges: conquered lands and enslaved peoples generated the wealth that enriched Europe even as the process impoverished Africa and America. That violent and exploitative Atlantic world supplied the means by which Portugal and Spain established a presence in Asia.

According to standard narratives of U.S. history, Atlantic civilization is the wellspring of national formation. This view renders the United States as essentially and centrally a European state and people, ignoring the black Atlantic and African diaspora. In that historical narrative of nation, then, the Atlantic world is the familiar self, while the Pacific world is the alien other. Yet the Atlantic world splashed into the Pacific world precisely because of Europe's efforts to find and plunder the treasury of Asia, and America was an accident of that ancient pursuit.

SEEKING ASIA

The search for wealth drew Europeans to Asia. By the fifteenth century, a few Europeans had crossed the Eurasian continent to reach the Pacific. China and India remained fabulous in the European imagination largely because of their resources—mainly raw silk from China, which fed the expanding textile industries of northern Italy, but also spices and slaves from India. A possible consequence of that traffic with Asia was the Black Death, or plague, of the first half of the fourteenth century, which decimated many European cities. In addition to that pandemic, wars, like the Hundred Years' War (1337–1453), waged mainly for control of France, destroyed much of the countryside and significantly reduced and displaced the population. Europe clearly was not in a position of global dominance.

Asia was the dominant partner in the east-west trade from the days of ancient Greece and Rome until at least the sixteenth century. Asians controlled the products desired by Europeans, and they managed the nature, volume, and prices of trade. In 1428, for instance, when the sultan of Alexandria, Egypt, raised the price of pepper by more than 60 percent, the change reduced the profits enjoyed by Venetian merchants who traded in the commodity. Europeans sought new avenues to escape the intermediate gatekeepers and gain direct access to Asia's goods.

At the western edge of Eurasia, the peoples who became the Portuguese and Spanish were at a disadvantage relative to those of the Italian city-states, which had capitalized on their location in the overland trade with Asia. However, their perch on the Atlantic shore conferred an advantage in charting a route to China and India by sea. Since the time of the ancient Greeks, who had hypothesized the world as a disk and then later as a sphere, Europeans had surmised that Asia could be reached by crossing the Atlantic or by sailing around Africa and through the Indian Ocean world.

Until about the fifteenth century, Muslim caravans from West African kingdoms like Mali, Ghana, and Songhai had transported gold, ivory, and slaves to the southern Mediterranean. That trans-Saharan trade had supplied most of the gold held by Europeans, who in turn traded it for Asian silks, spices, and slaves. Led by its Arab and Jewish merchants, Catalonia, situated on the Mediterranean bordering present-day Spain and France, prospered from that commerce, but the Catalans could not surpass Venice and Genoa in the Asian trade. Like the Genoese, the Catalans tried in the fourteenth century to reach Asia by sailing around Africa, but they failed. In 1469, with the marriage of King Ferdinand II of Aragon and Queen Isabella of Castile, Catalonia became a part of Spain, and the Catalan project of finding a route to Asia became a Spanish project.

It was Portugal that took up the ambitious business of circumnavigating Africa for the Asian trade. The effort began with Portugal's wars against the African peoples called Moors ("dark people")— Berbers, Arabs, and West Africans who had invaded and occupied much of the Iberian Peninsula, starting in A.D. 711, and imposed Islamic rule. The Africans ruled until the Portuguese and Spanish succeeded in the "reconquest" of the peninsula in the fifteenth century. The fall of Granada in 1492 marked the end of Muslim rule in Iberia, and the Portuguese and Spaniards carried the war to the African continent.

In 1415, shortly after the Portuguese conquered the African city of Ceuta, across the Strait of Gibraltar and a terminus of the trans-Saharan gold caravans, Prince Henry assumed the task of leading the Portuguese effort to reach Asia by sailing around Africa. The young prince assembled geographers and astronomers and books, charts, and maps at his headquarters at Sagres on the southern tip of Portugal, and from there he sent expeditions to the West African coast. From these Henry amassed details of winds, currents, tides, and sailing directions to aid the next voyages, and his captains used these to reach Africa south of the Sahara. There, in 1441, the Portuguese traded goods for African slaves. The prospect of a lucrative traffic in slaves and gold lured agents from Venice and other Italian trading cities to Sagres. Over the next five years, Henry imported about a thousand African slaves, whose sales helped to support his enterprise, and he formed a company with Italian shareholders to generate more income for his expeditions.

Prince Henry, "the Navigator," died in 1460 before realizing his dream of reaching Asia, but the effort continued. Bartolomeu Dias rounded the Cape of Good Hope at the southern tip of Africa in 1487, and in 1498 Vasco da Gama arrived at Calicut, on the southwest coast of India, with the help of a Gujarati pilot he captured on the East African coast. Thus the Atlantic world's intrusion into the Indian Ocean world was not a Portuguese achievement alone: it was underwritten in large part by the enslavement and sale of thousands of Africans and aided by African and Asian seamen who steered the Portuguese vessels through unfamiliar waters and contrary winds and currents.

When the triumphant da Gama discovered that the Indians were reluctant to give away their trade, he shelled Calicut and took Indian hostages to obtain his full cargo of spices. On his return to Portugal in 1499, the goods paid for his expedition six hundred times over and reaped a profit of over 3,000 percent. He returned to Calicut in 1502 and again bombarded the town and sank the anchored ships of his Indian and Arab competitors. The Portuguese selected Goa as the base from which their superior sea power would bring about the conquest of the Indian Ocean world and a monopoly over the Asian trade. By the sixteenth century the Portuguese controlled the sea lanes and extended their reach from India and Ceylon to Indonesia and Macao, China.

The chief architect of Portugal's commercial empire in Asia, Alfonso de Albuquerque, aimed not only to capture the Asian spice trade but also to initiate a reconfiguration of

European power relations in the process. Named viceroy of the Indies in 1508, Albuquerque captured Malacca, a key trade city on the Malay Peninsula, in 1511. "The first aim is the great service . . . to our Lord in casting out of this country and quenching the fire of the sect of Mohammed," he wrote in anticipation of the battle. "And the other is the service we shall render to the king," which was the taking of the city that is "the source of all the spiceries and drugs which the Moors carry every year." On capturing Malacca, he boasted, "Cairo and Mecca will be entirely ruined, and Venice will receive no spiceries unless her merchants go and buy them in Portugal."[1] A man of his word, Albuquerque slaughtered all of Malacca's Muslims and other "heathens"—Hindus and Buddhists—in the names of his god and king and used torture to win converts to Christianity.

Meanwhile, the Portuguese demonstrated a way of generating the income necessary for the Asian trade. On their island possessions off the African coast, including Madeira and the Azores, the Portuguese imported African slaves to cultivate sugar and wheat, which they sold to Italy and Spain. From 1450 to 1500, some 150,000 African slaves filled the holds of Portuguese ships bound for those island plantations and for sale on the European continent. Portugal's Asian goods were thus purchased with enslaved African laborers who served European masters, extracting "green gold" on plantations built on expropriated land. In addition, Portuguese manufactures undermined African producers, and the enslavement of Africans resulted in a net loss of labor for Africa. Portugal's producers in turn gained new markets in Africa, and its plantations profited from their exports to Europe, financing the commerce with Asia.

FINDING AMERICA

Before sailing as a representative of Spain, Christopher Columbus, a Genoese, first petitioned Portugal to outfit an expedition to sail westward to Asia. The Portuguese king had no interest in Columbus's proposal because his sailors had already progressed far down the African coast, and profits from slave sales made those voyages viable. Spain's agreement with Columbus renewed an enmity and a rivalry between the two nations. The conflict over dominion of new territories was resolved by Pope Alexander in Rome, who was a Spaniard. The pope, disregarding any rights of native peoples, awarded Africa to Portugal and America to Spain. Two years later, the Treaty of Tordesillas divided the Spanish and Portuguese claims with a vertical line down the map of the known world: Portugal claimed Brazil on the other side of the Atlantic, but Spain assumed rights to the lands west of the line.

Other European powers, like England and France, ignored that arbitrary division and pursued their own projects of colonization. But their efforts were mainly confined to what became known as North America and islands of the Caribbean. Spain retained most of the initiative in colonizing America. Spaniards called the people *indios* or Indians because Columbus had believed them to be natives of India. In their global expansions, the Spaniards used the word *indios* to designate native peoples wherever they encountered them in America and Asia.

The Spaniards soon learned that their newly colonized lands were not a part of Asia but a "new world," as was described by Pietro Martir de Anghiera in his 1493 account of Columbus's achievement, *De Orbe Novo* (Of the New World). On his second voyage, Columbus established settlers on Hispaniola, the island that today comprises Haiti and the Dominican Republic. He forced the Indians to forsake food cultivation to dig for gold, an order that led to famine, revolts, harsh reprisals, and many deaths. On his third crossing, in 1496, Columbus transported back to Spain 550 Taino Indians, 350 of whom survived the transatlantic Middle Passage to be sold as slaves to defray the costs of his expedition.

Spanish conquerors captured Mexico, with the aid of native allies, in 1521, and Peru in 1533. From Mexico City, the representative of the Spanish crown ruled "New Spain," which covered much of the American continent and the islands of the Caribbean. The Spaniards brought diseases like smallpox and measles that infected and spread quickly among the peoples of the islands and then the continent, killing millions in what some called "the great dying." Another deadly introduction, malaria, infiltrated the tropical and coastal lowlands. Hundreds of thousands more deaths resulted from raids to capture slaves. In Mesoamerica alone, the pre-Spanish population numbered an estimated 25 million, but by 1650, it had fallen to 1.5 million.

The Spaniards' brutal mission of expansion and conquest in America was driven by the quest for gold and silver. Over a 150-year period beginning in 1503, gold from Colombia alone increased the entire European supply by about 20 percent. Silver, however, was the bullion that sustained the Spanish empire: during the period 1503–1660, more than seven million pounds of silver from America were shipped to Spain. Mined in Mexico, Bolivia, and Peru, silver mining required hundreds of thousands of Indian workers and tens of thousands of pack animals. It led to countless deaths in the mines, along the roads, and from the toxic nature of the smelting process.

Silver also found its way from Acapulco, Mexico, to Manila, in the Philippines, to purchase the Asian goods so coveted by the Spaniards. The Manila galleon trade, begun in 1565, finally connected Spain with Asia. American silver bought Chinese silks, satins, and porcelain, along with Southeast Asian spices that were transported back to New Spain and from there to Spain and Europe. The trade brought Chinese and Spanish merchants to Manila, which grew into an urban trade hub, supported by the agricultural production of Filipino farmers in the rural hinterland. In 1597, an exceptional year, more American silver went to Manila than to Seville in Spain; and from 1570 to 1780, an estimated four thousand to five thousand tons of silver were delivered into Asian hands. The galleon trade ended in 1815 during the Mexican War of Independence, but its influences were transformative in Asia, America, and Europe. They included the introduction of American Indian crops—maize, potatoes, beans, squash, and pineapples—into Asia, which changed Asian diets and economies.

The Manila-Acapulco galleon trade was so lucrative that other merchants in Spain petitioned the king to limit it to two ships per year. To compensate, galleon traders increased the size of their ships to 1,700–2,000 tons. Built of Philippine hardwoods, they were capable of carrying up to a thousand passengers. Scores of Filipinos died from the forced labor imposed by the Spaniards to build those galleons.

Carried along with the loads of textiles, spices, porcelain, and furniture on board the Spanish galleons from Asia to America were Asians, mainly Filipinos and Chinese, and possibly South Asians and Arabs, who for hundreds of years had negotiated Southeast Asian waters. Those Asians worked on board the galleons, and Spanish masters enslaved some of them for sale in New Spain until the slave trade ended in 1700. Spaniards also took Filipina concubines to America, where they produced mestizos who blended into Mexico's Indian population, along with Asian seamen who deserted the galleons. Asians and American Indians alike were of the subject class, labeled as *indios* by their Spanish colonizers, and a century later, in 1810 to 1821, when Mexico rose up in rebellion against Spain, hundreds of Mexican Filipinos joined the struggle for freedom as soldiers and as military commanders, like Ramon Fabie.

IMPERIAL ORDER

European expansion involved the disciplining of what Europeans perceived as an unruly, chaotic world. European sciences named, classified, and described lands and peoples, and through conquest Europeans exploited the abundance of those distant, largely tropical shores. They extracted precious metals using American Indian and African labor, exchanged that gold and silver to obtain Asian products, and deployed African, Asian, and Pacific Islander labor in the Indian, Atlantic, and Pacific worlds to farm vast plantations of spices, tea, sugar, and other tropical produce. Imposition of an imperial order enabled that systematic exploitation of the world, called the world-system, that led to European development and to the reciprocal underdevelopment of the rest of the world.

The initiatives begun by the Portuguese and Spaniards at the end of the fifteenth century in the Atlantic world were not trade in the usual sense. As Spain's viceroy in Peru observed in 1736, the colonial economy was not based on trade or exchange, because the colonizers held a monopoly over the forces of production and goods. Instead, he wrote candidly, the Spanish empire's extraction of America's wealth was an "inheritance." The English, Dutch, and French soon followed the Spanish example by establishing outposts along the coasts of Africa, America, and Asia to defend and advance their national interests. Their ships stopped at those ports to replenish their water and food supplies and also their crew, many of whom died from diseases or deserted. Powerful trade monopolies, like the English and Dutch East India companies, had private navies, armies, and bureaucrats, effectively imposing imperial order within their domains.

European nations staked out and claimed African, American, Asian, and Pacific Islander lands to profit the imperial powers, often claiming royal prerogatives. European expansionists required colonial settlers, like expeditions, to cover their own expenses and generate material returns. These were produced using coerced labor. By the eighteenth century, the rapacious Atlantic world encircled the entire globe in a world-system with Europe at the core.

Conquest was both ideological and material. The European taxonomies imposed on lands, peoples, plants, and animals served to discipline their subjects, which the colonizers saw as wild and unruly. Claiming to replace superstition with rational explanation, Europeans mapped, surveyed, and assigned natures to waters and lands, and they understood the life forms of those lands as determined by their geographies. They saw native peoples as undifferentiated inhabitants, like the plants and animals, of their environments. Such discourses served to justify the conquest and exploitation of the lands, their resources, and peoples as a divinely ordained dominion of superiors over inferiors.

The world-system's core, then, dispatched expeditions to plunder the wealth of the periphery. Ships conveyed slaves and products from Africa, America, and Asia to Europe, and colonial plantations were cultivated by workers, both enslaved and indentured, who were transported from Europe, Africa, and Asia. Factories in the core processed raw materials like silk, cotton, and sugar from the periphery, and they manufactured products to sell in the periphery, transforming Europe's economy from a mercantile or trade economy to one based on industries and manufacturing.

As in the urban and rural areas of Europe, discrete pockets of poverty and plenty prevailed in the periphery. Europe and industrial capitalism were in large part built on profits generated from the Asian traffic, from lands expropriated in Africa, America, and Asia, and from laborers coerced and transported to produce surplus value in factories in the field. Asians and Pacific Islanders arrived in America as commodities carried on the fierce winds of the imperialist world-system.

ASIANS AND PACIFIC ISLANDERS IN AMERICA

Scattered references to Asians in European documents offer hints of their early presence and activities in America. As early as 1635, Spanish barbers in Mexico City expressed their displeasure with the presence of Chinese competitors. They petitioned the viceroy to impose a limit of twelve Chinese barbers in the city and banish the rest to outside districts. Together with Chinese seamen, carpenters, metalsmiths, and merchants, the Chinese barbers had arrived in Mexico by way of the Manila galleon trade. They settled in Mexico City, married Mexican women, and took on Spanish names. The seaport of Acapulco, called the "city of the Chinese," also flourished and teemed with American Indians, Chinese, Filipinos, and mestizos. From New Spain, Filipinos and probably some Mexicans sailed into the Gulf of Mexico and fished Louisiana's southeastern coast as early as 1765, before the United States declared its independence from Britain. A Filipino or Chinese, Antonio Rodriguez, was among the Spanish founders of Los Angeles in 1781.

The expanding capitalist world-system induced labor migrations from places of underdevelopment in Africa and Asia not only to regions of surging industrial and agricultural activity in America but also to Europe and other European colonies. The transatlantic commerce of enslaved Africans grew from 275,000 sent to Europe and America between 1451 and 1600 to over 1 million in the seventeenth century and then to over 6 million the following century, due mainly to the boom in sugar and tobacco production in America's plantations.

Asian and Pacific Islander migration was characterized by indentured labor. European settlers in Mauritius in the Indian Ocean drew indentures from India, and by the end of the eighteenth century, South Asian workers, contracted for periods of two to three years, were present in most major ports throughout Southeast Asia. At the beginning of the nineteenth century, the end of the African slave trade led to a "new system of slavery," according to the British imperial historian Hugh Tinker, in which Asians and Pacific Islanders replaced enslaved Africans. South Asian indentures labored in cane fields in Fiji and South Africa; Chinese contract workers worked tropical plantations, South African mines, and guano deposits along Peru's coastal islands. Traffickers captured Melanesians and Polynesians and sold them to planters in Australia and Peru.

Labor recruiters procured Hawaiians to work in Peru, where many of them perished from diseases and unforgiving work conditions. Their recruitment in the early nineteenth century followed a practice begun decades earlier by ship captains who relied on Hawaiian sailing skills and labor. Among the first were Ka'iana, born of a chiefly line, and Winee, a woman, who sailed to China and the Philippines in 1787–88 on board the *Nootka,* under the command of John Meares. Winee died at sea, but Ka'iana continued across the Pacific with Meares. On his return voyage from China, about half of the crew on Meares's two ships were Chinese sailors who had helped steer his ships from China to the Philippines and then across the Pacific to the Aleutian Islands off Alaska and to Canada's Vancouver Island, where the Chinese built the first ship of European design on America's West Coast.

Between 1845 and 1847, nearly two thousand Hawaiians served on foreign ships, and by 1850 that total reached four thousand, or almost one-fifth of the Hawaiian kingdom's total population. By midcentury they were toiling on ships and on land from Tahiti and Peru to the south to the Pacific Northwest and Alaska to the north. Hawaiians served in the Mexican navy and worked on Russian holdings along the West Coast. To benefit from that labor migration and limit the loss, the kingdom imposed a poll tax on foreign employers of Hawaiians.

Hawaiians also sailed Oceania, forming the majority of the crews on U.S. ships on the West Coast by 1830, and they also traveled to the port cities on the Atlantic coast. "We have heard that there is no port in this ocean [the Pacific] untrodden by Hawaiians," declared the Hawaiian kingdom's minister of the interior in 1846, "and they are also in Nantucket, New Bedford, Sag Harbor, New London and other places in the United States."[2]

Wynee, a Native of Owyhee,
One of the Sandwich Islands.

Publish'd Aug.26 1790 by J.Walter N.169.Piccadilly.

FIGURE 4

Winee, from John Meares, *Voyages Made
in the Years 1788 and 1789, from China to
the North West Coast of America* (London:
Logographic Press, 1790). Courtesy of
Rare Book and Manuscript Library,
Columbia University.

When American Indian and African slavery was abolished in Peru in 1854, the nation's planters recruited Chinese laborers, and later, during a brief ban on Chinese indentured labor, they sent ships to capture Polynesian workers. The *Adelante*, with barred hatches and compartments and swivel guns to sweep the deck, returned to Callao, Peru, in 1862 with 253 Polynesian captives, whose sale reaped their owners a profit of $40,000, or a 400 percent return. Men sold for US$200 each, women $150, and children $100.

For those gains, Pacific Islanders were hunted down and captured, marched in chains to waiting ships, thrust into crowded, unsanitary ships' holds, and sold to the highest bidder. Along the way, many died from violence and introduced diseases, ranging from

FIGURE 5

Newly arrived coolies in Trinidad, 1897. Between 1838 and 1917, some 149,939 South Asian coolies were transported to this British colony.

24 percent of one island's total population to 79 percent of another's. Rapa Nui (Easter Island) had an estimated population of 4,126 in 1862, but it lost 1,386 to labor raids and about 1,000 to disease and thus suffered a 58 percent population decrease. Moreover, the island's social order was devastated by the loss of its leaders and of elders who were the repositories of history, law, and culture.

To fill their labor needs, British sugar planters in the Caribbean turned to British holdings in the Indian and Pacific oceans. In India, the system involved both British colonizers and South Asian accomplices. Agents, including Jews, Armenians, Indian Christians, and Eurasians, contracted recruiters to scour the Indian countryside in search of indentures. Working through local bosses or headmen, recruiters offered cash advances as enticements to recruits who were in debt or in trouble. As the British colonizers privatized land in India to encourage agricultural production for export, rural peasants were displaced, making them ideal hired hands and migrant workers. Over a million South Asians served on tropical plantations, and about half a million labored in America, where their descendants today make up significant proportions of the populations of Guyana, Trinidad, and Jamaica.

China, too, became a prime source for migrant labor, especially after its defeat by Britain in 1842 in the First Opium War and the subsequent treaty whereby Hong Kong became British until 1997. European entrepreneurs, working though Chinese brokers in Macao, Singapore, and Penang, tapped into China's pools of labor, which also included

Vietnamese and Filipinos. Village leaders identified recruits: some signed or were deceived into signing indenture contracts, which bound them to employers for a period of years, while others received credit for their transpacific passage from creditors who controlled their movements and the terms of employment. This human traffic was called "pig dealing" by the Chinese. Nearly all of those destined for America came from Guangdong Province, clustering around the British and Portuguese enclaves of Hong Kong and Macao. About 125,000 went to Cuba, 100,000 to Peru, 18,000 to the British West Indies, and the remainder to Panama and Costa Rica, the Dutch and French West Indies, Brazil, and Chile. An estimated 46,000 Chinese indentures went to Hawai'i, and, primarily via the credit ticket, some 200,000 made the passage to California.

Coolies were an invention of Europeans, beginning with the Portuguese, who used the term to mean "Asian laborer." By the nineteenth century the word generally connoted Indian or Chinese indentured workers bound for sugar plantations in America to replace enslaved Africans. In the sense that coolie labor replaced the labor of emancipated slaves, it signified freedom over bondage; yet the coolie trade, with its roots in slavery and its abuses, continued to be associated with slavery. Despite investigations, hearings, and regulations by the British government, the planters exercised harsh controls over the workers, and laws criminalized resistance by indentures as violations of civil contracts. The coolie trade itself involved kidnappings, debt servitude, ships outfitted as prisons, and rapes, floggings, and corporal punishment.

In the 1850s, one out of six South Asians bound for the Caribbean died before making landfall. Of the first group of 396 South Asian indentures taken to British Guiana in 1838, one-fourth failed to survive their five-year contract, and only sixty chose to remain in the colony. The overall mortality for Chinese indentures during the second half of the nineteenth century was between 12 and 30 percent, a rate higher than that of the Middle Passage of the African slave trade. In some cases it was as high as 50 percent. Conditions on board the ships and the length of the crossing—three to four months from India and four to eight months from China—might account for those staggering figures. And while nearly all of the Chinese were men, South Asian indentures included men, women, and children; women were more susceptible to rape and children to malnutrition and disease. Of the 324 South Asian coolies from Calcutta on board the *Salsette* bound for Trinidad in 1858, more than half died. According to court papers, a woman on a different ship died en route after having been gang-raped by the crew.

Yuan Guan, a Chinese coolie in Cuba, testified that he was kidnapped and taken to Macao in 1858. He was put on a ship with more than a hundred other captives on board and arrived in Havana in April 1859. About two months later he was sold to a white sugar-plantation owner who had sixty Chinese working for him. After the owner's death in 1864, the new managers and overseers were "as vicious as wolves and tigers," and their hearts were "like snakes," Yuan recalled. Because of the cruelty, Yuan reported, two Chinese committed suicide: Chen jumped into boiling sugar and died, and Lian hanged himself. Liu and several others died after having been beaten by overseers. In his testimony, Yuan detailed the conditions of coolie oppression and also named men who would have been otherwise lost to history.[3]

That act of remembering is one of the main purposes of this version of American history. While men like Henry "the Navigator" and Columbus "the Admiral" are routinely commemorated as shapers of world history, it was the so-called ordinary people, like Ka'iana, Winee, Yuan, Chen, Lian, and Liu, who supplied the labor that ultimately transformed the world. Their deeds, although small when considered individually, literally moved mountains when seen collectively. Agricultural workers produced the foods and commodities that enabled social aggregations and specializations. Enslaved American Indians and Africans and indentured Asians and Pacific Islanders built and sailed the transport ships that circled the globe. American Indian, African, Asian, and Pacific Islander laborers extracted from the earth precious metals, as well as crops such as sugar, cotton, tobacco, and coffee, that changed the course of human history.

The world-system was created by European demand for the commodities and wealth of Asia. Resource extraction in the peripheries enriched the core and impoverished the colonies. The expropriation of land and resources in the colonies alienated and displaced peasants, compelling them to seek industrial employment. Factories hummed in the urban centers of Europe and later the United States, while in the periphery, mines, plantations, and fisheries supplied raw materials for the core's industries and markets. The expansion of capitalism and its discourses of imperial order led to the entry of Asians and Pacific Islanders into the United States.

SUGGESTED READINGS

Look Lai, Walton. *Indentured Labor, Caribbean Sugar: Chinese and Indian Migrants to the British West Indies, 1838–1918*. Baltimore: Johns Hopkins University Press, 1993.

Mintz, Sidney W. *Sweetness and Power: The Place of Sugar in Modern History*. New York: Penguin Books, 1985.

Yun, Lisa. *The Coolie Speaks: Chinese Indentured Laborers and African Slaves of Cuba*. Philadelphia: Temple University Press, 2008.

PRIMARY DOCUMENT
DOCUMENT 3

John Cummins, *The Voyage of Christopher Columbus: Columbus' Own Journal of Discovery, Newly Restored and Translated* (New York: St. Martin's Press, 1992), passim.

In his daily journal, Christopher Columbus describes his first landfall in America in 1492. His impressions of the islands and peoples reflect his belief that he had indeed found Asia. Not only would his "discovery" bring untold wealth to Spain and Europe, Columbus predicted, but it would also free Christianity from the commercial stranglehold of Muslims and eventually liberate Jerusalem and the Holy Land from the "infidels." Through eyes trained by European images of Asia, the admiral describes the new lands as green, lush, and flowing with abundant streams, and the people as peaceful and ready for conversion to the Christian faith through reason and not coercion. Still, Columbus takes Indian "prisoners" with him to serve as guides and specimens for his royal patrons. He is single-minded in his search for gold. When he arrives on the island of Cuba, he thinks he has reached Japan (Cipangu), the fabled land of gold and spices. Besides landing in Paradise, Columbus expects to encounter monstrous humans and perversions of nature, such as the Amazons, warrior women who had little need of men.

Such was his conviction that throughout his four voyages to America (1492–93, 1493–96, 1498–1500, and 1502–4), the admiral insisted that the lands of his "discovery" were abundant and rich and their peoples cowardly "savages." In a letter dated July 7, 1503, to Ferdinand and Isabella, Columbus defended his views: "When I discovered the Indies, I said they were the world's wealthiest realm. I spoke of gold, pearls, precious stones, spices and of the markets and fairs. But, because not everything turned up at once, I was vilified. These reproaches constrain me now to say nothing but what I hear from the natives of the country. One thing I dare say, since there are so many witnesses, is that in this land of Veragua I saw more signs of gold in my first two days, than in Hispaniola in four years; and that the lands of this region could not be more beautiful or better cultivated, or the people more cowardly. Moreover, there is a fine harbor and a beautiful river. . . . All this means security for the Christians, certainty of dominion, and splendid prospects for the glory and increase of the Christian religion."[4]

Wednesday, 10 October. Sailed WSW at about eight knots, sometimes up to nine and a half, occasionally only five and a half. Sixty-two and a half leagues in the twenty-four hours; I told the men only forty-six and a half. They could contain themselves no longer, and began to complain of the length of the voyage. I encouraged them as best I could, trying to raise their hopes of the benefits they might gain from it. I also told them that it was useless to complain; having set out for the Indies I shall continue this voyage until, with God's grace, I reach them.

Thursday, 11 October. Course WSW. A heavy sea, the roughest in the whole voyage so far. We saw petrels, and a green reed close to the ship, /and then a big green fish of a kind which does not stray far from the shoals./ On the Pinta they saw a cane and a stick, and they picked up another little piece of wood which seemed to have been worked with an iron tool; also a piece of cane and another plant which grows on land, and a little board. On the Niña too they saw signs of land, and /a thorn-branch laden with red fruits, apparently newly cut./ We were all filled with joy and relief at these signs. Sailed twenty-eight and a half leagues before sunset. After sunset I resumed our original course westward, sailing at about nine knots. By two o'clock in the morning we had sailed about sixty-eight miles, or twenty-two and a half leagues.

When everyone aboard was together for the *Salve Regina*, which all seamen say or sing in their fashion, /I talked to the men about the grace which God had shown us by bringing us in safety, with fair winds and no obstacles, and by comforting us with signs which were more plentiful every day. I urged them to keep a good watch and reminded them that in the first article of the sailing instructions issued to each ship in the Canaries I gave orders not to sail at night after we had reached a point seven hundred leagues from there; I was sailing on because of everyone's great desire to sight land./ I warned them to keep a good lookout in the bows and told them that I would give a silk doublet to the man who first sighted land, as well as the prize of 10,000 *maravedis* promised by Your Majesties.

I was on the poop deck at ten o'clock in the evening when I saw a light. It was so indistinct that I could not be sure it was land. . . . After I had told them, the light appeared once or twice more, like a wax candle rising and falling. Only a few people thought it was a sign of land, but I was sure we were close to a landfall.

Then the Pinta, being faster and in the lead, sighted land and made the signal as I had ordered. The first man to sight land was called Rodrigo de Triana. The land appeared two hours after midnight, about two leagues away. We furled all sail except the *treo*, the mainsail with no bonnets, and jogged off and on until Friday morning, when we came to an island. We saw naked people, and I went ashore in a boat with armed men. . . . I took the royal standard, and the captains each took a banner with the Green Cross which each of my ships carries as a device, with the letters F and Y, surmounted by a crown, at each end of the cross.

When we stepped ashore we saw fine green trees, streams everywhere and different kinds of fruit. I called to the two captains to jump ashore with the rest . . . , asking them to bear solemn witness that in the presence of them all I was taking possession of this island for their Lord and Lady the King and Queen, and I made the necessary declarations which are set down at greater length in the written testimonies.

Soon many of the islanders gathered round us. I could see that they were people who would be more easily converted to our Holy Faith by love than by coercion, and wishing them to look on us with friendship I gave some of them red bonnets and glass beads which they hung round their necks, and many other things of small value, at which they were so delighted and so eager to please us that we could not believe it. Later they swam out to the boats to bring us parrots and balls of cotton thread and darts, and many other things, exchanging them for such objects as glass beads and hawk bells. They took anything, and gave willingly whatever they had.

However, they appeared to me to be a very poor people in all respects. They go about naked as the day they were born, even the women, though I saw only one, who was quite young. All the men I saw were quite young, none older than thirty, all well built, finely bodied and handsome in the face. Their hair is coarse, almost like a horse's tail, and short; they wear it short, cut over the brow, except a few strands of hair hanging down uncut at the back. . . .

They are all the same size, of good stature, dignified and well formed. I saw some with scars on their bodies, and made signs to ask about them, and they indicated to me that people from other islands nearby came to capture them and they defended themselves. I thought, and still think, that people from the mainland come here to take them prisoner. They must be good servants, and intelligent, for I can see that they quickly repeat everything said to them. I believe they would readily become Christians; it appeared to me that they have no religion. With God's will, I will take six of them with me for Your Majesties when I leave this place, so that they may learn Spanish.

I saw no animals on the island, only parrots.

Saturday, 13 October. In the early morning many of the islanders came to the beach, all young, as I have said, tall and handsome, their hair not curly, but flowing and thick, like horsehair. . . . They brought us balls of cotton thread and parrots and darts and other little things which it would be tedious to list, and exchanged everything for whatever we offered them.

I kept my eyes open and tried to find out if there was any gold, and I saw that some of them had a little piece hanging from a hole in their nose. I gathered from their signs that if one goes south, or around the south side of the island, there is a king with great jars full of it, enormous amounts. I tried to persuade them to go there, but I saw that the idea was not to their liking.

I decided to wait until tomorrow and then to set off to the southwest, for many of them seemed to be saying that there is land to the S and SW and NW, and that the people from the NW often come to attack them, and continue to the SW in search of gold and precious stones. This island is large and very flat, with green trees and plenty of water, there is a large lake in the middle, no mountains, and everything is green and a delight to the eye. The people are very gentle.

Monday, 15 October. Last night I lay to for fear of approaching land. . . .

From this island I sighted another larger one to the west. . . . I anchored off the western cape just before sunset to find out if there was any gold there. The prisoners I took on San Salvador kept telling me that the people of this island wore great gold bracelets and legbands, but I thought it was all invention to enable them to escape. However, my intention being not to pass by any island without taking possession of it.

The islands are very green and lush, with sweet breezes, and there may be many things here which I do not know about, because rather than lingering I wish to explore and investigate many islands in search of gold. As these people tell me by signs that the folk wear it on their arms and legs—and it is gold they mean, for I showed them some pieces of my own—with God's help I cannot fail to find the source of it.

Tuesday, 16 October. I left the islands of Santa María de la Concepción about noon for the island of Fernandina to the west. . . .

The island is very large. I determined to sail all round it, for as far as I understand there is a gold mine either in or near it.

Sunday, 21 October. I reached this headland of the islet at ten o'clock and dropped anchor. . . .

I should like to fill all our water containers while we are here, and then, if I have time, I shall set off to sail round this island until I find and talk to the king, and see if I may obtain from him some of the gold which I am told he wears. Then I shall set off for another, very large island which I think must be Cipango, judging by the indications given me by these Indians I have on board. . . . From there I shall go to another island called Bohío, also very large, according to them. The ones in between I shall observe in passing, and depending on what store of gold or spices I find I shall decide what to do. But I am still determined to continue to the mainland, to the city of Quinsay, and to give Your Majesties' letters to the Great Khan and return with his reply.

Monday, 22 October. I have been waiting all last night and today to see if the king of this place or anyone else would bring me gold, or any other thing of importance. Many of the people have come, naked like those of the other island and painted in the same fashion, some white, some red, some black, in many different ways. They brought spears and some balls of cotton to barter with, and exchanged them with some of the crew for bits of glass, broken cups and pieces of earthenware dishes. Some of them were wearing little pieces of gold hanging from their noses.

Tuesday, 23 October. I should like to sail today for the island of Cuba, which I believe to be Cipango from the description these people give me of its size and riches. . . .

It is only sensible to go where there is good potential for trade. To my mind there is no point in lingering when one can set off and explore a large area until one finds a country which offers profit.

Wednesday, 24 October. At midnight last night I weighed anchor from where I was lying . . . and set sail for Cuba, which these people have told me is very large and busy, with gold and spices, and large ships and merchants. . . . I believe it to be the island of Cipango, of which such wonders are told, and which lies in this region on the globes and the maps of the world which I have seen.

Sunday, 28 October. I sailed SSW for the nearest point of the island of Cuba. . . .

I never saw a lovelier sight: trees everywhere, lining the river, green and beautiful. They are not like our own, and each has its own flowers and fruit. Numerous birds, large and small, singing away sweetly. There are large numbers of palm trees. . . . The land is very level. . . .

The Indians tell me that there are gold mines and pearls on this island. . . . I understand that large vessels belonging to the Great Khan come here, and that the passage to the mainland takes ten days.

Sunday, 4 November. Immediately after daybreak I went ashore in the boat to catch some of the birds I saw yesterday. . . .

I also showed them gold and pearls, and some of the old ones told me that in a place called Bohío there are endless quantities of gold. . . . I also understood them to say that there are large ships and a trade in goods, all to the SE, and that a long way away there are men with one eye, and others with noses like dogs who eat human flesh; when they capture someone they cut his throat and drink his blood and cut off his private parts . . .

The people here are very timid and gentle, naked as I have described, with no weapons and no religion. The land is very rich, and is planted up with *niames,* which are like carrots and taste of chestnuts, and they also have various kinds of beans, quite different from our own, and plenty of cotton, not sown but growing wild. I think it must be there for the picking all the time. . . . There are hundreds of other kinds of fruit, more than I can describe, and it must all be useful.

Monday, 12 November. At the end of the dawn watch we left the harbour of the river Mares to sail to an island which the Indians on board have told me is called Babeque, where according to their signs the people gather gold on the beach at night with torches and then beat it into bars with a hammer. . . .

Your Majesties should therefore determine to convert them to Christianity, for I believe that once this is begun a host of peoples will soon be converted to our Holy Faith, and great domains and their wealth and all their peoples will be won for Spain, for there is no doubt that these lands hold enormous quantities of gold. Not for nothing do the Indians I have on board tell us that there are places on these islands where they dig up the gold and wear it in their ears and round their necks and arms and legs, thick bands of it, and there are also precious stones and pearls and endless spices. . . .

One could also obtain great quantities of cotton, which I think could very well be sold here (rather than taking it to Spain) in the cities of the Great Khan. . . .

Moreover, the mouth of the river I have described is the finest harbour I ever saw, broad and deep and clean-bottomed, with a good location and site for building a town and a fortress where ships of all kinds could berth alongside the walls, and the land is high and temperate, and good fresh water.

Sunday, 6 January [1493]. I have learned that beyond the island of Juana, to the south, there is another large island which has far more gold than there is here, and they gather lumps of gold bigger than beans, whereas on Española the mines produce pieces only as big as grains of wheat. Its name is Yamaye. To the eastward there is an island inhabited solely by women; I have heard this from many people.

[*Columbus returned to Europe, first landing in Portugal on March 4, 1493.*]

Wednesday, 6 March. When it became known that I had been to the Indies an astonishing number of people came from the city of Lisbon to see me and to look at the Indians, all expressing amazement and praising God.

SIGNIFICANT EVENTS

4000 B.C.	Egyptian civilization
3000 B.C.	Indian civilization
2000 B.C.	Chinese civilization
A.D. 7th century	Islam
711	Africans bring Islam to Iberian Peninsula
1450	Portuguese convey enslaved Africans to Europe and Atlantic islands
1492	fall of Granada
	Columbus "discovers" America
1494	Treaty of Tordesillas divides the world between Spain and Portugal
1498	Vasco da Gama reaches India
16th century	Asian and African slaves serve on European ships in the Indian Ocean
1511	Portugal takes Malacca
1521	Hernán Cortés and Indian allies conquer Montezuma's Tenochtitlán
	Ferdinand Magellan names the Philippines
1533	Francisco Pizarro captures Cuzco, the Inca capital
1565	Filipinos, Chinese, and Asian mestizos settle in New Spain
	Spaniards rule Guam from New Spain
1600	British East India Company formed
1602	Dutch East India Company formed
1635	Chinese barbers in Mexico City
1760s	Filipino "Manilamen" settle near New Orleans
1781	Antonio Rodriguez in Los Angeles
1787	Winee and Kaʻiana sail for Asia

19th century	Polynesians captured and enslaved
	Chinese and South Asian coolie trade
1810–21	Mexican War of Independence
1815	end of Manila galleon trade
1838	South Asian indentures arrive in British Guiana
1839	First Opium War begins
1842	Britain defeats China in the First Opium War
	Treaty of Nanjing legalizes coolie traffic
1854	slavery abolished in Peru
1859	Yuan Guan in Cuba

3

THE UNITED STATES

America, "discovered" and named by Spaniards on their way to Asia, gave rise to these United States. The nation emerged from the imperialist world-system, beginning as a plantation colony on the European periphery. But like many other settler colonies the world over, the colony rose up in rebellion against its masters, gained its independence, and became a core nation itself through its concentration of capital, deployment of labor, and imperial powers.

Long before English settlers first established a beachhead on Virginia's shore—the prelude for the creation of the United States—America was principally a Spanish domain. Columbus, who died in 1506, failed to find the fortunes of Asia, but Spanish explorers who came after him found riches in America that facilitated Spain's traffic with Asia. Hernán Cortés plundered the treasury of the Aztecs of Mexico, while Francisco Pizarro similarly robbed the Incas of Peru. Tenochtitlán (Mexico City), the Aztec capital, fell to Cortés in 1521 after a devastating smallpox epidemic a year earlier, and from there he extended his rule southward over the Mayan people of Yucatán and Central America. Pizarro captured Cuzco, the Inca capital, in 1533, after smallpox weakened the empire, and from there pursued the seams of precious metals to other Inca cities.

Spurred on by the millions of pounds of gold and silver dug from mines in Mexico, Peru, Colombia, and Bolivia by enslaved Indians and Africans during the sixteenth century, Spanish expeditions invaded Indian lands to the north—the areas that became California, Arizona, New Mexico, and Texas—and on the east coast from Florida up to North Carolina. They cut paths of destruction in their greed for the fabled cities of gold.

Their introduction of horses, cattle, and sheep transformed a host of indigenous societies. The Spaniards also brought and spread diseases, devastating Indian nations and rendering them vulnerable to conquest and colonization. Spanish colonizers, including Indians and Africans as well as their mixtures—mestizos and mulattos—occupied the region that would later become the U.S. Southwest. Through the agency of colonization, which strove to supplant American Indian sovereignty and self-determination, they imposed on the indigenous peoples foreign religions, not only Catholicism but also Judaism; an alien tongue, Spanish; and Spanish architecture. A disparate and diverse collection of lands and peoples were collapsed under the colonial name of New Spain, and then, after 1821, under the name of the independent nation of Mexico. Parts of those lands would in turn fall to the United States, thereby becoming "American."

Yet the Spanish conquest of America was hampered by American Indian resistance. A notable example was the Pueblo Indian revolt of 1680, led by a religious healer, Popé, from San Juan Pueblo, in the area now known as New Mexico. The Pueblos endured an onerous tax on their labor, but when Franciscan priests also tried to destroy their religion by confiscating and destroying religious sites (kivas), masks, and prayer sticks and banning sacred dances, about two dozen Pueblo villages rose up in rebellion. They burned Spanish ranches, government buildings, and churches and killed settlers, soldiers, and priests, driving the invaders back toward Mexico. It took the Spaniards over a decade to return and reestablish their rule in colonial New Mexico.

New Spain figured prominently in the Manila galleon trade, which transported precious metals and furs—especially sea otter pelts obtained by California Indians—from the Pacific coast to the Philippines. There they were traded for Asian spices, silks, ceramics, and furniture, which were carried back to New Spain and Europe, along with American gold and silver, lumber, and crops such as corn (maize), beans, cacao, tobacco, and pineapples. The ships then returned to America laden with Spanish settlers, African slaves, and market plants from Europe, Africa, and Asia: sugarcane, coffee, wheat, and bananas. Those exchanges of peoples and products—and accompanying diseases—led to significant changes in both the Atlantic world and the Pacific world.

ENGLISH AMERICA

During the sixteenth century, the English, Dutch, French, and other Europeans poached in waters formerly held exclusively by Spain and Portugal. They, like the Spanish before them, searched in vain for a maritime route to Asia through America's landmass, and in the process they charted the waters, lands, resources, and peoples along America's Atlantic coastline, which was eventually settled by the English and French. After the defeat of Spain's Armada off its coast in 1588, Protestant England looked westward for an opportunity to ransack the New World at the expense of its Catholic Iberian rivals. English nobles sought to expand their estates on America's "free" land, while merchants saw the potential for abundant resources and new markets. The English failed in their first attempts to establish colonies in Newfoundland, North Carolina, Guiana, and Maine, and even their eventual success at Jamestown in 1607 and Plymouth in 1620 entailed great struggles.

Unlike like their government-backed Spanish and Portuguese counterparts, the English colonies were projects of companies funded by private investors. The London Company, chartered by King James I, established Jamestown in the region called Virginia in 1607. In order to turn a profit on its initial investment, the company directed its colonists to find gold, trade with Indians for skins and furs, and find a route to Asia. According to John Smith, who emerged as the colony's leader, the religious conversion of the native peoples was simply a covering motive for the colony "when all their aim was profit."[1] Despite its objective, the colony floundered even as the London investors poured more money and settlers into the venture.

After tobacco, procured from Indians and shipped to Europe, addicted a generation of European men, its successful cultivation for a time helped to stabilize the financial life of the Jamestown colony. By 1624, the colony had exported two hundred thousand pounds of what was described variously as the "jovial" or the "vile and stinking" weed.

The tobacco plantations required a large pool of laborers, obtained mainly as indentured servants. English indentures, both men and women, were bought and sold, and they were subjected to harsh masters and abuse. Rape was commonplace, and the Jamestown courts routinely deprived mothers of their illegitimate children and fined them severely for lost days of work during pregnancy and childbirth. Reproduction for women of that class was a matter of the master's property and labor rights. Indenture, unlike slavery, was for a limited time, although few indentures actually gained their freedom to become landowners. Most succumbed to diseases or the physical privations of work and punishment.

Africans, familiar as enslaved and bound laborers in the Mediterranean and Atlantic worlds, first arrived in the colony on a Dutch ship in 1619 to serve alongside English indentures in Virginia's tobacco plantations. For over fifty years, English servants outnumbered Africans by three to one: Africans totaled only three thousand in Virginia, although about thirty thousand toiled on sugar plantations in English Barbados. Although the Virginia planters preferred indentures to slaves, by the 1670s the supply of laborers from England had diminished and grown expensive, while the flow of workers from Africa became larger and cheaper. That shift, along with the rising demand for laborers in the tobacco fields, helped to fortify the related ideas of English freedom and African bondage.

The "free" land of America was, in fact, purchased by blood. Tobacco quickly depleted the soil and thus required continuous expansion of cultivated lands. That process came at the expense of American Indians, who resisted the invasion. Even the temporary truce gained through the marriage of Chief Powhatan's kidnapped and Christianized daughter, Pocahontas, to the settler John Rolfe in 1614 failed to quell the fires of armed resistance. As Powhatan, the leader of the confederation that opposed the foreigners, pointedly told

FIGURE 6

English artist's representation of Matoaka (Pocahontas), the Powhatan Pamunkey Indian captured by Jamestown settlers in 1613. Four years later, she died in England at the age of twenty-one or twenty-two.

Ætatis suæ 21. A°.1616.

John Smith, the Europeans had come not for trade but to expel his people from their land and take possession of Indian country. Some twenty thousand Powhatan Indians struck back at the colonists in 1622 when the English murdered Nemattanew, a Powhatan military and religious leader. They dealt the colony a severe blow, killing more than a quarter of the population, including John Rolfe. The settlers retaliated, continuing to see the Indians merely as obstacles to their acquisition of land and resources.

Like Virginia, the English colony at Plymouth, Massachusetts, was a business investment. The Massachusetts Bay Company, controlled by Puritans, set out to establish "a city upon a hill," in the words of the expedition's leader, John Winthrop, to show the watching world the rectitude of their mission and calling. That 1630 proclamation would resonate throughout the nation's history. But the Plymouth plantation, settled by the Puritan Pilgrims ten years earlier and financed by the London Company, was no utopia. The colony denied the rights and even the humanity of the original inhabitants, declaring them to be "savages" and threats to the well-being of the Plymouth community. With that in mind, Winthrop armed and trained male colonists, and the colony's laws punished Europeans who sold guns to Indians and prohibited Indians' entry into Puritan towns.

Introduced diseases decimated Indian nations, and settler encroachments on their lands provoked resistance. Using superior arms, the invaders prevailed, as in the 1637 war with the Pequots. Enabling the city upon a hill to shine as a beacon to a decadent world required conquest, removal, and land alienation.

Racial segregation began in English America when the English colonizers installed a divide, ideological and physical, between themselves and the indigenous peoples. The Proclamation of 1763 established on a larger geographical scale what individual colonies had already delineated: a border that separated settlers from Indians. Drawn by lawmakers in London to roughly follow the Appalachian mountain range, the proclamation declared the lands to the east as English and those to the west as Indian. Although unenforceable, the divide, like the line drawn by the Treaty of Tordesillas, was an expression of power over place. Within the English domain, it conferred legitimacy and the rule of law.

SOCIAL FORMATION

The discourses of purity and impurity, civilization and savagery, Christian and heathen, citizen and alien, along with the material conditions of life and livelihood—the plantations of the New World—did not merely reflect the emerging world-system; they also produced a nation, the United States. Understood as a social formation, the United States is a creation of land and labor. Its ideologies and apparatuses, such as laws and institutions, serve to preserve and advance the enterprise. Crucial to that order are the binaries (and hence hierarchies) of race, gender, and sexuality. These, like the inventions of Europe and Asia, are theoretical constructs, but they have material consequences when people enact them.

The laws of Virginia Colony illustrate how the apparatuses of the state produced subjects, social categories, and relations. In the service of upholding the colonists' claims to land and labor, those laws defined whites and blacks, men and women, the normative heterosexual family, classes of workers, and the citizen. The creation of those categories, based on the means and relations of production, reveals the workings of power and constitutes the social formation.

Antonio, an enslaved African, arrived in Virginia Colony in 1621, shortly after the first Africans landed. There he worked on a tobacco plantation along the James River, and about a year later he was among the five survivors of the fifty-seven occupants of the Bennett plantation after a Powhatan Indian attack. Over the next twenty years, Antonio became Anthony Johnson; married an enslaved African woman, Mary; and became the father of four children. Anthony and Mary Johnson gained their freedom during the 1640s and farmed some 250 acres on the colony's eastern shore. They kept cattle and had two African servants. But after Anthony's death in 1669, a settler jury of white men ruled that because he "was a Negroe and by consequence an alien," his son could not inherit his land.[2] Instead, the jury awarded the property to a white settler. In this court ruling, which gave substance to the social formation and subjectivities of that time and place, issues of race, citizenship, and property rights intersected: the categories of white, citizen, and propertied formed polar but mutually constituting opposites with the categories of black, alien, and without property.

In the same vein, a 1639 statute directed the Virginia governor to provide guns and ammunition to "all persons except Negroes," indicating that Virginia excluded African Americans from the prerogatives and responsibilities of men and citizens. Arms enabled men to protect and provide for their dependents and were instruments of war against Indians. Citizens were responsible for the creation and defense of the colony. Without arms, African Americans were thus incapable of acting as men or citizens. The 1639 act was the first law in the English colonies to identify a racialized group in order to deprive it of rights.

As Virginia relied increasingly on tobacco cultivation, which required large tracts of land and pools of labor, its laws produced a class of African laborers. Beginning in 1643, a head tax on all African women was instituted to coax their masters (whether owners or husbands) to send them to work outside the home. English women were expected, as wives or future wives, to serve within the home. The law defined and preserved the heterosexual white family and maximized the utility of the working class by dividing it by race and gender.

In 1662, the colony ruled that children of African women inherited the status and condition of their mother, not their father as was usual under English law. That ruling aimed to increase the labor force by decreeing that these children were born into slavery and to absolve European men of responsibility for rape of or intercourse with African women. Moreover, through the devices of blood and inheritance, the 1662 statute naturalized a racialized class position—the condition of bondage—and moved the idea of race toward the one-drop rule for Africans and alleged purity for Europeans. Thus race, gender, and sexuality intersected in this statute to create a subordinate class of workers.

By the 1670s, the colony had imposed a comprehensive tax on all European males above the age of sixteen, along with African men and women and Indian women, who, like African women earlier, were drawn into the class of laborers. The tax on European men hints at an unemployed class that required incentives to work. Laws thereby helped to regulate labor, the working class, by establishing and differentiating within categories of race, gender, and sexuality.

For several months in 1675 and 1676, Nathaniel Bacon mobilized colonists in Virginia who were discontented with declining tobacco prices, a perceived need for more land, anxieties over manhood and property, and additional restrictions on slaves and servants. He created a coalition and then a rebellion united in a hatred of Indians and a desire for more land and the restoration of patriarchal honor and rights. The force of four hundred armed men—English and African, landowners, servants, and slaves—pressed Virginia's governor from Jamestown to the sea, whence he sailed for England and returned with reinforcements.

The revolt was suppressed by English troops after Bacon died from dysentery in October 1676, but the movement's goals of property and rights prevailed for the privileged class. Land, the colony's rulers declared, was a right of white men, or citizens, and not of Africans or Indians, who were nonwhites and "aliens." As the dependents of white men, white women belonged to their husbands and fathers. Although men had joined Bacon's rebellion without regard to racial and class lines, the divide between white and black subsequently grew as a result of a strategy pursued by the colony's governors. As the seventeenth century progressed, what had been an amorphous set of beliefs about race, gender, sexuality, and citizenship cohered and took legal and institutional form. The social formation comprising white supremacy, patriarchy, the normative heterosexual family, enslaved African labor, and racialized citizenship prevailed in Virginia Colony as legacies of Bacon's rebellion.

In 1705, Virginia's colonizers determined that Indians and Africans, not being Christians, were "incapable in law." They thus excluded them from the courts to testify for or against Englishmen or citizens. The category *Christians* was equated with *white* despite the fact that Africans and Indians could and did convert to Christianity. This racialization of religion and citizenship continued, as we will see, in nineteenth-century California, when Asians, specifically the "heathen" Chinese, were similarly barred from testifying for or against a white man or a "citizen."

In the postcolonial United States, Virginia's precedents of Indian land alienation and deployment of Indian, African, and women's labor influenced the processes of incorporation of those rendered "white" and the exclusion of others, including Asians and Pacific Islanders. These events and practices are as relevant to this Asian and Pacific Islander history as Europe's search for and representations of Asia and the Pacific. They gave rise to the U.S. social formation, in which power is located and articulated around the axes of race, gender, sexuality, class, and nation.

REBELLION

Systematic regulation by England of its colonies worldwide, which began as private businesses, gained impetus in England during the seventeenth century with the realization that profits and prestige could accrue to the nation through the creation of an empire, as Spain and Portugal had demonstrated. In the imperialist view, colonies produced raw materials for the homeland while providing markets for domestic manufactures. Monopolies and taxation controlled the flows of goods. However, the extractive nature of that system impoverished the peripheries, which existed only to profit the metropole. This produced a tension in the relations between the colonial power and its settlers, who chafed at their exploitation and the circumscribing of their liberties. The situation was ripe for rebellion.

It is true that settlers derived some benefits from being within the empire: military protection and political stability. Moreover, areas unregulated by imperial troops provided opportunities for private gain. Membership in a global imperial community also had its ideological and material privileges. But by the 1760s, changes in local and global

FIGURE 7
Depiction of the Boston Tea Party. Playing Indian to dump tea from India.

conditions conspired to sever the ties of empire. The wars that England waged to protect and enlarge its empire saddled the nation with an enormous debt, which it tried to shift to its dependencies. To some who shouldered this burden, those exactions smacked of tyranny.

The British East India Company and its trade monopoly with Asia helped to fan the flames of discontent. In 1773, when Parliament passed the Tea Act, the company was on the verge of bankruptcy. The act allowed the dumping of the company's huge surplus of tea on the colonies tax-free, bypassing middlemen and their commissions. Enraged colonial merchants, denied their middlemen profits, feared the loss of their livelihoods at the hands of a powerful monopoly, and a protest against taxation without representation gained wide popular appeal. The tea trade involved nearly everyone across the colonies as merchants and consumers, and the calls for a tea boycott mobilized large segments of the population. White women were key figures in that movement.

In December 1773, the Boston Tea Party, involving white men dressed as Mohawks, staged a spectacle of revolution that riveted a large, surging crowd along the harbor. (The Mohawks themselves actually sided with the British in the war that followed.) The white actors in redface assumed the subjectivities of native Americans, as if to cement their claims to the land, while the object of their wrath (as well as their desire) was tea from the Asian trade. Those claims to land and capital, invoking the symbolic figures of American Indians and Asians, were necessary conditions for the rebellion and subsequent independence.

Although the rhetoric of the Revolutionary War (1775–83) foregrounded "universal" rights to "life, liberty, and the pursuit of happiness," it was a settlers' war, involving

British and European settlers who sought independence from their colonial overlords. The war failed to bestow those prized universal freedoms on the American Indians and African Americans who fought on the revolutionary side. After the British signed the treaty of capitulation with the Americans in Paris on September 3, 1783, the new nation established itself as a sovereign state with rights to land—at the expense of American Indians—and the right to delimit its citizens to "free white persons"—excluding American Indians, African Americans, and peoples of color.

SOVEREIGNTY

The new nation declared its independence on July 4, 1776, and promptly sought its destiny not only in westward conquests across the continent but also in Asia, following in the footsteps of Spain, Portugal, and the British East India Company. Both moves were crucially related to the constitution of national sovereignty, which involves lands, peoples, and political and economic autonomy.

One of the first acts of the fledgling state was to claim and parcel the lands west of the Appalachians, a border drawn by the British in 1763. The lands between that 1763 line and the Mississippi River had been claimed by several states, including Massachusetts, Connecticut, New York, and Virginia, without regard to the presence of the American Indians who lived there. During the 1780s, those states ceded their claims to the Confederation. In a series of ordinances passed in 1784 and 1785, the Confederation carved out districts and townships and made provisions for land purchases that favored speculators and large land holdings in what became the nation's Northwest Territory.

Congress tried to coerce Indian nations to surrender their lands in the Northwest Territory through treaties, but they largely resisted those pressures. Little Turtle led the Miami confederacy of Indian nations in securing their homeland against white invaders in the area that became Ohio and Indiana, and he defeated them at the Wabash River in 1791. Three years later, the Miami capitulated to the U.S. Army. While losing much of their land, the Miami Indians gained U.S. recognition of their sovereignty within their remaining territories. The 1795 Treaty of Greenville was the first acknowledgment of Indian sovereignty by the United States.

The new nation's thrust toward Asia began nearly at its inception. About a year after the Treaty of Paris ended the Revolutionary War, the *Empress of China* slipped out of New York's harbor for Canton, laden with 57,687 pounds of ginseng, a root known to Iroquois Indians as a medicine that grew in profusion from the Adirondacks to the Appalachians. The venture was financed by Robert Morris of Philadelphia, one of the most important patrons of the American Revolution; Daniel Parker, a merchant from New York; and others, including a Caribbean plantation owner who had served the British in colonial India.

The *Empress* set out expressly in quest of China's tea. Sailing on February 22, 1784, in the midst of winter, the *Empress* was commanded by John Green and carried his son, crew, and a commercial agent named Samuel Shaw, who wrote in his journal that

Americans "must have tea" and predicted that its consumption would increase with the rising population. The ship returned on May 11, 1785, carrying black and green tea, chinaware, and silks. In Canton, Samuel Shaw had arranged to have a Chinese artist paint on chinaware the eagle of the Order of Cincinnati, an elite society of French and U.S. officers who had served in the Revolutionary War and of which Shaw was the secretary. George Washington, the president of the order, bought a set of the Shaw-designed china with the eagle, called Cincinnati china. For about a hundred years, the patriotic eagle design on Chinese porcelain remained popular in the U.S. market.

When Robert Morris and his partners first conceived of their tea business, they thought grandly of forming an American India Company to rival the great English and Dutch monopolies. They had to scale back their ambition when the *Empress of China* returned with only a modest profit of 25 to 30 percent on their initial investment. Nevertheless, the *Empress* inaugurated the infant nation's trade with Asia, which was dominated at the time by Europe's leading empires.

Like driftwood, Asians made landfall in America on board U.S. and British trade ships. A few months after the *Empress* returned from China, another U.S. ship, the *Pallas,* docked in Baltimore with a crew of, according to one account, "Chinese, Malays, Japanese and Moors, with a few Europeans." A contemporary wrote to George Washington that the crew were "all Natives of India" and added that there were four Chinese on board, whose hair, color, and features reminded him of American Indians.

South Asians with new, English names—like John Ballay, Joseph Green, George Jimor, and Thomas Robinson—arrived in Boston, Salem, and Philadelphia in the 1790s. Some served their indentures; others were sold and bought as slaves. On attaining their freedom, the men perhaps married African American women and became members of the North's free black communities. We know of James Dunn, from India, because he filed a petition with the Pennsylvania Abolition Society around the 1790s, appealing for help in securing his freedom. Indentured to an English sailor in Calcutta when he was eight years old, Dunn was passed on to other owners until he found himself in Georgia. His owners considered him to be a slave, despite his protests that he had served the period of his indenture; the historical record of his story ends with his appeal, leaving us to guess at the outcome.

Meanwhile, U.S. merchants plied their prosperous trade. In 1797, the *Betsy* returned from China with a cargo that yielded $120,000 in profits. By the 1830s, the U.S. trade with China totaled nearly $75 million, a sum greater than the total debt of the American Revolution. Individual and family fortunes, like those of the Cushing, Forbes, and Perkins families, were made in the trade. Augustine Heard of Ipswich, Massachusetts, built on his father's business, trading New England lumber and fish for West Indian sugar, molasses, coffee, and other tropical products—a practice common in the eighteenth century. The molasses was distilled and sold as rum; it was also used to brew stout and ale. The son extended his father's business dealings in the Caribbean to India and China during the first half of the nineteenth century. Working for the large firm Russell & Co.

and then establishing his own, Augustine Heard & Co., Heard took hundreds of thousands of dollars' worth of bullion and gold and silver dollars on voyages to buy silk, spices, teas, and other Asian products in Calcutta and Canton. In retirement, his son declared that Augustine Heard & Co. was "rich and second to no other American house in China," and a poem published in a Boston newspaper after his death in 1868 boasted:

> Those noble merchants without steel or banners
> Carried truth East—and now the East is ours.

CITIZENSHIP

Establishing the new nation's sovereignty entailed not only delineating its borders but also defining its subjects or peoples. Article 1 of the U.S. Constitution, ratified in 1787, specified the nation's citizens, or those counted for full government representation, as "free Persons" (all whites, including indentured servants), American Indians who were taxed, and "three fifths of all other Persons," referring to African Americans and those not free. It excluded American Indians who were not taxed. Citizenship thus hinged on race and taxation. The first U.S. Census, of 1790, enumerated just three categories: "free whites," "slaves," and "all other free."

The first U.S. Congress, in 1790, passed the Naturalization Act, which declared the nation's members as limited to "free white persons." Any foreigner "being a free white person" of good character and a resident of the United States for two years could apply for naturalization, and on swearing to uphold the Constitution, "such person shall be considered as a citizen of the United States." Thus, in this foundational law, race (specifically whiteness) was a condition of citizenship, but so was freedom. In fact, at least since colonial Virginia, whiteness had been equated with freedom, while blackness was equated with bondage.

Three-quarters of a century later, in 1857, the Supreme Court's Chief Justice Roger Taney frankly explained the racialization of U.S. citizenship in his majority position in *Dred Scott v. John F. A. Sandford*. As the chief justice put it, the question before the court was simply this: "Can a negro, whose ancestors were imported into this country, and sold as slaves, become a member of the political community formed . . . by the Constitution . . . and as such become entitled to the rights, and privileges, and immunities, guaranteed by that instrument to the citizen?"

American Indians, Taney reasoned, were a free and independent people but "under subjection to the white race." African Americans were "regarded as beings of an inferior order, and altogether unfit to associate with the white race, either in social or political relations; and so far inferior, that they had no rights which the white man was bound to respect." Moreover, Taney contended, the 1790 Naturalization Act affirmed Congress's intention to limit citizenship to "free white persons" and not extend it to American Indians, who were members of alien nations, or African Americans, who were slaves and thus property. The distance and distinction, he concluded, was clear between "the citizen race," or whites, and "persons of color," or those "not included in the word citizens" but who were of "another and different class of persons."

As nonwhites, Asians and Pacific Islanders too were excluded from citizenship by the 1790 act. Three years before *Dred Scott,* California's supreme court had ruled in favor of a white man, George Hall, who petitioned to overturn a conviction of murder. An immigrant to California, Hall had killed a Chinese miner while trying to extort gold from the man, and his conviction was based on testimony from Chinese witnesses. Hall's petition flowed from a long tradition, beginning in colonial Virginia, holding that Indians and Africans were "incapable in law." Hall's attorney pointed out that California law disallowed American Indians and African Americans from testifying for or against whites and argued that Chinese witnesses should be debarred on the same grounds. In his decision in *The People v. George W. Hall* (1854), Chief Judge Hugh Murray agreed: "A free white citizen of this State" had had his rights abridged by having been subjected to a trial contaminated by evidence provided by aliens "not of white blood." The "European white man," Murray reasoned, must be shielded from the testimony of "the degraded and demoralized caste." Moreover, if given equality and the rights of citizenship, the Chinese would constitute "an actual and present danger" to the nation's stability.

The phrase *free white persons* thus defined citizenship as a matter of race. (It was also a matter of gender, insofar as freedom was a virtue possessed by men.) In the U.S. social formation, American Indians signified land, African Americans signified property and labor, and Asians signified labor. The classification of Indians, Africans, and Asians and Pacific Islanders as "another and different class of persons" purchased white men's citizenship and freedoms and with them the rights to life, liberty, and property, including dependents—women, children, servants, and slaves. Herein we find the intersection of race, gender, sexuality, class (freedom as opposed to bondage), and nation.

African Americans, considered "aliens," "property," and "other Persons" for nearly the first century of the nation, became "persons" only in 1868, with the adoption of the Fourteenth Amendment, which allowed that "all persons born or naturalized in the United States . . . are citizens." In 1924, Congress granted citizenship to American Indians, formerly classified as aliens, who were born after that year. In 1940, all American Indians were absorbed as U.S. citizens. Asians remained "aliens ineligible to citizenship," according to the 1790 Naturalization Act, until 1952, when Japanese and Koreans were the last Asians to receive naturalization rights.

CONQUEST

Like American Indians, Pacific Islanders fell within the grasp of the U.S. nation-state through conquest. Their loss of land and their loss of sovereignty were the means of their incorporation.

FIGURE 8

Davida Malo. Before his death on October 21, 1853, Malo requested burial on a mountain overlooking Lahainaluna on the island of Maui, high above the rising tide of foreign invasion. From Davida Malo, *Hawaiian Antiquities,* Special Publication no. 2, trans. Nathaniel B. Emerson (Honolulu: Bernice P. Bishop Museum, 1951).

About the time of the U.S. Declaration of Independence, Britain sent one of its most famous explorers, Captain James Cook, on expeditions to the South Pacific to find, name, classify, and collect the region's flora and fauna. On his third voyage, Cook was directed to explore America's northwest coast in search of a Northwest Passage. Although he failed to find the passage, Cook did encounter the Hawaiian islands and, on the west coast of America, animals whose pelts were valuable commodities in the China trade, as the colonists of New Spain had long known. Both Hawai'i and the fur trade would figure prominently in the new nation's expansion westward and its Asian and Pacific destiny.

The coming of whites to Hawai'i signaled a new phase in the life of the Hawaiian people. "If a big wave comes in," prophesied the Hawaiian scholar Davida Malo in 1837 of the European incursion, "large and unfamiliar fishes will come from the dark ocean, and when they see the small fishes of the shallows they will eat them up." Although educated by Christian missionaries and a convert to that religion, Malo lamented the swift decline of Hawai'i's sovereignty . "The white man's ships have arrived with clever men from the big countries," he wrote. "They know our people are few in number and our country is small, they will devour us."[3]

Called "Indians" by some foreigners, Hawaiians suffered population losses comparable to America's indigenous peoples. Variously estimated at 250,000 to 800,000 in 1778 when the first Europeans arrived, the Hawaiian population had plummeted by more than 50 percent by about the time of Malo's prediction. That was just the beginning.

Among the company of scientists and artists on Cook's third and final Pacific expedition was John Ledyard, born in Groton, Connecticut. Although his mother wanted him to become a missionary among American Indians, Ledyard fled Dartmouth College to take up voyaging on a U.S. trade vessel that carried goods between North Africa and the West Indies. Later, he enlisted in the British army and navy and somehow managed to secure a position on board one of Cook's ships as a corporal of the marines.

After Cook's death in Hawai'i in 1779, Ledyard published an account of the voyage in 1783: *A Journal of Captain Cook's Last Voyage to the Pacific Ocean, and in Quest of a North-West Passage, Between Asia & America.* Even before it appeared, Ledyard had tried to gain support from Robert Morris, among others, for a trade expedition to the Northwest to obtain furs to exchange for China's tea, silk, and porcelain, which he promised would reap "astonishing profit." After failing to attract sponsors, Ledyard traveled abroad to promote his scheme. In Paris he met the U.S. minister to France, Thomas Jefferson, who showed an interest in his account and commercial venture.

That contact, according to a biographer, later fired President Jefferson's desire to find a direct route across the continent when France offered to sell the Louisiana Territory. In April 1803, the nation nearly doubled in size when Jefferson purchased Louisiana, an area of some 830,000 square miles, for $15 million. Both the sale and the purchase disregarded the rights of indigenous peoples and nations who occupied the land. About two months after the acquisition, Jefferson directed Meriwether Lewis, his personal secretary, and William Clark, an army officer, to open a highway to the Pacific Ocean "for the purposes of commerce" and report on the availability of furs in the Northwest.

The U.S. fur trade with China had started earlier. In 1787, about a year before Ledyard's death in Egypt, the *Columbia* left Boston for the Pacific Northwest, where it took on a load of furs, sailed west to China to trade them for Asian goods, and returned to Boston in 1790. The voyage inaugurated a trade that, as Ledyard predicted, enriched many of America's merchants and bankers. And stepping from *Columbia*'s deck onto Boston's streets when the ship returned, embodying the connections represented by this trade among New England, the Northwest, Hawai'i, and Asia, was a Hawaiian who probably joined the voyage when the American ship stopped in the islands to rest and resupply on its way to China.

Conquest made these United States. Spanish conquistadores with their guns and germs invaded and subdued American Indians. Using Indian and then African labor, they extracted and harvested American silver, gold, and furs for their trade with Asia. Centuries later, the United States would annex a large chunk of the northern territories of Mexico, formerly New Spain, following their conquest by American settlers.

English implantations on America's East Coast were likewise achieved through the force of warfare, germs, and expropriation. The colonizers declared sovereignty over the lands they claimed and generally excluded American Indians, whom they considered as alien nations and peoples, from their property. By this means, European foreigners became natives, and American natives became aliens.

To produce wealth from the land requires labor. As Virginia's tobacco plantations grew in importance, the distance between whites and nonwhites increased, and enslaved Africans replaced white indentured servants as the mainstay of the colonial economy. Those changes lent force to divisions and hierarchies of race, gender, sexuality, class, and citizenship, shaped the social formation, and were influential in the constitution of the postcolonial nation.

Settler interests clashed with those of the colonial power, and Asia's teas and trade were involved in the rebellion. A border separating white from Indian America defined the new nation's lands, and its citizenship was limited to "free white persons." American Indians and African and Asian Americans, constituting "another and different class of persons," were thereby denied the rights of life, liberty, and property.

Not content with the nation's self-proclaimed limits and with an eye toward Asia, President Jefferson expanded the nation through a purchase of land from Europeans—not the land's peoples—to reach the continent's western shore, where China's wealth beckoned across the Pacific.

SUGGESTED READINGS

Brown, Kathleen M. *Good Wives, Nasty Wenches, and Anxious Patriarchs: Gender, Race, and Power in Colonial Virginia.* Chapel Hill: University of North Carolina Press, 1996.

Gutiérrez, Ramón A. *When Jesus Came, the Corn Mothers Went Away: Marriage, Sexuality and Power in New Mexico, 1500–1846.* Stanford, CA: Stanford University Press, 1991.

Wolf, Eric R. *Europe and the People without History.* Berkeley: University of California Press, 1982.

Yokota, Kariann Akemi. *Unbecoming British: How Revolutionary America Became a Postcolonial Nation.* New York: Oxford University Press, 2011.

PRIMARY DOCUMENTS

DOCUMENT 4

Nicholas Biddle, ed., *The Journals of the Expedition under the Command of Capts. Lewis and Clark,* vol. 1 (New York: Heritage Press, 1962), xviii–xix, xx, xxi, xxiii.

> Thomas Jefferson, writing on August 18, 1813, after the death of Meriwether Lewis, recalled the origins of his idea for the Lewis and Clark expedition, which began with his encounter with John Ledyard. At the end of this note, Jefferson appended his instructions to Lewis and Clark to chart the territory's geography, find the quickest way by water across the continent, and collect the furs of the Pacific Northwest "for the purposes of commerce."

In compliance with the request conveyed in your letter of May 25, I have endeavoured to obtain, from the relations and friends of the late governor Lewis, information of such incidents of his life as might be not unacceptable to those who may read the narrative of his western discoveries. . . .

Meriwether Lewis, late governor of Louisiana, was born on the 18th of August, 1774, near the town of Charlottesville, in the country of Albemarle, in Virginia, of one of the distinguished families of that state. . . .

While I resided in Paris, John Ledyard of Connecticut, arrived there, well known in the United States for energy of body and mind. He had accompanied captain Cook on his voyage to the Pacific ocean; and distinguished himself on that voyage by his intrepidity. Being of a roaming disposition, he was now panting for some new enterprise. His immediate object at Paris was to engage a mercantile company in the fur-trade of the western coast of America, in which, however, he failed. I then proposed to him to go by land to Kamschatka, cross in some of the Russian vessels to Nootka Sound, fall down into the latitude of the Missouri, and penetrate to, and through, that to the United States. He eagerly seized the idea. . . .

[*Ledyard failed to complete that journey across Russia, and returned to France.*]

The fatigue of this journey broke down his constitution; and when he returned to Paris his bodily strength was much impaired. His mind, however, remained firm, and he after this undertook the journey to Egypt. I received a letter from him, full of sanguine hopes, dated at Cairo, the 15th of November, 1788, the day before he was to set out for the head of the Nile; on which day, however, he ended his career and life; and thus failed the first attempt to explore the western part of our Northern continent.

In 1792, I proposed to the American Philosophical Society that we should set on foot a subscription to engage some competent person to explore that region in the opposite direction; that is, by ascending the Missouri, crossing the Stony [Rocky] Mountains, and descending the nearest river to the Pacific. Captain Lewis being then stationed at Charlottesville, on the recruiting service, warmly solicited me to obtain for him the execution of that object. I told him it was proposed that the person engaged should be attended by a single companion only, to avoid exciting alarm among the Indians. This did not deter him. . . .

In 1803, the act for establishing trading houses with the Indian tribes being about to expire, some modifications of it were recommended to congress . . . , and an extension of its views to the Indians on the Missouri. In order to prepare the way, the message proposed the sending an exploring party to trace the Missouri to its source, to cross the Highlands, and follow the best water-communication which offered itself from thence to the Pacific ocean. Congress approved the proposition, and voted a sum of money for carrying it into execution.

Captain Lewis, who had then been near two years with me as private secretary, immediately renewed his solicitations to have the direction of the party. I had now had opportunities of knowing him intimately. Of courage undaunted; possessing a firmness and perseverance of purpose which nothing but impossibilities could divert from its direction; careful as a father of those committed to his charge, yet steady in the maintenance of order and discipline; intimate with the Indian character, customs, and principles; habituated to the hunting life; guarded, by exact observation of the vegetables and animals of his own country, against losing time in the descriptions of objects already possessed; honest, disinterested, liberal, of sound understanding, and a fidelity to truth so scrupulous, that whatever he should report would be as certain as if seen by ourselves; with all these qualifications, as if selected and implanted by nature in one body for this express purpose, I could have no hesitation in confiding the enterprise to him. . . .

In April, 1803, a draught of his instructions was sent to captain Lewis, and on the 20th of June they were signed in the following form:

To Meriwether Lewis, esquire, captain of the first regiment of infantry of the United States of America. . . .

The object of your mission is to explore the Missouri river, and such principal streams of it, as, by its course and communication with the waters of the Pacific ocean, whether the Columbia, Oregan [sic], Colorado, or any other river, may offer the most direct and practicable water-communication across the continent, for the purposes of commerce. . . .

Your observations are to be taken with great pains and accuracy; to be entered distinctly and intelligibly for others as well as yourself. . . .

Should you reach the Pacific ocean, inform yourself of the circumstances which may decide whether the furs of those parts may not be collected as advantageously at the head of the Missouri (convenient as is supposed to the waters of the Colorado and Oregan or Columbia) as at Nootka Sound, or any other point of that coast; and that trade be consequently conducted through the Missouri and United States more beneficially than by the circumnavigation now practised.

THOMAS JEFFERSON.
President of the United States of America.

DOCUMENT 5

Frank Bergon, ed., *The Journals of Lewis and Clark* (New York: Viking, 1989), 350, 351–52.

In his journal entries of February 1806, at the mouth of the Columbia River and in sight of the Pacific Ocean, Meriwether Lewis reported triumphantly that he had found, per Jefferson's instructions, "the most practicable and navigable passage" across the continent to the Pacific, and encountered the sea otter.

Friday, February 14, 1806. I completed a *map* of the Countrey through which we have been passing from the Mississippi at the Mouth of Missouri to this place. . . . We now discover that we have found the most practicable and navigable passage across the Continent of North America. . . .

Sunday, February 23, 1806. The Sea Otter is found on the sea coast and in the salt water. this anamal when fully grown is as large as a common mastive dog . . . the colour is a uniform dark brown and when in good order and season perfectly black and glossey. it is the riches[t] and I think the most delicious fur in the world at least I cannot form an idea of any more so. it is deep thick silkey in the extreem and strong. the inner part of the fur when opened is lighter than the surface in it's natural position. there are some fine black and shining hairs intermixed with the fur which are reather longer and add much to it's beauty.

DOCUMENT 6

The People, Respondent, v. George W. Hall, Appellant (1854), California Supreme Court, as published in *The Columbia Documentary History of the Asian American Experience*, ed. Franklin Odo (New York: Columbia University Press, 2002), 19–21.

Section 394 of the Civil Practice Act provides, "No Indian or Negro shall be allowed to testify as a witness in any action in which a White person is a party."

Section 14 of the Criminal Act provides, "No Black, or Mulatto person, or Indian shall be allowed to give evidence in favor of, or against a White man."

Held, that the words, Indian, Negro, Black and White, are generic terms, designating race. That, therefore, Chinese and all other peoples not white, are included in the prohibition from being witnesses against Whites.

Mr. Ch. J. Murray delivered the opinion of the Court. Mr. J. Heydenfeldt concurred.

The appellant, a free white citizen of this State, was convicted of murder upon the testimony of Chinese witnesses.

The point involved in this case, is the admissibility of such evidence.

The 394th section of the Act Concerning Civil Cases, provides that no Indian or Negro shall be allowed to testify as a witness in any action or proceeding in which a White person is a party.

The 14th section of the Act of April 16th, 1850, regulating Criminal Proceedings, provides that "No Black, or Mulatto person, or Indian, shall be allowed to give evidence in favor of, or against a white man."

The true point at which we are anxious to arrive, is the legal signification of the words, "Black, Mulatto, Indian and White person," and whether the Legislature adopted them as generic terms, or intended to limit their application to specific types of the human species. . . .

Can, then, the use of the word "Indian," because at the present day it may be sometimes regarded as a specific, and not as a generic term, alter this conclusion? We think not; because at the origin of the legislation we are considering, it was used and admitted in its common and ordinary acceptation, as a generic term, distinguishing the great Mongolian race, and as such, its meaning then became fixed by law, and in construing Statutes the legal meaning of words must be presumed.

Again: the words of the Act must be construed in *pari material*. It will not be disputed that "White" and "Negro," are generic terms, and refer to two of the great types of mankind. If these, as well as the word, "Indian," are not to be regarded as generic terms, including the two great races which they were intended to designate, but only specific, and applying to those Whites and Negroes who were inhabitants of this Continent at the time of the passage of the Act, the most anomalous consequences would ensue. The European white man who comes here would not be shielded from the testimony of the degraded and demoralized caste, while the Negro, fresh from the coast of Africa, or the Indian of Patagonia, the Kanaka, South Sea Islander, or New Hollander, would be admitted, upon their arrival, to testify against white citizens in our courts of law.

To argue such a proposition would be an insult to the good sense of the Legislature.

The evident intention of the Act was to throw around the citizen a protection of life and property, which could only be secured by removing him above the corrupting influences of degraded castes. . . .

In using the words, "No Black, or Mulatto person, or Indian shall be allowed to give evidence for or against a White person," the Legislature, if any intention can be ascribed to it, adopted the most comprehensive terms to embrace every known class or shade of color, as the apparent design was to protect the White person from the influence of all testimony other than that of persons of the same caste. The use of these terms must, by every sound rule of construction, exclude every one who is not of white blood. . . .

We are not disposed to leave this question in any doubt. The word "White" has a distinct signification, which *ex vi termini,* excludes black, yellow, and all other colors. It will be observed, by reference to the first section of the second article of the Constitution of this State, that none but white males can become electors, except in the case of Indians, who may be admitted by special Act of the Legislature. On examination of the constitutional debates, it will be found that not a little difficulty existed in selecting these precise words, which were finally agreed upon as the most comprehensive that could be suggested to exclude all inferior races. . . .

We have carefully considered all the consequences resulting from a different rule of construction, and are satisfied that even in a doubtful case we would be impelled to this decision on grounds of public policy.

The same rule which would admit them to testify, would admit them to all the equal rights of citizenship, and we might soon see them at the polls, in the jury box, upon the bench, and in our legislative halls.

This is not a speculation which exists in the excited and over-heated imagination of the patriot and statesman, but it is an actual and present danger.

The anomalous spectacle of a distinct people, living in our community, recognizing no laws of this State except through necessity, bringing with them their prejudices and national feuds, in which they indulge in open violation of law; whose mendacity is proverbial; a race of people whom nature has marked as inferior, and who are incapable of progress or intellectual development beyond a certain point, as their history has shown; differing in language, opinions, color, and physical conformation; between whom and ourselves nature has placed an impassable difference, is now presented, and for them is claimed, not only the right to swear away the life of a citizen, but the further privilege of participating with us in administering the affairs of our Government. . . .

For these reasons, we are of opinion that the testimony was inadmissible.

The judgment is reversed and the cause remanded.

SIGNIFICANT EVENTS

1588	Spanish Armada
1607	Virginia Colony founded at Jamestown
1614	Pocahontas marries John Rolfe
1619	enslaved Africans in Jamestown
1620	Plymouth Colony established
1622	Powhatan Indians defend Indian country
1637	Puritans wage war against the Pequots
1639	"all persons except Negroes" in Virginia permitted to own guns and ammunition
1643	tax imposed on African women in Virginia
1658	Asian slaves taken to Africa's Cape of Good Hope
1662	Virginia ruling that offspring of African women inherit status and condition of mother, not father
1669	Anthony Johnson declared "a Negroe" and thus "alien"
1675–76	Bacon's rebellion
1680	Pueblo revolt
1705	Indians and Africans declared "incapable in law"
1763	Proclamation separating settlers from Indians
1773	Tea Act
1775–83	U.S. Revolutionary War
1783	Treaty of Paris
	John Ledyard publishes his *Journal*
1784	*Empress of China* sails for Canton, China
1785	*Empress of China* returns; *Pallas* docks in Baltimore
	Asians on the East Coast
1787	Article 1 of U.S. Constitution sets out "three-fifths" rule of representation
1790	Naturalization Act
1795	Treaty of Greenville
1803	Louisiana Purchase
1804–6	Lewis and Clark expedition

1854	*People v. George W. Hall* (California)
1857	*Dred Scott v. John F. A. Sandford*
1924	U.S. citizenship extended to American Indians born after 1924
1940	U.S. citizenship extended to all American Indians
1952	naturalization extended to all Asians

4

IMPERIAL REPUBLIC

The purchase of the Louisiana Territory from France in 1803 by President Thomas Jefferson opened up new lands for the young United States. Previously, settler lands had been constrained by a line drawn in London in 1763, roughly paralleling the Appalachian Mountains, which assigned territories east of the border to whites and those to the west to American Indians. That artifice segregated the English settlers from the indigenous peoples and justified the sovereignty of what within two decades became the new nation, the United States.

In this chapter, I refer to the United States as an "imperial republic" because the nation began as a product of English expansion into the Atlantic world and as a settler colony that appropriated lands from American Indians through treaties as well as through the violence of conquest. In the 1780s shortly after independence, Congress claimed and mapped the area west of the Appalachians, labeling it as the Northwest Territory and declaring it open for white settlement. That opening act was just the start of the nation's westward spread. Imperialism is a central feature of American history.

The Louisiana Purchase added not only land but also new populations to the nation: French citizens, Spaniards, Africans, American Indians, Filipinos, and their mixed offspring. The treaty ceding the territory stipulated that its inhabitants "shall be incorporated in the Union of the United States" as quickly as possible in order to enjoy "the rights, advantages and immunities of citizens of the United States; and in the meantime they shall be maintained and protected in the free enjoyment of their liberty, property, and the religion which they profess."[1]

With the treaty, France sought to protect former French citizens who possessed property, including enslaved Africans. Religious freedom was important because many of the incorporated French were Catholics, not Protestants. Those former citizens of France, the empire builders expected, would eventually assimilate into the nation. American Indians of that territory, however, were excluded. They were seen not as citizens or potential citizens but as foes and targets of conquest and removal. After 1795, they were considered foreign nations subject to treaties.

The nation's westward expansion and the absorption of novel lands and peoples posed serious challenges to the founding narrative of a common descent and racial homogeneity. That narrative established the nation's people as a homogeneous race of whites. American Indians and Africans, classified respectively as aliens and property, did not fully count. The French immigrant J. Hector St. John de Crèvecoeur described American citizenry, this "new race of men," as a fusion of Europe's nations and races: English, Dutch, and French. John Jay, a coauthor of *The Federalist Papers* and the first chief justice of the U.S. Supreme Court, added that Americans were "one united people—a people descended from the same ancestors, speaking the same language, professing the same religion, attached to the same principles of government, very similar in their manners and customs."[2]

Social forces unleashed by the territorial expansion and the burgeoning, rapidly changing economy challenged that idea of a white nation. The first half of the nineteenth century witnessed the rise of cities and industries in the Northeast and the related expansion of cotton production and slavery in the South. The nation's population grew through reproduction and immigration, mainly from Ireland but also from England and Germany. Those immigrants supplied the labor required for the economic transformation that included the rise of factories and manufacturing industries and an expanding network of roads, canals, and railroad tracks. Mercantile or trade capitalism had run its course, and the day of industrial capitalism was dawning. The shift reflected the change from an exchange-based to a manufacturing-based economy.

Between 1840 and 1860, Boston's population grew from 93,000 to 177,000 and New York City's from 312,000 to 805,000. While many German immigrants moved to agrarian regions in the West, the Irish generally settled in cities along the East Coast. Young girls and women made up significant proportions of the immigrant wave and workforce, and the Irish, colonized and held in contempt by the English, found themselves regarded in the United States as impoverished, foreign laborers akin to alien African and Chinese Americans. Depictions of the Irish as apelike, savage, dirty, and lazy circulated widely in popular culture. A Boston clergyman's sermon warned against "negroes, Indians, Mexicans, Irish, and the like," and referred to them as "inferiors" and "dangerous classes" of peoples.

The Irish, once called the "niggers of Europe," eventually attained whiteness by distinguishing themselves from African and Chinese Americans. They initiated and joined in noisy mass campaigns against both groups, although others, like some Irish women, worked with and married African and Chinese American men. In lower Manhattan, amid a culture of polyglot mariners and migrants, Irish women and Chinese men drank, danced, slept together, and married. The Chinese ship steward William Brown, living in New York City in 1825, wed Irish Rebecca Brown. The Chinese seaman John Huston, a resident of New York in 1829, married Margaret, an Irish woman, and they had two daughters. Of an estimated 150 Chinese in New York City in 1856, 11 were married to Irish women. Apparently many of those Chinese were former coolies from Peru, while others were seamen in the U.S.-China trade. New York's Chinese men mostly arrived in the United States through mercantile capitalism, while Irish women mill workers signified the transition from mercantile to industrial capitalism.

Linked to the economic transformation in the Northeast were the expanding fields of cotton, cultivated by enslaved African American labor, in the Deep South. Textile mills in the Northeast required the South's cotton production, which grew from five hundred thousand bales in 1820 to nearly three million in 1850 and five million bales a decade later. Slavery prospered: in Alabama, the number of enslaved African Americans soared from 41,000 in 1820 to 435,000 in 1860, while in Mississippi it leaped from 32,000 to 436,000. The acquisition of new lands in which slavery was legal in the South and west of the Mississippi River was a factor in the cotton boom.

MANIFEST DESTINY

In 1845 the writer John O'Sullivan coined the phrase *manifest destiny* to describe the ideology that contended that God and history had preordained the spread of the United States across the entire continent. O'Sullivan claimed that U.S. expansion was undertaken "by the right of our manifest destiny to overspread and to possess the whole continent which Providence has given us for the development of the great experiment of liberty and federative self government entrusted to us."[3] Fanned by those flames of nationalism and the imperatives of capitalism in the 1840s, manifest destiny drove the nation's border westward to the Pacific.

President Theodore Roosevelt echoed this sentiment at an exposition celebrating Jefferson's purchase of Louisiana. "We have met here today," he declared in 1903, "to commemorate the hundredth anniversary of the event which more than any other, after the foundation of the Government and always excepting its preservation, determined the character of our national life—determined that we should be a great expanding nation instead of relatively a small and stationary one."[4] Roosevelt spoke with the advantage of hindsight and experience, having participated in the nation's late-nineteenth-century expansion beyond its continental limits, as a Rough Rider cavalryman in Cuba during the 1898 Spanish-American War.

The first period of manifest destiny was the first half of the nineteenth century, as the nation engulfed Mexico's northern territories and lands to the north that had been settled by American Indians but were claimed by Mexico, Russia, and Britain in disregard of their inhabitants. In 1846, the United States and Britain signed a treaty that fixed a division between British and American territory at the forty-ninth parallel, which today forms the border between the United States and Canada. The fruits of that land grab were named the Oregon Territory, which became the states of Washington, Oregon, and Idaho.

The principal instigators in the conquest of Mexican lands in the U.S. Southwest were American settlers seeking agricultural landholdings cultivated by enslaved laborers. Initially invited by Mexico to settle Texas in the 1820s, white Americans came to dominate the area and then fomented rebellions against their newly independent host nation. The causes of settler discontent included Mexico's ban on slavery. In 1836, the white settlers defeated the Mexican army, declared an independent Texas Republic, and promptly petitioned for annexation by the United States.

Congress admitted Texas as a state in 1845, and President James Polk dispatched an army to Texas as well as a naval expedition to California to secure Mexican lands for the United States. The provocation led to a U.S. declaration of war against Mexico in 1846. After an invasion of Mexico and military offensives in New Mexico and California, where American settlers had declared a republic independent of Mexico under the "Bear Flag," Mexico agreed to surrender its lands to the United States. The Treaty of Guadalupe Hidalgo in 1848 ceded lands north of the Rio Grande River to the United States for $15 million. It also stipulated that former Mexican citizens would become U.S. citizens and thus effectively be racialized as whites.

Critics of expansionism in the United States, who lived mainly in the Northeast, feared that the nation's westward march was being driven by Southern interests to acquire new slave lands, and this sectional debate intensified in the years after the conquest and annexation of Mexican territory. Moreover, as other critics of manifest destiny were eager to point out, the reality of acquiring all those new lands threatened the national narrative of racial homogeneity, Mexican "whiteness" notwithstanding. Expansion also hastened the impending conflict over slavery.

Another dramatic demographic shift resulted from the quest not for land but for gold, after the discovery of gold in 1848 at a sawmill owned by John Sutter in the Sierra Nevada foothills of California. Hundreds of thousands of fortune seekers flocked to the goldfields. The Compromise of 1850 admitted California as a free state and the rest of the former Mexican lands—today's New Mexico, Arizona, Nevada, Utah, and parts of Colorado and Wyoming—as territories without restrictions on slavery.

Expansion was simultaneously overland as well as overseas. Throughout this period, U.S. trade with China, initiated soon after U.S. independence, continued. President Millard Fillmore instructed Commodore Matthew Perry to "open" Japan to U.S. vessels and trade. Since 1638, Japan, under the Tokugawa shogunate, had closed its doors to foreigners, fearing erosion of its sovereignty. After consulting with U.S. businessmen involved in the Asian commerce, Perry headed for Japan with an expeditionary force of four ships, having been granted executive powers to use arms if necessary to accomplish his mission. After a "dress rehearsal" in Okinawa, Perry arrived in Tokyo Bay on July 1853. Japan's government delayed negotiations, and Perry sailed away, promising to return the

ペルり像

FIGURE 9
A Japanese view of Matthew Perry. Woodblock print, 1854.

following year. On February 1854 Perry arrived with seven warships, determined to wrest a treaty from Japan. He succeeded with the Treaty of Kanagawa, which opened the ports of Shimoda and Hakodate to U.S. vessels. Later that year, the British, Russians, and Dutch also gained access to Japan's ports.

The acquisition of new lands during this first phase of manifest destiny, in violation of American Indian sovereignty, reveals the debris of imperialism—the nonwhite peoples in those territories. Whites assimilated into the nation as citizens, but nonwhites, with the exception of Mexicans, remained aliens . Territorial expansion during this period also reveals the tensions between enslaved and free labor, and between industrial capitalism in the Northeast and the plantation economy of the South. The conflicts would lead to a rupture between regions and cultures and to a brutal war between brothers.

CIVIL WAR

The U.S. Civil War transformed the nation. Among the consequences most pertinent to this history of Asians and Pacific Islanders in the United States were the passage of the

Constitution's Thirteenth Amendment (1865), which abolished slavery; the first Civil Rights Act (1866), which declared African Americans to be citizens; the Fourteenth Amendment (1868), which conferred citizenship on those born in the United States and ensured to "all persons" equal protection under the law; and the Fifteenth Amendment (1870), which guaranteed the right of citizens to vote regardless of "race, color, or previous condition of servitude."

Those advances in U.S. democracy illustrate the complexity of the intersections and articulations of race, gender, and class. The National Woman Suffrage Association, led by Elizabeth Cady Stanton and Susan B. Anthony, opposed the Fifteenth Amendment because it gave political power to "the lower orders of Chinese, Africans, Germans, and Irish, with their low ideals of womanhood."[5] That opposition divided the suffragist cause from the abolitionist movement, although the two had worked together for decades, and it underscored a longstanding positioning of race against gender and class.

The 1866 Civil Rights Act and the Fourteenth Amendment, although they failed to extend full political and civil rights to African Americans, redressed some 250 years of exclusion and their relegation to "another and different class of persons." The "citizen race" henceforth included a people of color, and that change was truly revolutionary. For most Asians, the Fourteenth Amendment was the only means of acquiring U.S. citizenship before 1952, when the final barrier to Asian naturalization was removed.

The importance of the Fourteenth Amendment's guarantee of equality under the law for all persons cannot be overstated. African and Asian American citizenship put to rest the prior state and fiction of a solitary nation and people or race. Equal protection under the law and voting rights in disregard of race were now enshrined in the Constitution, even if they were not always observed.

Asians and Pacific Islanders, and indeed all of the nation's peoples, benefited from that advancement of democracy. They were also instrumental in securing it. Asians were present in America long before the Civil War. About the time of the Jamestown colony, Filipinos and Chinese had arrived in New Spain with the Manila galleon trade. Asians and Pacific Islanders were living in the United States by the late eighteenth century. They, like African Americans, earned their claims to equality through the blood they shed on the nation's battlefields during the Civil War. Hawaiians, Chinese, Filipinos, South Asians, Mexicans, and Puerto Ricans served in the African American U.S. Colored Troops (USCT), and a few served in white units.

Among the Hawaiian soldiers known to have served in the USCT is Samuel Watt in Company A of the 20th Regiment. He was discharged in New Orleans in 1865, after about a year of service, possibly because of a wound suffered during the war. The Hawaiian John Brown enlisted at New Bedford, Massachusetts, and served in the 11th USCT, and Charles Heatley and Prince Romerson were enlisted in the 5th Massachusetts Colored Cavalry. Other Hawaiians, like Peter Adams, William Bill, Johnny Boy, William Brown, Mariano Flores, George High, John Ourai, Antonio Perez, John Smith, and

Henry Williams, served as mariners, sailors, seamen, barbers, cooks, and laborers in the Union Navy. In all, about fifty-four men from Hawai'i fought in the war.

Hawaiians served under the Confederate flag as well. The Confederate raider *Shenandoah* wreaked havoc in the Pacific against Yankee whalers. On board that warship were the Hawaiians James California, Henry Givens, Joseph Kanaca, Joseph Long, and John Mahoe. The Hawaiian kingdom, although neutral in the war, outlawed the *Shenandoah* as a pirate ship because its depredations ate away at the profits of the whaling business, and the government demanded its surrender.

Twenty islanders from Guam, including Jose Aglur, Joseph Carter, Thomas Andrews, Joseph Brown, Leon Cepeda, Vincente Leon, Peter Mindola, Joseph Perez, and Andreas Rodgers served in the Union Navy; from Tahiti were seamen Jacob Banyan, Charles Beeb, John Foster, Joseph Kanaka, James Rontongo, Joseph Rontongo, Robert Tahiti, and James Williams; from the Philippines Stephen Amos, a seaman; Felix Baker, a steward; and Felix Cornelius Balderry, Caystana Baltazar, Joseph Banards, Andrew Bellino, Joseph Bernard, Joseph Bernardo, and John Brown. From India came John Anderson and John Bank of the 31st USCT; Henry Bell, Morris Bird, and Andrew Brown of the 26th USCT; John Burnes and George Burton of Company G, 69th New York Infantry; George Buttery of Company B, 7th New York Infantry, and many others. From Sri Lanka came Peter Blake, Charles Boultbee, George McMillan, Thomas Palmon, and Arnold Pierce; and from Indonesia, John Brown, who served in Company F of the 40th New York Infantry. Other Asians and Pacific Islanders included men from Indonesia, Turkey, Japan, Malaysia, Myanmar, Persia, Samoa, Singapore, Tonga, and other Pacific islands.

Research also reveals that about fifty-five Filipinos and nearly eighty South Asians (from India, Pakistan, and Sri Lanka) served in the Civil War. The most prominently documented were some seventy-four Chinese who served both the Union and the Confederate causes. Private Joseph Pierce was born in Canton, sold by his father to the ship captain Amos Peck, and taken to Connecticut to work as a family servant. He served for three years in the 14th Connecticut Regiment. Promoted to corporal in 1863, he survived the war and returned to Connecticut, where he worked as an engraver. Another Chinese, Corporal John Tommy of Company D, 70th New York Regiment, lost both arms and legs during the battle of Gettysburg in 1863 and died of his wounds. In the South, Chinese and Filipinos served in Louisiana units, fighting on the Confederate side along with Christopher Bunker, the son of Chang, one of the original Siamese twins.

DESTINY'S CHILD

Historians agree that the first period of manifest destiny ended with the treaty with Mexico in 1848. There was a second period of manifest destiny during the late nineteenth and early twentieth centuries. Because both phases involved the acquisition of territories populated by nonwhite peoples, both tested the imperial republic's original intention to limit citizenship and therewith membership in the nation to "free white persons." White

FIGURE 10

Felix C. Balderry in his Union Army uniform. Balderry was born in the Philippines in 1842, enlisted in Company A of the Eleventh Michigan Volunteers on December 1863, and was mustered out on September 1865. After the war, Balderry worked as a tailor in Colon, Michigan. He married Ada May Burns, had a son, Frank, and died on August 18, 1895. Courtesy of Michigan Historical Center, Archives of Michigan.

settler machinations in Hawai'i and a war with Spain expanded the nation beyond the continental limits, opening the United States to other peoples of color and their island homes in the Caribbean and Pacific.

In the late nineteenth century, unprecedented numbers of immigrants, this time largely from southern and eastern Europe, flocked to cities in the Northeast. Working alongside African Americans arriving from the postbellum South, they supplied the muscle for the booming industries that mass-produced goods for a consumer market. Workers struggled against trusts and monopolies, and out West farmers set up cooperatives and organized against government controls and railroad barons. Often the white working class blamed immigrants and peoples of color for their troubles, especially during the economic crisis and resulting panic of the 1890s.

Between 1865 and 1915, twenty-five million immigrants streamed to these shores, more than four times the total of the previous fifty years. By 1890, foreign-born immigrants and their children made up 80 percent of the population of New York City and 87 percent of Chicago's. While industrialists welcomed them as workers, nativists agitated against their entry. United in a hatred of foreigners were the five hundred thousand or so members of the American Protective Association, and in 1894, the Immigration Restriction League began clamoring for laws to bar new immigrants. In his classic 1904 study *Poverty*, Robert Hunter observed: "The poor are almost entirely foreign born." These people, he wrote, formed "colonies, foreign in language, customs, habits, and institutions" and were distinguished from "Americans" by ethnicity and race, such as the Irish, Jews, Italians, Russians, Poles, Greeks, Syrians, Chinese, and African Americans. "To live in one of these foreign communities," Hunter wrote, "is actually to live on foreign soil. The thoughts, feelings, and traditions . . . are often entirely alien to an American."[6]

In 1886, in Chicago, police killed four strikers, and the next day a bomb exploded in Haymarket Square, killing seven police officers and injuring sixty-seven other people. Labor strife was commonly depicted as un-American, and the bombing came to symbolize to many Americans the alien menace posed by recent immigrants, radicals, and anarchists. "These people are not American," a Chicago newspaper reported of the Haymarket strikers, "but the very scum and offal of Europe."

Mirroring that wider fear of aliens, in 1882 Congress passed the Chinese Exclusion Act because, in the framers' words, "the coming of Chinese laborers to this country endangers the good order of certain localities within the territory thereof." The language of the act suggests that order is the preferred state, and Chinese workers, as perpetual aliens, introduce disorder and danger.

The 1890 U.S. Census declared that the nation had been fully settled or, in the choice language of the historian Frederick Jackson Turner, that "the task of filling up the vacant spaces of the continent" had been completed. He and many others saw this achievement as "the closing of the frontier." Yet they saw the frontier as central to the constitution of the nation and its people because it was the site that had sired and fostered the American spirit—rugged individualism, initiative and self-reliance, and democratic values. Moreover, the fuel for the nation's economic growth was the energy generated by the constantly expanding frontier, with its seemingly limitless resources and opportunities. Its closure, thus, was a cause for alarm. The economic crisis of the 1890s served to reinforce those fears. Markets, land, and labor abroad seemed to offer alternative opportunities. Pressed from within by population growth and a hunger for land, the U.S. sought to expand its reach abroad.

Justifications for expansion overseas included the need for naval bases to protect commercial interests in the oceanic worlds. In his widely read book *The Influence of Sea Power upon History* (1890), Alfred Thayer Mahan argued that the pattern of European empires demonstrated that sea power led to national greatness. Domestic production required overseas markets, a strong navy to protect the sea lanes, and colonies to provide

FIGURE 11

John Gast, *American Progress*, 1872. A new day dawns as America drives before her Indians, buffalo, and wild horses, bringing with her white settlers and industry (railroads). On her forehead shines the "star of empire."

anchorages and sources of materials and labor. As a nation bounded by the Atlantic and Pacific, Mahan pointed out, the United States must turn to the sea and its two ocean worlds. His argument merged the republic's economic and strategic interests and made a convincing case for extending imperialism.

Ideology fortified such imperialist arguments for material gains. Racism justified the conquest and colonization of inferior, backward peoples, and these projects were further infused with religious fervor. Josiah Strong, a Christian minister and author of the best-selling *Our Country: Its Possible Future and Its Present Crisis* (1885), declared in the language of manifest destiny that the "Anglo-Saxon race" was "divinely commissioned" to spread. This powerful race "will move down upon Mexico, down upon Central and South America, out upon the islands of the sea, over upon Africa and beyond." In a dramatic gesture toward social Darwinism and the final reward, he demanded, "Can any one doubt that the result of this competition of races will be the 'survival of the fittest'?"[7]

Expansion also soothed the patriarchy in the late-nineteenth-century United States, which had been bruised by the assertions of the "new woman." That idea had emerged as white working-class women toiled outside the home in field and factory and white middle-class women pursued education and engaged in social-reform movements directed at immigrants and the urban poor. Women's wage labor and uplift projects diminished the distance between the private and public spheres, enhanced the independence of white women, and thereby threatened white men's dominance both inside and outside the household. Imperialism offered a way to reconstitute white masculinity. This attitude was exemplified by the British author Rudyard Kipling's widely circulated poem "The White Man's Burden: The United States and the Philippine Islands." Published in 1898 and addressed to the United States, the poem urged the conquest of the womanly, childlike Philippines:

> Take up the White Man's burden—
>   Have done with childish days—
> The lightly proffered laurel,
>   The easy, ungrudged praise.
> Come now, to search your manhood
>   Through all the thankless years,
> Cold, edged with dear-bought wisdom,
>   The judgment of your peers![8]

Not to be outdone, the suffragist Anna Garlin Spencer feminized the U.S. colonization of the Philippines, in the midst of a brutal war of subjugation, by paraphrasing Kipling's popular racialized and gendered taunt:

> Take up the White Man's burden!
> Go, pilot as you may
> Your new-caught, sullen peoples
> Who do not know the way.
> Go, teach them not with cannon,
> Those fluttered folk and wild;
> But lead them, as, with yearning,
> A mother leads her child.[9]

Thus fortified with discourses—the language and ideology of manifest destiny, national greatness, and the white man's and woman's burden—the imperial republic materialized those justifications for extraterritorial conquest of ocean worlds.

THE SPANISH-AMERICAN WAR

The nation's expansion beyond the continent began with the war with Spain over Cuba and then Puerto Rico in 1898. This conflict was an outgrowth of American economic interests in various Caribbean islands since the colonial period, as well as the nation's

FIGURE 12

Theodore Roosevelt (center) and his Rough Riders, July 1898. Photo by William Dinwiddie. Courtesy of Library of Congress.

flexing of powers in the Western Hemisphere, as exhibited by the Monroe Doctrine (1823), which warned Europe against meddling in American affairs, including events in the Caribbean and Latin America. In 1897, the annual U.S. trade with Spanish-ruled Cuba totaled $27 million. The U.S. animus over Spain's "uncivilized and inhuman" conduct in Cuba, as President William McKinley described it in 1897, and its brutal suppression of Cuban anticolonial movements also fueled the war.

When the U.S. battleship *Maine* exploded in Havana harbor, killing more than 260 on board, the chant "Remember the *Maine!* To hell with Spain!" echoed in the halls of Congress. At the time, many held Spain responsible for the ship's sinking, but later evidence suggested the cause was an accidental explosion in the ship's boiler room. War on Spain was declared in April 1898 and ended by August the same year. It was, Secretary of State John Hay pronounced, "a splendid little war"—one in which many more U.S. soldiers died from tropical diseases, malaria, dysentery, and typhoid than from bullets.

Theodore Roosevelt, then assistant secretary of the navy, an ardent imperialist and Mahan follower, ordered Commodore George Dewey and the Pacific Squadron to Manila immediately after the declaration of war to battle the Spanish there as well—even though the Monroe Doctrine had not mentioned involvement in the Pacific. Roosevelt, not content to remain an armchair imperialist, quit his position to don the uniform of a soldier and lead a volunteer regiment called the Rough Riders. Their much-publicized charge up Cuba's San Juan Hill made Roosevelt a national hero. But the myth was made galling by accounts that were slighting of the role of African American troops who were pivotal in that battle.

In May 1898, Commodore Dewey steamed into Manila Bay and destroyed the anti-quated Spanish fleet anchored there, securing his promotion to admiral and his national fame. As in Cuba, in the Philippines the Americans walked into an anticolonial revolution against a teetering Spanish empire. The Filipinos had driven the Spaniards into the city of Manila and surrounded them. The U.S. forces lay anchored in the bay awaiting the arrival of ground troops to complete the Spanish defeat. After several months, the army arrived. The Spaniards, caught between the Filipinos and Americans, eagerly capitulated to the latter to avoid the humiliation of surrendering to their colored subjects.

Under the terms of an armistice and the 1898 Treaty of Paris, which ended the war between Spain and the United States, Spain recognized Cuba's independence and ceded Puerto Rico, the Philippines, and Guam to the United States for $20 million. During the Senate debate over ratification of the treaty, a mixed group of anti-imperialists opposed the acquisition of the Philippines, which some feared might lead to a pollution of pure American blood by the "inferior" and "mongrel" races of Asia and Puerto Rico. Others warned of the flood of cheap Asian laborers, while U.S. sugar interests resented potential competition from plantations in the Caribbean and Pacific.

Whitelaw Reid, the owner of the *New York Tribune* and a member of the U.S. delegation that concluded the Treaty of Paris, inveighed against the incorporation of motley peoples of the former Spanish colonies. "Their people," he declared of the new possessions, "come from all religions, all races—black, yellow, white, and their mixtures—all conditions, from pagan ignorance and the verge of cannibalism to the best products of centuries of civilization, education, and self-government." In another context, Reid raised the alarm that "the enemy is at the gates . . . [and] may gain the citadel." "The enemy," he explained, was Puerto Rico's "mixed population, a little more than half colonial Spanish, the rest negro and half-breed, illiterate, alien in language, alien in ideas of right, interests, and government." Their assimilation, he predicted, would lead to the "degeneration and degradation of the homogeneous, continental Republic of our pride."[10]

In response, proponents of the treaty cited as a model the historical treatment of American Indians, who were annexed territorially but not politically or socially. The senator from Massachusetts, Henry Cabot Lodge, reminded his anti-imperialist detractors that from the beginning American Indian lands had been acquired by purchase, and American Indians, though treated as subjects, were excluded from citizenship. The Fourteenth Amendment's provision of citizenship by birth failed to apply to American Indians who formed "domestic dependent nations," as the Supreme Court had ruled in *Cherokee Nation v. Georgia* (1831). Filipinos, Lodge assumed, were organized as "tribes" like the "uncivilized" American Indians. They were unfit to rule themselves and would be denied admission into the U.S. political and social community.

TROUBLES WHICH MAY FOLLOW AN IMPERIAL POLICY.

FIGURE 13
A representative from the Philippines persuades Congress for funds. Antiwar cartoon by Charles
Nelan, 1898.

THE INDIAN WAR

The Senate ratified the Treaty of Paris on February 6, 1899. According to President
McKinley, the "gift" of the Philippines troubled him at first, but after prayer it came to
him that he should "take them all, and to educate the Filipinos, and uplift and civilize
and Christianize them." However, the "little brown brothers" who were the objects of this
"benevolent assimilation" failed to recognize the transaction between the two imperial
powers. They continued their war for independence—now against the United States—a
war that was prolonged, bloody, and costly for the United States and for Filipinos.

A U.S. commander in the field justified the conquest of the Philippines as an application of the Monroe Doctrine in Asia, as a way of saying to European nations, "Hands off,

FIGURE 14

Mass burial of the Sioux dead at Wounded Knee, 1890. Courtesy of Library of Congress.

this is our foster-child, a republic in Asiatic waters." The U.S. is "a leaven to overcome tyrants and monarchs in the orient." At the same time, he admitted, "a month's campaigning against the Niggers so-called is very demoralizing, and bad for discipline. To the victor belong the spoils as an aphorism," he confessed, "has perhaps done more harm than the saying that No Indian is a good Indian, except a dead one."[11]

This comment brings to mind the massacre of over two hundred Sioux men, women, and children by the U.S. Army at Wounded Knee, South Dakota, in 1890. The rhetoric justifying the U.S. war of conquest in the Philippines cast it as a war in which, in the words of Secretary of State Hay, America's Far West became the Far East. Many of the same troops who had fought against the Sioux and chased and captured the Apache chief Geronimo in the U.S. West marched against Filipinos. Major General Adna Romanza Chafee, who led the 1901 invasion of the Philippines, had spent decades fighting against the Kiowas, Comanches, Cheyennes, and Apaches. A contemporary said of Chafee that he "brought the Indian wars with him to the Philippines and wanted to treat the recalcitrant Filipinos the way he had the Apaches in Arizona—by herding them onto reservations."[12]

FIGURE 15
Confronting the enemy, ca. 1899–1900. U.S. Army photo. Courtesy of National Archives.

Filipino soldiers, unable to match U.S. firepower in the open, resorted to hit-and-run tactics and guerrilla warfare. The invaders responded in kind, demolishing crops and burning villages, corralling civilians into concentration camps, and executing those suspected of being or collaborating with the enemy. "Kill and burn, the more you kill and burn the better it will please me," and "Shoot anyone over the age of ten," a U.S. commander directed his troops. Torture, such as the "water cure," which simulated and induced drowning, was routine. In the war, genocide was defensible because, as John Burgess, a Columbia University professor, declared, "there is no human right to the status of barbarism."

U.S. African Americans both at home and in the Philippines saw a connection between the conditions of racism and segregation in the United States and U.S. policy abroad "to rule earth's inferior races, and if they object make war upon them." These are the words of Frederick McGee, a founder of the Niagara movement, which sought equal rights for African Americans. In 1883, the Supreme Court voided the Civil Rights Act of 1875, which had ensured equal rights for all in public places. In 1896, in *Plessy v. Fergu-*

son, the court held that racially segregated, "separate but equal" facilities did not violate the Fourteenth Amendment. "Jim Crow" laws separated blacks from whites and endorsed inferior facilities for blacks in a variety of settings, including railroad cars, schools, hospitals, restaurants, theaters, and parks. The *Wisconsin Weekly Advocate* of May 17, 1900, published a letter from an African American soldier in the Philippines to his family in Milwaukee. White soldiers, he reported, "began to apply home treatment for colored peoples: cursed them [Filipinos] as damned niggers, steal [from] and ravish them, rob them . . . desecrate their church property . . . looted everything in sight, burning, robbing the graves."

The war in the Philippines continued from 1898 to 1902, despite a robust antiwar movement in the United States and disenchantment among the troops in the field. The conquest required approximately two hundred thousand U.S. soldiers and resulted in over 4,300 American deaths. Tens of thousands of Filipinos perished; some figures put the number of deaths as high as nearly a million, including those who died of disease and starvation as a result of the fighting. Property destruction was widespread. The capture of Emilio Aguinaldo, the leader of the Filipino republican army, in March 1901 was a factor in the war's end. That same year, the U.S. installed a civilian government headed by William Howard Taft, who would later become president of the United States. But fighting continued, especially in the southern, Muslim islands. As with the use of American Indians in the Indian wars in the U.S. West, the army inducted Filipinos as "scouts" and then as ground soldiers. The U.S. commander in the Philippines imposed press censorship, held those suspected of aiding the enemy in indefinite detention, and exiled prominent "agitators" to Guam, which was formally ceded to the United States in 1899.

The Muslim peoples of the island of Mindanao were especially effective in resisting conquest by both the Spaniards and Americans, and the U.S. Army framed its campaign against them as a war between Christianity and Islam. In March 1906, the army trapped some one thousand Taosug Muslims in Bud Dajo, an extinct volcano, on Jolo Island. For four days troops shot, bayoneted, and threw grenades at the men, women, and children, killing them all. A week after the massacre, President Theodore Roosevelt sent a telegram to the U.S. commander, Major General Leonard Wood, to congratulate him and his men "upon the brave feat of arms wherein you and they so well upheld the honor of the American flag."[13]

Meanwhile, in the Caribbean, the United States installed a colonial governor in Puerto Rico in 1900. After the 1901 passage of the Platt Amendment, which gave the United States control over Cuba's foreign relations, it granted independence to Cuba. Still, the U.S. military remained on the island to suppress dissent and protect U.S. economic investments in sugar plantations, refineries, and railroads, which had soared during the occupation. Guantanamo Bay Naval Base, built by the U.S. during the war with Spain, was obtained from Cuba under a permanent lease agreement in 1903. Originally a coaling station, the base would later serve in the twenty-first-century "war on terror."

FIGURE 16

Bud Dajo massacre. U.S. Army photo.

FIGURE 17

School Begins. The schooling of colored peoples, represented by an "educated" American Indian and African American, and the unruly, yet-to-be-educated children of Cuba, Puerto Rico, Hawai'i, and the Philippines. Behind, a Chinese stands at the door. Cartoon by Dalyrmple, *Puck* ,1899.

The United States established itself as an economic and military presence in other overseas locations as well. A busy Secretary of State Hay declared an "open-door" trade policy with China in 1898, and in 1899 the United States gained the coveted harbor and naval station of Pago Pago on Tutuila Island, Samoa. Hawai'i presented yet another opportunity for Yankee imperialists in the tropical zone. The frontier was again open for business.

HAWAIIAN KINGDOM

In 1893, the U.S. minister to the Hawaiian kingdom, John Stevens, advised his superiors in Washington, DC: "The Hawaiian pear is now fully ripe, and this is the golden hour for the United States to pluck it." Stevens had been a key agent in that "ripening." Earlier, the minister had warned Washington that in the absence of U.S. annexation, the islands would fall to Asians. The events of 1893 were the outcome of the choices made by Hawaiian elites, in particular, and the foreign inundation foreseen by Davida Malo.

Hawai'i's loss of sovereignty had begun over a century earlier with the arrival of the first Europeans—the advent of Malo's "large and unfamiliar fishes" from the "dark ocean," and the feasting that followed. The stratification of Hawaiian society, which had commenced before James Cook's arrival in the islands in 1778, increased with Kamehameha I, who conquered and ruled all of the islands in 1819, establishing the Hawaiian kingdom. Kamehameha promptly instituted a royal monopoly over foreign trade. Commoners, formerly called on for military service, were now required by chiefs to fell and haul sandalwood from the mountain forests to waiting foreign ships at anchor below. The work diverted labor away from subsistence activities, causing famine. But sandalwood was valuable in the U.S.-China trade, and the revenue enabled Hawaiian rulers to purchase guns, ships, and luxury items such as imported clothes, furniture, and houses.

Those material temptations caused the kingdom's foreign debt to soar to US$200,000 by 1826, and when Hawaiian clients of U.S. merchants in the islands neared bankruptcy, the United States dispatched two warships to investigate and enforce the merchants' claims. Thus threatened, the chiefs imposed Hawaii's first written tax law, dated December 27, 1826. The law required every able-bodied man to deliver each year a specified load of sandalwood or its cash equivalent of $4 (Spanish), and every woman to provide either a mat or a tapa (a cloth made of bark) or $1 in cash. Pressed, thereby, into the exchange economy, many men and women sold their labor, with men commonly working as sailors and women as prostitutes. During the 1840s, so many Hawaiians joined the crews of passing ships that the government levied a tax on ship captains to compensate for the labor lost. In 1850, about 12 percent of all working-age Hawaiian men still served on board foreign ships.

According to an estimate in an 1829 report, U.S. commerce with the Hawaiian kingdom involved some 125 ships each year, some carrying sandalwood from the islands and furs from the Northwest, others in transit between America and Asia, and still others in pursuit of whales in Hawaiian waters. The total annual value of their cargo exceeded $5 million. The once-dense stands of sandalwood trees, like the native peoples, diminished rapidly, and the trade in that aromatic wood—so closely associated with the islands that the Chinese knew Hawai'i as the "Sandalwood Mountains"—came to an end by the 1830s.

Whales supplied the next extractive resource and industry. Between 1852 and 1859, 484 whaling ships on average each year converged on Hawaiian ports, and the business supplying those ships was brisk, exceeding $150,000 each year. At first managed by Hawaiian chiefs, the provisioning of ships increasingly fell under the control of foreign trading companies such as C. Brewer & Company, begun by an agent for the Boston firm Bryant & Sturgis, which was involved in the U.S. China trade. Brewer, along with Alexander & Baldwin, Castle & Cooke, Theo. H. Davies, and H. Hackfeld (later renamed American Factors), were called the "Big Five" because those companies controlled Hawai'i's economy and polity. All of them began as mercantile houses.

New England missionaries, too, were empire builders, commissioned to recreate Hawaiian society in their own image of Christianity and capitalism. As the nation had turned from continental to oceanic destinies, missionaries redirected their ministrations away from alien, domestic Indians and toward peoples overseas. "You are to aim at nothing short of covering those islands with fruitful fields and pleasant dwellings, and schools and churches; of raising up the whole people to an elevated state of Christian civilization," the American Board of Commissioners for Foreign Missions (ABCFM) instructed its first company of missionaries dispatched to Hawai'i in 1819.

That burden, the missionaries soon discovered, involved converting natives into subjects of the kingdom of capitalism. In 1836, the ABCFM's Hawaiian mission proposed an ambitious plan for a Christian colony in the islands, not unlike the plantation at Plymouth, a spiritual kingdom on earth in which commercial plantations and manufacturing industries would employ the masses in useful labor and supply revenues for the government and mission. The colony failed to materialize, but the missionaries' message of "profitable exertions" captured thousands of Hawaiian converts to Christianity and planted the seed that made the islands ripe for the harvest.

White settlers and missionaries, mainly from the United States, seized the opportunity to realize their own material interests when the nine-year-old Kamehameha III ascended the throne in 1824. The child relied for guidance on his missionary teachers, and as a young man he signed the Constitution of 1840, which installed a constitutional monarchy with executive, legislative, and judicial branches of government. From 1842 to 1880, foreigners occupied twenty-eight of the thirty-four cabinet seats and 28 percent of the legislature despite accounting for a mere 7 percent of the population. Treaties with England in 1836 and France in 1837, secured during visits of those nations' warships, promised property rights to British and French citizens, despite the Hawaiian belief that land was not private property but the body of Papa, mother earth, and the ancestors, and was thus a sacred trust.

In 1848, the Board of Commissioners to Quiet Land Titles, created three years earlier, announced the Great Mahele or land division, which reserved about 24 percent of the land for the crown, 39 percent for 245 chiefs, and 37 percent for the government. Commoners filed claims against chiefly lands, and those claims were finalized by an 1850 Act that allotted to 8,205 commoners 28,600 acres, or less than 1 percent of the land. Although all adult males were eligible, only 29 percent had their claims validated, leaving 71 percent of the kingdom's subjects landless. The law required claimants to prove that their plots were "really cultivated," inviting interpretation and abuses.

As a complement to that dispossession, another 1850 act granted foreigners the right to buy, own, and sell land in Hawai'i. That same year, the ABCFM Hawaiian mission petitioned and received from the government 560 acres for each missionary, and between 1850 and 1860 the government auctioned off some of its holdings, 64 percent of which went to foreigners. By 1864, a mere 213 foreigners owned more than 320,000 acres of Hawai'i, and a year later, a single entrepreneur bought the entire island of Ni'ihau, more than 61,000 acres. That land coup, a legal study later concluded, was a triumph of Western imperialism "without the usual bothersome wars and costly colonial administration," and it sealed the fate of the Hawaiian nation.

Gone were the chiefs who served the people, wrote the historian and statesman Samuel Kamakau; instead, foreigners had the king's ear, and they influenced him to act against the interests of the chiefs and subjects. The constitutional changes begun in 1840 under Kamehameha III met with Hawaiian resistance. In 1845, commoners petitioned the king to adhere to "the old good ways of our ancestors" and not listen to men "who will devastate the land like the hordes of caterpillars the fields." Hawaiians were now debased, they lamented, while foreigners were elevated, and "the dollar is become the government for the commoner and for the destitute. It will become a dish of relish and the foreign agents will suck it up."[14]

Deaf to that advice, the legislature allowed foreigners to become naturalized citizens of the Hawaiian kingdom in 1845. In protest, fifty-two Hawaiians signed a petition to the king: "Do not sell the land to new foreigners from foreign countries," they pleaded. That prospect, they confessed, "aroused within us love and reluctance to lose the land, with love for the chiefs, and the children, and everything upon the land. We believe we will soon end as homeless people."[15]

Drawn into capitalism's spreading net, the Hawaiian kingdom's compass shifted from its ancient north-south axis, with the islands positioned at the apex of the Polynesian triangle, to a modern, east-west alignment with the commercial traffic between America and Asia. The gold rush in California strengthened the ties between the islands and continent as the kingdom began supplying the miners with pickaxes and shovels, clothing, boots, and provisions. Potatoes that sold for two dollars a barrel in Honolulu sold for twenty-seven dollars in San Francisco. The boom was short-lived because Oregon and then California began to produce cheaper goods for the miners, but the Royal Hawaiian Agricultural Society, formed in 1850, correctly credited the developments in California with moving Hawai'i more fully into the embrace of the empire of "civilization and prosperity."

Agriculture was the mainstay of the Hawaiian kingdom, and so it remained, despite the transformations effected by settler rule. In fact, that conversion from subsistence to commercial cultivation was a factor in the kingdom's end. The subsistence economy was a hindrance to "the progress of civilization, industry and national prosperity," asserted William Hooper of Boston and other white settlers.[16] Hooper predicted in 1835 that his sugar plantation at Kōloa on the island of Kaua'i would serve as "an entering wedge" into Hawaiian society to "upset the whole system." Financed by a Honolulu merchant firm, Ladd & Company, Kōloa plantation set the pattern for the boom that followed. Planted on land leased from Kamehameha III for fifty years at $300 per year, the plantation paid a tax to the chief and governor of Kaua'i for its supply of workers. By the year's end, the plantation boasted twenty-five acres of sugar cane under cultivation, a camp for workers, a superintendent's house, carpenter's and blacksmith's shops, a boiler, a sugar mill, and a reservoir for water.

Hooper paid his Hawaiian workers not in cash but in coupons, which could only be redeemed for goods at his plantation store. In that way, he profited from both their labor and their wages. Hooper employed men and women but preferred women because he paid them less for equal work: twelve and a half cents per day to men but only six cents to women. Like the tax levied by chiefs on the labor of commoners, wage work drew the masses into capitalist relations, while subsistence activities fell by the wayside. Under a colonial economy, the sacred land, became property, the basis of capitalism, producing a single crop for export. The requirements of labor regimented the workers' world according to the time clock and seasonal growing cycles.

By 1846, there were eleven sugar plantations, two of which were operated by Chinese, in the Hawaiian Islands. Sugar exports rose quickly from 4 tons in 1836 to 180 tons in 1840 and nearly 300 tons in 1847. After a brief setback in the 1850s, production and prices climbed again during the U.S. Civil War, which crippled the South's sugar industry and cut off the supply of sugar to the North. Hawaiian sugar exports ballooned from 702 tons in 1860 to 9,392 tons by 1870. The 1876 Treaty of Reciprocity exempted Hawaiian sugar from U.S. customs duty. That agreement secured the place of King Sugar in the islands, leading to the establishment of the industrial plantation; it also tied Hawai'i to the United States so closely that by 1886, the United States accounted for 90 percent of the kingdom's exports and 80 percent of its imports.

Reciprocity also tightened the grip of the Big Five on the economic and political life of the kingdom. Firms like C. Brewer and Castle & Cooke, which had begun as suppliers of passing ships, turned to financing and developing sugar plantations. Others supplied tools and machinery to plantations; built roads, ports, and railroads to transport sugar; and controlled the shipping lanes to U.S. markets. In 1910, the Big Five controlled 75 percent of Hawai'i's sugar; by 1933, the figure had risen to an astonishing 96 percent. Through the formation of alliances and interlocking directorates, the Big Five established an oligarchy that eroded and then usurped the Hawaiian kingdom's sovereignty.

Elected king by the Privy Council and legislature, Kalākaua (1874–91) had to rely on his sponsors to keep him in power. The Treaty of Reciprocity, favored by sugar interests and acquiesced to by Kalākaua, rendered the kingdom economically dependent on the United States and the Big Five. The dominant partner in that relationship was the United States, which set the prices for sugar and the goods purchased by the kingdom. Moreover, the concentration on a single crop reduced the kingdom's ability to compensate for low sugar prices by producing other crops. As the fortunes of the Big Five rose, the kingdom's powers diminished.

In 1881, Kalākaua visited Japan, his purpose being to invite a "cognate and friendly race" into the kingdom to secure the demographic and political future of Hawaiians, who were declining in numbers. He had the idea of forming a "Union and Federation of Asiatic Nations and Sovereigns" with other nations in Oceania as a counterweight to the common threat of European colonization, but the effort failed. The king also tried to forge a Pacific Islands confederation with Samoa, Tonga, and others at about the time Germany, Britain, and the United States were discussing the division of Samoa. This initiative also failed.

Although he submitted to economic dependency, Kalākaua fostered Hawaiian nationalism in politics and the arts. He established the Hale Naua Society to give prominence to Hawaiian learning, a Board of Genealogers to affirm the rule of chiefs and deny foreign claims to indigeneity, and a Board of Health to license native healers. He promoted music and dance, sacred arts that missionaries had tried to suppress as pagan. Under his reign the Hawaiian nation came to life again. However, those developments made members of the white elite nervous. In 1886, they formed the Hawaiian League, thereby staking their claim to the nation. Previously, the term *Hawaiian* had been reserved for the kingdom's indigenous peoples. The following year the league forced upon Kalākaua a new constitution known as the Bayonet Constitution, which reduced the king's powers, gave the vote to white men, limited the power of the Hawaiian electorate, and excluded all Asians from the franchise. At a protest rally two months later, a Hawaiian leader exhorted the crowd: "Now tell me, have any of you been endangered by this new constitution?" To which the people shouted: "We are greatly oppressed."

Mass rallies were held against the 1887 Bayonet Constitution, and in 1889 the Hawaiian Robert Wilcox led an insurrection, in which seven nationalists were killed, a dozen wounded, and about seventy arrested. Charged with treason and conspiracy, Wilcox was subsequently acquitted by an all-Hawaiian jury. In 1891, the king, on his way to Washington to renew trade reciprocity, died in San Francisco. Kalākaua's sister and regent, Lili'uokalani, an opponent of the Bayonet Constitution and an ardent Hawaiian nationalist, was named queen.

Thousands of registered voters promptly petitioned the queen to enact a new constitution "for our country and our people." Those signatures, the queen noted, were "the voice of the people," and "no true Hawaiian chief would have done other than to promise a consideration of their wishes." While the queen drafted a new constitution to restore the powers of the monarchy, members of the white elite conspired with John Stevens, the U.S. minister, to overthrow the kingdom. In 1892, they formed the Annexation League, and in January 1893, when the queen announced her intention to abrogate the 1887 constitution, the league and U.S. marines used the force of arms to install a provisional government and held the queen under house arrest.

Stevens, having plotted with conspirators against the queen and directed U.S. troops to assist in the illegal overthrow of the monarchy, justified those acts as required to preserve public order and protect American lives and property. On January 17, 1893, the league's provisional government imposed its rule, declared that the Hawaiian kingdom was "hereby abrogated," and applied for U.S. annexation. It was at this point that an eager Stevens reported the Hawaiian pear ripe. But the new president, Grover Cleveland, withdrew the treaty of annexation from the U.S. Senate and directed an investigation into the queen's removal and arrest. Stevens was relieved of his post, and the U.S. secretary of state, after having read the investigative report, recommended against annexation, admitting that a "great wrong [was] done to a feeble but independent State by an abuse of authority of the United States." The president agreed, adding that the revolution was achieved through "unjustifiable methods" involving "an act of war . . . without authority of Congress" and the "lawless occupation of Honolulu under false pretexts by the United States forces." The entire affair, he admitted, inflicted a "substantial wrong."

The provisional government's president, Sanford Dole, one of the "mission boys" (descendants of missionaries), rebuked President Cleveland, charging him with interfering in "our domestic affairs," and refused to return power to the deposed queen. Instead, on July 4, 1894, the provisional government announced the establishment of the "Hawaiian" Republic. Six months later, a military tribunal tried 191 Hawaiians for participating in a failed insurrection to restore the monarchy, sentencing most of them to prison for one to five years and exiling more than two dozen to the United States and Canada. The republic put the queen on trial, in order, the queen recounted, "to humiliate me, to make me break down in the presence of the staring crowd" and "to terrorize the native people."

While under house arrest, Lili'uokalani translated into English the Hawaiian creation hymn, the *Kumulipo,* which established her legitimate claim to custody over Hawaiian lands and waters against the false claims of foreign imposters. After her release in 1896, Lili'uokalani sailed to the United States to plead her case and that of her people. The queen paid visits to Boston and New York City, following in the footsteps of the many Hawaiians who had labored and lived in those cities since the late eighteenth century. She also spent time in Washington, DC, calling on President Cleveland and members of Congress. She wrote to the state department, charging U.S. annexation as "an act of wrong toward the native and part-native people of Hawaii, an invasion of the rights of the ruling chiefs, in violation of international rights[,] . . . the perpetuation of the fraud whereby the constitutional government was overthrown, and, finally, an act of gross injustice to me."

FIGURE 18
Queen Liliʻuokalani, 1913. The queen died at
the age of seventy-nine on November 11, 1917.
Bishop Museum Archives, Honolulu.

But when William McKinley succeeded Cleveland as president, Congress stood ready
to embrace a tropical empire. In the summer of 1898, the same year that the Treaty of
Paris awarded Cuba, Puerto Rico, Guam, and the Philippines to the United States, Congress voted to annex Hawaiʻi. Queen Liliʻuokalani returned to her dominion on August
2, 1898, about a month after annexation. An eyewitness at the wharf reported that as the
queen stepped off the boat, "it was strange because it was so quiet. Nobody cheered. But
when the queen raised her hand and said Aloha! A great shout of Aloha came from the
crowd. But that was all. Most people were crying."

EMPIRE AND NATION

As many white supremacists had feared, manifest destiny changed the face of the nation.
The white or "citizen" race was joined by other races who were not seen as entitled to

citizenship. That distinction was upheld in the differential treatment extended to the peoples of the overseas acquisitions. In 1900, Congress formalized the incorporation of Hawai'i as a territory, a move that anticipated its eventual absorption into the union as a state. By contrast, Puerto Rico, Guam, Samoa, and the Philippines remained "unincorporated" U.S. territories. The distinction was crucial for the rights extended to those peoples, whether as "citizens" or "nationals." Their status as "wards" of the U.S. government derived from the state's policies toward American Indians.

Within the continental United States, the Treaty of Guadalupe Hidalgo in 1848 had assimilated Mexicans as citizens and effectively rendered them white. The extension of citizenship to African Americans in the wake of the Civil War terminated the narrative of a single race and nation, and the Jones Act of 1917 bestowed a second-class citizenship to Puerto Ricans. The Dawes Act of 1887 sought to dismantle the structure of American Indian nations by privatizing land holdings and granting U.S. citizenship to adult landowners. The act reversed a nearly one-hundred-year-old policy recognizing American Indian sovereignty, beginning with the Treaty of Greenville (1795). The decision of the Supreme Court in *Elk v. Wilkins* (1884) ruled that American Indians were not U.S. citizens by birth, as guaranteed by the Fourteenth Amendment, but citizens of their tribal nations. In 1924, Congress declared American Indians born after that year to be U.S. citizens, and in 1940 it extended citizenship to all American Indians with the Nationality Act. Expansionism and the imperial republic produced a modern army and navy sharpened through wars and endowed the United States with international powers, but they also resulted in the "darkening" of the nation's peoples.

Asians and Pacific Islanders were particularly problematic to the processes of expansion and incorporation. Their lands, waters, and their resources were vital to the imperial republic, and their labor sustained the nation's economy, but they also posed a threat to the nation as alien competitors in Oceania and as an imagined imminent danger to domestic tranquility. Those problems and their attendant threats evolved over time, as did their solutions, which were extensions of earlier policies applied to all "persons of color." But peculiar to Asians and Pacific Islanders were the effects of the language of the 1790 act, which limited naturalization to "free white persons." Their status as "aliens ineligible to citizenship" until the mid-twentieth century made them especially well suited to serve as migrant laborers.

SUGGESTED READINGS

Bederman, Gail. *Manliness and Civilization: A Cultural History of Gender and Race in the United States, 1880–1917*. Chicago: University of Chicago Press, 1995.

Kramer, Paul A. *The Blood of Government: Race, Empire, the United States and the Philippines*. Chapel Hill: University of North Carolina Press, 2006.

Osorio, Jonathan Kay Kamakawiwo'ole. *Dismembering Lāhui: A History of the Hawaiian Nation to 1887*. Honolulu: University of Hawai'i Press, 2002.

Silva, Noenoe K. *Aloha Betrayed: Native Hawaiian Resistance to American Colonialism.* Durham, NC: Duke University Press, 2004.

PRIMARY DOCUMENT

DOCUMENT 7

"Women of the Philippines," an address by Clemencia Lopez at the annual meeting of the New England Woman Suffrage Association, May 29, 1902, published in *The Woman's Journal* (Boston), June 7, 1902, 184.

> Clemencia Lopez traveled to the United States to appeal to the president for the release of her brothers, imprisoned in the Philippines by U.S. forces. She addressed the New England Woman Suffrage Association on May 29, 1902. Lopez spoke to her audience of white feminists "on behalf of the women of my own country" and tried to establish a bond of sisterhood between the two disenfranchised groups of women. But she also took an anti-colonial stance: both men and women, Lopez declared, were soldiers in the Philippine war for independence because colonization oppressed Filipino women and men alike. She appealed to her audience in the name of liberty, a cause that, she said, united the peoples of the Philippines and the United States.

It gives me very great pleasure to greet the Massachusetts Woman Suffrage Association on behalf of the women of my own country. I have yielded to your kind invitation to tell you something about the condition of women in the Philippine Islands, in spite of my inexperience and lack of literary skill, for which I pray your indulgence, and have had the courage to speak to you [so you] may form a different and more favorable opinion of the Filipinos, than the conception which . . . the American people have formed, believing us to be savages without education or morals.

I believe that we are both striving for much the same object—you for the right to take part in national life; we for the right to have a national life to take part in. And I am sure that, if we understood each other better, the differences which now exist between your country and mine would soon disappear.

You will no doubt be surprised and pleased to learn that the condition of women in the Philippines is very different from that of the women of any country in the East, and that it differs very little from the general condition of the women of this country. Mentally, socially, and in almost all the relations of life, our women are regarded as the equals of our men. . . .

Long prior to the Spanish occupation, the people were already civilized, and this respect for and equality of women existed. . . .

Before closing, I should like to say a word about the patriotism of the women. This is a delicate subject, for to be patriotic to our country means that we must oppose the policy of yours. But patriotism is a quality which we all ought to be able to admire, even in an opponent. I should indeed have reason to be ashamed if I had to come before this Association with the admission that our women were indifferent to the cause of their country's independence. You would have a right to despise me and my countrywomen if we had so little love for our native land as to consent that our country should be governed by foreign hands. . . .

In conclusion, in the name of the Philippine women, I pray the Massachusetts Woman Suffrage Association to do what it can to remedy all this misery and misfortune in my unhappy country. You can do much to bring about the cessation of these horrors and cruelties which are to-day taking place in the Philippines, and to insist upon a more humane course. I do not believe that you can understand or imagine the miserable condition of the women of my country, or how real is their suffering. Thousands have been widowed, orphaned, left alone and homeless, exposed and in the greatest misery. It is, then, not a surprising fact that the diseases born of hunger are increasing, and that to-day immorality prevails in the Philippines to an extent never before known. After all, you ought to understand that we are only contending for the liberty of our country, just as you once fought for the same liberty for yours.

SIGNIFICANT EVENTS

1819	first company of U.S. missionaries departs for Hawaiʻi
1820s	Chinese in New York City
	slavery prospers in U.S. South
	U.S. trade vessels arrive in Hawaiʻi for sandalwood trade
1823	Monroe Doctrine declared
1835	Kōloa plantation built
1836	U.S. settlers declare an independent Texas Republic
1844	Treaty of Wanghia, giving the United States most-favored-nation status in China trade
1845	John O'Sullivan coins phrase *manifest destiny*
	U.S. admits Texas as a state
	Hawaiian commoners petition king against foreigners
1846	U.S. declares war on Mexico
1848	Treaty of Guadalupe Hidalgo
	gold found in California
	Great Mahele
1850	foreigners allowed to buy and sell land in the Hawaiian kingdom
1850s	U.S. whalers in the Pacific and Hawaiʻi
1853	Matthew Perry arrives in Tokyo Bay

1854	Treaty of Kanagawa
1860	U.S. Civil War begins
1865	Civil War ends
	Thirteenth Amendment
1866	Civil Rights Act
1868	Fourteenth Amendment
1870	Fifteenth Amendment
1870s–80s	Kalākaua revives Hawaiian culture
1875	Civil Rights Act
1876	Treaty of Reciprocity between United States and Hawai'i
1878	U.S. gains access to Pago Pago, Samoa
1881	Kalākaua visits Japan
1884	*Elk v. Wilkins*
1885	Josiah Strong publishes *Our Country*
1886	Haymarket Square bombing, Chicago
1887	Bayonet Constitution in Hawai'i
	Treaty of Reciprocity renewed; U.S. gains exclusive use of Pearl Harbor
	Dawes Act
1889	Hawaiian insurrection
1890	Wounded Knee
	Alfred Thayer Mahan publishes *Influence of Sea Power upon History*
1893	U.S. aids in the overthrow of the Hawaiian kingdom
1894	Hawaiian Republic declared
1898	Rudyard Kipling publishes "The White Man's Burden"
	U.S. declares war on Spain
	Treaty of Paris ends U.S.-Philippine war
	U.S. annexes Hawai'i
	U.S. declares "open door" in China
1898–1902	U.S. wages war in the Philippines
1899	U.S. and Germany divide Samoa
1903	*Lone Wolf v. Hitchcock*
1917	Jones Act

PART 2

MIGRANT LABOR

Pacific Islanders and Asians did not go to America; Americans went to Asia and the Pacific. Asians and Pacific Islanders did not go to take the wealth of America; whites, Europeans and Americans, went to take the wealth of the Pacific and Asia. Pacific Islanders and Asians came to labor in the ocean worlds and systems created by whites, serving on ships and building railroads, trading for furs, cultivating plantations, orchards, and vineyards, and working in manufacturing.

According to world-systems theory, migrant labor arises when the core (a place of high capital concentration) extracts resources and labor from its periphery (places of low capital concentration). The intentional results of that relationship are development in the core and underdevelopment in the periphery. The pool of laborers in the periphery is accordingly wide and deep, and the cost of labor is low. With the onset of colonialism, the lands and waters of Africa, Asia, and Oceania were opened for capitalism and Christianity, and their peoples became the targets of labor exploitation. The colonizers in the tropical zones installed an empire of plantations and built a network of naval bases to secure trade.

Successive waves of Asian and Pacific Islander laborers arrived in Hawai'i and the United States: Hawaiian, Chinese, Japanese, Korean, South Asian, and Filipino. Employers applied the strategy of divide and rule, engaging each new group to break the strikes of and work for less than the preceding one. Men predominated in all of the Asian migrant groups, in keeping with the labor requirements of agriculture, the railroads, and the lumber and heavy manufacturing industries, and encouraging their eventual return to Asia. The absence of women, together with miscegenation laws, discouraged the conception of children, who were seen as unproductive and, because they were U.S. citizens by birth, as defeating the purpose and benefits of migrant labor. Migrants were in their prime years, and U.S. exclusion laws and repatriation schemes, instituted first for Asian women and then for Asian workers generally, limited the numbers of Asian migrant laborers when they were no longer needed or sufficiently productive. In addition, anti-Asianism, of which the system of migrant labor was a prominent part, made their continued stay in the United States difficult. Asian resistance strove to mitigate those discourses and material conditions of oppression.

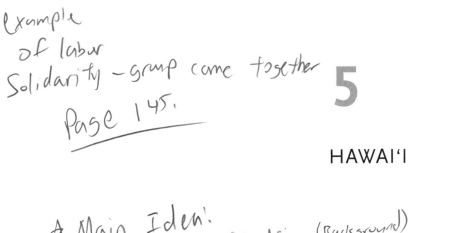

Example of labor solidarity — group came together
Page 145.

5

HAWAI'I

☆ Main Idea:
- European Imperialism in Asia (Background)
- Asian labor foundation of plantation economy in Hawaii
china → Japan → korea → phillippines (laborers in order)
- why in waves?
plantation owners ≠ laborers → chinese strike
- waves many → Japanese came in also strike
wants single job and so on.....

Like the Atlantic world created by Europeans, the Indian and Pacific ocean worlds involved the movement of capital and labor and the implantation of European settler colonies and naval bases to police the commerce. Tropical plantations of sugar, spices, tea, cotton, opium, coffee, jute, and rubber consumed, captured, enslaved, indentured, and recruited Pacific Islander and Asian workers. Located in the mid-Pacific and along the Pacific's eastern shores respectively, Hawai'i and America were outposts of that world-system.

In the United States, expansionists proclaimed their "manifest destiny" as a continental and oceanic imperial power. Shifting from its position on the periphery of Europe, the United States became a member of the core. Once the imperial republic secured land or the frontier, a demand for labor followed. Taming the American wilderness at first employed mainly indentured white workers to alienate and settle American Indian lands, but with the rise of the plantation economy, American Indian and, increasingly, enslaved African labor were used to purchase white freedom. Beginning around the mid-sixteenth century, Asians and Pacific Islanders—Filipinos, Chinese, and possibly South Asians from the Philippines and Chamorros from Guam—similarly served white masters on Spanish galleons and in New Spain. In Mexico and Louisiana, those migrant laborers formed the nucleus of an Asian and Pacific America on the continent.

In the eighteenth century, South Asians, Chinese, and Hawaiians, traveling on board U.S. and European ships, arrived in Philadelphia, New York City, Boston, and New Bedford, and on the Pacific coast in the Northwest. Some of those who settled formed hybrid families with African Americans, American Indians, Irish, and whites. In the following century, as replacements for enslaved Africans, indentured Pacific Islanders and Asians worked tropical plantations.

THE ASIAN PERIPHERY

The world-system, with its transits of goods and labor, precipitated and benefited from turmoil in Asia. The nineteenth century in East Asia—China, Japan, and Korea—witnessed discontent among peasants over government corruption, abuses, and taxes. It was also marked by widespread anxieties over the incursion of European capitalists, military expeditions, and Christian missionaries. Colonization in the Philippines and India introduced changes in the domestic economy and in the minds of colonial subjects.

In China, following China's defeat by Britain in the First Opium War (1839–42), a peasant uprising against the central Qing government and the foreigners admitted by that weakened state coalesced into the Taiping Rebellion of 1850. Led by Hong Xiuquan, who claimed to be the younger brother of Jesus Christ, the rebels attracted a wide following and won a series of victories, but they were finally routed by Qing forces in 1864. As many as forty million people died in the rebellion, and much of the countryside in the productive lower Yangtze River region was devastated. The resulting losses made China vulnerable to incursions by foreign ships, diplomatic missions, and Christian missionaries. By 1910, Western merchants operated in over one hundred treaty ports in China, and Westerners dominated in many major cities even though the Chinese vastly outnumbered them.

In Japan, the capitulation to U.S. commodore Perry's iron ships and soon thereafter to other European powers divided the Tokugawa shogunate. Remembering the Tokugawa persecution of Catholic missionaries and Japanese Christian converts of the late sixteenth and early seventeenth centuries, some Japanese leaders saw the intrusion by foreigners and their teachings as threats to the unity and well-being of the people and state. Others, however, perceived Westernization as the only way for Japan to avoid the humiliation and loss of sovereignty that had been inflicted on China. The success of the latter faction led to the restoration of the emperor, Meiji, in 1868 and set the nation's course toward modernization, in emulation of Western nations. Industrialization transformed Japan, and merchants supplanted the warrior class. The peasantry was heavily taxed, rice riots were frequent, and peasants faced conscription into the imperial army. Like its models in the West, Japan launched an empire, starting with an invasion of Korea in 1894–95. China, having failed to protect Korea, its tributary state, recognized Korea's independence, ceded the island of Taiwan to Japan, and opened some of its ports to Japan's factories.

Korea had suffered invasions from China and Japan during the Koryo (918–1392) and Choson (1392–1910) kingdoms, and Western ideas, including Christianity, had entered Korea from China. Catholic missionaries had slipped into the country by the end of the eighteenth century, and many Koreans converted to the religion despite state persecution. Drought, flood, disease, and famine stalked the land, and legions of the afflicted died as in the epidemic of 1749, which left about half a million dead. Peasant uprisings, such as the 1811 revolt led by Hong Kyongnae, threatened the state and revealed deep-seated discontent among the dispossessed class. English, French, Russian, and U.S. warships arrived in Korean waters during this period of internal strife, and the Korean state resolved that all foreigners must be repulsed. Stone slabs erected by the government warned, "If we do not fight we must make peace; those in favor of peace are traitors." While European imperialists were preoccupied elsewhere, Japan forced Korea to sign the Treaty of Kanghwa in 1876, opening Pusan and two other ports to trade. The Sino-Japanese War (1894–95) left Korea vulnerable to Japanese domination of the peninsula. Japanese goods flooded Korean markets, and Korean rice and other produce supplied Japan's consumers. Korea thereby came to depend on Japanese capitalism.

The Indian war in the Philippines extinguished Filipino aspirations for freedom from Spain and the United States. On July 4, 1902, the United States declared an end to the war, even though conquest of the southern, Muslim islands continued until 1913. The U.S. colonizers introduced the English language in schools, government, and business; diminished the influence of the Catholic Church, including its landholdings; and granted a limited self-government with an appointed colonial governor-general. The government sent promising students to study in the United States, and in the Philippines, mainly through the schools, Filipinos learned to admire the United States as a land of democracy and opportunity, making many eager to migrate there. At the same time, Filipino peasants were largely untouched by the language and ideology of the colonizers and had few incentives apart from poverty to leave subsistence farming for the uncertainties of migrant labor.

In South Asia, British colonial rule predominated after the collapse of the Mughal Empire in 1707. Describing the ensuing chaos, the Muslim Indian historian Khafi Khan wrote in the 1720s: "Revenue collectors have become a scourge for the peasantry. . . . Many townships which used to yield full revenue have, owing to the oppression of officials, been so far ruined and devastated that they have become forests infested by tigers and lions, and the villages are so utterly ruined and desolate that there is no sign of habitation on the routes."[1]

From the time of Vasco da Gama's landing at Calicut in southwest India in 1498, Portugal had dominated Western trade with India and Asia, but it had lost ground to the Dutch and English by the early seventeenth century. The Dutch drove the Portuguese from Ceylon, and the English displaced them in India. At first, Indian rulers and suppliers held the upper hand over English merchants, but after invasive and civil wars, a British colonial government imposed itself over India with Parliament's India Act of 1784.

Those conditions of factionalism and peasant unrest in much of Asia, coupled with the foreign invasion of ideologies and capitalism and, in some places, conquest, facilitated and compelled the region's entry into the world-system of capital, labor, and culture. The same was true of Oceania. The U.S. core drew Asian and Pacific Islander workers, and thus a certain interval of Asian and Pacific Islander history can be characterized as the period of migrant labor.

CHINESE

Hawaii's sugar plantations, first established in 1835, initially employed Hawaiians. By 1873, 2,627 Hawaiian men (about half of all adult males) and 364 women worked for sugar plantations, a group constituting nearly four-fifths of the total workforce. Their precipitously falling numbers and the expanding plantation system nonetheless rendered Hawaiians an unlikely long-term source of cheap labor, so plantation owners turned to imported laborers from Asia. The "Indians," William Hooper reported (referring to the Hawaiians), were difficult to manage, so he turned to "Chinamen," Chinese workers who had arrived in the islands on passing trade vessels as early as 1794.

Chinese were already processing Hawaiian sugar when Hooper established his Kōloa plantation. Wong Tze-Chun started his short-lived sugar works in 1802 on the island of Lana'i, and by the 1830s there were several Chinese-owned sugar mills. Many of those sugar entrepreneurs married Hawaiian women and became citizens of the kingdom. The best known was Fong Chun, or Afong, as he was known in the islands, who owned several businesses in Honolulu and became the major shareholder of a sugar plantation on the island of Hawai'i, which by 1888 had about 1,200 acres under cultivation and employed 326 workers. Afong was perhaps the first Chinese millionaire in Hawai'i. He married a Hawaiian woman, Julia Fayerweather, and they had twelve daughters and four sons. One of those sons, Anthony Afong, became governor of China's Guangdong Province in the 1920s.

Chinese workers were less favored. China's defeat by the British in the First Opium War opened Chinese ports and labor pools to foreign traders and recruiters. Chinese coolies came to work sugar plantations alongside Indian coolies in the Indian Ocean and Caribbean. In 1852 the Royal Hawaiian Agricultural Society, formed two years earlier to advance planter interests in Hawai'i, imported the first group of Chinese on the *Thetis*, which departed Amoy (modern Xiamen), a south Fukien port. Indebted for their passage and bound by contract, the 175 laborers destined for field work agreed to serve at three dollars per month for five years, and the twenty who would become domestic servants were contracted to work at two dollars monthly for the same period. During the fifty-five days under sail, four or five men perished. Once the ship arrived in Hawai'i, the rest were dispatched in groups of twenty-five to sugar plantations on three islands. Later that year, the planters imported nearly a hundred more Chinese indentures. During the 1850s, with a dip in the demand for sugar, the number of imported laborers diminished, averaging a mere thirty-four annually.

Another ship that transported Chinese migrants to Hawai'i later in 1852 was the *Robert Bowne*, captained by Leslie Bryson of New Haven, Connecticut. According to its departure papers, it sailed from Amoy with 410 Chinese bound for San Francisco. Ten days out to

FIGURE 19

Tojin-baka, memorial to Chinese coolies on Ishigaki Island in the Ryukyus Islands, erected in 1971. Their names are inscribed on the memorial. Photo by Gary Y. Okihiro.

sea, Bryson ordered the men on deck for a washing and scrubbing. The ship's steward testified: "The Captain . . . cut off the tails of a great many of the coolies and obligated them to come on deck and be washed all over. The coolies evinced much concern at losing their tails, many of them crying."[2] The tail, or queue, was a braid of hair worn at the back; it symbolized loyalty to the Manchu government, and its removal signified rebellion or an act of treason. The cutting was intended to erase the owners' identities as Chinese and as men, like shaving the heads of Africans during the Atlantic slave trade.

In response to these abuses, there was a scuffle, and some of the crew grabbed muskets, fired at the coolies who had gathered on deck, and charged them with bayonets, killing eight. The rebellious and more numerous Chinese armed themselves with axes, a saw, and spikes. They killed the captain, his second mate, and several crew members and convinced the rest to surrender. The triumphant Chinese then forced the crew to steer the ship back to China, but four days later, the ship ran aground on a reef offshore of Ishigaki Island of the Ryukyus chain. Abandoning ship, the Chinese rebels met with a hospitable reception from the islanders, who took them in, fed and housed them, and gave them medical care.

Meanwhile, the crew regained control of the ship and, eight days after the rebellion, returned to Amoy. Intent on punishing the rebels, British and U.S. ships tracked them to Ishigaki Island and killed and wounded many. About forty committed suicide rather than submit to recapture. Only 148 of the original 410 were accounted for, living or dead.

The *Robert Bowne* rebellion was the first such incident on board an American coolie ship, and the U.S. commissioner in Canton was thus determined to make examples of the men. He demanded that the "pirates" be put to death. Instead, Chinese officials released the coolies after concluding that the *Robert Bowne* was headed not for California but for Hawai'i, that its captain had fashioned contracts that would bind the laborers to the highest bidder practically for life, and that the captain and crew had subjected the Chinese to cruel and inhumane treatment.

During and after the U.S. Civil War, the sugar boom in Hawai'i encouraged Hawaiian planters to procure more Chinese migrants. In 1865, their recruiter, Wilhelm Hillebrand, returned from China with two shipments of 522 Chinese laborers, including 52 women and 3 children, to the islands. In 1876, the year of the Treaty of Reciprocity, Chinese migration exceeded one thousand for the first time, and for the next decade it averaged 2,596 per year. By the census of 1884, there were 17,068 Chinese men but only 871 Chinese women in Hawai'i. Chinese men totaled nearly half of the entire adult male population of the kingdom, and they outnumbered Hawaiian men between the ages of fifteen to fifty, who numbered a mere 12,412.

Kidnapping was a common means of obtaining Chinese indentures, Hillebrand testified. He admitted that the difference between a coolie and a slave was one of degree, not of substance. After scouring the labor pens in Macao and Canton, Hillebrand filed a lengthy report with his employers, the planters, on the labor potential of India, Malaysia, and Japan. In that report, he recommended that Chinese migrants be required to work to pay off the cost of passage. Hawai'i's planters agreed and extended the term of indenture.

Working conditions for laborers in Hawai'i, as in other parts of the world-system, were patterned after Britain's Masters and Servants Act of 1850, which bound servants to their employers for a period of years for specified wages and guaranteed their civil liberties. But the application of the law often favored the masters. Servants in Hawai'i, like the coolies in Cuba, had little recourse against physical abuse such as whippings except to fight back, desert, or strike. In 1873, a Chinese worker in Hawai'i was sentenced to five years in prison for retaliating against his employer after having been hit. Following his prison time, he was forced to return to his abusive master to complete his contract term. The kingdom's court records indicate 2,099 cases of desertions and refusals of service in 1876, the lowest yearly total for such charges, and a high of 5,876 in 1898, despite an 1892 law that imposed three months' hard labor and imprisonment for repeat offenders. Since the plantations employed 10,243 workers in 1882 and 20,536 in 1892, those numbers of desertions were significant.

Plantation owners preferred young, strong laborers in order to extract the maximum possible labor for their money. Most migrant labor contracts stipulated ten hours of labor per day, with twenty-six working days per month. Of the 6,894 Chinese contract workers in Hawai'i in 1895–97, almost half were under twenty-five years old and nearly all under thirty-five. Opium, pushed by British colonizers in China, was legal in Hawai'i at the time and widely used by the men working on plantations. It might have provided not only pleasure but also temporary release from the aches and pains of hard physical labor, the psychological distress of separation from loved ones, and feelings of alienation in the planters' world. In 1873, the Custom House reported imports of more than 2,700 pounds and 900 "pills" of opium.

FIGURE 20
Chinese cane workers watched by *lunas*, or supervisors, on horses. Courtesy of Hawai'i State Archives.

An 1899 report by the secretary of the immigration board described one plantation's "Chinese camp." The laborers lived in barracks with six to forty men in a room. The structures were rough frame buildings roofed with shingle or iron, with porches that extended the length of the building. The interior rooms had no ceilings and so were open to the roof. The men slept on platforms six to eight feet wide, raised two feet above the floor, running the length of the room or building and stacked three to four tiers high. As in the beds on a coolie ship, each man had a section three feet wide. Those quarters supplied no more than shelter and a place to rest, the report conceded. After all, the object of the plantation was "compulsory work under a master," which "the law compels."

Even though the punishment of recalcitrant workers was swift and severe, Chinese laborers frequently protested their abuses. In 1897, Chinese workers on Kauai's Lihue plantation rose up against a manager and his overseer. The overseer was fired, but the manager was merely reprimanded. Fifteen of the Chinese who "rioted" were ordered by the court to be returned to China. On the island of Hawai'i that same year, Chinese plantation workers were fined for "riotous conduct in resisting the Police": two were sentenced to one year's hard labor; eight were given six months; ten were given four months; and twenty-three were given three months. The rest were fined "for deserting contract service" and ordered back to work.

In 1883, the year after the United States passed the Chinese Exclusion Act barring Chinese laborers, the Hawaiian kingdom began passing a series of statutes restricting the number of Chinese men migrants. The Hawaiian statutes allowed entry to a limited number of Chinese contracted to serve on sugar and rice plantations. They imposed few restrictions on Chinese women, in part because many planters saw women as pacifying agents among men workers. Moreover, women enabled the reproduction of the workforce. During the

FIGURE 21

Chinese rice fields in Waipahu, O'ahu, ca. 1912. Chinese preferred self-employment to working for white masters. Photo by R. J. Baker. Courtesy of Hawai'i State Archives.

period of migrant labor, however, women made up less than 10 percent of Hawai'i's Chinese population, which comprised 110 women and 1,196 men in 1866; 231 women and 5,814 men in 1878; and 1,090 women and 16,367 men in 1890. Between 1879 and 1886, perhaps because of California's anti-Chinese movement, over one-third of the Chinese migrants to Hawai'i were from the U.S. West Coast, especially San Francisco. Although their numbers fluctuated, Chinese arrivals in the islands steadily declined: 2,464 in 1878, 3,812 in 1879, 4,243 in 1883, 2,708 in 1884, 1,766 in 1886, 654 in 1890, and 975 in 1899, the year after Hawai'i's annexation, when U.S. exclusion laws applied to Hawai'i.

With the "opening" of Japan to Western contact, Japanese migrants represented a new and more attractive source of labor, and at the end of the 1880s the Hawaiian legislature passed two pieces of legislation to restrict Chinese entry and control their productive labor. The first, passed in 1888, limited the number of Chinese migrants and imposed a licensing system to regulate all "common laborers." The second, passed in 1890, restricted the entry of Chinese to five thousand per year for agricultural or domestic work for a term of five years. This act also required that seventy-five dollars from each laborer's wages be withheld to pay for their return to China at the end of their service. When Hawai'i's supreme court invalidated both acts as unconstitutional, the legislature amended the constitution in 1892 to create a class of bound workers based on race.

The period of migrant labor for Hawai'i's Chinese ended in the 1890s, when the planter-dominated government further restricted Chinese entry and labor. Chinese plantation desertions and their movement into urban trades and businesses, as well as independent farming, worked against the interests of migrant labor and rendered the free Chinese unwelcome to the master class. In addition, the cost of their labor had risen to eight and nine dollars per month by the 1870s. Now both intractable and expensive to the planters, Chinese laborers were replaced by the cheaper Japanese. By 1894 Japanese laborers outnumbered their Chinese counterparts by 21,294 to 2,734 on the sugar plantations.

JAPANESE

Having had its doors pried open by the United States in the 1850s, Japan offered new opportunities for Hawai'i's plantation owners to recruit labor. Robert Wyllie, Hawai'i's foreign minister and the master of the Princeville sugar plantation on the island of Kaua'i, wrote in 1865 to Eugene Van Reed, an American businessman in Japan and the Hawaiian kingdom's consul general there, regarding Japanese laborers: "We are in much need of them." On May 17, 1868, the *Scioto* set sail from Japan for Honolulu with 141 men, 6 women, and 2 children on board. According to Van Reed, the contracts specified a term of three years at four dollars per month, or about half the wages paid to Chinese sugar workers.

When the ship arrived in Honolulu on June 19, 1868, the king, Lota Kapuāiwa (Kamehameha V), presented the laborers with salted fish. Once the Japanese had recuperated from their ocean voyage, plantations on Maui, O'ahu, Kaua'i, and Lana'i paid seventy dollars for the contract of each worker. Within a month, both planters and Japanese had lodged complaints with the kingdom's Bureau of Immigration. The masters petitioned for refunds and compensation for workers in ill health, including one who collapsed in the field and died. Workers complained of physical abuses, fines for work infractions, and wages withheld by planters. An agreement with Japan allowed forty of the indentures to return before the completion of their contracts. Another thirteen worked for the contracted three years and then returned to Japan. The remainder stayed in the islands where, like the Chinese before them, a number of the men married Hawaiian women.

Plantations were often isolated communities, encircled by fields of cane, with working and living conditions harshly policed by a manager. On Maui's Waihe'e plantation, the rules specified that "laborers are expected to be industrious and docile and obedient to their overseers." More specifically, they required workers "to retire to rest and rise at the appointed hours. . . . No fires will be allowed after 6 P.M. and no lights after 8 P.M. and to rise at 5 A.M., the hours before breakfast to be devoted to habits of cleanliness and order about their persons and premises." In addition, "gambling, fast riding, and leaving the plantation without permission are strictly forbidden."[3]

On the Nu'uanu plantation, workers could be fined one-fourth of a day's wage for reporting ten to fifteen minutes late, twenty-five cents for each curfew violation, and two days of extra work for an unexcused absence or illness caused by the laborer's "own imprudence." Deductions were made from their wages for broken, lost, or stolen tools, and they were charged twenty-five cents for each stalk of cane taken.

Robert Walker Irwin, Hawai'i's consul general and special agent for immigration in Japan from 1884 to 1894, renewed Japanese labor migration to the Hawaiian kingdom by arranging for the Convention of 1886, which allowed for government-sponsored contract workers. Years of diplomacy preceded that agreement, such as the state visit by King Kalākaua to Japan in 1881 and two special envoy missions led by John Kapena in 1882 and Curtis Iaukea in 1884. Some of the kingdom's rulers hoped the Japanese would be not simply workers but a "cognate race" to repopulate and assimilate with the native peoples. Kapena told Japan's Emperor Meiji, "Hawaii holds out her loving hand and heart to Japan and desires that your people may come and cast in their lots with ours and repeople our Island home." Iaukea offered a three-year contract with monthly wages of nine dollars for men and six for women and twenty-six workdays each month. The workday was ten hours for field hands and twelve hours for mill workers.

On February 8, 1885, the *City of Tokyo* arrived in Honolulu harbor with 676 Japanese men, 159 women, and 108 children on board. The king gave each migrant a gift of one dollar and enjoyed a day of music, sake, and a sumo tournament with his guests. Irwin, who sailed with that first group, issued directions to plantation managers that the Japanese were "not to be driven" but "be led by a silken thread of kindness." They must not be whipped, he urged, and they should be encouraged to rise to the rank of overseer.

The recruiter's advice failed to impress planters who believed that workers had to be seasoned, or broken in. On Maui's Pā'ia plantation, for example, before the end of the year, five men died from maladies likely sustained or exacerbated by cruel treatment.

The planters formed an office called the Japanese section, with a staff of ten interpreters and seven physicians to handle workers. Joji Nakayama, the head of the section, had served as Japan's consul general in Rome before moving to Hawai'i. He received a generous monthly stipend of $100 at first, then $250, and finally $6,000 per year, demonstrating his usefulness to his employers managing the workforce. Nakayama's approach was to "act firmly with the laborers who are generally ignorant men." His physicians were authorized to decide whether workers were truly sick or simply feigned illness to avoid work. The section's staff toured plantations to resolve conflicts and increase worker productivity, acting as firemen in preventing and stamping out labor conflagrations.

In 1886, at Kōloa plantation, fifty of the ninety-two Japanese laborers refused to work and were jailed. They were protesting the plantation's practice of forcing workers to labor even when sick, irregular payment of wages, and a ban on cooking. Nakayama spoke with the strikers and convinced them to return to work after he negotiated on their behalf with the manager. Instead of advocating for his fellow Japanese, however, Nakayama advised the overseers to exercise "a certain amount of benevolence in manipulating Japanese, though it is our desire that there be strictness in making them carry out a proper amount of work."

After 1887, the planters imposed a thirty-five-cent monthly tax on all Japanese plantation workers to pay Nakayama and his staff, including bonuses. In the fields, Japanese
workers sang:

> The laborers keep on coming
> Overflowing these Islands
> But it's only Inspector Nakayama
> Who rakes in the profits.[4]

In 1890, about 170 Japanese workers at He'eia plantation rose up against their overseers,
who, they claimed, kicked and beat them and fined them for not following orders. Three
representatives of the strikers walked ten miles, climbing the rugged Nu'uanu Pali, to
meet with Nakayama in Honolulu. The section head showed them no sympathy: "He was
haughty and irate. He threw their petition on the floor without even reading it and berated
them for having the temerity to make complaints and told them that they should realize
that they were nothing but mere contract laborers."[5]

Between 1885 and 1894, under the terms of the Convention of 1886, twenty-six ships
deposited about twenty-nine thousand Japanese in the Hawaiian kingdom. At first, passage was free, but after 1887, migrants paid seventy dollars for transportation and handling, charged against their wages. Although the fee gradually decreased over the years
to $13 in 1891, monthly wages also fell in that year, from $15 to $12.50.

Government-sponsored migration ended in 1894. From 1894 to 1908, private emigration companies in Japan managed the flow of laborers to the islands, providing ample
opportunities for profits at the expense of the 125,000 Hawai'i-bound migrants under
their charge. Advertisements and rumors fomented "migration fever," which benefited
not only emigration and shipping companies but also banks, notably the Keihin Bank. A
1902 editorial in the Osaka *Asahi Shimbun* accused the companies of looting migrants
for "self-centered profit making." One migrant, Ko Shigeta, recalled his experience: "I
was from . . . Hiroshima Prefecture, and went to Hawaii as an immigrant worker at the
age of seventeen. . . . I wanted to save money in Hawaii and go back to Japan as soon as
possible. It was 1903 when I arrived at Honolulu with my two comrades. . . . I had borrowed 100 yen from Keihin Bank."

Shigeta worked on O'ahu's 'Aiea plantation for fourteen dollars a month, working from
6 A.M. to 4 P.M. "Fifty of us, both bachelors and married couples, lived together in a hum-
ble shed—a long ten-foot-wide hallway made of wattle and lined along the sides with a
slightly raised floor covered with a grass rug, and two *tatami* mats to be shared among us."
For that housing he paid seven to eight dollars per month, about half his salary. Tired and
overworked, Shigeta fell ill, but "since I owed 100 yen to the bank, I could not afford to
rest. . . . I worked hard, and in two years I was able to pay back the 100 yen. I often wished
I was back in Japan instead of enduring this hardship in Hawaii. The lives of all the Japanese working on the sugar farms were the same as mine, more or less."[6]

FIGURE 22
Laborers' quarters, Hilo Sugar Plantation, n.d. Courtesy of Hawai'i State Archives.

In May 1905, workers formed the Japanese Reform Association to petition the Japanese government to take steps against the emigration companies, Keihin Bank, and Japanese officials, who conspired to exploit them. In response, the government recalled its consul general in Hawai'i, Miki Saito, who had collaborated with the planters, closed the Keihin Bank, and imposed new restrictions on emigration companies. In September 1906, the association dissolved itself, claiming: "The Reform Association, formed . . . to extricate the 70,000 Japanese from the clutches of the Keihin Bank and the immigration companies, has fulfilled its mission." Emboldened, the association promised: "We 70,000 strong can easily unite again if the need arises. This is to declare that the dissolution of the Reform Association does not mean the demise of its fighters."

Like field hands on plantations in the U.S. South, sugar workers sang songs to voice their sorrows and distress and to share their burdens. In the process, they created an ideology and a class consciousness that sustained solidarity and action against perceived injustices and inequities. The Japanese called their songs *hole hole bushi*, combining the Hawaiian term *hole hole*, referring to the work of stripping cane stalks of their razor-sharp leaves, and the Japanese *bushi*, or tune. Toma Misa called her songs *setsunabushi* or "songs of pain," similar to African American blues:

> Starting out so early
> Lunches on our shoulders
> Off to our holehole work
> Never seems to be enough.[7]

One *hole hole bushi* likened the sound of the work bell to the call of birds and the toll of temple bells—both associated with misfortune and death, especially of a family member.

FIGURE 23
Japanese woman carrying cane, *hapai ko*.
Courtesy of Hawai'i State Archives.

Worse than the birds crying
Or the temple bells tolling
Is the plantation bell
Calling us to another day.[8]

Baishiro Tamashiro remembered his first day of work as a *kachi kane* (cane-cutting)
worker at Lihue plantation on Kauai. "Since we used knives," he began, "our hands were
blistered. . . . It sure was hard work. We had no time to rest. We worked like machines.
For 200 of us workers, there were seven or eight *lunas* [overseers] and above them was a
field boss on a horse. We were watched constantly." Tamashiro came to Hawai'i from
Okinawa, which was an independent kingdom before its conquest and occupation by
Japan in 1609. Okinawans were discriminated against by the Japanese, Tamashiro
recalled. "They [Japanese] thought that the Okinawans had tails," he said. "They looked

down on Okinawans, therefore we had much hostility." They discouraged intermarriage between Okinawans and Japanese. "They would say Okinawans are just nothing."[9]

Women commonly accompanied their husbands to the fields as well as working in the home. Many felt vulnerable to crude sexual remarks and harassment, and few had the opportunity for female companionship or escape. Tsuru Yamauchi was so afraid of men that she insisted that her husband accompany her in the early morning darkness to the outdoor kitchen where she prepared their lunches. "That was because it was uncivilized in those days, you know," she explained. "The hardest thing to get used to was the bachelors saying this and that. I hated it."[10]

Before 1900, Chinese and Japanese workers usually arrived in the islands by way of labor contracts. Despite the kingdom's 1839 declaration of rights, which guaranteed "life, limb, liberty, freedom from oppression," and the its constitution, which outlawed slavery and involuntary servitude, the system of contract labor, as governed by the Masters and Servants Act, devolved into a form of bondage. Workers' or servants' contracts were bought and sold, servants were obliged to obey all lawful commands of masters and their overseers, planters and managers assumed a proprietary interest in labor-contract disputes , and the master class appointed judges who were attentive to their interests.

A Japanese worker known to us only as Mioshi challenged a pillar of the contract labor system in 1891 before the Hawaiian supreme court, arguing that the assignment of his contract from the Bureau of Immigration to Hilo Sugar Company constituted a form of involuntary servitude. The court ruled against Mioshi, but in his dissenting opinion, Justice Sanford Dole, who later became the renegade republic's only president, supported Mioshi's argument that he did not possess the freedom to choose his employers. Wages alone, Dole argued, failed to place him in the category of free labor or remove him from "that condition of involuntary servitude or semi-slavery which is inconsistent with our Constitution and laws."

Of course, the rule of law gave way to coercion, which extended far beyond the plantation to the oligarchy of which Dole was a part—the same oligarchy that extinguished Hawaiian sovereignty. An instruction to workers on the Waiheʻe plantation— "Laborers are expected to be industrious and docile and obedient to their overseers"—was the planters' golden rule. Their organ, the *Pacific Commercial Advertiser*, editorialized on July 26, 1904 on the psychology of the "plantation coolie": "Yield to his demands and he thinks he is the master and makes new demands; use the strong hand and he recognizes the power to which, from immemorial times, he has abjectly bowed. There is one word which holds the lower classes of every nation in check and that is Authority."

To repress strikes, troublesome workers could be imprisoned en masse solely on the word of the plantation manager. If such measures proved insufficient, the Citizens Guard stood ready "to check any trouble or uprising that may occur amongst the ever increasing number of Asiatics," as the attorney general of the planter-dominated government asserted in 1894. Even entertainment did not escape the surveillance of the territory's rulers. In 1905, the authorities arrested five Japanese actors for performing plays that

FIGURE 24

Katsu Goto gravesite. His memorial, "In Memory of Katsu Goto," erected in Honokaʻa town, reads in part: Goto "used his bilingual skills to achieve human dignity and fair working conditions for sugar workers. Many consider him a pioneer labor leader. His spirit lives on." Erected by the Katsu Goto Memorial Committee, December 10, 1994. Photo by Gary Y. Okihiro.

contrasted the impoverished condition of plantation workers with the lives of opulence led by a plantation manager and the wife of Japan's consul general. The planters' *Hawaiian Gazette* agreed with the action because the performances were "decidedly menacing to the labor situation."

On October 28, 1889, the trussed-up body of Katsu Goto, a storekeeper and an outspoken advocate of Japanese workers in the Honokaʻa area of the island of Hawaiʻi, was found hanging from a telephone pole. Five white *lunas* on a nearby plantation and a Hawaiian were charged with the killing, but many believed that Goto's lynching was instigated by the planters to make an example of him because of his defense of Japanese laborers. The five whites were found guilty of the lesser charge of manslaughter and were released on bail pending an appeal, before which they vanished from the islands.

The annexation of Hawaiʻi as a U.S. territory in 1898 invalidated contract labor, which was illegal in the United States. Annexation also made it easier for the workers on Hawaiian plantations to remigrate to the U.S. West Coast. Advertisements promised wages of $1.50 per day for picking fruits and vegetables in California, more than double the $16 a month plantation laborers made in Hawaiʻi. A notable exodus resulted. Between 1905 and 1916, 62,647 Japanese arrived in Hawaiʻi, 30,119 returned to Japan, and 28,068 left the islands for the West Coast, leaving a net gain of only 4,460 in the islands. The labor recruiter for Laupāhoehoe plantation on the island of Hawaiʻi expressed his frustration over the situation; the same ship that carried 1,300 Portuguese to Hawaiʻi, he observed, sailed from Honolulu with 1,000 to 2,000 Japanese bound for Vancouver.

Seeking to halt the loss of labor, planters seized workers' passports and offered them monetary inducements to stay. The legislature required labor recruiters to buy $500 annual permits, and Hawaiʻi's planters lobbied Congress for a modification of the Chinese Exclusion Act to allow the importation of Chinese workers into the Territory. Those efforts failed. What finally stemmed the flow of Japanese workers to the U.S. West Coast was the rise of anti-Asianism on the continent. Examples included the formation of the Japanese and Korean Exclusion League, later called the Asiatic Exclusion League, in 1905, and the San Francisco school board decision of 1906 to relegate Japanese students, like Chinese children before them, to segregated public schools.

In March 1907, President Theodore Roosevelt signed an executive order to prohibit aliens whose passports had been issued for travel to U.S. territories, including Hawai'i, the Panama Canal Zone, or any foreign country such as Canada and Mexico, from entering the continental United States. This measure effectively ended the labor remigration from Hawai'i to the West Coast. In 1906, 12,221 Japanese left Hawai'i for the West Coast; in 1907, the number decreased to 5,438; a year later, the total dipped to 69 and in 1909 to 28. Japanese workers denounced the president's order as a sentence to permanent servitude in Hawai'i.

During the winter of 1907, the U.S. ambassador to Japan negotiated an assurance from the Japanese government, known as the Gentlemen's Agreement, that it would stop issuing passports to laborers bound for Hawai'i and the U.S. continent. The accord, which, took effect in the summer of 1908, amounted to an exclusion of Japanese migrant workers. During those negotiations, Hawai'i's governor, Walter Frear, held independent discussions with Japan's representatives to continue the flow of laborers to the territory. The governor's initiative embarrassed the Roosevelt administration, and the president expressed his dismay over planter reliance on "Asiatic coolies" and the subordinating of the territory's interests, as he understood them, to those of the planter class.

The only exemptions to the Gentlemen's Agreement were made for former Japanese residents of Hawai'i and their parents, spouses, and children. The impact was immediate and dramatic. In 1906, 17,509 Japanese arrived in Hawai'i; in 1907, 14,742; in 1908, 4,202; and in 1909, 1,310. Women were among the exempt categories, and "picture brides"—women in Japan whose marriages to men in Hawai'i or the continental U.S. were arranged mainly by the couple's parents—were significant in the post-1908 flow of migrants from Japan to Hawai'i. In 1908, 755 picture brides arrived in Hawai'i; by 1911 their numbers had risen to 865, in 1912 to 1,285, and in 1913 to 1,572. Overall, between 1908 and 1915, picture brides constituted more than 58 percent of all Japanese women migrants to Hawai'i.

That infusion of women, together with reproduction among the Japanese resident in the islands, resulted in greater gender parity. In 1890, there were 10,219 Japanese men and 2,391 women in Hawai'i; in 1900, 47,508 men and 13,603 women; in 1910, 54,784 men and 24,891 women; and in 1920, 62,644 men and 46,630 women.

The entry of women and formation of families ushered in a new phase of Japanese history in Hawai'i. Migrant workers, until then temporary, established roots and greater permanence. While the planters generally preferred a settled and self-reproducing workforce, Japanese migrant workers, like the Chinese before them, frustrated the planters' plans for them. They organized strikes to improve their wages and working conditions, and their children fled the plantations for other opportunities. The period of migrant labor for Japanese lasted from 1868, when the first group of migrant workers arrived, until the 1908 exclusion.

KOREANS

Although a handful of Korean diplomats, students, and merchants landed in Hawai'i in the 1880s, beginning in 1883, the vast majority began arriving a decade later, having been recruited for the sugar plantations. First proposed in 1896 by one of the Big Five companies, Korean migrant labor began after U.S. annexation of the islands and in response to planter anxieties over Chinese exclusion and growing Japanese numbers and labor militancy. A planter noted in 1901: "The reason we would like to get Koreans here is that some of the planters fear that getting so many Japs here as we have, they will combine against us in strikes."[11]

Assured by the federal government that Koreans were not subject to the Chinese Exclusion Act, Hawai'i's planters found their point man in Horace Allen, the U.S. minister to Korea. The Kanghwa Treaty imposed on Korea by Japan was modeled on Western trade treaties with China. Through China's mediation, the United States obtained similar rights to operate in Korea. Other European nations followed suit, eroding Korean sovereignty while competing with Japan for business opportunities in Korea. American investments in Korea included railroads, mines, and trading companies, and missionaries helped to colonize Korean minds by spreading Christianity and education. Allen was one of those missionaries. He had formed a friendship with Korea's King Kojong and, as a U.S. official, was a staunch advocate for U.S. business interests in Korea.

Allen met with Hawai'i's oligarchy in 1902 and promised to negotiate an agreement with Korea's rulers to allow the recruitment of Korean workers, whom Allen compared favorably with African Americans. Allen delivered on his promise after Kojong issued an edict based on the Japanese government's regulation of its migrants. On Allen's recommendation, the king granted recruiting rights to David Deshler, a businessman and a member of a prominent banking family in Ohio. Allen was indebted for his position as U.S. minister to Korea to Deshler and his stepfather, the governor of Ohio, both of whom had intervened on Allen's behalf with their personal friend President William McKinley. In return, Allen's connections led Deshler to the American Trading Company and the U.S.-owned Unsan Gold Mines in Korea.

Deshler created the East-West Development Company to handle the recruitment of Korean migrant workers and arranged for the Deshler Bank to funnel the capital supplied by Hawai'i's planters. He hired Korean recruiters and placed advertisements in Korean newspapers about opportunities "for the purposes of education, observation and engagement in commerce, industry and agriculture." Despite its deceptiveness, the effort failed until the missionary George Jones, a friend of Allen's, advised his church members to join the move to Hawai'i not only to work but also to evangelize and establish churches there. He held tent meetings to inspire his followers. Fifty-eight heeded his call, along with twenty workers from Inchon harbor.

In December 1902, 102 Koreans boarded the Japanese steamer *Genkai Maru* for Nagasaki, from where, after inspection and vaccinations, they sailed on the *Gaelic* for Honolulu. Deshler gave the migrants fifty dollars each to show immigration officials on landing (to prove that they would not become public charges), and, contrary to U.S. law, had them sign "work agreements" that bound them for three years' work on sugar plantations. The group consisted of fifty-six men, twenty-one women, thirteen children, and another twelve infants. On landing in Honolulu after ten days at sea, the migrants were greeted by the missionary George Pearson, who shepherded them through the immigration process while the planters arranged for their transport to Waialua plantation on Oʻahu's north shore. Deshler, after seeing his migrants off from Nagasaki, had returned to Korea to recruit more workers.

By the first week of February 1903, Deshler had three additional groups of migrants. The second group of ninety Koreans left Inchon on February 10 and arrived in Honolulu on March 2, 1903. These were destined for the Kahuku plantation, where they would earn sixteen dollars a month for working six days a week, ten hours a day. Back in Korea, Deshler expanded his operations by opening branch offices of his labor-recruiting company in Korea and hiring a Japanese handler in Yokohama to arrange their transport. The third group, consisting of seventy-seven men, four women, and two children, left Inchon on March 1. More groups followed: during the first six months of 1903, Deshler's efforts landed 450 Korean men, 60 women, and 60 children in the islands. He received fifty-four dollars from the planters for every man and forty-one for each woman migrant.

For the migrants, the voyage was long and exhausting, and many fell seasick. As one of them vividly described, "As soon as the ship was out in the open sea it began to rock and roll, and I was already getting a dizzy spell. . . . The boat was now rolling violently, tossing around all the movable things in it from side to side. I was one of them. It made me very sick, indeed, and it made everybody else sick." The planters, through Deshler, paid for the migrants' passage and also provided them with the "pocket money" to prove to the immigration inspectors in Honolulu that they had means of supporting themselves. The fiction that they were free immigrants and laborers had to be maintained, and their interpreters, who earned over twenty-five dollars a month, paid by the planters, ensured that immigration officials heard from the Korean migrants that they fulfilled U.S. requirements for entry.

There were about 1,200 Koreans in Hawaiʻi by the end of 1903, and another 3,500 arrived the following year. In the final six months of Korean migration, January to June 1905, more than 2,800 made the passage to the islands, yielding a total of 7,226 Koreans arriving in sixty-five separate shipments. Like the Chinese and Japanese migrant laborers before them, most of the Koreans were single men between the ages of twenty and thirty, with about ten men for every woman. Unlike the Chinese and Japanese, an estimated 40 percent of all Korean migrants were Christians, indicating the importance of missionaries in the Korean labor traffic. Also, whereas Chinese and Japanese originated from specific regions of their countries, Korean migrants came from all over the peninsula, mirroring the locations of Deshler's eleven recruiting offices in cities north and south.

The pocket money given to the migrants had to be recovered. In addition, Deshler tried to extort payment from the migrants for travel costs incurred during their transit from Korea to Japan to Hawai'i—about fifty dollars each. Some apparently acquiesced, making monthly payments to his agents on the plantations, but others refused to pay, believing these costs to be the planters' responsibility. Besides, some noted, the conditions of plantation labor were strenuous and exploitative enough. In 1904, on O'ahu, irate Korean workers assaulted one of Deshler's agents who tried to wring payments from them.

Following the pattern for controlling Japanese workers, the planters hired Korean interpreters like Chi Pum Hong, a store manager in Korea and an early convert to Christianity. Hong became an itinerant preacher, and when an agent of the sugar planters offered him a position in Hawai'i, Hong left Korea to work for the Baldwin family on their Maui estates in 1903. There he attempted to keep Korean workers productive and contented, and he served as a translator for the courts whenever Koreans were brought to trial. Another, Hyung-soon Kim, who had learned English at an American missionary school in Korea, served as an interpreter and labor mediator on Maui. For his work, Kim received seventy-five dollars per month, while Korean workers received fifty-four cents for every ten hours of hard labor. In the planters' view, interpreters earned their keep; as a manager testified, interpreters acted "as a luna over the people." A Korean interpreter described his job as exhorting his countrymen, "Let us be happy and work hard in the fields."

Ekpo Pyun arrived in Honolulu on board the *Mongolia* in 1904 among some 350 Koreans and 550 Japanese migrants. After a lunch of rice and fish, the migrants were divided into groups and dispatched to plantations. He and others boarded a train for 'Ewa plantation, whose facilities included separate Chinese Japanese, and Korean camps surrounding the sugar mill, administration buildings, and a plantation store. "It took us but a few minutes to get to our camp which was found right by the railroad tracks and bound by the cane fields on two sides," Pyun discovered. "I saw the rows of the whitewashed cabins in the camp." Boss Jung greeted them. "He was an all round man there; he was everything; he did everything," Pyun reported. "He was the interpreter, camp boss, social leader, preacher, language teacher, mail carrier, and what-not." Because he had intended to be a scholar, Pyun's hands were "as soft as silk," but on his first day of work he was given a pickaxe to clear bushes from the field. "That pickaxe was big and heavy, and my hands so small and tender, that pretty soon both of my palms blistered and began to bleed. To be sure, I was too small for that kind of work, and my hands were never used to any rough stuff like that. The only things I was accustomed to were pen and paper, and nothing else."[12]

Hei-won Kang went to Hawai'i with her mother, two brothers, and a sister-in-law. Kang's mother had left her father when he acquired a concubine, saying: "I am no longer

FIGURE 25
Korean girls and women, n.d. Courtesy of Hawai'i State Archives.

going to live with you, I am going to take my three children to America and educate them. I shall become a wonderful woman!" She signed a labor contract to go to Hawai'i. After arriving in Honolulu in 1905, the family went to 'Ewa plantation, where they endured wretched living conditions and unforgiving labor in the fields. Kang recalled, "At first we were unaware that we had been 'sold' as laborers. . . . We didn't know how we were going to survive. There were not many Koreans there. We shed many tears."

"If all of us worked hard and pooled together our total earnings," Kang said, "it came to about $50.00 a month, barely enough to feed and clothe the five of us." The women earned extra income by washing, ironing, and mending clothes during their off hours, and their fingers became raw and swollen from the harsh soap. They hid the younger brother from the planters to spare his delicate body from fieldwork. "He had the brains of an Edison but was not fit to be a laborer," Kang explained. She dreamed of attending school, but poverty kept her from fulfilling that ambition; instead, she worked to support the education of her brother, who eventually earned a law degree but was forbidden from practicing law because he was not and could not become a U.S. citizen.

By leaving for Hawai'i, Kang's mother, a child of the aristocracy, had defied her husband, a high official. When she left her husband, Kang recalled, her mother "was

42 years old and a real beauty, much prettier than I was. Mother was truly beautiful." She was among some seven thousand Korean migrant workers in Hawai'i who labored under the hot tropical sun and amidst choking dust, fearing the lash of overseers and the uncertainties of life for her children. The Koreans on 'Ewa plantation, Kang remembered fondly, "all asked us to stay around Ewa and that we'd all take care of each other."[13]

Korean workers, if sufficient in numbers, were housed in their own camps to serve the planters' purpose of dividing the labor force by ethnicity. A Korean migrant recalled, "Ours was the smallest camp, so far as our own population was concerned. There were six by six rows of cabins in the whole camp, and we occupied only three rows on the east end. The rest was partly occupied by some Portuguese and Puerto Ricans." Couples and families had cottages, while single men lived in barracks or "longhouses" and slept on the wooden floors. A migrant said his longhouse lacked privacy, and the men slept "like animals" in barns. Out of necessity, the migrants planted gardens to supplement their diet, and they had to buy the cheaper parts of animals, such as heads and offal, for stewing. Rice, soup, kimchi, dried fish, and vegetables were staple fare.

A Korean woman recalled: "Workers were under the constant supervision of the luna . . . who always watched the movement of each. If he spotted any irregularity, such as standing straight to ease the pain, he would shout at or whip the deviant one." Another described her *luna* as knowing "all the cuss words in the world" and riding his horse and cracking his whip while calling the workers "lazy" and commanding them to work faster. Laborers were not allowed to talk, smoke, or stretch and straighten their backs. When the *luna* spotted an infraction of the rules, "he whipped the violator without mercy. If the worker showed any signs of resistance, he would be fired at once."[14]

Plantation labor attempted to strip workers of their humanity. They worked and lived like animals, Korean migrants remembered. "We worked like draft animals, cows and horses, in the plantation fields," one testified. Another reflected, "The plantation owners treated Korean workers no better than cows or horses, as animals rather than as human beings. Every worker was called by a number, never by name."[15] This anonymity was perhaps the greatest indignity. Every worker wore a brass tag around the neck, called by the Japanese a *bango,* with a number stamped on it, which was the bearer's principal identity. Indeed in 1910, in testimony before the U.S. Congress, the Hawaiian Sugar Planters' Association (HSPA) secretary, Royal Mead, boasted: "The Asiatic has had only an economic value in the social equation. So far as the institutions, laws, customs, and language of the permanent population go, his presence is no more felt than is that of the cattle on the ranges."[16]

The planters used Koreans as strikebreakers against Japanese workers, as in December 1904, when about 1,500 Japanese workers on Waialua plantation walked off the job. Yet Korean migrants, like all laborers, resisted abuse and exploitation. By the end of their first year in Hawai'i, Koreans from Waiākea and Wainaku plantations on the island of Hawai'i traveled to Honolulu to complain of ill-treatment, and a month later, the Kīlauea plantation on Kauai reported that sixty-two Koreans "suddenly quit work with a view to coming to Honolulu." In the summer of 1904, 200 Koreans on Waipahu plantation mobbed the physician, who, they claimed, had killed a Korean worker, and in June 1905, some 160 Koreans on Maui's Pā'ia plantation struck over the dismissal of 80 of their fellow laborers for beating an abusive overseer.

Picture brides changed the demography of Korean America, which had consisted principally of men. Women added labor and thus income to the household, and their children, born in the territory, were U.S. citizens. Korean picture brides, like their Japanese counterparts, began arriving in the islands after 1908. They were sometimes disappointed with their husbands. John Young-Ahn Kim recounted the moment when his mother first met his father at the dock in 1912. "My father said that when my mother actually saw his face, she cried and wanted to go back to Korea. The picture he had sent her didn't show all the smallpox marks he had on his face. Finally, she would have to get over that and accept him." Other men abandoned their wives at the harbor. Eun-Ai Cho told how her mother, who arrived in Honolulu in frail health, was left at the docks. "In those days Korean men watched and waited at the docks. Since no one claimed my mother, a man named Kim took her to the Big Island." She later married another man, Cho's father.[17]

Many picture brides had heard success stories in Korea but experienced bitter disappointment in Hawai'i. "This man [a marriage broker] told me to expect to see money growing on every tree. My eyes were dreamy. I believe him because he said everybody in Hawaii was rich." Another remembered: "The go-between said there would be so much food we'd never be hungry. That stuck in my mind. On the farm there was never enough to eat." But on the plantations, they encountered a different reality. "[My] first stove was a tin can with a hole cut out for the pot [and my] home was constructed of wooden slats which offered no privacy at night when the lights were on." Another regretted: "Oh what a destiny! How come I have to work in this strange cane field! I cried many nights but soon I gave up."[18]

Koreans, like the Japanese, sought better opportunities on the U.S. West Coast. At first, only 90 men, 9 women, and 4 children remigrated, but in 1905, 373 men, 16 women, and 10 children departed for California, and 219 returned to Korea. Labor recruiters from the Great Northern and Northern Pacific railroads in the Northwest promised Koreans daily wages exceeding $1.10 per day—about double their plantation earnings. Likewise, agricultural recruiters from California lured Koreans with daily wages of $1.50 when Hawai'i's plantations offered only 70 cents a day.

The period of Korean migrant labor to Hawai'i ended in 1905, after Japan won the Russo-Japanese war, which resulted in greater controls exercised by Japan over Korea. Because of its inability to protect its migrants abroad, the Korean government temporarily suspended labor migration. Japan saw that outcome as a convenience, sparing it from having to care for Koreans in transit and in America. Despite the ban, Korea could not stop the labor traffic to Hawai'i and to Mexico: over a thousand Korean migrants made the trip between 1904 and 1905. In 1905, Japan declared its "right to protect Korea" by taking charge of "all Korean foreign relations," including "the protection of Korean emigrants." That exertion of "rights" formed the basis for the protectorate in November 1905, usurping Korean sovereignty and establishing Japan's hegemony over the peninsula.

Annexed in 1910, Korea became a colony of Japan. At the time, some five thousand Koreans remained in Hawai'i, and between 1910 and 1924 about one thousand Korean picture brides added to their number. In 1905, Japanese constituted about 62 percent of the plantations' workforce, Koreans 11 percent, and Chinese 9 percent. A year later, the proportion of Koreans dropped to less than 9 percent, in 1909 5 percent, and in 1910 4 percent. Like many of the Chinese who fled the plantations, Koreans settled in urban areas. As colonial subjects of Japan, they suffered not only the indignity of holding Japanese passports issued by their colonizers but also the sting of anti-Japanese hatred. Although Korea's colonization by Japan continued for the next thirty-five years, Korean communities in the United States became the centers of Korean nationalism and the liberation movement against imperial Japan.

FILIPINOS

Even as the planters used Chinese to displace Hawaiians, Japanese to replace the Chinese, and Koreans to counter a perceived Japanese labor monopoly, they sought another group of migrants to compete with and ultimately supplant Korean and Japanese workers. They found them in the Philippines, where the U.S. imperial republic was beginning to transform the Far East into the nation's Far West. Their efforts were at first disappointing. As a frustrated recruiter put it, the Filipinos had "enough to occupy their time and mind, and enough to eat," and were thus uninterested in laboring as migrants. In 1906, after wrestling with the U.S. colonial bureaucracy and reluctant Filipinos, the planters' recruiter, Albert Judd, returned to the islands with only fifteen men. By 1907, only 150 had been recruited. E. Faxon Bishop, the HSPA president, conceded that the plan to recruit Filipino migrant workers was "all but a failure."

The first *sakadas,* or Filipino migrant workers, arrived in Honolulu on December 20, 1906 on the *S.S. Doric,* escorted by their recruiter, Judd. Five members of the Gironella family were among that group: Simplicio, the oldest at fifty-six, and his four sons, of whom Antonio was the youngest at fourteen. Another son, Francisco, an eighteen-year-old, spoke English and served as interpreter. The Gironellas were selected to tour the plantations and return to the Philippines to promote the idea of working in Hawai'i. "These men," Judd assured the reporter covering the migrants' arrival, "will be found quiet, industrious, temperate fellows without any pronounced vices." The *Pacific Commercial Advertiser*'s reporter added, as if surveying a labor auction block, "The newcomers are all small men, smaller than the Japanese who come here, but they are an intelligent looking lot. All are young men, most of them under twenty years old and all look very wiry and willing."

In the wake of the Gentlemen's Agreement, which curtailed the influx of Japanese workers, along with the outflow of Japanese to the West Coast and a massive Japanese strike in 1909, Hawai'i's planters redoubled their efforts to recruit laborers from the Philippines. As colonial subjects, Filipinos traveled as U.S. nationals and were thus unaffected by anti-Asian exclusion laws. The planters hoped that the Filipinos, like the Koreans, would disrupt the Japanese labor movement, which was reducing profits and challenging planter dominion over the working class. As a plantation manager wrote in 1913: "I should very much like to get say 25 new Filipinos to put into our day gang. . . . In this way perhaps we can stir up the Japs a bit." On receiving thirty Filipinos twenty days later, he reported his delight and observed that he intended to use them to bring Japanese workers to "their senses."

In the Philippines, recruiters concentrated their efforts in the Ilocos regions of Luzon in the north and Cebu (Visayas) in the south, among rural, agricultural peoples familiar with work in the fields. As outsiders, recruiters were met with suspicion. Filipinos in the town of Tacloban attacked them with sticks and clubs, driving them off to reclaim their townsmen, and a crowd from Tobaco stopped Filipino recruits from leaving on board the steamer *Cebu*. In 1915, the Philippine colonial legislature, fearful of losing laborers, imposed a tax of six thousand pesos on agents recruiting for labor overseas, charging another five hundred pesos for each province the recruiters visited. It also specified that recruits must receive written contracts and be guaranteed free passage back to the Philippines after the completion of their service.

Despite those obstacles, by the end of 1910, HSPA recruiting yielded 3,554 Filipinos for Hawai'i, where they numbered 21,031 by 1920. An additional 74,026 arrived during the 1920s and 7,388 more between 1930 and 1934. Sixty percent of those Filipino migrants were Ilocano-speaking, and about 30 percent were Cebuano-speaking. Overall, between 1909 and 1934, a total of 118,586 Filipino migrants arrived in Hawai'i: 103,544 men, a mere 8,952 women, and 6,091 children. The first two Filipinas arrived with the second group of *sakadas* on February 25, 1907. Eight more women came with the third group later that year.

A Filipino migrant described the labor recruiters and their ploy. Two well-dressed men worked together, and one of them "was always jingling the silver pieces in his pockets." They said they came from Hawai'i, and they asked if anyone wanted to accompany them back to the islands. "There was plenty of gold paid to laborers in Hawaii, they said. No one need worry about clothes or having to work hard for them either. People lived in houses made of lumber, a luxury which only wealthy people could enjoy in the Philippines. People could not believe that water could be gotten by turning a little handle instead of drawing it from a spring. . . . Everyone became fascinated by the tales told them of Hawaii." Word of a land filled with gold and quick wealth spread quickly throughout the village.[19] The agents received seven pesos for every laborer recruited from the Visayas or Ilocos regions but only five pesos for recruits from around Manila because Tagalogs, reputed to be "resentful of strict supervision," were less desirable.

The Hawaiian sugar planters, disregarding U.S. law as they had done in recruiting Koreans, required each Filipino migrant to sign a three-year labor contract for free passage

FIGURE 26

Sakadas Juan Baloran, Juan Pagoyo, Cipriano Barragado, and Julio Silga, n.d. Courtesy of Hawai'i State Archives.

to the territory. These contracts were modified in 1915 to conform to Philippine legislation of that year by providing return fare to the Philippines at the end of the contract period. Laborers were given a signing bonus of ten pesos for single men and twenty pesos for families. The labor agreement specified a ten-hour day in the field, or a twelve-hour day for office work, and twenty-six workdays per month for a salary of seventy-five pesos a month.

A Filipino migrant described the selection process. The recruiters, he noted, disqualified those who were educated and who had soft hands. They looked for rough, callused hands as indicative of a manual laborer. They checked for tuberculosis and other diseases, and they gave the selected migrants ten pesos each for signing the labor contract and then kept them on board the ship. The next morning, they sailed for Manila, where more recruits, "a large number of Ilocanos and a few Tagalogs," joined the group. From Manila, the ship sailed to Hong Kong, Shanghai, Kobe, and Yokohama before crossing the Pacific to Hawai'i. "One of the passengers in the boat died on the trip to Honolulu and they calmly threw his body into the sea. I felt very sad," the migrant reported. On arrival, agents formed Visayans, Ilocanos, and Tagalogs into separate groups and dispatched them to plantations. "The work in the plantation was very difficult!" the migrant declared. "I sometimes went to bed at night crying and wishing I were back in the Philippines."[20]

Juan Kihano arrived in Hawai'i in 1911 as a twenty-two-year-old and was assigned to Waipahu plantation on the island of O'ahu. Kihano remembered: "Work was hard in the plantation. All the lunas carried sticks. They said, 'Do this, Do that' and if you don't they beat you on the leg. They put me to work weeding and after that cutting the small cane. The work was very hard but I never complained."[21]

Segregated in a Filipino camp, which as the lowest stratum in the plantation hierarchy often sat in the least desirable place, *sakadas* attempted to restore some of their dignity by beautifying their homes. As Becky Ebat recalled: "We went to a certain plantation. That was 1919. At that time, it wasn't a pretty sight. It wasn't very clean where we stayed. The whole family, the whole clan got together and cleaned it all up. . . . It was beautiful to us. The clan decorated it, planted plenty of flowers, trees around it and painted. It was beautiful." Henceforth, their home was known as "Flower Village."[22]

Some planters wanted women to accompany the men, believing that women made men more docile workers and that reproduction added to the workforce. Theophilus Davies, head of one of the Big Five companies and an HSPA representative, consulted with the Catholic bishop of Honolulu about a plan to create a model community of Filipino families from a barrio in the Philippines, accompanied by their priest and village leaders. The planters offered to transport and house the priest, give him a comfortable stipend, and build a chapel for his services. That example, Davies proposed, would encourage more Filipinas to migrate and increase the number of Filipino migrant workers. The scheme failed, but it showed some planters' desire for a stable labor force. Additionally, planters used women and children as workers, especially seasonally, paying them less than men while exploiting their labor.

Other planters held that women and children were unproductive and sapped profits by requiring housing, medical attention, and schooling. According to one historian, nurses reported instances of forced sterilizations of women who were considered to have too many babies. Some men preyed on women and girls. As Alberta Alcoy Asis remembered: "My mama said, 'If we live in that Filipino camp, too much trouble' . . . not enough women, not enough women." Men, she reported, met newcomers to see if women were among them and, if so, to seduce them, "because they want to take the women. We call that 'cowboy-cowboy.'"[23]

A ten-year-old girl arrived in Hawai'i with her contract-worker parents in 1924. She married there when she was only fifteen years old. In 1936, she and her husband returned to the Philippines with her parents. There she had eight children, and after her husband died in 1946, she returned to Hawai'i as the nominal wife of her cousin's husband, who was a contract laborer. "We were afraid because we had falsified our names, but I told myself that if they were going to deport us, I would just jump from the boat. I have plenty of brothers and sisters in Hawaii, so I had come to stay with them."[24]

FIGURE 27

Filipina and children, ca. 1906. Courtesy of Hawai'i State Archives.

Filipinas bore the burdens of field and home. Juan Dionisio gave his impression of the blur of activity upon first arriving in Honolulu. "I remember the beautiful smell of the orchids," he began. "All the Sakadas were herded directly towards the trucks. . . . Some . . . the women wore 'camisas' and skirts; barefooted. They had big bundles on their heads. You know these sheets full of clothes. Big bundles on their heads. One child, hanging to the skirt; another child hanging on in here; one child with . . . a coconut shell where we put the water." Dionisio added, significantly, that besides wearing the alienating plantation *bango*, these people were also known by name: "They had numbers and they had names."[25]

West Coast recruiters posed a threat to a stable plantation workforce. As early as 1910, labor recruiters for Pacific Coast fruit companies and Alaska salmon canneries descended on Hawai'i to pluck Filipino workers, who were not subject to the nation's Asian exclusion laws. In response, the territorial legislature passed a law in 1911 that made it illegal to recruit contract-bound laborers for work outside the islands, and it enacted a requirement for agents to deposit a bond of $25,000 each and an additional $100 for each recruit. To circumvent the laws, one ship, the *Senator,* anchored beyond the three-mile territorial limit and boarded more than a hundred Filipinos, who reached the ship on small boats and barges. It then sailed for San Francisco under the cover of night.

The planters' purpose of displacing Japanese with Filipino migrants succeeded: Japanese gradually left the plantations. In 1902, Japanese constituted about 74 percent of the work force, but that figure declined to 38 percent in 1922 and 19 percent in 1932, while the proportion of Filipinos rose to 41 percent in 1922 and 70 percent in 1932. A divide-and-rule strategy failed, however, because Japanese and Filipino workers alike resisted exploitation, insisted on their humanity, and organized strikes across ethnic divides.

In the midst of the Great Depression, in 1931, the HSPA drastically reduced the number of recruits from the Philippines to twenty-five each month, and the following year the planters, faced with a labor surplus and growing unemployment, offered free return passage to the Philippines to 1,700 Filipinos. In 1933, another group returned to the Philippines, as did a group of about 6,500 in 1937. Despite those efforts to rid the territory of "excess" labor, independent recruiters and shippers continued to bring Filipino migrants into Hawai'i, exacerbating the unemployment problem.

The Tydings-McDuffie Act, passed by Congress in 1934, ended the period of migrant labor for Filipinos by imposing a quota of fifty Filipino migrants per year, though Hawai'i's plantations were exempted, and prohibiting Filipino remigration from Hawai'i to the U.S. continent. The Philippine Commonwealth was established in the same year, with the promise of independence for the Philippines ten years later. As a result, Filipinos lost their status as U.S. nationals and became "aliens," like other Asians, within the imperial republic.

MIGRANT LABOR

The relations of production helped determine the demographic profile of Asian and Pacific Islander America. The presence of Asians and Pacific Islanders in the United States depended on their utility as laborers and, for Hawaiians, Chamorros, and Samoans, their incorporation was an outcome of U.S. designs on their lands and waters.

Each place had a unique social formation. Plantation owners in Hawai'i, for instance, generally preferred a relatively stable labor force and accommodated migrant families. By contrast, the farm labor and work projects along the U.S. West Coast were more seasonal and transient in nature. Women were useful to many of Hawai'i's planters, providing cheap labor and enabling the reproduction of labor. But a settled workforce also had disadvantages for planters: it invariably included less productive members, like children and the elderly, who needed housing, schools, and social services. More important, stability might drive wages upward due to recognition of seniority and the needs of growing families, and it could create a labor monopoly, breed discontent, and thus pose a threat to the social order. Dividing the workforce by race, ethnicity, and gender was thus a key strategy for planters.

To the planters, Asian and Pacific Islander contract laborers were little more than necessary inputs, like machinery and fertilizer. The historian Ronald Takaki has found among plantation records orders and receipts for tobacco, Portuguese workers, lumber, and olive oil and bone meal, canvas, Japanese laborers, macaroni, and mules and horses. An inventory from Grove Farm Plantation on the island of Kauai listed fertilizer and Filipinos in alphabetical order.[26]

Shipping companies, like the ships and captains of the coolie trade, transported and thus profited from Asian and Pacific Islander migrant workers of various ethnicities. The *S.S. Doric,* for instance, which carried the first fifteen Filipinos to Hawai'i's plantations, also carried 288 Japanese destined for the sugar plantations, 139 Chinese—nine of whom were destined for Hawai'i and the others for the West Coast—and a few South Asian Sikhs bound for California.

Largely because of U.S. antipathy toward Asian laborers even before annexation, Hawai'i's planters tried to whiten and "Americanize" their workforce by recruiting Portuguese—some 17,500 between 1878 and 1886—and smaller numbers of Germans and Norwegians. The Portuguese, many recruited from islands off the west coast of Africa, formed a middle group, the class of *lunas,* or overseers, between the white planters and the Asian and Pacific Islander laborers. Although they were white, they occupied a lower tier than planters in the plantations' racialized hierarchy. The planters also speculated about employing formerly enslaved African Americans and "Hindu" workers from India and the Malay Peninsula, but attempts to recruit them failed. Hawaiian nationalists, seeking to replenish their people with a "cognate race," directed labor recruitment toward Asia and Polynesia, importing some 2,500 Polynesians to the plantations between 1878 and 1885. Most found the work unsavory and soon returned home.

Like the planters of the slave South, who saw free blacks as threats to their hold over the enslaved workforce, Hawai'i's planters by the 1890s perceived the growing numbers of laborers free from the bondage of contracts as a source of danger. In 1894, the secretary of the Planters Labor and Supply Company estimated that about seventeen thousand free Japanese and similar numbers of Chinese and Portuguese were present in Hawai'i. Alarmed, the planters' provisional government barred entry to "idiots, insane persons, paupers, vagabonds, criminals, and persons with a loathsome disease." Aliens without contracts or a visible means of support had to show they had at least fifty dollars in cash to gain admittance. Annexation and the termination of contract labor rendered this legislation superfluous, but its passage renders bare the planters' scheme of controlling migrant labor through punitive contracts.

Despite histories of conflict in Asia and the planters' strategy of divide and rule, Hawai'i's plantations nurtured an incipient and growing class consciousness among Pacific Islander and Asian workers. As Hawaiians, Chinese, Japanese, Koreans, and Filipinos interacted daily, they came to see that the principal divide was not between ethnic groups but rather between workers, on the one hand, and the ruling class and their allies, the overseers and *lunas,* on the other. On his visit to Hawai'i in 1905, during the period of Japanese hegemony in Korea, Ch'i-ho Yun, Korea's vice minister, recommended to Koreans that "the most cordial relations be kept up with the Japanese and other fellow Orientals," and a Korean migrant added that in the islands, "Orientals go with other Orientals, whether or not they like each other, their appearance, their tastes, their backgrounds, and their living standards being very much alike."[27] That solidarity would eventuate into worker actions and strikes that hastened the transition in the relations of production from the state of migrant labor to that of dependency.

SUGGESTED READINGS

Felipe, Virgilio Menor. *Hawai'i: A Pilipino Dream.* Honolulu, HI: Mutual Publishing, 2002.

Glick, Clarence E. *Sojourners and Settlers: Chinese Migrants in Hawaii.* Honolulu: Hawaii Chinese History Center and University Press of Hawai'i, 1980.

Kawakami, Barbara F. *Japanese Immigrant Clothing in Hawaii, 1885–1941.* Honolulu: University of Hawai'i Press, 1993.

Rhodes, Daisy Chun. *Passages to Paradise: Early Korean Immigrant Narratives from Hawai'i.* Los Angeles: Academia Koreana, 1998.

Takaki, Ronald. *Pau Hana: Plantation Life and Labor in Hawaii, 1835–1920.* Honolulu: University of Hawai'i Press, 1983.

PRIMARY DOCUMENT

DOCUMENT 8

Hashiji Kakazu, excerpts from an oral history by Michi Kodama-Nishimoto, translated by Linda Enga, edited by Alice Matsumoto, and published in *Uchinanchu: A History of Okinawans in Hawaii,* Ethnic Studies Oral History Project and the United Okinawan Association of Hawaii (Honolulu: Ethnic Studies Program, University of Hawai'i at Mānoa, 1981), 482–87.

I was born in the 23rd year of the Meiji Period (1891) on November 7th in the place called *aza*-Maezato of Takamine-*mura* (Takamine Village).

My parents were farmers. Potatoes [sweet] were planted for food, and our sugar cane was made into sugar to make money. That's how we lived in Okinawa.

I was the third one in the family. My eldest sister was quite healthy, but the sister right above me died even before I knew her. Her name was Utoru but I couldn't pronounce it. My grandparents used to laugh since I used to call her "Tōru, Tōru."

I started school from age nine for five years. The Japanese school was centered around the emperor and the boys were supposed to become military men. Ever since I was a child I didn't like fights and the Japanese militaristic education. Since they taught militarism at school I didn't feel good and couldn't stand it. So instead of going to school I used to help my parents. And since my dad said he was coming to Hawaii, I came with him, and I've been in Hawaii until now. My mom tried very hard not to have me come and tried to stop me with all her might. But I said, "What do you know? I may be drafted in five or six years!"

She thought it was better for me to go rather than be drafted, so my mother said, "All right."

Well, everyone then came to Hawaii to earn some money. I just followed my dad. For the cost of transportation to come to Hawaii we borrowed some money, about $100, from the moneylender. After we came to Hawaii we sent money back. If we didn't pay it back, our land would have been taken away. So before anything else our main task was to quickly pay back the money. I don't think it took too long, maybe about two years.

[In 1906,] we went from Okinawa to Kobe and came directly to Honolulu so it took only about one week. I got quite seasick. I couldn't eat for about four days. And after about four days a person named Takamine from my village came to visit me when I was sick. And even now, I won't forget that person. She was sick, too, and after she came to see me, that night, she died. Sometimes, even now I wonder if she knew she was going to die and came to say farewell to me.

At the immigration office there were some (physical) exams and people who had bad eyes couldn't pass. There were some who had to go back even after finally getting to Honolulu.

From there, we went to a hotel called Kyushu-ya. We didn't even stay there overnight because we got on a boat to go to Maui in the evening.

There were some Okinawans in a place called Paia, in Maui. We saw a letter written by them in Okinawa and came to seek them.

The houses at Camp 3 were really junk houses. A house was made of rough wood. It was a tenement house built long and big. It was partitioned and in one room there would be three or so people.

There were mostly Okinawans, and I can still remember one guy who was really strong. When the camp policeman came around, everyone feared him because he'd use a whip. But this guy was stronger than us. When the camp policeman came around with the whip to make him go to work he just took away the whip. The camp policeman couldn't even get angry.

[*Kakazu moved from Maui to another sugar plantation in Kukuihaele on the island of Hawai'i.*]

I was just an ordinary laborer, doing *kachi kane* (cutting cane) and *ho hana* (weeding). The pay was better in Kukuihaele than in Maui. Maui was about $18 for an adult, and I got less because I was a boy worker, but Kukuihaele was giving $23. There was a man named Furukawa who cooked, and I think I paid six dollars for the cooking. I think I still had some spending money left, but after paying for the cooking I sent the rest back to Okinawa.

[*Kakazu fell ill and was confined at Papaaloa Hospital. After his release, he worked as a horse handler in Papaaloa.*]

Here I heard about the infamous three. Papaaloa's "Hachi" was one of the three tough *lunas*. *Hachi* is a bee and it stings right away so you're afraid of it. Papaaloa's "Hachi," Ookala's "Tora" (tiger), and Kohala's "Aka" (red), these were the infamous three. Each nickname was probably given to these *luna* by the Japanese laborers. The Papaaloa big *luna* fell off a horse and died, so "Hachi" became the big *luna*, and finally he became the Papaaloa boss.

[*Kakazu married his cousin, Tokusato Tama, and they had a daughter. He tried farming but failed. He took up charcoal making, and that too failed.*]

So I thought I had to do something more unusual. I went to Waipio to make *okolehao* (*ti* plant liquor).

Making *okolehao*—well—there's nothing harder than that. And it's very dangerous. The plants used to make *ti*-root liquor are difficult to dig.

As for brewing the liquor, there were others who were doing it before so I'd go there and ask about brewing. Those who were brewing from before would often talk about things they'd one. So I'd listen to these talks and one by one ideas like I should do this or that would come to my head. So, it never happened that my brew was too weak. Everyone liked the liquor I made and the *kanakas* (Hawaiians) used to lie and say the ones they made were Okinawan, mine, since everyone knew that my brew was good.

Well, brewing liquor was a violation and it was being banned by others. If you were caught you couldn't help but be put in jail. I took too many risks and went a little too far. I was sent to jail. But even when I went to jail, there was no suffering. Only, I felt it was good to see the other side of the world.

[*After prison, Kakazu tried his hand at growing coffee in Kona during the 1920s.*]

[*Kakazu wrote about the onset of World War II.*] You see, I believe my body is mine and your body is yours. Each person should be able to do as one pleases. The Earth was created naturally and man didn't make it. The Okinawans didn't make Okinawa, the Japanese didn't make Japan, the Americans didn't make America. The Earth was made naturally, and man is just living under the kind auspices of the Earth.

SIGNIFICANT EVENTS

1784	British Parliament passes India Act
1802	Chinese begin producing sugar
1835	Kōloa plantation established
1850	Taiping rebellion
	Masters and Servants Act (U.K.)
1852	Chinese contract workers arrive in Hawai'i
	Chinese coolie revolt on the *Robert Bowne*

1865	Hawaiian planters recruit 522 Chinese laborers
1868	*Scioto* arrives with 149 Japanese laborers
1869	Meiji restoration
1876	Treaty of Kanghwa
	Treaty of Reciprocity
1878	Polynesian labor recruits arrive in Hawai'i
1881	King Kalākaua visits Japan
1883	Hawai'i enacts entry restrictions on Chinese men
1885	*City of Tokyo* arrives in Hawai'i with Japanese laborers
1882	Chinese Exclusion Act (U.S.)
	Planters Labor and Supply Company forms
	U.S. and Korea sign treaty allowing Korean migration
1883	Korean diplomats, students, and merchants arrive
1886	Convention between Hawai'i and Japan for laborers
1889	lynching of Katsu Goto
1891	Mioshi challenges contract labor
1892	Hawaiian Sugar Planters' Association forms
1894–95	Sino-Japanese war
1900	Organic Act (Hawai'i
1902	Korean laborers arrive in Hawai'i
1905	Japanese Reform Association formed
	Japan defeats Russia
	Japan declares protectorate over Korea
1906	Filipino *sakadas* arrive
1907	Theodore Roosevelt's executive order restricting migration
1908	Gentlemen's Agreement
	Japanese and Korean "picture brides" arrive in Hawai'i
1909	sugar plantation strike on O'ahu
1910	Japan colonizes Korea
1921	Japan denies passports to "picture brides"
1934	Tydings-McDuffie Act

6

CALIFORNIA

The U.S. continent supplied a different context and social formation for Asian and Pacific Islander migrant labor than Hawai'i, where the plantation economy, the Big Five, an oligarchy, and a colonial relationship with the United States prevailed. On the continent, other forces were at work. In particular, California, with its large landholdings (a legacy of the Spanish period), its numerous and diverse indigenous inhabitants (a consequence largely of geography), and its expansive, fertile valleys, enriched by rivers, produced a distinctive social formation.

The sequential nature of Asian labor migration in the United States as a whole suggests a design. The exemptions and specifications of the various migration laws passed in the nineteenth century reveal their purpose: regulating Asian labor. For instance, Hawai'i was exempted from provisions of the various Asian exclusion acts on the continent because the plantations required laborers; Asian women and prostitutes were specified in the 1875 Page Act; and laborers were specified in the Chinese Exclusion Act of 1882. Broadly, on the continent, unlike in Hawai'i, Asian women were unwelcome as laborers, in part because their reproductive abilities could result in children, an unwelcome presence to employers among this type of migrant labor. The fact that the 1882 act excluded Chinese laborers but not businessmen signaled the end of the laborers' utility as migrant labor. The 1935 Filipino Repatriation Act made the object of migrant labor especially clear by offering Filipinos free passage back to the Philippines during the Great Depression, when their labor was no longer required. Like other Asian migrant laborers, Filipino laborers were recruited by U.S. employers when required, and

TABLE I. Chinese and Japanese population in
Santa Clara County, 1860–1940

Year	Chinese	Japanese
1860	22	—
1870	1,525	—
1880	2,695	—
1890	2,723	27
1900	1,738	284
1910	1,064	2,299
1920	839	2,981
1930	761	4,320
1940	555	4,049

SOURCE: Timothy J. Lukes and Gary Y. Okihiro, *Japanese Legacy: Farming and Community Life in California's Santa Clara Valley* (Cupertino: California History Center, 1985), 19.

when they were no longer useful, they were discharged and repatriated by the nation-state.

The significant gender imbalance among all Asian migrant groups, more marked on the continent than in Hawai'i, testifies to the gendered work requirements of railroad construction and agricultural labor and the desire to reduce the social costs of Asian labor by culling members of the community considered unproductive by employers, such as women, children, and the elderly. Later, however, as on the plantations of Hawai'i, women and children formed a class of superexploited workers. Miscegenation laws policed reproduction, and the low numbers of women in the labor force suppressed the numbers of U.S.-born Asian and Pacific Islander children, who were eligible for U.S. citizenship under the Fourteenth Amendment.

How labor migration operated becomes clearer when we examine patterns in specific locations. In Santa Clara County, California, for example, the number of Japanese rose as the number of Chinese fell, and the former gradually replaced the latter in the county's agricultural labor force. As increasing numbers of Chinese agricultural workers left the county, growers attracted greater numbers of Japanese to replace them. These workers were the mainstay of the county's seed farms, which grew selected varieties of garden plants to produce seeds. The work was demanding and tedious. White men who operated machinery for plowing, cultivating, and hauling were paid thirty-five to fifty dollars per month with lodging and board. Chinese and Japanese men did the intensive handwork of caring for the seed stock, for which they received 80 cents to $1.75 per day, usually with lodging but without board, which amounted to $12 to $15 monthly. Both growers and white workers profited from that racialized labor hierarchy.

When Chinese left the fields beginning in the 1900s, seed growers tried to replace them with Portuguese and Italians but found these workers difficult to manage and unreliable. The Chinese worked as an organized crew, unlike the white laborers, who operated as individuals; and the Chinese returned year after year, whereas the whites were less predictable. So the growers turned to the Japanese, who, like the Chinese, organized themselves into work gangs.

As on the seed farms, so also in fruit picking and orchard work, Japanese workers replaced the Chinese, who had dominated orchard labor since the 1880s. Here too, orchardists first turned to white women, men, and children but eventually preferred Japanese labor crews for their efficiency. By the early twentieth century, the Chinese were virtually gone. On visiting thirteen orchards in Santa Clara County, a 1908 federal commission found 351 persons employed, including 46 white men, 66 white women, and 47 white children. The rest were Japanese: 187 men and 5 women.

Some Chinese, of course, remained in the county, just as Koreans, South Asians, and Filipinos later interacted with the Chinese and Japanese who had arrived before them. They cooperated and competed as workers, as Asians, and as distinctive ethnic and religious groups. Hawaiians, too, shared this condition of racialized labor and separation from political power. Those attributes, in fact, made Pacific Islanders and Asian workers desirable to the ruling class.

HAWAIIANS

Throughout the nineteenth century, Hawaiians worked America's West Coast, from Russian possessions in the north to Spanish and Chilean waters in the south. California was one workplace among many. John Sutter, a German immigrant who had crossed the Atlantic and the American continent to reach Vancouver, facilitated the arrival of Hawaiians on the West Coast. Sutter met James Douglas, the governor of Vancouver Island, who was an ardent booster of trade between the Northwest and Hawai'i. In 1838, Sutter sailed for Hawaii with a letter from Douglas, and in Honolulu he met with U.S. businessmen, one of whom wrote a letter of introduction to Mariano Vallejo, the Mexican commandant general of what was then Mexico's Alta California. After about five months in Hawai'i, Sutter departed for California, taking with him eight Hawaiian indentured laborers to serve him for three years at ten dollars per month.

When Sutter arrived in San Francisco, Hawaiians were already a presence on the West Coast: they had dominated the coastal carrying trade at least since the 1830s. Their work entailed piloting ships through treacherous waters, manning smaller transport vessels between ships anchored offshore and the beach, and navigating rivers. The Hawaiian William Davis captained the riverboat that took Sutter and his Hawaiian workers up the Sacramento River to his farm and tannery. Sutter's business contacts in Honolulu provided the funds to build his fort and houses, and his eight Hawaiian servants and their offspring supplied him with labor. They later became gold miners, river boatmen, fishermen, and farmers in the U.S. West.

In 1847, shortly before the discovery of gold at Sutter's mill, there were forty Hawaiians, thirty-nine men and one woman, in San Francisco, where they represented nearly 10 percent of the town's total population. Most of these worked on boats in the bay. Other Hawaiians caught up in the 1849 gold rush included Thomas Hopu and William Kanui, veterans of the War of 1812 on the U.S. side and former students at Cornwall's Foreign Mission School, established by missionaries in Connecticut for native youth. Kanui settled for a time in San Francisco and Hopu in Sacramento.

In 1850, white immigrants imposed a tax on miners whom they called foreigners, notably Chinese but also Hawaiians and miners from Mexico and Latin America, in apparent indifference to the fact that whites too were foreigners to California. Under the law, whites, including state employees, could extort payments from foreign miners and force them from land claims, as happened with the Hawaiians at Kanaka Dam in 1850. As early as 1852, some of California's politicians sounded the alarm over "the concentration, within our State limits, of vast numbers of the Asiatic races, and of the inhabitants of the Pacific Islands, and of many others dissimilar from ourselves in customs, language and education."[1] Accordingly, in that year, although they constituted less than 10 percent of California's population, Hawaiians and Chinese were the targets of a state senate resolution that sought the exclusion of Chinese and Pacific Islander carpenters, masons, and blacksmiths, who were said to be present in the state "in swarms under contract" and in competition with white artisans.

In California, as in other regions of the continent, Hawaiians faced a white racism that equated them with Indians, "Negroes," mulattoes, and nonwhites, and they were thus ranked as inferior. That common condition of exclusion and exploitation produced identifications and solidarities across the borders of racial classifications. For instance, during the 1850s, when the state forced the removal of the Maidu Indians near Sacramento to Round Valley Reservation, Ioane Ke'a'ala O Ka'iana, the grandson of the famed eighteenth-century traveler Ka'iana and one of Sutter's original Hawaiian workers, shared his Maidu wife's lot and sorrow by making the journey on foot with her into exile.

White hostility impelled Hawaiian workers to organize themselves into self-defense groups and to settle in segregated communities. Some Hawaiians arrived as couples, while other Hawaiian men married American Indian women. An 1863 newspaper report noted that Hawaiians tended to settle near Indian camps, marry Indian women, and share with Indians their way of life. Along Indian Creek in El Dorado County, Kenao's village consisted of twenty-four Hawaiians, including two women, and three Indian women and four *hapa,* or biracial children. At John Kapu'u's settlement, called Pu'u Hawai'i (Hawaiian Haven) at Vernon on the Sacramento River, eight Hawaiian men, one woman, and three children, together with Pamela Clenso, the Maidu Indian wife of John Kapu'u, fished for pike and sturgeon, which they sold to markets in Sacramento. Kapu'u was the son of two of John Sutter's contract workers, Sam Kapu'u and his wife. John Makani, a California Indian, went to Hawai'i for a mission education and returned to serve in a school for Indian children in Colfax, in the Sierra Nevada foothills. Like many of the Indian wives of Hawaiian men and the children of Hawaiian-Indian marriages, Makani was bilingual, speaking both his native tongue and Hawaiian.

In his memoir *Two Years before the Mast* (1840), the American writer Richard Henry Dana Jr. described Hawaiians in what was then Mexican California. In 1834, Dana sailed for California on the *Pilgrim* from Boston to acquire cattle hides for the leather factories in the Northeast. In San Diego, he wrote, Hawaiians hauled stacks of the stiff, smelly hides from the shore to waiting transport ships anchored in waters beyond the reefs. On the shore, Hawaiians processed the hides, soaking them in salt water for two days, boiling them in huge brine vats for another two days, and then stretching them out on platforms and scraping them. Along the harbor, in places like the Kanaka Hotel and the Oahu Coffee-House, Dana noted, the Hawaiians lived in a polyglot community, including Hawaiian, American Indian, Spanish, English, and French speakers, and communicated in a creolized trade language.

California's tallow and hide trade was important to both Mexico and the U.S. Northeast. Until the 1850s, in fact, Mexican California depended almost entirely on those exports to pay for its imports and state expenditures. Reciprocally, the Northeast's shoe and boot factories relied heavily on that source of leather, and ship owners realized profits that approached 300 percent from the commerce. Exports such as clothes, shoes, boots, jewelry, and cutlery manufactured in the Northeast and traded for tallow and hides in California also boosted the Northeast's economy. Hawai'i, too, produced cattle hides as well as meat and benefited from their export, which exceeded sugar exports in 1855 and continued to flourish during the second half of the century despite being dwarfed by sugar. Hawaiian boatmen and tanners and Mexican *vaqueros,* or cowboys, who raised the cattle in Mexico and Hawai'i, supplied the raw materials for the manufacturers of leather products in the Northeast. Those transoceanic exchanges of trade and labor underscore the separations and convergences of nations, regions, and peoples.

CHINESE

On January 24, 1848, James Marshall, a supervisor working for John Sutter, found gold at Sutter's lumber mill near Coloma, California. News of the find spread quickly, and California's gold rush drew miners from around the world, including the United States, Hawai'i, Mexico, Peru, Chile, Australia, and South Africa. Chinese workers from across the Pacific, long involved in the commercial traffic between America and Asia, joined the rushing tide. The First Opium War and the 1842 Treaty of Nanjing, which settled that war, had legalized the coolie trade, which transported thousands of Chinese to America. Because of environmental, demographic, economic, social, and political conditions during the mid-nineteenth century, southeastern China supplied a vast pool of overseas labor. European ships plied the waters, and port cities like Amoy (Xiamen), Canton (Guangzhou),

Fuzhou, Ningbo, and Shanghai became conduits for the global traffic, together with the European enclaves at Hong Kong and Macao.

Most Chinese workers required assistance to get to "Old Gold Mountain," as they called California. (Australia became "New Gold Mountain" after gold was found there in 1851.) The infrastructure involved labor recruiters, shipping companies, and credit suppliers to pay for the cost of transportation and ensure the repayment of the loans advanced. The costs and profits were considerable. In 1860, the boat fare from Hong Kong to San Francisco was about fifty dollars. Recruiters charged fees to shipping companies and the employers of their recruits, advanced money for the ship passage, and collected interest on those loans. The indentures, in turn, agreed to work for an employer for set wages and a specified term of years. The vast majority of Chinese migrants to California during the nineteenth century arrived by way of that credit-ticket system.

Cantonese songs told the tale of Old Gold Mountain. One is composed from the point of view of a wife left behind:

I am still young, with a husband, yet I'm a widow.
The pillow is cold, frighteningly cold.
Thoughts whirl in my mind, as chaotic as hemp fibers.
Separated by thousands of miles, how can I reach him?
Thinking of him tenderly—
I toss and turn, to no avail.
He's far away, at the edge of the sky by the clouds.
At midnight, I long all the more for his return now.[2]

In another song a Gold Mountain man boasted of his heroic exploits:

In the second reign year of Xianfeng [1852], a trip to Gold Mountain was made.
With a pillow on my shoulder, I began my perilous journey:
Sailing a boat with bamboo poles across the seas,
Leaving behind wife and sisters in search of money,
No longer lingering with the woman in the bedroom,
No longer paying respect to parents at home.[3]

The transpacific voyage could last one to three months, and conditions varied widely from ship to ship. Particularly horrible was the *Libertad,* which berthed in San Francisco in 1854 after losing about a hundred of its five hundred Chinese passengers en route. That statistic calls to mind the mortality rates on board coolie ships. In 1869, a San Francisco journalist described the Chinese migrants who streamed down the ship's gangplank as "blue coated men" carrying their luggage on bamboo poles across their shoulders. The men appeared to be in their twenties, the reporter estimated, and noted, as if

FIGURE 28
Chinese migrants in California, 1880.

describing livestock, that they were "healthy, active and able-bodied." Chinese business agents greeted and sorted the laborers and led them to Chinatown.

In 1851, a mere 2,716 Chinese entered San Francisco, but a year later the number rose to 20,026. In 1853 it dropped to 4,270, then increased to 16,084 the following year. By 1860, 73,890 Chinese had passed through San Francisco, and 112,362 arrived between 1860 and 1874 as the Central Pacific Railroad Company, eager to complete the western portion of the transcontinental railroad, actively recruited Chinese workers.

While these fluctuating numbers of Chinese migrants were driven by the demand for labor, they were boosted by a publicity campaign. In the early 1850s, Hong Kong newspapers reported that gold could be easily found on U.S. streets, and by the 1860s advertisers peddled the allegedly plentiful and lucrative jobs to be had in agriculture and on the railroads. Although those dreams of abundance quickly evaporated in the realities of the Golden State, they formed enduring myths about the land of opportunity.

During the second half of the nineteenth century, California was the most likely destination for Chinese migrants working in mining, railroads, and agriculture. Thus in 1860 about 84 percent of all Chinese in the state were in mining counties, but because of anti-Chinese hostility and declining quantities of gold in surface deposits, those numbers diminished rapidly to 45 percent in 1870, 32 percent in 1880, and a mere 12 percent in 1890. According to the 1870 census figures, that year Chinese made up about 25 percent of all miners in California and Washington and nearly 60 percent in Idaho and Oregon. Like other miners, the Chinese moved from one gold rush to another, including Pike's Peak, Colorado, in 1858; Nevada's Comstock Lode in 1859; Idaho in 1860; and Montana in 1864.

Some of the Chinese miners might have worked metal mines in Southeast Asia and so arrived in California experienced in the techniques required to extract gold. It seems that a recurrent event was the occupation by Chinese miners of claims abandoned by white miners who, because of racism and xenophobia, maintained first rights to the most promising rivers and lands. From the already sifted earth, known as tailings, Chinese miners worked the edges, a technique called "scratching," in search of gold. At Long Hollow Camp, California, four Chinese miners bought an abandoned claim for a few hundred dollars. In just two days, they reportedly extracted $4,000 worth of gold. News of their find led to the return of white miners, who promptly drove the Chinese away and reoccupied the camp.

Chinese, like other people of color in the United States, possessed no rights except those that whites chose to give them. According to the California supreme court ruling in *The People v. George W. Hall* (1854), Hall, the "free white citizen," was entitled to protection from the testimony of "the degraded and demoralized caste." The Chinese, after all, were "a race of people whom nature has marked as inferior, and who are incapable of progress or intellectual development beyond a certain point . . . differing in language, opinions, color, and physical conformation; between whom and ourselves nature has placed an impassable difference."[4]

The 1850 California foreign miners tax imposed on non-U.S. miners a twenty-dollar monthly tax, which decreased to three dollars in 1852 and rose to four dollars in 1853 and six in 1855. Not only was the tax onerous in itself, but whites, like George Hall, also used it to extort money from Hawaiian and Chinese miners. The law authorized the state's tax collectors to receive a commission on the amount they collected and authorized them to seize and sell property to pay the tax. The collectors readily did so. "I was sorry to stab the poor creature," one said of a Chinese miner, "but the law makes it necessary to collect the tax, and that's where I get my profit." Another admitted: "He was running away and I shot to stop him, I didn't think it would hit." "I took all the dust the rascal had," another collector explained. "There were seven beside him. And they didn't pay me last month."[5] By 1862, according to a report by the California legislature, the state's tax collectors had murdered eighty-eight Chinese, and only two of the killers had been found guilty and hanged. Generally, the perpetrators escaped scot-free.

Besides harassment from the state, Chinese miners faced hostility from both individual white miners and groups. In 1849, at Chinese Camp, Tuolumne County, white miners drove off about sixty Chinese working for a British mining company. In 1852, mass meetings in mining counties drew up resolutions to expel and bar Chinese and Hawaiians from their areas, and the Marysville mining district banned some three hundred Chinese from the North Fork of the American River and another four hundred from Horseshoe Bar. Yet self-interest militated against complete removal of the Chinese. Many counties drew much of their revenue from Chinese miners through the state miners' tax, and white-owned mining and other companies employed and benefited from Chinese labor.

The immediate cause of conflict was the resentment of individual white miners toward mining companies. The capitalists, white miners commonly held, employed cheap Chinese labor that undercut the wages of whites and drove them from the field. In fact, over time the depletion of surface gold had led to the need for large waterworks and machinery—which only large mining companies could afford—to find and extract gold. By 1860, independent miners and small mining companies were scarce, and standardization and consolidation were the norms.

Chinese miners survived by working the tailings and working for companies. They moved on frequently, driven by anti-Chinese statutes and hostile whites. Like Hawaiians, they operated in groups to ensure their safety and gather enough capital to establish claims. For instance, during the 1850s, a group of Chinese in Calaveras County paid $70,000 for a mining claim, along with protection money to forestall attacks and expulsion by whites. Chinese miners persisted in independent works long after most whites left for other opportunities, and Chinese capital financed Chinese mining companies when surface or placer mining came to an end. But other enterprises began recruiting Chinese workers and drawing them away from the pursuit of gold dust.

The railroads were a major employer of Chinese migrant labor. An 1858 notice reported that contractors for a California railroad had hired some fifty Chinese to labor "from sunrise until sunset." The Central Pacific Railroad began hiring Chinese in 1865. Contracted to build the western portion of the transcontinental railroad in 1863, in the midst of the Civil War, the company needed five thousand workers but had only eight hundred and had completed less than fifty miles of track when it decided to turn to the Chinese. The construction superintendent initially refused to hire them, but the situation was desperate, so an experiment began with fifty Chinese hired to fill dump carts. Having shown their capacity for hard work, the Chinese were pursued by agents of the company both in the U.S. West and in China. By the fall of 1865, there were three thousand Chinese on the Central Pacific payroll, and their numbers grew to some fourteen thousand, or four of every five men hired by the company at its peak.

Organized into labor gangs of fifteen to twenty laborers under a headman, the Chinese worked from dawn to dusk for a dollar a day, six days a week. Wages rose to thirty and then thirty-five dollars per month. The cook and headman took money from the men's wages for food, supplies, and their labor, leaving the workers between twenty and thirty dollars each month. Chinese merchants and a trail of pack teams likely supplied foodstuffs such as dried oysters, cuttlefish, fish, pork and poultry, rice, crackers, noodles, mushrooms, peanut oil, and salted cabbage and vegetables. Drinking hot tea protected laborers against contaminated water, and the varied diet helped to prevent vitamin deficiencies.

Conditions were desperate, especially in the high Sierra. Despite record snows in the winter of 1866, the company drove its workers to tackle construction of the railroad over Donner Summit, where in the winter of 1846–47 eighty-seven white settlers had been trapped by snow, and only forty-eight survived after having resorted to cannibalism. Snow buried the Chinese miners' cabins, requiring them to build chimneys and air-shafts, and the workers tunneled their way under the snow to their place of work, where they dug through the rock of the Sierras. It took two winters to break through the mountain. The winter of 1867 proved worse than the previous winter, and countless Chinese workers perished. Avalanches were frequent. About twenty thousand pounds of human bones were shipped back to China for burial there. Years later, the construction supervisor testified before a federal investigating commission: "The snow slides carried away our camps and we lost a good many men in these slides; many of them we did not find until the next season when the snow melted."[6]

On June 24, 1867, after enduring those conditions and tending their dead, some five thousand to seven thousand Chinese workers struck for better conditions: they demanded wages of forty dollars a month and a workday of ten hours for general work and eight for tunnel work. Eight hours was the standard for white men. The strikers also demanded an end to whippings by overseers. The men simply failed to report to work, a company official noted on the first day of the strike. They stayed in their camp. The company broke the strike within a week by cutting off the strikers' provisions, but it was alarmed enough to consider replacing the Chinese with ten thousand African Americans.

Other railroads besides the Central Pacific sought out Chinese workers. Between 1875 and 1876, as many as a thousand Chinese tunnel diggers bored the San Fernando Tunnel, which provided a way from the east through the mountains to Los Angeles. They also extended the tracks of the Southern Pacific eastward from Los Angeles, across the Mohave Desert through Arizona and New Mexico to San Antonio, Texas. Many perished in the extreme heat of the desert. The California and Oregon Railroad employed Chinese workers to lay tracks between San Francisco and Portland in 1887, and smaller lines within California hired Chinese construction gangs in the late nineteenth century. About 15,000 Chinese put down tracks in Washington, Idaho, and Montana during the 1880s, and the Canadian Pacific Railroad recruited 6,500 Chinese from the United States to work on its lines. In Canada, hundreds of workers perished because of the physical dangers, which matched conditions in the high Sierra. Beyond the American continent, a Seattle labor contractor, I-hsi Ch'en, recruited experienced Chinese railroad workers in the United States to build the Sunning Railroad in Toishan district, China, which was completed in 1909.

These skilled Chinese railroad workers were indispensable to U.S. economic and territorial expansion. Thaddeus Stevens, a Republican from Pennsylvania and one of the most powerful members of the U.S. House of Representatives, grandly described the importance of the transcontinental railroad during a debate: "The Western soil is but a platform on which to lay the rails to transport the wealth of the furthest Indies to

Philadelphia, Boston, and Portland, scattering its benefits on its way to St. Louis, Chicago, Cincinnati, Buffalo, and Albany. Then our Atlantic seaports will be but a resting place between China, Japan, and Europe."[7] Besides linking America's ocean shores, the railroad cut through the heart of Indian country, forcibly and artificially dividing that formerly borderless land and its communities of peoples, animals, and plants.

Chinese migrant labor was crucial not only for railroad construction but also for the development of the agrarian West. California's agriculture followed the pattern set during the Spanish and Mexican periods. Large land grants and holdings predominated, requiring masses of laborers to tend and harvest the pastures and fields. Livestock and grains formed the staple products, and American Indians and mestizos supplied the skills and labor. The completion of the transcontinental railroad in 1869 conveyed migrants and manufactures to the state and opened eastern markets to California's agricultural products, which shifted from grains to fruits and vegetables. The change required massive transformations of the land and rivers for irrigation. Chinese superseded American Indian and mestizo labor in that conversion.

Land-reclamation projects in the wetlands or tule lands of the Sacramento and San Joaquin valleys resembled railroad work: they required hauling and dumping tons of earth. From the early 1850s, white farmers hired Chinese laborers to build levees to reclaim rich farmland from the Sacramento River, and the work expanded as Chinese fled the mining regions during the following decade. Land-reclamation companies competed with the railroads for Chinese laborers, who organized themselves into supervised work gangs, as in railroad work. Chinese workers received about a dollar a day, while their reclaimed land increased in value a hundredfold. A report in the 1870s estimated that Chinese labor on railroads and reclaiming tule lands increased the state's property value by $290 million.

As in mining, Chinese agricultural workers were both independent producers and contract laborers. Mining and farming were related occupations. Miners needed food, and Chinese gardeners and peddlers met their needs and dietary preferences. Sometimes Chinese grew vegetables on the land of their mining claims, farming while panning the river for gold. As the Chinese left mining for other types of employment, gardeners and peddlers followed them to railroad construction sites and cities and towns. Those Chinese truck farmers grew fruits and vegetables, often on leased land or as sharecroppers, to supply local markets and tastes.

Chinese entrepreneurs also developed the state's fishing industry, which had begun with California's Indians. As early as 1854, Chinese fishing villages lined San Francisco Bay, and by the 1860s, Chinese fishermen had spread as far north as Humboldt Bay, where they established a fishing colony, and south to San Diego. They built Chinese sampans; their Chinese-designed nets swept the waters for sturgeon, squid, rock cod, halibut, and mackerel; and they sliced and dried their catch for export to Chinese settlements all over the state and abroad. They were also prominent in shrimping, their dried shrimp reaching markets in Hawai'i, China, and Japan. Before whites took a liking to abalone, the Chinese ranged the coast from San Diego to San Francisco for that shellfish. They salted and dried the abalone meat and exported it to China, together with the shell, which was used for the mother-of-pearl inlay for lacquer work.

While independent producers were key figures in Chinese California, many more worked as migrant laborers in wheat fields, on cattle and sheep ranches, and in the vineyards and orchards of the state. They provided essential labor for an industry that required large pools of capable, dependable, mobile workers. The labor demands of agriculture fluctuated widely with the seasons. Fruit trees and grape vines required pruning and vegetable seedlings needed thinning. The frequency of weeding depended upon the rainfall. Picking strawberries and cutting asparagus began early in the spring, while harvesting melons and picking apples came later. The ideal workers for these conditions were skilled, disciplined, and mobile in that they arrived in the numbers required, finished the job on time, were content with low wages, and moved on when no longer needed.

Besides working in the fields, Chinese built roads, bridges, rock walls, wine cellars, and irrigation ditches in rural areas, providing the infrastructure for the agricultural industry. Despite the value of their work, Chinese laborers' wages fell below those paid to whites. In the 1870s, winter wages were twenty-two dollars per month for Chinese and thirty for whites; during the busy summer season, Chinese received thirty and whites forty to fifty. The racial hierarchy and division of labor that favored whites mirrored the world of politics, in which whites were the citizen race and Chinese were excluded from power. Dividing the working class by race also reduced wages and class-based strikes, much as it had done on Hawaiian plantations.

Because of the nature of labor demand, the nineteenth-century Chinese California population was overwhelmingly male. Women were scarce, except for sex workers. A few of the first Chinese sex workers were independent entrepreneurs, such as a twenty-year-old from Hong Kong, Ah Toy, who arrived in San Francisco in 1849. Reputedly, white men formed a block-long line to pay an ounce of gold to see her, and within a year she opened a brothel on Waverly Place, staffed with Chinese women. She served mainly white men, accumulated enough money to leave the business, and married a wealthy Chinese man.

Most of the women, however, were part of an organized trade, lured and bound by contract, and transported to the United States for sex work in mining, railroad, and agricultural camps. The indentured and forcible nature of this traffic resembled the coolie trade rather than migrant labor. San Francisco's Hip Yee Tong was a leading organization in the traffic of women. From 1852 to 1873, the tong imported an estimated six thousand prostitutes, charged a forty-dollar fee to each buyer, and reportedly paid each white policeman ten dollars protection money. From that, the tong made an annual net profit of about $200,000. In 1870, a sex worker fetched $50 in Canton and sold for $1,000 in San Francisco, and by the 1890s, a prostitute allegedly sold for $3,000.

Most of these sex workers were in their twenties. They were divided into high- and low-class prostitutes: the former serviced only Chinese men, while the latter served working-class Chinese and white men. Their only wages were a small fraction of the charge for each sexual encounter, and they likely lived on tips and gifts from their customers, although they earned their owners thousands of dollars each year. Their lives were precariously brief: many full-time sex workers survived only four to five years, their deaths hastened by venereal disease.

Prostitutes made up about 3 to 7 percent of the Chinese population from the 1850s to 1870s, when the number of wives increased. Still, in 1870, Chinese prostitutes made up about 80 percent of Chinese women in rural California. A decade later, the number of wives increased, to about 30 to 40 percent of the total. The rise of families evidenced a more settled community and the end of the period of migrant labor, marked by the 1875 Page Act, which excluded bound or contract workers and Asian women and prostitutes from entry into the United States, and the 1882 Chinese Exclusion Act, which prohibited entry to Chinese laborers.

The numbers of Chinese migrant laborers followed the ebb and flow of California's industries and their needs. From 1850 to 1863, surface mining drew and employed Chinese migrants in considerable numbers, but from 1864 to 1867, as large company works superseded placer mining, more Chinese left than entered California. The boom in construction, agriculture, and the manufacturing industries from 1868 to 1876 led to another large influx of Chinese workers, which subsided during the depression years from 1877 to 1880. The geographic distribution of Chinese in California during these years reflects those employment patterns: initially, most Chinese were clustered in in mining counties, then along railroad lines, in rural farm districts, and in the manufacturing cities. Yet the story of Chinese in nineteenth-century California unfolded largely in rural areas, where the majority resided, worked, and built lives. Most were of the working class who depended on white employers. As Chinese displaced American Indian and mestizo laborers in California's fields, they in turn were replaced by other migrants.

JAPANESE

In California, as in Hawai'i, Japanese migrant laborers followed Chinese migrants. Decades before, however, the first Japanese had arrived in California not as migrant laborers but as political refugees and settlers. Katamori Matsudaira was a citizen of the city of Aizu Wakamatsu, which fell, with the Tokugawa shogunate, after Matthew Perry's "opening" of Japan. Seeking a new base, Matsudaira, at the suggestion of his German retainer, John Schnell, sent an exploratory party of samurai, farmers, tradesmen, and four women to establish the Wakamatsu Tea and Silk Colony on 640 acres of land near Placerville, California. On May 27, 1869, they landed in San Francisco. From there they proceeded up the Sacramento River with mulberry trees for silkworm cultivation, bamboo for food and furniture, tea seeds, and other plants native to Japan.

At the time, tea was one of Japan's major exports, and the United States was the largest market for Japanese tea. Water in the Placerville area was scarce, however, and the mulberry tree seedlings, weakened by the long journey, failed to thrive in the alien California soil. The colony lasted less than two years, despite an influx of new immigrants in 1870. There were twenty-two Japanese: fourteen men, six women, and two children. A few of the settlers returned to Japan; others drifted away. Okei Ito, a nineteen-year-old girl, died in 1871. Her tombstone near the site of the colony bears the simple inscription "A Japanese girl." Another settler, Kuninosuke Masumizu, chose to remain in California. He married Carrie Wilson, an African American–American Indian woman, had three children, and lived near Sutter's mill, where gold was discovered. After 1880, the family moved to Sacramento, where Masumizu worked as a farmer, miner, cook, barber, and fisherman.

The Japanese who came to California after the Wakamatsu colony experiment, however, were predominantly migrant laborers. Even the first students who arrived in San Francisco in the mid-1880s were workers, called *dekasegi-shosei*, or "student-laborers." Like the Yokoi brothers Saheita and Daihei, who arrived in New York City in 1866, they came to learn about "big ships" and "big guns" (in their words) to preserve Japan's sovereignty against the incursion of European nations. The Meiji government had determined that sending young Japanese to study abroad would bolster Japan against the West and advance Japan's modernization. Between 1882 and 1890, 1,519 of 3,475 passports issued by the Japanese government for migration to the United States were for *dekasegi-shosei*. The March 1890 *Japan Weekly Mail* reported that the Japanese population in San Francisco had grown rapidly, and that the new arrivals were chiefly student-laborers, "youths who have rashly left their native shores. . . . Hundreds of such are landed every year, with miserably scant funds in their pockets. . . . Their object is to earn, with the labour of their hands, a pittance sufficient to enable them to pursue their studies in language, sociology, and politics."

Japanese *dekasegi-shosei,* called "schoolboys," often suffered abuse from their employers. One Japanese applied for a job at a white home on Sutter Street after having borrowed money for a white coat and apron, the uniform of domestic servants. There the woman of the house insisted on calling him "Charlie" and set his wages at a dollar and a half per week. She immediately put him to work scrubbing floors and washing windows, and when she found him after hours of work sitting on a kitchen chair "thinking what a change of life it was," she was furious and screamed at him. Putting the silverware away after washing the dinner dishes, this student-laborer saw his reflection in the dining-room mirror. "In a white coat and apron!" he exclaimed. "I could not control my feelings. The tears so freely flowed from my eyes, and I buried my face with both my arms."[8]

From 1894 to 1908, the migration of Japanese laborers to California was handled by private Japanese migration companies that also shipped workers to plantations in Hawai'i, Australia, Fiji, Peru, Mexico, and Brazil. Their role in labor migration to the United States is shown in the dealings of the Hiroshima Kaigai Tokō Company, one of the biggest firms. Established in 1893, the company had branch offices throughout

Hiroshima and seven other prefectures, and it formed close ties with other migration companies elsewhere in Japan. In the year of its formation, the company signed an agreement with the Nichibei Yōtatsuha of San Francisco to recruit and employ laborers. One contractor for the San Francisco company was Tadashichi Tanaka, a seaman who had jumped ship in Seattle in 1885. There, Tanaka persuaded a Japanese prostitute to accompany him to Ogden, Utah, where he put her to work. A Chinese labor contractor from Rock Springs, Wyoming, fell in love with the Japanese woman and convinced Tanaka to allow him to take her as his mistress in exchange for subcontracting work for Tanaka. Operating from Nampa, Idaho, with student-laborers from San Francisco, Tanaka broke away from his Chinese employer and supplied five hundred workers to the Oregon Short Line, a subsidiary of the Union Pacific Railroad.

Labor contracting for railroads flourished first in the Northwest, where Japanese companies and contractors supplied thousands of workers for the Oregon Short Line, Northern Pacific, Great Northern, and other railroads. The Oriental Trading Company of Seattle, for instance, supplied between 2,500 and 3,000 railroad workers, and the S. Ban Company of Portland managed as many as 3,000 railroad and construction laborers. In California, the biggest contractor of railroad labor was the Japanese American Industrial Corporation, founded in 1902 and based in San Francisco. The company supplied laborers for not only railroad but also mining and agricultural work in California, Nevada, Idaho, Utah, and Wyoming, and at its peak, managed about 3,000 workers. As in Hawai'i, labor contractors exploited their workers, withholding daily commissions from their wages and monthly fees for translation and handling services. Contractors typically levied ten cents a day from men who earned $1.10 to $1.25 daily, yielding lucrative incomes of $2,500 or more each month.

Like the Chinese before them, Japanese labor contractors supplied workers for California agriculture. These operated on a smaller scale than the railroad contractors but were more numerous. Student-laborers first worked California fields in 1888, and by the 1890s Japanese began to replace Chinese migrant laborers. By 1908, the Japanese had become the main source of agricultural labor. The Japanese name for these workers— *buranke-katsugi,* or persons who carried a blanket—alluded to the bedding they carried with them as they moved from one agricultural job to the next.

Masuo Akizuki remembered arriving in San Francisco in 1912 and proceeding down the peninsula to San Jose to join his father. "When I came to San Jose the day after my arrival," Akizuki reported, "everybody was working in the countryside. The boarding houses in San Jose Japantown found jobs for us. They brought us by horse carriage to the place to work, and we each were given one blanket. Our living conditions were miserable. . . . We slept next to a horse stable on our blankets and some straw."[9] A *Shin Sekai* reporter agreed. After touring a Japanese labor camp in Fresno in 1900, he wrote: "The camps are worse than dog and pig pens. They are totally unfit for human beings to sleep in. Rain and moisture seep down from the roofs. Winds blow nightly through all four walls. It's like seeing beggars in Japan living beneath bridges."[10]

FIGURE 29

Japanese migrant workers packing cauliflower near Centerville, California, 1942. Photo by Dorothea Lange. Courtesy of National Archives.

Perhaps because of those circumstances, death certificates from 1898 to 1907 revealed that 182 Japanese workers died in the vicinity of Fresno; between 1900 and 1902, 99 died in the area around Sacramento. Most of the dead were young men in their twenties and thirties who expired from heatstroke, tuberculosis, or general "sickness." Between 1906 and 1913, according to Japanese consular statistics, 3,836 Japanese died in California. The total included 138 suicides and 476 deaths attributed to "other external causes," such as accidents and murders. The remainder were due to illnesses, led by tuberculosis, pneumonia, typhoid, and intestinal disorders, diseases usually associated with poor, unsanitary living conditions.

As among Chinese migrant workers, men accounted for the vast proportion of Japanese migrant laborers in California. From 1868 to 1900, the Japanese government issued only 2,036 passports to women destined for the United States, and according to the 1900 U.S. Census, there were only 958 Japanese women on the continent, of whom 553 were in California. They constituted a mere 5 percent of California's Japanese. In 1910, they numbered 6,240, or 15 percent of the total. Those figures reflected the gendered nature of migrant work.

Many of the women, perhaps a majority, were sex workers, who could be found in virtually every Japanese settlement in the state as well as in neighboring states. They were migratory, like most of the men, shadowing the places of men's employment.

Unlike the men, however, nearly all the women were bound and forced into prostitution by procurers who sometimes rose to positions of wealth and influence, like Genji Hasegawa, a San Francisco labor contractor who was also a brothel operator.

Waka Yamada was born in 1879 in a small fishing village near Yokohama. Her parents married her at age sixteen to a man ten years her senior. Her unhappy marriage might have made her susceptible to a stranger's stories of fabulous wealth in the United States, and she followed the stranger to Seattle in 1902. Instead of finding streets paved with gold, Yamada was forced into prostitution. Working in a brothel for white men only, she was known as Oyae of Arabia because of her dark complexion and ample buttocks, which apparently reminded some men of an Arabian horse. Yamada fled to San Francisco with the help of another man, only to be forced back into sex work in a Chinatown brothel by her rescuer.

Yamada eventually managed to escape to Cameron House, a Presbyterian mission established for Chinese prostitutes, where she served as a translator. There she met Kakichi Yamada, who taught English. They married and returned to Japan after the devastating San Francisco earthquake of 1906. Their home in Tokyo became a haven for intellectuals and feminists, and Yamada joined the feminist group Seitosha and began publishing her essays and translations in Seitosha's journal, *Seito*. Yamada was a prolific writer throughout the 1920s, and in the 1930s she published a popular advice column in Tokyo's *Asahi Shimbun*. She became a champion of mothers, founding the Motherhood Protection League in 1934, helping to pass a law providing relief to impoverished mothers of young children, and building the Hatagawa House for Mothers and Children in 1939.

Yamada, of course, was exceptional. Most Japanese sex workers, like their Chinese sisters, suffered abuse that lasted a lifetime. They were exhibited in cages and confined to filthy rooms, and they suffered venereal diseases. Many died young. But Yamada's will to survive and recover a sense of human dignity were unexceptional: they are reflected in the lives of countless women and men.

Expressions of self-determination were both individual and collective. In Oxnard, California, Japanese and Mexican sugar-beet field hands joined to form a historic union, the Japanese-Mexican Labor Association (JMLA) in 1903. Many of the Japanese were student-laborers from San Francisco. Under its president, Kozaburō Baba, the JMLA struck for higher wages, an end to labor-contractor commissions, and relief from the monopoly of company stores. On March 23, a Mexican striker was shot and killed, and two Mexicans and two Japanese were wounded. After negotiations a few days later, the union won most of its demands.

Despite the JMLA's membership, which exceeded 1,300, representing 90 percent of the workforce, and despite having shown the ability to organize agricultural migrant laborers across racialized lines, the American Federation of Labor (AFL) denied the union a charter because it enrolled Asians as members. Expel the Japanese, the AFL president Samuel Gompers told the union, and the JMLA will receive its charter. JMLA's secretary, J. M. Lizarras, a Mexican, responded: "We would be false [to the Japanese] and to ourselves and to the cause of Unionism, if we . . . accepted privileges for ourselves which are not accorded to them [Asians]." Workers should unite, Lizarras concluded, "without regard to their color or race."[11]

Between 1891 and 1900, some 27,440 Japanese, mainly workers, entered the United States, but in 1900, because of West Coast anti-Japanese agitation, Japan's government suspended labor migration to the United States and Canada. Two years later it relented, allowing laborers who had been in the United States but had returned to Japan to remigrate. From 1901 to 1907, 42,457 more Japanese entered the United States from Japan, along with 38,000 Japanese from Hawai'i who left the islands for the prospect of higher wages.

Most of the migrants from Japan came from districts in the southeast, where the migration companies had offices. U.S. restrictions also regulated—and terminated—the labor flow. In 1875, the United States banned Asian women and prostitutes, and in 1885, it outlawed contract labor. In 1907, President Theodore Roosevelt issued an executive order forbidding aliens, including Japanese, from entering the United States from Hawai'i and other insular possessions, although labor contractors vigorously opposed the presidential order that spelled the end of their lucrative business. Finally, the Gentlemen's Agreement in 1908 ended Japanese labor migration.

KOREANS

Initially, Koreans migrated not to California but to Hawai'i to work in the sugar plantations. There, the numbers of Korean migrants rose as Japanese migrants dwindled between 1903 and 1905, and declined steeply as Japanese migration picked up again from 1905 to 1907. The relationship likely reflected the planters' recruitment strategies, Japan's protectorate over Korea, and the Korean government's ban on foreign migration in 1905. Like the Japanese, however, Koreans eventually migrated from Hawai'i's plantations to California and the West Coast in search of better wages and working conditions. Still, in 1910, about 92 percent of all Koreans remained in the islands, while a mere 6 percent were on the Pacific Coast, mostly in California. The distribution tilted slightly a decade later, when 80 percent were in Hawai'i and 15 percent were on the West Coast. Koreans numbered 304 in California in 1910 and 772 in 1920.

In 1905, 1,039 Korean migrants went to Mexico, again indicating the pivotal role played by migration companies in Asian labor migration. The Continental Settlement Company, established in Seoul by a British citizen, John Meyers, and a Japanese businessman, Genichi Taisho, contracted with agricultural employers in Mexico to supply laborers. After their first efforts in China and Japan failed, they turned to Korea, where they tried to entice migrants with false promises: "Recently, many Japanese and Chinese people went to Mexico, some with their families, to make money and they are all rich now. Koreans can also become rich in Mexico if they emigrate."[12] The company succeeded in luring 702 men, 135 women, and 196 children from eighteen cities throughout

FIGURE 30

Korean contract workers at a Mexican hacienda. Museo Conmemorativo Inmigración Coreana a Yucatán.

Korea. Their ship left Inchon in April 1905, just before the government ban on foreign migration.

After a month-long voyage, during which two Koreans died, the migrants landed at Salina Cruz and proceeded to Yucatán, where they were divided among twenty-four henequen farms. Their contracts specified a term of four years and a wage of thirty to thirty-five cents a day. Under the scorching sun, they cut henequen for twelve to seventeen hours a day. Managers beat recalcitrant workers and held them in locked barracks under guard. A Chinese visitor, Hui Ho, described the conditions: "In rags and worn sandals, the Koreans are laughed at by Mexicans. You can't watch them without tears, going in groups to henequen farms, men holding the hands of their children and women carrying their babies on their backs. They are worse than animals."[13] Records show that at least ten committed suicide, and those who attempted to escape were severely punished on recapture.

Made aware of the migrants' plight, Korea's government appealed to Japan, which had declared a protectorate over Korea. Japan's embassy in Mexico inquired about the Korean workers, and Mexico responded that the allegations of mistreatment and slavery were untrue. A Korean newspaper depicted the migrants as inferior classes and fools.

Migration companies, the editorial stated, are able to recruit "many ignorant and stupid people, such as the Negro people of Africa and the peasants of Korea. . . . They lure stupid Koreans with sugar-coated words and many Koreans have crossed the sea. . . . It is lamentable that our brothers and sisters have become slaves like African Negroes in a strange land."[14] With that, the matter of Mexico's Koreans was put to rest.

Korean students were among the first Koreans to arrive in the continental U.S., beginning in about 1880. They, like the Japanese student-laborers, worked as domestic servants, waiters, gardeners, and field hands, taking whatever jobs were open to them. Between 1899 and 1909, sixty-four Korean students arrived. Most of them completed their college degrees, and five received doctoral degrees. The majority chose to remain in the United States to avoid Japanese repression and colonialism at home. The 541 students who arrived between 1910 and 1918 were called "refugee students" because most were active in the decolonization struggle and were fleeing Japan's rule in Korea. Few graduated from college, unlike the members of the previous group, and many became leaders of the U.S. Korean community and remained active in movements dedicated to the liberation of Korea.

Like other Asian migrants, Koreans followed work opportunities. California agriculture was their main employer, and they accordingly moved around the state throughout the year. A Korean farm worker described that life and livelihood: "About ten days after I arrived in San Francisco (in 1916), I went to Stockton, and through a Korean contractor I went to work on a Caucasian-owned bean farm. There were about 20 other Koreans working there." The work involved hoeing the bean fields. After finishing there, the labor gang moved to the next farm. "It was hard work. . . . Then we went to Dinuba to pick grapes. I was flocking with other Koreans, and I went wherever they went for available farm jobs."[15]

The organization of Korean farmhands, similar to the organization of Chinese and Japanese, involved a labor contractor who assembled labor gangs according to ethnicity. The contractor negotiated with white farmers for employment, wages, and hours. On completion of the contract and receiving payment, he distributed the earnings to his workers, taking a commission for his efforts. Work crews usually numbered between thirty and fifty but could include as many as three hundred members. Korean laborers, at times, worked under Japanese contractors. A 1911 government report noted that during the busiest time in Fresno, raisin-grapes harvest, there were "some 200–300 Koreans, who ordinarily work with Japanese and can not be distinguished from them."[16]

Because of Japan's colonization of Korea, there was ample cause for antagonism between the groups. Yet they also found causes for unity in opposing white racism and the racial division of labor that relegated Asian workers to the lowest level of work and wages. While whites earned wages of two dollars or more a day, Koreans received between $1.30 and $1.75, depending on whether board was included. Those rates increased during World War I, when there was a shortage of manpower, but the seasonal nature of agricultural work, with its periods of unemployment and underemployment, tended to keep incomes low.

In 1913, a white farmer in Hemet, California, contracted a thirteen-member Korean crew to pick his cherry crop. But before they could start, about six hundred white workers and businessmen confronted the Koreans and told them: "This town doesn't want any Koreans, Chinese, Japanese or Orientals. Leave now."[17] Thus ordered, the Korean migrants left the job, losing a day's wages. When the Japanese consulate offered to intervene, the Korean workers declined, not wanting to acknowledge Japan's hold over Korea and its subjects.

The starting point for social organization was ethnic solidarity. Cha'ng-ho Ahn, a noted nationalist leader and patriot who arrived in the United States in 1899, founded the Chin'mok-hoe (Friendship Society), the first Korean social organization in San Francisco, in 1903. The society amalgamated with the Kongnip Hyop-hoe (Mutual Assistance Society) when it was founded in 1905. Mutual Assistance officers often greeted and sponsored Korean migrants on their arrival in San Francisco, guiding them through the immigration bureaucracy and the required medical examination. The Kongnip Hyop-hoe also acted as employment agents. Besides notifying businesses and farms of the availability of Korean laborers, the society secured jobs by creating opportunities in fields closed to others by earlier labor contractors like the Japanese.

The orange growers of Riverside preferred Asian over white pickers because of their lower wages and efficiency, but Japanese contractors held a virtual monopoly there. The Kongnip Hyop-hoe assembled a highly selective team of able-bodied and experienced men to demonstrate the superiority of Korean over Japanese orange pickers. The society bought train tickets for the group, and before their departure, they instructed the men to be honest and "work diligently without wasting time, whether your employer watches you or not," because they would be working not for themselves alone but for other Koreans who would follow.[18] The demonstration succeeded, and thereafter the Kongnip Hyop-hoe sent Korean orange pickers regularly to Riverside.

Some Korean migrants supplemented their income with railroad work during slack periods in the agricultural cycle. Railroad work paid less than farm labor, ranging from $1.25 to $1.50 a day for repairing track in 1909.

Some Korean women joined their husbands in labor migration. There were perhaps fewer than one hundred Korean women on the continent in 1910. Despite their low numbers, women contributed significantly to economic life, serving as cooks and washing and ironing men's clothes. A wife of a laborer reported that in 1916 she made between eighty cents and a dollar a day washing and ironing clothes for whites and Korean bachelors. Another who cooked for a labor gang described her work: "When we were in the citrus orchards in Redlands, I was in the kitchen cooking food, Korean foods. I was one of the cooks for Korean farm workers. A hundred workers needed a lot of women cooking. . . . In Colusa, there were fifteen to twenty Koreans working, and I cooked their meals. At the same time, I had to raise ten children. Oh, it was pretty hard, but what could you do?"[19]

Women, and children when they came of age, earned income from their work outside the home, which enabled a crucial escape from the confines of migrant labor. Between

1908 and 1912, more Koreans returned to Korea than entered the United States. But from 1913 to 1920, the direction of this flow reversed. Many of the new migrants, coming directly from Korea, were "picture brides" who not only added to the total number of Koreans in the United States but also anchored the community with their labor and reproductive capacity. Their children were U.S. citizens by birth. Those changes would play pivotal roles in the period to follow.

SOUTH ASIANS

Like most Chinese and Japanese migrants, nearly all of the South Asian migrants came from a particular region—Punjab, a northwestern province of British India. Unlike migration from China, Japan, and Korea, where recruiters and companies were influential, Punjabi migration was more broadly the result of British colonial and imperial rule.

The British created a transportation infrastructure in Punjab, mainly to defend the western borders against Russian advances into India and Afghanistan. The system of roads and bridges, railroads and irrigation systems stimulated the rise of commercial agriculture where subsistence production had once predominated. Export crops like grains, cotton, sugarcane, flax, and tobacco were grown on large landholdings. The expanding economy, land reforms, and the change from collective to privately held land increased the land's value, enriched the propertied classes, and drove out the masses of peasants, who were reduced to either selling their labor or moving. As with the economic dislocations and peasant revolts in China, Japan, and Korea, those sweeping changes in the relations of production in nineteenth-century Punjab created large pools of labor.

Echoing the South Asian coolie traffic earlier in the century, in 1896 some nineteen thousand South Asian indentured laborers, more than half from Punjab, left India to work on railroad construction in British-held Uganda. They were recruited by labor contractors from the British colonies, along with workers for sugar plantations in Mauritius and Fiji.

Laboring abroad infiltrated popular culture, as seen in Punjabi songs that expressed skepticism over dreams of riches realized in foreign lands:

For twenty years you roamed abroad,
for what fortune?
What did you bring in return?

As in the songs of Cantonese women, Punjabi women expressed anxieties over long-absent husbands who had become strangers:

A crow on my roof,
might not the foreigner return today?[20]

The British imperial army provided an important avenue for Punjabi migration to America. The army was the largest employer of Sikh men outside Punjab: in 1920, about one-fifth of the British colonial troops in India were Sikhs, although they formed only 1 percent of the colony's population. The Sikh religion was founded in the late fifteenth century in an attempt to reconcile Islam with Hinduism. Largely as a result of religious persecution, the Sikh religion became a military theocracy with a distinctive identity. After baptism, men never shaved their beards or cut their hair. They covered their hair with turbans, a requirement for entry into a Sikh temple, or *gurdwara*. On the U.S. West Coast, the alleged peril posed by the Sikhs, erroneously called Hindus, was described as the "tide of turbans."

As soldiers in the imperial army, Sikhs traveled to and defended other areas of the British Empire, including Shanghai, Canton, Hong Kong, and Canada. It appears that substantial percentages of South Asian migrants in Canada and the United States arrived through Hong Kong, with its large Sikh community, and other Chinese cities. Two out of three Punjabis entering the United States between 1913 and 1923 cited Hong Kong as their point of departure. These men might have been following the trails cut by Chinese migrants before them, but they could just as easily have been drifting on the currents of the British Empire. Most came to the Americas by way of Canada, which at the time was a British dependency.

Peasants who possessed the means for travel abroad often left Punjab. At times, families mortgaged property to enable a son to migrate; nearly all the migrants were men. Migrants passed through Singapore, Manila, Hong Kong, and Nagasaki, utilizing Sikh networks often centered on temples, on their way to Vancouver. At the turn of the century the fare was at least two hundred rupees, roughly the price of two acres of fertile land. The migrants promised to send remittances to repay the mortgages, to buy land, to build brick houses, and to support wives and families left behind.

Lesser, though still significant, numbers arrived having signed labor contracts, which were legal for a time in Canada. The Canadian Pacific Railway was one of the employers that worked with Sikh middlemen to recruit contract workers in Punjab and Hong Kong. Agents of steamship companies, which profited from passenger fares, also worked Punjab, Bengal, and Gujarat with their promises of easy money to be made overseas.

Like the other Asians before them, South Asian migrants to Canada and the United States were mostly agricultural workers, with a sprinkling of students and intellectual and political refugees who became community leaders. Between 1899 and 1906, only 885 South Asians entered the United States, but in 1907, 1,072 were admitted, and in 1908 the number rose to 1,710. When anti-Asian laws effectively cut off Indian migration into Canada, in 1908, many moved to the United States. Migration fell to 337 in 1909; it rose again to 1,782 in 1910, when the Western Pacific Railroad required construction workers, and declined to 517 in 1911, 165 in 1912, 188 in 1913, 172 in 1914, and finally 82 in 1915. The 1910 census counted 5,424 South Asians in the United States, about half of whom were in California.

Anti-Asianism not only drove many South Asians from Canada into the United States but also encouraged a migration from Washington State south to California. Besides expulsions from Washington's lumber camps, South Asians faced residential segregation: in Port Angeles in 1913, white real estate brokers signed housing covenants prohibiting property sales to "Hindoos and Negroes" because their presence allegedly lowered land values and "injured" the reputation of the neighborhood. Anti-Asianism pursued South Asian migrants to San Francisco, where the Asiatic Exclusion League warned of the "Hindu invasion and menace" and urged South Asian exclusion. Immigration officials took heed, and between 1908 and 1920, 5,391 South Asians gained admittance, while 3,543 (58 percent) were turned away on the grounds that they would likely become public charges. The Exclusion League traced South Asian ancestry to a race "enslaved, effeminate, caste-ridden and degraded"—using racialized, gendered, and class-based terms familiar since the ancient Greeks.

At first, most South Asians worked for the railroads that had recruited them, helping to build the Western Pacific Railroad and serving as section hands on the Southern Pacific and Northern Pacific railroads. Later, California's growers actively recruited South Asian migrants in order to break the hold of Japanese farm workers. Moreover, agricultural work in California paid more than work on the railroads and sawmills in the Northwest. Like other Asians, South Asians agricultural workers were organized in work gangs under contractors; they moved into the Sacramento and San Joaquin Valleys and south to the Imperial Valley, following the seasons and crops. In the San Joaquin Valley, South Asian migrant farm workers gathered around Stockton, Fresno, and Bakersfield. Sacramento also attracted South Asians to work in adjacent rice fields and fruit orchards, and in the Imperial Valley, near the border with Mexico, they tended grapes, cotton, alfalfa, and melons.

The hours of work varied with the seasons and crops. Nine to ten hours a day might have been a standard, but when fruit and cotton had to be picked in a short time, a thirteen- to fourteen-hour day was commonplace. South Asian farm workers earned one to three dollars a day in 1909, a figure that rose to five and six dollars daily by 1920. Living conditions varied from farm to farm. In most cases workers slept in wooden shacks, though in hot weather sleeping outside was more comfortable. South Asian women were virtually absent, numbering perhaps fifty on the Pacific Coast; many of the men had wives and children in India. Some South Asian men married Canadian and American women, and in the Imperial Valley, a number of them married Mexican women.

South Asian migrant subjectivities centered on religion and culture, and religious and political organizations promoted their rights. These included the Moslem Association of America, formed in 1919 in Sacramento, and the Hindustani Welfare and Reform Society of America, founded in 1919 in the Imperial Valley. Teja Singh, a Sikh missionary who had studied at Columbia University, moved among the Sikh communities of British Columbia and California. In 1907, Singh played a major role in establishing a religious and educational organization, the Khalsa Diwan Society. In California, South Asians formed a parallel Pacific Coast Khalsa Diwan Society in 1910, based in the Sikh *gurdwara* in Stockton.

FIGURE 31
Sikh *gurdwara* in Stockton, California, 1912.

South Asian intellectuals, students, and workers engaged in political activity in in Canada and the United States against white racism and to promote the related cause of India's independence from Britain. Those missions intersected in the work of Taraknath Das, a community organizer in Vancouver during the 1907 riot of whites against Chinese, Japanese, and South Asians. Born near Calcutta, Das was selected for the colonial civil service, but he dropped out of university, began agitating for India's independence, was targeted for arrest, and fled to Japan. There, Das studied with South Asian and Japanese students at the University of Tokyo while the British ambassador petitioned for his deportation. In 1906, at the age of twenty-two, he arrived in Seattle. He wandered south to work California's celery fields and enrolled at the University of California, Berkeley. He won a position with the U.S. immigration services and was stationed in Vancouver.

A few days after the riot, the Vancouver *Daily Province* quoted Das, then secretary of the newly formed Hindustani Association, as saying that South Asians had migrated to Canada to flee high taxes and oppressive conditions in India. As Canada's government tried to remove and exclude South Asians, Das published the journal *Free Hindustan* in 1908, urging resistance against exclusion, for which he was dismissed from his U.S. immigration post. Das continued to publish and organize against racism in America and colonialism in India. He fled back to Seattle, where he restarted his paper, and then moved east, first to Vermont and then to New York City, where he collaborated with Irish Americans in advocating Ireland's independence from British rule. The United States tried and imprisoned Das for his political work in 1918. After his release in 1924, Das married Mary Keatinge Morse, a founding member of the National Association for the Advancement of Colored People (NAACP) and the National Woman's Party.

Like Das, Har Dayal, a Punjabi Hindu, linked the struggle for civil rights in America with the campaign for India's independence. In 1911, Dayal landed in San Francisco with a history of anticolonial activism in India and Europe. He taught Sanskrit and Indian philosophy at Stanford University but had to resign his position after a year. He became secretary of the San Francisco Radical Club; founded the Bakunin Institute of California, which was dedicated to anarchism; and agitated among California's South Asians for Indian independence. In 1913, the twenty-eight-year-old Dayal, with Das and others, helped form and lead the Ghadar Party, whose purpose was the expulsion of the British from India. Dayal became the editor of the association's weekly, *Ghadr,* published in Urdu. Its name, in Arabic, means revolution or mutiny.

In the *Ghadr*'s first issue, Dayal proclaimed: "A new epoch in the history of India opens today, the 1st November, 1913, because today there begins in foreign lands, but in our country's language, a war against the English Raj. . . . What is our name? Mutiny. What is our work? Mutiny. Where will mutiny break out? In India. . . . Why? Because the people can no longer bear the oppression and tyranny practiced under British rule, and are ready to fight and die for freedom."[21] Revolt was directed at the British in India because, the Ghadarites pointed out, the governments of Canada and the United States conspired with the British against the interests of South Asians in India and America.

In fact, Ghadar began as a transnational South Asian movement, not an ethnic, religious, or caste one. Its immediate origins can be traced to the 1907 riots of whites against Asians in Bellingham, Washington, and Vancouver, Canada. More broadly, the roots of the struggle can be found in Japan's defeat of Russia in 1905 and the revolutions in Russia and Mexico, which advanced the spirit of anticolonialism and freedom. The movement acquired its symbol in 1909 when Bhai Bhagwan Singh, a former Bengali lancer, publicly burned his certificate of honorable discharge from the British Army. Singh was a Sikh leader of the South Asian community in Vancouver, and his act recalled the mutiny of Indian soldiers in 1857 that severely threatened British rule in India. (In that rebellion, Sikhs were used by the British to quell the revolt.)

The spirit of mutiny spread through the work of G. D. Kumar, a former college teacher in India and a shopkeeper in Vancouver, who published calls for Sikh rebellion within the British Army and for an end to British colonial rule in India. Fleeing Canada in 1911, Kumar joined Das in Seattle. Together they established United India House, which became a center of intellectual activity among students and workers. The following year, Kumar went to Portland, Oregon, to join Sohan Singh Bhakna, a Sikh farmer and lumberman, and Kanshi Ram, a Hindu labor contractor. Together they formed the Hindustani Association of America and mobilized Sikh workers in Oregon lumber mills.

Kumar, Bhakna, and Ram invited Har Dayal to visit the workers in Astoria, at the mouth of the Columbia River. There on May 30, 1913, the Sikhs of Astoria and representatives from both inland and coastal areas of Oregon established the Ghadar Party, which moved its headquarters to San Francisco. The founding meeting was held at Astoria's Finnish Socialist Hall. The Finns had followed the Chinese in Astoria's fishing industry; in 1880, Chinese constituted more than 30 percent of Astoria's population, and in 1905, the Finns totaled nearly 20 percent. The Ghadar movement thus extended its influence to India, Canada, and the United States and touched Hawaiians, Chinese, and Finns. The South Asian rebellion involved intellectuals and workers, Hindus and Sikhs.

Like Das, Har Dayal worked among students at the University of California, Berkeley, and visited the dispersed South Asian communities in California's agricultural valleys. San Francisco became the center for Ghadar activities. Dayal reported that in the first year of its existence the party received $2,000 in donations from South Asian migrant laborers in the United States and Canada.

In Vancouver, the arrival of the *Komagata Maru* in May 1914 stirred Indian nationalism, debate, and fervor. The ship carried South Asian activists to protest Canada's restrictions on South Asian immigration. That August, pro-grower vigilantes fired at, attacked, and beat workers in Wheatland, California, targeting South Asians who were on strike in the hop fields. Those events highlighted for South Asians their oppression based upon race and class in America and as colonial subjects in India.

In 1915, five boats carrying propaganda, weapons, and Ghadarites left California for India. The Ghadarites had planned to instigate a revolt among the Indian Army, with its large contingent of Punjabis. However, they were intercepted and hunted down. The government charged and tried 291 rebels, hanged 42, meted out life sentences to 114, and imprisoned 93 others. The majority of those tried and convicted were Ghadarites from America.

Back in the United States, informers and constant police harassment decimated the Ghadar movement. In 1917, the federal government charged 105 persons with conspiracy to violate U.S. neutrality laws, but only 35 of them, including 17 South Asians, were actually tried. On the last day of the five-month trial, as two hundred spectators, attorneys, and the defendants were leaving the courtroom for the noon recess, Ram Singh, a codefendant, fired four shots at the Ghadar leader Ram Chandra, mistakenly believing that Chandra was a British agent. Chandra was killed. A U.S. marshal immediately shot and killed Singh. That afternoon, all but one of those charged were found guilty.

In the rebellion and freedom struggle, the worker Sohan Singh Bhakna languished in Indian prisons for some twenty years, and the labor recruiter Kanshi Ram was hanged. The intellectual Taraknath Das renounced revolution and became a professor of political science at Columbia University. After his arrest in California and exile in Switzerland and Germany, Har Dayal, too, apparently had a change of heart: in 1919 he wrote that British colonial rule was best for India's people, and he was subsequently granted permission to return to England.

In 1917, the U.S. Congress passed the Immigration Act, called the Barred Zone Act because it specified a "zone" that included India, Southeast Asia, Polynesia, and parts of Afghanistan, Arabia, and Russia from which immigrants were denied entry into the United States. The act left intact earlier laws that restricted Asian migration. The 1917 act effectively ended the period of South Asian migrant labor.

FILIPINOS

Filipinos, like South Asians, followed the course of empire. The first Filipino migrants sailed the Spanish empire and established footholds in Mexico and Louisiana. When the Philippines became a U.S. territory in 1898, Filipinos were "nationals" and could move largely unrestricted into the United States despite Asian exclusion laws.

Spanish and U.S. colonial rule in the Philippines encouraged the cultivation of export crops like sugar, coffee, and tobacco. The cultivation of these crops on large plantations displaced peasants, producing labor pools ripe for labor recruiters and their tales of quick riches. As the U.S. "pacification" campaign wound down in the Philippines, Hawai'i's sugar planters began recruiting Filipino migrant laborers to replace and discipline unruly Japanese plantation workers. Later, like the Japanese and Koreans before them, Filipinos moved in significant numbers from Hawai'i's plantations to fields and canneries on the continent, drawn by the promise of better opportunities. The 1930 U.S. Census counted 45,208 Filipinos on the continent. Of those, 19,524 had come from Hawai'i.

Some of the earliest Filipinos in the United States were students, as was true for all the other Asian groups. The *pensionados* were sponsored students chosen by the U.S. colonial government to study in the United States and return to the Philippines to govern and modernize the islands. They agreed to work one year for the government in the Philippines for every year they were sponsored in the United States. In 1903, the first contingent of 104 men departed the Philippines to study while living with host families. Between 1903 and 1910, over two hundred *pensionados* studied at the University of California, Berkeley, the University of Washington, the University of Iowa, Notre Dame, Northwestern, Cornell, Columbia, and Yale, among others. All but eight were men, and all, in the eyes of the colonial government, were investments in and exemplars of the project of colonial uplift.

The opportunity to demonstrate their transformation came early, at the Louisiana Purchase Exposition in St. Louis in August 1904. The *pensionados* spent a month at the fair, guiding tourists through the ethnography of human evolution while themselves serving as exhibits who testified to the power of colonization. In the same spirit as the Chicago World's Fair of 1893, which commemorated the four-hundredth anniversary of Columbus's "discovery" of America, the St. Louis Exposition recalled Jefferson's Louisiana Purchase one hundred years earlier, which had led to the occupation of American Indian country and thrust the nation toward the Pacific and Asia. Both fairs were designed to showcase the achievements of modern nations, particularly European civilization, and to instill in white American fairgoers a sense of comity and pride.

At the St. Louis Exposition, the Philippine Reservation exhibit, sponsored by the U.S. colonial government, was designed to show the benefits of manifest destiny through the civilizing of "our little brown brothers," as Filipinos were widely known. The exhibit began with the villages of "non-Christian tribes" as the baseline—assemblages of peoples of every type, but especially those considered lowest on the chain of human evolution, represented by the ethnic Negritos and Igorots. U.S. scientists went to the Philippines to select models from a group of eight hundred representatives, measuring, photographing, and finally choosing a handful for the journey to St. Louis. Their frank nakedness—both women and men wore loincloths—scandalized the delicate sensibilities of fairgoers and even the U.S. president.

The ways of life of these "savages" were intended to contrast with the dress and decorum of the "civilized tribes" and beneficiaries of Christianity and education. As the fair's secretary observed of the Philippine exhibit: "The civilization and barbarism of the Archipelago are shown side by side. . . . Igorot braves bow to the rising sun, kill a dog and dance on one side. . . . while on the other side . . . the neatly uniformed Scouts [a U.S.-trained Filipino militia] from the civilized tribes stand at attention as the United States flag is raised to American music by a Philippine band."[22]

In addition to the *pensionados*, more Filipinos arrived in the United States without scholarships but with the intention of studying while working. Those students, like the Japanese, were called schoolboys. They typically worked in service industries as domestic and personal servants, and in restaurants, hotels, and private clubs. According to the *Filipino Student Bulletin*, a bimonthly publication of the Committee on Friendly Relations among Foreign Students and then of the Filipino Students' Christian Movement, there were roughly 2,000 Filipino students from 1920 to 1925, 1,000 in 1928, 800 in 1932, 500 in 1935, and 300 in 1939. Apparently rising fees, work, and the Great Depression forced many out of school. Spread across 116 campuses in thirty-four states, the student-laborers favored California, followed by Illinois and Washington State.

The military, another apparatus of the colonial regime, also recruited Filipinos. During the conquest of the islands, the U.S. Army recruited and trained Filipinos for a unit called the Philippine Scouts. By 1901, there were over 5,500 Filipinos serving under U.S. officers and fighting against Filipino nationalists. The colonial government shipped some of those Scouts to the St. Louis Fair as vital objects in the Philippine exhibit. The U.S. Navy admitted its first Filipino recruits in 1904, some three hundred of them, to serve as stewards and musicians. They remained in those capacities and were denied mobility. By 1922, there were 5,018 Filipinos in the Navy, constituting about 6 percent of all enlisted men. Navy service deposited numbers of Filipinos in and around U.S. naval bases at San Diego and Long Beach, California, and Norfolk, Virginia.

Luis Reyes Acuzar, a U.S. Navy man, described his career, which began in 1932. At Long Beach, Acuzar trained at a school for naval chefs and stewards. He studied for seven to eight weeks to become a steward, and on completion of the course, he was assigned to a captain who took him to Honolulu. For years he served the captain, who, became an admiral in the 1940s; like his superior, Acuzar rose through the ranks, earning promotions from mess boy to third-, second-, and first-class steward. Finally, the admiral promoted Acuzar to chief steward, with the pay of a chief petty officer. Another chief steward, Angelo Pascual, described his daily tasks and sole concern: "I take care of the captain, his sleeping place, make the bed, polish the shoes."[23]

The 1910 U.S. Census counted 160 Filipinos in sixteen states. Louisiana had the most with eighty-four, although Louisiana's Filipinos believed there were over two thousand descendants of the original "Manilamen" in the state. The census found seventeen Filipinos in Washington State, and the number of Filipinos in Montana, Washington, DC, and Texas exceeded the total in California—a surprising distribution, considering that 21,123 Filipinos entered the United States through California ports during the 1920s. By 1930, by contrast, 30,470 of the 45,208 Filipinos on the continent were in California. Of that total, 42,268 were men and only 2,940, or about 7 percent, women. Like the student laborers and navy men, these Filipinos were migrant workers.

Alfonso Perales Dangaran recalled his arrival in California from Hawai'i: "I was twelve. . . . We landed in San Francisco. An uncle met us . . . [and] took us to Stockton . . . [because] that's the center of labor for our kind of people, that work . . . in the field. We lived there for a couple of years."[24] Stockton was also a gathering place for Punjabi farm workers; Filipinos flocked to the town's Eldorado Street, which turned out, despite the name, not to be paved with gold. Stockton was the transportation hub for the agriculturally rich Central Valley, and there Filipino farm laborers organized into work crews under a leader, like other Asian migrants, and fanned out to the fields.

Work crews completed contracts or agreements reached by their bosses in an arrangement called the *barcada* system. "In the old days," Joseph Arriola recalled, the crew leader "would go around to the different farmers, and say, 'Do you need some work done? I can bring in my crew. My company comes out to over forty, fifty people.' If we did ten thousand [heads of lettuce], we would be out there from five o'clock to maybe eight, eight-thirty in the evening."[25] The task completed, the work gang moved on to the next farm and job. Filipino migrants followed the well-trodden trail cut by Asian migrant laborers for over seven decades: reclaiming fertile land from rivers, planting vineyards and orchards, and cultivating garden crops.

"We traveled. I mean moved from camp to camp," Josephine Romero Loable explained. "You start out the year, January . . . you'd find a place and it was usually an asparagus camp. My mother cooked and my stepfather ran out in the fields and worked from four o'clock in the morning until they finished, usually around one o'clock. I remember them going out with flashlights on their heads just like miners so they could get the asparagus before it grew . . . the whiteheads. From asparagus season, we would migrate to Fairfield, to Suisun and there the men worked out in the orchards picking fruits while the women and even children, as long as they could stand on their boxes, cutting fruits."[26] White growers, a migrant laborer explained, favored Filipinos in the asparagus fields because the shoots had to be cut low to the ground: in their racist view, short men were best fitted for stoop labor.

Alfonso Yasonia was born in the Philippines in 1906.[27] He completed middle school before leaving for the United States "to study—but when I got here I changed my mind." With three hundred Pinoys, or Filipinos, on board the ship, the *President Madison* docked at San Francisco on May 3, 1928. Like many other Pinoys, Yasonia stayed at the International Hotel in Chinatown, where he heard of work in Stockton. A friend took him to the Ferry Building and told him to stay on board the ferry to the end of the line for Stockton.

On landing, Yasonia saw a Filipino restaurant and ate breakfast there. A man entered and announced he had work for anyone who wanted it. Yasonia followed the recruiter and group to nearby Turlock, where a Filipino called Tivan became their crew boss. But after two days, Tivan gave Yasonia five dollars and told him he was fired. He was not yet skilled in agricultural work. For about a week, he stayed with Japanese workers in a Stockton boardinghouse. Again a man recruited Yasonia at a Filipino restaurant, this time driving him to Concord to plant cucumbers. He lasted two days on that job before being delivered back to Stockton.

It was June, and the Alaska canneries were hiring Pinoys. Yasonia had read in a book that canneries rarely fired workers, even inexperienced ones, which suited him, given his record in fieldwork. So he and other men headed for Seattle, where the cannery recruiters housed and fed them, and on June 15 they sailed to Alaska, where Yasonia worked until September. Back in Seattle, the recruiters charged the men for their June lodging and food, which Yasonia had thought was free. Although he made sixty dollars a month in Alaska, deductions for his June expenses left him with only eighty dollars for the entire summer. "I must have eaten plenty when I was there!" he remarked.

By the end of the week, Yasonia was broke, so a friend suggested they pick hops at Sumner, about forty-eight miles from Seattle. Their employer charged them seventy-five cents a day for meals, and they made less than that for daily piecework, so they took their bags from the shed and sneaked away. Penniless, they had to walk all the way back to Seattle. With grape season in full swing, Yasonia left for Fresno, where he lasted a week picking grapes, literally eating his profits.

In 1929, Yasonia moved to Los Angeles, where a Filipino employment agent placed him in a restaurant as a busboy. "I was so happy—I made seventeen dollars a week," Yasonia remembered. But after six months, he was fired. He worked for a period at a Chinese gambling house and then moved to San Francisco to work in a similar establishment. When it closed, Yasonia worked as a janitor, making forty-five dollars a month. The year was 1937 or 1938.

The gambling houses, Yasonia noted, offered patrons free coffee and doughnuts twenty-four hours a day. The food, along with the prospect of striking it rich (however unlikely), attracted Filipino men. "The Filipinos go to the gambling houses in the daytime and about six o'clock they go home, dress up, and go to the barbershop," Yasonia said of their daily routine. The barbershop was a place not only to get their hair done but also for socializing and gossiping. In the evening, the men went to the dance halls, like the Hippodrome in Los Angeles. There white women charged them a dime a dance. Because there were occasional fights over women, it was common for men to arrive at the dance hall as a "gang."

Police harassed Pinoys everywhere, Yasonia testified, not only at dance halls but also at pool halls. "I see the police mistreat Filipinos many times too," he said. "Sometimes without warning they go into your room and beat you up—especially if you have a [white] girl in your room. I know a few boys who got beat up by cops, got TB, and died—maybe because they got hurt inside. The cops hit you in the stomach."

Alfonso Yasonia was just one among tens of thousands of Pinoys who, during the first half of the twentieth century, wandered the continent in search of work. But his account reveals experiences shared by many other migrant laborers—constant movement, impermanence, poverty and exploitation, friendships and betrayals, detention and escape. Networks, boardinghouses, and small businesses offered employment prospects and a sense of community. Interethnic solidarities among Asians were shaped by common conditions of race, gender, class, and nation. White women were important to Filipino heterosexual men's lives, but such associations were seen as racial transgressions that triggered hatred and violence in white men.

The 1934 Tydings-McDuffie Act ended the period of Filipino migrant labor by reclassifying Filipino nationals as "aliens," making them subject to the immigration restrictions on Asians. In the following year Congress passed a companion law, the Filipino Repatriation Act, which provided free return passage back to the Philippines for Filipinos on the continent—but not for those in Hawai'i, where their labor was still needed. Some 2,200 Pinoys were thereby removed. The Great Depression rendered Filipinos, like Mexicans, excess labor and hence disposable.

The experiences of Asian immigrants in California are, of course, specific to place and time. Yet, as these histories show, they have connections to the experiences of Asians in Hawai'i, other regions of the United States, and the rest of the world.

SUGGESTED READINGS

Azuma, Eiichiro. *Between Two Empires: Race, History, and Transnationalism in Japanese America*. New York: Oxford University Press, 2005.

Chan, Sucheng. *This Bitter-Sweet Soil: The Chinese in California Agriculture, 1860–1910*. Berkeley: University of California Press, 1986.

Cordova, Fred. *Filipinos: Forgotten Asian Americans* Dubuque, IA: Kendall/Hunt, 1983.

Jensen, Joan M. *Passage from India: Asian Indian Immigrants in North America*. New Haven, CT: Yale University Press, 1988.

Lee, Mary Paik. *Quiet Odyssey: A Pioneer Korean Woman in America*. Edited by Sucheng Chan. Seattle: University of Washington Press, 1990.

Sarasohn, Eileen Sunada. *Issei Women: Echoes from Another Frontier*. Palo Alto, CA: Pacific Books, 1998.

SIGNIFICANT EVENTS

1830s	Hawaiians dominate the coastal carrying trade
1838	John Sutter sails for Hawai'i
1847	Hawaiians total 10 percent of San Francisco's population
1848	gold discovered at John Sutter's mill
	Marie Seise, first Chinese woman, in San Francisco
1849	whites expel Chinese miners from Chinese Camp, Tuolumne County
1850	Foreign Miners' Tax enacted
1854	*Libertad* arrives in San Francisco with Chinese laborers
	The People v. George W. Hall
	Chinese fishing villages established along San Francisco Bay
1857	San Francisco opens a school for Chinese children
1865	Central Pacific Railroad hires Chinese laborers
1867	Chinese laborers strike against the Central Pacific Railroad
1868	U.S. and China sign Burlingame-Seward Treaty, affirming the right of free migration between China and the United States to citizens of those nations
1869	transcontinental railroad completed
	Wakamatsu Tea and Silk Colony established
1871	Okei Ito dies
1875	Page Act
1880s	Japanese and Korean students on the West Coast
1882	Chinese Exclusion Act
1896	Punjabi railroad workers leave for Uganda
1903	Japanese-Mexican Labor Association formed
	Cha'ng-ho Ahn founds the Chin'mok-hoe in San Francisco
	first *pensionados* arrive in United States
1904	St. Louis World's Fair
	U.S. Navy admits Filipino stewards
1905	Korean migrant laborers in Mexico
	Japanese protectorate over Korea
1907	President Theodore Roosevelt's executive order barring aliens from entering United States

	Khalsa Diwan Society formed
1908	Gentlemen's Agreement
1910	Japan colonizes Korea
1911	Har Dayal in San Francisco
1913	Ghadar Party formed
1915	Ghadar revolutionaries leave San Francisco for India
1917	Immigration Act (Barred Zone Act)
1917–18	trial of South Asians charged with violating U.S. neutrality laws
1919	Moslem Association of America formed
	Hindustani Welfare and Reform Society of America established
1920s	Filipino migrant laborers on the West Coast
1934	Tydings-McDuffie Act
1935	Filipino Repatriation Act

7

NORTHWEST, NORTHEAST, SOUTH, AND NORTH

While California's demand for Asian migrant labor arose from the state's cultivation of extensive tracts of land, employers in other parts of the United States sought Asians to meet a variety of other labor demands. In the Northwest, Asians worked in railroad construction, lumber, and fishing; in the Northeast, Asians were engaged to work in manufacturing trades. The regional divisions I specify in this chapter are widely used in discussions of U.S. history and culture, including the histories of Asians in the United States; but, like all such geographical distinctions, they are arbitrary human constructs. It is important to keep in mind that Asian and Pacific Islander migrant laborers regularly traversed other regions as well, including the Southwest and Midwest, and that many individuals and groups crossed and recrossed the continent in response to changing economic conditions, legislation, and personal circumstances.

NORTHWEST

By *Northwest,* I mean the region known in the 1840s as Oregon Country, which included the present-day states of Washington, Oregon, and Idaho, parts of Montana and Wyoming, and British Columbia. This region was the homeland of diverse American Indian nations, and was New Spain and Mexico's *El Norte.* Spain, Russia, Britain, and the United States contested for supremacy in the region. It was drawn into the U.S. orbit by the search, initiated by President Thomas Jefferson, for a route to the Pacific along waterways following the Louisiana Purchase.

Against the expansions of Russians from the north and the Spaniards and then Mexicans from the south, Britain and the United States both claimed the Northwest, and an 1818 treaty between them allowed their citizens equal access to the territory, without regard for the indigenous peoples. That joint occupation lasted for twenty years. During the 1820s and 1830s, missionaries from the United States sought to convert Indians to Protestantism in order to counter Catholic missions from Canada, and substantial numbers of white settlers from the United States invaded the region during the early 1840s, the first period of manifest destiny. While Texas and Mexico's northern territories loomed large in the nation's imperial vision, so did Oregon Country. In 1846, the United States and Britain agreed on a border at the forty-ninth parallel that divided Canada from the United States.

HAWAIIANS

Migrant labor in the Northwest first involved Hawaiians, then other Pacific Islanders, and then, in turn, Chinese, Japanese, South Asians, and Filipinos. Their main employers were extractive industries: the fur trade, timber, and fishing. Hawaiians served whites as imperial soldiers and settlers in the conquest and expulsion of indigenous peoples. At the same time, they interacted with the region's Indians, and their hybrid cultures and biracial descendants helped to establish Pacific Islander and Asian America.

In 1899, workmen unearthed a coffin while excavating on Newcastle Island, British Columbia. The body inside, according to those who remembered, was that of Kanaka Pete, or Peter Kakua, a Hawaiian who had been hanged for murder thirty years earlier. His story uncovers a wider tale of Hawaiian migrant labor in the Pacific Northwest. Kakua, who came from Honolulu, left the islands in 1853. He worked for the Hudson's Bay Company, the governor of the region, and, at the time of his arrest, the Vancouver Coal Company. Kakua was accused of killing his Canadian Indian wife, Que-en, their infant daughter, and his in-laws, Squash-e-lik and Shil-at-ti-Nord.

Kakua testified that he returned home drunk the night of the murders and remembered a domestic dispute, swinging an axe wildly, and falling down and passing out. The next morning, he awoke to find his wife, child, and mother- and father-in-law all dead. He fled the scene and met an African Canadian friend named Adam Stepney, and the two of them spent the next night drinking under the wharf. A search party eventually captured the pair, and an inquest charged Kakua with "willful murder" and ordered him imprisoned to await trial.

The Indian nation to which Kakua's wife and family belonged pressed for his execution, and the trial proceeded, contrary to his attorney's pleas for a delay to prepare his defense. His fate was deliberated by an all-white jury, although there were six Hawaiians on the jury list, and the court failed to provide him with a translator, although he understood English imperfectly. The jury, while declaring that Hawaiians were "not Christians," so "killing men may not be such an offense in their eyes," found Kakua guilty of murder; the court agreed and sentenced him to be hanged.

After rejecting an appeal from the Hawaiian consul, Henry Rhodes, on the grounds that Kakua's testimony in the Hawaiian language was disallowed during the proceedings, at 7 A.M. on March 10, 1869, Peter Kakua ascended the scaffold "unflinchingly, made no remarks, and struggled but slightly after the drop fell," according to the Victoria *Daily Colonist*. His neck broken, Kakua was pronounced dead and buried.

Peter Kakua's presence in the Northwest was unexceptional and followed on the path trod by Kaʻiana and two other Hawaiians who arrived in the vicinity in 1788. John Meares was the U.S. ship captain who took Kaʻiana, Winee, and two other Hawaiians to China and then, after Winee's death at sea, back across the Pacific to Vancouver Island. There, the fifty or so Chinese on board his vessels used Canadian timber to build a forty-ton schooner, the *North West America*, the first such ship built in that part of the continent. Meares returned to China to get more workers for his outpost, which was a collection point for furs for the China trade, a scheme proposed by John Ledyard to Thomas Jefferson just three years earlier. Meares intended to bring wives from Hawaiʻi for those Chinese migrants, but his plan failed when the Spaniards who claimed the area seized his vessels. Meares estimated he had seventy Chinese in his colony, but the Spaniards counted twenty-nine.

Despite their value to their employers, Hawaiians at first received nothing in exchange for their labor save food and shelter. Some of those workers might have been kidnapped and serving terms of involuntary servitude. By the nineteenth century, however, with a declining labor pool in Hawaiʻi and regulation and taxes imposed by the Hawaiian kingdom, Hawaiian seamen were paid with trade objects like cloth and Chinese goods as well as in cash. In 1811, twenty-four Hawaiians were hired to establish a trading post at the Columbia River mouth, named Astoria after John Jacob Astor of the American Fur Company. They received food, clothing, and merchandise worth $100 on completion of their three-year term of service. A year later, twenty-six Hawaiians bound for Astoria agreed to wages that included a suit of clothes and ten dollars a month, while their supervisor received fifteen dollars a month.

Among the 1811 group was Naukane from the island of Hawaiʻi. Chosen by the king to supervise the migrants, Naukane helped to secure Astoria and then joined an expedition to set up a string of fur-trading posts extending upriver along the Columbia. Along the way, the Americans encountered their British rivals from the British Northwest Company, whose leader traded one of his men for Naukane. Under the British flag, Naukane (known to the British as John Coxe) and his companions canoed and portaged their way to Fort William, the Northwest Company's hub on the shore of Lake Superior, and sailed to England.

The War of 1812 pitted Britain against its former colony, the United States, and Naukane's new masters planned to seize the U.S. factory at Astoria to monopolize the American fur trade. Naukane, with his knowledge of Astoria and the turbulent waters of the Columbia River, was selected to join the British force assembling in Portsmouth, England. On March 25, 1813, the Northwest Company's *Isaac Todd* left England and sailed

FIGURE 32

Paul Kane, *Old Cox, a Sandwich Islander, who was present at the death of Captain Cook.* Portrait of Naukane by Paul Kane, 1846–47, watercolor with graphite on paper. Kane painted many of Canada's American Indians. With permission of the Royal Ontario Museum.

south to Rio de Janeiro, around Cape Horn, and up the west coast to Astoria. By the time they arrived, however, an overland party had already taken the factory and renamed the post Fort George. Naukane worked there for the Northwest Company until August 1814, when all thirty-two Hawaiians, former employees of the rebuilt Pacific Fur Company, returned to their island home on the *Isaac Todd,* manned fittingly by Hawaiians.

Naukane's journeys were not over. When Liholiho, or Kamehameha II, sailed for London in 1823 seeking an alliance with the English, Naukane accompanied his king. When the king and queen contracted measles and died in London, Naukane brought their remains home. He departed Hawai'i again for the Northwest, where at Fort Vancouver (in present-day Washington State) he worked for the British Hudson's Bay Company. He retired a few years later to raise pigs and succumbed to tuberculosis sometime between 1836 and 1838. In his honor, the company gave the name Coxe's Plain to the grasslands on which his cabin stood and his pigs grazed, between Fort Vancouver and the Columbia River.

Using names not of their own language and likely not of their own choosing, Hawaiians such as John Coxe, Boatswain Tom, Bill King, Charley, John Bull, Negro, Honolulu,

Maui, Rice, and Pig left the islands for the continent to produce wealth for others who, although they needed Pacific Islander labor, despised the laborers as racially inferior. By 1817, when the Northwest Company's *Columbia* took on sixty Hawaiians for work on the Columbia River, their value had been established. The company's Fort Walla Walla, founded in July 1818, was manned by twenty-five Canadians, thirty-eight Iroquois, and thirty-two Hawaiians.

Hawaiians built ships, conveyed passengers and goods between the land and ships anchored offshore, and sailed coastal vessels along America's western shores, with their many rocks, dangerous tides, and thick, blanketing fogs. On land, they served as soldiers, as on the punitive expedition of 1828 against the Klallam nation; erected buildings and forts; operated sawmills; cleared forests; and cultivated food crops. Moreover, their labor produced goods that connected the Northwest with Hawai'i, Asia, America's West Coast, and the U.S. Northeast.

The U.S.-China fur trade depended on capital supplied by banks in the U.S. Northeast, where shipyards launched the ships; suppliers outfitted the expeditions; factories manufactured the glass, cloth, and metalware vital for the trade in furs with American Indians; and investors reaped profits from the commerce between America and Asia. Moreover, the resources of the Northwest, primarily its furs, reduced the usual demands of gold and silver by Asian suppliers.

Profits were considerable. Prominent among U.S. fur traders was William Sturgis of Boston, whose single venture netted a $284,000 return on a $50,000 investment. In 1811, fifteen US ships collected and transported to Canton eighteen thousand sea-otter pelts valued at more than half a million dollars. However, as was typical of extractive industries, this resource was soon depleted: rapacious hunting led to the decline and virtual extermination of sea otters around Nootka Sound, just as reckless cutting of the fragrant sandalwood tree, valuable in China for making incense, resulted in its near extinction in Hawai'i.

The loss of labor to America's West Coast was another aspect of Hawai'i's impoverishment. Nearly two thousand Hawaiians enlisted on foreign ships as seamen between 1845 and 1847, and by 1850 the number had risen to about four thousand, which represented almost 5 percent of the entire Hawaiian population and 12 percent of all Hawaiian males eighteen and older. By 1830, Hawaiians were the principal seamen on U.S. fur-trading ships along the West Coast, and in 1842 a contemporary traveler reported that Pacific Islanders, mainly from Hawai'i but also from Tahiti and New Zealand, were indispensable to the ship traffic along California's coast.

In 1834 the British-run Hudson's Bay Company opened an agency in Honolulu to sell the products of the Northwest, mainly lumber and salted salmon, which became important in the Hawaiian diet. The agency also recruited Hawaiian workers for the company. In Vancouver, British Columbia, Hawaiians settled along a road that led from the wharf to the town at a place called Kanaka Village. There, Hawaiians, together with Indians, whites, and those of mixed race, lived with their families as employees of the Hudson's

Bay Company. Other Hawaiians, led by William Naukana, built homes on Salt Spring Island; still others settled in Nanaimo, where Peter Kakua, or Kanaka Pete, lived; and still others inhabited Kanaka Row on Victoria's waterfront. According to an 1844 report, the company employed three to four hundred Hawaiians on the Columbia River. They signed three-year contracts and earned monthly wages of ten dollars. They split rails for fences and animal pens; repaired canoes and salmon barrels; tilled acres of wheat, oats, barley, and potatoes; herded sheep and cattle; and worked as domestics in the homes of the wealthy. A few had Hawaiian wives, but more took Indian wives.

White missionaries complained that the company treated their Hawaiian indentures little better than slaves, whipping and imprisoning them frequently and overcharging them for food and clothing to keep them indebted to the company. An Anglican missionary reported to the Aborigines' Protection Society of London that a Hawaiian accused of loafing was confined in irons for five months, even though he was later cleared of the charge. Hawaiian laborers, like Chinese contract workers on sugar plantations in the islands, routinely ran away to escape the harsh conditions. Most headed south for California as soon as they could, especially after the discovery of gold in 1848. Ten years later, the company closed its shop in Hawai'i, and a year later the military dismantled Kanaka Village in Vancouver to turn it into an artillery range.

By the mid-nineteenth century, Hawaiians had ventured not only to the Northwest but as far south as Acapulco, where they served as sailors on Mexican ships in the Manila galleon trade. They also made up a significant number of the employees of the Russian-owned Russian-American Company, whose holdings stretched from Alaska's Aleutian Islands to northern California. An 1850 report showed that in the company's employ were 4,051 Aleuts, 1,703 "creoles," 1,070 Hawaiians, and 505 Russians. Following the demographic pattern for settler colonies, native peoples far exceeded the number of Russians.

The period of migrant labor for Hawaiians in the Northwest, which began in 1788, continued until the 1850s, when whites imposed restrictions against them. As early as 1844, whites limited the vote to free white men and sought the exclusion of African Americans and Hawaiians from the area. Those who remained were to be auctioned off and removed from the territory within six months of completion of their term of labor. A year later, white leaders deliberated an act to impose a five-dollar tax on anyone introducing Hawaiians to the region and an additional three-dollar levy on employers of Hawaiians who failed to return them to the islands. Clearly, whites sought to restrict the role of Hawaiians in the region to that of racially inferior migrant workers. Two years after the formation of the Oregon Territory in 1848, Samuel Thurston, the territory's delegate to Congress, favored the expulsion of Hawaiians from the territory because they were "a race of men as black as your negroes of the South, and a race, too, that we do not desire to settle in Oregon." At the same time, he endorsed the U.S. takeover of Hawai'i and favored expansion across the U.S. continent as divinely ordained—"the gift of God." In 1849, Hawaiians petitioned the territory for U.S. citizenship and the vote, but they

FIGURE 33
Polly Bemis on the porch of a friend's cabin, 1923. Bemis, a Chinese migrant, arrived in Idaho Territory in 1872, married Charlie Bemis in 1894, and lived along the Salmon River on a mining claim. Courtesy of Idaho State Historical Society.

continued to be viewed, like Asians, as aliens and thus were denied land ownership and equal protection under the law.

SOUTH ASIANS

As British subjects, India's labor migrants followed the course of empire to British holdings in Africa, islands in the Pacific and Caribbean, and Canada. The first South Asians in British Columbia arrived in the late nineteenth century, likely unaware of the Hawaiians who had helped to lay the foundations of the region's modern economy earlier in the century. South Asians remained a small group, perhaps totaling 45 by 1905, but during the following two years they increased by 4,747. The Canadian government curtailed Asian migration after an anti-Asian riot in Vancouver in 1907, and from 1909 to 1920, only 118 South Asians entered Canada. Many South Asian migrants, along with Japanese, headed south shortly after landing in Vancouver: in 1907 alone, 1,072 South Asians and some 3,600 Japanese crossed the Canadian border into the United States.

The South Asians who remained in British Columbia joined the more numerous Chinese and Japanese migrant laborers who left Vancouver for outlying lumber and railroad camps and towns. For work in the sawmills, men received between $1.35 and $2 a day. They worked long hours, from sunrise to sunset, seven days a week, for nine months each year.

Lumber-mill work also enticed migrant laborers over the border into Washington State. By the fall of 1907, there were several hundred South Asians in the Bellingham area, where they worked in mills such as the Bellingham Bay Lumber Mill, Morrison Mill, and Larson's Mill. In the United States, they earned more than their counterparts in Canada, two dollars a day, though they received twenty-two cents a day less than whites. Despite earning higher wages, white workers perceived South Asians as a threats to their livelihood.

White racism homogenized nonwhites. Lumped together as "Orientals," South Asians, Chinese, and Japanese were the objects of hatred and fear, especially among white workers, and these sentiments translated into violence. On Labor Day, September 2, 1907, over a thousand white union supporters marched down Bellingham's streets, beat a few South Asian onlookers, and continued their violence against South Asians and their dwellings days after the parade. "Drive out the cheap labor!" was the rallying cry. On September 5, a mob estimated at five hundred attacked South Asians, pulling them from their beds, destroying and stealing their possessions, and burning their bunkhouses. About seven hundred South Asians fled Bellingham and crossed the border back into Canada.

This reverse migration did not protect them from violence. The Bellingham precedent spread to white Canada, which included large numbers of white immigrants from the United States, and to other parts of Washington State, including Seattle and the lumber town of Everett. In Bellingham, a group of fifty Japanese refused to leave and armed themselves, trying to avoid being "Hindued," but they too finally capitulated and fled the town.

Two days after the Bellingham riot, some ten thousand whites staged a big anti-Asian parade in Vancouver. The Vancouver *Daily Province* set the stage by announcing the expected arrival of the *Charmer,* with 400 Japanese on board, together with the *Monteagle* and its "oriental hordes" of 900 Sikhs, 1,100 Chinese, and a few Japanese. The events in Bellingham gave license to the Vancouver riot of September 7, 1907, in which a white mob swept through the town's Chinese and Japanese quarters, causing a few minor injuries and thousands of dollars' worth of property damage. "Stand for a white Canada," one of their banners declared. Three days after the Vancouver riot, the *Monteagle* arrived: contrary to the newspaper announcement, it carried 914 South Asians, 149 Chinese, and 114 Japanese.

FIGURE 34

South Asian antiracist, anticolonial activists on board the *Komagata Maru* in Vancouver harbor, 1914.
Canadian Photo Company, Vancouver Public Library.

South Asians organized in self-defense against the sentiment "White Canada forever," a phrase from a popular song. The Khalsa Diwan Society, one of whose founders was the Sikh missionary Teja Singh, who worked also among California's Sikh community, lobbied the Canadian government for South Asian civil rights and equality under the law.

Canada's anti-Asianists pursued a twofold approach. The government tried to induce those already in Canada to leave with an offer of free transportation to the British West Indies or Honduras as indentured laborers, and it initiated rules to restrict South Asian entry. Expulsion failed, but Canada's bar on contract labor and its requirement that each migrant possess at least $25 on landing—an amount increased to $200 in 1908—reduced South Asian entry to a trickle. The nation state's continuous-passage rule, adopted in 1908, was especially restrictive of South Asian migration. It required that all immigrants entering Canada come from the country of their birth or citizenship by "a continuous journey and on through tickets" purchased in their home country. There were, however, no commercial passenger ships that sailed directly from India to Canada.

To oppose the ban, Gurdit Singh, a wealthy Punjabi born businessman from Singapore, chartered a ship, the Japanese *Komagata Maru*, to transport 376 South Asians—340

Sikhs, 24 Muslims, and 12 Hindus, all British subjects— to Canada. Anti-Asianists in Canada were infuriated, and on May 23, 1914, when the *Komagata Maru* arrived in Vancouver harbor, the government refused landing rights to all the passengers except twenty who were previous Canadian residents. Officials boarded the ship, which was forced to anchor hundreds of yards from shore, and after inspecting the passengers, pronounced ninety medically unfit for entry. A legal challenge to the government's exclusion order took seven weeks and was denied by the provincial court.

Turned back, the *Komagata Maru* went to India, where, at Budge Budge harbor near Calcutta, the British tried to arrest Gurdit Singh and other leaders as dangerous political agitators. In the melee, the police shot and killed twenty of the passengers, and two white and two Punjabi officers and two bystanders were killed. Singh and others escaped, but those detained were held in prisons and under house arrest. The *Komagata Maru* incident and the massacre at Budge Budge exemplified the rule of white supremacy and British colonialism that prompted the anticolonial, antiracist struggles in India and America. The turning back of the *Komagata Maru,* affirming anti-Asian exclusion laws, ended the period of South Asian migrant labor in the Northwest.

NORTHEAST

Ships, again, were the vessels by which Pacific Islanders and Asians arrived in the U.S. Northeast. Soon after the nation's independence, the first U.S. ships made their way to China, fulfilling an ambition and "destiny" of European peoples at least since the fifteenth century. The *Empress of China* returned to New York harbor laden with tea in 1785, and the *Pallas* arrived the same year in Baltimore with an Asian and African crew. We know little about the lives of those sailors, but we can speculate that some probably settled in the Northeast, while others continued as sailors.

HAWAIIANS

The Atlantic world's contact with the Pacific was facilitated by Hawaiian seamen who worked the trade vessels on their way to Asia and eventually landed in port cities in the Northeast. Perhaps the first was the *Columbia,* which departed New England in search of furs in the Northwest in 1787 and returned three years later with a Hawaiian on board, who astonished onlookers as he walked Boston's streets. Such also was the lot of Hopu and ʻŌpūkahaʻia, who in 1807 were assigned by King Kamehameha to Caleb Brintnall's ship. The two left their island home for the Northwest, where the crew collected furs, then sailed across Oceania to China to acquire trade goods, stayed in Macao and Canton for about six months, and then made their way across the Indian Ocean, around Africa's Cape, and across the Atlantic to New York, where they stepped ashore in 1809.

Christian missionaries found Hopu and ʻŌpūkahaʻia and instructed them. After two or three years under a tutor, Hopu returned to sea. He participated in the War of 1812 but, unlike Naukane, served on the U.S. side. The British captured and imprisoned him on the Caribbean island of St. Kitts, where he witnessed the brutality of slavery and American Indian and African bondage. Slave masters, Hopu reported, drove the enslaved to labor, starved them, and shackled them with chains around their necks and legs. He was sickened by the sight. Hopu returned to New Haven, Connecticut, and soon left again for the Caribbean, where for two months he was marooned on an island where Africans treated him with great kindness. He eventually made his way back to Nantucket, Massachusetts, and New Haven, where he worked as a domestic servant, and in 1815 he moved with his master to New York State. Eager to return home, Hopu ended up at the newly founded Foreign Mission School in Cornwall, Connecticut, in the spring of 1817, along with ʻŌpūkahaʻia and another Hawaiian, William Kanui.

Kanui was born on Oʻahu but grew up in Waimea, Kauaʻi, where foreign ships were a common sight during the early nineteenth century because of their need to resupply with water, food, and crew. Kanui was eleven or twelve years old when he, his brother, and four other Hawaiians joined the crew of a Captain Davis of Boston. After a voyage that continued to Africa, the Hawaiians reached Boston in 1809. In the Northeast, Kanui and his brother worked as family servants and farmhands. They joined the U.S. Navy and fought in the War of 1812. After the war, Kanui's brother fell ill and died in Providence, Rhode Island. While in New Haven, ʻŌpūkahaʻia met Kanui and persuaded him to join the company that had assembled at the Foreign Mission School to prepare for the return to Hawaiʻi.

ʻŌpūkahaʻia had been instrumental in the founding of that school. He was about fifteen years old when he boarded Brintnall's ship. After he landed in New York, a missionary tale recounts, Yale College students found him weeping on the steps of one of the buildings. ʻŌpūkahaʻia was distraught, the youths discovered, because he longed for an education. Touched, the students resolved to teach the Hawaiian castaway. Up to this point, evangelical labors had been directed mainly at American Indians and whites in the U.S. West. This new effort, its founders resolved, would advance the cause of missions overseas, and Hawaiian youth, ʻŌpūkahaʻia especially, supplied an opportune moment. Because of his ardent desire for learning and his abilities, according to his teachers, ʻŌpūkahaʻia disproved the widely held notion that "heathens" were incapable of learning.

Established on October 29, 1816, the Foreign Mission School was to be a "school for the education of heathen youth" to train them as missionaries, teachers, interpreters, and physicians "to promote Christianity and civilization." The school's patron was the American Board of Commissioners for Foreign Missions (ABCFM). This was a product of the Second Great Awakening, an evangelical movement that swept early-nineteenth-century New England. Samuel Mills, a founder of the ABCFM and one of the Yale students who befriended ʻŌpūkahaʻia, argued in favor of establishing missions overseas. The presence of natives from foreign lands provided an excellent opportunity to spread the gospel to those far-off places, he contended, because they knew the language and their bodies were better suited for living in the hot, moist tropics.

FIGURE 35

'Ōpūkaha'ia's gravestone in Cornwall, Connecticut, lies horizontally, unlike those of the good citizens of Cornwall. Visitors placed items from Hawai'i on his tombstone. In July 1993, his family took his remains home to Hawai'i. Photo by Gary Y. Okihiro.

Similarly, Mills believed, African American teachers could uplift the race and serve as native missionaries to Africa. He thus proposed an African School to parallel the Cornwall Foreign Mission School, and he received financial support from slaveholders who saw free blacks as a cause for unrest among the enslaved. Mills was also an enthusiastic booster and fundraiser for the American Colonization Society, which was formed in 1817, following the 1800 slave rebellion in Virginia led by Gabriel Prosser, to relocate free blacks to a colony in Africa. Mills perished off the coast of Sierra Leone in 1818 while pursuing his object of "redemption and emancipation," searching for a site for that colony.

About two years after its founding, the Foreign Mission School had a student body of six Hawaiians, two Society Islanders, a Chinese, a Malay, and eleven American Indians— seven Cherokees, two Choctaws, one from Pennsylvania, and another from Canada. In 1825, there were six Hawaiians, four Chinese, fourteen American Indians, a Portuguese from the Azores, and a Jewish student from England. One of the Chinese was Wu Lan from Guangdong Province. The school's Hawaiians, like the migrant laborers in the Northwest, were given names that hid their identities: David Brainerd, John Phelps, Samuel Mills, and George Tyler. 'Ōpūkaha'ia worked on creating a Hawaiian grammar, dictionary, and spelling book, but he fell seriously ill and had to quit his studies. On February 17, 1818, he died.

On October 15, 1819, at the Park Street Church in Boston, a company of seven missionaries and their wives and children, together with three Hawaiians, were formed into a "Church of Christ" to spread the gospel among the heathen in the Pacific. One of the Hawaiians, now known as Thomas Hopu, addressed the assembly. A reporter for the *Boston Recorder* noted the irony of a native of Hawai'i calling on citizens of Boston to believe in Jesus Christ. Hopu would disappoint his shepherds soon thereafter by backsliding, but on this day he bore powerful witness to the transformative power of Christianity and civilization's benevolence. More than five hundred souls received Holy Communion at the farewell service, and on Saturday morning, October 23, at Boston's Long Wharf, the crowd lifted their voices to sing "Blest Be the Tie That Binds" and "When Shall We All Meet Again? "as the first missionary contingent departed the Northeast for the Hawaiian Islands.

These missionaries, others who followed them, and their descendants would help to revolutionize Hawaiian history, but the Hawaiians in the Northeast also brought about changes in U.S. society. Not only did they inspire the evangelical turn from the interior of the continent to expansions overseas, which prodded and accompanied the imperial republic under the banner of Christianity and civilization, but they also fought in the War of 1812 and facilitated the commerce that tied the U.S. Northeast to Asia and the islands of Hawai'i. They were the forerunners of other migrant laborers who visited and eventually settled in the region: Hawaiian whale men.

In the nineteenth century whale oil was the principal fuel for lighting, and whalebone was used in women's undergarments and as ivory. Whale hunts had long preceded the Revolutionary War, and ports like Nantucket and New Bedford, Massachusetts, became hubs for the industry. Many of the whalers were African Americans, who had settled in New Bedford especially after 1716, when the Quaker majority attracted and sheltered freed slaves and runaways. Along with other blacks, including West Indians, Cape Verdeans, and West Africans, they manned New Bedford's whaling ships and occasionally captained them. Crispus Attucks, the African American patriot killed by the British in the 1775 Boston Massacre, worked as a New Bedford whaler and merchant seaman for twenty years. In all, more than three thousand African Americans sailed on New Bedford whalers between 1803 and 1860. The toggle harpoon head, which became an industry standard, was invented in 1848 by an African American blacksmith, Lewis Temple. Whites, notably Portuguese who were racialized variously in categories from white to black, gradually displaced African American whale men in the years leading up to the U.S. Civil War.

Whaling work was dirty and dangerous, and conditions on board ships were foul. The large numbers of African Americans and foreigners on whaling crews was a testament to the occupation's low status among white seamen. Hawaiians and Pacific Islanders constituted as much as 20 percent of the overall whaling workforce at the industry's peak, around the middle of the nineteenth century; perhaps one-third of the crew on whaling vessels operating in the Pacific in the 1840s; and half during the 1860s. The men signed contracts specifying a fixed period of service for set wages and requiring a promise to serve as "good and obedient seamen." Their earnings were diminished by charges for essential items such as shirts, pants, socks, boots, and knives. For instance, Kahoau (Jim Maui) earned $90.56 for a term at sea, but his expenses totaled $53.25, leaving him with $37.31; Kapuahiloa (Isaac) earned $131.10, but his expenses reduced his returns to $8.78 after a year's labor.

In 1845, New Bedford was the nation's fourth leading port, behind New York City, Boston, and New Orleans. That year its 736 whaling vessels brought in 158,000 barrels of sperm oil, the finest grade of whale oil; 272,000 barrels of other whale oil; and 3 million pounds of whalebone. Outfitting the fleet generated an income of more than $10.5 million for merchants and suppliers, and income from whale products brought in more: in 1841, for instance, the revenue totaled more than $7 million. The fleet employed ten thousand crew members, and the workforce employed in constructing, repairing, and provisioning whale ships totaled an estimated fifty thousand. Clearly, the industry was consequential for the nineteenth-century U.S. economy.

New Bedford on the Atlantic and Honolulu and Lahaina, Maui, in the Pacific were the whaling capitals of the world during the 1840s and 1850s. The first whaling vessel arrived in Hawaiian waters in 1819. With the opening of hunting grounds off the coast of Japan and in the Arctic Ocean, visits to Hawaiian landings by whalers increased rapidly, from an annual average of 104 between 1824 and 1827 to 419 from 1843 to 1854. During its heyday, whaling was the leading source of revenue for the Hawaiian kingdom.

Whale men from Hawai'i and Guam migrated to and settled in the New Bedford area and in Cold Spring Harbor on New York's Long Island. Racialized as "mulatto" and "black," these Pacific Islanders probably lived as and among African Americans and other peoples of color. In New Bedford, for example, the 1860 U.S. Census found the Hawaiian seamen George Adams, William Grey, Henry Jones, John Maroin, and William Mohee, all classed as black, and John Booth and John Swain, classed as mulatto. Likewise, the Chinese Sit Afoo and John Apho were considered mulatto. The 1870 census listed the seamen Domingo Carder and George Nichols, both from Guam, as black. Carder lived with his Massachusetts-born African American wife and their six-year-old son.

Nantucket Island, offshore from New Bedford, also drew Hawaiian seamen. As early as 1825, the *Nantucket Inquirer* estimated that there were more than fifty Pacific Islanders on Nantucket, all employed on whale ships. Perhaps they stayed at the New Zealander William Whippey's Canacka Boarding-House or, as blacks, in "New Guinea," a racially segregated quarter reserved for African Americans. And when they died far from home— like one unnamed Hawaiian whale man whose body was found under a barn in 1832, or the Hawaiian seaman Joseph Dix, who died of tuberculosis in 1843—they were almost certainly buried in the island's Colored Cemetery.

Whereas in the Northwest Hawaiians constituted a distinctive race and class of people, excluded and exploited as migrant workers, the rigid black/white divide of the Northeast disallowed those nuances, so Hawaiians and other Pacific Islanders generally fell into the company of African Americans and "colored" folk. Like American Indians, they were seen by whites in the Northeast as heathens ripe for conversion. Whether because of their small numbers or the prominence and persistence of the black/white divide, Pacific Islanders in the Northeast became members of the black community in both life and death.

SOUTH ASIANS

South Asians, like Pacific Islanders, arrived in the U.S. Northeast on board ships employed in the Asian and Pacific trade. However, trade goods and European images of South Asia preceded them. The *Virginia Gazette* of 1739, for instance, carried a news item about Goa, India, a "rich Settlement belonging to the Portuguese." Indian tea, china, pearls, baskets, and chests appeared regularly in advertisements. Moreover, India's conquest generated individual fortunes and American institutions. Elihu Yale was born in Boston in 1649 but grew up in England, where his father was a man of property and social standing. The powerful East India Company selected Yale to represent its interests in India, and he rose quickly to become a merchant prince and the governor of Madras. Back in New Haven, the Connecticut Collegiate School petitioned Yale, by then retired in London, to endow the school in "your native country." The governor donated two trunks of mostly Indian textiles that, on their sale in Boston, brought in a sum sufficient to erect a college and a rector's house. In 1718, in anticipation of more to come, the school's trustees named the new building and later the institution after its benefactor. About a century later, Yale College, was the site of ʻŌpūkahaʻia's encounter with Christian missions. When Yale died in 1721, his tombstone inscription reduced his life to its essentials:

Born in America, in Europe bred,
In Africa travell'd and in Asia wed,
Where long he liv'd, and thriv'd.[1]

South Asians made landfall in the United States as early as the 1790s with the rise of traffic between Northeastern ports like Salem, Massachusetts, and Asian ports like Madras (today's Chennai), Bombay (Mumbai), Calcutta (Kolkata), and Canton (Guangzhou). On meeting an Indian from Madras in December 1790, a Salem clergyman noted in his diary that the man's complexion was "much darker than any native Indians of America," without apology for a conflation based on a gross error of geography. This Indian arrived on board a British trade ship from Europe, the American wrote. Other South Asians landed and apparently settled, as "colored" folk, among African Americans and married African American women.

South Asian indentures like James Dunn shared the experience of slavery with African Americans. Dunn petitioned the Pennsylvania Abolition Society for his freedom in the 1790s, and South Asians like John Ballay, Joseph Green, and unnamed others served indentures of twelve to fifteen years. Many probably married African American women and became "black."

CHINESE

Chinese, like South Asians, arrived in the Northeast's port cities as laborers. The first Chinese to make landfall were probably the seamen who arrived in Baltimore on the *Pallas* in 1785. Other Chinese followed them to the Northeast and mingled among seamen, migrants, and African Americans in the early 1800s. Around midcentury, we find Chinese students at the Foreign Mission School in Connecticut, as well as Chinese sailors, cooks, stewards, peddlers, cigar makers, former opera performers, and small businessmen in New York City; three Chinese students at Monson Academy in Massachusetts; and Chinese seamen in New Bedford. A number of Chinese men in New York and New Bedford married Irish women.

Representative of the commercial ties with Asia and the Northwest that brought Asian immigrants to the Northeast was the New Yorker John Jacob Astor, a German immigrant who capitalized on the pelts and furs of the Northwest (and on American Indian and Hawaiian labor). His American Fur Company dispatched at least one ship a year to the Northwest between 1802 and 1812, and it sold its receipts in the United States and Europe.

When furs became scarce due to overhunting, Astor, like other U.S. traders in China, turned to smuggling opium, a traffic pioneered by the British. This highly lucrative operation reversed the drain of precious metals from America and Europe to Asia; sustained the enterprise of British colonial India, whence the drug derived; and amassed personal fortunes for the traders. Opium crippled its addicts and impoverished the Chinese nation, leading to the Opium War of 1839–42. On retiring from the China trade, Astor invested his fortune in New York real estate, making him the city's richest man, with an estate valued at $20 million when he died in 1848.

SOUTH

The nation's Northeast was the principal but not the sole gateway for foreign trade. In the late nineteenth century, New Orleans was the South's leading shipping hub and a major port for international trade. Trains and barges from the Mississippi River converged on the city, and vessels from the Caribbean and Central and South America made New Orleans the second busiest harbor in the country. City boosters promoted New Orleans as a tourist attraction for its mix of peoples and goods from far-off lands, and Mardi Gras drew tens of thousands of visitors each year.

Beginning in the late 1880s, South Asian Bengali peddlers made New Orleans a base of their business in the United States, especially in the winter, the off-season for New York City. They found customers at Mardi Gras, which featured Orientalist fantasies and lavish Indian processions, Asian goods, and pavilions like those of the International Cotton Exhibition in 1884–85. So popular was the display that an Oriental Exhibition store opened on Canal Street, selling Oriental rugs, silks, and porcelain. Their opulence and sensuality adorned some of the finest brothels in New Orleans.

In the 1890s, South Asian vendors joined Chinese on the streets of New Orleans, selling silks, rugs, and other wares. Many of them were veterans of the tourist trade and refugees from New Jersey's winters. Most of them shared apartments in the Storyville section of the city, and they were regulars at the French Market stalls and in the commercial district along Canal Street. The 1900 U.S. Census recorded them as Alef Ally, Aynuddin and Solomon Mondul, Ibrahim Musa, Jainal Abdeen, Abdul Subham, Sofur Ally, and Eshrack, Bahadoor, and Majan Ali. Mostly in their mid-thirties to late forties, the men were peddlers by trade.

The presence of South Asian and Chinese entrepreneurs in the postbellum South illustrates that not all Asians were migrant laborers. New Orleans bustled with exchanges both material and cultural, not from the north Atlantic European world, which predominated in the Northeast, but from the hybrid Caribbean world. Even so, situated within the black and white racial formation of the South and Northeast, South Asians were racialized and classed as blacks. In the South, they served white masters as indentured and enslaved laborers.

Those intersections of race, class, and nation or citizenship—the social formation—were a prominent feature of Asian migrant labor in the United States. Asian migrant labor was efficient and inexpensive for employers, not only because Asians were classified as aliens without the rights of citizenship but also in large part because they were racialized as nonwhites. Those intersections manifested themselves differently among different groups and locales, as shown in the contrasting articulations of race, class, and nation involving Chinese migrant labor in the U.S. South and North.

SOUTH AND NORTH

Prior to the Civil War, the North and the South were distinguished by the type of labor that prevailed: free or unbound labor in the North, and slave labor in the South. Globally, the Chinese coolie was associated with slave labor, while in the North, Chinese laborers, who could be paid low rates, undermined "citizen laborers." In popular discourse, then, *coolie, slave,* and *cheap* referred to nonwhites, while *free* and *citizen* referred to whites.

SOUTH

In the South, Asian migrant labor, widely seen as a form of bound labor, formed connections with enslaved labor and its emancipation. During the Civil War, in 1862, Congress made U.S. participation in the coolie traffic illegal. As shown by the historian Moon-Ho Jung, nineteenth-century debates over African American slavery and freedom were instrumental in the passing of the nation's first exclusion laws involving Asian women and prostitution (the 1875 Page Act) and Chinese labor (the 1882 Exclusion Act). Political discourse reduced both these varieties of labor to slavery. Some white, middle-class women made it their mission to save Asian women from the bondage of prostitution and the clutches of Asian men. White planters in the British Caribbean and U.S. South endeavored to extricate Chinese migrant labor from the category of the coolie, which was equated with slave labor.

Sugar planters in the U.S. South closely followed developments on sugar plantations in the Caribbean. Even before the Civil War, they watched the Caribbean experiment of moving from African enslaved to Asian indentured labor. After the war, Louisiana planters blamed the war and Emancipation for the sugar industry's precipitous fall, and they tried to recoup their fortunes by importing Chinese migrant laborers, following the British West Indian planters in referring to them as "free" workers and "immigrants" to avoid the taint of slavery. At the same time, the state passed laws called the Black Codes in 1865 to undermine the freedoms of African Americans and compel them into contracts and indentures in agricultural work. Employers attempted to pit Chinese against African American laborers. As a newspaper reporter stated: "To bring coolie labor in competition with negro labor—to let the negroes see that laborers can be had without them—is the main feature of the plan."[2]

Radical Reconstruction, begun in 1867, opposed coolie importation as a species of slavery; yet the first group of Chinese from Cuba landed in New Orleans in that year, recruited by Louisiana planters and merchants. One shipment of fifteen and a second of fifty-five Chinese migrants agreed to a term of service, wages, and subsistence. Edward Wyches, a resident of Louisiana and Cuba and a labor recruiter, drew up agreements that specified eighteen months of service at fourteen dollars per month, a six-day work week from sunrise till dark, a ration of ten pounds of rice and three and a half pounds of pork each week, and the pledge "to render strict obedience to my employer, and submit myself to the regulations of the plantation or household, and in all things to conduct myself as a good and faithful servant."[3] Wyches brought in fifty Chinese "servants" in May 1867.

Word of the experiment in Louisiana spread throughout the South. In July 1867, Memphis businessmen sponsored a Chinese labor convention to discuss the best and cheapest means to procure Chinese workers. The plan was to form the Mississippi Valley Immigration Labor Company to import as many Chinese migrant laborers as possible in the shortest period of time. Some five hundred delegates met, representing agriculture, railroad, and business interests in Alabama, Arkansas, Georgia, Kentucky, Louisiana, Mississippi, Missouri, South Carolina, Tennessee, and California. One of the delegates was Nathan Bedford Forrest, president of the New Selma, Marion and Memphis Railroad and the first grand wizard of the Ku Klux Klan. Also present was Cornelius Koopmanschap, a San Francisco importer of Chinese goods and a major West Coast recruiter and contractor of Chinese labor. Koopmanschap was one of the suppliers of Chinese workers for the transcontinental railroad.

To avoid middlemen charges, the Arkansas River Valley Immigration Company sent its own agent directly to China to recruit laborers. In June 1870, a ship landed in New Orleans with 169 men, 20 having died en route. The Chinese migrant laborers were distributed among cotton plantations in Arkansas and Mississippi. Another shipment of about 220 Chinese arrived in New Orleans in October 1870 as a result of direct recruiting by Southern planters. Although efforts in China continued, agricultural labor recruitment shifted to California because it was cheaper, and recruiting labor from within the United States avoided the expense and legal entanglements of importing coolies. The railroads in the South also recruited Chinese migrants from California: in 1870 the West Coast contractor John Walker delivered some 250 laborers for the Houston and Texas Central Railroad and over 900 for the Alabama and Chattanooga Railroad. Those experienced hands, having worked on railroads in the West, agreed to three-year contracts for twenty dollars per month.

The net result of all those efforts was the northward and eastward flow of Chinese migrant laborers to fill the needs of the developing postbellum South. Workers were drawn from Cuba, China, and California to replace and discipline formerly enslaved African Americans.

To employers, Asians represented an ideal source of labor because they were plentiful and efficient. Moreover, as one white planter put it bluntly, Chinese migrants, unlike other laborers, had "no women, no children, no hogs, no ponies, no 'forecastle lawyers,' and no howling preachers."[4] Another crucial difference was that whereas African Americans, as citizens, could vote and thereby pose a challenge to white supremacy, Asian migrants, as "aliens ineligible to citizenship," could not vote.

Contrary to Royal Mead's memorable allusion to "cattle on the ranges," Asian migrant workers, like all peoples of color, resisted their oppression and exploitation. In fact, by contesting perceived injustices, Chinese migrant laborers in the South were soon cast not as "docile" workers but as "heathens" with long queues dangling down their backs, "their dark yellow countenances distorted, their black eyes flashing fire and fury, brandishing their cane knives and other weapons."[5] Betrayed by false promises, Chinese workers attacked a Chinese labor recruiter, they cornered an abusive white overseer, they filed complaints with the police, they ran away, and they stopped working.

In 1871, after a planter whipped a Chinese servant, all twenty-three of his Chinese laborers protested by striking. A scuffle broke out, and shots were fired, killing one Chinese and wounding two others. As a result, although bound by three-year contracts, all of the Chinese deserted the plantation. Corporal punishment generally failed to coerce laborers, and running away was common. A writer for the *Louisiana Sugar-Bowl* charged that the Chinese were "fond of changing about," ran away "worse than negroes," and left "as soon as anybody offers them higher wages."

Especially at critical times like the harvest, Southern planters depended heavily on Chinese labor crews. As African Americans were migrating northward and contractors drove up their prices for labor deliveries, Chinese crew leaders could negotiate favorable terms for themselves and their men. By the summer of 1871, some planters paid Chinese workers twenty dollars per month plus rations, and others twenty-two dollars without rations, at a time when the standard pay for African Americans was eighteen dollars per month with rations. Without the kind of solidarity common among planters in Hawai'i, plantations competed with each other for workers, even encouraging them to desert to new masters offering more favorable contracts. Given those conditions, Chinese migrant laborers refashioned themselves into mobile labor gangs, like seasonal African American workers and their Chinese counterparts in California, to maximize their earnings by offering their labor to the highest bidder.

Those acts of Chinese resistance operated within Louisiana's social formation, which positioned Asians against African Americans. At the same time, racial segregation promoted white supremacy and solidarity, even as class distinctions separated white planters and capitalists from the white working class. Segregation was the instrument of installing whiteness and white privilege while excluding, oppressing, and exploiting African Americans and distinguishing them from Asians on the basis of citizenship. In his lone dissent in *Plessy v. Ferguson* (1896), the Supreme Court justice John Marshall Harlan declared liberally that "our Constitution is color-blind, and neither knows nor tolerates classes among citizens." At the same time, he noted, African American citizens suffered segregation, while aliens of the "Chinese race," restricted from entry to the United States, were granted privileges denied to citizens. Those alignments of race, class, and nation reveal the workings of the social formation and its articulations of divide and rule.

Chinese and Asians generally, although labeled as "immigrants" and thus putative citizens for purposes of employment, were also racialized as coolies or cheap labor. By contrast, European immigrants were seen as supplying "citizen" labor. Those discourses are related: Asian connoted bound, nonwhite, and alien, and European connoted free, white, and citizen. In that relational sense, freedom was purchased by bondage, whiteness by nonwhiteness, and citizenship by "aliens ineligible to citizenship" in the U.S. social formation. Moreover, privileging whiteness served the interests of workers and capitalists alike in the crusade for the South's "redemption" from the black peril and Radical Reconstruction. White supremacy would perhaps find its highest expression in the large, urban centers of the postbellum South, with their manufacturing and industrial bases, which mirrored the social changes in the North.

The interests of the South's sugar planters extended beyond the region and nation. They contended that sugar grown in the tropical zone threatened their livelihood and way of life in the temperate zone, especially after the Reciprocity Treaty with Hawai'i in 1876, which allowed Hawaiian sugar to enter the continent duty-free. The Louisiana Sugar Planters' Association protested those "invasions" by sugar cultivated by slave and coolie labor. The state's representative in Congress argued that protective tariffs on sugar imports were necessary because at stake were "freedom and justice against slavery and injustice, American freedom against Cuban slavery and Hawaiian coolyism."[6] Louisiana planters claimed that the imperial republic, through its extensions beyond the continent to islands in the Caribbean and Pacific, threatened its domestic tranquility. According to some, global competition, such as sugar produced more cheaply in India, would spell the end of the U.S. industries. Those concerns reflected the rearticulations in the social formation under way around the world.

Insofar as the U.S. Civil War was waged over slavery and freedom, Asian migrant labor both troubled and calmed regional disagreements. In the South, the figure of the Chinese coolie conjured the specter of enslaved, black labor, while in the North, the image of cheap, alien Chinese labor threatened free, white citizen labor. In the West, as the historian Alexander Saxton has shown, the Chinese were the "indispensable enemy" of free, white citizen labor. Nationally, the anti-Chinese movement united whites as a race despite divisions of ethnicity and class.[7]

The figure of the Chinese coolie sutured the fractured union in the common cause of abolition of this "new system of slavery." As Moon-Ho Jung reveals, Asian migrant labor marked the nation's progress from slavery to freedom, from a nation of exclusion to a nation of immigrants, and from a young, immature nation to an international imperial power.

The U.S. Civil War produced a boom in manufacturing in the Northeast in towns like North Adams, Massachusetts. Shoemaking was one of the industries that profited from the war, with huge, lucrative Army contracts for boots. Factories ran day and night to fill the orders, as did textile mills that produced soldiers' uniforms. Even after the war, orders continued to grow. One of those who benefited from the boom was Calvin Sampson, whose boot and shoe factories and store carried on a brisk trade. Although New England's towns drew on labor from the surrounding countryside, the war's demands required recruiting workers from Canada, Wales, and Ireland. North Adams bulged with those immigrant laborers, and some residents, like members of the town's Temperance League, longed for quieter and more sober times.

The French Canadians Sampson recruited were one of the first groups to organize and strike. Mechanization threatened their jobs, and when Sampson purchased a new factory in 1869 and tried to fill it with more machinery and regimentation, the French Canadians founded a local Order of the Knights of St. Crispin, a union named for a Christian martyr and a medieval French shoemakers' guild. There were other Crispin lodges in Massachusetts and elsewhere in the United States, the first having started in Wisconsin in 1867. Ignoring the Crispin demand for a closed shop (that is, a factory with only union workers), Sampson hired a non-Crispin shoemaker. The Crispins struck, and Sampson fired them all. The unionists cornered and beat the sole nonunion employee and drove him out of town. Sampson retaliated by hiring inexperienced shoemakers, and he sent recruiters to Maine and Canada to find more workers. The Crispins succeeded in convincing the new recruits to join the union. In 1870, after the Crispins struck a second time, Sampson dispatched his superintendent to San Francisco to obtain Chinese workers.

About a year before, the shoe manufacturers' trade journal had noted that with the completion of the transcontinental railroad, the introduction of Chinese workers was not only possible but might "open the eyes of the Crispins, and be most effectual in bringing them to their senses."[8] As in the South, recruiting Chinese labor was seen as a way to discipline other intractable workers. Sampson's recruiter quickly succeeded in signing up a crew of seventy-five men, many of them teenagers, including a boss and two cooks. In June 1870, the group left San Francisco (traveling by train on tracks laid, in part, by Chinese laborers). When they arrived in North Adams two weeks later, a mob primed for violence against "scabs" awaited them. Thousands, both men and women, lined the streets outside the station. Sampson, who had boarded the train some distance from the town's station, alighted with seven armed men, and they pushed their way through the crowd, escorting the Chinese laborers to the factory. The crowd parted and let them pass.

The specter of enslaved and coolie labor haunted the struggle between capital and labor in the North as it did in the postbellum South. When the *New York Tribune* reported that the Chinese had arrived under coolie contract, Sampson insisted, like Louisiana's sugar planters, that the Chinese were voluntary "immigrants" in search of work. Still, as for migrant labor, Sampson's labor contract specified free room, heat, and water; free transportation from and back to California on completion of the contract; three years of service; eleven hours of work per day during spring and summer and ten and a half hours during fall and winter; and wages of twenty-three dollars per month the first year and twenty-six dollars the second and third years. Crispins commanded roughly double these wages.

The arrival of the Chinese broke the strike, and after about a week the Crispins returned to work. In 1871, Sampson recruited forty-eight more Chinese men, in 1873 an additional thirty-seven, and in 1874 forty-one. A few died, and a number were dismissed. Sampson built a fence around his factory and provided bunks for his nearly two hundred Chinese workers. He tried to isolate the Chinese from the Crispins, in keeping with the strategy of divide and rule. Meanwhile, white tourists flocked to witness the spectacle of Chinese workers stitching modern shoes for white women's feet in a Yankee factory. Sampson served as tour guide.

The Crispins distanced themselves from the Chinese and refused to recruit them for the union, although they had made efforts to recruit the white scabs. In fact, the French Canadian Crispins did not yet count as fully white. Their whiteness was dependent on their status as free, potential citizen workers, set against the bound, alien Chinese. As a unionist declared, the arrival of the Chinese heralded the beginning of a "new system of slavery," a phrase reserved for coolie labor, and was the opening wedge employed by capitalists against American workers. Labor leaders from the Atlantic to the Mississippi River sounded a similar theme, condemning Chinese migrant labor as a return to slavery and a move to cheapen and degrade white workers. If the North Adams experiment succeeded, they warned, it would spread and infect the nation as a whole. American freedom was at stake.

Although bound by contract, Sampson's Chinese laborers pursued their interests as workers. A festering discontent with Sampson and their crew boss, Chung Tang Sing (aka Charlie Sing), came to a head in 1873, when their three-year term expired. The workers wanted to negotiate wage increases and more storage space for their rice. In August, suspecting that Sing had conspired with Sampson and capitulated too easily during contract renegotiations, about a dozen men, led by Ah Coon, staged a sit-down protest, refusing to work. The protest was an embarrassment to Sing, whose leadership was being questioned, and Sampson, who tried to keep the disturbance from the press. The factory owner quietly sent for more Chinese laborers from San Francisco to replace the striking men. At the same time, the Chinese rejected Sing and elected a new leader.

In October, with no satisfactory resolution of their grievances, the men openly defied Sampson and Sing, charging their former boss with collusion. Sampson fired the strikers, several of whom threatened to kill Sing. When Ah Coon acquired a pistol, Sampson had him arrested. About forty Chinese accompanied Ah Coon to the jail, where a scuffle broke out, and the police, overwhelmed, called for help from citizens in the vicinity. The result was a riot in which, according to a reporter, the crowd, using clubs, stones, and brass knuckles, "fell upon the Chinamen and . . . a shocking scene of brutality and wanton cruelty ensued."[9] By evening, two Chinese were near death, Sing was given an armed guard, and the striking men were confined to the factory. Ah Coon was fined nearly a month's wages and forced to leave town. When fifteen new Chinese recruits arrived a few days later, Sampson kept them separate from the others.

In 1880, when the last Chinese contract expired, Sampson failed to renew any of the contracts. He did so despite the wealth that the Chinese workers had generated for him: the factory produced 12,500 cases of shoes in 1877, compared with 4,800 cases in 1870, when they first arrived.

In July 1870, about a month into Sampson's Chinese labor experiment, the U.S. Senate debated a pending naturalization bill to replace the 1790 Naturalization Act, which defined citizenship as white and free. Massachusetts Senator Charles Sumner, an ardent abolitionist, proposed to remove the word *white* from the original act. Sumner's amendment sparked a debate around Chinese labor and migration, freedom and slavery, equal rights, and manhood. Ultimately, the Senate rejected Sumner's modification and kept the original formulation of naturalization for "free white persons" only.

By contrast, the Civil Rights Act of 1870, prompted by Ku Klux Klan violence in the South and intended to protect African American voting rights, as promised by the just-ratified Fifteenth Amendment, provided that "all persons within the jurisdiction of the United States shall have . . . full and equal benefit of all laws." In this context, the phrase "all persons" encompassed U.S. citizens and noncitizens alike, including the alien Chinese. That wording was the achievement of Nevada Senator William Stewart, who explained that his intention was to protect especially Chinese aliens, who were treated as if they were outside the law. In Nevada, Stewart claimed to have been the first to introduce Chinese testimony and translators in court. "It is as solemn a duty as can be devolved upon this Congress," he declared, "to see that those people are protected, to see that they have the legal protection of the laws. . . . They, or any other aliens, who may come here are entitled to that protection." And, he added, "Justice and humanity and common decency require it."[10]

That common decency was wanting in both the South and North. Positioned against African Americans in the agrarian South and mainly French Canadian immigrants in the industrial North, Chinese laborers were racialized as coolies and as aliens in social formations involving race, class, and nation. They could neither vote like African Americans nor naturalize like French Canadians. Their outsider status and their efficiency made them consummate migrant laborers.

SOCIAL FORMATION

The period of Pacific Islander and Asian migrant labor begins around the time of the founding of the United States and extends to 1934, with the passage of the Tydings-McDuffie or Philippines Independence Act. The practice of employing migrant labor was anti-Asian and anti–Pacific Islander in that it emerged from the capitalist world-system of European national development and Pacific Islander and Asian underdevelopment. This disparity was achieved through conquest, colonialization, extractive industries, and forced "openings" for trade that impoverished the periphery to enrich the core. Moreover, migrant labor was devised to control and exploit Pacific Islander and Asian land and labor.

The social formation of migrant labor involved constraints—indentures, contracts, and credit tickets. Contract terms reduced individuals to units of labor recruited for specific jobs, periods, and wages. The categories and salaries of workers were determined by hierarchies of race, ethnicity, and gender. Low numbers of women and miscegenation laws retarded the formation of families and, after the passage of the Fourteenth Amendment (1868), affected generations of people who were U.S. citizens by birth. The system exerted controls over reproduction and sexuality and citizenship. Racialized classes pitted white workers against nonwhite laborers, conferring white privilege but also weakening class consciousness, and Asian ethnic nationalisms resisted oppression but also weakened solidarities of race. The racial prerequisite for membership in the nation excluded Pacific Islanders, except in Hawai'i, and Asian migrants were classified as "aliens ineligible to citizenship."

MATERIAL CONDITIONS

During the migrant labor phase of Asian and Pacific Islander history in the United States, remarkable changes in material conditions were under way in the nation at large. Following the divisive Civil War in which Pacific Islanders and Asians participated, the nation plunged headlong into occupying the continent and expanding overseas, moving from a largely agrarian and agricultural to an urban, industrial society. The economic change drew new immigrants from Europe and deployed their labor to propel the United States to global industrial supremacy. Corporate America prospered on the "gospel of wealth," a term coined by the steel baron Andrew Carnegie. Monopolies built by magnates such as J. P. Morgan, John D. Rockefeller, and Cornelius Vanderbilt thrived. The captains of industry took comfort in the social Darwinism of intellectuals and writers like Herbert Spencer and Horatio Alger, who preached the survival of the fittest and the success of the self-made man. Their discourses underwrote the material conditions and relations.

Contrary to the gospel of wealth, these men were not self-made: their wealth was generated by the labor of the masses, often castigated as the unfit. The unprecedented numbers of immigrants—some twenty-five million—who streamed to the United States came not from the British Isles and northern Europe but from southern and eastern Europe, with their "strange" tongues, religions, habits, and cultures. Labor brokers recruited many Greeks, Italians, Poles, and Russians, who served under contracts until 1885, when the Labor Contract Law was repealed. Prominent in the New England mills were French Canadians, who, like the new immigrants, worked for low wages under harsh conditions.

By 1900, women accounted for about 17 percent of that pool, and at least 1.7 million children under sixteen years of age worked in factory and field. The average annual wage for men was $597 for men and $314 for women. Unions like the Knights of Labor and the American Federation of Labor (AFL) rose to protect and advance workers' rights, but mainly for men because, as the AFL's Samuel Gompers held, women and children workers lowered the wages of men, the family breadwinners. Strikes were often massive and influential, like the Chicago Pullman strike of 1894, led by Eugene V. Debs of the American Railway Union, which required some two thousand federal troops to quell the uprising.

While the labor of those huddled masses was indispensable to the industrial barons, the influx was threatening to many of the old immigrants, the so-called native Americans, who saw the new immigrants as troublemakers, radicals, and aliens. Social movements tried to assimilate them through "Americanization" programs, in evidence especially in the public schools, and also in housing reforms, temperance movements, public hygiene and health care initiatives, and "rescue" missions for women and youths. Others, particularly nativists, sought the exclusion of new immigrants, whom they saw as "degraded races" and Europe's outcasts because of their cultural differences, which supposedly made them unassimilable.

DISCOURSES

Accompanying, indeed validating, the material conditions were the discourses of the period. The notion of eugenics was particularly ideologically potent. Coined in 1883 by Francis Galton, a cousin of Charles Darwin and a pioneer of modern statistics, the term refers to the science and practice of retaining and passing on "good" genes while excluding and eliminating "bad" genes from a population. The vigor and purity of the nation's "native stock," eugenicists believed, were being threatened by the infusion of inferior blood from southern and eastern Europe. In 1907, the U.S. Congress established the Dillingham Commission, a joint investigating body chaired by Vermont's Senator William Dillingham, to study the new immigration and its effects on the nation. It concluded its work in 1911, reporting that southern and eastern Europeans imperiled the nation's health and recommending a limit on their numbers.

Exclusion laws were proposed as a way of combating racial decline, as described by the lawyer and scientist Madison Grant in his book *The Passing of the Great Race* (1916) and by his colleague and friend Lothrop Stoddard in *The Rising Tide of Color against White World-Supremacy* (1920). Harry Laughlin, the director of the Galton Society's Eugenics Institute at Cold Spring Harbor, New York, advised Representative Albert Johnson, chair of the U.S. House committee on immigration, and fed him data supposedly demonstrating crime, insanity, and racial inferiority among new immigrants. The 1924 Johnson-Reed Act, which established national quotas on immigration, was an outcome of those ideas.

A parallel and equally influential ideology was the fictive distinction between white and nonwhite. That racial formation was an instrument of the colonial and postcolonial state, and it became transnational during the noonday of imperialism, when Kaiser Wilhelm II of Germany proclaimed a "yellow peril." A painting he commissioned in 1895 depicted the "civilized nations" (Austria, England, France, Germany, Italy, Russia, and others) confronting the Chinese dragon and the Buddha. It bore the inscription: "Nations of Europe, defend your holiest possession." Although competitors in the project of imperial expansion, the work suggested, Europeans, as whites and heirs to a common "possession" —Christian civilization—stood united against the peril of barbarism and heathenism.

That racial ideology of whiteness, as the African American scholar W. E. B. Du Bois understood, lent credence to the material condition of empire; that is, white supremacy propped up the edifice of colonialism and exploitation in Africa, Asia, and Oceania. Conversely, the main work of the decolonization and liberation movements of the twentieth century was to promote Asian, Pacific Islander, and African resistance to colonialism and racism. Accordingly, as Du Bois famously declared in 1900, the problem of the twentieth century was the color line. This problem was instigated not by the colonized but by white racism.

Race relations as a field of study emerged from the colonial project to understand and better manage colonized subjects, particularly when they posed problems for their colonial masters. In the mid-twentieth century, the sociologist Robert Park, one of the field's founders, explained: "One speaks of race relations when there is a race problem." To illustrate, he wrote of the "race problem" in South Africa where "the African does, to be sure, constitute a problem."[11] Of course, from the point of view of for the indigenous San, Khoikhoi, and Bantu speakers of the region, the problem was the invading and colonizing Dutch and British. Race relations proposed to study "racial tensions" and "racial conflicts" as social problems in order to ameliorate them. Called "racial adjustments," those solutions were gradual and sought conformity to the will of the dominant group.

In the United States, the Institute of Race Relations was charged with studying "native peoples" to install "effective government" and thereby continue their subjection. The Institute of Pacific Relations, established in 1925, had as its prime objective "to prevent a possible Oriental-Occidental war arising . . . out of increasing bitterness over racial, religious, economic and political differences."[12] That "bitterness" was, in reality, generated not by "differences" but by the hierarchical power relations of hegemony and subservience.

This thinking fell out of favor when African and Asian elites in the colonial world not only subscribed to the tenets of the European Enlightenment such as equality, fraternity, and rights but also crafted racial identifications and solidarities that emulated the idea of a global whiteness. To demand "Africa for Africans" and "Asia for Asians" threatened to disrupt the racial imperial order. Japan's 1905 victory over Russia, the first defeat of a white by a nonwhite nation in modern warfare, was particularly potent in that regard. In 1908, in the wake of Russia's defeat, President Theodore Roosevelt's "Great White Fleet," consisting of sixteen battleships, visited Japan. The visit's purpose was to impress on Japan and other potential upstart nations the U.S. resolve to enforce white imperial supremacy. This visit to Japan also followed the 1906 San Francisco school board controversy. Amidst newspaper warnings of a "yellow peril," the city's school board voted to require Japanese children to attend segregated Oriental schools, but President Roosevelt intervened to have the board rescind its vote in exchange for establishing migration restrictions on Japanese workers. The Gentlemen's Agreement was an outcome of that incident.

Meanwhile, during the first decades of the twentieth century, the U.S. anthropologist Franz Boas and his colleagues and students were working to disentangle race, or physical type, from culture, or patterned behavior, disproving the assumption that race was identical with culture. Thereafter, social scientists abandoned race as a way to explain society and social organization and instead searched for such explanations in ethnicity or culture. Cultural assimilation or Americanization was the process by which diversity, as embodied by the new immigrants, devolved into unity (equated with homogeneity), and ethnicity or culture was the object of conversion.

If ethnicity prevailed as an explanatory concept for European immigrants, it failed to dislodge the concept of race for non-Europeans. When the southern and eastern European immigrants conformed to the dominant culture, they assumed a whiter cast in comparison with their nonwhite racialized others. The poor whites in the South and the French Canadians in the North became white, in contrast to African Americans and Chinese. Likewise, the Irish by the late nineteenth century and Jews and Southern and Eastern Europeans in the following century gradually became white people. In this way, nonwhites produced whites.

TRANSITIONS

With the decline and demise of Pacific Islander and Asian migrant labor, coupled with the growth of agriculture, mining, and railroads in the U.S. Southwest, an influx of

Mexican migrant laborers arrived to fill those labor needs. During the 1920s, close to a million Mexicans streamed across the contrived border, more than doubling the number of Mexican Americans in the region. About half of those migrants, according to a 1920 Bureau of Labor report, were women and children. Cotton growers and railroad companies preferred to employ married men with children because they believed single men were more likely to jump contracts than men with families. Despite fears of racial pollution by a flood of "mongrel" immigrants, Mexican migrant labor was valuable for those who held power, and the border consequently went virtually unguarded, despite the formation of the understaffed Border Patrol in 1924. The Great Depression would later reverse the tide and the fortunes of the Border Patrol.

African Americans, too, were on the move. The 1890 census found 90 percent of all African Americans living in the South, 85 percent of whom lived in rural areas. With the rise of urban industries in the South, African Americans moved from the rural to urban South. From 1910 to 1920, more than half a million African Americans left the South for the North in the Great Migration, and nearly a million more headed north in the following decade. Like other people of color, they were lured by the promise of work, and labor agents peddling high wages and good living conditions accelerated the exodus. African Americans were driven by threats of lynching and Jim Crow segregation in the South and drawn by prospects of opportunities in the North.

Military service in World War I achieved little by way of claims and rights for African Americans. Some 380,000 of them served in segregated units and returned to the United States to face continued racism and unemployment. Race riots in twenty-six cities and towns across the United States resulted in so much bloodshed that the summer of 1919 was called the Red Summer. Blamed for white unemployment, African Americans were the targets of postwar labor strife. In July 1919, after two weeks of violence in Chicago, fifteen whites and twenty-three African Americans lay dead.

The northward exodus did create some opportunities for freedom and self-expression. During the 1920s, New York blossomed with African American art, dance, literature, and music in what became known as the Harlem Renaissance. The writer Alain Locke described that renewal as the work of the "New Negro," who embraced blackness and eschewed the colonizer's stigma of inferiority. The Great Depression, however, would retard those advances in African American self-determination.

Impelled by the changing material conditions and discourses, the next stage of Asian and Pacific Islander history, the period of dependency, promised to be more complicated than the years of migrant labor. Despite exclusionary laws and closed borders, the migrants were still in the United States. The new strategy of dependency sought to assimilate people of color culturally, rendering them "ethnic" rather than "racialized" subjects, while restricting their upward social mobility.

Dependency signaled that Pacific Islanders and Asians, despite the white republic's founding proposition, had become citizens and members of the nation's peoples, like their fellow persons of color. No longer were they migrant workers who could be discarded, consumed, or returned like commodities or chattels. Imperial expansions, as some whites had feared, had made Asians and Pacific Islanders permanent members of the nation. Ultimately, their location within the social formation would be conditioned by the forces at work in the United States, including the rise of industries and cities, the responses to the immigration of the late nineteenth century, and by the longer global history of relations along the color line.

SUGGESTED READINGS

Bald, Vivek. *Bengali Harlem and the Lost Histories of South Asian America*. Cambridge, MA: Harvard University Press, 2013.

Jung, Moon-Ho. *Coolies and Cane: Race, Labor, and Sugar in the Age of Emancipation*. Baltimore: Johns Hopkins University Press, 2006.

Lee, Anthony W. *A Shoemaker's Story: Being Chiefly about French Canadian Immigrants, Enterprising Photographers, Rascal Yankees, and Chinese Cobblers in a Nineteenth-Century Factory Town*. Princeton, NJ: Princeton University Press, 2008.

PRIMARY DOCUMENT

DOCUMENT 9

Madison Grant, "Introduction," in Lothrop Stoddard, *The Rising Tide of Color against White World-Supremacy* (New York: Charles Scribner's Sons, 1920), xi–xxxii.

> Madison Grant (1865–1937) was the chairman of the New York Zoological Society, a trustee of the American Museum of Natural History, a councilor to the American Geographical Society, and the author of *The Passing of the Great Race* (1916). Grant was influential among the New York elite, a cohort that included Theodore Roosevelt. Lothrop Stoddard received a doctorate from Harvard. In F. Scott Fitzgerald's classic *The Great Gatsby*, the character Tom Buchanan talks about having read *The Rise of the Colored Empires*, by "Goddard," and advises: "Everybody should read it," because "the idea is if we don't look out the white race will be—will be utterly submerged. It's all scientific stuff; it's been proved."

Mr. Lothrop Stoddard's "The Rising Tide of Color," following so closely the Great War, may appear to some unduly alarming, while others, as his thread of argument unrolls, may recoil at the logic of his deductions. . . .

In our present era of convulsive changes, a prophet must be bold, indeed, to predict anything more definite than a mere trend in events, but the study of the past is the one safe guide in forecasting the future.

Mr. Stoddard takes up the white man's world and its potential enemies as they are to-day. A consideration of their early relations and of the history of the Nordic race, since its first appearance three or four thousand years ago, tends strongly to sustain and justify his conclusions. For such a consideration we must first turn to the map, or, better, to the globe. . . .

Without attempting a scientific classification of the inhabitants of Eurasia, it is sufficient to describe the three main races. The first are the yellow-skinned, straight black-haired, black-eyed, round-skulled Mongols and Mongoloids massed in central and eastern Asia north of the Himalayan system.

To the west of them, and merged with them, lie the Alpines, also characterized by dark, but not straight, hair, dark eyes, relatively short stature, and round skulls. These Alpines are thrust like a wedge into Europe between the Nordics and the Mediterraneans, with a tip that reaches the Atlantic Ocean. Those of western Europe are derived from one or more very ancient waves of round-skulled invaders from the East, who probably came by way of Asia Minor and the Balkans, but they have been so long in their present homes that they retain little except their brachycephalic skull-shape to connect them with the Asiatic Mongols.

South of the Himalayas and westward in a narrow belt to the Atlantic, and on both sides of the Inland Sea, lies the Mediterranean race, more or less swarthy-skinned, black-haired, dark-eyed, and long-skulled.

On the northwest, grouped around the Baltic and North Seas, lies the great Nordic race. It is characterized by a fair white skin, wavy hair with a range of color from dark brown to flaxen, light eyes, tall stature, and long skulls.

These races show other physical characters which are definite but difficult to describe, such as texture of skin and cast of features, especially of the nose. The contrast of mental and spiritual endowments is equally definite, but even more elusive of definition.

It is with the action and interaction of these three groups, together with internal civil wars, that recorded history deals. . . .

All wars thus far discussed have been race wars of Europe against Asia, or of the Nordics against Mediterraneans. The wars against the Mongols were necessary and vital; there was no alternative except to fight to the finish. But the wars of northern Europe against the south, from the racial point of view, were not only useless but destructive. Bad as they were, however, they left untouched to a large extent the broodland of the race in the north and west. . . .

To what extent the present war has fostered this tendency, time alone will show, but Mr. Stoddard has pointed out some of the immediate and visible results. The backbone of western civilization is racially Nordic, the Alpines and Mediterraneans being effective precisely to the extent in which they have been Nordicized and vitalized.

If this great race, with its capacity for leadership and fighting, should ultimately pass, with it would pass that which we call civilization. It would be succeeded by an unstable and bastardized population, where worth and merit would have no inherent right to leadership and among which a new and darker age would blot out our racial inheritance.

Such a catastrophe cannot threaten if the Nordic race will gather itself together in time, shake off the shackles of an inveterate altruism, discard the vain phantom of internationalism, and reassert the pride of race and the right of merit to rule.

The Nordic race has been driven from many of its lands, but still grasps firmly the control of the world, and it is certainly not at a greater numerical disadvantage than often before in contrast to the teeming population of eastern Asia. . . .

The great hope of the future here in America lies in the realization of the working class that competition of the Nordic with the alien is fatal, whether the latter be the lowly immigrant from southern or eastern Europe or whether he be the more obviously dangerous Oriental against whose standards of living the white man cannot compete. In this country we must look to such of our people—our farmers and artisans—as are still of American blood to recognize and meet this danger. . . .

Democratic ideals among an homogeneous population of Nordic blood, as in England or America, is one thing, but it is quite another for the white man to share his blood with, or intrust his ideals to, brown, yellow, black, or red men.

This is suicide pure and simple, and the first victim of this amazing folly will be the white man himself.

SIGNIFICANT EVENTS

1718	Yale College named for Elihu Yale
1785	Chinese in Baltimore
1788	Hawaiians and Chinese in British Columbia
1790	Hawaiian in Boston
	Indian from Madras in Salem
1809	ʻŌpūkahaʻia and Hopu in New York City
	Kanui and other Hawaiians in Boston
1811	Hawaiians help establish Astoria
1812	Hawaiians serve in the War of 1812
1816	Foreign Mission School established
1818	U.S. and Britain jointly "occupy" Northwest
	ʻŌpūkahaʻia dies
1819	missionaries leave Boston for Hawaiʻi
	U.S. whaling vessel in Honolulu
1823	Liholiho sails for England
1825	Hawaiian seamen in Nantucket
1834	Hudson's Bay Company in Honolulu
	Afong Moy (Chinese woman) exhibited in New York City

1846	boundary set between Canada and the United States
1854	Yung Wing becomes the first Chinese student to receive a degree from a U.S. higher education institution (Yale College)
1860	Civil War begins
1862	U.S. involvement in coolie trade outlawed
1865	Civil War ends
	Black Codes passed
1866	Japanese students arrive at Rutgers University
1867	Radical Reconstruction begins
	Chinese migrant laborers in Louisiana
	Memphis Chinese labor convention proposes Mississippi Valley Immigration Labor Company
1869	Peter Kakua executed
1870	Civil Rights Act
	Calvin Sampson recruits Chinese laborers
1871	Chinese strike on a Louisiana plantation
1872	Yung Wing establishes Chinese Educational Mission to educated students from China in New England schools
1873	Chinese walkout at the Sampson shoe factory
1877	Radical Reconstruction ends
1883	theory of eugenics proposed
	Kil-jun Yu, a Korean, studies in Massachusetts
1885	Labor Contract Act repealed
1894	Pullman strike, Chicago
1895	Kaiser Wilhelm II's "yellow peril" painting
1900	W. E. B. Du Bois defines the color line as the "problem of the twentieth century"
1905	Japan defeats Russia
1906	San Francisco school board controversy
	Taraknath Das in Seattle
1907	Dillingham Commission formed
	Bellingham and Vancouver anti-Asian riots
1908	Roosevelt's "Great White Fleet" visits Japan
1908	Canada imposes restrictions on South Asian migration
1910–20s	African American Great Migration
1911	Dillingham Commission report
1914	*Komagata Maru* in Vancouver harbor

1919	Red Summer
1920	Lothrop Stoddard publishes *The Rising Tide of Color against White World-Supremacy*
1920s	Harlem Renaissance
1924	Johnson-Reed Act
	Border Patrol established

PART 3

DEPENDENCY

The African American intellectual W. E. B. Du Bois understood conditions in the United States as manifestations of relations in the world. The color line, the "problem of the twentieth century," was simultaneously a domestic and an international issue. The conquest, subjugation, and exploitation of peoples of color in the United States were aspects of the material condition of colonization in Africa, Asia, Latin America, and Oceania and its discourse of racism. In the Third World, white supremacy and race relations gave way to neocolonialism and assimilation. For peoples of color in the United States, exclusion and segregation flourished even as citizenship and Americanization enticed a new generation called "new Americans."

Under the system of migrant labor, race and racism justified the exploitation of alien labor. As "aliens ineligible to citizenship," Asians could never attain the status of citizen labor. But Asian migrants remained in the United States despite exclusion laws, anti-Asian movements, and expulsion and repatriation drives. They labored and formed communities. Their children became U.S. citizens by birth, as guaranteed by the Fourteenth Amendment, bringing greater permanence and some rights to Asians on U.S. soil.

With the rise of the second generation, intellectuals who studied race relations posited the "Oriental problem." Some of them proposed the solution of cultural assimilation. Thus ethnicity, not race, became the dominant discourse. That erasure of race, even as racial segregation expanded, advanced the prospects for white supremacy into the twentieth century. That gentler, more complex strategy of soft racism and social formation offered another means for subjugation: the state of dependency. Under this regime, ostensibly free subjects remained economically, politically, and culturally subservient to and dependent on the normative, ruling order and group. As with migrant labor, dependency was upheld by segregation. In addition, assimilation, called *Americanization*, paralyzed movements for self-determination and deferred dreams of full equality.

Oppression, nonetheless, inspired resistance, and that dialectic of conflicting agencies continued to shape the course of history.

8

DEPENDENT HAWAI'I

In 1930, standing before an audience of "new Americans," most of whom were second-generation Japanese, or *nisei,* the president of the University of Hawai'i, David Crawford, counseled his young listeners: "Do not count on education to do too much for you, do not take it too seriously. Do not expect a college degree, an A.B. or a Ph.D., to get you ahead unduly in this world." Education was important, Crawford explained, but "it must be education in the proper sense."[1] The recipients of his advice could not have missed the educator's point: lower your ambitions and defer your dreams of upward mobility.

By education "in the proper sense," Crawford meant an education of the hand and not of the mind. That brand of education was designed to colonize subjects and keep them contented under subjection. Dependency is a pedagogy of powerlessness, a curriculum of relationships of superior over inferior, a teaching of reliance on the economic, political, and social conditions imposed by those in power. Dependency retards possibilities and constrains freedoms. Self-determination is not an option.

Schools for African American and American Indian children in the later nineteenth century had those objects in mind. They began not on the continent but in Hawai'i, with missionaries from New England. The Foreign Mission School in Connecticut, established as a ministry to American Indian, Hawaiian, and Chinese pupils, was a forerunner of the schools in Hawai'i. At first, missionaries in the islands directed their conversion efforts at the *ali'i,* or chiefs, and their children; later, they established schools for commoners to convert them to Christianity and to promote civil and literary learning.

The earliest mission schools in Hawai'i trained boys and girls from the elite to become teachers who could minister to the masses, thus accelerating the propagation of religion and culture. The missionary David Lyman, who grew up on a farm in Connecticut, firmly believed in the value of manual labor and its ability to elevate a race from barbarism to civilization. Accordingly, his Hilo Boarding School, founded in 1836, emphasized training for manual labor. Having his students grow food to feed themselves and sugar cane to sell for a profit not only served their course of study but also defrayed the school's expenses.

Lyman's fellow missionary Richard Armstrong described his educational philosophy for Hawaiians in 1846: "I think an effort should be made to connect some sort of manual labor, especially agriculture, with all the schools," he wrote. "Early habits of industry will supply their wants, make their homes comfortable and remove the temptation to wander about and commit crime in order to get money or fine dress."[2] When he became the Hawaiian kingdom's minister of public instruction a year later, Armstrong instituted a manual labor and industrial curriculum that became the standard for Hawai'i's public schools.

Armstrong's son Samuel, born in Hawai'i, took those lessons of Christian education with him when he left for the U.S. continent. He studied at Williams College in Massachusetts, near North Adams and Calvin Sampson's shoe factory. During the Civil War, Armstrong commanded African Americans of the 8th and 9th U.S. Colored Troops. After the war, he worked with the Freedmen's Bureau to assist formerly enslaved African Americans and displaced poor whites. In 1868, continuing his labors among "the darkies" (his term for Hawaiians and African Americans), Armstrong founded the Hampton Normal and Agricultural Institute in Virginia under the aegis of the American Missionary Association.

As lesser peoples, Armstrong reflected, Hawaiians and African Americans shared a common educational need. His daughter and biographer testified: "As he meditated upon the development of the plan [for Hampton], the Hilo Manual Labor School for Native Hawaiians, which he had observed in his boyhood, often occurred to this mind as an example of successful industrial education for an undeveloped race."[3] In Armstrong's own words, "It meant something to the Hampton school, and perhaps to the ex-slaves of America, that, from 1820 to 1860, the distinctively missionary period, there was worked out in the Hawaiian Islands the problem of emancipation, enfranchisement, and Christian civilization of a dark-skinned Polynesian people in many respects like the negro race."[4]

Like the Hilo school, Hampton trained boys for the field and girls for the home. It subscribed to the belief that education began with rooting out "every vestige of their former manner of living" and implanting new habits of deed and thought. "The temporal salvation of the colored race for some time to come is to be won out of the ground," Armstrong reiterated. "Skillful agriculturists and mechanics are needed rather than poets and orators."[5]

Education for dependency conveyed the discourses of colonization that, in turn, created domesticated subjects and the social formation of race, gender, sexuality, class, and nation. Other colonizing discourses emanated from science, religion, and the nation-state. Those ideologies of the social formation were supported by the means and relations of production, namely land and labor. By *land,* I mean the physical means of production, including land and water and all of their resources to which humans assign value. The idea of privatized land or property, a cornerstone of capitalism empowered by law and enforcement, justified conquest, colonization, and appropriation. By *labor,* I mean human exertions on land (resources) that produce value (as determined by humans).

LAND

Dependency for Hawaiians, as for Chamorros and Samoans, involved foremost their loss of sovereignty or self-determination. Hawaiian sovereignty ended with the illegal U.S. takeover and annexation of the islands. Leading up to that theft, traders, missionaries, whalers, and planters snared Hawaiians in the expanding net of global capitalism, at first through exchanges of essential items such as water and food for manufactured cloth, wood, and metal. Ship captains captured laborers for their voyages and loaded their holds with the resources of Hawaiian land and waters, such as sandalwood and whale parts, and settlers monopolized the best lands, especially with the rise of the sugar-plantation economy. Missionaries introduced beliefs and ideologies, including a written language and literate culture and religion, trying to convince Hawaiians to forsake their own traditions.

Yet Hawaiian history did not end with the demise of Hawaiian sovereignty. Instead, Hawaiians engaged the new order in a variety of ways. While Sanford Dole, the territory's first governor, opposed the vote for Hawaiians, Portuguese, or any class of "irresponsible people," the Organic Act (1900) that incorporated the islands stipulated that citizens of the renegade "Hawaiian" Republic were citizens of the territory and thus of the United States.

Despite their drastic population decline, Hawaiians held a numerical advantage over whites. They mobilized to become a political force in the territory, which was dominated economically by white planters and the Big Five. In the first territorial elections, Hawaiians rallied behind the Home Rule Party led by Robert Wilcox, the revolutionary and Hawaiian nationalist. Wilcox had organized and joined two failed insurrections to restore Hawaiian sovereignty in 1889 and 1895. The Home Rulers won fourteen seats in the territorial House, constituting a majority; they also won nine of the thirteen Senate seats and elected Wilcox to serve as the territory's delegate to Congress. Those results were remarkable because of white supremacy in the islands and the fact that Wilcox had a prison record for having opposed white rule. In addition, the Home Rulers ignored the Organic Act's instruction that legislation be conducted in the English language and insisted on speaking in Hawaiian.

Incensed, Dole dissolved the legislature after two months and called for a special election. Appointed by the U.S. president for a four-year term, the territory's governor held extraordinary powers. He could not be impeached, he could suspend the writ of habeas corpus and impose martial law, he could veto items in the budget, and he controlled education, welfare, sanitation, health, and public works. But because the Hawaiian electorate commanded two-thirds of the vote, they had to be divided and swayed in order to be overcome. The white oligarchy found their man in Jonah Kuhio Kalanianaole, Queen Kapiolani's *hānai* (adopted child), who was, ironically, a fellow rebel of Wilcox's in the 1895 revolt.

In the election of 1902, Prince Kuhio, at the invitation of the Republicans, the party of the oligarchy and conspirators against the Hawaiian kingdom, ran against Wilcox for delegate to Congress. Kuhio gained enough Hawaiian votes to win the election and bring the Republicans to power. In fact, so popular was Kuhio that he was reelected ten times before his death in 1922, and he brought key Hawaiians into the Republican fold, including royalists. In turn, Kuhio expected political patronage that would enable him to distribute favors to his followers. This arrangement suited the islands' white rulers. Although they were a numerical minority, they maintained political control of Hawai'i for fifty years.

The Republicans secured their hold on power through patronage, particularly in the form of government jobs. By 1927, Hawaiians held 46 percent of the executive positions, 55 percent of the clerical posts, and over 50 percent of the judgeships and elective offices. In 1935, when Hawaiians numbered less than 15 percent of the total population, they held almost one-third of all public-service jobs in the territory. For his part, Kuhio diligently served his patrons—the Hawaiian Sugar Planters' Association (HSPA), the Honolulu Chamber of Commerce, and the Merchants' Association—despite the insults they directed at him, such as bypassing him by appointing their own lobbyists in Washington.

Kuhio was not deceived by his compromising political position. As he pointedly noted, the Republicans, while needing the Hawaiian vote, had an attitude of "We don't want no Niggers."[6] To the U.S. interior secretary, the prince charged: "The vital trouble is that the people who control the industrial life of Hawaii have been so blinded by long continued prosperity and the habit of controlling everything from their own standpoint that they, themselves, do not realize how deadly that policy is to the ultimate welfare of the Territory."[7] The political alliance of Hawaiians with whites was a fragile one, and it hinged, to a large degree, on the influence and judgment of Kuhio.

In the name of Hawaiian sovereignty, Kuhio opposed the planters' plan to import Filipino migrants, believing it would advance only the interests of the white oligarchy. Instead, he favored attracting white settlers from the continent and creating a large middle class to challenge the planters' power monopoly. An Asian flood, he feared, would prompt the U.S. to end "self-government" and corral Hawaiians, like American Indians, onto reservations.

The prospect of Hawaiian extinction was, for Kuhio, fundamentally a matter of land and its alienation. "This is our land," a Hawaiian noted. "It belongs to us. Strangers have come here from the other side and have fattened on the land. . . . Everybody gets rich through the Hawaiians, and we are thrown out." In 1920 the prince predicted: "If conditions remain as they are today, it will only be a matter of a short space of time when this race of people, my people, renowned for their physique, their courage, their sense of justice, their straight-forwardness, and their hospitality, will be a matter of history."[8]

That same year, with the oligarchy's consent, Kuhio proposed to restore the lands lost since the Great Mahele of 1848 through a Hawaiian Rehabilitation Bill, which passed Congress as the Hawaiian Homes Commission Act. The law set aside land for Hawaiian homesteaders on places unclaimed and unproductive for sugar and pineapple cultivation. The act also denied Asians access to government jobs, thereby protecting the Hawaiian patronage system, and made it difficult for Asians to get homestead land. In exchange for Hawaiian rehabilitation, the provision of the 1900 Organic Act that stipulated a one-thousand-acre limit for corporate landholding (which sugar plantations had routinely violated) was removed. In practice, the land law benefited few Hawaiians because of the remote and arid nature of the areas set aside for them. Its main beneficiaries were the planters. The law, in fact, was drafted by their lawyers.

Hawaiians were drawn, and often compelled, to sell their labor to survive under capitalism, but many also retained their cultural values of sharing and working for the common good. Ida Kanekoa Milles was born in 1913 and grew up on Maui, where her father was a taro farmer and her mother a weaver.[9] She attended the public school but had to drop out after the fifth grade because of her father's illness. She worked as a maid for a white family in Kahului town, and the following year she married John Milles and gave birth to the first of her seven children.

In an oral history, Milles recalled her childhood and early life of labor. In Nahiku village, she began, her father built a grass shack for his wife and two children. "Nothing on the floor, just dirt. My mother used to weave about three or four mats to lay on the ground. That's our bed." With her brother, Milles explored their surroundings. "I enjoy living there because fruits were plentiful. Lots of bananas and sugar cane—it grows wild—and lots of passion fruit. You know those purple ones? Where we live they have spring water and the water flow freely. I go to the river to catch shrimps and I enjoy it."

She remembered her father as a hardworking man. "He tried to do what he could to keep his family." He planted taro, sweet potatoes, corn, cabbages, cucumbers, and watermelons to feed the family. In addition, her father worked for the county, cutting grass and bushes along the sides of roads for about five dollars a week. Her mother wove hats out of bamboo strips and sold them to buy the few things the family needed, like salt, sugar, flour, and shoyu.

When she began working, Milles gave all of her earnings to her parents. As a thirteen-year-old, Milles worked as a maid for a banker and his wife, a businesswoman, who had two children. She lived in a cottage at the back and worked constantly, starting at seven in the morning. After breakfast, she saw the children off to school, cleaned the house, and prepared all of the family's meals. "While I was working," Milles regretted, "I wanted

FIGURE 36

Women cane workers of various ethnicities, Kilauea Plantation, Kaua'i, 1888. Courtesy of Hawai'i State Archives.

to go back to school, but the maid pay was very little. Twenty-one dollars a month. So I stay home take care of the house and take care whatever I have to do."

The children were her companions, Milles confessed. She was about their age, and so she played with them, and they taught her English, arithmetic, geography, and how to use the washing machine. "But to tell you the truth," Milles said, "at the beginning, I didn't like the job. Because they were white people. Only when I moved to Kahului, I seen lot of *haoles*. I seen Chinese, Japanese, too." In Nahiku, where she grew up, Milles observed, she rarely saw non-Hawaiians.

Her parents called her home in 1927 because they were getting old and needed her nearby. Shortly after returning, she married, at the age of fifteen, and had a child nearly every year. Her husband worked for the Nahiku Ranch for a dollar a day, and when their son was eight years old, he began working with his father cutting guava trees. Milles joined them, clearing pastureland of bushes and small trees. For extra money, she and her husband caught freshwater shrimp to sell to plantation workers.

Her next job was with the Hana Sugar Company, where she joined Japanese women and Filipinas weeding rows of cane. After she learned how to grip and use the hoe, Milles remembered, the work was easier, and talking with the other women helped to pass the time. "I made friends with these ladies," she recalled, "we all worked together. Then, if I get through first and see that person have couple more rows, I go there and give them a hand. Of course, I don't have to help the next person, but it's better to help each other. So everybody can go home together."

After two or three summers of plantation work, Milles's husband told her to quit working. He earned enough, he said, and they were satisfied with what they had, feeling no envy of those who had more material possessions. "So, I stayed home to raise my children, and in between 1936 and 1941, we used to go catch wild shrimps in the river and sell. On Saturdays, my husband sell and with the money, he used to buy dresses for the children, clothes for myself and him, or something that we need." Her life was full, and reflecting on her years of labor, Milles remarked simply, "My working life, I have no complaint."

Some Hawaiians found ways of escape from dependency. Perhaps preeminent for its location, resources, and history is Waipiʻo on the island of Hawaiʻi. Watered by five streams that descend from high mountains at the head of the valley, Waipiʻo is nearly a mile wide at its broadest and over three miles long, extending from the mountains to the breaking surf. The streams converge on the valley floor, bringing life to the land and depositing rich silt on their way to the sea. The freshwater and alluvial soil make Waipiʻo ideal for growing taro, the staple of Hawaiian life.

According to Hawaiian history, the valley is sacred ground. Its first occupants were gods, beginning with Wākea of the sky, whose mating with Papa, the earth, produced the islands of Hawaiʻi. In his old age, Wākea retired to the haven of Waipiʻo. Kāne and Kanaloa, brothers associated with freshwater springs and cultivation, fought Maui, the fisherman, in Waipiʻo, and killed him there when he tried to steal their bananas. Lono, god of the heavens and agriculture, met his wife, Kaikilani, by a waterfall in Waipiʻo valley, and his remains were buried there after his death.

Waipiʻo supplied the needs of Hawaiians. Even during times of severe drought and famine, the waters flowed, and the land enabled the chiefs to fulfill their responsibility of providing food. When land became property after the 1848 Mahele, much of the valley fell into the possession of the Bishop Estate, a holding of Bernice Pauahi Bishop, a descendant of King Kamehameha. By the time of her death in 1884, it was the kingdom's largest landowner, holding some 5,800 acres of the valley, while maka'ainana (commoners) received 102 plots totaling only 374 acres.

At the beginning of the territorial period, about 150 Hawaiians farmed the valley. Over the next two decades, the population swelled to over a thousand, due largely to an influx of Chinese, who moved into Waipiʻo after leaving the sugar plantations. The two groups carried on parallel farming practices, and they married and produced hapa, or mixed offspring, who became Hawaiians. In that way, the native peoples absorbed the migrants and always outnumbered them. The Chinese mainly grew rice in the lower valley, where the water was slower-moving and warmer; Hawaiian farmers cultivated wet taro higher up, where the water was cooler and faster-moving. The Chinese were tenant farmers, subletting from companies that rented the land from the Bishop Estate.

David Makaoi, a resident of Waipiʻo during the first decade of the twentieth century, described the valley and its shifting colors. "We had rice patches near the ocean. And

FIGURE 37
Waipiʻo Valley, where gods dwell, and its taro patches. Photo by Gary Y. Okihiro.

then, taro patches further up in the valley. Hardly any trees on the [valley] floor. Course there were guava groves along the edges of the stream." The young rice fields were "nice and green. You see green patches down there along near the beach. And then, before harvest time they were all yellow. So, it was one color one time, and another the next time."[10] The Chinese also grew taro, Makaoi recalled, to produce poi in their poi factories. When their crop was short, they bought taro from their Hawaiian neighbors upstream.

Chinese rice farmers prospered at first, but when cheaper California-grown rice entered the market in the late 1920s, it drove them out of business. Gradually the Chinese abandoned their fields, and by 1930 the valley's population had declined to 271. The Chinese left a legacy of rice cultivation and a cash economy: the single valley store sold sugar, salt, rice, flour, cooking oil, canned goods, salted fish, matches, kerosene, soap, and clothing. The Chinese operated three poi factories, which employed Hawaiian women at fifty cents a day for cleaning and pounding the taro.

During the 1930s, Hawaiians in the valley numbered 178, Chinese 63, Filipinos 19, Japanese 9, and Koreans 2. Taro was the staple crop for Hawaiians, but they also planted fruit trees like avocado, banana, breadfruit, coconut, guava, lemon, mango, orange, and papaya. They fished in the streams for ʻoʻopu and shrimp, and they also gathered seaweed along the shore and caught fish in the ocean. They kept chickens, pigs, and cattle, built their homes with thatched roofs of coconut fronds, and covered their floors with woven pandanus mats. Each house had a shrine to the family's guardian spirit, their *'aumakua*. Many traced their ancestry to the shark who circled them in the ocean, others to the sea turtle or the lizard. Waipi'o's Hawaiians conducted their lives in balance with nature; they only planted and took what was necessary for their daily sustenance. At a time when the plantation economy was consuming increasing amounts of land and labor and the U.S. military was engaged in fortifying the "loveliest fleet of islands," in Mark Twain's memorable words, for the anticipated Pacific war, Hawaiians in Waipi'o planted, tended, and harvested their taro patches in concert with the changing phases of the moon.

LABOR

Hawai'i's annexation by the United States made trade reciprocity unnecessary because the territory's exports were domestic and not foreign commerce. This change allowed the sugar trade to flourish. In 1900, plantations produced 289,544 tons of sugar from 66,773 acres of Hawaiian land. By 1920, that yield had nearly doubled, to 556,871 tons cultivated on 114,100 acres, and by 1930 it had grown to 930,627 tons on 136,136 acres.

Sugar occupied increasing amounts of alienated Hawaiian land, and its irrigation needs drew freshwater from Hawaiian wet taro farms. An immense system of ditches diverted millions of gallons of water from the mountains to the dry side of the island to saturate vast fields of sugar and pineapple. Small farmers thereby lost land and freshwater, and many were forced out of independent production into tenancy and wage labor.

Sugar production profoundly affected the territory's demographics. The Hawaiian and Asian population increased, primarily through reproduction among Chinese and Koreans and more dramatically through labor recruitment among the Japanese and Filipinos (see table 2).

CHINESE

Chinese created institutions parallel to those of whites to reduce their economic dependency on the white oligarchy. They established rice plantations and businesses that supplied the Hawaiian and Asian markets and moved into urban trades that were open to them. Chinatown, Chinese-language schools, and mutual aid and voluntary societies shielded them from the full force of cultural assimilation efforts. The cause of China's sovereignty forged the islands' disparate Chinese linguistic and ethnic groups into a single people and connected the islands to China and the global Chinese diaspora.

Chinese sugar-plantation workers behaved like the Hawaiians who fled the plantations for independent farming. At first, the Chinese pursued familiar niches such as rice cultivation, having come from the rice-growing regions of South China, but they also moved from subsistence production to the market economy under capitalism. They were

FIGURE 38
Paniolo loading cattle onto a ship anchored off Kailua-Kona, n.d. Hawai'i State Historic Preservation Division, Department of Land and Natural Resources.

able to take advantage of the plight of Hawaiian taro farmers, who had abandoned their fields for other pursuits. The Chinese rented former taro lands that were well watered by springs and rivers and planted rice.

Although whites were the first to grow rice commercially in Hawai'i, the Chinese held a virtual monopoly on its production for fifty years, mainly on O'ahu. Chinese rice fields grew from about a thousand acres in 1875 to 7,420 acres in 1890, 9,130 acres in 1900, and 9,425 acres in 1909. Thereafter, the acreage under cultivation declined. Rice growing employed 3,710 men in 1890 and 5,643 in 1900. At one point, the rice crop, with a value estimated at more than $3 million in good years, was second only to sugar, and it supplied the local market and the U.S. West Coast. Rice fields occupied smaller patches of land than sugar plantations, and their cultivation required fewer workers and less machinery. Hand tools and draft animals like the donkey and water buffalo sufficed.

Some Chinese rice growers attracted workers from the sugar plantations, including runaways and those whose contracts they bought. Other laborers were independent, like the brothers Yee and Leong Ho, who paid their own passage to Hawai'i in 1876. Yee went to 'Ewa to work on a rice plantation, while Leong settled in Honolulu to form a business. For fifty-one years, Yee remained at the rice farm, starting as a worker and ascending to

TABLE 2.   Hawaiian and Asian populations in Hawai'i, 1900–1940

	1900	1910	1920	1930	1940
Hawaiian	39,656	38,547	41,750	50,860	64,310
Chinese	25,767	21,674	23,507	27,179	28,774
Japanese	61,111	79,675	109,274	139,631	157,905
Koreans	—	4,533	4,950	6,461	6,851
Filipinos	—	2,361	21,031	63,052	52,569

SOURCE: Andrew W. Lind, *Hawaii's People* (Honolulu: University of Hawai'i Press, 1967), 28.

the position of manager. He later moved to Honolulu for other work opportunities and the education of his children.

Groups of migrants frequently came from the same villages in China, and thus, although the profit motive was central, the relations of production were tempered by those of kinship and community. Merchants in town owned many of the larger rice plantations, which their hired managers oversaw. Laborers often lived, ate, and worked together with their managers, and the entire business consisted of Chinese who cultivated a community of mutual obligation. The two main arrangements were *fun kung* (divide work), or sharecropping, in which the landlord received 50 to 60 percent of the returns and the workers the remainder, and *wai* (partnership), in which the partners (*fo pun*) shared equally in the expenses and profits.

An example was Punalu'u on O'ahu's windward side, where several hundred Chinese from the same district in China developed rice plantations. One of them, Wah See Leong, leased some six acres, and in cooperation with others built terraces and banks. Leong built a house of rough pine lumber, a stable for his horses, a pigpen, and a chicken coop. He also planted vegetables for subsistence. After a few years, Leong returned to his home village with his savings to marry, and his wife later joined him in Hawai'i.

Besides family farms like Leong's at Punalu'u, there were four or five *wai* farms consisting of ten or more men, operating plantations of fifty or more acres. Doo Wai Lung had some twenty partners, and together they cultivated about sixty acres of rice. The *wai* invested in an artesian well to supplement water from the stream. As on Leong's family farm, the *wai* devoted land to vegetables and animals for subsistence. These small farmers were largely self-sufficient, but they had to rely on outside brokers for loans, supplies and equipment, rice mills, and access and transportation to the market. These needs were supplied by Chinese merchants in Honolulu.

A few growers, like Ah In Young, accumulated great wealth from the rice business. Young arrived in the islands at the age of nineteen to work as a truck farmer near Honolulu in 1872. With the support of a number of relatives who pooled their resources, and the backing of a white financier whose Hawaiian princess wife owned the land he leased, Young began the Tung Sun Wai Plantation at Pālama. As his profits grew, Young amassed several hundred acres of rice, including acreages in Waikīkī, Moanalua, Hālawa, and

Waipiʻo on Oʻahu and other fields on Kauaʻi. He built two rice mills, one at Pālama and the other, in ʻEwa. Young's Chin Wo Company in Honolulu distributed and exported the rice and imported an immense quantity of provisions and merchandise from China. Young owned stores throughout the islands and bought and leased property, including buildings and homes.

Most Chinese were not so fortunate. They moved from job to job seeking to improve their economic position. Following his father, who had been a sugar-plantation laborer, Bow Yuen left China for Hawaiʻi in 1888. For his first three months in the islands, Yuen worked on a rice plantation on Oʻahu, and for another eight years he worked on sugar plantations on Oʻahu and Kauaʻi, earning fifteen to seventeen dollars monthly. For the next several years, Yuen worked full-time on a Kauai rice plantation, and during the harvest season he also worked part-time at a nearby sugar plantation. He left that work for a year on a sugar plantation to earn eighteen dollars a month. Yuen returned to Oʻahu to work at a Chinese-run fish pond at Puʻuloa (Pearl Harbor) for a monthly wage of twenty-two dollars with room and board. He later moved to the Hawaiian Pineapple Company at Wahiawa for wages of $2.50 a day and stayed there for about two years. Probably nearing retirement in the 1930s, Yuen became a casual day laborer in Honolulu.

Other Chinese migrants grew vegetables for the local and continental markets; farmed coffee, bananas, and pineapples for export; and, like those in the Waipiʻo valley, moved into growing taro for poi. Perhaps most successful was Yip Kee Lum, the so-called taro king of Hawaiʻi. At the age of nineteen, Lum landed in Hawaiʻi in 1884, and for three years he worked as a taro farmer in the Mānoa and Pālolo valleys. He returned to China in 1887, married shortly thereafter, spent a few years in Saigon, and returned to the islands as a twenty-seven-year-old, leaving his wife behind in China. Lum resumed taro operations on Oʻahu, employing relatives and fellow villagers on his plantations and in his poi factory. After his import firm Wing Tuck Chong suffered losses during the Chinatown fire of 1900, Lum sailed for China to consult with relations in business.

In 1902, Lum established a second store in Honolulu, which, like his taro and poi enterprises, capitalized on kinship ties to attract employees and patrons. With Chinese partners, Lum built the Oahu Poi Factory in 1905, the Honolulu Poi Factory in 1913, and the See Wo Poi Factory two years later. By the 1930s, his Oahu Poi Factory was the largest in the territory, and Lum and his partners held a virtual monopoly over poi production. Lum also acquired large interests in rice production. In 1916, he was one of the founders and directors of the Chinese American Bank. Lum helped establish the ʻAʻala Market in Honolulu, which leased stalls to Chinese and Japanese fish dealers, butchers, and grocers in 1920, and two years later he helped organize and then served as president of Liberty Bank.

In that same year, the Hawaii Suisan Kaisha, a Japanese fishing organization, began, and Lum served for a time as its treasurer. Such instances of cross-ethnic engagements mirrored some of the changes under way in the social formation. Even before the advent of competition from cheaper California rice, Japanese began to erode the Chinese

FIGURE 39

Chinese woman (aunt) and child, 1914–15.
Photo by R. J. Baker. Courtesy of Hawai'i State
Archives.

monopoly in rice growing. By 1932, Japanese farmers produced 62 percent of Hawai'i's
rice, and Japanese entrepreneurs gradually took over the rice mills as well. During the
1930s, Japanese and Koreans also became the largest taro farmers, while the Chinese
maintained control over the poi factories.

By that time, most of the Chinese workers had left the rural areas for the urban centers. Whereas in the 1890s four-fifths of Chinese men labored in the agricultural sector,
by 1930 only one-fourth of all Chinese laborers were farm workers. In 1900, about 35
percent of all Chinese lived in Honolulu; by 1930 that figure had grown to 71 percent.
Peddling and bartering in markets in South China supplied an entrepreneurial tradition
for the transition to Hawai'i, and many Chinese importers and traders migrated with the
intention of setting up shop in Honolulu. Even in the rural areas, former plantation
workers peddled fish and garden produce.

Small retail stores, which required only a modest amount of capital to start, were
within the means of some Chinese migrants. Many began as partnerships similar to

Chinese agricultural arrangements. While white businesses clustered in urban areas, Chinese opened stores in rural settlements and plantation towns, selling a variety of goods, from groceries to clothing and general merchandise. Chinese retail businesses increased from 54 in 1866 to 393 in 1889, when they represented 63 percent of the total number of such establishments; their number peaked at 1,067 in 1910. Despite this apparent success, the monthly salaries of store proprietors might not have exceeded those of agricultural laborers, according to a 1900 estimate. Depending on their size, stores earned salaries for their owners of between twenty and forty dollars a month, but the investment over several years might have amounted to thousands of dollars.

Chinese worked as laundrymen, tailors, dress and shoemakers, domestic servants, and restaurant workers, occupations widely avoided by other groups. The 1884 census listed 325 Chinese and no other "washermen" in Honolulu, and in 1896, the Chinese operated all of the laundries in Honolulu except one. Even as their numbers declined during the territorial period, Chinese laundrymen were the norm. Around 1930, non-Chinese women began to replace them, and by 1950, women did most of the laundry work. Chinese men throughout the late nineteenth century were likewise overrepresented in domestic service until non-Chinese women replaced them. In 1910, Chinese men made up 20 percent of the total 5,317 servants in the territory; in 1930 12 percent; and 1940 a mere 1 percent.

Chinese migrants dominated Hawai'i's prepared-food industry. In 1889, they operated 85 percent of all the islands' restaurants, bakeries, and food establishments. Because of competition from others, notably the Japanese, this figure declined to 59 percent in 1910 and 31 percent in 1930. Still, Chinese restaurants surged between the 1930s and the 1950s with the growing popularity of Chinese food, and two became institutions in Hawai'i: the Wo Fat Chop Sui restaurant in downtown Honolulu, started in 1885 by six migrants from Chung Shan district in China, and the Lau Yee Chai restaurant in Waikiki, begun by the popular chef Pang Yat Chong. Situated in the heart of the tourist district since 1926, Lau Yee Chai offered visitors Chinese food served in a setting of Chinese architecture, interiors, and decor, promising a total and authentic Chinese experience.

The social life of Hawai'i's Chinese, most without families, revolved around Chinese-owned stores and locales where old-timers gathered to gossip and hear news from home brought by visitors. "The appearance at the store of an immigrant who had been home to China for a visit was as important as a personal letter," a Chinese resident recalled. "He also brought news and family tidings from the village to the immigrants in Honolulu. . . . Sometimes he brought small bags of herbs, beans, yam flour, or sweets from the wives, parents, mother-in-laws, or godparents to the immigrants." Moreover, the Chinese store was a refuge from daily racism. In such places, for a Chinese migrant, "words found meaning; he could be understood and his conversation appreciated. He could talk at length and be listened to."[11] By 1900, about 40 percent of Honolulu's Chinese lived in Chinatown.

Chinatown offered markets with familiar foods and Chinese drama to feed the mind and senses. Chinese movies thrilled audiences, and herbal medicines calmed frayed nerves and restored bruised bodies. Temples offered solitude and assurances of divine protection and assistance. Honolulu's Chinatown was a conduit to China, the United States, and the rest of the world. Businesses facilitated those global exchanges, transmitting letters and remittances, serving as post offices and banks, and importing and exporting goods and culture.

In 1900, following a public health scare over bubonic plague spreading from Chinatown, Hawaiʻi's Board of Health ordered a controlled burn of some buildings. The fire spread into a conflagration that reduced all of Chinatown to ashes and rubble, destroying homes and businesses and leaving at least four thousand people homeless. "To a great extent," a white eyewitness at the scene remarked, "these crowds [of the displaced] were in a state of panic, as well as anger at the whites, who, as they believed, had deliberately burned them out."[12] Most of Chinatown's residents were Chinese, Japanese, and Hawaiian, and the businesses alone claimed losses totaling $3 million. Honolulu's example sent several West Coast cities inspecting their Chinatowns and Japantowns for similar contagions.

The relative absence of Chinese women during the period of migrant labor was mitigated during the period of dependency. As the sugar planters had anticipated, women, marriage, and families brought greater stability to an otherwise mobile population of men. Chinese family formation, however, was largely a matter of class: merchants could afford to bring their wives and children to Hawaiʻi, whereas workers could not.

As a Hawaiian-born generation came of age in the islands, the reduced gender imbalance led to more marriages and children. In 1900, Chinese women numbered 3,466, or over 13 percent of all Chinese in the territory. That percentage rose to 21 percent in 1910, 31 percent in 1920, 39 percent in 1930, and 40 percent in 1940. Correspondingly, marriages of Chinese men to Chinese women increased. Of the 18,595 men over twenty-one years of age in 1900, 13,449 were single, widowed, or divorced; 3,362 had wives in China; and 1,409 had Chinese wives in Hawaiʻi. By 1920, of the 11,223 Chinese men over twenty-one, only 5,763 were single, widowed, or divorced, while 2,576 had wives in China, and 2,576 had Chinese wives in the islands. Some 350 Chinese men had Hawaiian wives in 1900, and 650 in 1920. Most of the children of Chinese-Hawaiian marriages became Hawaiian through their mothers and their Hawaiian relatives.

As on Punaluʻu's rice plantations, Chinese families formed alliances according to their home districts in China. Life-cycle rituals drew them together in celebration and remembrance, and they participated in community-wide observances such as Chinese New Year, the Moon Festival, and Qingming, or ancestral remembrance. Those observances helped to shape their subjectivities as Chinese against the forces of Americanization, which sought to assimilate especially those born in Hawaiʻi.

Language was a key element of contention between Americanizers and Chinese parents, who feared the assimilation of their children into a foreign culture, mainly through the public schools and use of the English language. As a Chinese-language school explained in its founding statement in 1911: "Our youths of school age number several

FIGURE 40

Chinese Women's Tea Club, August 27, 1928. Courtesy of Hawai'i State Archives, Anne Sunn Collection.

thousands. Because they are brought up here in an American cultural milieu, their speech, contacts and experiences tend to be foreignized. Concerning Chinese customs and manners they possess no knowledge, and we are forced to bear seeing the process of a racial transformation."[13] Two Chinese-language schools, Wah Mun School and Mun Lun School, opened that year near Honolulu's Chinatown, and over the years twenty others opened on O'ahu, Kaua'i, Maui, and Hawai'i. The Chinese-language schools operated after public-school hours and on Saturdays, teaching the language together with Chinese history and culture.

Chinese and American subjectivities are constructs, as we know, and centering the former by alienating the latter was consistent with the Chinese strategy in Hawai'i of creating parallel economic structures to mitigate the power of the white oligarchy. Of course, the dominant discourse and material conditions were impossible to ignore: they ruled the territory and affected everyone's lives and prospects. While being subject to and resisting the prevailing social formation, Chinese migrants conceived institutions of their own design and making.

In the islands, isolated from China and treated as an undifferentiated group, diverse peoples melded to become Chinese. Initially, most of the migrants saw themselves as members of kin and village groups, but their world grew. From Hawai'i, Chinese workers sent remittances to support not only their families but also the construction of buildings and roads in China, and they raised funds for flood and famine relief in Canton and Guangdong Province.

As they moved to urban centers in China and from there to places abroad, Chinese migrants had to innovate to thrive. They organized mutual aid societies, fictive kinship and family associations, linguistic and political unions, and occupational guilds and networks. The Chinese in Hawai'i formed more than two hundred such organizations. Perhaps most prominent were the district associations, which tended to the needs of members from the same district in China. Also vital were the cemetery associations, which managed the bodies of migrants who died in the islands, performed Qingming services to honor them, and cleaned their bones for shipping back to China for reburial in their ancestral homes.

Concerned about anti-Chinese laws and regulations, some twenty-five Chinese merchants met in Honolulu and formed the Chung Wah Wui Goon, translated into English as the Chinese Union and later the United Chinese Society. The organization came to represent Hawai'i's Chinese community as a whole. Its objects, the society's charter declared, were to promote amity among the islands' diverse and at times conflicting Chinese ethnicities and to mediate relations between Chinese and non-Chinese. The society hired white attorneys to handle members' cases in court and passed resolutions like the 1894 action against a proposed discriminatory licensing fee. "We, the Chinese residents of Honolulu," the resolution began, "do solemnly protest against the injustice, degradation, and insult threatened to be imposed upon us and our race. . . . We respectfully assert our right . . . to dwell in Hawaii and be accorded the protection of the law upon terms of equality."[14]

Nationalism thrived among those who argued that a weak, colonized China could not effectively counter or restrain anti-Chinese racism abroad. Sun Yat-sen, the father of modern Chinese nationalism, joined his older brother in Hawai'i as a thirteen-year-old to enroll in 1879 in a mission school, which later became Iolani. But when Sun expressed his desire to become a Christian, his brother sent him back to China. Sun returned to Hawai'i as a revolutionary to promote the cause against the ruling Manchus in China and to raise funds to support the insurgency. In 1896, he organized the Hing Chung Wu or Save China Society, which declared: "China is weaker day by day. Those who are invested with the central power are indifferent and unscrupulous while the masses are ignorant and incapable of any deep thought. Unnecessary indignities and insults are suffered from many foreign nations. . . . The Hing Chung Wu has been organized solely for the purpose of saving the country."[15]

Before leaving Hawai'i, Sun raised about $6,000 in support of the revolution. Sun's Save China Society was just one of several nationalist organizations in the islands, some devoted to revolution while others focused on reform. Sun's wife had lived in Hawai'i for more than a decade. When he became the provisional president of the Republic of China in 1912, there was much enthusiasm among the islands' Chinese for the couple, Sun's

Guomindang political party, and the new republic. Sun's death in 1925 and continued civil strife in China divided Hawai'i's Chinese, and local concerns grew more pressing, especially with the rise of an American-born generation. Still, nationalism and China's sovereignty were key issues in the Chinese struggle for civil rights and equality under the law in the United States, and ethnic solidarity and creation of a unified Chinese people were responses to the dominant discourse and material condition of racism, assimilation, and political and economic dependency.

JAPANESE

Unlike Hawaiians and Chinese, the Japanese continued to live and work mainly within the system of plantation labor. Perhaps this was because when the Japanese arrived in the 1880s and 1890s, there were few alternatives. By 1902, they constituted 74 percent of the plantation workforce. Yet Japanese, like Chinese, fled the plantations when they could, and, like Hawaiians, they left the islands for the prospect of better wages on the U.S. continent. When the planters and Hawaiian government erected barriers to block those means of escape, Japanese chose to pursue self-determination by resisting the plantations from within.

Collective work action began even while Hawai'i's workers fell under the rule of masters and servants and before labor contracts ended through U.S. law. In 1890, some 400 Japanese marched to Hilo to protest overwork; the following year, 150 walked off a Maui plantation when the management failed to pay them, and about 200 marched from 'Ewa to Honolulu to voice their grievances. Numerous other Japanese work actions took place throughout the 1890s. In 1900, the first year of the territory, a government report listed twenty strikes. The largest involved 1,350 strikers. In all, 7,806 field hands, cane cutters, and mill laborers struck in that year. At Kīlauea plantation on Kaua'i, 43 Japanese and Portuguese women workers were locked out for demanding a wage increase from eight to ten dollars a month, which they ultimately won.

Women's presence on the plantations and their insistence on better wages and work conditions indicated a change from a pattern of migration to settlement. That was shown in the great strike of 1909, when 7,000 Japanese workers from all major O'ahu plantations joined in a four-month-long strike for higher wages and full equality in the workplace. Motoyuki Negoro, a Honolulu attorney, opened the campaign for higher wages with an article published on July 31, 1908 in the Japanese *Nippu Jiji*. In subsequent essays, he argued that the Japanese were no longer migrants and desired to make their homes in Hawai'i. There were, he noted, 21,500 married Japanese women, 12,500 children under six years old, and 4,966 school-age children. Japanese communities worshipped at thirty-three shrines and temples and twenty-six Christian churches. They were treated like slaves, he asserted, and forced to live in "pigstylike homes" on wages of $18 a month, while Portuguese and Puerto Rican laborers lived in "family cottages" and received monthly salaries of $22.50. Besides that racial inequality, Negoro argued, the prosperity enjoyed by the sugar industry had not trickled down to the Japanese, "who are suffering from the steadily rising living costs and weighted down by a practice of a discriminatory wage system."[16]

Sometaro Shiba, the editor of the rival *Hawaii Shimpo,* disagreed, saying this was not an opportune moment to stir up discontent among Japanese plantation workers. The two newspapers debated the issue for months. By the end of 1908, some of the urban elite had formed the Zokyu Kisei Kai, or Higher Wages Association. Under the leadership of Kinzaburo Makino, a businessman, they set out to mobilize the masses. Some 1,700 Japanese attended a rally for higher wages in Honolulu in December 1908, and they also adopted a resolution against coolie wages and demanded a meeting with the planters.

A month later, the Higher Wages Association submitted to the planters a letter asking for the same wage earned by Portuguese and Puerto Rican workers, $22.50 monthly. They cited not only the need for fairness but also the rising cost of living, the growing number of dependents, and the expenses associated with children's education. Additionally, the association alleged, poor housing and sanitation services threatened the health of workers and their children. Workers deserved a "living wage," the letter asserted, appealing to the planters' sense of justice and equity through language quoted from the U.S. Constitution's Fifteenth Amendment: "Is it not a matter of simple justice, and moral duty to give [the] same wages and same treatment to laborers of equal efficiency, irrespective of race, color, creed, nationality, or previous condition of servitude?"[17]

Far from accepting these arguments, the planters arranged the arrest of the *Nippu Jiji*'s publisher, Yasutaro Soga, for sedition conspiracy, although he was released shortly thereafter. The higher-wage leaders knew that a strike was imminent. In anticipation, the Hawaiian Sugar Planters' Association (HSPA) vowed in May 1909 to share strike expenses: this represented an unprecedented show of unity, for plantations had sometimes competed over workers. On May 9, 1,500 workers at 'Aiea plantation walked off the job; Waipahu laborers joined them three days later. Workers at four other O'ahu plantations joined the strike before the month's end. "Just as if with the force of wildfire," wrote Soga, "7,000 compatriots, from each of Oahu's plantations, launched the great strike in the month of May."[18] Plantation managers promptly evicted striking workers from their jobs and homes, and over five thousand of them converged on Honolulu seeking food and shelter.

The planters refused to negotiate with the Higher Wages Association, calling its leaders agitators and the strikers loafers. Japan's consul general scolded the strikers for damaging relations between the United States and Japan, accused them of being disloyal to the emperor, and urged them to return to work. Police rounded up strikers to force them back to work and arrested leaders for inciting unrest. Strike sympathizers worked feverishly to provide shelter and food, using vacant buildings, theaters, and private homes and organizing four outdoor kitchens in different parts of the city to serve three meals a day. Japanese businesses donated funds and supplies for the evicted strikers. Meanwhile, the planters recruited scabs from among Hawaiians, Chinese, Koreans, and Portuguese by offering them twice the daily wages paid to Japanese laborers.

The planters succeeded in breaking the strike. They employed Japanese spies to monitor the higher-wage movement; they harassed its leaders and even strike supporters and had them arrested and imprisoned on conspiracy charges. It was later revealed that the planters had loaned Shiba $1,500 to purchase the *Hawaii Shimpo* in 1908 and gave him a $100 monthly subsidy, and that Shiba had used planter money to bribe the *Hawaii Nichi Nichi,* another Japanese newspaper, to side with the planters' during the strike. In addition, for one year, starting a month before the strike, the *Shimpo* and *Nichi Nichi* received bonuses from the planters totaling $11,700, and Shiba had plans for a takeover of the *Nippu Jiji* while its editors and reporters were in prison. The sheriff, in the course of his duties, explained his stand: "I took the position in making these arrests, that the Higher Wages Association, together with its organ, the Nippu Jiji, was a criminal organization." He later candidly admitted that his actions were intended to keep in motion "the systematic coercion of thousands of Japanese laborers."[19]

With their funds dwindling and their leaders in prison, the strikers quietly returned to work. At the trial of the strike leaders, Tomekichi Mori, a Higher Wages delegate from Maui, stabbed and seriously wounded Shiba outside the courtroom. Two days later, on August 5, Higher Wages Association representatives met in Honolulu and voted to end the strike.

The aftershocks of the strike were felt for years. The workers had had a demonstration of the planters' powers, but they also witnessed what they could achieve through collective and organized resistance. For the first time in Hawaiian labor history, plantation workers had organized an industrywide strike. They gained the support of workers on other islands and the nonstriking community, raised a strike fund of about $42,000, and inflicted losses to the planters of an estimated $2 million.

Although most strikers returned to their former plantations on Oʻahu, more than a thousand left for the neighboring islands, and the number and percentage of Japanese sugar plantation laborers steadily declined thereafter, from 28,106 (64 percent) in 1910 to 24,046 (54 percent) in 1915, and 19,474 (44 percent) in 1920. Correspondingly, the numbers of Filipinos rose: their recruitment, the HSPA admitted, was to supplant "the Jap," "to clip his wings," and "to keep the more belligerent element in its proper place."[20]

Despite formally conceding nothing to the strikers, the planters recognized that the days of absolute masters and abject servants were over. A leading HSPA official described the change to a plantation manager: "In times past we got too much into the habit of treating the Japanese and Chinese as if they were more animals than men. We can not do this now, and it is not likely that the Japanese will stand being so treated. . . . So, while you must not give way to loafers for a moment, it would be well to be firm in a more kindly manner than was the custom ten years ago." During the strike, the HSPA trustees urged managers to adopt paternalism "to get our house in order before a storm breaks," they forecast. "Once the great majority of the laboring classes are busy under conditions which breed contentment and eliminate grievances, then we can expect a gradual and effectual diminution in the power of the agitating element."[21]

About two months after the strike's end, representatives of six conservative Japanese newspapers met as the "true" leaders of Hawai'i's Japanese to condemn the Higher Wages Association for having misled "our innocent workers" into "foolish agitation." They urged patience on the part of workers and advised them to perform their tasks faithfully while petitioning the planters for necessary improvements. On their part, the planters conceded to the strikers' demands in a sequence of face-saving, orchestrated events. On November 29, 1909, the HSPA thanked the newspaper leaders for their "respectful consideration" and announced that the planters would raise Japanese monthly wages to twenty-two dollars and institute a bonus system for day laborers.

In recognition of U.S. Independence Day, July 4, 1910, in an act of benevolence, the jailed strike leaders received pardons and were released to a welcoming crowd of several hundred supporters. The group passed through 'A'ala Park, once a campground for the evicted strikers, to the Yamashiro Hotel, the strike headquarters, where nearly a thousand greeted them with rousing cries of "Banzai!" As a Higher Wages Association strike pamphlet had pointed out, the strike and its demands were thoroughly American, whereas the planters and the oligarchy were undemocratic and anti-American at their core. Their demands for a living wage and decent housing were a measure of the workers' Americanization, the pamphlet noted—the realization of the "high ideal of Americanism." It proposed a "new" Hawai'i, wherein the regime of "plutocrats and coolies" would end and in its place emerge racial equality and democracy.

The planters and oligarchy depicted the strike less as an act by organized labor than as a "Japanese strike:" in Governor Walter Frear's words, it was an action that was "racial, and perhaps partly political." He saw it as the work of outside agitators, including urban editors and businessmen, who had stirred up the contented rural masses for their own political ends. At stake, the planters claimed, was the economic, political, and cultural supremacy of whites, "Americans," over Japanese "aliens." Racialized citizenship precluded Japanese inclusion within the nation-state, and in an order of white supremacy, clamor for inclusion by people of color was dissonant, even subversive.

The entry of the United States into World War I led to rising prices for staple commodities like rice and shoyu. Despite soaring sugar prices, wages were frozen at seventy-seven cents a day for men and fifty-eight cents for women. Bonuses, a benefit of the 1909 strike, were paid only to workers who had spent at least a year on one plantation, and to men who had worked at least twenty days a month and women who worked fifteen days. In 1914, bonuses amounted to 5 percent of a worker's earnings; a year later they rose to 20 percent. However, fearing that inflated bonuses would lead to expectations of permanent raises, planters unilaterally reduced the bonus and withheld half until the year's end.

Once again, faced with rising prices, growing families and expenses, and lagging salaries, plantation workers organized a higher-wage movement across the islands. In 1917 they formed the Association for Higher Wages and proposed wage increases, reforms to the bonus system, and day-care facilities for the children of workers. With child care, they reasoned, both parents could work. About a month later, the HSPA reduced the bonus by about 20 percent and then expressed surprise over the association's proposals, which the planters rejected. Especially because of wartime calls for patriotism and the oligarchy's representations of Japanese labor agitation as anti-American, the association was vulnerable, and it disbanded. But the wage problem persisted.

In October 1919, nearly a year after the war's end, Japanese plantation workers throughout the territory resumed the campaign for higher wages. This time, the leaders came from the working class, not the urban elite, and not from the first generation, or issei, but the second generation, the nisei, many of whom belonged to the Young Men's Buddhist Association (YMBA). On October 19, YMBA members representing five plantations on the island of Hawai'i declared their intention to organize a mass movement to fight for higher wages, an eight-hour day, and reform of the bonus system. Less than a week later on O'ahu, the Waialua YMBA held a mass rally for higher wages, and by November, workers had organized higher-wage associations on 'Aiea, 'Ewa, Waialua, Waimānalo, and Waipahu plantations and on the islands of Kaua'i and Maui.

During the first week of December 1919, fifty-eight higher-wage delegates met in Honolulu to consolidate their efforts. They formed the Federation of Japanese Labor, which described itself as if to a watching nation and world: "We are laborers working on the sugar plantations of Hawaii. People know Hawaii as the paradise of the Pacific and as a sugar-producing country, but do they know that there are thousands of laborers who are suffering under the heat of the equatorial sun, in field and in factory, and who are weeping under 10 hours of hard labor and with the scanty pay of 77 cents a day?" They further proclaimed: "We consider it a great privilege . . . to live under the Stars and Stripes, which stands for freedom and justice."[22] That patriotic invocation played on the planters' tactics in the 1909 strike, when the planters reminded the white nation of its racial kinship with the oligarchy and of U.S. imperial ambitions in the Pacific.

That global stage, "the problem of the twentieth century," was the defining significance of the 1920 strike. The federation and its ally, the Filipino Labor Union, presented demands to improve the lot of workers: wage increases to $1.25 a day for men and 95 cents for women; bonuses to men who worked at least fifteen days each month and women who worked ten days; an eight-hour day for field and mill workers; eight weeks of paid maternity leave for women workers; twice the regular wages for work on Sundays, legal holidays, and overtime; 60 percent returns for sharecroppers instead of the prevailing 40 percent; wage increases and bonuses for independent cane growers; and expanded and improved health-care and recreational facilities for workers and their families.

The strike began on January 20, 1920, when 2,600 Filipino and 300 Puerto Rican and "Spanish" workers struck. A week or so later they were joined by 5,400 Japanese workers, . The HSPA claimed that the strike was the work of "alien agitators" and, in the words of its president, John Waterhouse, was "an anti-American movement designed to obtain control of the sugar business of the Hawaiian Islands." Ten days after the strike's start, in an editorial titled "The Hand across the Sea," the *Pacific Commercial Advertiser* charged: "The inference is plain and unmistakable: The Japanese government . . . is back of the strike, it is back of the organization of Japanese labor in the American Territory of Hawaii; it reaches out its arm and directs the energies and activities of its nationals here in these American islands, just as it directs those at home."[23]

Meanwhile, as in 1909, Japan's consul general condemned the 1920 strike and urged Japanese workers to return to the plantations. Instead, some three thousand Filipino and Japanese men, women, and children marched in downtown Honolulu holding portraits of President Abraham Lincoln and banners that read: "We Want to Live like Americans; How Can We Live like Americans on 77 Cents?" and "God Has Created Us Equal. "Lincoln's picture bore the inscription, "We Believe in Lincoln's Ideas," a reference to his Emancipation Proclamation and the freeing of enslaved plantation laborers in the South.

In unity, the Japanese strikers sang:

We don't like to strike
    But it can't be helped
    Because our wages aren't increased
Will you raise them, until you raise them
    Unless you raise them, we'll have to
Strike, *don don*
77 cents is cheap
    But we can't eat on it
    So it can't be helped
We'll launch our strike
    Until our cries can he heard above
Don don[24]

As it had during the 1909 strike, the HSPA recruited scabs—Chinese, Koreans, Hawaiians, Portuguese, and even Filipinos and Japanese—to replace the striking workers. Managers evicted strikers from the plantations, sealing their houses and leaving them homeless. An estimated 12,020 were displaced, including 5,087 men, 2,796 women, and 4,137 children; of the total, 1,472 were Filipinos who had cast their lot with Japanese workers.

The situation of the Filipino strikers was complicated because they had acted on their own initiative, beginning the strike on January 20 without the prior approval of the Filipino Labor Union leader, the Honolulu attorney Pablo Manlapit, who wavered, urged his members to return to work, and then called for an end to the strike. In addition, there was poor coordination between the Japanese and Filipino unions, and Filipinos had to contend with widespread Japanese prejudices against them. Yet, in solidarity across ethnic divides, many Japanese joined the Filipino strikers on their picket lines.

The homeless families of strikers shared horrific conditions. The evictions took place at the peak of an influenza epidemic, over the protests of Acting Governor Curtis Iaukea, a Hawaiian. Among the crowded, makeshift shelters, tent encampments, vacant buildings, and churches in Honolulu, the flu spread quickly and with deadly results. By April 20, ninety-five Filipinos and fifty-five Japanese had died as a result of the epidemic, according to a Federation of Japanese Labor estimate. At Waialua alone, there were eight hundred patients, and deaths daily; forty-three died in ten days. There was one Japanese physician to care for the sick in the plantation hospital and a temporary infirmary in a school building. The report described "wives weeping with their sick babies over the loss of their husbands, children made orphans overnight,husbands burying sons and wives on the same day. . . . Lives went out like candle flames in a gust of wind."[25]

As the strike dragged on, morale and money ran low. On July 1, at the behest of the Buddhist bishop Hosen Isobe, John Waterhouse of the HSPA met with workers at a Honolulu hotel. That same day, the renamed Hawaii Laborers' Association met and declared an end to the strike. They called for "the spirit of Aloha" to prevail because, they observed, capitalists needed workers, and workers depended on capitalists. In valediction, they addressed the strikers: "You have faithfully stood to the last of this long strike, as inhabitants under the rule of the United States, respecting and obeying its laws, as members of this association, and as laborers, preserving your honor and dignity."[26] The strike, which cost the workers $600,000 and the planters an estimated $11.5 million, was over.

Unknown to most workers, the U.S. military monitored the strike, which they saw as a national defense concern. Democracy, an Army intelligence officer complained, placed unfortunate constraints on the military: what Hawai'i needed was a military government and stricter laws to root out espionage and protect the nation's strategic interests. During the strike, some members of the oligarchy favored calling in the military to suppress the workers, but Acting Governor Iaukea, mindful of the role played by U.S. forces in the Hawaiian kingdom's overthrow, refused. U.S. marines were used to "over-awe" Hawaiians, Iaukea noted, and he would not employ them again as an instrument of "intimidation." The army, however, was unimpressed by Iaukea's history lesson and principled stand for democracy, and its intelligence officers appealed directly to plantation managers to inform them of any "emergency arising from the Strike." The military's eclipse of state powers would be more fully realized after Japan's attack on Pearl Harbor.

The strikers resumed their position under planter hegemony without any concessions or even recognition of their right to organize and bargain collectively. But as before, three months after the strike and without fanfare, the HSPA raised wages by 50 percent and allowed monthly bonuses. In addition, the planters expanded worker recreation and social-welfare programs and made extensive improvements in housing and sanitation, using paternalism to convert intractable workers into docile ones.

Increasingly, efforts to recruit and retain contented workers focused on the second-generation Japanese, who were coming of age during the interwar period. While constituting 43 percent of Hawai'i's population in 1920 and 38 percent in 1930, the Japanese were leaving the plantations to pursue education and other employment opportunities. By 1932, the number of Japanese plantation laborers reached a low of 9,395, or 19 percent.

The educational campaign launched by the Japanese elite in January 1921, which was endorsed by prominent members of the Japanese government and business community and select members of Hawai'i's oligarchy, aimed to convince Japanese workers to see the value of plantation labor, to remain in the places assigned them, to avoid "ugly racial disturbances" like strikes, and to have their children, the nisei, follow in their footsteps. A key figure in that campaign was Takie Okumura, a Christian minister, who advised: "Forget the idea 'Japanese' and always think and act from the point of view of the American people."[27]

In the first seven months of the HSPA-financed campaign, Okumura and his son visited forty-seven plantations on the islands of Kaua'i, O'ahu, Maui, and Hawai'i. In addition, Okumura started the Conference of New Americans, a series of conferences. Its focus was the second generation, who were replacing their aging parents as the principal wage earners. The sugar industry and its employment opportunities were discussed at every session of the conference, and political topics included the importance of registering and voting, party affiliation, and the danger of Japanese bloc voting. Population projections predicted that nisei would cast 47 percent of the territory's votes by 1940.

It was at one of those conferences that President Crawford of the University of Hawai'i made his remarks about not taking education too seriously. Realistically, the educator claimed, "a great number of our young people must go into the agricultural industry—sugar, pineapples, coffee and general farming."[28] Nisei must not scorn "rough work," and they should be satisfied with what they had instead of aspiring to white-collar jobs. Crawford offered these new Americans just two choices: either develop a "proper attitude" toward plantation labor or leave the islands for Japan or the U.S. continent. Not all the nisei agreed. In fact, according to one, the consensus among nisei was that the plantations were at odds with Americanism.

Whether as a result of those efforts or because of the lack of opportunity elsewhere, the numbers of Japanese plantation laborers rose to 10,397 or 31 percent in 1942. As a nisei declared in 1936: "I am a true son of the plantation. My father came here from Japan about forty years ago and worked on the plantation the entire period and is still on the plantation pay roll in spite of his old age. I was forced to quit school early in life and for the past fifteen years have been employed by Papaikou plantation. It is my intention now to work for the plantation for the rest of my life."[29]

While the Conference of New Americans instilled patriotism in the most amenable members of the second generation, education played a key role in securing their dependency. A federal Bureau of Education survey of the territory's schools concluded, in a report issued two weeks after the end of the 1920 strike, that education should serve the nation by producing "dependable, patriotic, and worthy citizens" by educating "competent leaders and efficient workers."[30] To achieve that goal, it recommended, elementary schools should devote much attention to handwork, manual labor, cooking, simple sewing, the making of beds and housework, and the organizing of pig and poultry clubs. High schools should have well-stocked farms for boys to run, and girls should be taught the duties of farmers' wives. This manual training was not intended to encourage independent farming, the survey noted, but to provide labor for the sugar and pineapple industries.

At the height of the 1920 strike, the territory's school superintendent, at the request of mainly white parents, initiated a two-track school system that effectively created racially segregated schools. The nominal dividing line was language: children were assigned to schools on the basis of whether they spoke "standard" English or "nonstandard" or "pidgin" English, which was widely spoken by nonwhites.

In 1925, Central Grammar School, a standard-English school, had a student body of 546 white children, 135 Hawaiians, 78 Portuguese, and only 27 Chinese and 16 Japanese, at a time when Chinese and Japanese children made up 60 percent of all students enrolled in public schools. Moreover, schools were unequal in educational outcomes. As late as 1941, tests comparing children's achievement in the two educational tracks invariably showed the standard-English schools to be superior to the other track. The islands' segregated schools operated from 1920 to 1947.

Not all of Hawai'i's whites favored the segregated schools. One of the most influential was Miles Cary, the principal of McKinley High School. During his long tenure as principal, Cary worked to instill self-reliance and independent thinking in his students. He rejected vocational education and introduced classes in art, journalism, languages, mathematics, social sciences, and science. During World War II, Cary interrupted his duties as principal to work with Japanese students in a U.S. concentration camp in Arizona.

The anti-Japanese campaign intensified after the 1920 strike and expanded to include attacks against Japanese-language schools and "paganism," or Buddhism. These institutions were related: most Japanese-language schools were associated with Buddhist temples, and priests often served as teachers. Moreover, Buddhist priests and youth organizations were among the leaders of the 1920 strike. The legislature took up the matter of Japanese-language schools and passed Act 30 in November 1920, ostensibly to regulate them but in practice to dissolve them.

In response, eighty-seven Japanese-language schools challenged Act 30 in the courts. The case worked its way up to the U.S. Supreme Court, which rendered its unanimous ruling on February 21, 1927. The Court acknowledged the "problem" of a "large alien population" in Hawai'i and the prevalence of mainly Japanese but also Korean- and Chinese-language schools but ruled that the Constitution "must not be transcended."[31] Act 30, the court declared, was unconstitutional. Kinzaburo Makino, a leader of the court challenge, told supporters: "We must never forget that we have to stand up for our rights as guaranteed under the Constitution."[32]

Meanwhile, a power struggle was under way among Hawai'i's rulers. On one side was the military, which advocated for a commission form of government headed by the military. Its proponents saw the islands mainly as a vital strategic outpost in the Pacific. On the other side were the planters, who argued that the Americanization and assimilation of the nisei would secure the islands against the large "alien" population while profiting from their labor.

In the winter of 1932, Connecticut Senator Hiram Bingham introduced a bill in Congress aimed at placing Hawai'i under the Department of the Navy and a governing commission. As Admiral Yates Stirling Jr. had warned that same year, U.S. democracy was ill equipped to deal with the Japanese problem. Stirling's argument was unabashedly racist: "If these Islands were populated . . . by American citizens, comprised in large measure of the Caucasian race," he intoned, "their allegiance and loyalty to the welfare of the whole Nation might not be questioned." Instead, "several claimed unassimilable" races predominated in the territory, giving the situation "a decided element of doubt, if not of actual alarm." Moreover, under a democracy those alien races would inevitably win control of the government. "The safety of the United States is far too important for us to close our eyes and refuse to appreciate the importance of this fact in the military problem in these islands."[33]

Bingham's bill failed, but the following year the Rankin bill, endorsed by President Franklin Roosevelt, proposed allowing the president to appoint a nonresident governor of Hawai'i. That bill likewise failed, but those instances of federal concern hinted at deeper workings in the nation-state. The army and navy intelligence services, together with the civilian Bureau of Investigation (the forerunner of the FBI) had been secretly investigating Hawai'i's Japanese at least since World War I. Those efforts intensified during and after the 1920 strike, and their concern was the doubtful loyalty of that "alien race," especially given the increasing likelihood of a war with Japan. Various war scenarios emerged from those efforts, and the plans alternated between the mass confinement of all the Japanese and the selective internment of "disloyals" and community leaders. Martial law or military control of the islands was the essential condition for Hawai'i's defense, which by the 1930s was seen as integral to the security of the U.S. homeland and its empire abroad. In that sense, the nation stood prepared despite the surprise attack on Pearl Harbor.

KOREANS

Whereas Hawaiians and Chinese quickly fled the sugar plantations, and Japanese and Filipinos stayed while deploying union organizing and strikes to loosen the bonds of plantation paternalism and dependency, Koreans chose to follow the pattern set by the Hawaiians and Chinese.

Although recruited as migrant laborers for Hawai'i's plantations and thus expected to return home, most Koreans chose to remain in the United States. Unlike the Chinese and Japanese, Koreans felt they had no homeland to which to return, especially after Japan declared a protectorate over the peninsula in 1905 and later annexed Korea. Migration estimates show that about half of Hawai'i's Chinese and more than half the Japanese returned to China and Japan, but only one-sixth of Korean migrants returned to Korea.

Like all plantation laborers, Koreans rebelled against perceived injustices. Besides striking and lodging complaints, Korean workers shifted from plantation to plantation, seeking better opportunities. A survey found that nearly a third of the Korean respondents had been employed at five or more plantations; they readily moved for better prospects. Their swiftly declining numbers on the plantations testify to Korean mobility. In 1906, there were 4,700 Koreans on sugar plantations, constituting about 10 percent of the workforce; in 1909, they numbered 2,229, or 5 percent; in 1922, their number fell to 1,170, or 3 percent; and in 1932, they diminished to a mere 442, or less than 1 percent. Contrarily, the lure of higher salaries as strikebreakers during the 1909 and 1920 strikes brought increases in the number of Koreans on plantations. Those, however, were temporary.

Organizations were important for social cohesion and survival. The most basic was the *dong-hoe,* or village council, which adjudicated conflicts among Koreans in plantation camps. The *dong-hoe* drew up rules mandating respect for women and prohibiting gambling, alcohol consumption, and prostitution, and it provided aid to those in need. The councils, along with Korean brotherhoods, looked after the welfare of their members and acted in place of kin-based affiliations in Korea. The Sinmin-hoe (New People's Society), founded in 1903, similarly sought to advance the common interests of Koreans, including the goal of rebuilding the homeland through the regeneration of Koreans abroad. Although factionalism divided, weakened, and then destroyed the Sinmin-hoe a few months later, several other, similar societies arose in its place.

The United Korean Federation absorbed most of the various societies and *dong-hoe* in 1907. The Federation maintained an office in Honolulu, published a newspaper from 1907 to 1909, and in 1909 merged with the Mutual Assistance Society of San Francisco to form the Korean National Association (KNA). The KNA became the leading Korean organization in the islands and on the continent. In California it was composed mainly of Korean migrants from the islands. In Hawai'i there were seventy-eight local KNA branches. The annual membership dues purchased textbooks for Korean-language schools, funded a weekly newspaper, provided welfare for needy members, and supported the liberation movement in Korea.

Christianity brought many Koreans to Hawai'i and united them on and off the plantations. The planters and Americanizers alike encouraged the religion. On 'Ewa plantation in 1904, Koreans raised $300 and the manager contributed $750 to build and furnish a church. The following year, the church opened its doors to about one hundred parishioners. The Hawai'i Methodist Mission strove to bring independent Korean churches, like the one at 'Ewa, into its fold. After frequent visits to plantations, one Methodist Mission leader had enrolled over 1,600 Koreans and seven chapels, including the Korean Methodist Church in Honolulu, by 1905. Other Christian denominations, like the Episcopalians, competed for Korean members. Episcopalians reportedly tried to recruit Sun Hyon, an itinerant Methodist minister, promising him a salary increase (from twenty-five to forty dollars) and a house for his family. Hyon accepted the offer, but the Methodist head countered, pleading with him to stay with the Methodists. There were over eight thousand Koreans without a shepherd, the Methodist missionary reminded him; could Hyon abandon them? Hyon replied: "I will remain with you for my people."[34]

The Methodist Mission, knowing that their pastors played a mediating role among Korean workers, appealed for and received financial support from plantation managers and the HSPA. When the mission fell short of funds, its head went to the HSPA to solicit contributions, and Hyon received monthly stipends from plantation managers to cover his travel expenses. Besides preaching, Hyon taught English classes to Korean workers. When Koreans left the plantations for better opportunities, the Methodist Mission began a "back to the plantations" movement, similar to the efforts of the Christian minister Takie Okumura among the Japanese. Planter subsidies made its work possible.

Funds dried up with the departure of Koreans from the plantations. Rather than work directly for the plantations, Koreans took to contracting, a form of tenancy in which the contractor cultivated several acres of plantation land for an agreed wage, with a bonus on completion of the harvest. In 1915, Korean contractors received average incomes of twenty-four dollars per month, while plantation day workers earned twenty dollars. Others pursued coffee, tobacco, and macadamia growing on the island of Hawai'i, and, like the Chinese, farmed rice, garden vegetables, chickens, and pigs. By the 1930s, drawn by higher wages, more Koreans worked in pineapple than in sugar. In 1938, they constituted 3 percent of the men and 5 percent of the women working in the pineapple fields, with men earning an average of nineteen dollars weekly and women thirteen. Pineapple cannery work in Honolulu also employed Korean men and women, paying higher wages than fieldwork and offering better labor conditions.

As they had for the Chinese, entrepreneurial endeavors offered Koreans an alternative to agricultural work. They operated grocery stores on plantations and in the rural areas. They also moved to Honolulu, where a Korean community took root and grew. Tailoring and dressmaking, laundry work, and service industries were Korean niches, and the city lights appeared irresistible. "We didn't like the work," a Korean laborer recalled of the plantations. "The hours were long and the work was hard. We heard there were better-paying jobs in Honolulu. We imagined Honolulu was a big, glamorous metropolis. . . . So we took the boat to the big city." On landing, however, he found that jobs were scarce, so he eagerly accepted work as a yard boy.[35]

By 1910, about 10 percent of all Koreans lived in Honolulu. A decade later, that number reached 27 percent, and by around 1930, nearly two-thirds of all the territory's Koreans lived in or around Honolulu. The migration of Koreans from the plantations to the city generally improved incomes, allowing families to buy homes and invest in small businesses. Besides operating shops in town, Koreans worked as carpenters, clerical and office employees, sales and service workers, and domestic helpers. They settled in certain neighborhoods but frequently interacted with non-Koreans in their business and personal relations.

Their flight from Japanese colonialism in Korea failed to dim the fire of freedom for Koreans in Hawai'i. Most were refugees from Japanese brutality, and many of their family members continued to live under colonial rule. Notable nationalist leaders like Syngman Rhee lived and worked in the islands. Born into an upper-class family, Rhee participated early in political reform and antigovernment activities, for which he was jailed for seven years. He left for the United States to study at Harvard and then Princeton, where he earned his doctorate. After he returned to Korea, a friend invited him to Hawai'i to teach at the Korean Community School, where he soon became the principal. Built for children of Korean plantation workers, the school taught Korean history, culture, and language as well as English language and Western civilization. From his base in Hawai'i, Rhee participated in numerous international conferences and lobbied tirelessly for Korea's independence. After Japan's surrender, he became the Republic of Korea's first president in 1948. Exiled in 1960, Rhee returned to Hawai'i, where he died in 1965.

Yong-man Park, like Rhee, engaged in antigovernment protests at an early age, served a prison term, and migrated to the United States as a student in 1904. He attended the University of Nebraska. Convinced that Korea's freedom could be attained only through armed struggle, Park founded the Korean Youth Military Academy in Hastings, Nebraska. The academy began by training twenty-seven Korean cadets using wooden guns. Park's academy inspired four other military centers, each with about twenty trainees, in California, Kansas, and Wyoming. Jong-lim Kim, a wealthy Korean rice farmer in California, donated the funds to build a pilot training center in Willows. In 1910, the KNA in Hawai'i set up military training camps on O'ahu, Maui, and Hawai'i and recruited about two hundred volunteers. Park visited those camps in 1912 and the following year merged them to form the Korean National Brigade. Park was assassinated on October 17, 1928, in Beijing.

Many ordinary Korean migrants, not just leaders, bore the scars of Japanese colonialism. Sam-il, or "three-one" (March 1), was a turning point for many migrants. A nationwide demonstration against Japanese colonialism was planned for March 3, 1919, the day of the funeral for the deposed King Kojong, but it was moved up two days. Inspired in part by calls for national self-determination after World War I, Korean patriots in Korea and abroad planned a day of protest and the announcement of a declaration of independence signed by thirty-three leaders. Over the next several days, an estimated two million people participated in about 1,500 demonstrations. One eyewitness, Peter Hyun, recalled: "Countless thousands of Koreans—men and women, young and old, defying the Japanese police—poured out into the streets of Seoul and, shouting and dancing, proclaimed their national independence. . . . Long Live Korea! Long Live Korea! Long Live Korea!"[36]

The Japanese military responded with great brutality, killing about seven thousand people, wounding fifteen thousand, and arresting forty-six thousand. Although the movement failed to win independence, it galvanized the Korean people's resolve and showed the repressive nature of Japanese colonialism. Independence groups in Hawai'i and on the U.S. continent joined in the movement for national unity, suspending their factionalism and echoing President Woodrow Wilson's call for national self-determination during World War I.

The March 1 movement involved many Koreans in Hawai'i, like Margaret Pai and her mother, Hee Kyung Lee, who was imprisoned by the Japanese for her participation in the

FIGURE 41

March 1 parade in Dinuba, California, 1920. Waving Korean and U.S. flags, Korean Red Cross nurses commemorate the first anniversary of the uprising against Japanese colonization in Korea. Courtesy of the Korean American Digital Archive, University of Southern California Libraries.

demonstration. Lee first arrived in the islands as an eighteen-year-old picture bride in 1912, hoping to pursue a college education. That dream quickly vanished when she encountered the reality of poverty in Honolulu. Pai recalled of her mother, "For many days she cried when alone. Her life was nothing like what she imagined or what her parents wanted for her."[37] Lee's husband, Do In Kwon, worked as a yard boy for a wealthy white businessman and supplemented his meager earnings by growing and peddling vegetables.

The Methodist church and the Methodist Ladies Aid Society, the Youngnam Puin Hoe, which Lee helped to form, brought meaning to her mother's circumscribed world, allowing her to socialize with other Korean women. Its main purpose was to help the poor, sick, and needy. The women also spoke constantly about the need for freedom in Korea. When plans for the March 1 movement became known among Hawai'i's Koreans, Lee determined to sail for her homeland to participate in the struggle for Korea's independence. The society named Lee its representative at the demonstration and entrusted her with donations from its members. Thus, in the summer of 1918, Lee and her daughter, Pai, then three years old, departed for Korea.

In Korea, Lee enrolled in Ewha College, a women's institution begun in 1886 by the U.S. missionary Mary Scranton, fulfilling her deferred ambition. Ewha was alive with Korean nationalism, and its students played a central role in the March 1 movement. Pai stayed with her grandparents in Taegu while her mother studied and plotted for freedom in Seoul. Lee marched, the colonizers arrested her, and after ten months in prison, she

FIGURE 42
Students with their teacher, Gertrude Ko Min (back row, far right with scarf), at the Korean Christian Church's Korean Language School, Honolulu, ca. 1936. Photograph from the Agnes Rho Chun Collection, Center for Korean Studies, University of Hawai'i, Mānoa.

returned, a shell of her former self, to her parents' home in Taegu. On July 1921, Lee and Pai returned to Hawai'i on a ship with other Korean migrants. In Honolulu, Lee reported to the society that had sent her. Some of the women, Pai recalled, were "overcome with emotion, wiped away tears and blew their noses," stirred by Lee's exhortation to continue the struggle for freedom.[38]

Japanese colonialism was an affront to Korean history and culture. Like colonialism everywhere, it sought to strip its subjects of their basic human rights, aspirations, and abilities. Korean nationalism, accordingly, was a clear expression of the people's essential humanity. As Hawai'i born Nam-Young Chung observed: "Deep in the heart of every Korean immigrant, as poor as they were, was the knowledge that they were in a foreign land not by chance but by choice. They had it in their hearts that some day they would liberate their country. I saw them working toward this day after day, month after month. Furthermore . . . they had their hopes in the younger generation. They did everything within their power to educate and provide for the well-being of their offspring."[39]

By the 1930 census, Hawai'i's Korean population had shifted from a predominantly migrant group to one in which a majority were island born. While many of the second generation pursued careers in education and the professions, others fell into poverty, mental illness, and suicide. Among men between the ages of twenty and fifty-four in Honolulu, 13.3 percent were on the public dole in 1934, a rate twice that among the Chinese and three times that of the Japanese (and second only to that of Puerto Ricans).

Perhaps many of those Korean men were aging bachelors who had no families to support them. Koreans also suffered the highest rate of mental illness of any group in the islands. Their suicide rate of 75 per 100,000 was high when compared with the Chinese at 32 per 100,000, the Japanese at 27 per 100,000, and the overall average of 23 per 100,000.

Koreans were targets of particular forms of racism. Employers almost invariably preferred whites over Asians except for menial work, which was reserved for Asians. In sugar-plantation labor, Koreans benefited from taking the jobs of striking Japanese, but among the territory's financial institutions, according to a study, there was a tacit understanding that businesses would not hire Koreans to handle large amounts of cash. Additionally, fellow Asians discriminated against Koreans even as they formed intimate and lasting friendships with others.

In time, however, Koreans made Hawai'i their home. Sue Kim Shin was born in 1916 and lived with her parents on a farm in Waimānalo. There, she remembered, the streams cascaded down the steep, rugged Ko'olau mountains. Her mother, Soo-Yee Lim, who had come to the islands as a sixteen-year-old picture bride, was "a serious type" for whom "duty was most important." She was also exceedingly hard-working and frustrated because her husband, Tai-Ho Kim, refused to help her with the domestic chores. "She always mentioned paying debts to society so I remember my upbringing, which was very strict. I knew only work, work, work." There were six children in the family and plenty of spankings for all of them except the youngest boy.

Shin's mother was a Buddhist in Korea but converted to Christianity in Hawai'i. After her mother's death, Shin searched through her things and discovered for the first time that her mother knew how to write. "I didn't know about life. My mother never told me about life. Instead she compared my intelligence to a pig! I was so miserable I wanted to die. Even when I married in 1939 I was always looking to run away. . . . I had to face up to my husband's macho-samurai ways." Years later, Shin confronted her husband, and frankly told him she regretted catering to him and being a dutiful wife. "I admitted how dumb and stupid I had been."

After living in Honolulu and Wahiawā, Shin returned to Waimānalo "near the mountains where I lived when I was but a year old." There, a stream "hugs the mountains," and it runs pure day and night, never stopping. Its waters bring health and meaning, Shin noted. "Sometimes when a memory of my mother's trials and tribulations comes to me I know what makes me happy and whole. I think of the land, the stream and the beautiful scenery of God's nature my home is on. This is very close to me. I hear it, see it, and touch it."[40]

FILIPINOS

Both in Hawai'i and on the U.S. West Coast, Filipinos were leaders in the Asian and Pacific Islander labor movement, especially in agricultural work. Through mobilizing as a class of workers, they overcame the divides of language, religion, and regionalism common in the Philippines to emerge with a strong Filipino identity. In addition, in their struggles against U.S. colonialism in the Philippines and dependency in the United States, they developed ties across Oceania as Filipinos. Most Filipinos in Hawai'i, a U.S. military intelligence report found in 1929, favored Philippine independence.

Following the 1909 strike, the HSPA recruited increasing numbers of Filipinos to remove the "belligerent" Japanese and to keep them in their "proper place." But as their numbers grew and they were confronted with the same conditions of oppression and exploitation, Filipino workers rose up against the planter class. They initiated the 1920 strike that was subsequently supported by Pablo Manlapit and his Filipino Labor Union and then the Federation of Japanese Labor. During the strike, more Filipinos died than Japanese, mainly as a result of the devastating flu epidemic.

By 1924, Filipinos outnumbered Japanese on the sugar plantations. They launched the strikes of 1924–25, which cost many lives and led to the banishment of Manlapit from the territory. As before, their main goal was higher wages, but they also demanded other progressive reforms, such as an eight-hour day (as opposed to the prevailing ten hours), equal pay for men and women engaged in the same work, overtime pay and double pay for working on Sundays and holidays, and recognition of the right of workers to organize and bargain collectively.

Once again, the planters ignored the workers and began a campaign of intimidation, targeting the leaders. The Philippine colonial governor appointed a conservative resident labor commissioner to Hawai'i and pointedly warned Manlapit to refrain from striking. Thus Filipino workers' strikes for equality challenged two U.S. colonial regimes, that in the Philippines and the oligarchy of the territory.

Despite the Philippine labor commissioner's intervention, Manlapit issued a manifesto on January 2, 1924 warning of an impending strike, and on March 14 he declared "a silent strike, staying on the job, but doing only enough work to earn the wages." He appealed "to all races and nationalities on the sugar plantations to join the strike. It is a strike for American standards and American ideals." The High Wages Movement claimed ten thousand members, which represented about half of the Filipino plantation workforce and a quarter of the total. A steady stream of new migrant laborers from the Philippines softened the movement's bite, and Japanese workers, while perhaps sympathetic to the strikers' demands, did not strike. Because the strike leaders were divided and poorly organized, workers struck haphazardly on different plantations and islands, and plantation managers easily infiltrated and undermined the movement.

The 1924–25 strikes were notable less for the workers' actions than for the range and severity of the repression, which perhaps reflected a fear of the racist stereotype of the violent Filipino. In anticipation of and during the strikes, government officials beefed up their local police forces with uniforms, guns, and ammunition supplied by the HSPA, which had a generous strike fund. The job of the police was to isolate the strike leaders and to discourage the strikers. George Wright, a coleader of the High Wages Movement and a white man, was fired from his civil service job at Pearl Harbor for his alleged political activities. Kinzaburo Makino, the publisher of the *Hawaii Hochi* and a labor activist, promptly hired Wright as editor. In that capacity, Wright's son recalled, "he became a more powerful voice for labor and against the HSPA than he could have been while a civil service worker for the Navy."[41]

Police violence flared up on Kaua'i, where strikers were the least numerous. At Hanapēpē on September 9, 1924, as the police escorted two young Filipinos who had been beaten and held hostage by the strikers, shots rang out, and the police responded with a volley directed at the assembled crowd. According to a National Guard report, "The strikers kept pressing closer and closer on the officers as they neared their cars, when finally a shot was fired at the police by the strikers which was returned by the police, which started a hand to hand battle resulting in the death of four Police Officers, sixteen Filipinos, the wounding of Sheriff Crowell and nine strikers, and the arrest of one hundred and one strikers."[42]

The police and National Guard began a systematic search for weapons, and over a hundred alleged strikers were arraigned and imprisoned. The HSPA donated five hundred dollars to the families of each slain police officer. The Filipino victims were buried together in a trench in Hanapēpē's Catholic graveyard. Donations from the Filipino community amounted to $82.35 for the strikers' funeral and $75.95 for the widows and orphans of the dead.

The *Honolulu Star-Bulletin,* published by Hawai'i's governor, editorialized on the Hanapēpē riot: "If the strike murders at Hanapepe are not to be repeated elsewhere, the people of this territory must line up at once and unmistakably for law and order and against the criminal labor agitators and all their ilk." "On one side," the paper claimed, "we have a majority of liberty-loving and law-abiding Americans. On the other side we have, first the labor 'leaders' and their deluded, ignorant followers; second, their alien backers; third, the fringe of hangers-on—the professional agitators, the 'reds,' the I.W.W.'s [Industrial Workers of the World]—who are egging on the Filipino leaders and preaching class warfare and the destruction of American institutions."[43] By contrast, Japanese-language newspapers urged sympathy for Filipino strikers, perhaps as a result of the Filipino-Japanese coalition formed during the 1920 strike.

Manlapit, the sole Filipino attorney in the territory, was charged with and convicted of perjury. On August 13, 1927, he was paroled on condition that he spend the remainder of his two- to ten-year sentence on the U.S. continent. His Hawai'i-born wife and children visited him briefly in Los Angeles. On April 16, 1932, Manlapit returned to Hawai'i. During his absence, the islands' Filipino community remained mired in agricultural labor and poverty.

Filipino numbers in the islands declined during the Great Depression, when planters trimmed their payrolls by shipping some 7,200 "excess" Filipinos back to the Philippines at industry expense. That repatriation mirrored the contemporary eviction of Filipino and Mexican migrants on the continent.

In 1935, according to a study, there were eight Filipino newspapers, twenty-nine Filipino Protestant churches, and thirty-four small businesses in Honolulu. A survey two years later found about forty-two Filipino-operated small businesses, including tailors, barber shops, and stores, and a dentist and an attorney. The vast majority of Filipinos remained on the sugar plantations, their number peaking at 34,915, or 70 percent of the workforce, in 1932 and dropping to 53 percent by 1942. On the sugar plantations, Filipinos received the lowest salaries of all groups of workers. Like Koreans, thousands of Filipinos left for higher-paying work in the pineapple fields and canneries. By 1938, Filipinos made up about 60 percent of the male workers on pineapple plantations, with Japanese constituting 25 percent. In pineapple canneries, Filipino men were second only to Japanese, making up about 23 percent of the workforce. That concentration in agricultural labor reflected a system designed to restrict Filipino upward mobility, but the shift from sugar to pineapple showed that Filipinos, like other Asian workers, acted in their best economic interests.

Over time, Filipinos strengthened their roots in the islands. The Manila entrepreneur Gregorio Labrador ran an import/export business in Kalihi starting in 1933, and the Luviminda Commercial Corporation, a branch of the Filipino union and secret society Vibora Luviminda on Maui, bought fifteen acres of land in Kalihi in 1939 and sold it in perhaps the first Filipino real estate deal in the islands. The corporation also bought and sold land in the Philippines. Some of the oldest Filipino community organizations were labor and mutual-aid societies, like the secret Legionarios del Trabajo, formed in 1921; the Gran Oriente Filipino, begun two years later; and the Caballeros de Dimas Alang, which Patricio Belen brought from the Philippines to Hawai'i and thence spread to the U.S. continent. The Filipino Women's Club of the Honolulu YWCA, established in 1935, held territory-wide annual conventions and sponsored activities for women.

Hilario Camino Moncado was twenty-one when he arrived in the islands in 1914 to work for the Kōloa sugar plantation. A year later, he joined hundreds of Filipinos seeking better opportunities on the U.S. West Coast to work as migrant laborers from Alaska to California. Moncado graduated from high school and entered the University of Southern California law school. In 1924, he edited a Filipino newspaper and gained influence in the Los Angeles Filipino community. In 1925 he founded the Filipino Federation of America, headquartered in Los Angeles. It soon grew to twelve lodges with dues-paying members. Representing himself as the shepherd of an exiled "chosen people" in an inhospitable land, Moncado preached against gambling and prostitution and in favor of Filipino pride and Philippine national independence. His organization combined mysticism with nationalism: some members grew their hair and beards long, ate no meat or salt, practiced numerology, and held that Moncado was the incarnation of Jesus Christ. The Filipino Federation spread to Hawai'i and the Philippines and was influential in the lives of many Filipinos before Moncado's death in 1956.

Such movements created and advanced a distinctively pan-Filipino subjectivity rooted in syncretistic religion and in national liberation. Similarly, Filipino labor organizers formed connections between agricultural labor movements in California and in Hawai'i. Pablo Manlapit was an example of such a link. During his exile in California, Manlapit joined other Filipino labor leaders, like Antonio Fagel, who had been in the state since 1917 to organize Filipino agricultural laborers in the central and coastal valleys. On his return to Hawai'i in 1932, Manlapit brought Fagel with him to rebuild the flagging Filipino labor organization and movement. Together with Epifanio Taok, they renewed the Filipino Labor Union in 1932. This undertaking led to their arrest and a second banishment of Manlapit, who returned to the Philippines.

Fagel continued the work by forming the secret Vibora Luviminda, named for the Filipino patriot general Artemio y Recorte, who was known as Vibora, or serpent, because of his ability to attack U.S. troops suddenly and without warning. The name Luviminda comes from a contraction of the names of the three main Philippine island groups: Luzon, Visayas, and Mindanao. Fagel's Vibora Luviminda aimed to create pan-Filipino unity in the struggle against labor exploitation in Hawai'i. The last major ethnic labor union in the islands, it was based on Maui. Vibora Luviminda's involvement in the strike of Filipino sugar workers on Maui in 1937 resulted in the first HSPA-negotiated agreement with a union, although Vibora Luviminda was not mentioned in the document.

While forging a Filipino subjectivity based on a common condition of colonialism in the Philippines and the United States, Filipino labor organizers also sought to mobilize across ethnic lines. Along with Japanese, Hawaiians, Chinese, Koreans, and Portuguese, Filipinos worked as longshoremen throughout the islands. The shipping industry, controlled by the Big Five, sought to divide them with tactics like racist baiting and differential wages. Still, seamen and dockworkers, unlike sugar-plantation laborers, were connected across the Hawaiian Island chain, and they forged links between Hawai'i and the U.S. West Coast and other global ports. Hawai'i's longshoremen participated in the U.S. labor movement, joining John Lewis' Congress of Industrial Organization (CIO), rather than the racist American Federation of Labor (AFL) led by Samuel Gompers. They were also a part of the International Longshoremen's Association (ILA) and later the International Longshoremen's and Warehousemen's Union (ILWU) led by Harry Bridges.

Like Pablo Manlapit and Antonio Fagel, Harry Kamoku exemplified efforts to forge class solidarities across geographic and ethnic divides. Kamoku, a Hawaiian-Chinese seaman, worked on the U.S. West Coast during the 1920s and 1930s. In Seattle and San Francisco, he developed a deep interest in labor movements, and he brought those ideas home with him to Hilo, where he organized the multiracial, multiethnic Hilo Longshoremen's Association in 1935. He was promptly fired and blacklisted by employers on Hilo's waterfront.

Labor organizing for Kamoku was a family affair, involving not only the longshoremen but also their wives and families. He invited women to meetings, over the objections of the men, who later voted to exclude women from their discussions. The Hilo union walked off the job when a dock foreman mistreated a longshoreman, and in 1935 the men struck over members fired for joining the union. In both instances, the union won.

Kamoku wanted to integrate all of the Big Island labor unions, which were divided by ethnicity and race, into a single council of unions under his Hilo Longshoremen's

FIGURE 43

Harry Kamoku and demonstrators surge past police line. Courtesy of Hawai'i State Archives.

Association. "To consolidate the many races of workers into one solid organization," Kamoku reported, "is something of a miracle, which is happening here in the Port of Hilo."[44] On February 1938, the Inland Boatmen's Union, representing sailors, struck for a closed shop and for pay comparable to that earned on the West Coast. In May they were joined by two other unions of machinists, boilermakers, carpenters, and dry-dock workers, Dockworkers along the West Coast had won the closed shop in 1934. The strike dragged on through June and July 1938 while the company refused to bargain and instead hired scabs and strikebreakers.

On July 22, 1938, when the interisland steamer *Waialele* docked in Hilo, about 250 union supporters met the ship and heckled the strikebreakers. Attempting to disperse the crowd, a police lieutenant lobbed a tear-gas bomb, which exploded in the face of a child, Onson Kim, who was rushed to the hospital. In the ensuing panic, the fleeing bystanders trampled three other small children.

When the ship returned about a week later, the longshoremen determined to picket it, despite an order from the sheriff to stay away. The unionists planned a peaceful demonstration on August 1 but were also prepared to use force to prevent the ship's unloading. Sheriff Henry Martin lined up his sixty-eight police officers, some armed with shotguns and bayonets, behind an advance line of firemen with hoses. Behind them an additional ten to fifteen officers with shotguns and three with machine guns waited inside a warehouse.

The strikers arrived at the pier and advanced slowly. Troubled by the presence of women in the front line, the police tried to move them to the rear. The police dragged one of them, nineteen-year-old Theresa Hamauku, to the back, but she promptly returned to the front, to the applause of her union brothers and sisters. All the while, the police taunted the protesters with the racist, sexist threat to throw the strikers' women and wives to the Filipinos. At this point, the police lieutenant who had thrown the tear gas on July 22 lunged at Kai Uratani with his bayonet and hit Red Kupukaa with his rifle butt. He then fired a shot, and the police began firing into the crowd. After the guns fell silent, fifty-one protesters, including two women and two children, had been shot. Most suffered back wounds, indicating that the police had fired while the protesters were fleeing.

August 1, 1938, known as Bloody Monday and the Hilo Massacre, was remembered by Hawai'i's workers. Many subsequent labor agreements declared that day a workers' holiday in memory of the victims. It was significant that the massacre involved a class of workers across the divides of ethnicity, race, and gender. Their leaders were part of that class, men such as Harry Kamoku, Harry and Levi Kealoha, and Jack Kawano, rather than outside agitators.

In testimony to the U.S. House of Representatives following the devastating 1920 strike, the HSPA secretary, Royal Mead, boasted: "I do not think that there is any contest as to who shall dominate; the white race, the white people, the Americans in Hawaii are going to dominate and will continue to dominate—there is no question about it."[45] Most historians have agreed with Mead. The white elite, one social historian observed, constituted an oligarchy with extraordinary powers. For forty years, he wrote, from the islands' annexation to World War II, Hawai'i's oligarchy "skillfully and meticulously spun its web of control over the Islands' politics, labor, land, and economic institutions, without fundamental challenge."[46]

But Hawaiians defied attempts at their physical and social extinction. Together with the Chinese and Koreans, they left the plantations in pursuit of self-sufficiency, while Japanese and Filipinos remained on the plantations but resisted exploitation through unions based upon ethnic and then class solidarities. With the notable exception of Filipinos, most Pacific Islanders and Asians during those years of dependency became U.S. citizens. They shed their assigned status of migrant laborers and became permanent members of the island community.

As citizens, they could vote and hold office, threatening white supremacy. To the territory's rulers, that move from alien to citizen was the "second-generation problem." Attempts at Americanization or cultural assimilation and a back-to-the-plantations movement, sponsored by the planters, tried to convince the "new Americans" to follow their parents' example by remaining on the plantations. Although in competition with the planters for power, the military agreed with the need to contain the "alien menace." The mutual reinforcement of dependency and white supremacy would become patently clear at the onset of World War II.

SUGGESTED READINGS

Fuchs, Lawrence H. *Hawaii Pono: A Social History*. New York: Harcourt, Brace & World, 1961.

Jung, Moon-Kie. *Reworking Race: The Making of Hawaii's Interracial Labor Movement*. New York: Columbia University Press, 2006.

McGregor, Davianna Pōmaika'i. *Nā Kua'āina: Living Hawaiian Culture*. Honolulu: University of Hawai'i Press, 2007.

Merry, Sally Engle. *Colonizing Hawai'i: The Cultural Power of Law*. Princeton, NJ: Princeton University Press, 2000.

PRIMARY DOCUMENT
DOCUMENT 10

Angeles Monrayo Raymundo, diary excerpts, *Lost Generation: Filipino Journal* 1, no. 1 (1991): 31–40.

Riz Raymundo, the daughter of Angeles Monrayo Raymundo, was born in Modesto, California, and grew up during the 1930s. Her mother began her diary on January 10, 1924, when she was eleven years old. At the time, she had only three years of schooling. Remarkable are her childhood recollections of the Filipino strikes of 1924–25, including life in a "strike camp" in Honolulu after the family's displacement from their plantation home in Waipahu.

Waipahu, Oahu, January 10, 1924.

Dear Diary:

Christmas and New Year is now over and the month is the beginning of the New Year of 1924, and I think this is the best time to start a diary my teacher told us about a book that she wrote about herself. And this is why I got my idea to start one for myself because, I would like to read about me—what everyday things happen to me—when I am old woman, right now I am only 11 years, 5 months.

I have been in School just this past few years but god gave me the mind to catch on how to learn my alphabets and to put them together so can read and write like I do now. I'm thankful.

Waipahu, Oahu, March 3, 1924.

Dear Diary:

Mary and her folks have moved to Honolulu. I feel so lonely now without her. The reason why they went to Honolulu, because it's been heard that all Filipinos must strike for higher pay. Mr. Pablo Manlapit is the leader of this strike. Mr. Manlapit says that all Filipinos must strike or else there will be many hurt. So I think that's why they left and moved to Honolulu to stay. Oh why did this strike has to come up for, now no one to play with, now I have to sleep all by myself from now on go to school alone and eat my lunch alone and I'll have to go to shows alone. Gee, I don't think I'll have anymore fun, now that Mary is gone. I have other friends but they're not as close to me like Mary is.

Speaking of the Strike, I wonder if Tatay will go to Honolulu too. Gee Tatay is making good here tho' he is steadily putting money in the bank. Anyway I'll let you know if we do go to Honolulu.

Oh Diary, before I forget, father bought a new car. An Oakland touring car. Boy, it's nice to have, I mean, own a car. A friend of ours will drive it for us. And my brother will learn from him. Faustino will drive the car—and I'm scared of him some how, I do not like him.

Strike Camp, Middle Street, Honolulu, May 10, 1924.

Dear Diary:

We just arrive here today, here, at the "Strike Camp." There are so many Filipinos here, married-couples and unmarried men. They're from all parts of Oahu. There are five other young girls here too. I became friends with two of them already. Their first names are Esperanza and Victoria. They are, both, very nice girls. They showed me the place around here, as soon as we settled, I mean, found our sleeping quarters. You see, we all live in one big house, and so all we did was put curtains around our bed, and that will have to serve as our room for how long, we don't know. I guess we have to stay here until this strike is over. And Manlapit is going to feed the whole crowd. We're suppose to go down to his office, every other day to get our ration of food. Gosh I hope this strike won't last long. You see, Diary, Mr. Manlapit wanted the Plantation to give the laborers $2.00 a day and eight hours work. I certainly hope Manlapit wins, 'cause then it will be for our own good. Will tell you some more later on as the girls are draggin me, I told them I want to finish this.

Stirke Camp, Middle Street, May 11, 1924.

Dear Diary:

Another day had gone by, do you know, as soon as we finished breakfast, I went over to Esperanza's sleeping quarters and she was just finishing breakfast. I asked her if she has anything to do today, she said "no." And I asked her to show me the place again, and so that's what we did. We looked into everything. The bathroom, the toilet, the kitchen and do you know there are so many mangoe trees close by—boy! wait until the mangoe season is in full blossom, by that I mean when they get ripe, and that's not far-off—it is next month, and I'll surely do some climbing again, I haven't climb trees for so long, it seems. Oh well, it won't be long now. I told Esperanza about it, and she says "That's good, 'cause that means, we don't have to ask any boys to get mangoes for us we can get them ourselves.

And Esperanza introduced me to the other 3 girls—Sofia, Marcella and Trinidad. I don't know which of this girls is the oldest, but I know I am the youngest of them all. Triny is sort of snobbish—'cause she's better looking—but she has such mannish walk. But just so they are nice to me I'll be nice to them. And, Diary, the men here play basketball and volley-ball. And there are 3 woman here that "cooks" and "sells" "Maruya," you know, fried Bananas and other good things to eat. Oh, I just love "Maruya." I bought four today and gave 2 to Esperanza. Somehow Esperanza kind of fill in Mary's place, but I don't think I'll ever forget Mary, I do hope I'll see her soon. Well Diary that's all for now. If something new happens here I'll let you know.

Strike Camp, May 13, 1924.

Dear Diary:

Say, there'll be something going on here on every Saturdays and Sundays from now on. You know what, Well, I'll tell you. It's this; there's going to be dances here every Saturdays and Sundays, gee, won't that be fun. You see, Diary, I'm so crazy about dancing. And another thing we are going to charge the men 10 cents for 3 minutes dance. Gosh that's not bad is it? You know, Diary, someone thought of the idea, and it is for our own good, cause you see, we are very far from "Show-houses." This dancing business is for our benefit so that the place here won't be so dull every Saturday and Sunday. And I know we girls are going to have lots of fun when that day comes around. Gee, I hope all the girls will be in it. I'm sure Esperanza and Victoria and Sophia will join in—including myself.

Strike Camp, May 17, 1924.

Dear Diary:

Gee, the dance is tonight and I'm so glad; I can hardly wait for tonight. I wonder how much I'll earn. Maybe nobody will dance with me. Esperanza and Victoria are so excited as I am, gosh who wouldn't be, may I ask you? It's now 4 o'clock in the afternoon. Gee, I can not eat my supper; oh well, my dad and brother will have my share. Father doesn't care if I go dancing with the girls tonight, 'cause he knows it is all for the fun only, and adults will enjoy it as well as we children do. So until here, Diary dear, will let you know as soon as I can how I came out. Gee, but it's grand to have you, 'cause I can come to you and tell you what's in my heart, you know the things I feel and many other things too. I know, you'll keep it secret just as long as nobody is looking into my things and get hold of you. This is all for now.

Strike Camp, May 18, 1924.

Dear Diary:

Sorry, I couldn't tell you anything last night, when the dance was over because, I was so tired and sleepy, but I was happy, 'cause I made $7.20. I counted it before

I went to sleep and I gave it to father this morning. I kept just a dollar for myself to spend on something that I'd like to eat.

Gee, I didn't think I would make that much, but I did. And tonite there is going to be dancing again. Hope I'll make just as much as I did last night.

Oh, there were only four girls that danced last night. The other two didn't join in 'cause they say nice girls don't dance at all. Marcela didn't say that but Trinidad did; Gee, I wish one of these day she'd be real jealous about us making some money and she isn't, so that she will really join us, that way we'll make her eat her words without us forcing her to. Cause she says too, that it's bad for us girls to dance, 'cause dancing will lead us to something else later on. She's just evil-minded that's all. Gosh we just dance. I don't see any harm in it do you? These dancing isn't anything like they have in dance-Halls. The dancing we have here is just-clean-good-fun, for all of us here. Oh well, if that's the way she feels about it, well, that's up to her, eh Diary?

[Throughout the rest of May, the diary records more dancing and earnings, and a laundry business, begun with Esperanza, to earn additional money. Esperanza and her father left the strike camp on June 14, 1924, leaving Angeles behind.]

SIGNIFICANT EVENTS

1836	Hilo Boarding School founded
1847	Richard Armstrong becomes Hawai'i's minister of public instruction
1868	Samuel Armstrong establishes Hampton Normal Institute (Virginia)
1882	Chinese merchants form Chung Wah Wui Goon
1885	Wo Fat Chop Sui restaurant opens
1886	Ewha College founded (Korea)
1889	insurrection for Hawaiian sovereignty
1895	insurrection for Hawaiian sovereignty
1896	Sun Yat-sen establishes the Hing Chung Wu
1900	Organic Act
	first territorial elections
	Chinese laborers excluded from migrating to Hawai'i
	Chinatown (Honolulu) fire
1902	Republicans attain control of Hawai'i's territorial government
1903	Sinmin-hoe founded
1904	Yong-man Park arrives in U.S.
1907	United Korean Federation formed

1909	higher-wage strike by Japanese sugar workers
	Korean National Association formed
1910	Japanese strike leaders released from prison
1911	Sun Yat-sen becomes provisional president of the Republic of China
1914	Hilario Moncado arrives in Hawai'i
1917	Association for Higher Wages formed
1919	Sam-il uprising and movement (Korea)
1920	Hawaiian Homes Commission Act
	'A'ala Market established
	Filipino and Japanese sugar workers strike
	standard-English and non-standard-English schools instituted
	Act 30 regulates Japanese-language schools
1921	Educational Campaign launched
	Legionarios del Trabajo formed
1924–25	Filipino sugar plantation strikes
1925	Filipino Federation of America established
1927	Conference of New Americans begins
	U.S. Supreme Court extends protection to foreign-language schools
	Pablo Manlapit exiled to U.S. continent
1932	Senator Hiram Bingham's bill for navy control of Hawai'i
1934	Tydings-McDuffie Act
1935	Filipino Women's Club (Honolulu YWCA) formed
1937	Vibora Luviminda sugar and pineapple strikes
1938	Hilo Massacre
1947	standard-English schools close
1948	Syngman Rhee becomes president of the Republic of Korea
1960	Syngman Rhee exiled to Hawai'i

9

SAN FRANCISCO

On the continent, securing the dependency of Pacific Islanders and Asians was not as pressing an issue for the ruling class as it was in Hawai'i. In the islands, Hawaiians and Asians constituted over 70 percent of the population and thus a significant part of the labor force from the period of exclusion until World War II. On the continent, by contrast, with variations by region and state, they were never a large percentage of the total, so the "problem" of containing them economically, politically, and socially was not as critical for the maintenance of white rule. Moreover, segregation was the law until 1954, when the U.S. Supreme Court's *Brown v. Board of Education* dismantled not only school segregation but also the doctrine of separate but equal set forth in *Plessy v. Ferguson* (1896). In practice, however, even after 1954, peoples of color were still relegated to separate schools, housing, and jobs. This racism restricted their upward mobility and promoted inequality and inferiority.

For many Pacific Islanders and Asians, San Francisco, a colonial outpost first of Spain and then (after 1821) of Mexico, was the first point of contact with the continent. Hawaiians were among the first to arrive: as early as the 1830s, they were prominent fixtures of the West Coast carrying trade and constituted 10 percent of San Francisco's total population in 1847. The discovery of gold in the Sierra Nevada foothills in 1848 transformed the city, bringing not only gold seekers but also merchants and businesses providing goods and services to them.

Because Asians generally moved from rural to urban areas during this period of dependency, I focus on their history in cities. San Francisco, Seattle, New York, and

Chicago, the cities I discuss here, represent regions and illustrate the forces that affected Asian and Pacific America and the nation. Asian migration from the rural countryside to urban ghetto was in part a product of anti-Asian expulsions, but it also mirrored the industrialization and urbanization of the United States as a whole and a shift from an agricultural to a manufacturing economy. The rise of cities was largely the result of massive immigration from southern and eastern Europe in the late nineteenth century, the rapid growth of manufacturing and export trade, recruitment of African American laborers from the South to the North, and the emergence of monopolies and concentrations of capital.

New York City's population grew from one million in 1860 to over three million in 1900. Chicago grew from a city of one hundred thousand residents in 1860 to over one million by 1900. By 1920, for the first time in U.S. history, the urban population exceeded the rural.

For African Americans, moving from the rural South to the urban North offered new opportunities and an escape from poverty, Jim Crow segregation, and racial violence. They headed to Baltimore, Chicago, Detroit, New York City, and Philadelphia, where they encountered not the chance of upward mobility but instead menial, low-paying service jobs, persistent unemployment, and segregation that relegated them to another form of dependency. During the Great Migration from 1910 to 1930, Chicago's African American population increased from about 44,000 to 234,000 and Detroit's from 6,000 to 120,000. Cleveland's leaped eightfold. In a comparable migration, Mexicans moved from the rural Southwest to Midwest cities during the 1930s.

It was immigrants, not the U.S.-born, who populated the major cities. In 1890, Chicago's population was 87 percent foreign born and New York City's 80 percent. Those new immigrants arrived in unprecedented numbers, many from places not widely represented before, including Southern and Eastern Europe, Asia, Puerto Rico, and Mexico, bringing "foreign" tongues, religions, and cultures. They were largely working class and poor, seeking work as unskilled laborers in growing urban industries. Germans, Greeks, Hungarians, Italians, Poles, and Russians crowded into ethnic neighborhoods, where they ran and frequented restaurants, stores, theaters, schools, churches, synagogues, and social organizations. Mexicans, Puerto Ricans, Chinese, Japanese, South Asians, and Filipinos likewise established enclaves, usually in the poorest quarters of the city, around businesses such as boardinghouses and restaurants, and churches and temples, that catered to their needs.

CHINESE

Like Hawaiians, Chinese probably first arrived in San Francisco on European and U.S. vessels. Two Chinese men and one woman employed as servants by Charles Gillespie, a New York City trader, landed in San Francisco in 1848, just before the gold rush. The woman, Marie Seise, ran away from home in Canton, found work with a Portuguese family, and married a Portuguese sailor. After her husband abandoned her, she worked as a servant to an American family. In 1837, Seise accompanied her employers to Hawai'i. She returned to China six years later, when she joined the Gillespie family as their servant.

According to a study, there were fifty-four Chinese in San Francisco in 1849, mainly businessmen engaged in the import and export trade, and cooks and domestic servants. In 1850, their numbers grew to 787 Chinese men but only two Chinese women: one of the women was Ah Toy, the well-known sex worker and brothel owner. By the year's end, the total number of Chinese in the city had risen to 4,025. By 1860 that number had dropped to 2,719, including 587 women; it increased again to 12,022, including 1,410 women, in 1870, making San Francisco the largest Chinese enclave in America. In 1870, of Chinese women in San Francisco's Chinatown, the vast majority (1,132) were sex workers, and 18 operated brothels. The second largest employment category for Chinese women was the domestic sphere: 137 were homemakers and 68 domestic servants. Those in other trades included 35 in sewing and shoemaking, 6 actresses, and 3 boardinghouse operators.

San Francisco's Chinatown grew quickly. Centered on Sacramento Street, called "Chinese Street" by Chinatown's residents, in the mid-1850s it boasted thirty-three general merchandise stores. These were stocked with a variety of foods, such as tea, rice, dried fish and shrimp, seaweed, bamboo shoots, and mushrooms; they also sold pots and cooking implements. Fifteen apothecaries offered balms for tired and bruised bodies; five restaurants served familiar dishes. In addition, there were five butchers, five barbers, and five herbalists; three tailors, three boardinghouses, and three lumber yards; two bakers and two silversmiths; and one wood engraver.

To protect their property and rights in the face of anti-Chinese animus, Chinatown's businessmen met on December 1849 at the Canton Restaurant on Jackson Street to hire a white attorney to serve as a "counselor and adviser, to whom we may all appeal, with confidence, for wholesome instruction and advice, in the event of any unforeseen difficulties arising."[1] Because segregation extended its reach into the laws and judicial system, white attorneys were necessary to defend Chinese rights and prosecute crimes committed by whites against Chinese.

In addition to the state's foreign miners tax, which sought to limit and profit from Chinese labor, the city of San Francisco passed a series of restrictive ordinances that stifled Chinatown's economic life. From 1870 to 1873, a city ordinance directed at Chinese boardinghouses required rented rooms to have at least five hundred cubic feet of air per person, and an 1870 ordinance prohibited using poles to carry bundles, in the Chinese fashion, on city sidewalks. A laundry ordinance passed in 1873 taxed laundries for using horse-drawn vehicles and Chinese laundries for not employing horse-drawn vehicles. A year later, a court voided that Chinese laundry tax, but the city enacted it again in 1876 (and another court again nullified it). The city's laws regulating Chinese businesses showed a clear intention to limit Chinese self-determination and instill economic dependency.

A similar pattern followed Chinese initiatives in the urban trades. Cigar making in San Francisco grew to become a million-dollar industry during the U.S. Civil War, and by 1868 California surpassed Massachusetts as the fourth largest producer of cigars. Initially in 1859, white owners hired and taught Chinese workers to wrap cigars, and seven years later, Chinese owned about half of San Francisco's cigar factories. Chinese constituted 450 of the 500 cigar workers in the city in 1867, and 5,500 of 6,500 in 1876. Despite disguising their identities with Spanish names like Ramirez & Co., Chinese cigar manufacturers became the target of the white Cigar-Makers Union, which organized a campaign to boycott their products. By the late nineteenth century, Chinese-made cigars were a thing of the past.

The 1870s and 1880s were notable for anti-Chinese violence that, together with declining employment, drove Chinese from rural counties into urban Chinatowns. According to the U.S. Census, which probably undercounted Chinese, San Francisco's Chinatown in 1880 nearly doubled in size from the previous decade, to 21,475 residents, or over 20 percent of all the Chinese in the United States. The number grew to 25,833 in 1890, or 24 percent of the U.S. Chinese population. Although those totals and percentages decreased thereafter to 13,954 in 1900, 10,582 in 1910, and 7,744 in 1920, they increased dramatically in 1930 to 16,303 and in 1940 to 17,782, or 23 percent of all Chinese in the United States. Because of its centrality to their lives, many of the early West Coast Chinese called San Francisco the "First City."

San Francisco was not only a place of settlement but also a gateway for migrants to inland California (the Chinese "Gold Mountain") and other parts of the United States. The city was also their link with China: San Francisco was the departure point for the China traders and passenger steamers that conveyed goods, people, and ideas back to China. Shipping lines like the United States' Pacific Mail Steamship Company, the Canadian Pacific Steamship Company, and Japan's Tōyō Kisen Kaisha all maintained regular service between San Francisco and destinations in Asia and China, promising passengers delicious meals, clean rooms, and sometimes even a lounge for opium smoking.

Beginning with the 1875 Page Act, various U.S. immigration laws prohibited or limited entry to specific classes of migrants, particularly Asians. The acts necessitated a bureaucracy to detain, process, and allow or deny entry to migrants. After 1882, San Francisco began detaining Chinese migrants in a facility called the "shed," a two-story warehouse at Pier 40 on the waterfront. A missionary, Ira Condit, described conditions for Chinese migrants in the shed in 1900. On their arrival, he noted, "merchants, laborers, are all alike penned up, like a flock of sheep, in a wharf-shed, for many days, and often weeks, at their own expense, and are denied all communication with their own people, while the investigation of their cases moves its slow length along. The right of bail is denied. A man is imprisoned as a criminal who has committed no crime, but has merely failed to find a white man to prove his right to be here."[2]

Conditions in the shed were actually far worse than what Condit witnessed. Built to hold two hundred people, it often held twice that number, men on the ground floor and women on the second. The shed was located next to the outflow of the city sewer into San Francisco Bay. The smell was unbearable, and conditions inside were unsanitary. Chinese called their quarters an "iron cage" and "Chinese jail," and some of their white keepers called it a "fire trap" and "disgraceful." Detainees fell ill, several committed suicide, and in 1902 inmates threatened to riot and "tear the shed apart," in the words of the protest leader, Yuen Wing Loy. In 1908, thirty-two escaped.[3] The commissioner general of immigration appealed for a better facility, and in 1904 Congress allocated funds for an immigration station on Angel Island.

From 1910 to 1940, over a million people entered or departed the United States through the port of San Francisco, and about half of them passed through Angel Island Immigration Station. Although designed primarily for the Chinese (some 100,000 of them), during those years Angel Island's detention cells also held 85,000 Japanese, 8,000 South Asians, 1,000 Koreans, and 1,000 Filipinos. The island in addition held 8,000 Russians and Jews and 400 Mexicans, along with Asians from Formosa, Indonesia, and Singapore; Pacific Islanders from Borneo, Fiji, Samoa, and Tahiti; and Central Americans from El Salvador, Guatemala, and Honduras.

It took a natural disaster, the San Francisco earthquake and fire of April 1906, to open a window of opportunity for Chinese migrants. The fire destroyed most of the city's archives, including immigration and birth records, allowing migrants to claim U.S. birth and with it citizenship, as guaranteed by the Fourteenth Amendment. Citizens had the right to move freely between the United States and Asia, even under exclusion laws, and could return with or receive their children born abroad. Some used this opportunity to bring the children of relatives into the United States, or to profit from bringing in children from other families. These fictive offspring were known as "paper sons."

One San Francisco Chinatown resident explained: "My father came in as a laborer. But the 1906 earthquake came along and destroyed all those immigration things. So that was a big chance for a lot of Chinese. They forged themselves certificates saying that they were born in this country, and when the time came, they could go back to China and bring back four or five sons, just like that! They might make a little money off it, not much, but the main thing was to bring a son or nephew or a cousin in."[4]

Immigration officials knew of the practice, and thus Angel Island became a place of interrogation. White officials and Chinese translators and informants grilled prospective migrants about their nativity and kinship claims. Transcripts from Hoy Kun Fong's 1918 session illustrate the proceedings.

Q: Which direction does the front of your house face?

A: Face west.

Q: Your alleged father has indicated that his house in How Chong Village faces east. How do you explain that?

A: I know the sun rises in the front of our house and sets in the back of our house. My mother told me that our house and also the How Chong Village faces west.

Q: Cannot you figure this matter out for yourself?

A: I really don't know directions. . . .

Q: How many rooms in all are there on the ground floor of your house?

A: Three. . . . I mean there is a parlor, two bedrooms and a kitchen. There are five rooms in all downstairs. The two bedrooms are together, side by side, and are between the parlor and kitchen.

Q: Do you wish us to understand you would forget how many bedrooms are in a house where you claim to have lived seventeen years?

A: Yes, I forgot about it.

Q: Did you visit the Sar Kai Market with your father when he was last in China?

A: No.

Q: Why not, if you really are his son?[5]

The setting and tenor of the proceedings could easily intimidate migrants, whose entire futures must have raced through their heads during the interrogation, and a few questions were intentionally designed to confuse and at times trap the claimants. In response, paper sons learned their putative family histories from coaches and studied crib sheets before arriving in San Francisco, and the station's Chinese cooks and workers smuggled answers to the island from the migrants' sponsors in the city. Still, over 4 percent of Chinese petitioners between 1911 and 1932 were rejected and returned to China. South Asians had the highest rejection rate, at over 25 percent. Between 1910 and 1924, 76 percent of rejected Chinese migrants hired attorneys, and overall they won 39 percent of those cases.

Carved into Angel Island's barracks walls are the voices of some of those Chinese migrants. Their choice of inscriptions was both popular and profound, drawing on folk songs and poetic traditions.

In the quiet of night, I heard, faintly, the whistling of wind.
The forms and shadows saddened me; upon seeing the landscape, I composed
    a poem.
The floating clouds, the fog, darken the sky.
The moon shines faintly as the insects chirp.
Grief and bitterness entwined are heaven sent.
The sad person sits alone, leaning by a window.

America has power, but not justice.
In prison, we were victimized as if we were guilty.
Given no opportunity to explain, it was really brutal.
I bow my head in reflection but there is nothing I can do.

Imprisoned in the wooden building day after day,
My freedom withheld; how can I bear to talk about it?

FIGURE 44
State surveillance for entry into the nation. Angel Island, 1917. Courtesy of National Archives.

I look to see who is happy but they only sit quietly.
I am anxious and depressed and cannot fall asleep.
The days are long and the bottle constantly empty; my sad mood, even so, is not
    dispelled.
Nights are long and the pillow cold; who can pity my loneliness?
After experiencing such loneliness and sorrow,
Why not just return home and learn to plow the fields?[6]

San Francisco's Chinese laborers took the opportunities that were open to them. Domestic work, an undesirable niche for whites, employed Chinese men as cooks, servants, and gardeners to cater to the city's wealthy. Their entry into laundry services was an innovation driven by the demand from the huge influx of men connected with mining. When the first Chinese laundry opened in 1850, whites no longer needed to wait several months to have their clothes cleaned in Hawai'i or Canton, China, and the costs were far lower. By 1870, most of the city's some two thousand laundrymen were Chinese, and they owned about three hundred laundries.

Chinese laundries and laundrymen were scattered throughout San Francisco, but most Chinese businesses and residents were in Chinatown. By 1882, there were nearly one thousand Chinese establishments in Chinatown, with over 190 on Dupont Street, the center of Chinese economic activities in the city for many years. The business class formed Chinatown's elite, ruling through the Chinese Consolidated Benevolent Association (CCBA) or Chinese Six Companies, comprising six district-association members from the same region in China. The district associations were composed of family associations or individuals with the same surname.

The Six Companies represented China's imperial Manchu government in the United States and spoke for the Chinese in their dealings with whites. The organization kept census records, started a Chinese-language school, provided medical care for Chinese when the city's segregated medical facilities denied them treatment, and hired legal counsel to challenge anti-Chinese legislation. The Six Companies also exerted its authority over migrants, who were often indebted to merchants for loans to pay for their passage to the United States. That credit-ticket practice was closely regulated to ensure that the advances were repaid. In Chinatown and during certain periods, the only challenge to the Six Companies' dominance came from the tongs, or secret societies.

In 1905, intellectuals, merchants, politicians and high-ranking officials, women's rights activists, and students throughout China joined in a boycott of U.S.-produced goods to protest the pending renewal of the 1894 Sino-American treaty, which endorsed the exclusion of Chinese laborers and acknowledged the United States' right to deny naturalization to Chinese migrants. The main target of the protests was white racism in the United States, exemplified in a number of widely reported incidents. In October 1902, for example, police and immigration agents raided Boston's Chinatown and arrested 234 Chinese, merchants and laborers alike. Chinatown was alleged to be a haven for illegal immigrants and a site of pollution involving race, gender, sexuality, and vice. Fifty of those arrested were deported as illegals, and about 150 Chinese fled Boston. One of the fifty deported, Xiawei Feng, went to the Philippines. On returning to China, he wrote a book denouncing U.S. treatment of Chinese. Feng later committed suicide to become a martyr for the 1905 boycott.

Other provocations included the beating of the Chinese diplomat Jinyong Tan by two San Francisco policemen in September 1903. To humiliate Tan, the police tied him to a lightpole with his queue, which was a sign of loyalty to the Manchu government, and charged him with assaulting a police officer, despite his diplomatic credentials. Rather than face trial, Tan committed suicide. About a year later, a Chinese delegation en route to the 1904 Louisiana Purchase Exposition in St. Louis was detained and interrogated for possible immigration violations, and federal officials made certain its members left the country. The insult was reported widely in China, and Qichao Liang published a popular book exposing U.S. treatment of Chinese "as if they were criminals," which was "an insult to our nation's dignity."[7]

The 1905 boycott departed from earlier antiforeign movements in China in that it was an aspect of modern nationalism. Ultimately, it led to the overthrow of the Manchu government. It also linked the fate of the nation with that of its migrants overseas. "China for the Chinese" and the recuperation of the people's dignity were at stake. As a poster in Canton read: "The boycott movement concerns the life or death of our people's spirit."[8] In the United States, the boycott heightened Chinese national consciousness and commitment to China's sovereignty. Migrants came to believe that China's freedom was vital for Chinese liberties in the United States.

Chinatown's women were involved in the movement to secure China's national integrity and Chinese civil rights in the United States. As early as 1885, one of Chinatown's residents, Mary Tape, had protested against school segregation. Reared in a Shanghai orphanage, Tape arrived in San Francisco at the age of eleven under the auspices of missionaries. She married the Chinese migrant Joseph Tape, a labor contractor and interpreter, and had a daughter, Mamie Tape. When eight-year-old Mamie was denied entry into the city's public school, the Tapes sued the school superintendent and board. In 1885, a superior court judge ruled that "to deny a child, born of Chinese parents in this State, entrance to the public schools would be a violation of the law of the State and the Constitution of the United States."[9] The Fourteenth Amendment, the judge noted, secured equal protection for all persons.

Following the logic of "separate but equal" facilities affirmed in the *Plessy v. Ferguson* decision, San Francisco's school board urged the state legislature to provide separate schools for Chinese and, later, Japanese children. Public schools, the law stated, had the right to bar "children of filthy or vicious habits, or children suffering from contagious or infectious diseases" and, the 1885 revision added, "to establish separate schools for children of Mongolian or Chinese descent."[10] For many whites, filth and disease were synonymous with Asians.

Mary Tape rejected the contention that separate was equal. In a letter to the school board dated April 8, 1885, she declared, "Mamie Tape will never attend any of the Chinese Schools of your making! Never!!!" She condemned the racism that kept her daughter from the public schools, declaring racial segregation unjust and un-American, and promised she would work to expose the board's racist conduct. She concluded, "I guess she [Mamie) is more of a[n] American than a good many of you that is going to prewent [*sic*] her [from] being Educated."[11]

As many anti-Asianists had feared, the second generation, enabled by the Fourteenth Amendment, became citizens with claims on the promise of America. In 1895, San Francisco's second generation formed the Native Sons of the Golden State, which in 1915 became the Chinese American Citizens Alliance, to ensure their civil rights as citizens and to dismantle the tools of dependency, such as segregation in the workplace and labor exploitation. The alliance was also active in voter registration drives and in mobilizing voters to support candidates and issues favorable to the Chinese. This increased assertiveness of the second generation was reinforced by their numbers, which, according to the U.S. Census, increased from 18,532 in 1920 to 40,262 in 1940.

Chinatown's business elite tried to discourage unions such as the League of Labor, founded in 1919 to demand workers' rights. In 1938, women employed by the

FIGURE 45

Chinese Ladies Garment Workers Union on strike at the National Dollar Store, 1938. Courtesy of People's World and Labor Archives and Research Center, San Francisco State University.

Chinese-owned National Dollar Stores in Chinatown's largest sewing factory organized Local 341 of the International Ladies' Garment Workers' Union, and 108 of them struck for higher wages of fourteen dollars per week, a forty-hour work week, overtime pay, and health, sanitation, and fire regulations in the factory. For thirteen weeks the women picketed, while the Chinese Six Companies and most of the businesses opposed them. The strikers returned to work only after having achieved their major demands.

The National Dollar Stores strike was at the time the longest in San Francisco's Chinatown, and it led to improvements for other workers, such as those in restaurants, who won time off and shorter working hours. Having shown their mettle, Chinese workers were able to find jobs outside Chinatown in formerly whites-only industries. As one of the strikers, Sue Ko Lee, remarked: "In my opinion, the strike was the best thing that ever happened. It changed our lives. We overcame bigotry, didn't we?"[12]

During the Great Depression, Chinese entrepreneurs brought a new face to Chinatown, stimulating the economy by cashing in on Orientalism and white men's desires for the erotic exotic. By day, the Chinatown economy was operated mostly by and for its Chinese residents. At night, however, the lights went up and the bars, clubs, and restaurants catering to whites transformed Chinatown into fleshpots. Perhaps the most successful entrepreneur was Charlie Low, a Nevada native, whose Forbidden City served American drink and food and offered entertainment that was at once familiar—crooners and showgirls— but also foreign in that it exhibited Asian women's bodies. Likewise, Americanized Chinese cuisine catered to non-Chinese tastes and appetites while claiming exotic, Chinese ingredients and qualities. As Chinatown's Shanghai Café printed on its menu, "Please visit our café, it is equal to a trip to China."[13]

Japan's aggressions in China stirred Chinese America from Honolulu to New York City. Residents of San Francisco's Chinatown rallied to support China's war effort by organizing a boycott of Japanese goods and protesting Japan's 1915 Twenty-One Demands, which expanded Japan's role in China and eroded the nation's sovereignty. From the 1920s through the 1940s, Chinatown's residents and businesses held numerous fund-raising drives to support the nationalist cause. Some companies ordered their employees to contribute to the war effort, and the Association to Save China imposed fines on those who failed to meet their monthly quotas.

Chinatown's businesses had an economic as well as a patriotic motive to support China, because much of their import and export trade depended on China's markets and supplies. The Bowl of Rice movement, begun in the late 1930s, raised money to alleviate the plight of China's war refugees. Mobilizing both Chinese and whites, the movement was inspired by the story of a Chinese general, Xin Han, a founder of the Western Han Dynasty (206 B.C.-A.D. 220), who was saved by a bowl of rice given to him by a woman stranger, without any expectation of repayment.

JAPANESE

The U.S. "opening" of Japan and the Meiji restoration that followed brought to San Francisco the Wakamatsu tea and silk colonists of 1869 and later student laborers. San Francisco became a transit stop for Japanese migrant laborers dispatched by labor contractors for railroad and agricultural work in the interior. Most of the laborers came from Hawai'i, and that influx in part prompted President Theodore Roosevelt's 1907 executive order stopping that flow.

An additional reason for Roosevelt's order was the San Francisco school board incident of the previous year. Like the Chinese, Japanese children were required to attend the city's Oriental school and were barred from the public schools. At the time, there were ninety-three Japanese students in twenty-three of the city's public schools. Twenty-five of them were U.S. citizens by birth. But to the school board it was their race, not their citizenship, that mattered. Following a protest from Japan, the president sought a political settlement that involved a termination of Japanese labor migration, which he effectively achieved with his executive order and the 1908 Gentlemen's Agreement.

The U.S. Census counted 9,598 Japanese men and 553 women in California in 1900. With the recruitment of migrant laborers, this number rose dramatically by 1910. The pattern changed again by 1920 as picture brides led to an influx of women. Largely as the result of births, the percentage of women increased again in 1930 and 1940 (see table 3).

Following a San Francisco Board of Health announcement in March 1900 that bubonic plague had been found in Chinatown, anti-Asian rhetoric increased. In response, Japanese residents formed the Japanese Deliberative Council of America "to expand the

TABLE 3. Japanese population in California, 1900–1940

	Men	Women	Total	Women as percentage of total
1900	9,598	553	10,151	5
1910	37,356	6,240	43,596	14
1920	45,414	26,538	71,952	37
1930	56,440	41,016	97,456	42
1940	52,550	41,167	93,717	44

rights of Imperial subjects in America and to maintain the Japanese national image."[14] In 1908, at the request of Japan's consul general in San Francisco, the council dissolved and re-formed as the Japanese Association of America. The association and its many local chapters would channel Japan's controls over its migrants.

Like those of the Chinese Six Companies, the Japanese Association's leaders were nearly all businessmen. The association registered marriages, divorces, and births and, most important, issued certificates as specified by the Gentlemen's Agreement for travel outside the United States and for permission to bring wives and family members into the United States. The association also tended to the interests of Japanese migrants by promoting Americanization, which it saw as a way to deflect anti-Japanese hostility. By 1919, the Japanese Association had developed an independent stance. For example, it opposed Japan's decision to stop issuing passports to picture brides, a practice deemed essential for the welfare of Japanese in America.

For the Japanese, San Francisco served primarily as a hub for dispersal to jobs in rural areas. Although many of the Japanese work-study students in the city, like the Chinese, found employment as cooks, servants, and gardeners, most Japanese migrants went into agricultural work in California's rural counties. Thus Los Angeles became the center of Japanese America by 1910. The Japanese population in Los Angeles County grew from about 1,000 in 1900 to nearly 9,000 in 1910, 20,000 in 1920, and over 35,000 in 1930. There, Little Tokyo, like Chinatown, emerged as a segregated community but mainly represented an outgrowth of Japanese agricultural initiatives in southern California.

San Francisco's Nihonmachi, or Japantown, by contrast, remained small. The city's Japanese population totaled 1,781 in 1900, 4,518 in 1910, and just over 5,000 in 1940. At the same time, the city was a center for West Coast Japanese, with Japan's consul general and the Japanese Association based there. In 1903, the newly formed Japanese American Citizens League, a counterpart of the Chinese American Citizens Alliance, chose San Francisco as its headquarters.

San Francisco was a hub of anti-Japanese, anti-Asian agitation. The influential *San Francisco Chronicle* railed against the Japanese "menace" to white women, and the city was home to the Japanese and Korean Exclusion League (later renamed the Asiatic Exclu-

FIGURE 46
Japanese women arrive at Angel Island, ca. 1910. California State Parks.

sion League), which grew from San Francisco's building trades movement and festered anti-Asian sentiment up to World War II.

Some Japanese migrants became politically active. Sen Katayama, who later founded the Japanese Workers' Association in New York City, organized the Japanese Socialist Party, though it soon folded because of lack of interest. As one of the party's founders reflected: "Our minds had not progressed to the idea of starting a movement."[15] Before dissolving, however, party members met at San Francisco's Methodist Episcopal Church to discuss an antiwar campaign to end the conflict that pitted Japan against Russia over imperial ambitions in Manchuria and Korea. The Japanese socialist Shūsui Kōtoku arrived in San Francisco in 1905, hoping to make San Francisco a base of operations for Japanese socialists. Instead, after a six-month visit with U.S. socialist and labor leaders, he established the Social Revolutionary Party in Berkeley in 1906 to bring together Bay Area progressives regardless of race. One of the party's platform promised: "We shall eliminate national and racial prejudices and strive for true brotherhood and international peace."[16]

Despite those high ideals, individual migrants who experienced the world at street level met with bigotry and violence. "My first impression of San Francisco was bad," remembered Nisuke Mitsumori, who arrived in 1905. "There was a gang of scoundrels who came to treat the immigrants roughly as soon as they heard that some Japanese had docked. . . . There were a group of fifteen to twenty youngsters who shouted, 'Let's go! The Japs have come!'" They pelted the newcomers with crude racial epithets and horse dung. Even after months of working at the city's Japanese newspaper, the *Nichi Bei Times*, Mitsumori recalled, "I never went out at night, and even during the day I tried to avoid the streets where American youngsters might be. I felt very insecure, not economically but physically." So he headed south to Los Angeles and eventually to Pasadena.[17]

Largely because of white racism, Japanese migrants had to tend to their own needs. Kamechiyo Takahashi had heard that Japanese women in San Francisco required mid-wives, so she studied midwifery in Japan before leaving for California. After earning her license in 1917, she opened the Takahashi Clinic of Midwifery in San Francisco and soon had patients from as far away as San Jose, about fifty miles distant. Some mothers stayed at her clinic for two weeks. Takahashi also made house calls, and she was so busy that she fell ill in 1929. "Some of my patients were so poor that they couldn't afford electricity," Takahashi noted. "They used kerosene lamps instead. Being ignorant of sanitation, they didn't have any absorbent cotton, disinfectant, or ether. I couldn't believe this was actually happening in the United States."[18]

The second generation, unlike the issei, grew up in a divided world of home and white America. Atypical, for sure, but instructive nonetheless is the story of a Bay Area nisei whose father ran away from home at thirteen, went to sea as a cabin boy, and after nine years of sailing landed in San Francisco in 1900. In 1904, he joined the U.S. Navy, serving as a cook, and after that he worked as a fisherman, farm laborer, railroad section hand, and lumber mill worker before settling as a barber near a navy landing across the bay from San Francisco. There he received his picture bride, and they had eight children. The anonymous storyteller was their second child. born in 1917.[19]

The First World War brought prosperity to the family because the naval station teemed with sailors who were his father's prime customers. The family bought a small building to house both the shop and the family. The purchase required the help of a Japanese attorney in San Francisco. who put the title in the name of the oldest child because of California's alien land law, which prohibited aliens from owning property. The family lived in a neighborhood with Italians, Portuguese, Filipinos, and Mexicans. They ate Japanese food in good times and American food in bad. The father began drinking heavily and gambling and became abusive toward his wife and children.

When he was seven, this nisei went to school, but he could not understand the English language. His teacher accompanied him home to explain the language problem to his parents, who could not understand her either. His father, believing his son had misbehaved in school, accused his son of being stupid and his wife of spoiling the child. His outbursts in English, family members recalled, were shouted with contempt: "Japs, goddamn' Japs!—Japs, goddamn' Japs!" over and over again. He blamed his son for being a disgrace to Japanese, kicked him, hung him by his feet from the rafters, and beat him. His son later speculated that it was self-hatred, induced by white racism that made him feel unmanly, inferior, and inadequate, that prompted his father's anger.

Unable to endure the abuse, the narrator's mother took the children and fled to Nihonmachi in San Francisco, where she consulted with a Japanese divorce lawyer. The stigma of divorce and her husband's promise to reform his ways brought the family back together, but the mother, intent on saving her son, placed him in a home for abandoned children. It was no haven: the children slept on the ground at night and toiled in the fields by day. One child died while being held in solitary confinement. The police found that he had been abused and deprived of food and water. The authorities closed the home, and the nisei returned to his family.

Again to protect her son, the mother put him in another home for abandoned children, orphans, and delinquents. The nisei remembered: "On a lovely California spring day in 1925, as I was going on eight, I found myself in a red touring car and on the way somewhere. It was my first automobile ride, and I would have enjoyed it were it not for my inability to keep tears from my eyes. I sat alone in the back seat with no idea where I was going, and terribly lonely." When he arrived at "the Home," as the children called it, he found "several Negroes, a couple of Indians, an Egyptian, numerous Mexicans, and many orphans with nothing known about their origin," and the rest whites.[20] He was the sole Japanese.

The nisei attended the institution's school, learned English, and, having completed his elementary education, attended the local high school, which had a few Chinese and a South Asian. He graduated in 1934, worked to pay off his debts, and left for San Francisco. In the city, a white barber refused to cut "Jap" hair and threw him out despite his pleas. "I was born in this country, right here in California, and that made me an American. . . . I walked out, hurt and bewildered. Goddammit, I *was* an American, *not* a 'Jap.'"[21] More confusion ensued when the nisei visited Nihonmachi, where he felt a stranger because he was unable to read the Japanese signs or speak with the town's residents.

Though unable to land a job because of racism, the nisei stubbornly tried to ignore it because "damnit, I *was* an American! If not, *what* was I? I was no 'Jap'! This *was* my country. I *did* belong!"[22] He resented his sister's advice that he accept positions commonly held by Japanese, like houseboy, valet, or servant. He wanted to work in an office like other Americans, but poverty and necessity required him to take a job as a houseboy to wealthy whites. In 1935 he entered college. As a servant, the nisei felt contempt for his employers and work, and in college he disliked his fellow Asians, mainly Chinese and Japanese. He hated both pursuits equally, and he described himself as a "marginal man."

During his junior year in college, he recognized that he was not only an American but also a Japanese. "At first I felt queer about this," he confessed. "Then I said to myself: after all, my background *was* Japanese! Why pretend it wasn't? Why try to evade it and go around waiting for and dodging blows, feeling guilty as though I had a secret shame and sorrow; insisting I was an American, which of course I was anyhow, but by this insistence denying to others and myself that I was also of Japanese parentage—a pretty obvious fact? For the first time I saw myself."[23] His discovery led him to read and immerse himself in the study of Japanese in the United States and things Japanese, leaving him feeling free.

His sister remained a domestic servant. One brother, after finishing high school, supported the Chinese nationalist cause in the war against Japan and became a migrant laborer, working with Mexicans, Filipinos, and South Asians from Santa Clara, not far from San Francisco, to El Centro, in the Imperial Valley near the Mexican border. Another brother spoke fluent Japanese. While in high school he attended race-relations conferences, and as a student leader he insisted that Americanism required the racial and religious equality of all groups. Some of his fellow students branded him a communist.

All the while, the narrator continued, his mother was "a silent, helpless bystander in the struggle, with her sympathy largely on the children's side," and she "adapted herself as well as she could." Finally, "during my last two years in college," the nisei reflected, "I moved toward the pleasant realization that, when all is said and done, we [his family] were more or less all right; at least as good as could be expected. Our future was not rosy, but neither was it hopeless."[24]

The future for Asians and Pacific Islanders was, nonetheless, dimmed by dependency. The various alien land laws passed during the first half of the twentieth century in several western states illustrate efforts to curb nonwhite upward mobility. In California, the area of land cultivated by Japanese nearly tripled between 1909 and 1919, and although that expanse still represented only 1 percent of the state's agricultural land, Japanese farms generated $67 million, or about 10 percent of the state's total crop value.

In 1913, California passed its first alien land law, which denied "aliens ineligible to citizenship" the right to own land and restricted land leases to three years. Like earlier anti-Chinese statutes, although apparently race neutral, in practice the law discriminated against Asians because they were the only group that fell into the category of "aliens ineligible to citizenship." California's attorney general, the architect of the 1913 law, described the act as seeking "to limit the numbers who will come by limiting the opportunities for their activity here when they arrive."[25] Despite the law, Japanese-owned land expanded from 16,450 acres owned in 1909 to 74,769 acres in 1919, and land leased or sharecropped by Japanese increased from 139,234 acres in 1909 to 383,387 acres in 1919.

A 1920 proposition sought to plug the loopholes that allowed those increases. The campaign was led by white supremacist organizations like the Native Sons of the Golden West (and its affiliate, the Native Daughters), which was formed to preserve California "as it has always been and God Himself intended it shall always be—the White Man's Paradise."[26] In Santa Clara County, where the measure passed in a landslide, its representative declared: "These yellow peoples . . . have nothing in common with the people of this country. . . . Should they be free to come to the Pacific shores without restrictions numerically, it would only be a few years when the Americanism now in California would be completely submerged and Japanese ideals and practices would dominate the entire state. Let these people acquire vast tracts of land, which they are doing in spite of the Alien Land Law, and ambitious white Americans will be driven from their land."[27] The local newspaper added that the situation in Hawai'i, where "the yellow races" "overrun" the white population, was a lesson for Californians.

The 1920 law prohibited the transfer or lease of land to Japanese nationals. It also made illegal the formation of corporations in which Japanese held a majority of the stock and the practice of noncitizens' acting as guardians for citizens in matters of land tenure. Some of the law's proponents wanted more. The Japanese Exclusion League, for instance, proposed to alter the U.S. Constitution's Fourteenth Amendment to deny citizenship to those born in the United States to one or both parents of a race "ineligible to citizenship."

Exclusion was not the sole object of supporters of the alien land laws. There were profits to be reaped under a regime of dependency that created a vulnerable and hence exploitable people. When legal loopholes to Japanese land ownership were closed (such as the creation of farm corporations and the practice of registering property under the names of minor children who were citizens), verbal and unconventional agreements emerged that only heightened the exploitation of Japanese farmers.

The alien land laws were not consistently enforced because it was not always in the interests of white farmers and landowners to uphold them. For example, Japanese tenants in six agricultural counties paid in 1920 an average rent of $24.75 per acre, while whites paid $10.91 per acre; local law-enforcement officials had little interest in interfering with these lucrative arrangements. Additionally, Japanese tenants were forced to pay higher prices and accept unfavorable terms for short-term leasing arrangements. Under "quasi-leasing," for instance, the Japanese farmer agreed to pay a cash rent to the landowner, while the latter retained absolute control over the management and sale of the crops.

J. J. O'Brien, a white landholder in Santa Clara County, had thirty-five Japanese farm families on his property. Each tenant paid forty dollars per acre cash rent to O'Brien, plus an under-the-table commission of 5 percent of their gross sales. The commission was charged for the apparent risk O'Brien took for renting land to the Japanese. Ordinarily, sharecroppers sold their produce and split the earnings with the landowner. For his Japanese sharecroppers, however, O'Brien sold the crops, kept about 50 percent of the proceeds, and charged them a 5 to 7 percent commission on the sales. Under the alien land laws, thus, O'Brien managed a fictional farm with Japanese workers, not tenants, and grossly exploited them. To preserve his interests, O'Brien instituted a suit against California's attorney general to enjoin him from enforcing the terms of the 1920 Alien Land Law.

O'Brien was not alone in using these methods of exploitation. Shoji Takeda told how his father, Tomiju, produced "a beautiful crop, but the owner would receive the total compensation from the buyer and without his knowledge the owner would spend all of the money." Once, the landowner gave his father a cow instead of his share of the income.[28] Largely because of the land laws and their deployment by white landowners, the acreage of Japanese-operated farms decreased to 191,427 in 1930, less than half the area of a decade earlier. The upward mobility of Japanese was thereby restricted, and farming, their main means of livelihood, became an instrument for ensuring their dependency.

Before 1904, there were fifty Koreans living in San Francisco. Between 1904 and 1907, the year that Roosevelt's executive order stemmed migration from Hawai'i, about one thousand Koreans arrived. There, organizations such as Cha'ng-ho Ahn's Chin'mok-hoe and later the Kongnip Hyop-hoe greeted the migrants and found work for them in Chinese businesses and white farms. The Korean Women's Society was formed in 1908 to provide educational and social services to Korean women and children. Yet the city's anti-Asianism and segregation laws and practices limited Korean residential, educational, and occupational mobility, as was the case for Chinese and Japanese before them.

San Francisco was home to Korean mutual aid societies: a Korean-language newspaper, the *Shinhan Min-po* (New Korea), and the Korean National Association (KNA), which made the city its headquarters beginning in 1909. The association's purposes were to provide for the welfare of Koreans in the United States, promote Korean educational and economic activities, advocate equality and justice for Koreans in the United States, and work for the restoration of Korea's independence. Unlike the corresponding Japanese and Chinese organizations, it was led by intellectuals and political refugees, not businessmen. The KNA's had chapters in the Korean diaspora from Hawai'i to Siberia and Manchuria.

Nationalism was dominant among Koreans in the United States, and San Francisco was a major site for the independence struggle. In 1908, Durham Stevens, a U.S. citizen employed by the Japanese government, told a *San Francisco Chronicle* reporter that Japan's control over Korea was good for the Korean people. The statement outraged Koreans, and two of the city's nationalist associations sent four members to demand an apology from Stevens. At his San Francisco hotel, when Stevens refused to retract his statement, the delegates jumped and beat him. The following morning, in the company of Japan's consul, Stevens was about to board a ferry when In-whan Chang fatally shot him. Chang was a member of the Taedong Poguk-hoe (the Great Unity Fatherland Protection Society), one of the organizations that had tried to get Stevens to apologize. For Chang's legal defense, his Korean supporters raised $7,390 in donations from the U.S. continent, Hawai'i, Mexico, China, and Japan. The court, however, convicted Chang of second-degree murder.

In 1913, Cha'ng-ho Ahn established the Hung Sa Dan (Young Korean Academy) in San Francisco. Believing that the fight for national independence was a long-term struggle because of internal divisions within Korea's ruling class and Japan's hegemony over the peninsula, Ahn's academy trained future leaders of the freedom movement by stressing four virtues: truth seeking, deeds, loyalty, and courage. Students, intellectuals, and professionals adopted Ahn's teachings, and many became prominent leaders in the community and KNA.

Although most Koreans left San Francisco for California's rural areas, some stayed to work as waiters, janitors, and servants and to sell ginseng in Chinatown as street peddlers. Korean fishermen worked the Pacific from San Francisco to Seattle and Alaska during the fishing season. In 1910, Yong-man Choi opened the Korean Trading Com-

FIGURE 47

Meeting of the Hung Sa Dan in Los Angeles, 1916. Photo in front of the Ahn residence on Temple Street. Courtesy of Korean American Digital Archive, University of Southern California Libraries.

pany in San Francisco, but he had to close it soon thereafter, when Japan annexed Korea and stopped the Korean import/export trade. Because there were so few Koreans in the city, many of them lived and worked in Chinatown. Both Ahn's Chin'mok-hoe and Kong-nip Hyop-hoe were located there.

A second-generation Korean migrant, Dora Yum Kim, remembered growing up in Chinatown.[29] Her father, Man Suk Yum, arrived in San Francisco in 1904 and found work on the Union Pacific Railroad. Her mother, Hang Shin Kim, arrived as a picture bride and married at the Korean Methodist Church on Oak Street in 1920. At the time, her father was thirty-seven years old and her mother twenty-two. Her parents farmed in Dinuba, California. Kim was born in Manteca as the couple made their way north, and she came of age in San Francisco during the 1920s.

"I grew up with discrimination," Kim recalled. "Discrimination affected every aspect of my life. You're not born with it. It's a learned thing. But when you grow up with it, it's just part of life." Living in Chinatown, she said, seemed normal because "we just couldn't live anywhere else." Chinatown's borders were North Beach, where the Italians lived; Kearny and Bush Streets, which delineated the edge of the business district; and Powell Street, which marked the wealthy white neighborhood of Nob Hill. Asians had to stay within those limits. "Most of my earliest memories are about living in Chinatown. We weren't exactly immersed in the Korean community because there were so few Koreans around us." Instead, Kim celebrated Chinese festivals and associated with Chinese friends in school. "We didn't think about the world beyond Chinatown because it just wasn't accessible to us."[30]

During the 1920s, Kim remembered, there were no more than a hundred Koreans in San Francisco. Her father opened a cigar store in Chinatown, and the family lived in an alley off Jackson Street, between Grant and Stockton Streets. Their home had a gas burner but no refrigerator. In 1923, her father and a partner opened a restaurant next to his cigar store, with a pool hall at the back of the restaurant. Other Koreans opened three restaurants, two cleaning shops, two barbershops, a bathhouse, and a shoe repair store in Chinatown in the 1920s. The lone church, founded in 1906 and located on Powell Street during the 1920s, was the center of Korean activity.

The family's restaurant, Lee's Lunch, was a hangout for bachelor men—Filipinos, Chinese, Japanese, and a few Koreans. Her mother felt compassion for them and treated them as her sons. She worked sixteen-hour days waiting tables, washing dishes, and managing the restaurant. Kim and her brothers attended Chinatown schools. To learn about her budding Korean subjectivity, Kim had to ask her parents, and a few of the family's restaurant customers taught the children to read and write Korean. For a time, the children attended a Korean-language school at the church. Although her parents detested Japan and its colonization of Korea, the family had a Japanese physician, and Kim had a few close Japanese girlfriends, along with many Chinese.

After graduating from high school, Kim and a Japanese classmate enrolled at the University of California, Berkeley, in 1939. "There were very few Asians," she recalled, "and as an Asian girl I discovered that the white boys wouldn't speak to me. So I joined the Chinese Students' Club at International House."[31] As far as she knew, there were only two Korean women at Cal. Kim realized that she was fortunate to have attended the university, because under the Korean patriarchy, daughters were an extravagance. Midway through her university education, Kim dropped out and fell in love with a Korean man from Hawai'i, a customer at her family's restaurant.

World War II intervened, and "all the Japanese were shipped out, and we lost touch with a lot of childhood friends because of that. It was really bad. And because we were in Chinatown, we didn't know about it until they were already gone. It happened so quickly." Whites mistook Kim's father for a Japanese while venturing outside Chinatown, and he was nearly beaten. "After that," Kim recalled with a note of finality, "he never went out of Chinatown again until after the war."[32]

SOUTH ASIANS

South Asians, like Koreans, based their national-independence activities in San Francisco. The Ghadar Party spread its revolutionary message to the rural West Coast, where most

South Asians labored, as well as to the East Coast, Canada, and India. In California, the party that began as a South Asian collective came to reflect at least two streams of thought—the views of the students and intellectuals in the San Francisco Bay Area and those of the peasants and workers in the rural and farming districts. Those divergences apparently emerged from the class, regional, and religious divides within the first groups to arrive in California—the South Asian migrants who came from urban, middle-class, and Hindu backgrounds between 1903 and 1906 and those who came mainly from Punjab, with rural agricultural roots, from 1907 to 1910. The former were mobile, moving from the West to the East Coast, while the latter settled in farming communities in the West.

The Punjabis, who formed the vast majority of the South Asian migrants, were mainly unmarried Sikh men. Many migrated with other male relatives and fellow villagers. They were skilled agriculturalists; as migrant laborers, they also followed fellow Asian migrants into other employment open to them, such as work in the lumber mills and railroads of the Northwest and the orchards and fields of California's agricultural valleys, migrating north and south according to the seasons. By 1910, they were farming as far south as El Centro.

South Asians, like West Asians, occupied a precarious position within the U.S. racial formation. Some Europeans, like the Irish, came to be considered white after having been treated as racially inferior, and Mexicans, although of a "mixed" race and treated as colored peoples, were legally white by treaty. Asians, clearly, were neither white nor black, but as nonwhites they fell on the stigmatized side of the racialized binary.

South Asians, however, posed a particular challenge to the U.S. racial formation. Many Punjabi men married Mexican women who were legally white, although a few married African American women. Jim Crow toilets, restaurants, and barbershops denied service to South Asians. A Sikh in Marysville, California, told how a white man called out to him: "Come here, slave!" In many towns, real estate agents agreed not to sell property to "Hindus or Negroes," and the West's alien land laws included South Asians among those "aliens ineligible to citizenship." Still, at least sixty-eight South Asian migrants managed to acquire U.S. citizenship through naturalization in seventeen different states. Those contradictions were wrapped up in the case of a Punjabi man, Bhagat Singh Thind, who claimed but was denied whiteness and hence citizenship by the Supreme Court.

The legal context from which the *U.S. v. Bhagat Singh Thind* case arose was the tangled precedents of Armenians classified as Asians and later in 1909, as whites, and Syrians considered whites in 1909, 1910, and 1915 but nonwhites in 1913 and 1914. The 1909 ruling *In re Najour,* by a federal court in Georgia, involved the Syrian Costa George Najour. According to the judge's ruling, the term *free white person,* the criterion for naturalization eligibility in the 1790 Naturalization Act, referred to race, not skin color. Race, he ruled, was a scientific concept: since Syrians belonged to the Caucasian race, they were white. Thind's contention was in line with that precedent, pointing out that science

classified South Asians as Caucasians. Another context for the *Thind* case was the U.S. Supreme Court's decision in *Takao Ozawa v. U.S.* the previous year, in which the Japanese Takao Ozawa contended unsuccessfully that race was a matter of color and culture. Ozawa claimed that his skin was whiter than that of "the average Italian, Spaniard or Portuguese" and that he was thoroughly assimilated and a fervently patriotic American. He was thus white and eligible for citizenship. In rejecting Ozawa's arguments, the court relied on scientific opinion that denied skin color as a criterion of racial classification and held that *white* was synonymous with *Caucasian*.

A lower district court agreed with Thind in 1920, citing the reasoning of the *Najour* case, and granted him naturalization. On Thind's appeal, the Supreme Court took on the question: "Is a high caste Hindu of full Indian blood, born at Amrit Sar, Punjab, a white

FIGURE 49
Left: Bishan and Herminia Lozano Singh with children Lucy and Billy. Right: Karm and Francesca Singh with baby, ca. 1935. Courtesy of Karen Isaksen Leonard.

person?" Intersecting in that phrasing were race, geography, class, and religion, although Thind was not a Hindu but a Sikh. The court's decision vacated the notion of a Caucasian race, proposed by Johann Blumenbach in the late eighteenth century, and abandoned the hall of science for the precincts of the "common man" when it ruled: "What we now hold is that the words 'free white persons' are words of common speech, to be interpreted in accordance with the understanding of the common man, synonymous with the word 'Caucasian' only as that word is popularly understood." Moreover: "It may be true that the blond Scandinavian and the brown Hindu have a common ancestor in the dim reaches of antiquity, but the average man knows perfectly well that there are unmistakable and profound differences between them to-day." After all, the court pointed out, science also claims as Caucasian "some of the Polynesians, (that is the Maori, Tahitians, Samoans, Hawaiians and others)."[33] Americans, the court declared, would be "astonished" by that kinship.

South Asian challenges to segregation interrogated social categories and their borders. The *Thind* case destabilized normative ideas of race and citizenship. In the social sphere, as nonwhites, South Asian men's marriages to Mexican women, as whites, contested the social formation of race, gender, sexuality, and nation. Although such unions were theoretically subject to miscegenation laws, county clerks and local officials could exercise discretion in their enforcement. Most clerks, it seems, raised few barriers to marriages involving Mexican women and South Asian men because they considered both parties to be colored.

A study of California county records shows that of the 378 South Asian men's marriages between 1913 and 1949, the majority took place in southern California. Of these, 304 involved Mexican women, but they also included 48 whites, 15 African Americans, 9 South Asians, and 2 American Indians. It is possible that many of those marriages to whites involved urban, middle-class South Asians in cities like San Francisco and Los Angeles, whereas marriages to Mexicans involved Punjabi agricultural workers, mainly in the rural Imperial Valley. If that is the case, those South Asian divisions of class, region, and religion in marriage mirrored the politics of the decolonization movement, which was prominently led by urban Hindu intellectuals.

Antonia Alvarez married Sher Singh in 1916. The following year, Alvarez's sister, Anna Anita, married Sher's business partner, Gopal Singh. By 1919, two more Alvarez sisters and a niece had married Punjabis. According to one estimate, Punjabi-Mexican families averaged six children, although infant mortality was high. The children faced white racism in restaurants, swimming pools, theaters, and buses and trains well into the 1950s. In resistance, the families formed ties through both Mexican and Punjabi traditions, such as the Catholic tradition of godparents and the social networks centered on the Sikh temples that were central to the lives and global dispersion of Sikhs.

FILIPINOS

Filipinos posed another troubling challenge to segregation because, designated as "nationals" until 1934, they possessed a freedom of movement that was denied to other Asians. In addition, like West and South Asians, Filipinos straddled the U.S. racial fault line. They were Asians or Mongolians in the commonsense view, while they were classified as Malays under Blumenbach's scientific scheme.

As nationals and Malays, Filipinos were able to escape some of the strictures of anti-Asian laws and practices. As in the case of West and South Asians, courts vacillated over their racial classification. Some decisions ruled that Filipinos were Asians because "the Malay is a Mongolian," while others declared that Malays were distinct from Mongolians. The application of the state's miscegenation laws illustrated the disruption Filipinos posed to the domestic tranquility.

In 1931, a Los Angeles County clerk denied a marriage license to Salvador Roldan, a Filipino, and Marjorie Rogers, a white American. A few years earlier, such petitions would have been routinely granted at about the same rate as marriages between American Indians and Mexicans with whites. But the Great Depression and its dislocations

FIGURE 50

Racial, gender, and sexual anxieties on display at the beach. From Jesse Quinsaat, ed., *Letters in Exile: An Introductory Reader on the History of Pilipinos in America* (Los Angeles: UCLA Asian American Studies Center, 1976).

accentuated the rise of nativism and hatred, and Asian and Mexican migrant laborers were easy targets. According to Roldan, when he asked for a marriage license form, the county clerk asked him "whether I was a Filipino and . . . also whether I was white, or yellow, or brown, or red." When he replied he was Filipino, the clerk questioned him about his prospective bride, "whether she was an American girl."[34] Having established that the bride was white, the clerk denied Roldan the license.

Roldan consulted with a white attorney, Gladys Towles Root, who had successfully overturned a denial of marriage between Gavino Visco, a Filipino, and Ruth Salas, a Mexican. The exiled labor leader Pablo Manlapit had urged Root to take on that case. In Roldan's situation, both the state and the petitioners agreed that the central question was whether Filipinos were Asians or Mongolians. Root built her argument around science,. She invoked Blumenbach's five varieties or races of mankind: Caucasian, Ethiopian, American, Mongolian, and Malay. The state's 1880 miscegenation law specified Mongolians, but failed to mention Malays.

The state's attorneys likewise constructed their case around scientific claims, which, they contended, had advanced since Blumenbach's day. They argued that the law used *Mongolian* in the generic and not the specific sense of the term. The critical questions here were the shifting categories and meanings of race. That argument over the science of race approached the precarious position of the 1923 U.S. Supreme Court *Thind* ruling, that race was what the "average man" made of it (in effect, that race and science are social constructions). The superior court sided with Root, endorsing Blumenbach's racial classification system. The California District Court of Appeal subsequently upheld that ruling. The *Roldan* case, finally resolved in 1933, determined that Filipinos were Malays.

The victory was hailed as a "racial right" by a Los Angeles Filipino newspaper. Filipinos, the paper exulted, were "A MALAY or BROWN RACE and PROUD OF IT," and as Malays, "Filipinos can marry American girls."[35] On April 10, 1933, Salvador Roldan and Marjorie Rogers obtained a marriage license from the county clerk's office that had denied it to them nearly two years earlier. But the triumph was short-lived. About two months after the *Roldan* appeal, an amendment to the state's miscegenation law added "members of the Malay race" to the classes of people prohibited from marrying whites. Roldan and Rogers' marriage, the revised law pronounced, was thus "illegal and void." California was a latecomer to this specification of "Malays": South Dakota, Nevada, Arizona, and Wyoming already had laws against the union of whites with Malays. Utah and Maryland followed in California's wake.

After World War II, however, California took the lead in the desegregation movement with the case of *Pérez v. Sharp* (1948). The case involved the marriage of Andrea Pérez, a Mexican, and Sylvester Davis, an African American. Ruled a white woman by the marriage license bureau, Pérez contested the state's miscegenation law on the basis of religious freedom, contending that the Catholic Church blessed their proposed union. In addition, the Catholic Interracial Council of Los Angeles, formed in 1944, supported Pérez and Davis and called for integration and freedom of interaction among all peoples and an end to segregation. Church officials at the Los Angeles diocese, however, were appalled by the contention that the Catholic Church endorsed interracial marriage, and that argument quickly fell apart. Instead, the California Supreme Court (which had just months earlier affirmed the validity of the state's alien land laws as violating no fundamental civil liberties), ruled by a majority on October 1, 1948, that California's miscegenation law violated the Fourteenth Amendment's equal protection clause. Marriage, the court determined, was a "natural" right and "a fundamental right of free men."[36]

While the bustling urban centers of early twentieth century America might have brought diverse groups of immigrants into contact, they were not the cauldron that melted them into a single, "American" race and people. Whereas European immigrants were generally assimilated into whiteness and citizenship on the Atlantic seaboard, the experience was different for Asians and Pacific Islanders.

In San Francisco Bay, on the Pacific coast, Angel Island's detention cells held some Russians and Jews (putative and eventual whites), but the occupants were overwhelmingly Asians, Pacific Islanders, and Central Americans. Those detainees were persons of color, "a different class of persons" excluded from many constitutional protections guaranteed to "people of the United States" or citizens. Peoples of the Pacific world were refused admission to the United States by exclusion laws, border patrols, and expulsions. Even after entry, they languished under a regime of segregation and dependency.

To escape the full force of economic and cultural dependency, Asians capitalized on openings available to them, and they employed the legal system to claim their rights as persons and citizens. They connected the decolonization struggles in Asia with the movement for civil rights in America. Their freedom movement was premised on a global understanding. While they did not always succeed in their struggles for self-determination, Asians exercised agency and shaped the course of history.

SUGGESTED READINGS

Chen, Yong. *Chinese San Francisco, 1850–1943: A Trans-Pacific Community.* Stanford, CA: Stanford University Press, 2000.

Chin, Soo-Young. *Doing What Had to Be Done: The Life Narrative of Dora Yum Kim.* Philadelphia: Temple University Press, 1999.

Lee, Erika, and Judy Yung. *Angel Island: Immigrant Gateway to America.* New York: Oxford University Press, 2010.

Yung, Judy. *Unbound Feet: A Social History of Chinese Women in San Francisco.* Berkeley: University of California Press, 1995.

PRIMARY DOCUMENTS
DOCUMENT 11

Petition signed by Filipinos in Salinas, California, addressed to President Franklin D. Roosevelt, published in the *Philippines Mail,* October 8, 1934.

The Great Depression affected all Americans, but Filipinos faced particular hardships. As U.S. nationals, the president's petitioners pointed out, they were neither U.S. citizens nor foreigners represented by their nation and thereby protected under international agreements. (Although published in October, after passage of the Tydings-McDuffie Act that declared Filipinos to be aliens, this petition must have been written before the Act.) Unemployed, they were refused public assistance, and as a people of color, they were subjected to racism and social ostracism. Without relief, these Filipinos noted, even repatriation would be preferable to the injustices they faced in the United States.

Honorable Franklin D. Roosevelt
President of the United States
Washington, D.C.

Your Excellency:

We, the undersigned natives of the Philippine Islands, residing on the Pacific Coast and engaged in agricultural work, respectfully petition as follows:

Due to the fact that we are Nationals of the United States of America, but not entitled to the rights of full citizenship and not having representation through consular agencies or other duly authorized officials, we find ourselves, in the case of social or economic difficulties, without the facilities of protest or protection afforded to citizens of a foreign country, and though we owe allegiance to the United States government, we have no means through which our rights as a non-citizen group may be protected.

We find ourselves accused by the general public of lowering the wage scale by working for lower wages and yet forced by the growers to accept a lower scale than corresponding white labor. With the alternative of being subject to mob violence, the destruction of our homes by fire and to unwarranted arrest, if any action is taken to unite for the purpose of maintaining a higher wage scale.

We find ourselves losing thousands of dollars a year in unpaid wages for employment by citizens of foreign nations, who are well organized and duly represented and who take advantage of the fact that we, as a National group, have no representation.

We find ourselves subject to racial prejudice and discrimination in all social relationships, after having been educated in Americanized schools in the Philippine Islands and encouraged to esteem and strive for the civilization typified by Americans.

We have all emigrated to the United States, stimulated by the high ideals of Americanism and desirous of finding a higher and more worthy means of expression, only to be disillusioned on every hand by the experiences of our unsatisfactory social status.

We find ourselves, for the most part, forced to live in barns and outbuildings in direct violation of the State housing laws and when we secure camps of the most modern type, having such buildings subject to destruction by incendiary fires, because an attempt is made to demand higher wages through orderly and approved methods.

We therefore ask and beg of you, as President of the United States of America, to take the necessary steps through the proper agencies to set up means by which our interests may be represented and protection to our rights afforded.

If this is not possible, we petition you as President of the United States of America, that steps be taken immediately for our repatriation to our native land in the Philippine Islands at government expense, so that we may work out our destiny and future among our own people, where we hope and trust, that even though it may not afford all the seeming advantages of Western Civilization, it may be more conducive to our future happiness.

It is with the greatest esteem and respect for you, our Chief Executive, that we herewith attach our signatures.

SIGNIFICANT EVENTS

1848	Marie Seise arrives in San Francisco
1849	Chinese merchants hire a white attorney
1870	San Francisco carrying-pole ordinance
1873	San Francisco Chinese laundry tax

1875	Page Act
1880	Section 69, Civil Code (CA), prohibiting marriage between whites and "Mongolians, Negroes, mulattoes and persons of mixed blood"
1882	Chinese Exclusion Act
	opening of the "shed" detention center
1885	Mary Tape protests school segregation
1886	*Yick Wo v. Hopkins,* U.S. Supreme Court ruling that "facially neutral" legislation, if discriminating in its application, violates the Fourteenth Amendment's equal protection clause
1892	Geary Act
1895	founding of Native Sons of the Golden State
1896	*Plessy v. Ferguson*
1898	*Wong Kim Ark v. U.S.*
1899	"open door" policy in China
	U.S. war in the Philippines
1900	Japanese Deliberative Council of America founded
1902	Chinese threaten to riot in the "shed"
1903	San Francisco police violence against Jinyong Tan
1904	Sen Katayama founds the Japanese Socialist Party
1905	Asiatic Exclusion League
	boycott of U.S. goods in China
1906	San Francisco earthquake and fire
	Shūsui Kōtoku establishes Social Revolutionary Party
1908	Gentlemen's Agreement
	founding of Japanese Association of America
	founding of Korean Women's Society
	In-whan Chang assassinates Durham Stevens
1909	founding of Korean National Association
	In re Najour
1910	Angel Island Immigration Station opens; the "shed" closes
1913	Alien Land Law (CA)
	opening of Hung Sa Dan
1915	founding of Chinese American Citizens Alliance
1917	Barred Zone Immigration Act
1919	May 4 Movement

1920	Alien Land Law (CA)
	Nineteenth Amendment
1921	Japan refuses passports to "picture brides"
	Japanese farm workers expelled from Turlock, CA
1922	*Takao Ozawa v. U.S.*
	Cable Act
1923	Alien Land Law (CA, WA, Idaho, Montana, Oregon)
	U.S. v. Bhagat Singh Thind
	Terrace v. Thompson, U.S. Supreme Court ruling upholding alien land laws as constitutional
	American Loyalty League
1924	Johnson-Reed Act
1924–25	Pacific Coast Survey of Race Relations
1927	Filipino Federation of America
1929	Great Depression
	Japanese American Citizens League
1930	anti-Filipino riot in Watsonville, CA
	Filipino Federation of America office bombed
1931	Cable Act amended
	Japan invades Manchuria
1933	*Salvador Roldan v. Los Angeles County* (CA)
	National Industrial Recovery Act
1934	Tydings-McDuffie Act
	Filipinos strike in Salinas, Santa Maria, and Lompoc, CA
	Filipinos expelled from Turlock, CA
1935	Filipino Repatriation Act
	naturalization to Asian veterans of World War I
1936	Mexican, Japanese, and Filipino celery workers strike in Venice, CA
	Cable Act repealed
1937	Japan invades China
	Filipino Repatriation Act extended
1938	National Dollar Stores strike
1939	Filipino Repatriation Act extended
	Filipino asparagus workers strike in Stockton and Sacramento, CA
	Filipino Agricultural Workers Union
1940	Filipino repatriation ends

10

SEATTLE, NEW YORK CITY, CHICAGO

In the early twentieth century, Seattle, New York, and Chicago, although geographically separated, constituted a common field of study for social scientists, who viewed those cities as ethnic and racial frontiers and as social laboratories. Scholars of assimilation saw the ecology of the city as essential to the process by which foreigners became Americans.

The Chicago school of sociology, an approach associated with the University of Chicago's department of sociology, took a particular interest in that urban metamorphosis, and its researchers studied the patterns and effects of immigration in Seattle, New York, Chicago, and other cities. The European immigration of the late nineteenth century and its attendant "problems" were seen as aspects of U.S. exceptionalism. The Chicago school saw assimilation as an "ethnic cycle" of contact, conflict, accommodation, and assimilation.

The Chicago race riot of July 1919 forced a recalibration of this vision. The riot pitted whites against African Americans, who were, like most of the whites, new to the city. In more than a week of rioting, 15 whites and 23 African Americans died, 537 people were injured, and over 1,000 were left homeless.

The African American Charles Johnson, a University of Chicago graduate student of sociology at the time, led the city's investigation into the causes of the riot. The commission's report, *The Negro in Chicago*, adhered to the Chicago school's theory of the ethnic cycle, but it also documented the numerous and deleterious effects of racism against African Americans. It identified the roots of African American discontent as the pervasiveness and persistence of inferior housing, schools, and public facilities, along with poverty and an unstable family life. Those conditions did not support the concept of the ethnic cycle, which predicted temporary setbacks but eventual advances and assimilation, a pattern reflected in the European immigration experience. For African Americans, however, the commission concluded that race was a central and unchanging feature of African American life.

Robert Park, a Chicago sociologist who was a principal architect of the field of race relations, believed that these "problems" arose because of color. "The chief obstacle to assimilation of the Negro and the Oriental are [sic] not mental but physical traits," Park wrote. "It is not because the Negro and the Japanese are so differently constituted that they do not assimilate. . . . The trouble is not with the Japanese mind but with the Japanese skin. The Jap is not the right color."[1] Park's Pacific Coast Survey of Race Relations (1924–26), funded by the New York based Institute of Social and Religious Research with Rockefeller Foundation money, undertook to understand the "Oriental problem." The survey's list of sponsors shows that the period's social ills and their cures elicited the interest of Protestants who adhered to the notion of the "social gospel" and certain elements of the ruling class.

Both the survey and Chicago's school of sociology treated African and Asian Americans as exceptions and aberrations to the central narrative of U.S. history. In addition, assimilation theory blamed peoples of color for their inability to blend into the majority group and saw segregation as a natural, spontaneous, "more or less instinctive defense-reaction," in Park's words. The victims of racism, accordingly, were the social problem. By analogy to the natural world and the idea of ecological succession, peoples of color were the "invading race" that upset the social stability achieved through naturalization and assimilation.

Those discourses, dating from the so-called Age of the City in the first half of the twentieth century, still dominate conventional narratives of U.S. history. Insofar as they affirm the centrality of whites and marginality of nonwhites, those ideas have palpable, material effects in maintaining dependency and regulating people's lives.

SEATTLE

Pacific Islanders and Asian Americans began arriving in the Pacific Northwest during the Spanish and Russian periods. Hawaiian migrant laborers were soon joined by Chinese and then by Japanese, South Asians, and Filipinos. The anti–Pacific Islander and Asian movement pursued them across the Canadian-U.S. border. I highlight Seattle because it was the main entry point and distribution hub for Asian migrant laborers and settlers in the region, and its influence was felt across the Canadian border.

Seattle's importance had much to do with its strategic location on the Great Circle ocean navigation route, the most direct route between America and Japan. Seattle is the closest U.S. port to Yokohama, more than two hundred miles closer than San Francisco. Because of that geography, the U.S. military used Seattle (as well as San Francisco) to supply its troops in the conquest and colonization of the Philippines. In return, during the early 1900s, Filipino seamen and products such as hemp reached Seattle. When the U.S. Army laid communication cables between Seattle and Alaska from 1903 to 1904, about 80 of the cable ship's 175 crew members were Filipinos.

Seattle's commerce with Japan and China was substantial, amounting to over half of the port's total revenues from 1922 to 1931. From the late nineteenth century onward, the transcontinental Northern Pacific Railway connected the rest of the nation with Seattle. The region's lumber, wheat, fruit, and fish were loaded on ships for Asian markets in China, Hong Kong, Japan, and the Philippines. Its proximity to Alaska added to Seattle's importance in the transpacific trade. Those ties brought Asian migrants to Seattle.

CHINESE

Gold rushes in British Columbia's Fraser Canyon and Oregon's Rogue River Valley in the 1850s and construction of the Canadian Pacific and Northern Pacific railways during the 1880s drew Chinese migrant laborers from China and California to the Northwest. Labor contractors in San Francisco and Chinese contractors in China recruited thousands of Chinese workers for the gold mines and railroads. Most Chinese migrants were not independent but labored under bosses for Chinese and white companies. At the turn of the century, many were replaced by Japanese and South Asian migrants on the railroads and in lumber mills. Later, Filipinos worked in the canning industry.

In the Northwest, Hawaiians and Asians, like the Chinese and Japanese, engaged with America's native peoples. Hawaiians fought against, married, and settled among American Indians. In 1871, the Chinese "Jack" Gho, a cook hired by "Charley" Julles, a Snohomish Indian in Washington Territory, sued his employer over unpaid wages. Gho claimed he had an agreement with Julles, a logging-camp proprietor, to work for wages. Julles countered that territorial courts had no jurisdiction over Snohomish and Indians generally. The court disagreed, contending that American Indians, like all persons involved in "pursuits that occupy the attention of our race," were subject to the rules and agreements under U.S. law. In protecting this "natural right" of Indians, who were historically considered to be without rights and incapable of law, the court rendered a decision rare in the U.S. West while also ruling in favor of another oppressed group, the Chinese. Even so, Chinese miners invaded American Indian land. In a different form of engagement, one Chinese, "Chesaw," married an American Indian and settled into a life of farming along Myers Creek in eastern Washington.

In Washington Territory, Chinese were the objects of racist attacks. In 1885, a band of white and American Indian workers descended on a Chinese camp in Issaquah valley and fired indiscriminately into the tents of Chinese farm laborers, killing three of them. The same year, near Newcastle, a mob burned the barracks of thirty-six Chinese coal miners, and following a parade through Seattle led by Tacoma's mayor and the president of the territory's Anti-Chinese League, vigilantes murdered three Chinese men. On

October 24, 1885, hundreds of whites set fire to Seattle's Chinese district, and newspaper editorials ordered the Chinese to leave the territory by November 1. The governor declared martial law, and federal troops kept the peace, but when the soldiers left in February 1886, a mob of about 1,500 whites descended on Chinatown and forced its more than four hundred residents to leave. Hundreds boarded the *Queen of the Pacific* for San Francisco. Others were marched to the courthouse, where a mob lynched a Chinese man and injured four others. Despite protests from China's government, none of the perpetrators faced prosecution.

Around the same time, Seattle's rival city, Tacoma, also took up the cause of Chinese exclusion. Blaming the 1885–86 national recession and local unemployment on the city's Chinese, white workingmen formed a labor union and an Anti-Chinese League to protect their jobs. Class conflict between workers and employers, derisively called "American mandarins," devolved into a matter of race and citizenship. Chinese, the white workers claimed, were illegal immigrants whose "slave-labor" undercut the wages of American workingmen. Moreover, as aliens characterized by "ingrained heathenism," "vile habits," and "peculiar diseases," Chinese could not and should not be permitted to assimilate with the white race.

The movement swelled throughout the summer of 1885, aided by the city's anti-Chinese mayor and its newspapers. Workers' rallies and anti-Chinese demonstrations heightened the anxiety among Tacoma's Chinese community of about 700, causing some 150 to flee to Portland, Oregon, and across the Canadian border to Victoria. Restaurants, lumber mills, and canneries began to dismiss their Chinese employees, and by November only a few remained in Tacoma.

On November 3, a mob of five hundred armed men ordered the remaining Chinese to leave immediately; they gave storeowners an additional day to settle their accounts. Within hours, the Chinese, including women and children, assembled with their possessions, and guards escorted them in the pouring rain to a nearby train station, where they boarded trains that rode on tracks laid by Chinese workers. A Tacoma newspaper called the forced expulsion a "glorious victory" and a "peaceful and successful culmination" to the effort to "purge" the community of "obnoxious elements."

During the riot, Chinese merchants appealed in vain to the territory's governor and the city's mayor for protection. In fact, the mayor was a member of the mob. The merchant How Lung remembered that a crowd of several hundred men approached his shop, kicked down the door, and made their way into the living quarters. "They took hold of the Chinese that were in these houses, some of them were Chinese women, including my wife, and pulled them out," recalled Lung. "Some person in the mob pointed pistols at the Chinese but did not fire any pistols. The Mayor of Tacoma . . . was there . . . with the mob. He came to my house and said I must go."[2]

To board the trains that took them into exile, the Chinese had to pay the six-dollar fare to Portland. Others who had no cash were seen wandering southward along the tracks, carrying their meager possessions. Over the next several days, Tacoma's citizens looted the Chinese homes and stores and burned them to the ground. When the rampage was over, John Arthur, a white resident, reported triumphantly to the governor: "The Chinese are no more in Tacoma."[3]

When the federal government charged the mayor and riot leaders with conspiring to violate the rights of the Chinese to equal protection under the Fourteenth Amendment, the defendants cited two Supreme Court rulings on race, *Dred Scott v. Sandford* (1857) and *United States v. Harris* (1883), sometimes called the Ku Klux case. They also claimed that under the Chinese Exclusion Act (1882), all of Tacoma's Chinese were illegal immigrants. In *Dred Scott*, the court had ruled that African Americans were property and noncitizens, with none of the rights and privileges guaranteed by the Constitution. In Tacoma, the defense claimed that the Chinese were perpetual foreigners, aliens ineligible to citizenship, and thus likewise unprotected by the Constitution. The *Harris* case, decided just two years prior to the Tacoma expulsions, involved the lynching of an African American man and beating of several others by a sheriff and white mob in Tennessee. The court determined that the federal government could not intrude on the rights of states or territories to prosecute crimes such as assault and murder. The Washington court agreed with the defendants and dismissed the charges, but President Grover Cleveland, concerned over relations and trade with China, convinced Congress to indemnify China over $270,000 in 1888 for the anti-Chinese riots in the "Pacific States and Territories." Reparations were more a matter of commerce than of rights.

The Chinese refugees from Tacoma and Seattle became part of a larger Chinese community in Portland. At the time, there were 9,346 Chinese men and 164 Chinese women in Oregon, according to the 1880 census, while Washington had only 3,161 Chinese men and 25 Chinese women. A decade later the numbers were much the same: Oregon had 9,270 Chinese men and 270 women, while in Washington there were 3,210 Chinese men and 50 women. Portland, with its 1,612 Chinese in 1880, 1,547 men and 65 women, was one of three West Coast cities, including Tacoma and San Francisco, targeted for anti-Chinese agitation by labor organizers to advance the cause of white labor. Some of the leaders of the Tacoma riot followed the Chinese south to Portland.

Despite its larger Chinese community, Oregon did not have a history of welcoming nonwhite migrants. From its beginnings, Oregon Territory favored the exclusion of Hawaiians from citizenship and the vote. In its application to Congress for statehood, Oregon submitted documents that explained the restriction of rights for African Americans and Chinese proposed in its draft constitution of 1857. Oregon proposed restricting the vote to white men, including foreigners resident in the United States for a year, and explicitly denied the right of suffrage to the "Negro, Chinaman, or Mulatto." As a drafter of Oregon's constitution noted, Chinese were "practically slaves."

Despite that past, Portland's Chinese did not suffer the fate of those expelled from Tacoma and Seattle but were allowed to remain in the city's Chinatown. While white labor leaders agitated against the "Chinese menace," the city's white elites, through its newspapers, defended the Chinese presence because cheap Chinese labor benefited

Oregon's industries and did not threaten white workers. Other whites, concerned over law and order, warned against vigilante justice and the anarchy that might descend if citizens attempted to force the mass expulsion of Portland's Chinese. Those sentiments prevailed.

JAPANESE

Like the Chinese before them, Japanese were drawn to port cities like Victoria and Seattle by the prospect of work. Migration companies and labor recruiters facilitated the traffic, and by 1910 there were 6,127 Japanese in Seattle, 1,018 in Tacoma, and 352 in Spokane. Railroads, lumber mills, and salmon canneries hired them at wages lower than those for whites: $1.10 per day for Japanese railroad section workers, compared with $1.33 for whites. By the spring of 1899, some 800 Japanese worked for the Northern Pacific Railway, and a year later, the Great Northern Railroad employed 2,500. Oregon's Railway and Navigation Company also employed large numbers of Japanese, and those ranks increased with Hawai'i's annexation and Japanese migration from the islands to the West Coast.

Violence against Japanese migrants, like the earlier outrages against Chinese, attempted to protect white privilege against erosion. Japanese, white workers held, threatened their livelihoods, and patriots claimed that Americanism was tainted by Japanese bodies. In 1897, a white mob beat twenty Japanese railroad workers in Idaho, and a year later, a crowd threatened four Japanese in Portland. In Washington, hundreds of Japanese and white workers battled in bloody confrontations in 1899 and 1900. California's Asiatic Exclusion League, formed in 1905, opened a branch office in Seattle and held a convention there in 1908.

Segregation was a key instrument for maintaining white supremacy and nonwhite dependency. Heitaro Hikida of Seattle remembered that "colored people were excluded from restaurants, and so it followed that they would be excluded from public swimming pools and beaches. . . . Not a single Japanese was allowed to enter the Alki Beach or the shore at Ballard. Also, we were discriminated against in the high class movie houses and theaters." Banzo Okada recalled: "When we went shopping in department or drug stores and brought our items to the cashier's counter, the cashier purposely neglect us, looking the other way. Some told us directly, 'We don't sell to Japanese.' The situation was the same at the barbershop. We were refused with, 'If we take Japanese customers, then whites won't come here because they don't like it.' Also, when we went to restaurants the waiters and helpers neglected us."[4]

Washington's Yakima Valley offered the Japanese a haven from the oppression of the cities. But even here, in the "beautiful land" first inhabited by the Yakama Indian peoples, anti-Asianism reared its head. Japanese first farmed in the valley in the late nineteenth century. In 1905, Kishiro Sakai brought about forty men from Hawai'i to work on a nursery on the Yakama Indian Reservation. New markets for the valley's products opened in 1887, when the Northern Pacific Railway line was completed, linking Yakima with

Tacoma and the rest of the United States. The valley's town and hub, Wapato, located on Indian land, had a hotel and store, and its residents laid out streets and sidewalks.

The Yakama reservation was administered by the Bureau of Indian Affairs. The Dawes Act of 1887, which was designed to assimilate American Indians by giving them arable land, opened the reservation to non-Indian settlers. In 1904, Congress authorized the sale of Yakama tribal lands, and by 1919, 1,151 white tenants cultivated 72,832 acres on leased reservation lands; 119 Japanese farmed 6,334 acres; and 43 American Indians, the supposed beneficiaries of the act, held a mere 2,717 acres. Most of the land required irrigation to grow garden crops, and the Yakama Indian chief Kamiakin was among the first to channel water from a tributary of the Yakima River for his fields.

In 1920, a week before a Joint Congressional Committee on Immigration and Naturalization held hearings in Seattle, the *Seattle Star* asked its readers: "Will you help keep this a white man's country?" and urged them to testify before the committee against the "growing menace of Oriental aggression." The paper referred to the peril posed by Japanese "colonization" and economic competition in the state, spreading from strongholds in Hawai'i and California to Washington, Idaho, and Colorado. Congressman Albert Johnson of Washington chaired the committee hearings, and it was he who coauthored the Johnson-Reed Act of 1924, which established racist, national quotas that virtually ended Asian migration.

Washington instituted its alien land law in 1921 and, like California, passed a follow-up measure in 1923 to clamp down on Japanese attempts to escape the original restrictions. While federal lands such as the Yakama Indian Reservation were exempt from state law, the Bureau of Indian Affairs told whites and Japanese it would no longer lease lands to aliens. American Indians, however, apparently preferred leasing their land to Japanese because they paid five to ten dollars per acre more than whites. When leases expired, some Japanese left the reservation, but because of births their numbers actually grew during the 1920s.

Amidst the exclusionists' call for Japanese expulsion from "American" land (even when the land in question was Indian), Japanese farmers formed families, developed economic and social organizations, established stores and churches, and sent their children to the valley's schools. They weathered the Great Depression by subsisting on their fields. Beginning in the late 1920s, many employed Filipino migrants recruited from Seattle. The Filipinos, numbering some 150, met the same hostility as the Japanese. Whites targeted them as cheap labor and alleged that they posed sexual threats to white girls and women. Ranchers urged the removal of both Filipinos and Japanese from the valley because "their low standards of living make it impossible for white farmers to compete with them."[5]

As the anti-Asian rhetoric increased in the Yakima Valley, so did violence. On March 15, 1933, someone attempted to burn and bomb the home of Yasutaro Matsushita. Two days later, arson destroyed six tons of hay at Sataro Masuda's farm, and on March 20 Hikohachi Inoue lost seven tons of hay to arson. On April 6 a bomb destroyed Mitaro Masufuji's truck, and six days later a bomb exploded on a ranch west of Wapato. On April 13 and 16, bombs destroyed property on farms operated by Sanzo Ito and Jinmatsu Nishida. Most of the targets, a witness remembered, were Japanese places with Filipino workers. The terror ended when police arrested eight white men and uncovered a cache of dynamite.

Yuriko Ito, the wife of Sanzo Ito, described the bombing of her home and the fear it inspired. After a day weeding peas, Ito returned home exhausted, prepared dinner, and turned in as usual around ten o'clock. Nearly forty years later, she vividly remembered the night. "With loud cracking sounds the house was shaking. I suddenly woke up. My husband jumped out of bed, threw on his robe and ran out. Beside myself with shock, I followed him. Just as I took a couple of steps out of the house, the second explosion took place. As I watched, pieces of flying wood were landing within two feet of my husband, and I was scared to death! It was dynamite that caused the explosion." She went on: "I was most afraid for Mr. and Mrs. Kurihara who were sleeping in the hands' house. I was terrified that they might be hurt, and so we went to them at once. They were standing outside with vacant, shocked expressions."[6]

In 1936, the state, under the alien land laws, prosecuted the leasing of Indian land to Japanese and Filipino "aliens," despite the Filipino attorney John Ayamo's well-founded argument that Filipinos were nationals, not aliens. "The Filipinos are much the same as the Indians," Ayamo pointed out, "wards of the government."[7] The three Filipinos charged were found guilty and fined. Later, the state admitted that Filipinos were not aliens in the sense reserved for Asians, but the Yakama Indian Agency continued to refuse to lease land to Filipinos. In 1937, a judge ruled that Filipinos were subject to the state's alien land laws and found thirteen Filipinos guilty of violating their provisions by farming under American Indian landowners.

Far from a haven, Yakima Valley mirrored the social relations of the state, region, and nation. Other peoples and cultures, including systems of belief, were seen by whites as threats to domestic tranquility. They responded with racial segregation and efforts to limit economic opportunities for Asians. Conjoined herein were the discourses of race, gender, sexuality, class, and nation—the social formation. During the Great Depression, when the valley's whites rallied against the Industrial Workers of the World (IWW), the international socialist union founded in 1905, they rose as patriotic citizens of the nation-state against a threatening radical, alien ideology, namely socialism.

FILIPINOS

Seattle's ties to the Philippines brought Filipino migrants to the city. Many took the Dollar Line, which regularly docked in Seattle during the 1930s. Because other Asians and Pacific Islanders had preceded them in labor migration, Filipinos worked not only in Filipino work gangs led by Filipino bosses but also with whites and other Asians. In 1927, for instance, Felix Narte got his job on the Great Northern Railway from a Japanese employment office in Seattle, Teodolo Ranjo's section crew consisted of Filipinos and

South Asians, and Antonio Rodrigo rode boxcars with Filipinos and Japanese. Japanese farmers in the Yakima valley employed Filipino workers, and Filipino men and women picked strawberries with American Indians on Japanese farms on Bainbridge Island. Farther afield, the Filipinos who went to work in Alaska's salmon canneries became known as Alaskeros. By 1930, there were about 4,200 Alaskeros, and by World War II the number had grown to about 9,000.

Many of the first Filipinos in Seattle were students, both work-study and government-sponsored *pensionados,* who enrolled at the University of Washington alongside Chinese and Japanese students. Others began their studies in local high schools. Nearly all worked to support themselves. Roman Simbe remembered over a dozen Filipino students at Franklin High School, where he graduated in 1923. Belen Braganza, after graduating from Broadway High School in 1932, went on to the University of Washington and to Seattle College when the college opened its doors to women. Maria Abastilla Beltran enrolled at Firland Sanitarium in 1929 to train as a public health nurse. A U.S. education helped to ensure employment and upward mobility in the Philippines, although many graduates chose to remain in the United States after completing their course of study.

The University of Washington has claimed preeminence at least since the 1920s in recruiting Asian students and promoting Pacific Rim commerce because of its location and educational standing in the Northwest. Although they flocked to the university, Asian students felt the sting of racism on campus as well as elsewhere in the state and region. Housing segregation was a common feature of student life, and one professor publicly objected to living next door to "dark skinned students." Trinidad Rojo reported that only "brave" white women students dared to walk with Filipinos on campus, and he noticed that few African Americans attended the university. "American university students despise us and look down on us and refuse to allow us the representation our numbers should entitle us to," wrote Julius Ruiz, a Filipino freshman, in 1935. At the same time, Ruiz praised the university and its faculty for educating Filipino students.

Seattle, like many of the West Coast's cities and towns, served as a hub for Asian migrant laborers, as a transit point and a place to spend the winter during the offseason. Both men and women were employed in urban trades and service work: by 1930 there were 1,563 Filipinos and 51 Filipinas in Seattle. The number of Filipinas grew over the decade to 179 in 1940, while the number of men decreased to 1,213. Although many of the Filipinas were probably students, their increase might also indicate the beginnings of families and the second generation.

Seattle's Chinatown was home not only to Chinese and Japanese residents but also Filipinos, American Indians, African Americans, and white transients. Cheap hotels and rooming houses, gambling joints and brothels, nightclubs, and small stores and restaurants offered shelter, material comforts, and companionship. Although relatively safe, the Chinatown district was not immune from police harassment. Standing at street corners and public spaces invited police attention, Felipe Dumlao remembered. Police ordered men to move on and sometimes beat them for no reason other than their race.

Asian men were commonly charged with disturbing the peace and soliciting white women. Two officers shot and killed Mariano Marapoa in his hotel room. In 1926, a street fight erupted between whites and Filipinos during a New Year celebration, and the following year some a crowd of two hundred stabbed and beat each other in a racial melee. Especially volatile was the subject of relations, both real and imagined, between Filipino men and white women. Even in marriage, a Filipino migrant recalled, white wives invited white violence. At stake here were white men's privileges over white women, involving the social formation of race, gender, and sexuality.

Filipinos confronted racism and segregation by claiming their rights as U.S. nationals and as human beings. "They are men, not dogs, and deserve to be treated as men," wrote M. F. Bolima in 1911, protesting the treatment of Filipino workers. After all, he explained, "we were led to believe that this civilized land stood for liberty and freedom from tyranny and oppression."[8] They also engaged in nationalism and cultural revivals to assert their identity. The Balagtas Society promoted the Tagalog language among the migrants, and the Dimas Alang, a fraternal organization, sought the Philippines' independence from Spain and then from the United States. With many branches in Hawai'i and on the West Coast, including one in Seattle in 1923, Dimas Alang members nurtured dreams of independence from U.S. colonialism as late as the onset of World War II.

Labor organizing in Seattle, as in Hawai'i, mobilized Filipino workers as a race and class. The Great Depression and declining job opportunities and wages extinguished the hopes of many. Filipino student enrollments declined from eight hundred in 1932 to five hundred in 1935 and a mere three hundred in 1939. Many had to work full-time, leaving them little time for their studies. Between 1929 and 1933, unskilled cannery workers' wages fell 40 percent, and hop and apple picking, which usually supplemented summer cannery incomes, paid only pennies. Moreover, Filipinos, as the newest Asian immigrants, had to contend with white employers' established relationships with Chinese and Japanese workers and labor contractors.

In the winter of 1932, Filipino men organized the thousands of idle workers in Seattle's Chinatown area into the Cannery Workers' and Farm Laborers' Union (CWFLU). By June 1933, seven Filipinos were elected to head the CWFLU. The union was organized under the auspices of the AFL, which revealed its racism by trying to pit the Filipino members against the Japanese. The Filipino CWFLU, like the Japanese Cannery Workers Association and the Filipino Cannery Workers Association, was an ethnic union with little interest in recruiting non-Filipino members. Cannery and agricultural workers were in any case difficult to recruit into unions because of their mobility, and organizers had to contend further with ethnic, linguistic, and religious differences among Filipinos.

The CWFLU sought more than higher wages and improved conditions for its members: it also advocated for Filipinos in the political sphere. In 1935, when the state of Washington considered a miscegenation bill, the CWFLU sent lobbyists to the capital. Two years later, the union protested against a state law that made Filipinos subject to the alien land laws as "aliens" under the Tydings-McDuffie Act (1934). Despite its achievements, it made little headway in recruiting members, and factionalism and leadership conflicts weakened the movement. In December 1936, two CWFLU leaders, Virgil Dunyungan and Aurelio Simon, were assassinated in a Seattle Japanese restaurant. Placidio Patron, the nephew of a labor contractor, may have been responsible. Though the reason was unclear, many believed the killings involved a struggle between contractors and workers. Following the murders, the union rose in stature among Seattle's Filipinos. When it switched its affiliation from the AFL to the nonracist CIO in 1938, the union reached out to Japanese workers.

Because Washington had no miscegenation law, Filipinos were able to marry white or American Indian wives and thereby to obtain land. In addition, from the 1930s to World War II, despite the alien land laws, Filipinos gained access to land through labor agreements with American Indian landowners and white lessees by agreeing to cultivate their land for wages, thereby getting around the efforts of the Bureau of Indian Affairs to ban Filipinos from the Yakama Indian Reservation. In 1935, they formed the Filipino Farmers' Marketing Co-operative, but two years later the state closed it down. When the state arrested Filipino farmers after passage of the 1937 Alien Land Law, the Filipino Community of Yakima Valley was formed, vowing to "fight for justice." The group petitioned the Yakama Tribal Council to allow Filipinos to lease land, and in 1941 the council agreed. Set against "alien" Japanese farmers at the start of World War II, Filipinos rose in the estimation of whites, and in 1942 the Indian commissioner granted Filipinos the right to lease land on the reservation.

Other American Indians entered the lives of Filipino migrants. Alaskeros married indigenous women in Alaska, creating new communities. Cebuano Ricardo Lopez married Anecia Iyuptula, an Aleut and Yup'ik, in 1938, apparently at the request of his wife's dying father, Yako Iyuptula. The couple had ten children and lived next to Iyuptula's widowed mother. At Ekuk, Alaska, in the spring and summer, the couple fished for income and food, and Lopez learned from the native peoples how to handle dog teams and sleds and trap mink, fox, and beavers for their furs.

Filipinos confronted many of the same problems of migrant labor and dependency faced by other Asians and Pacific Islanders, but, because of their later arrival, new migrants from the Philippines also had to contend with the Great Depression and its aftermath and the solidarities and prejudices of Asians and other peoples of color.

NEW YORK CITY

The returns of the *Pallas* and the *Columbia* from their voyages in the late 1700s brought the first Asian and Pacific Islander migrants to the Atlantic coast. New York was one of the eastern ports through which exchanges with Asia were conducted. In the following century, New York and New England ship owners profited from the lucrative trade in humans—Chinese and South Asian coolies—who generated wealth for Caribbean planters and American mine owners, some of whom built fortunes and estates in New England.

During the first half of the nineteenth century, New York's poor congregated in lower Manhattan, in swampy areas near the docks. There, amid cheap boardinghouses, taverns, dance halls, tattoo parlors, and brothels, Irish, African American, and Chinese migrants moved and mingled. African Americans ran small businesses and built the African Methodist Episcopal Church and the African Free School. Chinese men, including many former sailors and a few former coolies, lived in boarding houses and worked as cooks, cigar makers, peddlers, and store clerks. Some had lived in New York City for over twenty years by the time of the 1855 city census, and significant numbers of them had married Irish women and formed families.

In 1855, New York City's Chinese numbered around 150. One of them, Lo Chee Ko, a boardinghouse operator and former ship's cook and steward, advocated for Chinese sailors' rights by checking on their condition on incoming ships during the 1860s. He reported on instances of unpaid wages and charges of cruelty, and in at least one case, he forced a captain to pay a Chinese cook $2,000 in back pay and as compensation for assault and battery. Ko was also a city booster, writing to Chinese in China and California to urge them to move to New York City. Chinese businesses such as Ko's boardinghouse were probably gathering places for the city's Chinese residents and visitors as well as distribution centers for news and mutual aid. Many of the city's Chinese lived in poverty; Chinese beggars were a common sight. A Chinese shopkeeper told a *New York Times* reporter in 1856 that Chinese unemployment reflected the migrants' inability to speak English and negotiate the host culture; but their predicament was no doubt aggravated by white racism.

During the Civil War, some Chinese men were employed in military service, mainly in the North but also in the South. After the war and Reconstruction, the underemployed Chinese population of New York City provided a pool of labor for recruiters from the Midwest. In 1870, for instance, a group of Chinese recruited from New York City arrived in St. Louis to work in the coalmines of F. A. Rozier & Company.

Southern planters' employment of Chinese migrant laborers and Calvin Sampson's 1870 experiment in his factory in North Adams, Massachusetts, stirred up anti-Chinese sentiment in the Northeast. Unionists rallied in New York City, and the city's newspapers covered their actions. Nevertheless, some employers defied public sentiment for economic reasons. James Hervey, the owner of the Passaic Steam Laundry in North Arlington, New Jersey, followed Sampson's advice and example. Finding it difficult to recruit Irish and German women to wash and iron shirts, Hervey employed a San Francisco Chinese labor recruiter to supply him with sixty-eight laborers bound to contracts of three years at thirty dollars per month. Unlike Sampson, Hervey smuggled the workers into his factory's storeroom, which became their sleeping quarters, under cover of night. Pleased with his Chinese laborers and despite protests from unions and the newspapers, Hervey brought about three hundred more to New Jersey between 1870 and 1872.

Many of Hervey's workers were unhappy with their situation. They conducted walk-outs and strikes and left as soon as their contracts expired. A few of Hervey's former employees opened their own laundries in New Jersey and New York. A brother of one of them, Ong Yung, began what was perhaps the first Chinese hand laundry in Manhattan and went on to establish several others. By 1879, there were at least two hundred Chinese hand laundries in New York City, according to a newspaper reporter, and they became the major source of employment for New York City's Chinese. By 1888, there were over two thousand Chinese laundries in New York City, and some eight to nine hundred in Brooklyn.

From the late 1880s to 1930s, those laundries employed an estimated seven to eight thousand workers. The facilities were distributed throughout New York City, their proprietors generally lived over the business, and they each employed one to several men. If there were two workers, one man washed the clothes, and the other ironed them. Typically, the washer began on Mondays, and the presser started ironing the washed clothes on Tuesdays. The washer ended his week on Friday and the presser on Saturday. Both worked five days a week, starting around 7 A.M. and ending near midnight.

The proliferation of Chinese laundries was a product of racism. In 1888, the journalist Chin Foo Wong observed that the Chinese became laundrymen "simply because there is no other occupation by which they can make money as surely and quickly. The prejudice against the race has much to do with it. They are fine cooks, neat and faithful servants, and above all, very skillful mechanics at any trade they have a mind to try. . . . But here in New York as yet there is no alternative."[9]

Chinese laundrymen faced anti-Chinese hate speech and vandalism every day. Lee Chew, a businessman in the city, told of "the street boys" who broke the windows of Chinese laundries "all over the city, while the police seem to think it a joke."[10] Chinese laundrymen were stereotyped as sexual predators of white women. The gender inversion of the solitary Chinese man working within the confines of the laundry, a domestic sphere, might also have been troubling to some whites. Even in the nascent U.S. film industry, movies such as *In a Chinese Laundry* (1897), *New Chinese Laundry* (1903), and *The Heathen Chinese and the Sunday School Teachers* (1904) suggested the laundry as a site of perversion manned by lecherous Chinese who plotted the fall and capture of virtuous white women. Herein, race, gender, and sexuality combined to produce a moral case against the main economic livelihood of New York City's Chinese.

The 1880 U.S. Census found 748 Chinese in Manhattan and 143 in Brooklyn and Newark, New Jersey, but this was surely an undercount. "Chinatown," wrote Chin Foo Wong, was small, consisting of about thirty grocery stores, most of them on Mott Street. On Sundays, when the city's laundries closed in observance of Sunday blue laws, Chinatown swelled as thousands of laundrymen from Manhattan, Brooklyn, Long Island, and New Jersey descended on the stores for groceries, clothing, and laundry supplies. As late as 1898, an observer described Chinatown's population as numbering four to five thousand on Sundays and "very much less" on other days. In lower Manhattan, with its racially mixed population and flourishing European immigrant working-class neighbor-hoods, Chinatown was a fluid space. Its development as a residential and commercial center mainly for Chinese was a development of the twentieth century.

The 1900 U.S. Census counted 6,321 Chinese in New York City: 6,189 men and 132 women, or about 47 men for every woman. Their total number decreased in 1910 to 4,614. After 1910, both the total Chinese population and the proportion of women stead-ily climbed: a total of 5,042 in 1920, 8,414 in 1930, and12,753 in 1940. Of the 1940 population, 10,967 were men and 1,786 were women, a ratio of 6 men for every woman. These demographic trends reveal the workings of the system of migrant labor and Chi-nese exclusion legislation, whose effects on the lives of individual, mainly working-class Chinese migrants were profound and in most cases permanent. Most men remained single; most women married.

Employment opportunities in New York City reflected that demography. In 1930, more than 70 percent of working-class Chinese men toiled in laundries and restaurants, while most Chinese women remained at home. Second-generation women had choices denied their migrant mothers. One woman born in Chinatown in 1907 worked while completing her high school diploma. She was then employed as a bookkeeper, and dur-ing the Great Depression she toured the country as a singer and dancer in the company of a Japanese acrobat and a Filipino comedian. In 1915, Alice Lee, born in the heart of Chinatown, became the first Chinese woman hired by a New York City hotel. The Great Depression probably forced most Chinese women to labor outside the home in the cash economy.

One of the jobs for Asians was to be exhibited as Oriental curiosities, as on Coney Island. Perhaps the earliest and best-known examples were Chang and Eng, the original "Siamese twins." They were first shown in 1829 in Boston, where a reporter for the *Boston Patriot,* after seeing the twins, called them a "strange freak of nature" and "one of the greatest living curiosities." Chang and Eng made great sums for their owners but insisted on their freedom when they reached twenty-one years of age in 1832, and they settled in North Carolina in 1839. There, they married white sisters, became landowners and sla-veholders, and fathered twenty-two children. P. T. Barnum, the showman, toured the twins as middle-aged men. In 1850 he opened a Chinese Museum in New York City, featuring such novelties as a "Chinese living family" and "Miss Pwan-Ye-Koo" with bound feet two and a half inches long.

In a state that had no miscegenation laws, the mid-nineteenth-century practice of interracial marriages continued into the twentieth century. The 1900 census showed that of the 133 marriages in New York City's Chinatown, 82 involved Chinese men and non-Chinese women. In 1910, such couplings totaled about half of all marriages in China-town. Most were between Chinese men and white women, such as the 1890 marriage of Que Ong and Lena Smith, a native New Yorker, and Ah Wah and Kittie Williams of Brooklyn. The white women in Chinatown, Lee Chew observed, were "excellent and faithful wives and mothers."[11] There were also Chinese-black couples, such as John

Archung and his African American wife, Barbara; Hon Chu and his Cuban wife, Laura; and Lok Chin and his wife, Ellen. In 1921, Olga Claudine Chin, a Chinese African, left her native Trinidad to join her Chinese husband in New York City.

Many mixed-race couples lived in Chinatown, although the Italian Teresa Ferrara and her Chinese husband, Young Lee, lived on the border between Chinatown and Little Italy in an apartment house with only Italian, working-class families. One building in Chinatown housed twelve Chinese and four interracial families. These included John Lum and Sarah Duncan, an African American, and their children. The couple had met and married in South Carolina in 1864. They promptly moved to New York City, where they had six children, although only three survived. One of them, Cynthia, married the Chinese migrant Mon Ki, and in 1890 Cynthia gave birth to her first child, a daughter named Sarah, after her mother. When Mon Ki died seven years later, Cynthia and her three children continued to live with her parents. Cynthia was the godmother to children of two other interracial couples in her building: Charles Toy and Josephine, a Chinese Cuban, and Joseph Bock and Sarah, an African American from Kentucky.

As early as 1874, a report noted the presence in New York of *gongsi fang*, or Chinese mutual-aid societies, remarkable institutions that shaped a sense of community amidst the dislocations of migration, labor exploitation, and racism. One of them, the Poolon Kun Cee, had fifty dues-paying members. The *fang* served its members by providing a place to meet, relax, and socialize; temporary sleeping quarters with eleven beds (often shared); loans and credit for those in need; and health care and burial arrangements. Some members arranged for the *fang* to return their bones to their home villages in China after death, while the indigent were buried in a *fang*-purchased plot at the Green-Wood Cemetery in Brooklyn. Members bore expenses equally, and the organization performed the functions of faraway family and kin. During the Great Depression, the *fang* provided food and shelter to its unemployed, impoverished members. The institution was so essential to the lives of Chinese migrants that it lasted until the 1940s.

Like all Asians in the United States, New York City's Chinese knew that their lives were connected with conditions in Asia. In 1919, the May Fourth movement in China sought to free China from Confucian status hierarchies and move the nation toward liberation by mobilizing the peasants and workers. Led by Sun Yat-sen, the Guomindang or Kuomintang (KMT) adopted the ideology of a people's revolution in 1924, targeting elitism and imperialism as the enemies. Many of New York City's Chinese came from Guangdong Province, Sun's birthplace and the KMT's base, and they watched these developments with great interest. The party established an Overseas Chinese Affairs Bureau and opened a branch office in New York City to solicit support. Like Chinese in Hawai'i, New York's Chinese contributed generously to the KMT.

After Sun's death, Chiang Kai-shek took over the party leadership, reconstituted the KMT as a party of elites, and purged it of communists. Similarly, in New York City, the KMT branch shifted from being a party of workers to one controlled by Chinatown's business elites, represented by the Chinese Consolidated Benevolent Association

(CCBA). In Chinese communities across the United States, communists, trade unionists, and leftists fled the party. The Alliance of Chinese Workers and Peasants (ACWP) was formed in San Francisco and soon established a chapter in Philadelphia's Chinatown. The Philadelphia ACWP changed its name to the Chinese Anti-imperialist Alliance, and in 1929 it moved its office and paper, the *Chinese Vanguard,* to New York City.

There, the Anti-imperialist Alliance worked closely with the U.S. Communist Party (CP-USA), sharing office space for a time, and the contents of the *Chinese Vanguard* mirrored the views of the CP-USA's *Daily Worker.* Besides opposing Japanese imperialism in China, the alliance organized workers in Chinatown, incurring the wrath of the KMT and CCBA, which banned the *Chinese Vanguard* and threatened to report its readers and sympathizers to the U.S. immigration authorities as communists to get them deported to China. The alliance's effort to raise the consciousness of Chinatown's workers met with little success, and in the midst of the Great Depression, it turned to the more pragmatic problem of Chinese unemployment.

In 1932, the alliance and a group of unemployed workers established the Chinese Unemployed Council–Greater New York. At the time, about 30 percent of Chinatown's Chinese were out of jobs, but according to federal statistics, while 9 percent of New York City's whites sought public assistance, only 1.2 percent of Chinese did so. Despite the high unemployment figures, the growing numbers of apartment evictions, and disturbing reports of old men dying from starvation or suicide, Chinese were reluctant to seek help from a government that excluded and regulated their migration, prevented them from becoming citizens, and threatened to expel them.

With several hundred members, the Chinese Unemployed Council raised money, collected and distributed donations of food and clothing, contested illegal evictions, and condemned racial discrimination. As the U.S. economy recovered and the need for relief declined, the council's membership dwindled to about forty in 1934, and its focus changed from assisting the unemployed to advocating for workers' rights.

New York City's Chinese laundrymen were at the forefront of organizing to advance their interests. In the late nineteenth century, they had formed guilds to resolve conflicts, fix prices, and oversee the establishment of laundries. By the early 1930s, however, there were no guilds, and Chinese laundrymen relied on the CCBA to defend their interests, a service for which they paid fees. The Great Depression brought matters to a head. With declining business, laundries had to lower their prices, work longer hours, and increase their services to survive. Moreover, white competitors began a smear campaign against Chinese hand laundries, employing racist cartoons, advertisements, and reports alleging unsanitary practices. In 1933, the New York city council proposed requirements for all laundry operators that included an annual $25 license fee, a $1,000 security bond, and U.S. citizenship. The fees were prohibitive for nearly all Chinese-run laundries, and the U.S. citizenship requirement meant their virtual eradication.

The CCBA's response to those threats was slow, condescending, and ineffectual, so in April 1933 the laundrymen formed the Chinese Hand Laundry Alliance (CHLA). The alliance's remarkable founding document, signed by 254 Chinese laundrymen, explained the circumstances of its formation. European and American "capitalist-imperialism," it began, had forced its way into China, impoverishing the nation's rural agriculture and destroying its urban industries. Those conditions "forced" Chinese to seek work overseas, resulting in the Chinese laundry business. Now, the city council's proposed ordinance would bankrupt Chinese laundrymen and cause their children and wives in China to starve. "That's why we have to fight against it with every effort," the CHLA's founding fathers declared. The CHLA was an organization "of our own" to "unite ourselves to fight the City government collectively so as to abolish the discriminatory ordinance" and "prevent such discrimination from occurring again in the future."[12]

Led by Zhuofeng Lei, the CHLA recruited more than two thousand members in its first month. In May, it sent its white lawyer and a delegation to the city council, whose public welfare committee heard their testimony and passed a revised version of the proposed laundry ordinance. It reduced the license fee to $10 and the security bond to $100. Although it kept the U.S. citizenship requirement, it added an exemption for "Orientals." The city's Chinese laundrymen celebrated the CHLA's achievement, calling it the "Victory of May," and its membership grew. From the CCBA's perspective, however, the Victory of May was a challenge to its sole authority in Chinatown. The split between the CCBA and CHLA revealed a mainly class-based divide in New York City's Chinese community.

As its founding statement shows, the CHLA understood world history and saw the importance of China's freedom for Chinese rights in the United States. The CHLA slogan, "To Save China, to Save Ourselves," recognized the connection between racism and imperialism in Asia and racism and oppression in the United States. When Japan's aggression threatened China's sovereignty during the 1930s, the CHLA campaigned to end it. The CHLA joined other Chinese organizations in parades and rallies, contributed funds for China's defense and relief, and protested the KMT's passive stance toward the Japanese invaders and aggressive pursuit of Communist forces in southern China. The CCBA, allied with the KMT, fell out of favor with many of the city's Chinese, and the CHLA rose in popularity.

Japan's full-scale invasion of China in July 1937 galvanized the resistance movement and united New York City's Chinese. When the elites in China tried to mobilize the overseas Chinese under the banner of "patriotism," meaning support of the KMT, most of Chinatown's masses rejected the party line, seeing the defense of China as a struggle against Japanese imperialism. That insight emerged from the recognition that China's humiliation was Chinese America's degradation and that China's sovereignty conferred dignity upon Chinese in the United States. It also reflected a spirit of independence among Chinatown's working people, who refused to acquiesce to the dictates of the CCBA business elites and the attempts of China's KMT government to control its overseas subjects. This idea of self-determination also served as a means of resisting white supremacy and its instruments, migrant labor and dependency.

From the 1930s through World War II, the Chinese Women's Patriotic Association cut an independent path through the thicket of Chinatown's politics. Operating within an overwhelmingly male, bachelor community, most of the few Chinese women were the wives of merchants and hence would be expected to side with the CCBA and KMT. But the Women's Association operated as a "patriotic" society while opposing the KMT's strategy of appeasement. Its members rallied with groups like the CHLA against Japanese imperialism, and they organized fund-raising auctions, bazaars, and charity balls. Like the CHLA, the Women's Association linked China's plight with the problems facing Chinese in the United States by demanding racial equality at home while working for China's freedom abroad.

JAPANESE

Japanese, like many of the city's Chinese, arrived in New York having worked on U.S. and European ships. By 1890, there were over a hundred Japanese in New York City. As with the Chinese, most of them were men. In 1900, there were 1,097 Japanese men and only 73 Japanese women, and in 1920 3,286 men and 640 women. Their numbers subsequently declined: the U.S. Census found 2,356 Japanese in New York City in 1930 and 2,087 in 1940. Most of the city's Japanese, unlike the migrant laborers in Hawai'i and on the West Coast, came from Tokyo and its environs, revealing a class difference, although many derived from the southern prefectures of Japan, including Hiroshima, Fukuoka, and Kumamoto, as was typical of the migrant laborers. The largest group of Tokyo residents arrived in the United States between 1902 and 1916, consisting first mainly of students and then of businessmen. During the first two decades of the twentieth century, those from the student and professional classes constituted nearly three-quarters of New York City's Japanese.

Despite their status at home, many of the Japanese were forced to turn to service work as they encountered the same kind of racism faced by the Chinese. Most whites made little distinction between the Chinese and Japanese. As a Japanese journalist reported, it was not uncommon for Japanese strolling in Central Park to encounter whites who screamed "Chinamen!" and threw stones at them. On another level, certain members of the white elite eagerly embraced the prospects for commerce that had led to the U.S. "opening" of Japan in 1854 and the presence of a Japanese governmental and business elite in the city.

Before 1914, over 90 percent of New York City's Japanese engaged in service work. By 1921, about 75 percent were domestic servants, despite the increasing numbers of Japanese businessmen and consular officials arriving with the rise of U.S.-Japan trade. One center for Japanese migrants was the Brooklyn Navy Yard, which employed them as kitchen workers, cooks, mess "boys," and stewards. A nearby boardinghouse catered to Japanese seamen. During the 1890s, over half of New York City's Japanese lived and worked in Brooklyn. But in 1907, when the navy prohibited the hiring of noncitizens, Brooklyn's Japanese filtered back to Manhattan.

An account by a Japanese student reveals some of the conditions faced by many of those migrants.[13] The seventeen-year-old landed in Victoria, Canada, and from there went to Tacoma, Portland, and New York City. Because of racism, he noted, Japanese work choices were "very narrow and limited." He thus became "a recruit of the army of domestic servants." Working in boardinghouses, in mansions, and on yachts, he soon lost his original ambition for a college degree in the exhausting grind of domestic labor. Moreover, the life of a servant demanded absolute obedience to the master, a trait he called "the unconscious servile habit of action." Independent thinking vanished. "To be a successful servant is to make yourself a fool," the writer observed bitterly. At the same time, he resisted being dehumanized, especially by his wealthy patrons. After an encounter with a particularly contemptuous woman, the migrant wrote: "You might bully me as you please and treat me like a dog . . . [but] I have a soul within me." Still, he reflected, New York City's sheer size can crush and defeat youthful dreamers, and he confessed, "I feel home-sick. I was so lonesome and so sorry that I came to America."

Frequent relocations were a way of life for many of New York City's Japanese, reflecting their tenuous positions and constant search for better opportunities. They were, a Japanese writer observed, "like nomads." A few moved up, but the vast majority remained mired in their assigned places. Japanese shops, like Chinese laundries, were scattered throughout the city, and domestic workers commuted to their employers' homes. During summer, many of them accompanied their wealthy patrons to the cooler mountains and seashore. In New York City, they stayed at Japanese boardinghouses like Senzō Kuwayama's establishment on West Fifty-Eighth Street, which in 1914 provided room and board to forty to fifty men, mostly domestic servants.

New York's Japanese elite criticized the workers as weak-willed, servile, and effeminate, and saw them as a blot on Japan's national image. Toyohiko Campbell Takami, a leader of New York City's Japanese, recalled a friend from his Navy Yard days who later became a Brooklyn laundryman. "I asked him how on earth he ever got into such a business. He said that he had obtained a job in a Chinese laundry and learned all about the laundry business in a month. Now, he could do the work better than a Chinese laundryman. I was very grateful that I did not come to America to be a laundryman."[14]

In 1921, some five hundred Japanese bankers, businessmen, and government officials belonged to the Nippon Club, enjoying privileges most of the workers could only imagine. In the view of the elite, those at the bottom were *imin*, or migrants of the coarse, laboring class, whereas those at the top were *hi-imin*, or Japanese nationals of the educated class who helped advance Japan's development. That social distinction was reflected in the 1908 Gentlemen's Agreement between Japan and the United States, whereby Japan agreed to stop issuing passports to the *imin*. Thereafter, only "gentlemen" were admitted.

Some members of this elite helped found the Japan Society in 1907 to promote goodwill between the United States and Japan. The society, although dominated by white businessmen, was a project of Jokichi Takamine, a prominent and wealthy medical doctor and researcher who discovered the hormone adrenalin, or epinephrine, in 1900. Takamine established a pharmaceutical company in New Jersey.

The few Japanese women in New York City faced challenges not only on account of race but also on account of gender, sexuality, and class. Haru was eighteen years old when she arrived in New York in 1922, the young bride of Eikichi Kishi, a man more than twenty years her senior, who had returned to Japan to find a wife.[15] Kishi had come to the city as a student in 1910 but, like many other young Japanese men, deferred his education for fulltime work. He was, Haru said, a scholar who detested manual labor. In the summer, Kishi managed a concession stand at Coney Island; in the winter, when the beach closed, he worked for a Japanese merchant. Haru cooked and cleaned for the concession workers who lived together in lodgings above the stand, a far cry from the life as the wife of "a businessman in New York," as Kishi had portrayed himself to entice her into marriage. "I knew nothing about cooking," Haru recalled. "I never cooked in my life . . . and I had to cook for all those people. At first I put the meat on the burners. Nobody told me what I was supposed to do. I was the only woman among fifteen men, sometimes more."

After spending three or four seasons at Coney Island, the couple ran a concession stand at Rockaway Beach in Brooklyn during the summer and a small gift shop in Washington Heights, Manhattan, in the winter. They moved to New Jersey during the Great Depression, but, like other legitimate businesses and concession stands, their business suffered when police raided and closed gambling joints. The couple returned to Manhattan. With mounting debts and unable to pay the rent, they were evicted from their apartment and had to move into a small place behind a laundry. Through those hard times, Haru bore four children. The first was born in 1924, when she entered a hospital with an English-language dictionary in hand to communicate with the physicians. "I really don't know how I did it," Haru exclaimed. "It was very hard. I didn't know anything about childbirth." Her husband visited Haru just twice during her ten-day confinement and failed to tell their friends, so she had no visitors. "I guess that's the way Japanese men are," Haru mused. Later, Kishi took a job as a domestic servant and was gone most of the time. Haru had a fifth child, and the couple tried to make lampshades and ran a lampshade store. The FBI closed this business down in January 1942, shortly after Pearl Harbor.

To the few Japanese women at the top of the class hierarchy, Haru Kishi's world was a foreign place. They, like their husbands, belonged to the Nippon Club, and the Japanese Women's Club of New York offered lessons on flower arrangement, the tea ceremony, and gardening. They might have mingled with the white wives of some Japanese businessmen and professionals, and they moved relatively freely among their husbands' Japanese peers and white Americans.

Most Japanese men in New York City either remained single or married interracially, like many Chinese men. New York, unlike Hawai'i and the West Coast, attracted few, if any, picture brides. Between 1909 and 1921, when Japan ceased issuing passports to picture brides, there were eighty-two interracial marriages recorded at Japan's consulate in New York City. One of them was between Kinichi Iwamoto and Elsa Konrad. Iwamoto grew up in Nagoya and migrated to the United States in 1920 to continue his medical training at Columbia University. Three years later, he earned his medical degree, and in 1924 he opened his practice on Manhattan's Upper West Side. Then in his thirties, Iwamoto dated an Irish woman for several years but later married Konrad, a German nurse at the hospital where he practiced. They remained in New York City and had two children. For Japanese men, marriage, especially to white women, was related to class and social standing, and the Japanese elite generally had more options than Japanese men of the laboring class.

Single Japanese working-class men frequented dance halls to seek the company of white women. During the 1920s, T. Takagaki ran several "dancing schools" throughout New York City, hiring young white women to teach Japanese and Filipino men to dance for a dollar a lesson. Police raids and a series of *Daily News* investigative reports in 1923 shut down Takagaki's enterprise. In one of his establishments, a reporter found sixty Japanese and Filipino men and nineteen white women, most under twenty years old, some dancing and others sitting on the laps of men. The police arrested all the white women and seized illegal liquor in the raid.

There were other venues for companionship. In the late nineteenth century, Nancy Campbell's Chinese Sunday School taught the English language and Christianity to Japanese as well as Chinese pupils, and Chinatown offered Japanese migrants a place to socialize with fellow Asians. White and Chinese sex workers spoke a halting Japanese with their customers. Chinatown offered a relatively safe space for Asian migrants, who otherwise dotted the city and were susceptible to white racism.

Even the Japanese elite, the *hi-imin*, who looked down upon the laboring class, commonly encountered anti-Asian insults and housing discrimination. As a consequence, in the late nineteenth century, they clustered in boardinghouses, like Delia Dudley's establishment at 55 West Ninth Street. Like working-class Japanese, they were not free to pursue their dreams but had to negotiate the limited opportunities open to them.

The *Japanese American Commercial Weekly* was established to serve the business community in 1910. Six years later its editor, Hajime Hoshi, a graduate of Columbia University, added an English-language section. The addition reflected the growing interest of U.S. companies in the Japan trade, as did the increase of Japanese firms in New York City, from about six in 1904 to over fifty by 1922, including the Bank of Japan, Mitsui Bank, and Sumitomo Bank. In 1911, the business-oriented Japanese Association sponsored a "campaign of education" to inform whites about Japan and to urge Japanese assimilation to white cultural norms.

Perhaps in response to white racism, which made no distinction between Chinese and Japanese, much less between the Japanese elite and laboring class, a few among the elite founded the Japanese Mutual Aid Society of New York to tend to their needy. The society, founded in 1907, offered medical care and funeral and burial plans for its members, which numbered over seven hundred by 1912. Instead of being buried at Potter's Field on Hart's Island with the city's indigents and criminals, the Japanese poor could be buried in Mount Olivet Cemetery in Queens, where the society bought 102 plots.

New York City's *Japanese American Courier,* an all-English language newspaper begun on January 1, 1928, heralded the coming of age of the nisei. Its editor, James Sakamoto, was a founder of the Japanese American Citizens League (JACL), which, among other causes, sought to ensure the civil rights of citizens. Also during the 1920s, radical issei like Sen Katayama, a devoted communist and anti-imperialist, began the Japanese Workers' Association of America to advance workers' rights in the United States and Japan. Like the Chinese Hand Laundry Alliance, the Japanese Workers' Association connected the fight against racism in the United States with the cause of freedom for oppressed classes and peoples across national borders.

SOUTH ASIANS

South Asians, like the Chinese and Japanese, arrived on the East Coast mainly on board U.S. and European ships, some as early as the late eighteenth century. The nineteenth-century coolie traffic transported South Asian migrant laborers to the Caribbean islands and thence to the edges of the American continent. Other South Asians served as sailors, cooks, and stewards on ships carrying Asian products and jumped ship when they made landfall in port cities like Galveston, New Orleans, Baltimore, Philadelphia, New York City, and Boston.

The shift from sail to steam shipping in the 1860s brought decisive changes in labor and migration patterns. British shipping companies recruited armies of men from British colonies in Africa and Asia to work below decks to stoke the coal furnaces that powered the steamships. Laboring in compartments without fresh air or sunlight and in oppressive heat, colored men shoveled coal and raked the fires. "Working in the coal bunkers through the Red Sea was such hell that the firemen had to pour buckets of sea water over their bodies before opening the furnace door," remembered Amir Haider Khan, a Pakistani seaman and later a labor leader. "Still, some firemen, scorched and asphyxiated, had to be carried to the deck by their workmates with others taking their places."[16]

Agents recruited most of those South Asian seamen in Calcutta and Bombay. Many of them were from the class of displaced peasants impoverished and made landless by British colonial land laws and taxes. They signed "Asiatic" or "lascar" contracts, which differed from contracts for European sailors by specifying the terms: fixed wages for six months to two years. More significant, the contracts bound sailors to the shipping company. In addition, they worked under bosses who took a portion of their wages, frequently several months' pay. Under such conditions, suicides at sea were common, as were desertion and jumping ship.

During the U.S. Civil War, over sixty South Asian men, classified as "Blacks," served in the Union Army in African American units, and many married African Americans or

Latinas and melded into those communities. Alef Ally, a peddler, arrived in New Orleans in 1882 and married Emily Lecompte, from a black Creole family. The couple had two daughters. Moksad Ali arrived in New Orleans six years later and married the African American Ella Blackman; they had six children. In the 1880s and 1890s in New York City and Atlantic City, South Asian seamen lived in African American neighborhoods, and many peddled "Oriental goods" in seaside resorts during the summer season.

In 1900, the *New York Post* estimated that there were more than five hundred "Malays and Lascars" in New York City. Most were Filipino seamen, but they also included Indonesians, Malaysians, and Singaporeans. The linking of "lascars" with "Malays" suggests that the two categories were identical in the minds of most whites. Over the next two decades, South Asians in the city increased as documented migrants trickled through Ellis Island: 109 in 1914, 55 in 1915, and 79 in 1916, before the 1917 Barred Zone Act that excluded West and South Asians.

Undocumented South Asian migrants escaped both immigration restrictions and the 1917 exclusion act. They constituted the largest portion of New York City's total South Asian population of 2,132 in 1917, 7,502 in 1918, 2,552 in 1919, and 1,914 in 1920. Between 1914 and 1924, an estimated twenty to twenty-five thousand South Asian seamen passed through New York's harbor, and many took the opportunity to jump ship. In the 1920s immigration agents in New Jersey swept through South Asian homes and white-owned factories to round up the undocumented for confinement on Ellis Island before deportation. Activists like the white American Agnes Smedley, the partner of the South Asian nationalist leader Sailendranath Ghose, hired lawyers to defend those arrested. Mohammed Abdou, an Egyptian nationalist, befriended and supported South Asian seamen, facilitating their desertions and helping them find employment in the city.

Asian seamen used the skills they learned at sea to find employment on land. Japanese men gathered at Brooklyn's Navy Yard, and South Asians and Chinese worked at railroad yards. Having labored in ship boiler rooms, South Asians found jobs at shipyards, steel mills, and automobile plants from New York City to Bethlehem, Pennsylvania; Youngstown, Ohio; and Detroit, Michigan. In July 1922, when the Erie Railroad hired some fifty South Asians and thirty-one Chinese, together with African Americans, to break a strike of white workers at its Jersey City yard, the strikers retaliated with the threat of mob violence against the colored workers. Many of those Asians were former seamen who, along with African Americans, were barred from membership in racist unions. The police kept the peace and escorted the Asians and African Americans out of town.

South Asians negotiated the U.S. color line as blacks but also as Orientals, and they associated with Arabs, Egyptians, and Syrians as purveyors of Oriental goods and culture. In 1899, Joe "Ranji" Smile, a "curry cook" from Karachi, caused a stir among New York City's white elite. Working the kitchen of a hotel on posh Fifth Avenue, Smile promised: "If the women of America will but eat the food I prepare, they will be more beautiful than they as yet imagine. The eye will grow lustrous, the complexion will be yet so lovely and the figure like unto those of our beautiful India women."[17] Customers flocked to savor his curries, and two years later he opened the Omar Khayyam restaurant on Fifth Avenue, near the renowned Waldorf Astoria Hotel.

In 1903 and 1904, Coney Island's Luna Park attracted the summer crowds with amusements and exotic delights that played on long-held European fantasies of the Orient. They included a Japanese teahouse with geishas and the "Streets of Delhi," featuring temples, shops, dancing girls, acrobats, elephants, and maharajahs. Yet most of New York City's South Asians, belying Orientalist fictions, led somber lives as service workers in hotels, restaurants, and laundries. They clustered in the Lower East Side and Hell's Kitchen during the 1910s, and by the 1920s many lived uptown in Spanish Harlem and Harlem with their Latina and African American wives and children. Nawab Ali, a laundry worker, married Frances Santos from Puerto Rico; Caramath Ali, a bellboy, married Carolina Green from the Dominican Republic; Kassim Ullah, a painter, married Frances English, an African American from North Carolina; and Eleman Miah, a cook's helper, married Emma Douglass, an African American from Indianapolis. Between 1922 and 1937, eighteen such marriages were recorded by the city's health department. All the South Asian men had Muslim names, and most of them hailed from Calcutta and elsewhere in Bengal. Eleven of the eighteen were marriages with Latinas: nine Puerto Ricans and one each from the Dominican Republic and Barbados. The remaining seven were with African American women from New York State, Florida, Maryland, South Carolina, and Indiana. Harlem's *Amsterdam News* carried notices of those marriages, and it also reported criminal activity involving South Asian men, including sexual assaults, thefts, and drug possession.

Single male workers and visiting South Asian sailors, intellectuals, and holy men frequented boardinghouses and restaurants catering to South Asians, like K. Y. Kira's Ceylon and East India Oriental Restaurant in Harlem. Kira first worked at Coney Island's Streets of Delhi exhibit as an animal handler. He then joined the Barnum & Bailey Circus and finally returned to settle in New York City. His Harlem restaurant and its later incarnation as the Ceylon India Inn in midtown Manhattan were gathering places for the city's South Asians through the 1930s.

The cause of Indian independence drew nationalists and anti-imperialists alike. In 1920, the Friends of Freedom for India held its first conference in New York City, which included speeches by the Ghadar Party leaders Taraknath Das and Sailendranath Ghose. The conference called for solidarity among freedom movements across the British Empire, in Egypt, Mesopotamia, and Ireland. Its attendees were united against colonialism and racism. Agnes Smedley and other white Americans were present, as well as several Koreans representing the freedom struggle against imperial Japan.

On the West Coast, the Ghadar Party had two branches, whose divergent aims were reflected in their respective publications. The *Ghadr* (Mutiny) was written by students and intellectuals in the San Francisco Bay Area whose primary focus was India's national liberation. The *Ghadr di Ganj* (Echoes of Mutiny), containing essays, songs, and poems by peasants and workers, was intended for the Punjabi farmers in the fertile valleys of Washington, Oregon, and California. Those complementary causes might have had counterparts on the East Coast and in New York City. The Friends of Freedom for India sought national self-determination and the end of imperialism, while the workers, especially those who had found solidarity with African Americans through being labeled as blacks, might have identified more with antiracism and the movement for civil rights and equality. African and Asian liberation movements gained traction during the period between the two world wars, and nationalist leaders understood their struggle as a two-fold fight against colonialism and racism because the latter, they knew, supplied the idea that justified the former.

CHICAGO

The region now called the Midwest was once the nation's west. The historian Carl Becker rhapsodized over Kansas and its people when he was a professor at the University of Kansas in 1910. The state, Becker noted, was located on "the frontier of human endeavor," and its people held "an identity of race, custom, habits, needs; a consensus of opinion in respect to morals and politics." Moreover, he claimed: "The Kansas spirit is the American spirit double distilled. . . . Within its borders, Americanism, pure and undefiled, has a new lease of life. It is the mission of this self-selected people to see to it that it does not perish from off the earth."[18]

Chicago emerged from that discourse and material condition. A hub first for canal and then for railroad transport, the city grew in size and importance to become an essential link between the East Coast and the Midwest. In 1848, the Illinois and Michigan Canal opened, allowing passage from the Great Lakes to the Mississippi River through Chicago. By the 1850s, railroads had eclipsed canals as the principal means of transportation for the Northeast and Midwest, financed by large corporations and wealthy individuals like Cornelius Vanderbilt, Andrew Carnegie, and John D. Rockefeller. As a center of commerce and transportation, Chicago attracted African Americans, Chinese, Filipinos, Japanese, and South Asians with the prospect of work, although racism relegated most of them to occupations considered demeaning for whites.

CHINESE

Perhaps the first Chinese to visit Chicago were members of a touring group of twenty jugglers, men and women, who arrived in 1852. The company landed in New Orleans and made its way up the Mississippi River to Chicago, probably through St. Louis, performing in cities along the way.

Less entertaining but just as revealing is the presence of two Chinese men in Chicago in 1858. One of them was John Dorming, who lived with his white wife and their biracial daughter, who was born in Kentucky. Dorming was a professional knife thrower and worked in one of the city's saloons. In 1863, a captured Chinese Confederate soldier, Charley Pang, was confined at the Chicago's Camp Douglas. Pang, who had served in the Orleans Light Guards Company, was captured by Union troops near Chickamauga, Georgia.

After the completion of the transcontinental railroad in 1869, Chinese from the West arrived in Chicago, and by the 1880s a Chinatown had begun to form. Around Clark Street in the Loop, an 1889 newspaper reported, there were eight Chinese grocery stores, two drugstores, two butcher and barber shops, two art studios that created portraits to send back to families in China, and a restaurant. Nearby were two Chinese farms that supplied fresh vegetables to the several hundred Chinese. The Hip Lung shop at 323 Clark Street sold furniture, textiles and clothing, musical instruments, tea, and foods like pickles, seaweed, sausages, salted fish, dried shrimp, and fresh produce.

As proof of a settled community, in 1892 several Chinatown businessmen bought plots at Rosehill Cemetery to bury Chinese dead. In 1926, when the cemetery evicted the Chinese, community members exhumed the remains of 412 Chinese and shipped them back to families in China. That racist exclusion continued through the 1940s.

Again because of racism, leases in Chinatown had to be procured through whites, such as the H.O. Sloane Company. In the early 1900s, rising rents forced many businesses to move from Clark Street to Chicago's South Side, which had seen a succession of European immigrants: Swedes, Germans, and Italians. Here Chinese businessmen hired white architects to give Chinatown an Oriental look, beginning with the On Leong Merchants Association building. Chicago's Chinatown, not unlike the bodily displays of the nineteenth century in circuses and resorts, was designed to make a profit by attracting and catering to whites.

As in New York City, Chinese laundries were a principal source of livelihoods for Chicago's Chinese. The first Chinese laundry opened for business in 1872, a year after the Great Fire and as Chicago was becoming an industrial center for the Midwest. Two years later, there were eighteen Chinese laundries, and by 1876 the number had grown to twenty-seven. The business took off the following decade, with 67 laundries in 1881, 97 in 1882, and 165 in 1883. Chinese laundries could be found in virtually every neighborhood, including the city center. The twentieth century, too, witnessed a boom in Chinese laundries, which increased from 209 in 1903 to 368 in 1913, 397 in 1923, and 704 in 1928.

Typically, laundrymen lived at the back of the shop. Their lives were circumscribed within that domestic enclosure, and loneliness was a frequent companion. Their customers rarely took much notice of them as individuals or took the trouble to speak with them. One customer said of the Chinese laundryman: "He seems hardly a part of the American community."[19] Yet the laundries were places of social interaction between the owner and employees, including Chinese and African American women who often worked part-time for hourly wages.

FIGURE 51
On Leong Merchants Association Building, Chicago.

Filipino men also patronized and socialized in the Chinese laundries, and Chinese and Filipino men found common ground in their isolation from women of their own ethnicity. Because there were so few women in either the Chinese or the Filipino community, most of the men's heterosexual encounters involved white and African American women and Latinas. From 1900 to 1940, a number of Chinese men married immigrant white women—Germans, Polish, Swedes, and Irish—and African Americans like Yee Sut Hong and Rose Chin, both Chicagoans.

FILIPINOS

Filipinos first arrived in Chicago as early as 1903, mainly as students—a few *pensionados,* others supported by their families, and still others as work-study students—to earn credentials from the city's numerous universities, colleges, and trade schools. Like the migrant laborers, most Filipino students were men: between 1903 and 1907, there were about two hundred Filipinos and fewer than twelve Filipinas in Chicago schools. By 1917, out of a total Filipino population of eight hundred in the city, an estimated six hundred were students. The Great Depression caused drastic reductions in student enrollment: at the University of Chicago, the number dropped from forty-six Filipino students in 1926 to ten in 1933. Unemployment rates were high among the city's Filipinos, and many were rendered homeless.

Education failed to translate broadly into economic mobility. Despite their average years of education—twelve years for Chicago's Filipinos over twenty-five years old, compared to seven years for California's Filipinos—segregation put them at the low end of the labor market. Filipinos could find jobs only in service industries, as butlers, gardeners, drivers, barbers, waiters, and dishwashers. A few of the elite graduated, returned to the Philippines, and entered medicine, education, law, and politics. Jose Abad Santos graduated from the University of Chicago and went on to become a chief justice of the Philippine Supreme Court. But most languished because of their socioeconomic position, and, like most other Asian students in the United States, they were forced into full-time employment by financial necessity. When the U.S. post office opened clerical positions to Filipinos during the 1920s, many took the civil service examination to qualify for those coveted jobs. The few who made it formed the Filipino Postal Club of Chicago.

The Pullman Company began hiring Filipino attendants for its train cars in 1925. African Americans had traditionally served in that capacity, but the train company saw an opportunity to divide its workers by race and began replacing African Americans with Filipinos. African Americans, led by A. Philip Randolph's Brotherhood of Sleeping Car Porters, were organized and posed a serious threat to the company's powers over them. By the 1930s, nearly four hundred Filipinos were working in Pullman club and dining cars.

Some African American workers, including Randolph at first, considered the Filipinos scab labor. In 1933, however, the Brotherhood began recruiting Filipinos into the union and hired Filipino field agents, like J. C. Brana in New York City and Cypriano Samonte in Chicago. "We must either align ourselves with the powerful reactionary forces—our employers . . . or . . . with the progressive forces of the country—our fellow employees and their trade unions," Brana reasoned. The Pullman Company appealed to Filipinos to ignore the Brotherhood's call, but they stood firm. In 1939, the union reiterated its position: "There can be no such thing as a colored labor union or a Filipino labor union. All unions are workers' unions, or should be."[20]

By 1947 Filipinos were joining the union at a rate nearly equal to that of African Americans, with 56 percent of Filipino and 57 percent of African American workers becoming union members. That solidarity was remarkable considering that in 1932 African American sleeping-car porters made a minimum monthly salary of $72.50 and Filipino attendants $85. The Pullman Company's labor and wage hierarchy was clearly intended to buy Filipino loyalty at the expense of African Americans. Labor and civil rights leaders like Randolph could have easily dismissed Asians as scab and cheap labor, as the white AFL did, and favor their exclusion. Instead they chose to unite workers.

The 1940 Census found 1,740 Filipinos in Chicago, mainly Ilocanos and Visayans, who formed separate social clubs. On the North Side rose a cluster of Filipino restaurants, pool halls, and barbershops. The many single men in the community found companionship in the numerous taxi-dance halls scattered throughout Chicago, and Chinatown and Chinese laundries offered familiar foods and places to socialize.

Taxi-dance halls, which started in San Francisco in 1913, became popular during the 1920s and 1930s in major U.S. cities. Dancers, usually young white women, earned commissions for dancing with male patrons, who commonly paid ten cents for a ticket to dance for the duration of a song. According to a study, at a time when they constituted a mere fraction of the city's population, Filipinos accounted for about 20 percent of the patrons of Chicago's taxi-dance halls, where their relations with white women drew undeserved suspicion. At stake was the alleged "purity" of white women, which was seen as coming under the protection and control of white men. When a Filipino dance-hall patron said of himself, "I'm a 'dangerous man,'" he was referring not only to his race but also to his gender and sexuality.[21]

Although sex workers rarely worked as taxi dancers, the two occupations were regarded as similar. To avoid police scrutiny, dance-hall proprietors agreed to the "Chicago plan" devised by the Juvenile Protective Association, a social work agency. Under the plan, owners agreed to have trained women supervisors on their dance floors to prevent "questionable conduct," and the Juvenile Protective Association monitored dance-hall owners' meetings and had the right to go through their records.

That racial policing also stigmatized relationships between Filipino men and white women. A 1927 Chicago survey found fifty-five such interracial couples. Public stares and insults were commonplace, but the couples were also at risk of violence. When John Cruz and his white wife dined at Chicago's Sunset Café, a white man announced for all to hear: "There is a Filipino with a white woman."[22] Outside, the man pulled out a gun and shot Cruz twice, leaving him in serious condition.

SEGREGATION AND DEPENDENCY

Segregation governed the lives of all peoples in the United States, bestowing privileges on whites and deprivations on nonwhites. Segregation was the principal means of securing the economic, political, and cultural dependency of Pacific Islanders and Asians after the period of migrant labor. Their economic activities were largely limited to occupations undesirable to white men. In industries that employed both whites and nonwhites, Asians were relegated to inferior and subservient positions. Asian men, and some women, were employed as domestic servants, cooks, and laundrymen—jobs commonly considered women's work. As a 1930s woman high school graduate recalled of growing up in San Francisco: "In those days there was no two ways about it. If you were Japanese, you either worked in an art store [Japanese gift store] . . . or you worked as a domestic. . . . There was no Japanese girl working in an American firm."[23] For Asians, as for African and Mexican American women, domestic service was an occupation with virtually no upward or outward mobility.

The Supreme Court's ruling in *Plessy. v. Ferguson* (1896) supplied a legal platform for the practice of segregation by declaring that "separate but equal" facilities were consistent with the Fourteenth Amendment's guarantee of equal protection under the law. Insofar as separate facilities and statutes such as miscegenation laws applied to all, courts and legislatures held, equal protection was achieved.

The Geary Act (1892) extended Chinese labor exclusion, refused Chinese (as non-whites) the ability to naturalize, and required all Chinese residents to register and carry identification cards or face imprisonment and deportation.

The anti-Asian movement's targeting of picture brides and the Cable Act, passed by Congress in 1922, revealed the social formation of race, gender, sexuality and nation in their focus on the central social institution of marriage. The act removed U.S. citizenship from women who married "aliens ineligible to citizenship." In 1931, Congress amended the Cable Act to allow women who had lost their U.S. citizenship through marriage to regain it through naturalization, as if they were immigrants. The law was finally repealed in 1936.

Segregation did not go unchallenged. Gong Lum, a Chinese grocer in Mississippi, opposed the South's Jim Crow school system when he sued to permit his daughter, Martha, to attend a white school. He was unsuccessful: in 1927, in *Gong Lum v. Rice*, the U.S. Supreme Court ruled that the state possessed the right to segregate whites from "the brown, yellow, and black" races. But school segregation was dealt a blow in California, where a federal court ruled in *Méndez v. Westminster School District of Orange County* (1946–47) that the segregation of Mexican children from white schools denied them equal protection under the Fourteenth Amendment. The petitioners and court, however, framed the case as a denial of white children's access to white schools, contrary to the arguments of African and Japanese Americans, who had urged that race and racial discrimination form the bases of the challenge.

The end of racial segregation had to await the U.S. Supreme Court's ruling in *Brown v. Board of Education* (1954), which dismantled not only school segregation but also *Plessy*'s separate-but-equal doctrine. Although segregation persisted within the U.S. social formation after 1954, requiring remediation through civil rights legislation in the 1960s, *Brown* effectively ended state-sanctioned segregation and weakened the foundation of dependency.

SUGGESTED READINGS

Fujita-Rony, Dorothy B. *American Workers, Colonial Power: Philippine Seattle and the Transpacific West, 1919–1941.* Berkeley: University of California Press, 2003.

Lui, Mary Ting Yi. *The Chinatown Trunk Mystery: Murder, Miscegenation, and Other Dangerous Encounters in Turn-of-the-Century New York City*. Princeton, NJ: Princeton University Press, 2005.

Wong, Marie Rose. *Sweet Cakes, Long Journey: The Chinatowns of Portland, Oregon*. Seattle: University of Washington Press, 2004.

Yu, Renqiu. *To Save China, to Save Ourselves: The Chinese Hand Laundry Alliance of New York*. Philadelphia: Temple University Press, 1992.

PRIMARY DOCUMENT
DOCUMENT 12

Paul G. Cressey, *The Taxi-Dance Hall: A Sociological Study in Commercialized Recreation and City Life* (Montclair, New Jersey: Patterson Smith, 1969), 157–58.

In the summer of 1925, Chicago's Juvenile Protective Association assigned Paul Cressey to study the city's taxi-dance halls. Cressey served as a caseworker and special investigator for the association. According to its executive director, Cressey's report revealed "the complexities which social agencies face in the urban situation, when in the interests of young people they are called upon to control and regulate doubtful social centers." Cressey's *Taxi-Dance Hall* reflects the interests and perspectives of the Chicago school of sociology in its approach to the phenomenon of rapid social changes promoted by the urban setting. Indeed, in the course of his studies, Cressey consulted with the Chicago sociologists E. W. Burgess and Robert E. Park and served as a research assistant for the university's sociology department and Local Community Research Committee. Cressey depended heavily on the case records of social agencies, including the Juvenile Protective Association, and from other reports and investigations. The following account by a Filipino subject is presented as case no. 44.

"Another Filipino and I attended a dance given in a downtown hotel. We saw a dance-hall girl who looked pretty good to us. We danced with her several times and she seemed clever. Then she asked me why she'd never met us before at Filipino affairs and I explained that we had our own life around the campus and didn't come to these dances often. Pacito took the cue and began bragging me up to her. He told her that I was a very rich fellow, that I had my own automobile and bought a car just because I didn't know what else to do with my money. Then he told her that I had several college girls who were crazy about me and that I didn't have to come to the dance halls. She became interested and invited me to come to the dance hall and see her.

"But I didn't go right away. I figured on disappointing her for a while so she'd be even more anxious when I did show up. About a week later my friend and I went around to the dance hall. She said she had a sister named Hazel and introduced us to her. So we decided to give the girls a rush. We laid our plans carefully, though. The only trouble was that they were too smart for us.

"He and I planned to 'talk up' each other to our girl, especially about the other's wealth, with the knowledge that each would tell the other what she heard, so we'd both profit. I guess our scheme worked because they surely began working on the principle that we had lots of money.

"After we left the dance hall, we drove to Chinatown. . . . The girls told us they'd get kicked out of their home if they were seen with a Filipino. That made us all the more interested because of course we thought they must come from a pretty good family if that were true. The next night my girl recalled that she was to have a birthday the following Friday. I told her I'd get her a present, even though I knew well enough she probably didn't have a birthday at all. The next day she called me to remind me of her birthday.

"I asked her for a date for a dance to be given the following week. But she said she already had a date with another Flip [Filipino]. She said she liked me better but that the other fellow was going to give her a dress. The implication was, of course, that if I'd buy her a dress she'd break her date and go with me. I told her that since she had already made this date with the other fellow that it wouldn't be right to break it. She seemed kind of nonplussed by that but finally intimated that I must not love her much or I wouldn't want her to go out with other fellows when she was already halfway engaged to me. I replied that I was liberal that way, that I always wanted my fiancée to have a good time.

"Then later in the week she phoned and asked if I wanted to go to a Filipino picnic. She said she'd go with me if I'd buy her a dress. Then she threatened to go with somebody else. I told her to go ahead, that I was broadminded that way. She wasn't satisfied; said she wanted to go with me and that the dress would be my birthday present to her. . . .

"I was sore but didn't want to give the impression of being a tight-wad. So I fixed up a story. I called her into a side room and said: 'It isn't because I don't want to give you a dress or because I don't want to spend the money. I don't like your principles. . . . You don't give me a chance to offer to make a present.' She was dumb with amazement. She probably didn't think a Filipino could talk like that. She just stood there with a blank look on her face for a minute or so and then turned and walked away."

SIGNIFICANT EVENTS

1829	Chang and Eng exhibited in Boston
1852	Chinese jugglers perform in Chicago
1863	Confederate soldier Charley Pang held as prisoner of war in Chicago
1870	Passaic Steam Laundry (New Jersey) recruits Chinese workers
1874	*gongsi fang* forms in New York City
1880	anti-Chinese riot in Denver, Colorado
1885	lynching of three Chinese in Issaquah Valley (WA)
	burning of Seattle's Chinese district

	expulsion of Tacoma's Chinese
	anti-Chinese riot in Rock Springs, Wyoming
1886	expulsion of Seattle's Chinese
1887	Dawes Act opens land on Yakama tribal lands
1888	Congress indemnifies China for anti-Chinese riots
1892	Chinese buy plots in Chicago's Rose Hill Cemetery
1894	*In re Saito* (Massachusetts), circuit court ruling affirming Asians as ineligible for naturalization
1896	*Plessy v. Ferguson*
1897	anti-Japanese mob violence in Idaho
1900	*Japanese American Commercial Weekly* (NY) begins
1901	Joe "Ranji" Smile's Omar Khayyam restaurant opens in New York City
1902	Boston Chinatown raid
1903	Filipino students arrive in Chicago
1907	Japan Society (NY) founded
	Japanese Mutual Aid Society of New York forms
1919	Chicago race riot
1920	Friends of Freedom for India holds first conference in New York
1921	Alien Land Law (WA)
1922	Erie Railroad hires South Asians, Chinese, and African Americans
	Alien Land Law (New Mexico)
1923	Revisions to Alien Land Law (WA)
1925	Pullman Company (Chicago) hires Filipino sleeping-car attendants
	Alien Land Law (KS)
1926	Rose Hill Cemetery (Chicago) expels its Chinese dead
1927	expulsion of Filipinos from Toppenish, WA
	Gong Lum v. Rice
1928	*Japanese American Courier* (NY) begins
	Filipino farm workers expelled from Dryden, WA
1929	Chinese Anti-Imperialist Alliance moves to New York City
1932	Cannery Workers' and Farm Laborers' Union (Seattle)
	Chinese Unemployed Council—Greater New York
1933	Chinese Hand Laundry Alliance (NY)
	Brotherhood of Sleeping Car Porters recruits Filipinos
1935	Filipino Farmers' Marketing Co-operative (WA)
1936	Virgil Dunyungan and Aurelio Simon assassinated

1937	Filipinos subject to alien land laws (WA)
	white vigilantes expel Filipinos from Yakima Valley, WA
1938	violence against African Americans at Wapato and Toppenish
1946–47	*Méndez v. Westminster School District of Orange County* (CA)
1948	*Pérez v. Sharp* (CA)
1954	*Brown v. Board of Education*

PART 4

WARS AND REALIGNMENTS

All of the major wars of the twentieth century in which the United States was involved, save World War I, also involved Asia, revealing the nation's pursuit of its manifest destiny. The masters of war deployed conventional, chemical, and nuclear weapons to destroy life and poison the waters and lands. The creation of militarized zones affected millions of Asians and Pacific Islanders.

Displacements were one of the consequences of wars as well as the global realignments of capitalism. Humans cause glaciers to melt, oceans to rise, and climates to change. Pacific Islanders lose their island homes, dislocated by nuclear tests and rising seas, and Asians join the new world order of transnational capitalism and imperialism and resist it in the name of religious fundamentalism.

In the United States of the 1960s, there were stirrings among people of color in favor of self-determination and against racism. The movement advocated an alliance with insurgent third world peoples. Those dreams died in the pursuit of national cultures, such as black power in the United States and the nation-state in Africa, Asia, and Oceania, which divided even as it mobilized.

The period also saw social movements by women, queers, workers, and immigrants all claiming rights that were denied them. Together, their demands for equality and justice on the bases of race, gender, sexuality, class, and nation testified to the realignments under way in the United States and world.

11

WORLD WAR II

Imperial wars in Asia are a salient feature of modern U.S. history, beginning in the Philippines at the start of the twentieth century; in Japan, Korea, and Southeast Asia thereafter; and in Iraq, Afghanistan, and Pakistan in the twenty-first century. In those wars, millions of people perished and millions more were dislocated and dispossessed. The wars had profound consequences for Pacific Islanders, whose homes became battlefields, nuclear test sites, and military fortresses and whose sons and daughters served in the U.S. military. They deeply touched Asians in the United States, whose families in Asia bore the brunt of those wars, who fought for the United States but were victimized as enemies of the state, and whose numbers swelled with "war brides," refugees, those called Amerasians, adoptees, and other casualties of those hostilities.

For many third world intellectuals, World War II was, like World War I, fought over territorial sovereignty at home and colonial possessions abroad—the material conditions. In addition, the war prominently involved the discourse of race and white supremacy—discourse. In Europe, Nazi Germany advanced the idea of Aryan supremacy in its determination to exterminate "inferior" peoples. In the Pacific, European and U.S. colonial powers defended white supremacy by defeating Japan and its siren call for Asian self-determination and decolonization.

THE COLOR LINE

European empires, wrote the African American scholar W. E. B. Du Bois in the midst of World War I, were built on colonialism and the economic exploitation of the lands and peoples of the "darker races"—"Chinese, East Indian, Negroes, and South American Indians"—justified by a belief in their inferiority, as affirmed by science and religion. The 1884 Berlin Conference, he noted, had parceled out Africa, synonymous with "bestiality and barbarism," for European colonization. The present conflict, Du Bois declared, was about the future of those colonies and the white supremacy that warranted them. Only after the abolition of racism and the granting of democracy across the color line would true peace descend upon the earth. The Caribbean intellectual Hubert Harrison elaborated this argument: World War I, ostensibly fought for democracy, was never fought for the benefit of peoples of color: rather, it was a war of the white race over possession of the lands and destinies of the earth's colored majority in Asia, Africa, and the islands of the sea.

Years earlier, in 1900, Du Bois had observed that "the problem of the twentieth century" would be the color line. Both the First and Second World Wars were global manifestations of that problem. Both wars were fought over European sovereignty, which included control of colonial possessions. They were entwined with sustained, anticolonial struggles that eventuated in the dismantling of European empires and the emergence of new, independent third world nations. Decolonization changed the course of more than four centuries of imperialism.

RACE WAR

Race figured prominently in the Second World War, epitomized by the Nazi project of producing a master race and the eradication of "undesirable" peoples and their genes. In its Pacific theater, the war tapped into the myths of a pure race and of simians, primitives, and the madmen of the yellow peril. It was part of the continuing decolonization struggles of Africans and Asians against their white rulers.

A March 1942 commentary in the London *Times* depicted Japan's attack on Pearl Harbor on December 7, 1941 as producing "a very practical revolution in race relations." The article referred to Japan's championing of peoples caught under European colonial rule, despite its own imperialist expansions into Manchuria and north China in the 1930s, which mimicked the European formula for national greatness. During the negotiations over the Treaty of Versailles (1918–19) that ended the First World War and founded the League of Nations, Japan had proposed an amendment to the league's covenant that would ensure "equal and just treatment in every respect, making no distinction, either in law or in fact, on account of their race or nationality." The European colonial powers rejected that proposition of racial equality, but Japan had gained the esteem of Asian and African anticolonialists as the "logical leader," in the words of Du Bois, of all colonized peoples of color.

Britain's prime minister, Winston Churchill, declared retrospectively that Pearl Harbor was "a staggering blow" and that "our prestige suffered with the loss of Hong Kong" to the Japanese three weeks later. A U.S. journalist in Hong Kong, who was among a group of civilians detained by the Japanese and paraded through the streets, confirmed the humiliation of defeat along the color line: "We were the perfect picture of the Fall of the White Man in the Far East." She added, "If you in America could see your own people being marched by those little monkey men with the big bayonets, you would realize what the Japs intend to do to all the white men."[1] Japanese conquests punctured the aura of white invincibility; they heightened race consciousness in a world divided by Europeans between West and East, white and nonwhite. While Nazi Germany affirmed the idea of white supremacy, Japan, at least discursively, threatened it.

The day after Pearl Harbor, on December 8, 1941, an Imperial Rescript described Japan's war aims: to ensure Japan's integrity and to remove European colonialism from and bring stability to East and Southeast Asia. These objectives were consistent with the calls of Japanese intellectuals during the 1930s to break the chains of dependence on the West. As Japan's army advanced into Southeast Asia, its generals proclaimed "Asia for Asians," and General Tomoyuki Yamashita promised to sweep away the arrogance of British colonizers and share the pains and joys of all peoples of color. On November 1943, as its prospects for victory dwindled, Japan called for a Great East Asia Conference that included representatives from Southeast Asia—Burma, the Philippines, and Thailand. There, the Japanese prime minister, Hideki Tojo, reiterated Japan's aim to wage war against "Anglo-Americans" who sought to perpetuate their colonial hold over Asia, and the conference concluded by urging cooperation based on principles of coexistence and shared prosperity, respect of national sovereignty and cultural diversity, the economic development of all, and the abolition of all systems of racism.

Those pronouncements were made despite Japanese atrocities committed against Asian soldiers and civilians alike. Imperial troops followed orders to "kill all, burn all, loot all" in China; bombed and massacred hundreds of thousands of men, women, and children; and repeatedly raped captive women. Throughout the Japanese empire, Koreans and Filipinas served as "comfort women," an obscene euphemism to be sure. Japan's militarists coerced civilians into work camps to labor in support of the war effort, drafted troops from their colonies in Korea and Taiwan to bolster their armies, and performed "experiments" on live prisoners.

Japan's stated intentions must have rung hollow for many of those who suffered under Japanese rule. Still, some anticolonial leaders among those peoples simultaneously condemned and cheered the Japanese advance. Mahatir Mohamad, a former prime minister of Malaysia, recalled that most Asians felt inferior to their British, French, and Dutch colonizers, and rarely did they consider independence a viable option. European masters, he explained, had structured their Asian colonies in order to exploit their raw materials and natural resources, and the colonies were thus dependencies. But, he observed, Japan's expulsion of the British "changed our view of the world," showing that "an Asian race, the Japanese" could defeat whites. That realization led to "a new awakening amongst us that if we wanted to, we could be like the Japanese. We did have the ability to govern our own country and compete with the Europeans on an equal footing,"

Mohamad wrote. Despite the suffering under Japanese wartime occupation and the "tremendous disappointment" over the return of the British after the war, the shackles of "mental servitude" had been broken.[2]

Indian nationalists were similarly divided in their defense of colonial India against a Japanese army ostensibly fighting to liberate them. The contradiction was heightened, remembered Jawaharlal Nehru, the first prime minister of India, when the British used the Defence of India Act to suppress everyday activities and arrest and imprison Indians without trial. "So instead of the intoxication of the thought of freedom which would unleash our energies and throw us with a nation's enthusiasm into the world struggle," Nehru wrote, "we experienced the aching frustration of its denial. And this denial was accompanied by an arrogance of language, a self-glorification of British rule and policy."[3]

On August 8, 1942, the anticolonial Indian National Congress passed the Quit India resolution, which called colonialism degrading and enfeebling of India and an offense to world freedom. The next day the British made numerous arrests. In response, acts of mass resistance spread throughout India. "As the war developed," Nehru observed, "it became ever clearer that the western democracies were fighting not for a change but for a perpetuation of the old order," and that both the Allied and Axis powers shared a common war interest: the preservation of white supremacy and the colonial status quo. Both sides, he noted, embraced legacies of "empire and racial discrimination," and after the war "the old imperialisms still functioned."[4] His view was confirmed in early 1942, amid widespread mass resistance to colonialism in India, when Churchill reassured a concerned House of Commons that the Atlantic Charter's provisions of sovereignty and self-government applied only to the nations of Europe and not to the colored, colonized races of the British empire. The Atlantic Charter, issued in August 1941, defined the Allied goals for the postwar world.

Conflict between imperial rule and the anticolonial, nation-building movement, which the colonizers painted as antiwhite, crested during World War II and continued through the Cold War of the 1950s and 1960s. Moreover, the Allies' rhetoric of freedom, equality, and self-determination, notwithstanding the outcome of the Second World War, simply reinstated European global dominance. From one side of the color line, then, World War II represented a continuation of and not a break with the past; while from the other side, the national liberation movements of the mid-twentieth century transformed world history with their demands for and achievement of freedom, equality, and self-determination.

THE DOMESTIC FRONT

Most U.S. histories celebrate World War II as the "good war," mainly because the war represented a new beginning for a nation mired in the Great Depression and led to its rise to world leadership. According to those histories, the war was launched not with imperial designs but in self-defense against fascist aggression, to protect liberty and democracy. The war also brought prosperity to the nation: weekly earnings rose by as much as 70 percent, manufacturing output doubled, and trade union membership increased by nearly 50 percent. In this view, the war offered women unprecedented economic opportunities and, in turn, greater freedoms from the bonds of marriage and domesticity. Similarly, the war granted African Americans, Latinos, American Indians, and some Asians greater employment mobility, and their contributions to the war effort gave them a powerful argument for civil rights.

The reality is otherwise. Although millions of women entered the workforce, many to hold jobs formerly reserved for men, the change was temporary: when the men came home from war, they displaced women from the workplace and expected wives to return to the domestic sphere. The federal government's push to engage African Americans and Latinos in military and civilian work was not intended to promote equal opportunity or even the beginnings of social equality: it arose principally from the need for their labor, especially in the secondary and service sectors of the wartime economy. In fact, it was only after A. Philip Randolph, the African American labor and civil rights leader, threatened a massive march on Washington, DC, in the summer of 1941 that President Franklin Roosevelt established the Fair Employment Practices Commission to investigate racial discrimination in the war industries. After the war, African Americans experienced high unemployment rates, indicative of the temporary and situational nature of their participation in the war economy.

The "good war" narrative neglects the racial fault lines and social upheavals at home that were exposed by the global conflict. World War II alerted African Americans to a resurgent internationalism and solidarity with peoples of color, based on their common condition of subjugation and exploitation. Walter White, the executive director of the National Association for the Advancement of Colored People (NAACP) during the war, testified: "World War II has given to the Negro a sense of kinship with other colored—and also oppressed—peoples of the world," and the realization that "the struggle of the Negro in the United States is part and parcel of the struggle against imperialism and exploitation in India, China, Burma, Africa, the Philippines, Malaya, the West Indies, and South America."[5]

The zoot-suit riots—named for their victims, Mexican, Filipino, and African American youths who adopted a style of dress called the zoot suit—as well as white race riots directed at African Americans and the mass removal and detention of Japanese, reaffirmed the racial cast of the war within the nation's borders. The weeklong zoot-suit riots, which began in Los Angeles on June 3, 1943, started when some Mexican youths fought with a few white sailors; the next night about two hundred sailors, calling themselves a "task force," descended on East Los Angeles and beat four Mexicans. Over the next several days, sailors and soldiers roamed through Mexican districts looking for male teenagers in order to strip off their clothes, cut the hair that distinguished them as "zooters," and beat them. On one night, the police arrested forty-four Mexicans, all of whom had been severely beaten, instead of apprehending their assailants. African and Filipino

FIGURE 52

Los Angeles, June 1943. The armed forces at work during the city's zoot-suit riot, defending their nation against "pollutions" of race, gender, sexuality, and nation.

Americans suffered the same fate as Mexicans when thousands of whites marched through other areas of Los Angeles ostensibly looking for zooters. Only after the military declared the downtown area out of bounds for those in uniform did the riots end.

Similar incidences of mob violence flared up in San Diego on June 9, Philadelphia on June 10, Chicago on June 15, and Evansville, Indiana, on June 27. Between June 16 and August 2, large-scale race riots occurred in Detroit, New York's Harlem, and Beaumont, Texas. The Detroit race riot of June 20–21 was one of the most devastating of the century: thirty-four people were killed, and property worth hundreds of thousands of dollars was destroyed. The Harlem riot of August 1–2 was the most severe in the history of the city's African American community: five people died, and approximately 565 received hospital treatment. Police arrested over five hundred, and property damage reached an estimated $5 million.

When President Franklin D. Roosevelt delivered his State of the Union address to Congress in January 1941, he told his audience that U.S. democracy promised "four freedoms": "The freedom of speech and expression—everywhere in the world. The second is freedom of every person to worship God in his own way—everywhere in the world. The third is freedom from want—everywhere in the world. The fourth is freedom from fear—anywhere in the world."[6] When the war came to the United States later that year, these freedoms supplied the rationale for fighting. Still, the war, while being waged in the name of freedom, curtailed the rights of many of America's peoples. A Jim Crow military, race riots, martial law and race-based detention, and American Indian reservations highlighted some of the incongruities.

African and Japanese Americans served in segregated units, were excluded from certain branches of the service, and were denied full equality in the military. While serving honorably in the war, Mexicans were attacked by uniformed sailors and soldiers. Draft boards routinely classified Japanese nisei as "enemy aliens," in violation of the Selective Service and Training Act of 1940. Among civilians, Japanese were held in concentration camps, African Americans were victimized by mob violence in U.S. cities, and American Indians were relegated to impoverished reservations. Hawai'i languished under martial law, the U.S. West Coast was a restricted military theater of operations, press censorship prevailed, and German and Italian aliens were held in detention on the suspicion—not proof—of Axis sympathies.

An African American soldier, Private Charles K. Wilson, wrote to Roosevelt on May 9, 1944: "It was with extreme pride that I, a soldier in the Armed Forces of our country, read the following affirmation of our war aims, pronounced by you at a recent press conference: 'The United Nations are fighting to make a world in which tyranny and aggression cannot exist; a world based upon freedom, equality, and justice; a world in which all persons, regardless of race, color and creed, may live in peace, honor and dignity.'" Accordingly, Wilson observed, that fight for "freedom, equality, and justice" for "all persons, regardless of race, color and creed" encompassed the world and the United States. But that view posed a paradox that required a resolution. "Let me give you an example of the lack of democracy in our Field, where I am now stationed," he wrote. "Negro soldiers are completely segregated from the white soldiers on the base. . . . How can we convince . . . the Negro members, that your pronouncements of the war aims of the United Nations means what it says, when their experience with . . . the United States of America, is just the opposite?"[7]

JAPANESE

As the possibility of war in the Pacific loomed, the U.S. military turned its focus onto the large Japanese population of Hawai'i. A federal commission sent to investigate Hawai'i's labor situation after the Japanese sugar workers' strike of 1920 had warned of the "menace of alien domination," and military intelligence concluded that Japan had embarked on a race war by organizing its nationals abroad. The Bureau of Investigation had predicted in 1921 that the rising tide of color would soon swamp "the white race" not only in California but also along the entire Pacific Coast. It painted a picture of a global threat to white supremacy led by Japan. Such hyperbole matched the most lurid "yellow peril" fantasies promulgated by journalists, writers, and filmmakers of the time.

During the 1930s, U.S. intelligence expanded its surveillance network and refined its prescription for containing the alleged Japanese contagion. In the midst of those preparations, President Roosevelt wrote a note to the military's Joint Board chief in Washington, DC, dated August 10, 1936: "Has the local Joint Planning Committee [Hawai'i] any recommendation to make? One obvious thought occurs to me—that every Japanese citizen or non-citizen on the Island of Oahu who meets these Japanese ships or has any connection with their officers or men should be secretly but definitely identified and his or her name placed on a special list of those who would be the first to be placed in a concentration camp in the event of trouble."[8]

The president's query and "obvious thought" had been prompted by an intelligence report from Hawai'i that discussed the arrival in Hawaiian waters of Japanese naval vessels and the entertainment of their officers and men by local Japanese. Although these were perfectly legal public events, in the eyes of U.S. strategists and the president, those encounters posed threats to national security: according to a Bureau report, "It is said, and no doubt with considerable truth, that every Japanese in the United States who can read and write is a member of the Japanese intelligence system."[9] The president asked the Joint Board chief and acting navy secretary, "What arrangements and plans have been made relative to concentration camps in the Hawaiian Islands for dangerous or undesirable aliens or citizens in the event of [a] national emergency?"[10]

The acting secretary of war responded that the army had established a "Service Command" in Hawai'i that linked the military with territorial forces such as the National Guard, police, and other civilian organizations for "the control of the civil population and the prevention of sabotage, of civil disturbances, or of local uprisings" of "potentially hostile Japanese." The Joint Board reassured the president: "It is a routine matter for those responsible for military intelligence to maintain lists of suspects, who will normally be the first to be interned under the operation of the Joint Defense Plan, Hawaiian Theater, in the event of war." But it underscored the need for continued vigilance and urged that the resources of government be pooled with those of the army and navy against the anticipated danger. Intelligence, the board noted, had "for years suspected espionage activities on the part of the indicated nation in the Pacific" and considered "the curbing of espionage activities in the Hawaiian area to be of the highest importance to the interests of national defense."[11]

While military and civilian intelligence disagreed over the potential for sabotage among Hawai'i's Japanese, they agreed that the people's loyalty to the United States could be coerced by interning their leaders. Thus, on the eve of Pearl Harbor, both military intelligence and the FBI maintained lists of Japanese "suspects" for their selective detention program. That strategy was especially important for Hawai'i, where Japanese labor was essential for the territory's economy, and where the military's concern was, as the army's chief planner put it, "to guarantee security to the islands and still maintain economic stability as well as adherence to the democratic principles of American government."[12] Accordingly, the army rejected as impractical and ruinous of the islands' industries the mass removal and detention of Hawai'i's Japanese, despite the insistence of the president, seconded by his navy secretary, on that course of action well into 1942.

Instead, the military's plan for Hawai'i, formulated as early as 1923, was to impose martial law, an extraordinary measure in U.S. history, to ward off the imagined Japanese peril. Military rule neatly bypassed "the democratic principles of American government"; it could impose a detention program, labor controls, and restrictions over freedoms of speech, religion, and movement. Martial law was designed to inspire fear and thus obedience. "Fear of severe punishment," an army document explained, "is the greatest deterrent to commission of crime." Hawai'i's governor observed in retrospect, "Internment of all suspected enemy aliens was the only safe course to put the 'fear of god' in the hearts of those who would assist the enemy."[13]

The Japanese attack on Pearl Harbor on the "day of infamy," December 7, 1941, marked a dividing line for Japanese in the United States. As smoke rose from the wreckage of the U.S. Pacific Fleet, martial law was declared in Hawai'i, and squads of FBI agents, military police, and local law-enforcement officers knocked on the doors of persons listed on index cards for apprehension in Hawai'i and on the West Coast. By December 9, 1,291 Japanese, 865 Germans, and 147 Italians were in custody.

Thus some 120,000 Japanese—two-thirds of whom were U.S. citizens, and the remainder excluded from citizenship under U.S. law—were summarily removed from their homes and placed in concentration camps for the duration of the war. They were not accused of any crime other than the presumed fact of their race. One drop of "Japanese blood" justified that racial profiling. As the general in charge of the defense of the West Coast explained: "The Japanese race is an enemy race and while many second and third generation Japanese born on United States soil, possessed of United States citizenship, have become 'Americanized,' the racial strains are undiluted." The *Los Angeles Times* added: "A viper is nonetheless a viper wherever the egg is hatched—so a Japanese-American, born of Japanese parents—grows up to be a Japanese, not an American."[14]

Yasutaro Soga, the Honolulu newspaper publisher, recalled that the events of December 7 filled him with apprehension. Instead of wearing his usual kimono at home, Soga put on his suit and wore shoes. In the evening, there was the anticipated knock on the door. "There were three, taller than six feet and young, military police," remembered Soga. "They told me to come to the immigration office. Without hesitation, I replied, 'surely' and went to my bedroom to wear my vest and coat." His wife went with him outside to the gate, and, in farewell, she whispered in his ear, "'Don't catch a cold.' I wanted to say something," he confessed, "but the voice couldn't come out."

He was hustled to Honolulu's immigration station, where the atmosphere was "bloodthirsty," the guards were "rough," and "things could have burst into bloodshed once a false step was taken." A young white military policeman treated the internees, many of whom were elderly and distinguished, with obvious contempt and brusquely ordered them around with his pointed bayonet. "I was so furious," Soga admitted, "as if my blood started flowing backward. I almost threw my mess kit at him." A fellow Japanese, Soga noticed, stared at the guard with "a pale face due to his anger," but they all had to restrain themselves because "if we had expressed our feelings, we would have died . . . a dog's death from the thrust of his bayonet."[15]

Japanese living on the West Coast were similarly rounded up. Yoshiaki Fukuda, a Konko church minister in San Francisco, was apprehended on December 7. "Although we were not informed of our destination," Fukuda recalled, "it was rumored that we were heading for Missoula, Montana. There were many leaders of the Japanese community aboard our train. . . . The view outside was blocked by shades on the windows, and we were watched constantly by sentries with bayoneted rifles who stood on either end of the coach. The door to the lavatory was kept open in order to prevent our escape or suicide. A gloomy atmosphere prevailed on the train. Much of this was attributable to the fact that we had been forced to leave our families and jobs with little or no warning. In addition, there were fears that we were being taken to be executed."[16]

Like Fukuda, forty-five-year-old Ichiro Shimoda, a Los Angeles gardener, was taken from his family on December 7. On the train to the Missoula detention camp, despairing over the fate of his wife and family back in Los Angeles, he attempted suicide by biting off his tongue. The other internees restrained him by putting a piece of wood in his mouth. At Missoula, Shimoda tried to asphyxiate himself. Transferred to Fort Sill in March 1942, he climbed the camp's inner fence. According to the FBI report, "One Jap became mildly insane and was placed in the Fort Sill Army Hospital. [He] . . . attempted an escape on May 13, 1942 at 7:20 A.M. He climbed the first fence, ran down the runway between the fencing, one hundred feet and started to climb the second, when he was shot and killed by two shots, one entering the back of his head. The guard had given him several verbal warnings."[17]

In the early hours of December 8, 1941, the FBI picked up Take Uchida and her husband, Setsuzo, in Idaho Falls, Idaho, because they were Japanese-language schoolteachers. "We were taken to the Seattle Immigration office immediately," she recalled. "We were not given a chance to store our belongings or furniture—just enough time to finish breakfast." From Seattle, her husband was sent to Bismarck, North Dakota. Uchida remained in Seattle until April 1942, when she was transferred to the Federal Women's Penitentiary in Seagoville, Texas. There she joined other Japanese internees, women and children, and hostages from Peru, Panama, and Hawai'i. "Most of the ladies were schoolteachers and the educated wives of influential businessmen engaged in business with Japan," Uchida explained.[18] The South American Japanese were in U.S. internment camps mainly because of pressure from the U.S. government, which intended to use them as hostages to exchange for U.S. prisoners of war in the Pacific theater.

As intended, these arbitrary and swift removals and detentions generated fear in Japanese communities. In Seattle, the Christian minister Daisuke Kitagawa remembered visiting the families of those who had been interned. "In no time," he wrote, "the whole community was thoroughly panic-stricken; every male lived in anticipation of arrest by the FBI, and every household endured each day in fear and trembling." Most believed that even a casual association with those taken away or their wives and children marked them, too, as targets. "Much of that fear can be attributed to the rumors, rampant in the community," Kitagawa reasoned, "about the grounds for those arrests, about the treatment the detainees were getting, and about their probable imprisonment for the duration of the war. No rational explanation could set their minds at ease."[19]

Across Honolulu harbor, within clear view of the immigration station, was Sand Island, a flat, desolate piece of land that had once served as a quarantine station. After Pearl Harbor, the army sought to isolate the internees from the rest of Hawai'i's people by transforming the station into a concentration camp. Told they were "prisoners of war" by the camp commander, the internees were strip-searched, forced outside into the pouring rain, and, in the gathering darkness, ordered to erect the tents that would house them.

Sand Island's terror worked on both the body and the mind. Strip searches were a common tactic of intimidation and humiliation. Citing that indignity, an internee exclaimed: "They stripped us down and even checked the anus. We were completely naked. Not even undershorts. They even checked our assholes." Another described how guards holding rifles lined a group up against a wall and threatened to shoot them if they refused to do as they were told. "With that threat," he remarked, "there was no need to say anything more."[20]

Women internees were detained separately. Unlike the men, they were racially integrated. At least eighteen Japanese and about ten German and Italian women were interned on Sand Island. The camp commander's wife served as matron. Like the men, Japanese women were held because they were community leaders, often connected with Shintoism or Buddhism. There were also women like Tsuta Yamane, who was apparently interned because she defended her husband as he was being arrested, and Umeno Harada, the wife of Yoshio Harada, who was accused of helping a downed Japanese pilot after the Pearl Harbor attack. Her husband and the pilot were killed. Before being brought to Sand Island, she had been separated from her three young children, placed in solitary confinement, watched constantly by armed guards, and handcuffed whenever she was led from her cell to the interrogation room. In protest, Harada refused to eat for five days. Her keepers summoned a minister to rekindle in her a desire to live.

On February 19, 1942, Roosevelt signed Executive Order 9066, authorizing the mass removal of all Japanese along the West Coast. The order gave the military the power to designate areas from which "any and all persons may be excluded" and to provide for such persons "transportation, food, shelter, and other accommodations as may be necessary . . . to accomplish the purpose of this order." The justification for Roosevelt's order was "military necessity."

Two days before the executive order, 172 Sand Island internees were told that they would be shipped to concentration camps on the U.S. continent. Early on the morning of February 20, military trucks, escorted by jeeps with machine-gun mounts, sped the internees through the back gate of the immigration station, past family members who had come to catch a glimpse of their husbands, fathers, brothers, and sons. On board the *Ulysses Grant,* the internees were hustled below deck for the one-week voyage to Angel Island in San Francisco Bay, the former detention center for migrants.

Throughout the spring and summer of 1942, Hawai'i's internees were scattered across the continent. In 1946, traces of the islands' Japanese could be found at Angel Island and Tule Lake (California), Camp McCoy (Wisconsin), Camp Forrest (Tennessee), Camp Livingstone (Louisiana), Camp Shelby (Mississippi), Fort Sill (Oklahoma), Fort Missoula (Montana), Lordsburg and Santa Fe (New Mexico), Crystal City and Seagoville (Texas), Jerome (Arkansas), and Topaz (Utah). Between 1942 and 1945, 1,875 Japanese from Hawai'i were detained on the continent. An additional 1,466 Japanese were held in camps in the islands, including Sand Island and Honouliuli on the island of O'ahu, which replaced Sand Island in March 1943 as the main detention camp for Hawai'i's internees. Japanese were also held in prisons and camps on the islands of Kaua'i, Lana'i, Maui, Moloka'i, and Hawai'i.

The forced removals in Hawai'i and along the West Coast had historical precedents. They recall President Andrew Jackson's expulsion of American Indians from the South, when thousands of Choctaws, Creeks, Chickasaws, and Cherokees walked the Trail of Tears to the "Great American Desert." Those who survived settled on land deemed unfit for human habitation. Japanese were similarly banished to deserts and barren lands, many on or bordering Indian reservations. Dillon Myer, head of the War Relocation Authority (WRA), the government bureaucracy that administered the World War II concentration camps for Japanese, would later become the director of the Bureau of Indian Affairs, in which capacity he launched a program of American Indian removal and assimilation called "termination."

When Japan launched an attack on the Aleutian and Pribilof islands off the Alaskan coast in the summer of 1942, the United States relocated other native peoples, the Unangan or Aleuts, to "abandoned facilities" in southeastern Alaska, where they were exposed to "a bitter climate and epidemics of disease without adequate protection or medical care." There, in the words of a U.S. government commission later charged with investigating civilian detentions, "they fell victim to an extraordinarily high death rate, losing many of the elders who sustained their culture." While the United States held the Aleuts in detention, its military "pillaged and ransacked" their homes on the islands. Those forced removals, the commission concluded, along with the "slow and inconsiderate" resettlement thereafter, sadly followed the historical pattern of "official indifference" that so many American Indian groups had experienced.[21]

Not all whites followed their government's example of racism. In Seattle, some called on Japanese homes to reassure families of interned men, located the internees and notified their families, and assisted those with frozen bank accounts. Their faith in their Japanese neighbors was vindicated by a comprehensive report on the Pearl Harbor disaster. The Army board of inquiry found that among Japanese "no single instance of sabotage occurred . . . up to December 7," and "in no case was there any instance of

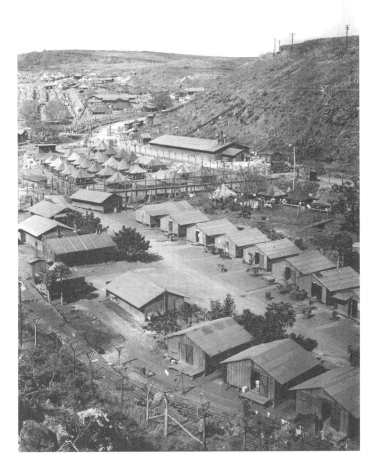

FIGURE 53

Honouliuli detention camp. After Sand Island closed in 1943, Honouliuli served as the camp for Hawaiʻi's internees (shacks in foreground). Some 2,700 noncombatant Korean prisoners of war were also confined at Honouliuli (tents in background). They were repatriated to Korea in December 1945. Photo by R. H. Lodge. Courtesy of Japanese Cultural Center of Hawaiʻi and Hawaiʻi's Plantation Village.

misbehavior, despite a very exhaustive investigation being made constantly by the FBI, and by G-2 [army intelligence], as well as by Naval Intelligence."[22]

In March 1942, Lieutenant General John DeWitt, head of the Army's Western Defense Command and the officer in charge of implementing Roosevelt's executive order, issued proclamations that divided up the command into a "prohibited zone"—essentially the coast and a strip along the Mexican border—and a "restricted zone"—a larger area contiguous with the former. The restrictions applied to German and Italian aliens but were extended to "any person of Japanese Ancestry." Japanese were advised to move "voluntarily" inland, away from the prohibited zone. Perhaps as many as nine thousand Japanese tried unsuccessfully to comply. "Those who attempted to cross into the interior states ran into all kinds of trouble," a government report noted. "Some were turned back by armed posses at the border of Nevada; others were clapped in jail and held overnight by panicky local peace officers; nearly all had difficulty in buying gasoline; many were greeted by 'No

FIGURE 54

Seven-year-old Helene Nakamoto (Mihara) (front, left), Mary Ann Itashiki (Yahiro) (front, right), and other children pledge allegiance to the flag at Raphael Weill Public School, San Francisco, 1942. Photo by Dorothea Lange. Courtesy of National Archives.

Japs Wanted' signs on the main streets of interior communities; and a few were threatened, or felt that they were threatened, with possibilities of mob violence." Residents of those interior states refused to become California's "dumping ground."[23]

DeWitt's first proclamations did not order any removals or confinements but designated restricted zones, established a curfew for "enemy aliens," and prohibited Japanese from leaving parts of Washington, Oregon, California, and Arizona, where most Japanese on the continent lived. On March 24, 1942, the general issued a "civilian exclusion order" that effected the complete removal of Japanese from the West Coast. The targets of this order were the several hundred Japanese who farmed on Bainbridge Island in Puget Sound, near Seattle. Soldiers dressed in battle fatigues tacked up the notices, bearing the heading "Instructions to All Persons of Japanese Ancestry," on the island's utility poles and at the post office and ferry landing. The Bainbridge Japanese, mostly berry and truck farmers, had six days to close their farms, settle their affairs, and pack their possessions. Some of the island's Japanese farmers were fortunate to have Filipino workers who managed their farms in their absence.

This order became the model for subsequent exclusion orders. The army and its civilian agency, the Wartime Civil Control Administration (WCCA), swept southward, forcibly evicting all Japanese living in California and parts of Washington, Oregon, and Arizona by August 1942.

Many Japanese believed they had to comply with the order . "We were herded onto the train just like cattle and swine," recalled Misuyo Nakamura. "I do not recall much conversation between the Japanese." Tei Endow added: "Our departure was somewhat quiet and reserved. Everyone seemed willing to express good feelings rather than bitter ones. Naturally we did not like what was happening," she explained, "but we tried to suppress our feelings and leave quietly and with goodwill. . . . My five-year-old son thought it was great to ride on a train! But my husband and I commiserated with Mr. and Mrs. Tamura, crying together about our fate."[24]

A few Japanese resisted the order. In April 1942, before the eviction notices were posted, Mary Asaba Ventura, a nisei married to a Filipino and a Seattle resident, filed a court challenge to the military curfew orders on the grounds that they infringed unreasonably on her rights as a loyal citizen. A federal judge denied her petition, trivializing her claim as "some technical right of [a] petitioning wife to defeat the military needs in this vital area during this extraordinary time." A fellow Seattle nisei, Gordon Hirabayashi, deliberately tested the constitutionality of the curfew order by failing to report for "evacuation." He was jailed for five months before his trial, at which he was found guilty of violating the curfew and "evacuation" orders by the same judge who had heard Mary Ventura's case. In Hood River, Oregon, native-born Minoru Yasui, like Hirabayashi, purposely violated the curfew order to challenge its legality. He was found guilty and sentenced to a year's imprisonment, of which he spent more than nine months in solitary confinement. When Fred Korematsu of Oakland, California, tried to avoid his forced removal, he was found guilty of violating the military exclusion order. The cases of Hirabayashi and Korematsu eventually reached the U.S. Supreme Court in 1943 and 1944. In both cases it ruled against the detained Japanese, and these rulings formed the legal basis for the entire program of mass removal and detention.

The government's actions sought to deprive Japanese not only of their civil liberties, property, and livelihoods but also of their dignity and humanity. After waiting in long lines, the detainees were registered, given numbers, and anonymously herded onto trucks, buses, and trains. They were dumped in makeshift "assembly centers," often county fairgrounds and horse racetracks; made wards of their government, which arbitrarily stripped them of their rights and possessions; and told nothing about their destinations or futures.

From assembly centers like Puyallup (Washington), Portland (Oregon), Tanforan, Marysville, Sacramento, Stockton, Turlock, Merced, Salinas, Pinedale, Fresno, Tulare, Santa

FIGURE 55
Tagged but defiant Sakutaro Aso and
children, 1942, just prior to confinement
in an "assembly center." Photo by
Dorothea Lange. Courtesy of National
Archives.

Anita, and Pomona (California), and Camp Myer (Arizona), the exiles were transferred to the ten concentration camps run by the WCCA's successor, the WRA: Tule Lake and Manzanar (California), Minidoka (Idaho), Topaz (Utah), Poston and Gila River (Arizona), Heart Mountain (Wyoming), Amache (Granada, Colorado), and Rohwer and Jerome (Arkansas).

To affirm their humanity, internees worked to transform the barren, cheerless barracks into tidy homes. They put up walls, papered and painted them, carved out niches and added shelves, and built window screens to shield them from the desert sun. Using scrap lumber, including shipping crates, skilled hands built tables, chairs, dressers, and other furniture.

Not content with detaining Japanese on the grounds of potential disloyalty, the government asked them to prove their worth by serving in the U.S. military. "The Army recruiting team came into Manzanar around the early part of 1943," Frank Chuman recalled.

We had a big meeting in this mess hall of all persons eligible for military duty with two white soldiers and a person of Japanese ancestry, and this guy was trying to persuade us all to volunteer for the Army, and I'm not too sure whether I got up and spoke back to him

FIGURE 56

Manzanar children's village, 1942. All Japanese orphans in the restricted zone, even babies in white foster homes and biracial children, were sent to Manzanar. Photo by Dorothea Lange. Courtesy of National Archives.

or whether I said it in my own mind, but I said, "Why should we fight for the United States Government as soldiers, when the United States Government distrusts us? Why do they now want us to serve when they consider us to be disloyal? Why do they want us to serve when they have taken us out of our homes and schools and businesses? . . . It doesn't make sense, and so far as I'm concerned I'm not going to do anything . . . until the United States Government does something to remedy this unjust situation."[25]

The Fair Play Committee at Heart Mountain concentration camp, begun by Hawai'i-born Kiyoshi Okamoto to protest against injustices, attracted large and eager audiences after Henry L. Stimson, Roosevelt's secretary of war, announced on January 20, 1944, that the nisei, formerly classed as "aliens not acceptable to the armed forces," would be subject to the draft. In a bulletin to the camp, the committee declared: "We . . . are not afraid to go to war—we are not afraid to risk our lives for our country. We would gladly sacrifice our lives to protect and uphold the principles and ideals of our country as set forth in the Constitution and the Bill of Rights, for on its inviolability depends the freedom, liberty, justice, and protection of all people including Japanese-Americans and all other minority groups." But, the committee noted, Japanese had been denied these rights. "Without any hearings, without due process of law . . . , without any charges filed against us, without any evidence of wrongdoing on our part, one hundred and ten thousand innocent people were kicked out of their homes, literally uprooted from where they have lived for the greater part of their lives, and herded like dangerous criminals into concentration camps with barb wire fencing and military police guarding it."[26]

Japanese subject to draft.

DENIAL

To make an example of those draft resisters, the government charged sixty-three of them and seven members of the Fair Play Committee's executive council with draft evasion and conspiracy to violate the law. The trial judge, Blake Kennedy, addressed the defendants as "you Jap boys." After finding the sixty-three guilty and sentencing them to three years' imprisonment, he assailed the men's loyalty: "If they are truly loyal American citizens, they should . . . embrace the opportunity to discharge the duties of citizens by offering themselves in the cause of our National defense."[27] As for the seven leaders, Kennedy found them all guilty and sentenced them to four years in Leavenworth Federal Penitentiary. After the war, an appeals court overturned those convictions, and on Christmas Eve 1947, President Harry Truman granted a presidential pardon to all draft resisters, including the nisei.

Some nisei chose to demonstrate their loyalty to the United States by volunteering for the armed services. After the Pearl Harbor attack, Hawai'i's military governor dismissed the 137 Japanese in the Territorial Guard, and the National Guard disarmed its nisei soldiers. Despite that obvious show of distrust, the nisei formed a volunteer labor battalion called the Varsity Victory Volunteers to "set out to fight a twofold fight for tolerance and justice," in the words of a prominent member. In May 1942, the military governor endorsed the mustering of a segregated unit of mainly Japanese, and in June of that year, the men of the newly created Provisional Battalion set sail for the continent.

The provisional battalion, renamed the 100th Infantry Battalion, confronted many indignities before facing their nation's enemies. They marched and trained with wooden guns before their commanders trusted them with firearms. White soldiers taunted them by calling them "Japs," and some of them were chosen to play the enemy in training exercises on Cat Island, Mississippi. Because of the belief that Japanese emitted a peculiar body odor that trained dogs could distinguish, nisei soldiers were ordered to hide and wait for the dogs to find them. "Most of us were transferred to Cat Island to pollute the island where the dogs were with the smell of 'Jap' blood," Yasuo Takata recalled. "Later results showed that this did not make any difference. . . . When the dog spotted us, the trainer would fire a shot and we would drop dead with a piece of meat . . . in front of our necks. The dog would eat the meat and lick our face. We didn't smell Japanese. We were Americans. Even a dog knew that!"[28]

About twenty-six thousand Japanese men and women served in the U.S. armed forces during World War II. The 100th Infantry was composed mainly of men from Hawai'i; the 442nd Regimental Combat Team consisted primarily of nisei from the concentration camps. In addition, Japanese members of the Military Intelligence Service and Office of Strategic Services served as translators and intelligence officers in the Pacific war. Over five hundred nisei women served in the U.S. military during the war, primarily in in the Women's Army Corps (WAC) and U.S. Cadet Nursing Corps.

The 100th and 442nd were among the most-decorated units of the war, garnering 18,143 individual citations. They also suffered some of the highest casualties, with 680 deaths, 67 missing, and 9,486 soldiers receiving Purple Hearts. "If you look at the 442nd boys," said Shig Doi, a veteran, "don't look at their faces, look at their bodies. Then you'll find out how much they've suffered."[29]

Of their sacrifice, President Truman told their depleted ranks when they assembled on the White House lawn in 1946, "You fought for the free nations of the world . . . you fought not only the enemy, you fought prejudice—and you won. Keep up that fight . . . continue to win—make this great Republic stand for what the Constitution says it stands for: 'the welfare of all the people, all the time.'" Spark Matsunaga, a veteran of the 100th and later a U.S. senator from Hawai'i, elaborated on that continuing struggle and its responsibilities: "If we the living, the beneficiaries of their sacrifice, are truly intent upon showing our gratitude, we must do more than gather together for speechmaking and perfunctory ceremonies. We must undertake to carry on the unfinished work which they so nobly advanced. The fight against prejudice is not confined to the battlefield, alone. It is still here and with us now." He concluded: "So long as a single member of our citizenry is denied the use of public facilities and denied the right to earn a decent living because, and solely because of, the color of his skin, we who 'fought against prejudice and won' ought not to sit idly by and tolerate the perpetuation of injustices."[30]

Despite President Truman's celebration of the nisei soldier, the government pursued the "repatriation" of Japanese to a defeated and occupied Japan long after the war's end. Public Law 405, an extraordinary measure passed by Congress in July 1944 to allow citizenship renunciation, was seen by some as a way to rid the United States permanently of its "Japanese problem." The state continued to seek "repatriation" by this means for more than two decades after the war's end. The San Francisco attorney Wayne Collins argued from 1945 to 1968 that the 5,766 Japanese who renounced their U.S. citizenship during the war did so under duress, and thus their action had no legal validity. "You can no more resign citizenship in time of war than you can resign from the human race," declared an indignant Collins.[31] Almost singlehandedly, Collins managed to restore the U.S. citizenship of all but a few hundred. In addition, as late as May 7, 1945, the U.S. House of Representatives passed HR 384, a bill authorizing the "repatriation" of native-born women who had lost their U.S. citizenship by marrying "aliens ineligible to citizenship" (issei).

Long after any pretext of military necessity could be sustained, Japanese were held in Justice Department internment and WRA concentration camps. Even after the war ended in August 1945, over forty-four thousand remained in those camps. Although groups of Japanese were gradually released to work in vital industries, to serve in the military, and to attend colleges and universities, the last camp closed only in March 1946, when the last internee left Tule Lake.

Japan's defeat and the U.S. military occupation of Japan and Okinawa held consequences for Japanese in the United States. As a result of the presence of U.S. bases and servicemen in devastated Japan, whether from love or power relations, there were marriages between U.S. servicemen and Japanese and Okinawan women. During the 1950s, an average of two to five thousand Japanese and Okinawan women entered the United

States annually as dependents or wives of U.S. servicemen, constituting about 80 percent of all Japanese immigrants in those years. Their numbers declined in the 1960s to about 2,500 each year, and during the 1970s to about 1,500. Wives of U.S. servicemen and their *hapa* children diversified and invigorated the U.S. Japanese population; yet racist and sexist stereotypes from those military encounters in postwar Japan and Okinawa haunted Asia and Asians in the United States

The practice of detaining potential spies and saboteurs did not end with the war: a rising tide of anticommunist sentiment led to continued violations of civil rights. In 1950, over President Truman's veto, Congress passed the Internal Security Act, Title II of which enabled the attorney general to apprehend and detain any person suspected of "probably" engaging in espionage or sabotage, without the rights of due process or trial by jury. One of the act's sponsors called Title II a program for "establishing concentration camps into which people might be put without benefit of trial, but merely by executive fiat . . . simply by an assumption, mind you, that an individual might be thinking about engaging in espionage or sabotage." From 1952 to 1957, the justice department maintained six concentration camps, including Tule Lake.

Some ten years later, the chairman of the House Un-American Activities Committee (HUAC) resurrected Title II because "black militants have essentially declared war on the United States, and therefore they lose all constitutional rights and should be imprisoned in detention camps."[32] Alert to the injustice and danger of the measure, Japanese led a repeal effort, joined by African Americans and civil libertarians, which succeeded on September 1971.

The Title II repeal effort was a part of the unfinished business of the World War II concentration camps. As was astutely noted by the civil rights activist Edison Uno, the campaign was an effort by the Japanese community to come to terms with a shameful past by acting as Americans with the full rights of citizenship. Japanese, he declared, had been held in "physical and psychological" concentration camps for too long. Further, he added, activism enabled a clearer sense of the group's place in the United States and a realization of its common ground with other oppressed minorities, including American Indians, who "for generations have been victims of the original American concentration camps which exist to this very day." In addition, poverty, hunger, disease, unemployment, mis-education, and racism "contribute towards the psychological concentration camps which continue to repress human beings as man practices his inhumanity to man. It is wrong to say 'it can't happen again,'" Uno warned.[33]

Prodded mainly by Japanese, Congress passed the Civil Liberties Act of 1988, which issued a formal apology for government mistreatment of Japanese during World War II, presidential pardons for those who resisted the eviction and detention orders, recommendations that government agencies restore to Japanese employees status or entitlements lost because of the wartime actions, and financial redress to Japanese individuals and communities: $20,000 to each survivor and the creation of a community fund to educate the American public about the experience. Never again, the act's sponsors resolved, should racism justify government infringements of civil liberties.

Civil liberties suffered a severe setback thirteen years later, when, following the September 11 attacks on the World Trade Center and the Pentagon, Congress passed the U.S.A. Patriot Act of 2001, enabling a secret and arbitrary government-sponsored program of racial profiling, registration, expulsion, and indefinite detention. As before, empire was pursued in the undeclared and extended "war on terror" on the basis of alleged threats to the nation's security, and protests against expansion abroad and lost liberties at home were condemned as unpatriotic.

CHINESE

War came to China years before Pearl Harbor. Japan's aggressions in China during the 1930s rallied Chinese patriots in the United States. "It is the sacred duty of the Chinese in America to resist Japanese aggression and save China," declared the Chinese student and activist Xueli Zuo in August 1936. In her speech, Zuo listed three tasks for Chinese America: enhance China's international standing; abolish unequal treaties and develop the economy of overseas Chinese; and publicize "the valiant contributions made by our forefathers to gold mining and railroad construction in order to help dispel discrimination against the Chinese in America."[34]

After Pearl Harbor, the U.S. wartime economy drew Chinese and other nonwhites into jobs formerly reserved for whites. Shipyards and aircraft factories were hungry for laborers. For the first time, many left the Chinatown laundries, shops, and restaurants for better-paying defense work. Both men and women answered the call. Dorothy Eng of Oakland, California, recalled: "Matronly women who had never worked outside of their homes before, got jobs as sweepers aboard ships. All they did was sweep. Sweep the decks. I remember seeing them get off the bus, going home to Chinatown carrying their broom and having their hair tied." Those jobs changed women's lives and loosened them from Chinatown. "So women were leaving homes just like everywhere else," Eng noted. "That was the big change. And then there were young women working in the shipyards. So there was a lot more mobility for the people."[35]

In 1942, an estimated 1,600 Chinese worked in the San Francisco Bay Area's defense industries, especially shipbuilding, and by 1943, Chinese made up 15 percent of the shipyard work force. These lucrative jobs came with the possibility of government-subsidized housing. May Lew Gee earned 25 cents an hour waitressing but $1.26 an hour working at the Kaiser shipyard in Richmond.

There were limits to the new acceptance of Chinese workers. Segregation was practiced at some shipyards, like Oakland's Moore Dry Dock, which apparently had a hierarchy of color and class with whites at the top, "Okies" and Chinese in the middle, and African Americans at the bottom. Also, like African Americans, Chinese were barred from certain crafts. They often worked in segregated crews, and few rose to supervisory positions.

San Francisco's Chinatown experienced a wartime boom, along with the national and regional economy. Restaurants saw a 300 percent increase in their revenues during the war years, and with sailors and soldiers passing through, Chinatown's bars and nightclubs carried on a brisk trade. A cocktail waitress at the Forbidden City club, Gladys Ng Gin, recalled: "During the Second World War, it was good money—fifty to sixty dollars a night in tips alone—wow!"[36]

Unlike African Americans, Japanese, and Filipinos, Chinese men and women served in integrated military units, as did American Indians and Mexicans. Private Charles Leong's account differs from the experience that Private Charles Wilson described in his letter to President Roosevelt. Leong wrote: "The average Chinese GI Joe likes and swears by the army. The most obvious reason, of course, is the fact that every Chinese would like to participate in defeating our common enemy—the Jap. . . . Perhaps more complex, but equally important . . . to GI Wong, in the army a 'Chinaman's chance' means a fair chance, one based not on race or creed, but on the stuff of the man who wears the uniform of the U.S. Army."[37]

Over 20 percent of all Chinese adult men in Hawai'i and the U.S. continent during the war years joined the U.S. Army. Of the 12,041 Chinese draftees, most saw combat duty, and 214 died. Chinese women served in the women's auxiliary units, the WAC; Women Accepted for Volunteer Emergency Service (WAVES); and the Army Nurse Corps. Two Chinese women, Maggie Gee from California and Hazel Ying Lee from Oregon, were among the 1,074 who made it into the elite Women's Airforce Service Pilots Program (WASP), flight-testing damaged and repaired aircraft and ferrying domestic deliveries.

Though many Chinese served in integrated military units, some served in the all-Chinese 115th Signal Company Service Group. Beginning in 1943, they also served with Chinese nationals and white Americans in a special support group called the Chinese-American Composite Wing on the China, Burma, and India war front. The U.S. 407th Air Service Squadron, led by white, Chinese, and Korean officers, served as a linguistic and cultural liaison between Chinese and U.S. forces.

Madame Chiang Kai-shek, the wife of China's wartime Nationalist leader, who was educated at Wellesley College in Massachusetts, made a well-received goodwill tour of the United States in 1943. She was supported by the powerful China Lobby, a group mainly composed of business interests, which influenced U.S. policy toward China for three decades. She was a guest of the Roosevelts and stayed at the White House, and she was the first private citizen and the second woman to address both houses of Congress. Besides stopping in major cities to call on prominent U.S. leaders, Madame Chiang visited with Chinese in New York City and San Francisco to thank them for their contributions to China's war effort.

The tour glossed over past U.S. actions in Asia and Asian migrant labor, exclusion, and dependency. Instead, Madame Chiang tried to foster friendship between wartime allies and boost the morale of Chinese America. An advertisement paid for by several businesses in San Francisco's Chinatown read: "For 100 years we Chinese have lived in California, working to make our community an integral institution of this region. . . . We welcome you, Madame Chiang, an outstanding Chinese leader. We welcome you as a woman who is proving the glory of womanhood. And, proving among leaders of both sexes, of all nations, of all times, you rank with the truly great."[38]

As it did for other peoples of color in the United States, the war provided an opening for Chinese to chip away at segregation at home by fighting for democracy abroad. A group of whites with interests in China formed the Citizens Committee to Repeal Chinese Exclusion and in 1943 lobbied Congress. They pointed out that the 1924 Johnson-Reed Act still imposed annual quotas on all Asians, which stood at 105 for Chinese, and it still banned "aliens ineligible to citizenship" and new Asian migrants. The timing was good for ending Chinese exclusion because of the wartime alliance with China. At a dinner she hosted for several key congressmen, Madame Chiang urged repeal of Chinese exclusion to boost Chinese morale in the war effort. Japan's propaganda, which embarrassed the United States with its accusations of racism, also played a prominent role in considerations of repeal. On December 17, 1943, President Roosevelt signed the act repealing the Chinese exclusion laws and allowing Chinese already in the United States to apply for U.S. citizenship.

The act not only rendered Chinese eligible for citizenship but also set a precedent for the naturalization of Filipinos and South Asians in 1946 and Koreans and Japanese in 1952. These naturalizations took place within the context of the Cold War and under the regime of dependency and assimilation in the United States. These developments paralleled decisions about U.S. citizenship and "termination" for American Indians during the 1940s and 1950s.

Other immigration laws further altered the status of Chinese in the United States. The War Brides Act of 1945 allowed admission to the United States of "alien spouses and alien children of citizen members of the United States armed forces." The Chinese Alien Wives of American Citizens Act (1946) amended the original act to allow the entry of Chinese wives unrestricted by the annual immigration quota of 105. In 1947, Congress passed a law admitting all alien wives of U.S. citizens on a nonquota basis. Many Chinese men who served in the U.S. military had family members in China, and some had married wives while in China during the war. But the majority of the wives and children who arrived in the United States under the 1945 and 1946 acts were resident in China and were reunited with their husbands and fathers after the end of the war. These family reunifications helped to close the gender gap and increase reproduction among U.S. Chinese. Under the War Brides Act, 5,132 Chinese women entered the United States, and the Chinese Alien Wives Act added 2,317 more. According to a study, from 1946 to 1950, the gender gap decreased from ratio of three men to every woman to a ratio of two to one, and the birth rate nearly tripled. Those increases also reflect the coming of age of U.S.-born Chinese women.

Japan invaded the Philippines, then a U.S. dependency, shortly after the Pearl Harbor attack. The Filipino and U.S. defenders fought until January 2, 1942, when Manila surrendered, but the army, four-fifths of whom were Filipino, retreated to the south of Manila on the Bataan Peninsula. There they continued their resistance until mid-April, when the Japanese Army overwhelmed them. Their commander, General Douglas MacArthur, had slipped out by submarine to Australia, but the captured survivors of his army were not as fortunate. The Japanese victors beat and bayoneted their prisoners and drove them on the Bataan Death March, in which up to ten thousand Filipino and over six hundred U.S. soldiers perished. The survivors were reduced to skeletons from starvation.

Filipinos, like the Chinese, sought to free their homeland by serving in the U.S. military, but with the Philippines still under the yoke of a colonial government, liberation was incomplete. On February 1942, the secretary of war announced the formation of the First Filipino Infantry Regiment to allow Filipinos in the United States to serve in the U.S. military in a segregated unit, like Japanese and African Americans The army needed to boost its troop levels, and the Filipino Regiment enabled noncitizens to serve. In California, some sixteen thousand, or 40 percent of the state's total Filipino population, quickly registered for the draft. That success prompted the formation of the Second Filipino Infantry Regiment, and together the two regiments totaled over seven thousand men. They undertook intelligence and scouting work and fought behind enemy lines. The First Reconnaissance Battalion, consisting of men from the Filipino regiments, provided valuable information for the return of U.S. forces under MacArthur.

Dominador Gobaleza, a member of the Reconnaissance Battalion, recalled training in Australia in 1943. After that, each man was posted to his home island and people, where he could speak the dialect and blend into the local population. That prospect excited Gobaleza and his comrades because, he said, he was eager to learn the fate of his family. Gene del Rosario remembered a morning in Seattle in March 1942 when he encountered two navy recruiters, a white and a Chinese, in Mary's Café, a Filipino hangout in the city's International District. With their encouragement, del Rosario joined the navy. "My thing [was] to avenge Bataan, the fall of Bataan. . . . I didn't want to sit down here and let the fight do it for me. I was happy to join any branch of service, but it just so happened that the Navy came and got me first. I just was so mad that the Japanese sneak attack on Pearl Harbor and the Philippines at that time." He served mainly as a ship's steward, like most other Filipinos before him, but he was also a gunner in combat. "Filipino veterans who enlisted from the United States are all forgotten," del Rosario sadly noted, and "even our own people, they forget us already. We Filipinos who served in the U.S. Armed Forces are veterans, but forgotten veterans."[39]

Bert Letrondo Sr. served in a different capacity. When the war came to the Philippines, Letrondo was a seventeen-year-old student at the Visayan Institute in Cebu. The first Japanese invaders arrived in his hometown of Palompon on Leyte Island in April 1942.

At first, Letrondo remembered, the Japanese tried to convince the people that they had come as liberators, not conquerors, but when the people opposed their town's occupation, the Japanese retaliated by "treating them like animals, beating them with guns, raping women and forcing both young and old men to act as their guides during patrols."[40] Letrondo joined a guerrilla band to drive the Japanese from their town. Lacking arms, they resorted to using pipes, slingshots, and poisoned arrows. He and his brother, Enrique, spied on Japanese troop movements and ambushed their patrols. On October 1945, when the U.S. forces landed on Leyte, they assigned Letrondo to building shelters for hundreds of displaced war victims. Later that year, he joined the U.S. Navy and, like other Filipinos, served white officers as a steward.

In the United States, Filipino farm workers made a critical contribution to the war effort, and Filipinas joined other women of color in the shipyards and defense industries. Children collected scrap metal and rubber, and adults purchased war bonds. Some Filipino men married First Nations women who had come from Canada to work, and their children were called Indipinos. Other young people, like Connie Amado Ortega, entertained the Filipino soldiers as they trained for duty. "When the war broke out, I was in high school," Ortega remembered. "We'd go to Fort Ord, Camp Cooke, Camp Roberts . . . on Greyhound buses. We used to sing a lot, doing Filipino folk dances for the troops."[41]

Tens of thousands of Filipino combatants died in the war, and an estimated one million Filipino civilians perished. Despite their sacrifice, the United States denied Philippine Army veterans, who had served under U.S. officers and alongside U.S. soldiers, the benefits that accrued under the G.I. Bill of Rights (1944), except for disability and death benefits. After the war, orphans made the journey to the United States along with war brides, many of them wives of Filipino American soldiers. "I was the first war bride to arrive in Seattle," said Magdalena Domingo Ruiz. "I landed in San Francisco from Manila in July 1946. It was a twenty-two day ocean voyage on the *S.S. Marine Jumper* . . . a troop ship loaded with returning servicemen and women from the Pacific War Theater together with repatriates, including kids. The fast tempo of living amazed me as compared with the slower pace in the Philippines."[42] In Seattle, mainly Visayan women formed the Philippine War Brides Association to assist in the transition for migrant women and to create a sense of community.

Filipina dependents of U.S. citizens entering the United States during the late 1950s totaled about 1,000 each year. Their numbers climbed to about 1,500 per year during the 1960s, and over 4,000 annually in the 1970s. Most of them were married to non-Asian servicemen and gained admission to the United States under the McCarran-Walter Act (1952) as nonquota immigrants or wives of U.S. citizens. Their numbers helped reduce the gender disparity among Filipinos in the United States.

KOREANS

Koreans' motives for joining the U.S. war effort were similar to those of the Chinese and Filipinos: to liberate their country of origin and claim their rights in the United States.

For Koreans, as for the Chinese, the war began long before Pearl Harbor, as their communities had rallied to the cause of Korea's independence from Japan since the start of the twentieth century. In April 1941, Korean leaders met in Honolulu and formed the United Korean Committee in America, with offices in Los Angeles and Honolulu. The committee was intended to unify all Korean nationalist activities under one organization.

More than two hundred thousand Korean refugees lived in China, and from that temporary shelter, Koreans waged a war against Japan's occupation of their country. In Los Angeles, on the evening of Japan's attack on Pearl Harbor, the Society for Aid to the Korean Volunteer Corps in China sponsored a fund-raising Korean Night, during which Koreans, Chinese, and whites alike cheered the U.S. entry into the war against Japan, and Koreans embraced it as a war for Korea's independence.

The U.S. government hired Japanese-speaking Koreans, including many students, as interpreters and translators of Japanese documents, and some served as teachers in Japanese-language training schools. Others joined the U.S. Army and were sent to Japanese-occupied areas in Korea, China, and Southeast Asia, where their language skills proved extremely valuable. Women volunteered for the Red Cross and sold war bonds. Between 1942 and 1943 Koreans bought defense bonds worth more than $239,000, and in Hawai'i, the United Korean Committee raised over $26,000 for the war effort in 1943.

Beginning in late December 1941, about a hundred men joined the Tiger Brigade, an all-Korean unit of the civilian, not regular, militia of the California National Guard in Los Angeles. Another unit was formed in San Francisco. Complicating the situation of Koreans was the U.S. government's prewar recognition of Japan's hegemony over Korea, which led to Koreans' being classified as Japanese. The United Korean Committee dispatched representatives to Washington, DC, to rescind that understanding between imperial powers, and the state and treasury departments agreed to reclassify Koreans as citizens of an allied nation rather than enemy aliens.

One exceptional Korean soldier was Young Oak Kim, who grew up in downtown Los Angeles with African American, Japanese, Korean, and Mexican neighbors. Kim's father was a grocer, and he attended local schools. On January 1941, he was drafted. Kim completed basic training and attended officer candidate school, where he graduated and earned the rank of second lieutenant. The only graduate without an assignment at first, Kim was eventually sent to the Japanese 100th Infantry Battalion. Kim's mother, on learning of her son's commission, voiced her objection, but Kim embraced the challenge. They were all Americans, he said, and he took command of the Second Platoon in Company B. He shared the horrors of war with his men, served with great distinction, and received the Distinguished Service Cross and Silver Star.

In anticipation of the war's end, Koreans in Hawai'i established the Post-war Assistance Society and collected seven hundred tons of relief supplies for Korea. On the continent, Koreans established another assistance society that operated until 1955. After Japan's surrender on August 15, 1945, the United Korean Committee met in Honolulu and sent a delegation to assist Korea in postwar reconstruction.

The victorious Allies agreed on the thirty-eighth parallel of latitude as the line dividing northern Korea, under Soviet occupation, and southern Korea, under U.S. troops. What was originally designated as a temporary division hardened with the onset of the Cold War and the installation of a communist government, led by Kim Il-sung, in the north and an anticommunist state in the south, headed by U.S.-educated Syngman Rhee. Both Kim and Rhee were hardliners and puppets of the two competing postwar superpowers. Korea, once again, became the battleground for foreign empire builders.

World War II profoundly affected peoples of color in the United States and the world. On the one hand, it was an imperial war waged to secure possessions and preserve white supremacy at home and abroad; on the other, it was an anticolonial war that brutalized even as it uplifted Asians and Africans. The U.S. concentration camps showed the racial and imperial cast of World War II, as W. E. B. Du Bois had predicted, and freedom movements in the United States were intimately tied to the anticolonial struggles in the third world. Like all wars, World War II failed to bring peace to the world. Instead it laid the foundations for new conflicts, empires, and militarized zones.

SUGGESTED READINGS

Camacho, Keith L. *Cultures of Commemoration: The Politics of War, Memory, and History in the Mariana Islands.* Honolulu: University of Hawai'i Press, 2011.

Fujitani, Takashi. *Race For Empire: Koreans as Japanese and Japanese as Americans during World War II.* Berkeley: University of California Press, 2011.

Kim, Elaine, and Chungmoo Choi, eds. *Dangerous Women: Gender and Korean Nationalism.* New York: Routledge, 1998.

Odo, Franklin. *No Sword to Bury: Japanese Americans in Hawai'i during World War II.* Philadelphia: Temple University Press, 2004.

Tateishi, John. *And Justice for All: An Oral History of the Japanese American Detention Camps.* New York: Random House, 1984.

Wong, K. Scott. *Americans First: Chinese Americans and the Second World War.* Cambridge, MA: Harvard University Press, 2005.

PRIMARY DOCUMENT

DOCUMENT 13

Mariano Bello Angeles, oral history, in *A Different Battle: Stories of Asian Pacific American Veterans,* ed. Carina A. del Rosario (Seattle: Wing Luke Asian Museum, 1999), 30–31.

Mariano Bello Angeles served in the segregated First Filipino Infantry during World War II. During his military service, from 1943 to 1947, Angeles rose to the rank of sergeant. The interviewer is Cynthia Mejia-Guidici.

Mariano Bello Angeles, Filipino promoted to sergeant in military service,

I arrived here in June 1927, at Victoria, Canada. We stayed there for one night and the next day we came to Seattle. It was always my ambition to go abroad. I had a friend over here, a townmate who was in Iowa during that time, who used to write to us over there in the Philippines about America. I was still a young man when the missionaries were boarding our home and they told us what America is, what kind of people they have and what government they have. . . . They describe America as a "dry" country and there is no drinking or something like that. They also say democracy and equality, justice and liberty and freedom—those are the American teachings there.

So when I came here I was surprised that the first person I saw was a drunkard on the street. And then at the same time, when I went and looked for a room or apartment, here I had a hard time. We had friends here already, other townmates of ours who came before me. I don't like to go and bother them so I have to go and look for my own room. Where I like to go, they don't like. Like the Olympic Hotel or something like that. They didn't like Orientals during those times. So again I like to eat, so I went to the restaurant to eat. Here again, it is disappointment that I really come across. And the first day, they don't like to serve me. So I said to myself, "This is America."

I worked and went to school from 1928 to 1930. Then I quit and I took a job again in the ship with the intention to go back to the Philippines. That is during the severity of the Depression and, at the same time, I did not like this place. From the experience I have—that's why. I look for a job in the ship and I was able to take a job in the ship as a captain's clerk or captain boy. They give me $45 as a wage each month at that time. The ship will travel around the world. I was very happy to get it but it happened that I was not a good sailor and got seasick. Got sick so then they dropped me in San Francisco.

I enlisted. I did not wait for my induction. I was just going into the military because the Philippines was involved. Then when I was in the Army, I was assigned on the medical department of the 1st Filipino Infantry. Before World War II, we Filipinos were fighting to become citizens. The Philippine and the U.S. government wouldn't give us that privilege except those who already are in the service. Those were the ones who were eligible only but us here, as a private citizen, we were not able to. Then during the World War II, when we were in the Army . . . then you can ask. In fact, they try to force you to get American citizenship. That was the thing that I fought. I resented it. Why do they have to become an American citizen now? But only they give it to the servicemen, see? Now I resented that. I refused to become an American citizen. When we were private citizens, we asked before and they didn't like us. In fact, they branded us. They even described us as barbarous. And why only the soldiers? So they mean to say that when my future is to die, that is the time when they give me the privilege to become American, so hell no.

How I came back. I was discharged in Fort Lewis, and came back to Seattle. I went back to Mrs. Perkins' place to be janitor again but different already. Different because there is a union and also different management already. I tried to take a job under the GI program, something like that, and I went and applied to the City Light, to the public health but they don't hire me. Frederick and Nelson, no, they still have that prejudice or discrimination. And the same attitude just after the war, the same attitude as before. Prejudice among Americans towards the Filipinos just gradually, year by year, became lax. But after the war—the same. One year after that, still the same. Then sooner or later, we were able to get our wives here, especially the service wives. Those men who came over here with the war brides now. They have no such trouble about discrimination anymore.

SIGNIFICANT EVENTS

1884	Berlin Conference
1900	W. E. B. Du Bois declares the "problem of the twentieth century"
1914–18	World War I
1919	League of Nations founded
1920	federal commission report on the sugar strike in Hawai'i
1923	military plans for martial law in Hawai'i
1934	Tydings-McDuffie Act
1936	President Franklin D. Roosevelt's concentration-camp memorandum
1939–45	World War II
1941	A. Philip Randolph threatens a march on Washington
	Fair Employment Practices Commission
	Japan attacks Pearl Harbor
	Japanese, aliens and citizens, and German and Italian aliens interned
	Sand Island internment camp opens
	"Tiger Brigade" of Koreans
	Public Law 360 allows Filipinos to serve in U.S. military
1942	Japan defeats U.S. in Philippines
	transfer of Hawai'i's Japanese to continent
	Terminal Island forced removal
	Executive Order 9066
	Public Law 503 enforces Executive Order 9066
	Mary Asaba Ventura and Minoru Yasui challenge military curfews
	First Filipino Infantry Regiment established
	Varsity Victory Volunteers established
	mass removal and confinement of Japanese on West Coast
	forced removal and confinement of Alaska's native peoples
	Gordon Hirabayashi and Fred Korematsu challenge forced removals

	100th Infantry Battalion formed
	Quit India Resolution
1943	zoot-suit and race riots
	Sand Island internment camp closes
	Honouliuli camp opens
	Chinese-American Composite Wing sent to Asia
	Kiyoshi (Gordon) Hirabayashi v. United States
	Minoru Yasui v. United States
	military volunteers recruited in concentration camps
	Madame Chiang Kai-shek tours the United States
	Chinese exclusion repealed
1944	nisei subject to military draft
	Fair Play Committee begins draft resistance
	Public Law 405 allows renunciation of U.S. citizenship
	G.I. Bill of Rights Act
	Fred Korematsu v. United States
	Ex Parte Mitsuye Endo, U.S. Supreme Court case involving forcible confinement of a U.S. citizen
1945	HR 384 and "repatriation" of women
	Japan surrenders
	United Nations founded
	Korea divided at the thirty-eighth parallel
	Honouliuli camp closes
	War Brides Act
	United Korean Committee helps with Korean reconstruction
1946	Tule Lake detention camp closes
	last shipment of "repatriates" to Japan
	Chinese Alien Wives of American Citizens Act
	Philippine independence
	Luce-Celler Act, allowing naturalization of some Filipinos and South Asians
1947	House Un-American Activities Committee hearings
1948	Japanese American Evacuation Claims Act, enabling redress for losses sustained in removal and detention
	Republic of Korea declared

1949	conviction of Iva Toguri d'Aquino, allegedly Tokyo Rose, wartime propaganda broadcaster on wartime Radio Tokyo
1950	Internal Security Act
1968	last Japanese American renunciation case
1971	Title II of Internal Security Act repealed
1976	Executive Order 9066 rescinded
1983	Commission on the Wartime Relocation and Internment of Civilians issues its report
1984	*Fred Korematsu v. United States* vacated
1987	Gordon Hirabayashi's conviction overturned
1988	Civil Liberties Act
1991	dissolution of Soviet Union
2001	U.S.A. Patriot Act

12

MILITARIZED ZONES

Having extended its grasp firmly into the Pacific and Asia, the United States established outposts to defend its interests. The future was not always in clear view, because the United States saw itself primarily as an extension of Atlantic civilization. But, like European nations before it, the United States had had Asia in mind when it first expanded across the American continent. The vision became clearer as the Far East became the nation's Far West. Theodore Roosevelt called the Pacific the nation's "ocean of destiny." Straddling the Atlantic and Pacific ocean worlds, the United States proclaimed policies of imperial right and installed colonies, dependencies, and militarized zones.

HAWAI'I

Pivotal to U.S. interests in the Pacific were the Hawaiian Islands. Fortification began with the naval base at Pu'uloa (Pearl Harbor), and with successive wars in Asia, U.S. military bases in the islands mushroomed. In central O'ahu, Schofield Barracks expanded to become the largest garrison in the United States. As the nation's air force developed, airfields were built to complement these fortifications. From World War II to the 1970s the military supplanted sugar as the leading industry, especially on O'ahu. In 1985, military spending accounted for $1.95 billion (15 to 20 percent) of the state's direct income, second only to the tourist industry. Moreover, military personnel in the islands, who were mainly haoles (whites), swelled with the tides of U.S. wars in Asia.

The long history of the white oligarchy and military occupation was offensive to locals, mainly Hawaiians and Asians. That enmity surfaced on the night of September 12, 1931, when Thalia Massie, the wife of Navy Lieutenant Thomas Massie, claimed that five or six "Hawaiian boys" had abducted and raped her. The police accepted Massie's testimony and quickly arrested Ben Ahakuelo, Henry Chang, Horace Ida, Joseph Kahahawai Jr., and David Takai, who had been involved in an automobile dispute and fight with a Hawaiian couple at about the time not far from where the alleged rape took place. At the police station, despite her earlier recollection that it was too dark to see her attackers, Massie positively identified three of the five suspects. The young men denied the allegation and claimed to know nothing of "the white woman."

At the trial held several weeks after the alleged assault, the attending physician and nurse testified there was no evidence of rape on Massie's body or clothing. Meanwhile, her husband claimed that Massie had become pregnant from the gang rape and had an abortion. A physician's report clearly stated that the patient was not pregnant. After four days of deliberation, the jury was unable to reach a verdict, so Judge Alva Steadman released the five defendants on bail. That decision, declared Admiral Yates Stirling, the highest-ranking navy officer in the territory and commander of the base at Pearl Harbor, was "a deliberate miscarriage of justice," and it "lessened the prestige of white peoples the world over wherever they are in contact with the darker stained races." He confided to a fellow Navy officer: "Our first inclination is to seize the brutes and string them up on trees."[1]

Six days after the youths' release, navy men forced Horace Ida, one of the five defendants, into their car and took him to the isolated, mountainous Pali, where they stripped him naked and beat him unconscious with leather belts. The police arrested no one. Feelings ran high, and fights between local men and sailors in Honolulu nearly led to a race riot. Finally, Thalia Massie's mother, Grace Fortescue, her husband, and two other navy men abducted Joseph Kahahawai, another of the five defendants, and shot him dead. One of his murderers later bragged: "I didn't fear this black bastard, although I had no use for him. To me, it was a challenge."[2]

The police caught and arrested Kahahawai's murderers in the act of taking his naked body to the ocean to dump it. Nearly two thousand mourners attended Joseph Kahahawai's funeral. "They shoot and kill us Hawaiians," David Kama exclaimed in his eulogy, and the mourners erupted in cheers as Kahahawai's four friends filed past his body.

Pending an indictment, the killers were released into the custody of the navy, and sailors quickly raised $7,000 for the defense of the four charged with the murder and kidnapping. Fortescue, the daughter of a prominent Washington, DC, banker, hired the noted labor and criminal lawyer Clarence Darrow for the defense. Despite Darrow's contention that this was an honor killing, the jury of six whites, three Hawaiians, two Chinese, and a Portuguese found the defendants guilty of manslaughter. Darrow later claimed that a white jury would have acquitted his clients "almost without argument."

The white oligarchy, the press, and over a hundred members of Congress urged Hawai'i's governor to pardon the convicts, and the governor responded by reducing their sentences from ten years to one hour, which they spent in his office drinking cocktails. Thalia Massie and her mother and husband fled Hawai'i for the safety of the continent, to be "among my own people," as Fortescue said. Nine months later, with no complainant, the charge against Ahakuelo, Chang, Ida, and Takai was dropped. But Kahahawai was dead, and justice had not been served. Locals understood well the different standards of justice for peoples of color and whites, especially those of the white elite and the military.

The imposition of martial law with the onset of World War II suspended democracy in the territory. The army issued decrees and dispensed justice through provost courts and military commissions. It regulated labor and froze wages, suspended union contracts, and banned strikes; it controlled prices and food production; and it censored the press, repressed criticism, defiled and occupied Buddhist and Shinto temples, and closed Japanese-language newspapers. Without the benefit of due process, the accused were tried, and some were convicted of violating the "spirit" of martial law. The territory's white elite took comfort in the repressive measures of military rule, and with wages frozen and military orders flowing, their businesses prospered.

The influx of defense workers during World War II caused the territory's population to leap from 258,000 in 1940 to 348,000 in 1945. Most of those, like the hundreds of thousands of U.S. servicemen who made stops in the islands, were single white men. By June 1945, there were about 253,000 soldiers on O'ahu alone, and the gender ratio resembled that of the bachelor societies of Chinese America. In the words of an army pamphlet given to soldiers on their way to the islands, "Girls are scarce in Hawaii . . . there simply aren't enough wahines (gals) to go around."[3] Although housed on military bases, soldiers on leave frequented the bars and brothels in Honolulu and towns adjacent to large military installations, like Wahiawa near Schofield Barracks.

Hotel Street in Honolulu's Chinatown, with its bars, tattoo parlors, brothels, and tourist shops, was the daily gathering place for over thirty thousand soldiers, sailors, and marines seeking the pleasures of the flesh during World War II. Men paid three dollars for three minutes with a woman an estimated 250,000 times. Although prostitution was illegal in the islands, there were about fifteen brothels in Honolulu, and between 1941 and 1944, about 250 sex workers registered with the Honolulu police, each paying a dollar a year for a license to operate as an "entertainer." Both the military and the police approved of organized prostitution as a way, ostensibly, to regulate and normalize men's sexual desires and protect elite white women from rape or seduction.

Most of the sex workers were white women from the continent, especially from San Francisco. With so many men and few women, sex workers serviced an estimated one hundred men daily, at least twenty days each month. Few women remained in the business for long more than six months. At a time when working women made about $2,000 a year, sex workers made $30,000 to $40,000, and madams made over $150,000. But disease was rampant, the lines of men were long, and the women had to work quickly.

As a patron said, "From the time you got in the room until the time you came didn't take three minutes."[4]

Contributions of Hawai'i's people to the war effort were substantial. More than forty thousand men from Hawai'i served in the U.S. military during World War II. About 806 died, and more than 2,200 were permanently disabled. Nearly half of the total were Japanese; 15 percent were white, 12 percent Hawaiian, 11 percent Chinese, 8 percent Filipino, and 2 percent Korean. Fifty-nine women, mostly Japanese, enlisted in women's auxiliary units. The territory's peoples invested millions of dollars in war bonds and contributed millions more toward war relief efforts.

For Hawaiians, as for the people of Korea, the Philippines, and Okinawa, the wartime military presence reopened old wounds. As the historian Jon Kamakawiwoʻole Osorio has written, Puʻuloa (Pearl Harbor) is a "visual and kinetic reminder not only of our loss . . . but of our hopelessness as well," and the U.S. warships in its placid waters are "the symbol of American power and the symbol of our dispossession."[5] The ships and armaments, with their effluents of waste and oil, pollute the bay fed by clear, freshwater springs and streams, and they exemplify the islands' dependency on war and imperialism for employment and revenues.

THE COLD WAR

The end of World War II engendered the beginning of the Cold War. The critical moment for some historians was the U.S. dropping of the atomic bomb on Hiroshima and Nagasaki on August 6 and 9, 1945, civilian targets attacked after most U.S. strategists knew that Japan had been defeated. The nuclear holocaust destroyed those cities and killed over one hundred thousand in Hiroshima and sixty-five thousand in Nagasaki, leading Japan to surrender unconditionally on August 15, 1945. Some have argued that racism facilitated those acts of inhumanity. The bombings alerted the Soviet Union to U.S. military might and the threat of nuclear war.

A strong though pliant China was vital to U.S. strategic planners, who, under the influence of the China Lobby, favored the Guomindang (KMT) government of Chiang Kai-shek despite its corruption and weakening hold against the surging tide of Mao Zedong's communist forces. By 1947, a full-scale civil war engulfed China. Initially the KMT held most major cities with a vast superiority in numbers and weapons. Yet an inept Nationalist government and Mao's appeal to China's peasant masses and his tactical acumen led to the KMT's swift collapse in 1949. Chiang and his followers, perhaps as many as two million officials, soldiers, and civilians, fled mainland China for the island of Taiwan. A Japanese colony since 1895, Taiwan was given to China after Japan's defeat. The KMT recolonized the island and brutally suppressed a rebellion in February 1947 by killing several thousand Taiwanese. The United States persisted in its recognition of Chiang's government in exile and refused to acknowledge China for more than twenty-five years.

With the loss of China as a client state, the United States turned to Japan and its development to secure its interests in Asia. During its occupation of Japan, the United States at first limited the nation's industrial recovery to prevent it from reemerging as a competing imperial power, but after Mao's victory in China, the United States lifted all restrictions on development and encouraged Japan's rapid economic growth. Henceforth, a strong and friendly Japan would serve U.S. strategic and economic interests in East Asia. These reversals of earlier U.S. relationships with China and Japan had ramifications for Chinese and Japanese in the United States.

The United States and the Soviet Union, although allies during World War II, had competing ideological and imperial objectives. The United States pursued an open-door trade policy to acquire resources and sell and purchase goods, while the USSR developed spheres of influence to bolster its war-ravaged nation and to buffer against future invasions. In the United States' "One World" vision, nations shaped in the image of the United States would fall under its dominion. The world of colored peoples, called the third world during the Cold War, was the ideological and material battlefield for these contending powers. The domestic analogue to the One World foreign policy of the United States was the assimilation of its peoples of color into the white majority.

In its contest with the Soviet Union, the United States subscribed to the containment policy known as the Truman Doctrine. The strategy, adopted in 1947, assumed an expansionist Soviet state that the United States should seek to contain. Later, Dean Acheson, Truman's secretary of state, observed that Soviet expansion would lead to what President Dwight Eisenhower likened to a row of dominoes falling, with one nation falling into communism and toppling another. For over forty years, the Truman Doctrine and domino-effect theory guided U.S. foreign policy.

The Marshall Plan, which poured over $12 billion into the postwar recovery and reconstruction of Europe, was a strategy for containing socialism. At home, the U.S. did not dismantle its wartime capabilities but in fact expanded them. The National Security Act of 1947 created a united military under a new Department of Defense, a National Security Council to advise the president on foreign and military affairs, and a Central Intelligence Agency (CIA) to collect information and conduct covert operations.

In a farewell address at the end of his presidential term in 1961, President Eisenhower, a war hero, cautioned against the nation's drift toward militarization. He warned against a "military-industrial complex" that threatened U.S. democracy. But civil liberties had already suffered since World War II in the government's crusade against internal subversion. Beginning in 1947, the House Un-American Activities Committee (HUAC) held widely publicized hearings to investigate the alleged communist infiltration of Hollywood and the government. Those accused were subject to intimidation, loss of their jobs, and imprisonment. Richard Nixon, a member of HUAC, and Joseph McCarthy, a senator from Wisconsin, made their reputations relentlessly pursuing suspected communists and making allegations of domestic subversion.

The strategy of containment effectively committed the United States to waging more wars in Asia, notably in Korea and Vietnam. This involvement in the affairs of other nations was justified in a 1950 National Security Council report known as NSC-68, which argued that the United States could no longer rely on client states to contain Soviet expansion but had to take the initiative to stop the contagion of communism within their borders. The report also called for a major expansion of the defense budget and U.S. military power.

THE PHILIPPINES

On July 4, 1946, the U.S. flags on Manila city buildings were lowered as bands played "The Star-Spangled Banner," and President Manuel Roxas hoisted the new Philippine national flag to the sound of "Marcha Nacional." General MacArthur flew from Tokyo, where he ruled occupied Japan, to proclaim "the end of mastery over peoples by force alone—the end of empire as the political chain that binds the unwilling weak to the unyielding strong." He then turned to a friend to say, without any apparent sense of irony, "America buried imperialism here today."[6]

Contrary to MacArthur's claim, the United States did not end its mastery of the Philippines but instead imposed twenty-two new military bases on the Philippine government, the main ones being Subic Bay Naval Base and Clark Airfield. The U.S. held ninety-nine-year leases on these bases and maintained jurisdiction over U.S. citizens in the Philippines as well as over Filipinos who worked on the installations. "Camptowns" sprouted up next to Clark and Subic bases (Angeles and Olongapo respectively), and their residents survived by catering to the needs of the U.S. personnel in bars, brothels, and massage parlors. Similar social relations emerged around other U.S. bases in Guam, Hawai'i, Okinawa, Korea, Thailand, and Vietnam, where local women and some men served the sexual desires of U.S. soldiers.

In a letter to President Roosevelt in August 1944, Manuel Quezon, president of the commonwealth, had stated what became the guiding principle of the nation's leaders: "One would be very blind indeed not to see that the postwar relationship between the Philippines and the United States should be as close, if not closer, than our relationship before the war."[7] The Philippines gained independence but remained dependent on the United States, as did Hawai'i, Guam, Okinawa, and Korea.

KOREA

In June 1950, North Korean forces invaded South Korea, rapidly occupying its capital, Seoul. Under U.S. prodding, the United Nations condemned North Korea's aggression and authorized an expeditionary force, composed mainly of U.S. troops, under the command of General Douglas MacArthur. The U.S. described its involvement as a "police action," as prescribed by NSC-68. UN, South Korean, and U.S. soldiers halted the North

FIGURE 57
Sister with brother on her back, Haengju, Korea, June 9, 1951. U.S. Navy photo.

Korean advance near the southern port of Busan and, after heavy fighting and much destruction, pushed the invaders back across the border at the thirty-eighth parallel. With Truman's agreement, MacArthur sent his troops into North Korea, to the border with China. In 1951, China retaliated by sending its armies into Korea and driving the allies to the far south of the Korean Peninsula. For the third time in a year, armies overran Korean cities and lands, and the fighting caused enormous destruction and loss of life.

In 1953, an armistice agreement suspended the war and imposed a demilitarized zone (DMZ) that roughly followed the thirty-eighth parallel. In all, about eight hundred thousand Korean soldiers, an equal number of Chinese, and fifty-six thousand UN combatants perished, four million civilians were killed or wounded, and over three million people were displaced and rendered refugees. Tens of thousands of Korean civilians found themselves in the United States as war brides and orphans. Between 1950 and 1989, Korean wives of U.S. servicemen totaled nearly one hundred thousand, and between 1955 and 1977, American families adopted about thirteen thousand Korean orphans.

In addition, many students became refugees, fleeing from an authoritarian South Korean government. Between 1945 and 1965, about six thousand Korean students left Korea and entered the United States to pursue their education. In the April 19 movement launched and led by students, tens of thousands took to the streets to protest against the police state of President Syngman Rhee. Many of the demonstrators were killed, and there were more than nine hundred casualties, but they won their cause, toppling the

Rhee government on April 27, 1960, and forcing him to flee to Hawai'i, where he lived until his death in 1965.

Yong-sook Chin was a fifteen-year-old high school student when she was killed by a police bullet during a demonstration in Seoul in the 1960 student uprising. Witnesses said she died shouting, "Long live democracy." Chin had left a note for her widowed mother on her way to the demonstration. In her letter, she apologized for leaving without saying goodbye but said she was determined to take part in the student demonstration "to show my love for my country and my people. All my school mates are ready to lay down their lives for our country," she reported, "and so am I. . . . Mother, I know you will feel grieved about my decision because you love me so much, but you should be cheerful when you think of freedom for the people and a bright future for our country. . . . Let me say again, I made up my mind to lay down my life for the cause of democracy. I have to close, time is short."[8] On hearing this story, concerned Koreans in San Francisco collected money to support Chin's mother and enable the schooling of her surviving children.

Koreans in the United States were not immune from surveillance by the Rhee regime. Korean diplomats collected information on Korean residents in their jurisdiction from a network of informers, and consul generals tried to infiltrate and control Korean student groups, churches, and social and political organizations through bribery and intimidation. The Rhee dictatorship branded critics of the Korean state as communists, in the language of the Cold War.

After the armistice, the United States kept its bases and military personnel in South Korea. The country effectively remained dependent on the United States, a status sustained through military dictatorships and coups. In 1966, South Korea and the United States signed a Status of Forces Agreement that gave the United States privileges such as free access to land deemed necessary for U.S. military activities. The agreement also permitted U.S. tanks, trucks, and hardware to rumble through rural towns and farmlands.

The U.S. military installations drove wedges into Korean culture, promoting consumerism and U.S. music, dress, and sensibilities. In the camptowns adjoining the bases, the gendered and imperialist binary of U.S. men and dependent Korean women was reinforced daily. In South Korea during the 1960s, more than thirty thousand Korean sex workers serviced some sixty-two thousand U.S. servicemen, and a 1997 study estimated twenty-five thousand women sex workers in camptowns. It was within those militarized zones that romance, marriage, and migration to the United States often began.

Even today, children born in Korea of U.S. paternity and their mothers remain social pariahs and noncitizens, according to the South Korean government. Many Koreans have removed sex workers from their family registries, effectively rendering them stateless. To be eligible for 7.S. citizenship, their children need documentation from their biological fathers, but these men frequently desert their pregnant partners. Relegated to the fringes of society, so-called Amerasian children have the highest school-dropout rates in

Korea. Many see orphanages and adoption as offering their best chance for a happy life. Even marriage fails to remove the stigma associated with "base women" in South Korea. In addition to looking down on them as impure, many Koreans see them as reminders of Korea's subservience.

One consequence of World War II and the U.S. war in and occupation of South Korea was the phenomenon of transnational adoptions. The first foreign-adoption program began when Harry and Bertha Holt of Oregon adopted eight Korean children in 1955. They later established Holt's Adoption Agency, renamed Holt International Children's Services. Between 1955 and 1965, the children who arrived in the United States from South Korea were mainly biracial children fathered by U.S. soldiers. In later years, they were Korean orphans, children of unmarried mothers, and children put up for adoption by impoverished families. The Amerasian Immigration Act of 1982 allowed U.S. entry to Amerasians born between 1950 and 1982 from Korea, Thailand, and the Philippines, but it required applicants to document their paternity and to have U.S. citizen sponsors willing to offer financial support for at least five years.

During the 1980s, over six thousand children were put up for adoption from South Korea each year, and they brought to the South Korean economy millions of dollars annually. Based on South Korea's Ministry of Health and Welfare statistics, there were 156,272 international adoptions between 1953 and 2004. The United States was by far the leading destination of those children, at 67 percent of the total. While most of the parents in the United States might have the best of intentions for their adopted children, South Korean transnational adoptions are rooted in U.S. Cold War history and the continuing occupation of U.S. troops.

GUAM

Since 1620, Guam's Chamorro people have negotiated Spanish and then U.S. conquest and colonization. After Spain's defeat in 1898, the United States established a coaling station on the island, as it did in Hawai'i, the Philippines, and Samoa, to supply its naval vessels and its growing Pacific empire. U.S. naval officers governed Guam, and American schools sought to inculcate in Chamorro children values and ideas promoting assimilation and loyalty to the colonial power. The U.S. military rulers aimed to instill dependency— political, economic, and cultural. Thus, the Guam Congress, created in 1917, held no legislative powers but was merely advisory to the U.S. Navy: from the naval governor's point of view, the Congress was a mock government for those unfit to rule themselves or participate fully in democracy. Chamorros were children, like Hawaiians, American Indians, and other indigenous peoples, maturing under tutelage.

With Germany's defeat in World War I, the League of Nations gave Germany's colonial hold over the Northern Mariana Islands, except Guam, to Japan. Although it saw the "South Seas" natives as inferior to Japanese and East Asians broadly, Japan promoted the islands' economic development and encouraged marriages between Japanese men and indigenous women to add vigor to the race. Between 1916 and 1918, Japan sent some two thousand Korean and Okinawan forced laborers to work the Mariana Islands' sugar plantations. By 1930, there were over 40,000 Japanese, Koreans, and Okinawans in the Northern Marianas, far outnumbering the estimated 4,300 native Chamorros.

In October 1941, in anticipation of war with Japan, the U.S. Navy evacuated some of its personnel and dependents from Guam to Hawai'i, leaving a force of about 160 men to defend the island. The Japanese invasion of Guam began on December 8, 1941, and two days later, the U.S. naval governor capitulated. Japan claimed to have "liberated" Guam from Western colonialism, declaring that its intention was to make the island self-sufficient and provide resources and labor. In reality, however, Japanese imperial soldiers searched for, interrogated, and executed suspected U.S. loyalists, raped Chamorro women, and demanded food from Chamorro farmers. They cultivated Chamorro dependency through assimilation, as advanced by Japanese-language instruction, schools, and cultural observances.

Whereas Guam's Chamorros were dubious about their U.S. and Japanese colonizers alike, Chamorros in the Northern Marianas held a more favorable opinion of the Japanese, having had a longer relationship of dependency with Japan. As the prospect of a U.S. invasion grew in 1944, the Japanese forced many of Guam's Chamorros into concentration camps to reduce the threat of internal subversion. U.S. planes bombed the island in June 1944, and, the United States reoccupied Guam in August. About sixteen thousand Japanese, Koreans, and Okinawans—soldiers and civilians—perished in the fighting, as well as nearly two thousand U.S. troops.

Chamorros to the north, on islands like Saipan, joined the Japanese in mobilizing against the United States, but in February 1944, when Japan's battle-hardened troops arrived on Saipan from China, Chamorros quickly came to see Japan as just another occupying power. When the United States invaded, Saipan's civilians—Chamorro, Japanese, Korean, and Okinawan—were caught between the contending armies. Some of those who could not escape, civilians and soldiers alike, leaped to their deaths from the cliffs fringing Saipan's northern coastline, facing Japan. By August 1944, the United States had secured Saipan, and it fortified huge airbases on Guam and the Northern Marianas to launch bombing raids against Japan, including the atomic missions over Hiroshima and Nagasaki.

From August 1944 to May 1946, the U.S. military imposed martial law on Guam, as it had done in Hawai'i. It decreed curfews, restricted movement, and regulated labor and food, justifying navy rule as promoting Chamorro welfare. The military forcibly removed Chamorros from their land to build and enlarge bases, affecting nearly fifteen thousand of Guam's twenty thousand inhabitants. Most of those lands were taken without compensation. The U.S. "rehabilitation" of Guam proceeded from martial law to the introduction of material objects like Spam and Tabasco sauce. The military built internment camps for civilian Japanese, Koreans, Okinawans, and Chamorro Japanese suspected of harboring pro-Japanese sentiments. Two years after Japan's surrender, those camps were still in operation. A legacy of that imposed segregation is the term *Guamanian*, which refers to Guam's Americanized Chamorros, distinguishing them from Chamorro Japanese and Chamorros from the Northern Mariana Islands.

With passage of the Organic Act of 1950, Guam remained an unincorporated U.S. territory but was granted a civilian government, ending half a century of U.S. Navy rule. Chamorros became U.S. citizens, and a nonvoting member represented them in the U.S. Congress. Like Hawai'i and other Pacific islands, Guam, Saipan, and Tinian are U.S. garrisons with military and naval bases to ensure their state of economic and social dependency.

OKINAWA

Okinawa, or the Ryukyus, an independent kingdom and a chain of islands, was invaded in 1609 and occupied by Japan from 1879. Okinawa Island was selected by Japan's militarists as the last battlefield of World War II. In the conflict, 90 percent of Naha City, the capital, was reduced to rubble by U.S. bombs, and some 150,000 Okinawan civilians, as many as one-third of the total population, perished in the invasion and from disease and starvation in its aftermath. As South Sea natives, Okinawans were considered primitive and uncivilized by the Japanese: these attitudes were evident in Japanese prejudices against Okinawans in Hawai'i before the war. After the war, Japan readily gave Okinawa over to the U.S. military, who governed the islands until 1972.

The "soft" occupation of Okinawa under U.S. military rule began with the education of its children, following a pattern of colonization practiced from Hawai'i to the Philippines and Guam. During the Cold War, the educational system was designed to produce dependent subjects as a bulwark against communism. Douglas MacArthur wrote about the military's establishment of the University of the Ryukyus in 1950: "Conceived in the aftermath of war and intended to flourish in the way of peace, the University is born as the champions of freedom rally once more to defend their heritage against those forces that would enslave the mind of man."[9] The university's main function was to educate teachers, who would help form the young minds of the islands, and all instruction was to be in English. Just as Japanese colonizers of Okinawa had insisted on the exclusive use of the Japanese language, the U.S. colonizers sought to eradicate the indigenous tongue. To underscore the U.S. conquest and triumph, the military chose to erect the university over the throne room of the ancient Ryukyu kingdom.

Okinawa Island supplied an ideal base for U.S. military operations in the Pacific and Asia. From Okinawa, the United States could police the tensions between Taiwan and China, the U.S. wars in Korea and Vietnam, and even the wars in the Persian Gulf. When Okinawa reverted to Japan in 1972, the U.S.-Japan Mutual Cooperation and Security Treaty of 1960 still ensured the United States free access to the prefecture's thirty-eight military facilities, occupying nearly 20 percent of all the real estate on Okinawa Island. In 2010, 75 percent of all U.S. bases in Japan were located in Okinawa. As in Korea and the Philippines, camptowns sprouted next to the bases, establishing a culture of dependency that included prostitution. According to a 1969 study, about 7,400 Okinawan women, or about 3 percent of all women between the ages of ten and sixty, were involved in sex work.

The U.S. military presence led to other crimes. Violent assaults committed by U.S. servicemen against Okinawans, mainly women, rose from 973 cases in 1964 to 1,003 in 1965 and 1,407 in 1966. Many more instances went unreported, and those charged with rape and murder were acquitted or sentenced to mild punishments such as transfers, salary reductions, and demotions in rank.

The U.S. military maintained jurisdiction over its own personnel. In September 1970, an intoxicated U.S. soldier driving in Itoman village struck and killed an Okinawan woman walking on the sidewalk, but the U.S. military found the driver innocent of any wrongdoing. Three months later in December, another drunk U.S. soldier hit an Okinawan pedestrian in Koza town. This time, an angry crowd of some two hundred Okinawans gathered, and some of them tried to prevent the U.S. military police from taking away the car from the crash scene. Removing the evidence, they believed, would lead to another whitewash. Others called out for a "people's trial" of the American driver.

Some began throwing stones at passing cars carrying Americans, and someone called out not to harm African American soldiers. By the time several military and Okinawan police arrived to restore order at the scene, there were over a thousand people in the streets. The police fired shots, the surging crowd retreated, and groups of them proceeded to overturn and burn cars with license plates designating them as American-owned vehicles, yelling "Yankee Go Home!" Protesters threw Molotov cocktails, and some ventured onto the adjacent Kadena Air Base and torched several buildings. Within six hours, the demonstrators had destroyed about seventy cars, and the police arrested nineteen Okinawans.

The 1970 Koza uprising appropriately occurred in a camptown of bars, strip clubs, and other amusements catering to the desires of the Kadena Air Base personnel. Koza did not exist prior to U.S. occupation: it represented the seething discontent of many of its colonized occupants over their economic, political, racial, and sexual subordination. To many of the white servicemen who were in transit to or returning from Vietnam, Okinawans were simply "Japs" or, like the Vietnamese enemy, "gooks."

Some African American soldiers, segregated to quarters in Koza contemptuously called the "bush" by white servicemen, had a different opinion of Okinawans. A group called the "Bush Masters," appropriating the slur, numbered over one hundred members in 1969. They met in a Koza bar to discuss black power and, as the Black Panthers taught, third world solidarity. The Bush Masters paid Okinawan businesses what was owed them by negligent African American patrons, and they coordinated a blood drive when an Okinawan woman needed blood transfusions.

Following the Koza uprising, African American servicemen distributed a flier addressed to Okinawans, written in English and Japanese. "We are both in the same situation," it began. "The Black GI's are willing to help and talk to the Okinawans in order to form much better relations between the oppressed groups, because we have so much in common." African Americans, the flier assured, were aware of the underlying causes of the uprising, which was "truly a RIGHT-ON-MOVE" because "that's the only way they'll [U.S. military] bend."[10] Back in the United States, the January 4, 1969, issue of *Black Panther* praised the courage of the three hundred Okinawan university students who rallied to demand the removal of U.S. B-52 bombers from their soil and the dismantling of U.S. bases.

Asian activists in the United States concurred. In New York City in April 1969, two nisei Japanese women activists, Minn Matsuda and Kazu Iijima, started the group Asian Americans for Action (AAA), consisting mainly of students at Columbia University and the City College of New York who had been politicized by the black power movement. AAA opposed racism, capitalism, and imperialism and was ardently against the U.S. war in Vietnam. In an undated publication, the AAA urged Americans to join "the people of Okinawa and Japan in demanding the complete removal of all U.S. bases, personnel and military equipment from Okinawa and Japan" and proclaimed that Americans "must insist on liberation and self-determination for the people of Okinawa as for all of the Third World."[11]

In the twenty-first century, the United States sees a resurgent China as a threat to its dominance in the Pacific and much of Asia. The continued militarization of Pacific islands points to that perceived challenge. In 2009, the United States and Japan signed an accord to transfer U.S. marines from Okinawa to Guam, making Guam a center for intelligence, surveillance, and strike operations. When that relocation is complete, the U.S. military presence in Okinawa will diminish even as the remilitarization of Guam, where Chamorros accounted for less than 40 percent of the population in 2010 and U.S. bases occupy nearly one-third of the island, will begin anew.

VIETNAM

To most Americans, the Vietnam War was a distant event, but to Vietnamese, the conflict was a vital decolonization struggle. Indochina, a French colony since the mid-nineteenth century, briefly fell to the Japanese during World War II. In 1941, the Viet Minh, led by Ho Chi Minh, a communist educated in Paris and Moscow, battled the Japanese. After Japan's defeat, he declared an independent Vietnam in 1945. In the same year, Cambodia and Laos likewise declared their independence. France, however, saw its former colonies as important for its postwar economic recovery and returned to reclaim Indochina. Britain and the United States supported France, and in 1949 a French cruiser shelled Haiphong, killing some six thousand civilians. The French army easily expelled the Viet Minh from Hanoi, and the colonial power installed their puppet, the former emperor Bao Dai, as the nominal head of the national government. The Viet Minh regrouped to press the French army, which the United States backed financially, and defeated them at Dien Bien Phu in 1954. The French granted Cambodia and Laos their independence in 1953.

The Geneva Conference (1954), involving principally Britain, China, France, the Soviet Union, and the United States, was originally planned to settle the conflict in Korea by uniting the peninsula. With the French defeat in Indochina, the conference turned to the consideration of Vietnam, which the conferring powers divided at the seventeenth parallel, leaving the North to Ho Chi Minh's Viet Minh and the South to a pro-Western regime headed by Ngo Dinh Diem. The Geneva Accords also promised an election in 1956 to reunite the country under a single government. As in the case of Korea, the Vietnamese people were largely excluded from these determinations of their destinies. Both Korea and Vietnam were artificially divided largely as a result of the Cold War.

With France gone, the United States stepped into the breach by supplying intelligence to the Diem government and providing military aid, which by 1956 was second only to the U.S. military aid supplied to Korea. With the 1949 Communist victory in China and the division of Korea, Vietnam became strategically important to the United States in its effort to contain communism in Southeast Asia.

The U.S.-supported Diem reneged on the Geneva Accords' promise of a 1956 election and instead pursued a campaign to eliminate Viet Minh supporters in the South. Driven underground, the Viet Minh formed the National Liberation Front (NLF) in 1959 to remove the remnants of Western colonialism and its collaborators and reunite the nation. With support from the North, the NLF pursued that war of national liberation.

The early 1960s went badly for the Diem government, which made little headway against the NLF and angered Buddhists by favoring Catholicism and Westernization. The United States tacitly supported a plot by South Vietnamese generals to topple Diem in 1963, which resulted in a coup and Diem's assassination. With a foreign policy dominated by the Cold War, the strategy of containment, and NSC-68, the United States poured money and armaments, advisers, and then troops into the escalating conflict. In 1964 Congress passed the Gulf of Tonkin resolution, which authorized the president to "take all necessary measures" to protect U.S. forces and prevent further aggression in Southeast Asia. Given that opening, President Lyndon Johnson began the U.S. military buildup that by 1967 involved over half a million U.S. military personnel, including over eighty-eight thousand Asian and Pacific Islander Americans. As in other U.S. wars in Asia, these troops experienced disquiet, looking like and sometimes sharing the ethnicity and cause of the enemy.

Teresita Iriarte Coalson was from Guam, where she saw armaments being assembled for shipment to Vietnam. She entered the WAC in 1968 "for God and country," she said, and became, according to a recruiter, the first Chamorro woman to serve in military intelligence. Coalson became an assistant instructor and "demonstrator," playing the roles of Vietnamese women—bar girl, guerrilla, wife—in practice interrogation sessions. Despite her strong sense of duty, she was shocked by an incident during a training session in which she played the enemy. A Special Forces veteran of two or three tours in Vietnam was to interrogate her with a monitor watching. When the monitor left them alone, the soldier without warning picked her up and slammed her against the wall. "In my mind

I was thinking, 'Geneva Conventions! Geneva Conventions!'" recalled Coalson. "I really didn't have a chance to get it out. I hit the board; he hit me against it pretty hard."[12] He was probably having a flashback, Coalson reasoned, a "gook" moment.

Another Asian serviceman, Ron Chinn, "never gave the military any thought." He believed the U.S. war in Vietnam "would blow over and never affect any of us." But one day, he received a letter, delivered by a postman and two FBI agents, informing him he had been drafted into the U.S. Army. The FBI agents were present because of a suspicion that Chinn was a draft dodger: he had failed to respond to an earlier notice, which had been returned unopened. Chinn explained that he had moved from Seattle to spend the summer working with his father and so never received the original letter.

The FBI agents escorted Chinn to Tacoma without giving him time to say goodbye to his father. During basic training, Chinn recalled, the drill instructors repeatedly called him "gook." "My name wasn't Pvt. Chinn; it was gook." Even in officer candidate school, his instructors believed "no gook should lead their men to combat. I was always treated that way; they never let up." When he arrived in Vietnam, Chinn was with fourteen other enlisted men when an African American major spotted him and "started yelling real loud and he called our command sergeant out and demanded . . . [to know] why there was a gook in his formation." He kept yelling and screaming and ordered the men to "lock and load. Shoot the son of a bitch. He cannot be on our base; this is a maximum security base."[13] Chinn's sergeant took him aside after that incident and told him that he and his team would have to stay in a segregated compound. Nevertheless, Chinn served for two years as an army Ranger and earned the rank of captain.

As in the U.S. war in the Philippines, U.S. soldiers carried out "pacification" campaigns aimed to isolate the enemy: they uprooted peasants from their homes and forced them into "refugee" camps. By 1967, those tactics had produced more than three million displaced people whose anger was directed primarily at the United States and not the Viet Minh. On New Year's Day or Tet, January 31, 1968, the Viet Minh launched a major attack that reached into the heart of Saigon, the South Vietnamese capital. Although U.S. troops soon repelled the advance, inflicting heavy losses, the Tet offensive was a tactical success for the Viet Minh.

Within weeks, opposition to the war in the United States nearly doubled, and the antiwar movement mobilized to challenge President Johnson. Facing certain defeat in his own party, Johnson withdrew from the 1968 presidential contest, and Richard Nixon won the White House, determined to restore order at home and abroad. During the campaign, Nixon promised "peace with honor" in the Vietnam conflict, which seemed endless and had claimed the lives of many U.S. servicemen, divided the nation, and undermined the nation's standing in the world.

Before negotiations in 1970, however, Nixon ordered an expansion of the war by invading Cambodia to destroy Viet Minh bases there and give the United States an advantage at the peace table. Instead, support for the war continued to drop, and by 1971 nearly two-thirds of all Americans favored an immediate U.S. withdrawal from Vietnam.

In December 1972, U.S. B-52s began the heaviest and most destructive bombing of the war, targeting North Vietnam's cities. The "Christmas bombing" must have inflicted high civilian casualties, and on January 27, 1973, the United States and North Vietnam signed an "agreement on ending the war and restoring peace in Vietnam."

The United States, though, refused to leave. In March 1975, the North Vietnamese army began its southward offensive, reaching Saigon a month later. U.S. personnel and South Vietnamese leaders fled Saigon in disarray, and Communist forces quickly occupied the city and renamed it Ho Chi Minh City. Vietnam was reunited.

Around the same time, the U.S.-supported military regime in Cambodia under Lon Nol collapsed, and the communist Khmer Rouge and its leader, Pol Pot, seized power. Similarly, in Laos, where a secret CIA-led mercenary army of some nine thousand Hmong under General Vang Pao carried on a war against the communist Pathet Lao, the communists assumed leadership in May 1975 when the U.S.-backed military and government fled.

Vietnam was left a wasteland, its forests destroyed by bombs and chemical defoliants, its fields cratered and harboring unexploded shells and mines, and its waters polluted with poisons. More than 1.2 million of its soldiers perished, along with countless more civilians, who to U.S. forces seemed indistinguishable from Viet Minh combatants. They were all enemies. Birth defects, cancers, and other legacies of the war continued to stalk the land long after the Americans departed.

The U.S. spent nearly $150 billion on the war. More than fifty-five thousand U.S. soldiers died, and three hundred thousand suffered injuries. Americans have not yet come to terms with the nation's defeat in Vietnam. The war's legacies of containment and interventions in the affairs of other nations were evident through the period of the Cold War, which ended with the Soviet Union's collapse in 1991.

Despite acknowledgment of the "quagmire" of Vietnam, it has not prevented U.S. presidents from ordering the nation's troops into seemingly endless conflicts, and the bitter memories of antiwar protests are reawakened for many Americans whenever U.S. young men and women are sent into harm's way. Patriotism and loyalty rise to the defense of U.S. imperial aggressions, stifling dissent and sacrificing democratic principles and freedoms for the sake of unity and support for the troops. Asian and Pacific Islander civil liberties are particularly vulnerable, especially when the United States perseveres in waging wars and installing military bases in the Pacific and Asia.

During and after the Second World War, deploying European discourses of freedom, self-determination, and national liberation and sovereignty, Africans and Asians overturned over four hundred years of imperialism and colonial rule. That achievement was mitigated by neocolonialism and renewed dependence on former colonial powers, as well as by autocratic, often military, and corrupt regimes in decolonized nations that came to resemble the colonial relations of a privileged governing elite and masses of impoverished and exploited workers. The European colonial world had passed, nonetheless, and global relations would never be the same.

In the United States, as in other parts of the world, momentous changes were under way. The African American–led civil rights movement and its demand for full equality under the law broke the back of legal segregation. *Brown v. Board of Education* (1954), a unanimous ruling of the Supreme Court, declared, in contradiction to the 1896 *Plessy* decision, that "separate facilities are inherently unequal" and that segregation violated the equal-protection clause of the Fourteenth Amendment.

The civil rights movement consisted of countless acts of individual and collective courage. On December 1, 1955, in Montgomery, Alabama, forty-two-year-old Rosa Parks refused to give up her bus seat for a white rider, sparking a yearlong bus boycott that targeted the city's segregated public transit system. The protest ended with a Supreme Court decision declaring that the Alabama and Montgomery segregation laws were unconstitutional.

The year 1965 was mixed with respect to the repression and advancement of democracy. On the one hand, the United States dispatched thirty thousand soldiers to the Dominican Republic to depose a democratically elected president, and President Johnson sent U.S. combat troops to Vietnam. On the other, Congress passed the Civil or Voting Rights Act that outlawed racial discrimination in voting practices. Like the Fifteenth Amendment's "right of citizens . . . to vote" without abridgment "on account of race, color, or previous condition of servitude," the 1965 act prohibited the denial of vote "on account of race or color."

In the same year, Congress passed the Immigration Reform Act, which terminated the racist "national origins" quotas that had begun with the 1924 Johnson-Reed Act. Under the 1952 McCarran-Walter Act, which the 1965 act amended, the total annual immigration quota for Africa was 1,400, for Asia 2,990, and for Europe 149,667. The 1965 act established hemispheric, not racial, limits on immigration and gave priority to family reunification and workers and professionals with skills needed by the United States. The act changed the face of Asian and Pacific Islander America and the United States as a whole. That, however, was not the intention of the act's sponsors.

One purpose of the act was to allow the recruitment of scientific and technical expertise from other countries. Starting in 1957, the Soviet Union had launched its Sputnik satellites, and there were fears that the United States was lagging in the arms and space races. The act was also intended as a piece of Cold War showmanship, demonstrating that U.S. democracy was nonracist. In practical terms, the act's sponsors expected European immigrants to continue to predominate because of the priority the act gave to family reunification in setting immigration quotas: most of the U.S. families likely to sponsor a relative were assumed to be white. Contrary to those expectations, Asian and Latino immigration soared, fundamentally reshaping the nation's demography and its racial formation.

On April 4, 1968, Martin Luther King Jr., who was in Memphis, Tennessee, to support striking African American sanitation workers, was shot and killed. Following his death, major riots broke out in over sixty U.S. cities, leaving forty-three dead and more than three thousand injured, and leading to some twenty-seven thousand arrests Two months later, on June 7, Senator Robert Kennedy died from an assassin's bullet after having won the primary election in California that might have propelled him to the Democratic presidential nomination. King and Kennedy had carried the aspirations of the poor, workers and students, migrants, peoples of color, and white liberals.

The lessons from the 1960s involving U.S. imperialism and the global and local struggles against its powers were carried forward by new generations of Pacific Islanders and Asians, who strived to reconstitute peoples and cultures, histories and national consciousness to break the chains of assimilation and dependency—a "colonized mentality," according to the Tunisian Jew and anticolonial intellectual Albert Memmi—for self-determination and liberation.

SUGGESTED READINGS

Chan, Sucheng, ed. *Hmong Means Free: Life in Laos and America.* Philadelphia: Temple University Press, 1994.

Cordova, Fred. *Filipinos: Forgotten Asian Americans.* Dubuque, IA: Kendall/Hunt, 1983.

Freeman, James M. *Hearts of Sorrow: Vietnamese-American Lives.* Stanford, CA: Stanford University Press, 1989.

McKelvey, Robert S. *The Dust of Life: America's Children Abandoned in Vietnam.* Seattle: University of Washington Press, 1999.

PRIMARY DOCUMENT
DOCUMENT 14

"Beyond Vietnam: A Time to Break Silence," a speech delivered by Martin Luther King Jr. to a meeting of clergy and laymen concerned about Vietnam, Riverside Church, New York City, April 4, 1967.

> In "Beyond Vietnam," Martin Luther King Jr. agreed with the concerned clergy and laity that "a time comes when silence is betrayal." "We must speak," he declared, and in so speaking King revealed a new direction in his thinking and political stance. There was a connection between civil rights and the war in Vietnam, King noted, and it went beyond the fact that black and white men were dying in the fighting. It was a cruel irony in that integration happened in death when in life black and white children could not sit next to each other in the nation's schools.

And as I ponder the madness of Vietnam and search within myself for ways to understand and respond to compassion my mind goes constantly to the people of that peninsula. I speak now not of the soldiers of each side, not of the junta in Saigon, but simply of the people who have been living under the curse of war for almost three continuous decades now. I think of them too because it is clear to me that there will be no meaningful solution there until some attempt is made to know them and hear their broken cries.

They must see Americans as strange liberators. The Vietnamese people proclaimed their own independence in 1945 after a combined French and Japanese occupation, and before the Communist revolution in China. They were led by Ho Chi Minh. Even though they quoted the American Declaration of Independence in their own document of freedom, we refused to recognize them. Instead, we decided to support France in its reconquest of her former colony.

Our government felt then that the Vietnamese people were not "ready" for independence, and we again fell victim to the deadly Western arrogance that has poisoned the international atmosphere for so long. With that tragic decision we rejected a revolutionary government seeking self-determination, and a government that had been established not by China (for whom the Vietnamese have no great love) but by clearly indigenous forces that included some Communists. For the peasants this new government meant real land reform, one of the most important needs in their lives.

For nine years following 1945 we denied the people of Vietnam the right of independence. For nine years we vigorously supported the French in their abortive effort to recolonize Vietnam. . . .

They ["primarily women and children and the aged"] watch as we poison their water, as we kill a million acres of their crops. They must weep as the bulldozers roar through their areas preparing to destroy the precious trees. They wander into the hospitals, with at least twenty casualties from American firepower for one "Vietcong"-inflicted injury. So far we may have killed a million of them—mostly children. They wander into the towns and see thousands of the children, homeless, without clothes, running in packs on the streets like animals. They see the children degraded by our soldiers as they beg for food. They see the children selling their sisters to our soldiers, soliciting for their mothers. . . .

We have corrupted their women and children and killed their men. What liberators? . . . .

Somehow this madness must cease. We must stop now. I speak as a child of God and brother to the suffering poor of Vietnam. I speak for those whose land is being laid waste, whose homes are being destroyed, whose culture is being subverted. I speak for the poor of America who are paying the price of smashed hopes at home and death and corruption in Vietnam. I speak as a citizen of the world, for the world as it stands aghast at the path we have taken. I speak as an American to the leaders of my own nation. The great initiative in this war is ours. The initiative to stop it must be ours. . . .

There is something seductively tempting about stopping there and sending us all off on what in some circles has become a popular crusade against the war in Vietnam. I say we must enter the struggle, but I wish to go on now to say something even more disturbing. The war in Vietnam is but a symptom of a far deeper malady within the American spirit, and if we ignore this sobering reality we will find ourselves organizing clergy- and laymen-concerned committees for the next generation. They will be concerned about Guatemala and Peru. They will be concerned about Thailand and Cambodia. They will be concerned about Mozambique and South Africa. We will be marching for these and a dozen other names and attending rallies without end unless there is a significant and profound change in American life and policy. Such thoughts take us beyond Vietnam, but not beyond our calling as sons of the living God.

In 1957 a sensitive American official overseas said that it seemed to him that our nation was on the wrong side of a world revolution. During the past ten years we have seen emerge a pattern of suppression which now has justified the presence of U.S. military "advisors" in Venezuela. This need to maintain social stability for our investments accounts for the counter-revolutionary action of American forces in Guatemala. It tells why American helicopters are being used against guerrillas in Colombia and why American napalm and green beret forces have already been active against rebels in Peru. It is with such activity in mind that the words of the late John F. Kennedy come back to haunt us. Five years ago he said, "Those who make peaceful revolution impossible will make violent revolution inevitable."

Increasingly, by choice or by accident, this is the role our nation has taken—the role of those who make peaceful revolution impossible by refusing to give up the privileges and the pleasures that come from the immense profits of overseas investment.

I am convinced that if we are to get on the right side of the world revolution, we as a nation must undergo a radical revolution of values. We must rapidly begin the shift from a "thing-oriented" society to a "person-oriented" society. When machines and computers, profit motives and property rights are considered more important than people, the giant triplets of racism, materialism, and militarism are incapable of being conquered. . . .

These are revolutionary times. All over the globe men are revolting against old systems of exploitation and oppression and out of the wombs of a frail world new systems of justice and equality are being born. The shirtless and barefoot people of the land are rising up as never before. . . . Our only hope today lies in our ability to recapture the revolutionary spirit and go out into a sometimes hostile world declaring eternal hostility to poverty, racism, and militarism. With this powerful commitment we shall boldly challenge the status quo and unjust mores and thereby speed the day when "every valley shall be exalted, and every mountain and hill shall be made low, and the crooked shall be made straight and the rough places plain." . . .

Now let us begin. Now let us rededicate ourselves to the long and bitter—but beautiful—struggle for a new world. This is the calling of the sons of God, and our brothers wait eagerly for our response. Shall we say the odds are too great? Shall we tell them the struggle is too hard? Will our message be that the forces of American life militate against their arrival as full men, and we send our deepest regrets? Or will there be another message, of longing, of hope, of solidarity with their yearnings, of commitment to their cause, whatever the cost? The choice is ours, and though we might prefer it otherwise we must choose in this crucial moment of human history.

1917   Guam Congress created

1931   Massie case and murder of Joseph Kahahawai

1939–45   World War II

1941   Japan attacks Pearl Harbor

          Japan takes Guam from United States

          Japan takes Vietnam from France

1944   Japan interns Guam's Chamorros

          United States launches airstrikes against Japan from Guam

          Navy imposes martial law on Guam

1945   atomic bombs dropped on Hiroshima and Nagasaki

          Japan surrenders

          Vietnam, Cambodia, Indonesia, and Laos declare independence

          United Nations established

          Korea divided at the thirty-eighth parallel

          War Brides Act

1946   Philippine independence

          U.S. martial law in Guam ends

1947   Taiwan rebellion

          civil war in China

          India gains independence

          Truman Doctrine

          National Security Act

          House Un-American Activities Committee hearings

1948   Republic of Korea declared

          Burma gains independence

1949   Kuomintang defeated

          People's Republic of China established

          Indonesia gains independence

1950   National Security Council Report (NSC-68)

          Internal Security Act

          North Korea invades South Korea

          Organic Act (Guam)

          University of the Ryukyus established

1951   China enters Korean war

1952	McCarran-Walter Act
1953	Korean armistice; demilitarized zone imposed
	Cambodia and Laos gain independence
1954	Dien Bien Phu (Vietnam)
	Geneva Conference; Vietnam divided at the seventeenth parallel
1955	Rosa Parks resists segregation, leading to Montgomery bus boycott
	Harry and Bertha Holt adopt Korean children
1959	National Liberation Front formed (Vietnam)
1960	United Nations affirms the right of national self-determination
	April 19 movement in Korea
	U.S.-Japan Mutual Cooperation and Security Treaty
1964	Gulf of Tonkin Resolution
1965	Voting Rights Act
	Immigration Reform Act
1968	Tet offensive in Vietnam
	Martin Luther King Jr. and Robert Kennedy murdered
	Robert Kennedy assassinated
1969	Asian Americans for Action forms in New York City
1970	Koza uprising, Okinawa
	United States invades Cambodia
1972	Okinawa reverts to Japan
1973	United States and North Vietnam sign agreement to end the war
1975	United States defeated in Vietnam and Laos
	Operation Babylift
	Indochinese Migration and Refugee Assistance Act
	Southeast Asian refugees arrive in the United States
1978	Vietnam invades Cambodia
1980	Refugee Act
1982	Amerasian Immigration Act
1987	Amerasian Homecoming Act
1991	Soviet Union collapses
2009	United States and Japan sign agreement to transfer U.S. bases from Okinawa to Guam

13

GLOBAL TRANSITS

American history is a global history, beginning with European contact. Starting as a colony at the English periphery, the United States expanded to become a member of the European core, with an empire and militarized zones along its periphery. The United States of the twenty-first century is an extension and modification of that modern world-system. Industrial capitalism has evolved into finance capitalism and corporations that exceed the reach of nation-states. That species of capitalism has multiple branches and claims no loyalty to any nation, only to shareholders and investors. It is, accordingly, transnational, composed of global actors who regard labor also as transnational in service to their needs. As the traffic of this form of capitalism crisscrosses the globe, its transits involve military, material, and ideological contests. As in the past, Pacific Islanders and Asians, as peoples and nations, are central figures in that essentially acquisitive world.

As we saw, the 1965 Immigration Act changed the complexion of the United States. Contrary to the intentions of its sponsors, the act swelled the ranks of Asian and Latino immigrants, leading to the "browning" of America. Asians were the fastest-growing group by percentage increase, and since the 2000 U.S. Census, Latinos have eclipsed African Americans as the largest nonwhite group in the United States. Chinese surged as the largest Asian group, numbering 4 million in 2010. The numbers of South and Southeast Asians also increased. In 2010, according to the U.S. Census, Filipinos were the second largest Asian group at 3.4 million, followed by South Asians at 3.3 million and Vietnamese at 1.7 million. These increases, along with the remarkable growth in numbers of Vietnamese, Cambodians, Hmong, Laotians, and Thai in the United States, were almost all the result of U.S. wars in Southeast Asia.

WAR REFUGEES

After the U.S. war in Southeast Asia ended, refugees, military brides, and so-called Amerasian children flowed into the United States. Vietnamese refugees streamed into Guam, where the U.S. military prepared a tent city to house fifty thousand. Thailand, the Philippines, Wake Island, and Hawai'i took in more refugees. By August 1975, there were over 130,000 refugees, mostly Vietnamese but also Cambodians. From those temporary shelters, refugees entered the United States through military bases in California, Arkansas, Florida, and Pennsylvania. The federal government contracted nine voluntary agencies, called volags, to resettle them. For each refugee placed, a volag received five hundred dollars. Resettlement required each refugee to have a sponsor who promised to provide food, clothing, and shelter until the refugee was self-sufficient. Nearly 60 percent of those sponsors were families, 25 percent were churches and other organizations, and the remainder were individuals.

In 1975, Congress passed the Indochina Migration and Refugee Assistance Act, which funded services provided by state governments and public and nonprofit agencies to refugees, including medical care and social services, English-language instruction, job placement, and mental health services. The act expired in 1977 but was extended for another year around the time the next group of war refugees arrived—mostly poorer, less educated, and ethnically Chinese. Over 250,000 Sino-Vietnamese refugees fled to China, and thousands more left Vietnam in small, overcrowded boats bound for Malaysia, Indonesia, the Philippines, or Hong Kong. An estimated 50 percent of those "boat people" died at sea.

In Cambodia, Pol Pot and his Khmer Rouge regime displaced, executed, and starved millions of its people, allegedly in a quest to root out undesirable elements. As many as three million, nearly half of the total population, died as a result. In 1978, the Vietnamese ended Pol Pot's reign of terror by invading and replacing the regime with a government favorable to Vietnam. Tens of thousands of Cambodian refugees crossed the border into Thailand, and by 1979, about six hundred thousand of them lived in camps supervised by the United Nations High Commission for Refugees along the Thai border.

In Laos, the Communists who had gained leadership in May 1975 pursued the Hmong people for their role in the U.S. war effort, rendering some twenty-five thousand of them refugees in neighboring Thailand. Thousands more followed, including Laotians from the lowlands fleeing from government relocation programs. By the early 1980s, an estimated three hundred thousand refugees from Laos huddled in Thailand camps.

In early 1979, the United States permitted about 7,000 Southeast Asian refugees a month into the country, and later that year raised the quota to 14,000 monthly. Their annual totals rose rapidly: 20,400 in 1978, 80,700 in 1979, and 166,700 in 1980. To

FIGURE 58
Vietnamese refugees awaiting rescue
from their thirty-five-foot fishing boat
350 miles off Vietnam after eight days at
sea, May 15, 1984. U.S. Navy photo.

regulate the inflow, Congress passed the Refugee Act of 1980, which adopted the UN definition of refugees as persons seeking shelter outside their country because of a well-founded fear of persecution on the basis of race, religion, nationality, membership in a social group, or political opinion. The act also provided funds to states for refugee-related expenses, and it authorized Congress to establish annual quotas on refugees.

Before the 1980 act, the United States had taken in refugees on humanitarian grounds, like the quarter million Europeans displaced by World War II. During the Cold War, the United States favored refugees fleeing communist countries in Eastern Europe, Cuba, and China. The United States admitted them under the attorney general's parole powers and presidential directives, which granted special permission to certain classes of people seeking asylum. The massive numbers of Southeast Asian displacements, also a feature of the Cold War, required a more systematic effort and hence the 1980 act. Since 1975, over 1.4 million Southeast Asian refugees have resettled in the United States, out of a total of 2.4 million refugees.

Southeast Asian refugees were generally able to make few preparations before fleeing their homelands. As a result, many experienced a period of loss and mourning in addition to the shock of arrival in an alien place among strange peoples. At a refugee center in the Philippines in 1985, Tran van Xinh lamented: "I am free now and many of my countrymen too. But we remember and we are full of sorrow for Vietnam because it is lost, my country."

Born in the rural village of Long Xuyen, Tran worked for the U.S. Army. When the Americans fled the country, he returned to work on his father's farm. In 1980, the Communists forced Tran into a reeducation camp in a forest with four thousand others. "In this camp I worked from six o'clock in the morning to five o'clock in the evening," Tran recalled. "I had no tools for working. I used my bare hands. I ate only one bowl of rice for lunch and one for dinner. We had to plant rice and prepare rice fields, pulling out wild grass with our bare hands. It was very sharp and after one week our hands bled all the time." Tran lived in that camp for eight months, "and for eight months I longed to escape."

One day, given the opportunity, Tran simply walked away and took a series of boats to Ho Chi Minh City. Without papers, Tran lived in the city as a fugitive. In 1983, he decided to leave Vietnam with his wife, two sons, and four daughters. A former student helped him plot their escape. They left at night on a boat whose engine failed after two days at sea. Adrift, they were attacked by Thai pirates, who robbed them, raped the girls and women, and beat the men. "After our suffering the wind blew our boat to shore in Songkhla Province in Thailand and there we were robbed again by Thai villagers," Tran remembered. "There were about a hundred of them. They were hidden near the shore and when they saw our boat wash up they ran out and took everything that we had left." The police arrived and placed them in a camp.

On July 4, 1984, the United States accepted Tran and his family as refugees, and in September they moved to another camp in Thailand and then to the Philippines, where they studied English and enrolled in a "cultural orientation" course to prepare for life in the United States. Despite his determination to contribute to the United States as a resident and citizen, Tran could not forget "our native country and our people there who are still suffering under the bloody hands of the Communist regime. We want to liberate our nation. There are two things we must do. First, we must preserve our ancient Vietnamese philosophy, which teaches that all Vietnamese are equal. And so we must love each other. If we follow this philosophy we will be in unity." Second, "we must fight . . . united by a strong ideology. . . . We can take back our nation."[1]

Him Mao was born in Cambodia and worked as a schoolteacher. After Pol Pot came to power, the people were forced to leave the cities to work on communal farms. "There

FIGURE 59
Cambodian refugee mother and child, Ban
Mai Rut refugee camp, Thailand, July 1, 1979.
UN photo.

was not enough food to eat," Him recalled. "On some days we got only one cob of corn for the whole day. It was very difficult for the people to live and to work with so little food." People died from malnutrition or were killed by the Khmer Rouge. Those included teachers and government workers: "They took them from the jail to kill them in the forest. They also killed the women, their wives. Sometimes the whole family, small babies, the whole family together." For the first year, Him and his wife lived together, but later their captors separated them. From 1975 to 1979, they cultivated rice and dug irrigation and transportation canals. Forced labor produced rice in abundance, Him recalled, but the Khmer Rouge tormented them by rationing the amount of rice they received.

During a battle between the Khmer Rouge and a band of Vietnamese soldiers in 1979, Him and many others escaped. Him located his wife and family, and together they headed to the Thai border. "We walked on small paths in the forest," he remembered. "It was about a hundred kilometers and it took two weeks, maybe three. Walking in the forest is not so fast." When they reached Thailand, they stayed at a refugee camp for about a month. For several years, in Thailand and later in the Philippines, Him taught Cambodian student refugees, many mentally retarded and others deaf from the torture inflicted by the Pol Pot regime. His goal, however, was to join his brother, a Buddhist monk in Boston.[2]

Khamsamong Somvong served in the Laotian military, having trained as an Airborne Ranger in Georgia and Kentucky in 1972. After the U.S. war ended and the Pathet Lao came to power, he and other former officers were sent to reeducation camps. "It was hard to live there," Khamsamong recalled. Everyone thought about escape. A small group succeeded, but when a second group of sixteen tried, all but one were killed. Everyone fell sick. "We had no medical care. We hadn't enough rice to eat. We were just working and working. We had to try to grow vegetables, to raise chickens in order to eat. Only about one meal a month did I manage to get enough to eat. Otherwise no more, no more. And I kept thinking about finding a way to escape."

After spending over eight years in the camp, in 1983 Khamsamong finally managed to bribe a Pathet Lao officer to give him a fifteen-day pass to visit his wife and family. Instead, he plotted to escape from Laos into Thailand. With his wife and baby, Khamsamong fled Vientiane City and headed across the Mekong River into Thailand. He and his family stayed for over a year in an overcrowded refugee camp before arriving in the Philippines in 1985. There they awaited passage to Portland, Oregon, to join Khamsamong's mother and sister.[3]

"My name is Zer Lo," began a Hmong woman living in Fresno, California. "My mother's name was Me Cha, and my father's Lu Chai. I am the youngest child in my family." Her family was poor, Zer Lo recalled, even by the standards of impoverished Laos. Everyone worked, tending the family's fields of rice, corn, vegetables, and sugarcane and raising pigs, chickens, and other animals. No one knew how to read or write. Water had to be carried in large bamboo buckets and wood gathered to provide fuel for cooking. Women performed most of that work. Zer Lo's parents and two of her four brothers died. When she was fifteen, Zer Lo married and lived with her husband as his second wife.

"We worked hard and our crops were very good," Zer Lo continued. "But at that time there was a big lake where demons lived who caused people to get sick and die. They did a lot of evil in our village, where many people died. So we had to go live in the jungle." There they lived for over a year, surviving on bananas and other wild fruits and plants. "Life was very hard in the jungle," so they moved to another village where conditions improved "until my children came." Despite her poor health, Zer Lo had six children. To feed them she had to work harder, "under the hot sun. There was very little time for rest. . . . Life was not easy at all."

The war made life even more difficult. Her husband went off to fight, and she had to fend for herself and her children. "My husband did not seem to care about us," Zer Lo said sadly. At last, when her two older sons became men, "we stopped going hungry." Their farming provided sufficient food. "They took care of me and did not allow me to go hungry and finally I felt happy." But the approaching war caused them to flee to

Thailand and "leave everything behind—everything that had taken us a whole lifetime to acquire."

After about five years in Thailand, Zer Lo and her family moved to the United States, where "our new life in America is not easy, either. My sons who are uneducated, because they never had a chance to go to school, have to work hard to earn a living. I did not get any support from the government such as social security when I first arrived. I was told I had to work to support myself even though I was already very old. I am tired of working and suffering." Only after her husband died did Zer Lo receive his social security check. She told her grandson, "Your grandpa never loved me. He never helped feed the children nor clothe them. . . . He was always unjust to me. If this is the life that every woman in this world has to live," she concluded, "then it's not worth it to be a wife."[4]

Chou Nou Tcha and his wife, Tchue Vue, like thousands of other Hmong, fled Laos for Thailand after the United States left the region. They spent about four years in refugee camps. "We lived in filth in the refugee camp and wanted desperately to leave," Chou Nou Tcha recalled. They applied to go to France, and after securing permission to enter as refugees in 1979, they settled in a small town near Marseilles, where Chou Nou Tcha worked making jewelry and then planting grapes in a vineyard. When the grower cheated him of his wages, Chou Nou Tcha sued him; in retaliation, the grower beat Chou Nou Tcha. The police jailed the man, but Chou Nou Tcha and his family had to move to another town to find work. He worked for about four years in a photography laboratory and a furniture repair shop. "We had a hard time in France," Tchue Vue noted.

In 1985, with their life savings, the family bought air tickets to the United States to enter as refugees. "After we arrived in America," Tchue Vue recounted, "we once again worked in the fields. We settled in Fresno, California, where we have grown sugar peas and strawberries. One summer we grew tomatoes, then we switched back to strawberries. That is what we have been doing ever since we came to the United States. Life is very difficult for us adults in the United States. We now live in a place that is strange to us. We do not know the language, nor are we educated. It is not easy to make a living here." By contrast, in Laos "we had land, we had water. We could farm as much as we wanted to." Still, "in our old country, we worked very hard, we were always very tired, and we got very little profit." Added her husband, Chou Nou Tcha, "I feel really frustrated about my hard life in the United States."[5]

By contrast, their son, Vu Pao Tcha, a college student, although born in Laos, finds his American routine familiar, hanging out with friends, playing basketball or volleyball, eating fried eggs and noodles, and crashing at a friend's house to study or "just to talk and share jokes and laughs." On Friday nights, Vu Pao Tcha and his friends "party like animals," and then on the weekends he catches up on lost sleep and house chores and has time to muse about college life.

Vu Pao Tcha only vaguely remembers his life in Laos, watching his parents till the land. Moving to France changed his worldview. "When I was in Laos, I thought that my life would be no different from that of my parents. I had no ambitions, no hope, but just the desire to stay alive and have a long and happy life. France opened a new door for me and gave me hope and inspiration and a strong desire to achieve many things I had never dreamed of." His father had told him he had the choice of picking up a hoe or a pen. He chose the latter and studied hard, with little time for a social life, sports, or field trips.

Just two years short of graduating in France, he moved with his parents to the United States. "I did not really want to come to the United States because I knew that by coming, I would have to give up all the goals that I had so carefully planned for my life in France." His family moved to Fresno, where the buildings, the cars and traffic, and the people, "a lot of blacks, Chicanos, and Central Americans," offered contrasts to his life in France. Many Asians, including Hmong, formed large communities that drew the enmity of some whites. Driving home from school one day, Vu Pao Tcha passed a pickup truck with white youth who yelled at and cursed him repeatedly. "I heard them say, 'Go back home! This is our country!'"

After four years of intensive study, Vu Pao Tcha still spoke English haltingly and with a French accent. He completed high school, however, and entered the university, where he began to feel at home, studying, playing sports, and partying. He and his friends, Vu Pao Tcha believes, have "similar values in life and share the same interests, goals, and dreams—to have a successful and happy life. I believe I am living an American life with an American dream today." Yet Vu Pao Tcha finds it hard to consider himself a genuine "American" because of racism and because he remains an Asian and a Hmong. But in the end, "I know I have become an American even though I am different from other Americans."[6]

A special category of persons from U.S. militarized zones in Asia and the Pacific are the orphans and children fathered by the occupying troops. These are children of the enemy, called by the Vietnamese *bui doi*, the "dust of life," and the poorest of the poor. Their biological parents often abandoned them to fend for themselves on city streets or in rural villages. They form a fractured community, suspended between Asia and America.

Like the debris of empire, *hapas* and so-called Amerasians are found clustered around U.S. bases throughout Asia and the Pacific, a testament to the legacy of imperialism. Chau, for example, is the daughter of a Vietnamese mother and a North African soldier in the French Army who died at Dien Bien Phu, the pivotal battle that led to the French exit from Indochina in 1954. She, in turn, mothered three children with three different U.S. soldiers—white, black, and Asian—and one with a Vietnamese man, and she also has an adopted daughter.[7]

Oanh was born in the central highlands of Vietnam to an African American father and Vietnamese mother who abandoned her at birth. She never knew them, although she had a picture of both. According to her foster grandmother, Oanh's mother came from a very poor family and worked on a U.S. base to make a living. There, she fell in love with Oanh's father, became pregnant, and was disowned by her family. Before her child was born, the father returned to the United States. Oanh's mother received only a single letter from him. Distraught and depressed, she left Oanh with the woman who became the child's foster grandmother.

Through a childhood friend of her mother, Oanh, then twenty years old, tracked her mother to an apartment building in Ho Chi Minh City. She made the long journey by bus, but when she arrived, neighbors told Oanh her mother had moved several months earlier and left no forwarding address. For a glimpse of her father, Oanh often visited the U.S. base where he had been stationed to pick through the ruins and scraps. Her father's photograph shows him standing in front of the base wearing his uniform. She often wondered about him.[8]

In 1975, Operation Babylift relocated Vietnamese children, many of them orphans and biracials, to adoptive homes in the United States. Although not included in the 1982 Amerasian Immigration Act, some 4,500 American-Vietnamese children entered the United States from 1982 to 1987. The Amerasian Homecoming Act of 1987 granted entry to biracials born between 1962 and 1976, along with certain members of their families. Under the legislation, about twenty-three thousand Amerasians and sixty-seven thousand of their family members entered the United States.

Unlike Oanh, who never left Vietnam, Tung Joe Nguyen was able to leave in 1983. Nguyen's father was a civilian from California, an employee of an appliance company doing business in Vietnam. His mother was seventeen when they met, and Nguyen was born in 1968. The couple had another boy and a girl, but before getting married, Nguyen's father returned to the United States, around 1972 or 1973, "and he never contacted us again, nothing at all."

Just before the war's end, a missionary church offered to evacuate Nguyen's brother and sister to the United States. They were classified as burn victims who needed treatment in the States. His mother lost touch with those children, and the church disclosed only that they had been adopted and were being reared by foster parents. "I have no idea why they would not tell her more," said Nguyen. An aunt in the United States was able to contact Nguyen's father, but when he was told two of his children were in the United States, he reportedly replied, "'I have my own family to take care of now.' And that was the end of that."

Nguyen lived with his mother, moving from one place to another. She had to beg for food and housing, and people called her "a prostitute, a whore, just because she had been with an American guy and had American kids. That's why Amerasians are called 'children of the unwanted.'" Some children harassed Nguyen and threw rocks at him, though others befriended and played with him. School officials prevented him from continuing past the fourth grade because he was half American. Nguyen and his mother thought about leaving Vietnam "constantly." "My mom dreamed about it almost every night, dreaming that she was in the States with me, and then waking up in tears, realizing that we were still in Vietnam, with not enough to eat, trying to make ends meet."

Nguyen and his mother made it to Rochester, New York, bringing his uncle's son, who they claimed was Nguyen's brother (a ploy reminiscent of the Chinese "paper sons" of the early twentieth century). There Nguyen attended school. Somehow Nguyen's mother managed to contact the foster parents of her children and learned that her son was in Washington, DC, and her daughter in Virginia. When they were reunited, "my mom cried all day long, everybody cried."

After graduating from high school, Nguyen attended the Rochester Institute of Technology. His girlfriend's Vietnamese family broke up their relationship, having retained the Vietnamese prejudice against so-called Amerasians. Nguyen transferred to the University at Buffalo, married Julie, a fellow biracial child of the war, and joined the U.S. Air Force. They were posted to Japan. "I'm Amerasian, you know," Nguyen reflected, "but I'm no different than anybody."[9]

Most Southeast Asians have made homes in California and Texas—many in Los Angeles, alongside substantial numbers of refugees and migrants from Mexico and Central America. Large numbers of Southeast Asians also moved to Orange County, San Jose, and Sacramento in California; Seattle and Portland in the Northwest; and Minneapolis-St. Paul in the Midwest.

To place the Asian refugee exodus in a more global context, significant numbers of refugees arrived in the United States from the Caribbean, Central America, Africa, and the former Soviet Union. During the 1980s and 1990s, thousands of Cubans fled the Castro regime. In the early twenty-first century, civil wars in Africa contributed to a growing number of refugees from Ethiopia, Liberia, and Somalia. From 1983 to 2004, refugees from the former Soviet Union led the list with 493,040, followed by Vietnamese at 387,741. Other Asian countries from which large numbers of refugees have settled in the United States include Laos with 113,504, Cambodia with 71,433, Iran with 61,349, Iraq with 35,252, and Afghanistan with 31,180.

GLOBAL WORKERS

Global capitalism involves large redistributions of capital, labor, and culture around the world. South Asians, particularly Indians, and Southeast Asians, notably Filipinos, exemplify those flows of migrant labor.

The post-1965 influxes of migrants to the United States involved mainly productive young people, lowering the median age of the migrant population in the United States. In the 2000 U.S. Census, for example, the Japanese, a group with few migrants, had a median age of 43 years, whereas the migration-heavy category of Filipinos had a median age of 36, Indians 30, and Pakistanis 28. The 2000 census gave other indications of migrant labor: 71 percent of Filipino men and 65 percent of Filipinas were wage laborers, and 79 percent of Indian men and 54 percent of Indian women were employed. Of the Pakistani migrants, 77 percent were men and 37 percent women, recalling the gender imbalances of earlier migrant groups.

The priority given to professional qualifications in the 1965 Immigration Act stimulated a brain drain from Asia. Again, according to the 2000 U.S. Census, 44 percent of

Filipinos, 64 percent of Indians, and 54 percent of Pakistanis had college degrees, as contrasted with 24 percent of the United States population.

FILIPINOS

There were about 6.5 million Filipino migrant laborers worldwide during the 1990s, reflecting the Philippines' export-based economy. More than half of those migrants were women, a majority of them in domestic service. In fact, Filipinas constitute the largest dispersion of women worldwide, to over 130 countries, from Hong Kong to Japan, Bahrain, Italy, Great Britain, Brazil, and the United States. By 2009, the total number of Filipino migrant laborers worldwide had increased to over 10 million.

U.S. colonialism in the Philippines was critical for the recruitment of *sakadas* for Hawai'i's plantations at the start of the twentieth century, just as it was instrumental in the outflow of Filipina nurses and service workers to the United States at the century's close. The service workers, unlike the *sakadas*, were not recruited but migrated to Hawai'i following the earlier precedents and patterns. Once those migrations began, they were sustained by informal and formal networks like family and kinship ties and popular magazines for Filipinas across the globe.

Filipino labor migration, like labor migration generally, is stratified by race and gender. Broadly, Europe, Canada, and the United States are the most desirable destinations because of better wages and working conditions, while other parts of Asia, the Middle East, and Latin America are less desirable. The demand for certain kinds of workers draws Filipino migrants to those places, but reaching the industrialized world requires greater investments, higher educational attainments, and more effort.

The gendered labor dispersal also reflects women's position in the Philippines. Poverty, domestic abuse, and family responsibilities drive many women to seek better opportunities abroad or simply to escape. Yet separation from children can cause mental anguish and depression, especially for domestic workers tending to the children of their employers. In supplying domestic labor, Filipinas nurture and support the social order of their former colonizers, thereby perpetuating the imbalance of the world-system: core development and peripheral underdevelopment.

After 1965, Filipinos were the largest group to migrate to Hawai'i, averaging about three to five thousand per year. The vast majority came from the Ilocos region of the Philippines. The migrants injected new life into an aging population of mainly male plantation laborers. Migration reduced the gender gap, and births to young migrants lowered the average age. More women were employed in wage labor. A 1985 study of the Ilocano migrants found higher educational attainments among post-1965 migrants than among the earlier migrants, but it also demonstrated downward mobility, with more migrants working in service industries and construction. In 2000 there were 170,635 Filipinos in the islands, constituting 14 percent of the state's population. Their numbers testify to Hawai'i's changing economy.

During the 1980s, tourism eclipsed the United States military as the single largest industry in the islands. In 1959, the year of statehood, 243,216 tourists visited Hawai'i, bringing in about $109 million; by 1987, the Hawai'i Visitors Bureau counted 5,799,830 tourists and expenditures of $6.6 billion, or 34 percent of the state's gross product. Between 1946 and 1987 the number of hotel rooms in the islands expanded from 1,572 to 69,012. Jobs in the tourist industry likewise increased from 71,000 in 1970 to 175,000 in 1985, representing 36 percent of all employment in the islands. By 1994, tourism had created some 232,900 jobs, mainly low-paying service positions, drawing thousands of migrants. In 2008, tourist expenditures dropped to 17 percent of the state's gross product and accounted for 18 percent of the state's employment.

In Hawai'i, Filipina domestic servants filled the tourism industry's labor demands. But because of the long hours, uncertainty of employment, and low incomes in tourist resorts—the "new plantations"—migrant laborers often required second jobs to make ends meet. An Ilocano-speaking Filipina who migrated to Hawai'i in 1992 found a hotel housekeeping job through word of mouth. She had held a similar position at a hotel in the Philippines, but the Hawai'i position paid higher wages and came with fringe benefits such as tips and "leftovers" from hotel guests. Besides, she loved the company of her fellow Filipina workers in the hotel. The industry preferred to employ Filipinas because of their reputation for hard work and docility.

Many of the first Filipina housekeepers were overqualified, suggesting that their migrant status and perhaps language difficulties made them susceptible to exploitation. Conchita Belmonte was a teacher in the Philippines for over twenty years. In 1972, she migrated with her husband to Hawai'i and accepted a housekeeping job in a hotel. Belmonte rose to a supervisor's position at the Sheraton Waikiki, along with three other Sheraton Filipinas who worked as housekeepers despite their college educations. Cleaning fourteen rooms a day, they all expressed their desire that their children not follow in their footsteps but complete college to enter professions.

The tourist industry, like the old plantations, taxes the environment. The millions of tourists who visit Hawai'i each year consume water, electricity, and other scarce resources; they add to overcrowding and vehicular traffic, especially on O'ahu and Honolulu, where most of them congregate; and they pollute the islands' beaches and streams and stress the few remaining forests and wilderness areas. Tropical islands are vulnerable worldwide, and in Hawai'i, tourism and its effects are constant reminders of Hawaiian sovereignty lost and the islands' state of dependency. For Filipina workers, the industry provides employment, but it also signifies their dislocation from their places of birth and their dependent position in the global economy.

SOUTH ASIANS

British imperial rule prompted the first, large labor migration of South Asians to America with the coolie traffic of the nineteenth century. Those migrants, mainly men, replaced formerly enslaved Africans on the sugar plantations of the Caribbean islands and the American continent. They also labored in Fiji, Mauritius, South Africa, and Malaysia. Later, from British India, migrants as "imperial auxiliaries" traversed the British Empire from East Africa to Hong Kong and Canada. After India's independence and partition in 1947, unskilled laborers from India and Pakistan migrated to fill the critical need for labor in Britain during the 1950s. The Commonwealth of Nations (previously the British Commonwealth), consisting of former British colonies, enabled the relatively free movement of people among member nations. South Asians living in British East Africa and the Caribbean thus moved to Britain and Canada, and many later moved from Canada to the United States.

On one hand, the migration of South Asian laborers, like that of their Filipino counterparts, has impoverished Asia and enriched Europe and America. On the other hand, remittances sent by migrant workers to their families in Asia represent a major source of much-needed foreign currency for the nation-state and its financial institutions. Millions, even billions, of dollars annually are transferred. India has created the tax status of "non-resident Indian" (NRI) to ensure the allegiance of Indians abroad and facilitate the return of their earnings. The Reserve Bank of India, for instance, offers favorable interest rates for NRI deposits, which amounted to $8.8 billion between 1986 and 1994.

At the same time, Indians abroad are sometimes seen as selfish and unpatriotic for having left their country of origin. Their relationship with the Indian government fluctuates from adversarial to mutually supportive. Indians abroad not only send currency home but also participate in multidirectional exchanges of technology, ideologies, and culture. South Asian subjectivities can embrace differing regional, religious, linguistic, and national affiliations.

Like the Filipinos who migrated to the United States after 1965, South Asians constituted a highly educated group of migrants through the 1970s. Between 1966 and 1977, fully 83 percent of Indian migrants entered as professional and technical workers, including tens of thousands of scientists with doctorates, engineers, and physicians. By the 1990s, however, South Asian migrants included increasing numbers of service workers granted entry through the family reunification category. They arrived from India, Pakistan, Sri Lanka, and Bangladesh, and from Guyana, Trinidad, Mauritius, Kenya, Uganda, South Africa, Fiji, Hong Kong, and Canada. Those divergent paths and histories exemplify the complexity and mobility of the Indian and Pakistani subject positions, along with their divisions and hierarchies of class, gender, and sexuality. Those subject positions are not simply diversely constituted; they are negotiated and shaped in changing contexts and over time and as such, are works in progress.

In India, for instance, food traditions are intimately connected with family and gender relations, as well as with region, religion, caste, and class. In the United States, those distinctions break down. Grocery stores catering to South Asians offer rice from Thailand, mangoes from Mexico, pineapples from Costa Rica, dried lentils from Washington State, and frozen samosas and chapatis made in Flushing, New York. South Asian restaurants serve and cater to a mixed customer base of Bangladeshis, Indians, Pakistanis, and Sri Lankans, broadening their menus to appeal to a wide range of tastes. These restaurants cater to other Americans as well, for instance by offering kosher and vegetarian dishes, and they influence American food ways in their turn. Foods labeled as "Indian" or "traditional" in fact reveal changes in their ingredients, preparations, and tastes that reflect a global marketplace.

Even as India's peoples and their initiatives continue to reshape India, the nation and its members abroad interact with the changing world around them. *India Abroad,* a widely read newspaper begun in New York City in 1970, keeps its readers in touch with developments in India; yet it is published in English and also carries news from Indian communities elsewhere. The paper circulates and thereby manufactures a sense of community among Indians in the United States, Canada, Great Britain, and other parts of the world. Likewise, Indian stores in dispersed communities commonly carry hundreds of videos made in India, but those communities also engender new and distinctive forms of art and culture. Bhangra music and dance, for instance, originated among South Asians in London, fusing Punjabi vocals with Jamaican reggae and African American hip-hop. That invention, which has spread throughout Europe and America, has become an expression and a marker of South Asian subjectivity. Other producers of culture, such as South Asian and Bollywood filmmakers and actors, have influenced U.S. media from film to cartoon, comedy, and advertising.

At the individual level, the lives of working-class migrants might evoke dreams of historical agency and self-determination, but many struggle to make a living. "A few weeks ago I visited a friend in an upper Manhattan hotel for transients," a letter writer related in 1992. "The hotel used to be a second home for immigrants from Eastern Europe at the end of World War II. . . . Today, Indians, Pakistanis, and Bangladeshis constitute about 50 percent of this hotel's population. Others come from Haiti and Dominican Republic." In that hotel and at least eight others like it, the writer noted, over five hundred South Asians rest from their labors throughout the city as grocery store clerks, taxi drivers, and newspaper sellers. Many of them have psychological problems, but "they do not know where to go for help; some of them are even beyond help."[10]

DEMOGRAPHY

The global forces of transnational finance capitalism, labor migrations, wars in Asia, and the 1965 Immigration Act reshaped the demography of Asian America by narrowing the gender gap between men and women, rapidly increasing the total numbers of Asians in the United States, and bringing greater ethnic and religious diversity.

In 1970, Japanese, Chinese, and Filipinos constituted nearly the entirety of Asian America, numbering 588,324 Japanese, 431,583 Chinese, and 336,731 Filipinos. The fourth largest group, Koreans, numbered only 69,510.

By 1980, reflecting the effects of the 1965 act, Japanese fell behind Chinese and Filipinos largely due to numbers of new migrants, and the census counted significant numbers of Asian Indians, Koreans, and Vietnamese. The Chinese population nearly doubled, to 812,178, and Filipinos increased to 781,894. With lower numbers of immigrants, the Japanese population fell to 716,331, while Asian Indians numbered 387,223, Koreans rose to 357,393, and Vietnamese totaled 245,025.

In 1990, the Chinese population more than doubled, to 1,645,472, Filipinos, rose to 1,406,770, and Japanese increased to 847,562; Asian Indians increased to 815,447, Koreans to 798,849, and Vietnamese to 614,547.

Overall, from 1970 to 1980, the population of Asians and Pacific Islanders grew by a remarkable 175 percent. From 1980 to 1990, their numbers increased by 95 percent. According to the Census Bureau, immigration accounted for about 86 percent of that increase. The total number of Asians and Pacific Islanders in 1970 was 1.4 million, in 1980 3.7 million, and in 1990 7.3 million.

The 2000 census was the first to allow respondents to select more than one racial category. Of the nearly 12 million Asians counted, 868,395 were distinguished as Asian and white *hapas* (biracial individuals), 138,802 as Asian and Pacific Islander *hapas*, and 106,782 as Asian and black *hapas*. Of the "Asian alone" categories, Chinese, including Taiwanese, totaled 2.4 million, South Asians (including Indians, Bangladeshis, Pakistanis, and Sri Lankans) numbered 1.9 million, Filipinos 1.85 million, Vietnamese 1.1 million, Koreans 1 million, and Japanese 796,700. Cambodians totaled 171,937, Hmong 169,428, Laotians 168,707, and Thai 112,989. Other groups included Indonesians, 39,757 and Malaysians, 10,690. The census failed, however, to account for West Asians, including Iranians, Iraqis, and others from Arab nations, who were subsumed under the "white" and "black" categories.

Asians, including Asian multiracials, totaled over 4 percent of the United States population in 2000. Their rate of increase between 1990 and 2000 was 72 percent, compared to 13 percent for the U.S. population as a whole. In 2010, Asians and Asian multiracials numbered 17.3 million, or 6 percent of the U.S. total.

The 2010 census found Asians living in all fifty states, including Puerto Rico. Of the total Asian population, 50 percent lived in the West, where they constituted 11 percent of the population: 21 percent, or 6 percent of the regional total, in the Northeast; 24 percent, or 3 percent of the regional total, in the South; and 12 percent, or 3 percent of the total, in the Midwest. Asians were clustered in particular localities, and especially in cities. For instance, Asians totaled 57 percent of Hawai'i's population, 15 percent of California's, 9 percent of Washington's, 9 percent of New Jersey's, 8 percent of New York's, 7 percent of Alaska's, and 7 percent of Virginia's. New York City, with the largest urban population in the United States, also had the most Asians, totaling 1.1 million, or 14 percent of the city's total. Los Angeles, the nation's second largest city, had the second largest number of Asians: 483,585 or 13 percent of the city's total. Other cities with significant Asian populations included San Jose, California, with 326,627 (35 percent of the city's total); San Francisco, with 288,529 (36 percent); and San Diego, with 241,293 (18 percent). Honolulu had the highest percentage of Asians in the population, at 68 percent.

The national census began to count Hawaiians only in 1970. In 1980, it counted 172,346 Hawaiians and added separate categories for Samoans, who numbered 39,520, and Guamanians (the term used in the census), numbering 30,695. Those totals increased in 1990 to 211,014 Hawaiians, 62,964 Samoans, and 49,345 Guamanians, while the total population of Hawaiian and Pacific Islanders was 365,024.

The 2000 census included separate categories for Hawaiians and other Pacific Islanders, enabling more detailed enumerations. Like the designation *Asian American,* the term *Pacific Islander* has an evolving membership and is a panethnic subjectivity and formation, encompassing peoples from numerous and widely separated island groups. The census counted a total Hawaiian population of 401,162. Among these, Hawaiian multiracials numbered about 261,000, while approximately 141,000 identified as "Hawaiian alone." Samoans numbered 133,281 and "Guamanians or Chamorros" 92,611, including about 42,000 Samoan multiracials and 34,000 "Guamanian or Chamorro" multiracials. Pacific Islanders from Tonga numbered 27,713, from Palau 2,228, and from Fiji 9,796. The total population of Hawaiian and Pacific Islanders was 874,414.

The 2000 census found that in the continental United States, 73 percent of Hawaiians and Pacific Islanders lived in the West, while 14 percent lived in the South, 7 percent in the Northeast, and 6 percent in the Midwest. Fifty-eight percent lived in Hawai'i and California. Honolulu was the city with the most Pacific Islanders, at 58,130, followed by New York at 19,203, Los Angeles at 13,144, and San Diego at 10,613. In 2010, Hawaiians and Pacific Islanders, including multiracials, totaled 1.2 million, or 0.4 percent of the total U.S. population.

The sweeping demographic changes in Pacific Islander and Asian America after World War II mirrored national and global realignments. The rise of the third world, the fall of the Soviet Union, the global supremacy of the United States and capitalism, and the transnational traffic in capital, labor, and culture rearticulated the locations and relations of power. Asia and Oceania were key battle zones and staging areas in what some have imaginatively called a "clash of civilizations," a continuation of the ancient, contrived oppositions of East and West.

Within the nation, colonialism, restrictive immigration laws, and segregation initially relegated Pacific Islanders and Asians to a state of dependency, but the post-1965 demographic shifts in the United States and revolutionary movements in the third world prompted challenges to this order.

SUGGESTED READINGS

Bonus, Rick. *Locating Filipino Americans: Ethnicity and the Cultural Politics of Space.* Philadelphia: Temple University Press, 2000.

Choy, Catherine Ceniza. *Empire of Care: Nursing and Migration in Filipino American History.* Durham, NC: Duke University Press, 2003.

DeBonis, Steven. *Children of the Enemy: Oral Histories of Vietnamese Amerasians and Their Mothers.* Jefferson, NC: McFarland, 1995.

Maira, Sunaina Marr. *Desis in the House: Indian American Youth Culture in New York City.* Philadelphia: Temple University Press, 2002.

Parreñas, Rhacel Salazar. *Servants of Globalization: Women, Migration, and Domestic Work.* Stanford, CA: Stanford University Press, 2001.

Prashad, Vijay. *The Karma of Brown Folk.* Minneapolis: University of Minnesota Press, 2000.

PRIMARY DOCUMENT

DOCUMENT 15

"Conclusions and Recommendations," chapter 8 of *Civil Rights Issues Facing Asian Americans in the 1990s* (Washington, DC: United States Commission on Civil Rights, February 1992), 190.

> The United States Commission on Civil Rights is an independent, bipartisan agency first established by Congress in 1957 and reestablished in 1983. It is directed to investigate complaints alleging that citizens are being deprived of their right to vote by reason of their race, color, religion, sex, age, handicap, or national origin, or by reason of fraudulent practices; study and collect information concerning legal developments constituting discrimination or a denial of equal protection of the laws under the Constitution because of race, color, religion, sex, age, handicap, or national origin, or in the administration of justice; appraise Federal laws and policies with respect to discrimination or denial of equal protection of the laws because of race, color, religion, sex, age, handicap, or national origin, or in the administration of justice; serve as a national clearinghouse for information in respect to discrimination or denial of equal protection of the laws because of race, color, religion, sex, age, handicap, or national origin; and submit reports, findings, and recommendations to the President and Congress.

This report presents the results of an investigation into the civil rights issues facing Asian Americans that was undertaken as a followup to the Commission's 1989 Asian Roundtable Conferences. Contrary to the popular perception that Asian Americans have overcome discriminatory barriers, Asian Americans still face widespread prejudice, discrimination, and denials of equal opportunity. In addition, many Asian Americans, particularly those who are immigrants, are deprived of equal access to public services, including police protection, education, health care, and the judicial system.

Several factors contribute to the civil rights problems facing today's Asian Americans. First, Asian Americans are the victims of stereotypes that are widely held among the general public. These stereotypes deprive Asian Americans of their individuality and humanity in the public's perception and often foster prejudice against Asian Americans. The "model minority" stereotype, the often-repeated contention that Asian Americans have overcome all barriers facing them and that they are a singularly successful minority group, is perhaps the most damaging of these stereotypes. This stereotype leads Federal, State, and local agencies to overlook the problems facing Asian Americans, and it often causes resentment of Asian Americans within the general public.

Second, many Asian Americans, particularly immigrants, face significant cultural and linguistic barriers that prevent them from receiving equal access to public services and from participating fully in the American political process. Many Asian American immigrants arrive in the United States with minimal facility in the English language and with little familiarity with American culture and the workings of American society. There has been a widespread failure of government at all levels and of the Nation's public schools to provide for the needs of immigrant Asian Americans. Such basic needs as interpretive services to help limited-English-proficient Asian Americans in their dealings with government agencies, culturally appropriate medical care, bilingual/English as a Second Language education, and information about available public services are largely unmet.

A third, but equally important, problem confronting Asian Americans today is a lack of political representation and an inability to use the political process effectively. Asian Americans face many barriers to participation in the political process, in addition to the simple fact that many Asian Americans are not yet citizens and hence ineligible to vote. Although some Asian Americans are politically active, the large majority have very little access to political power. This lack of political empowerment leads the political leadership of the United States to overlook and sometimes ignore the needs and concerns of Asian Americans. It also leads to a failure of the political leadership to make addressing Asian American issues a national priority.

This chapter lays out specific conclusions and recommendations. Many of the civil rights issues facing Asian Americans also confront other minority groups. For example, issues related to the rights of language minorities are equally important for other language-minority groups. Thus, many of our conclusions with respect to violations of Asian Americans' civil rights and our recommendations for enhancing the protection of their civil rights are applicable to other minority groups as well.

14

REGENERATIONS

"These are revolutionary times," Martin Luther King Jr. thundered in the sanctuary of New York's neo-Gothic Riverside Church in 1967. The world over, he said, was engulfed in flames in a revolt against the old systems of exploitation and oppression and in a movement to create new systems of justice and equality. The oppressed, the wretched of the earth were rising up, he continued, to eliminate poverty, racism, and militarism.

Although national histories associate King primarily with the movement for civil rights, his 1967 speech goes beyond the nation-state to embrace the third world and internationalism. The civil rights acts of 1964, 1965, and 1968 sought equality in employment, voting, and housing, but, as the black power activist Malcolm X pointed out in a speech three months before the passage of the landmark 1964 act, the objectives of the freedom movement should extend beyond civil rights and inclusion in the United States to embrace international human rights.

MLK's speeches go beyond just civil rights alone

Conversely, some groups within the United States reached out to international bodies to advance their rights at home. Recognizing their continuing colonial bondage in the United States, Hawaiians and American Indians joined indigenous peoples around the world to pursue human rights through international organizations like the United Nations and the International Court of Justice. Asian and Pacific Islander history emerged not from the civil rights, feminist, and queer movements of the 1960s but from the antiwar and peace movements that established ideological solidarity with third world peoples. The social formation for Asian and Pacific Islander history was the problem of the color line, and not the domestic movement for civil rights.

civil rights was not the problem, it was rather the social formation of Asian and pacific islanders

404

In consonance with the National Liberation Front in Vietnam and Algeria, students at San Francisco State College in 1968 initiated a project they called the Third World Liberation Front (TWLF). In a statement of its philosophy and goals, they announced: "The TWLF . . . has [as] its purpose to aid in further developing politically, economically, and culturally the revolutionary Third World consciousness of . . . oppressed peoples both on and off campus. As Third World students, as Third World people, as so-called minorities, we are being exploited to the fullest extent in this racist white America, and we are therefore preparing ourselves and our people for a prolonged struggle for freedom from this yoke of oppression."[1] The TWLF called their field "Third World studies." It was a precursor to the field misnamed "ethnic studies."

Revolutions in Africa and America, national liberation struggles in Asia, the writings of the anticolonialists Frantz Fanon and Albert Memmi, and the lives and deeds of the martyrs Patrice Lumumba and Che Guevara fortified a generation in the United States, Mexico, France, and Japan. Asians drew particular inspiration from the determined struggles of the Vietnamese peoples in their protracted wars for freedom and from the successful revolution in China, where Mao Zedong's "little red book," *Quotations from Chairman Mao Tse-Tung* (1964), and his ideas of global insurgencies inspired dread among some architects of the Cold War, imperialism, and the modern world-system.

Education was a crucial field of engagement, students of the TWLF knew, because education shapes consciousness and thereby action. Education can liberate, but it can also enslave. The African American educator Carter G. Woodson pondered the predicament of the "educated Negro" who seemed distant from the African American community in his study *The Mis-education of the Negro* (1933). Schooling, Woodson found, inspired the oppressor and crushed the spirit of the oppressed by teaching that whites possessed great civilizations and blacks had produced nothing of significance. "Lead the Negro to believe this and thus control his thinking," he wrote. "If you can thereby determine what he will think, you will not have to worry about what he will do. You will not have to tell him to go to the back door. He will go without being told; and if there is no back door, he will cut one for his special benefit."[2] Mis-education, "a colonized mentality," in Memmi's words, creates servants of dependency.

Education, however, like any apparatus of discipline, is not totalizing, and it contains contradictions. Mis-education can subject, but its tools, including literacy and critical thinking, can liberate the mind and body. Moreover, teachers and students can choose to reject an institution's designs. The discourses of race and their practices, the spread and workings of imperialism and colonialism, the system of migrant labor, and the instruments of dependency notwithstanding, people have always struggled to direct their own destinies. The global, anticolonial movements of the twentieth century and their kindred initiatives in the United States were the stirrings of a "revolution" and "revolutionary spirit," in the words of Martin Luther King Jr., and signs of regeneration.

HAWAI'I

The militarization of Hawai'i, like the militarization of Samoa, Guam, and Okinawa, designated the Pacific as an "American lake" in the schemes of U.S. imperial ambitions globally. During the Cold War, the second world, composed mainly of the Soviet Union and China, challenged those intentions, as did a rebuilt Europe and Japan later. Locally, Hawai'i's peoples conspired in but also resisted the militarization of their land, water, and air. As such, they formed a part of the third world peoples' liberation movement to decolonize their material conditions and ideological states.

LABOR

Critical to the islands' economy were labor and its exploitation, from migrant labor to dependency, which installed the Big Five business elite and kept them in power. Sugar and pineapple plantation workers organized at the start of the twentieth century to promote their interests against the Big Five. In 1945 and 1946, plantation workers voted to have the International Longshoremen's and Warehousemen's Union (ILWU), a maritime union from the West Coast, represent them. Under the ILWU, Filipino and Japanese sugar plantation laborers struck in 1946. After seventy-nine days they won their demands for wage increases and an end to paternalism.

Military rule during World War II advanced the interests of the territory's oligarchy by restricting labor mobility and strikes, and after the war, as on the continent, the Cold War fear of communists was used to discipline workers. In 1947, army intelligence gave to the governor a list of alleged communists in Hawai'i and cited the danger they posed to the territory's security and economic well-being. In response, the governor launched a sustained public attack against the dangers of communism, and in September 1947 he announced that there was a communist "master plan" for control of the territory.

The Communist Party, U.S.A. (CP-USA) began its work in Hawai'i during the late 1930s, concentrating on labor organizing, especially with the ILWU. The oligarchy's unfounded charge of communist infiltration and control of the unions, in particular the ILWU, threatened to disrupt the union movement. In December 1947, an ILWU leader, Amos Ignacio, formed the Union of Hawaiian Workers, dedicated to Americanism and anticommunism. The union leadership struck back, sponsoring a unity conference the following year, and promised that no political party or racial or religious group would govern the ILWU's affairs. The Ignacio initiative ultimately failed in 1948, when the membership voted overwhelmingly to remain within the ILWU.

The House Un-American Activities Committee (HUAC) conducted hearings in Hawai'i in April 1950. HUAC's visit followed in the wake of the 1949 dock strikes in the islands after the successful West Coast longshoremen's strike the previous year. The goal of the 1949 strike was greater wage equity between dockworkers on the West Coast and in Hawai'i, which maintained "colonial" wages, forty-two cents per hour lower. The solidarity of workers in the islands and on the continent led to an effective strike against Hawaiʻi's Big Five, despite the territorial government's seizure of the waterfront, and in 1950, the ILWU won its demand for a wage increase of twenty-one cents per hour. HUAC was determined to root out communism, especially among labor unions, and directed thirty-nine labor leaders to testify about allegations of communist infiltration of the unions. The union leaders refused to answer the committee's questions, earning them the name of the "Reluctant 39," and HUAC found them in contempt of Congress.

In addition, in June 1953 seven labor leaders were convicted of conspiring to overthrow the government and organize the CP-USA. The atmosphere of intimidation was such that the "Hawaii Seven" could not retain an attorney to represent them. Most unionists were simply motivated by a quest for justice, racial equality, and economic opportunity. The Hawaii Seven each received a sentence of five years in prison and a $5,000 fine, except for the lone woman, Eileen Fujimoto, who received a three-year sentence and a $2,000 fine. Five years later, the U.S. Circuit Court of Appeals in San Francisco vindicated them by ruling that communism, as an abstract teaching, did not constitute conspiracy to overthrow the government by force.

DEMOCRATIC "REVOLUTION"

Besides union organizing, Hawaiʻi's working masses mobilized to assemble a majority at the polls. For over fifty years, the oligarchy and the Republican Party governed the territory, but a new generation of leaders, confident in their proof of loyalty to the nation during the Second World War (many having served in the U.S. military), resolved to bring democracy to the islands through the ballot box. In the 1946 territorial elections, fourteen Democratic candidates won seats in the legislature. Two years later, public-opinion surveys indicated a trend toward the Democratic Party, especially among union members, nisei war veterans, and Hawaiians and Japanese. By 1950, Japanese comprised about 40 percent of the electorate.

Despite its rising popularity, the Democratic Party was split mainly within the ranks of labor, and the ILWU faction lost to the centrists led by John Burns, a white former police captain who formed alliances with nisei veterans and unionists. In 1954, as the party of the working class, the Democrats swept the territorial elections, capturing two-thirds of the house and senate. Described as a revolution at the polls, the 1954 Democratic triumph ended the political reign of the oligarchy and the Republicans, and it represented a reversal of sorts whereby the children of plantation workers governed over the children of the planter elite. Burns failed to win the position of delegate to Congress, but the rejuvenated Democratic coalition he forged was victorious.

Defense industries in the islands, which competed with the plantations for laborers during World War II, received a boost from the Cold War. In 1950, defense expenditures in Hawaiʻi were about $147 million; in 1959, they soared to $338 million and exceeded the total value of all exports, including sugar. Hawaiʻi served as a conduit for military personnel and supplies to Okinawa, Japan, and Guam. The military made up roughly one-sixth of the total population of Hawai'i, and nearly one in four workers in the islands depended on the military for employment. Pearl Harbor alone gave jobs to some six thousand workers. The military and tourism, the islands' most important economic sectors, mirrored a colonial economy dependent on and driven by external factors, not internal production. With the decline of sugar and pineapple, the Big Five moved to diversify their holdings. Some moved into construction, capitalizing on the boom in hotels, shopping malls, houses, and highways, and others moved their capital into retail and wholesale stores and away from the islands to other, more lucrative investments.

In 1959, Hawai'i joined the United States as its fiftieth state (after Alaska was admitted earlier that year). A poll taken the year before showed that only 33 percent of whites in Hawai'i supported statehood, while some 30 percent of all Hawaiians favored the change; the majority opposed U.S. annexation and loss of Hawaiian sovereignty. Statehood was another step in the alienation of Hawaiian lands and waters. Only among the Japanese did a majority, 62 percent, favor statehood: conversely, most of those who were against statehood, including whites, Hawaiians, Chinese, and Filipinos, cited a fear of the local Japanese as their principal concern. Yet in June 1959, Hawai'i's voters approved statehood by a large plurality.

At the time of statehood, Hawaiians, once the sole stewards of the land, had dwindled to approximately 16 percent of Hawai'i's peoples. They were plagued by poverty and social problems: about 80 percent of those in juvenile detention homes and 40 percent of the prison inmates were Hawaiians. Sensing his peoples' sorrow over the prospect of statehood, Abraham Akaka, pastor of the venerable Kawaiaha'o Church in Honolulu, held a special statehood service on March 13, 1959. Acknowledging that statehood for some conjured "silent fears," Akaka reminded his parishioners of a Hawaiian chant: "There is fire underground, but the firepit gives forth only smoke, smoke that bursts upward, touching the skies, and Hawaii is humbled beneath its darkness. . . . It is night over Hawaii, night from the smoke of my land . . . but there is salvation for the people, for now the land is being lit by a great flame."[3] The chant—Hawaiian poetry—called to mind Pele, the embodiment of volcanism, and the *Kumulipo*, the Hawaiian creation hymn, affirming the connections of the present with the past and the fact of Hawaiian rootedness in the islands pulled up from the sea. About the same time, at the Kamehameha School for Hawaiian boys, teachers agreed that "a psychological rebirth of the Hawaiian people" was under way.

THE HAWAIIAN MOVEMENT

If the 1954 revolution at the polls was the most significant event of the first fifty years following Hawai'i's loss of sovereignty, its counterpart during the second fifty years was the Hawaiian movement. One of the formative events of this movement was the protest to save Kalama Valley in 1970. The struggle began in 1968 when the Bishop Estate, the landowner, leased about eight hundred acres of Kalama Valley on the island of Oʻahu to the Kaiser Hawaii-Kai Development Corporation. Residents of the valley, mainly farmers, had no knowledge of the transaction, nor did they know of the Kaiser Corporation's plan to remove the farms and homes of the valley's residents—mainly Hawaiians, Portuguese, and Japanese—to build luxury houses, high-rise apartments, hotels, a golf course, and shopping facilities. The corporation set a June 30, 1970, deadline for the nearly seventy families to move out, but there was considerable resistance against the eviction order, led by the group Kōkua Kalama (*kōkua* means "help").

On July 1, the bulldozers moved in and began knocking down homes and clearing the land. When protesters and residents refused to leave, the state charged them with trespassing. Nine days later, police arrested seven of the protesters, but the bulldozing was halted. Fires broke out in the valley for several nights. The standoff continued while all of the valley's residents fled, except George Santos, a pig farmer, who defied eviction with about thirty Kōkua Kalama members. They were arrested.

Kōkua Kalama organized tours of the valley for an estimated two thousand people, including members of the media. In October, Kōkua Kalama rallied about a thousand people at the state capital to demand the return of the land to the farmers. The protesters noted that the Bishop Estate, begun in 1884 as willed by Princess Pauahi, was formed to hold lands in trust for education and charity work, especially among Hawaiians. The estate needed to fulfill its pledge to the Hawaiian people.

Kōkua Kalama articulated some of the main goals of the modern Hawaiian movement, distilled into the phrase *aloha ʻāina,* or love of the land. The group demanded a moratorium on confiscating agricultural land for tourism and urban development; immigration controls, necessary because "our local people must come first"; stewardship over the islands' waters, lands, and skies; an end to land monopolies; and a move toward economic self-sufficiency. The effort to save Kalama Valley ultimately failed, and expensive homes and businesses filled the development called Hawaii Kai, but the movement's ideas and commitments took root in numerous other ways, especially in the resurgence of Hawaiian culture and language and in the drive for Hawaiian sovereignty.

That drive for sovereignty had several sources. Many Hawaiians, like Myron Thompson, worked within the political system to claim and secure rights for their people. Thompson was the chief of staff of Hawaiʻi's first Democratic governor, John Burns, during his second term. Thompson consulted at the federal level with the state's congressional delegation and with American Indians to have Hawaiians included in the definition of "Native Americans," thereby releasing federal funds for numerous social and economic programs. Thompson was also a founder of Alu Like ("working together"), a state community-action program that tried to instill a sense of roots and culture among the dispersed Hawaiian community. Alu Like saw education and Hawaiian language revitalization as pivotal to that effort, and it also supported job training and placement, health care, housing, and small business loans to provide for the immediate material needs of Hawaiians.

Hawaiian activism within the political system culminated with the constitutional convention in 1978. Delegates like John Waiheʻe, later the first Hawaiian governor of the state, and A. Frenchy DeSoto, a community activist in Alu Like and Protect Kahoʻolawe ʻOhana (*ʻohana* means "family"), used the convention as a platform to promote environmental protections for the state's lands and waters and to further Hawaiian history, culture, and rights, including the founding of the Office of Hawaiian Affairs (OHA), chaired by DeSoto. The architects of OHA saw it as a state agency, yet distinctive from the state, to enable Hawaiians to govern themselves.

Other Hawaiian activists worked outside the state's political system and sought sovereignty based on a rejection of the illegal U.S. overthrow of the kingdom and an affirmation of the right to self-determination. In 1972, Louisa Rice began Aboriginal Lands of Hawaiian Ancestry (ALOHA) to seek reparations from the federal government for the loss of land, resources, and rights. Two years later, Peggy Haʻo Ross founded ʻOhana O Hawaiʻi to sue the United States in the International Court of Justice at The Hague for its role in the Hawaiian kingdom's demise. In 1987, the Hawaiian attorney Mililani Trask called for a constitutional convention for a Hawaiian nation, or Ka Lāhui Hawaiʻi. Delegates drew up a constitution and met again in 1989 to revise it.

Central to the Hawaiian movement has been the issue of land, as seen through the lens of *aloha ʻāina*. On January 4, 1976, inspired by the 1969 American Indian occupation of Alcatraz Island in San Francisco Bay, nine protesters, including Hawaiians and an American Indian, landed on Kahoʻolawe Island, used since the 1930s as a military site. Once peopled but long since abandoned, mainly because of a lack of freshwater, Kahoʻolawe became a symbol of the theft and dispossession of Hawaiian lands and their desecration by the U.S. military, which used the island for aerial practice bombing runs and dubbed it "Target Island."

Seven of the Kahoʻolawe Nine were quickly captured, but Walter Ritte Jr. and Emmett Aluli managed to escape and spent two days on the island. There they found shrines and petroglyphs testifying to the Hawaiian presence and affirming the claims of the Hawaiian nation. As Aluli later wrote: "Each time we pick up a stone that has fallen from a cultural site, we pick ourselves up as a people. We lay the foundation for a nation."[4]

Determined to stop the desecration, a group formed the Protect Kahoʻolawe Association and then the Protect Kahoʻolawe ʻOhana, led by the musician George Helm. After the group landed on the island on January 14, 1976, landing, the navy allowed another group of sixty-five people to land about a month later, on February 13, to conduct a religious ceremony of gift giving and aloha. Other landings and arrests, countless meetings and community forums, and even an archaeological survey that found twenty-nine sites eligible for inclusion in the National Register of Historic Places failed to stop the bombing.

On January 30, 1977, two men from Protect Kahoʻolawe ʻOhana began an occupation of the island. By March, Helm, concerned that the men needed help, persuaded Kimo Mitchell, a National Park Service ranger and participant in an earlier Kahoʻolawe landing,

FIGURE 60

Kahoʻolawe coastline. Once named Kohemālamalama O Kanaloa for the deity of ocean currents and navigation, the island is a sacred place of refuge and a navigation marker. Photo by Marc Hodges.

and Billy Mitchell from Maui to accompany him to find and rescue the pair. After failing to locate the occupiers, they entered the water on two surfboards to return to Maui, with George Helm and Kimo Mitchell sharing a board. Helm and Mitchell were last seen in rough waters near Molokini Island off Maui's coast, according to Billy Mitchell, the lone survivor. Helm had written prophetically long before his disappearance: "I dreamt of being in the ocean as if I was a part of it, like I belonged in the water—it gave me content[ment]."[5]

After years of protest, the U.S. Navy stopped live-fire training on Kahoʻolawe in 1990, and four years later the federal government transferred the island to the state of Hawaiʻi, which established the Kahoʻolawe Island Preserve. Its lands bore the scars of years of bombings, but the island and its powers kindled a rebirth of Hawaiian consciousness, and it became a site for Hawaiian spiritual, cultural, and subsistence activities.

Another significant moment in the Hawaiian movement appears to have been precipitated by an academic debate. Whites, including many scholars, held that Hawaiians and Pacific Islanders broadly possessed simple, primitive cultures and technologies. Although they acknowledged that Polynesian ocean voyages had crossed thousands of miles of open water, detractors held that these achievements were largely a matter of accident, because the islanders lacked the canoe technology, navigational instruments and skills, and provisioning abilities for long-distance sailing. The Hawaiian scholars Katherine Luomala and Mary Kawena Pukui disagreed, and a group of Hawaiian and white sailors set out to prove them correct.

In 1973, the group founded the Polynesian Voyaging Society to promote interest in building a canoe and sailing it from Hawai'i to Polynesia. The society stimulated a revival of ancient seafaring and, more broadly, of Hawaiian culture and its points of origin. Research and experimentation led to the building of the *Hōkūle'a* (Star of Gladness) two years later, and after testing and trial runs in Hawai'i's waters, the craft proved seaworthy. One of the ship's designers and builders, Herb Kawanui Kāne, saw the project as the catalyst for a Hawaiian cultural revival. A boat such as the *Hōkūle'a,* Kāne reasoned, was the central artifact of Polynesian culture, and the project might reawaken among Hawaiians a pride in their achievements despite the attempted erasure and denigration of their culture.

For some Hawaiians, however, the presence of whites and non-Hawaiians posed a contradiction in this project of race uplift. Thus, while the *Hōkūle'a*'s voyage drew wide interest among Hawaiians, the project also created divisions along race and ideological lines. Still, non-Hawaiians played pivotal roles in the formation of the Polynesian Voyaging Society. Its president, Ben Finney, was white. Its craft design team included the Korean Rudy Choy, and the navigator, Pius "Mau" Piailug, was a Micronesian who knew how to navigate on the open ocean without instruments, using the winds, currents and waves, ocean color, cloud formations and movements, and heavenly bodies.

On May 1, 1976, with a Hawaiian captain, Elia "Kāwika" Kapahulehua, at the helm and a crew of Hawaiians and non-Hawaiians, the *Hōkūle'a* sailed for Tahiti, a journey of 2,250 miles. After a month at sea, the *Hōkūle'a* made landfall on the western end of the Tuamotu chain, and on its arrival in Tahiti, some seventeen thousand people greeted the *Hōkūle'a* and its crew. The voyage, which received wide publicity, showed that ancient Hawaiians could have made the journey using Polynesian canoes and navigational techniques, and it boosted the surging Hawaiian movement of cultural revival. But the trip took a toll on Piailug, the navigator, who resigned, and several of the original crew returned home, leaving the ship's return to a new crew, including two women, flown in from Hawai'i.

In 1978, Myron Thompson became head of the Polynesian Voyaging Society, and his son, Nainoa, learned celestial navigation from the astronomer Will Kyselka and from Piailug. After months of intensive training, Nainoa Thompson steered the rebuilt *Hōkūle'a* with a crew of men and women to Tahiti in March 1980. The achievement was tempered by the loss of the crew member Eddie Aikau, a champion surfer and lifeguard, who, during a practice run in 1978, took to his surfboard to summon rescuers after the *Hōkūle'a* capsized in rough Hawaiian waters and was lost at sea. Aikau's selfless devotion

FIGURE 61

The *Hōkūleʻa* under sail off the coast of Molokaʻi, 1997. Photo by Monte Costa. Photo Resource Hawaiʻi.

was commemorated years after his death with a surfing competition and bumper stickers and T-shirts declaring, "Eddie would go."

For Hawaiians and other Polynesians, the 1980 and subsequent voyages of the *Hōkūleʻa* resurrected pride in their cultures and ways of knowing. Their success led to the building of a new vessel, the *Hawaiʻiloa,* in 1993, this time using traditional techniques to manufacture the canoe, sails, and cordage, along with recital of the prayers, rituals, and chants that accompanied voyaging. As Nainoa Thompson observed: "Two hundred years ago, we lost basically all that we knew about our traditions, and it's going to be through research and through projects like this that we can regain it. But we're not just regaining an artifact. We are regaining the pride in the culture of the people—a proud, courageous people."[6]

Because of the decimation of indigenous stands of koa trees on the islands, the wood traditionally used for making canoes, Nainoa Thompson went to Alaska, at the suggestion of Herb Kāne, to get the logs for the *Hawaiʻiloa.* Some years earlier, Kāne had met Judson Brown, a Tlingit elder and a member of Sealaska, a corporation of Tlingit, Haida, and Tshimshian nations involved in logging. When the Hawaiians approached Sealaska, its head, Byron Mallott, eagerly agreed to their request. Mallott hoped that renewing the historic ties with Hawaiians, who had been involved with America's native peoples since the eighteenth century, would help his people rethink the use of natural resources for cultural purposes.

Thus it was that on June 1990 on Shelikof Island, a magnificent spruce tree was felled, after having lived for 418 years, to provide the wood for the *Hawai'iloa*. Before cutting it, Paul Marks, a Tlingit, raised his hands and addressed the community of trees:

> We thank you trees, in Tlingit *askwani*.
> And the tree that we are going to use today.
> That we look at you as a symbol of strength and power.
> And that you would hold up in the storms and weathers to come.
> And that it would be a blessing to the Hawaiian nation.
> And that it would also serve as a link between the three nations,
> Haida, Tlingit, and the Hawaiians.
> And that our love would grow with one another.
> And that it would be an ongoing relationship.[7]

As Native Americans, American Indians and Hawaiians shared histories of conquest and dispossession. American Indians cleared a path for Hawaiian sovereignty by challenging the post–World War II federal policy of termination, which sought to end their status as nations, even "domestic dependent nations," and to assimilate them into the U.S. mainstream. Hawaiians, however, remain divided over identification as Native Americans, mainly because the designation would subject the Hawaiian nation, which they maintain was never legally dissolved, to the U.S. government.

Although diverse, Hawaiian sovereignty groups are united in demanding an apology from the U.S. government for the illegal overthrow of the Hawaiian kingdom in 1893 and financial reparations for the losses sustained by that act; the restoration of land and the exercise of Hawaiian sovereignty thereon; and guarantees of Hawaiian rights to beach access, fishing and hunting rights, freedom of religion and cultural expression, and the protection of historic sites. In 1993, on the one-hundredth anniversary of annexation, Congress passed and President Bill Clinton signed an apology resolution that acknowledged U.S. complicity in the demise of the Hawaiian kingdom.

The Hawaiian movement is essentially about sovereignty, but it also calls for the development of a national culture. Since the 1960s, Hawaiian language, literature, scholarship, music, and dance have blossomed. Credited by many as the source of that Hawaiian renaissance are the 1964 lectures by the Hawaiian writer John Dominis Holt, delivered at the renamed and reorganized Kamehameha Schools and published as *On Being Hawaiian*.

"What is a Hawaiian?" Holt asked probingly. "Who is a Hawaiian in the modern State of Hawaii?" Because of the political realities, Holt concluded: "I cannot be a Hawaiian politically, or nationally, for there is no longer a Hawaiian nation." *Hawaiian*, nonetheless, means more than a sovereign nation and people. "I am a Hawaiian in sentiment, perhaps in a sense aesthetically, for I am governed in my feelings as a Hawaiian by an ideal, an image, a collection of feelings fused by the connecting links of elements that go deep into the past, and which play in my consciousness. . . . I am seized with inordinate pride in knowing that some of my roots go to the aboriginal substratum upon which the dazzling achievements of our modern community have been constructed."[8]

Hawaiian-language immersion schools have produced a new generation of thinkers and scholars, and the Merrie Monarch Festival, begun in 1964 by George Na'ope, has prompted a revival in ancient and modern forms of the hula in the islands and across the Hawaiian dispersion. Music, including the distinctively Hawaiian *ki ho'alu*, or slack-key guitar, and innovations like Jawaiian (a blend of Jamaican reggae and Hawaiian music) and Hawaiian rap thrive. Those renewals require an appreciation and restoration of precontact Hawaiian culture even as they involve changes in that culture in response to contemporary conditions.

Contrasting statements by two Hawaiians offer a measure of the transformation wrought by the Hawaiian movement. One comes from a life history published in 1936. "A Hawaiian is always a Hawaiian—no matter how educated he is, he is always a Hawaiian," the writer declared. "He never succeeds in business. I don't like Hawaiians. . . . I don't care to mingle with them because most of them are not educated. They don't do anything; most of them are loafers. . . . They are so dirty. They eat just like pigs with their hands. Gee, there's one Hawaiian boy who sits right next to me . . . and his feet are full of dirt and mud. Gee! dirty, can't stand it! . . . I hate Hawaiian! Oh, Hawaiian kind of low. I wish I didn't have any Hawaiian blood. I regret I have Hawaiian blood."[9] The other is from an eight-year-old named Kelsey, a third-grade student at Kamehameha Elementary School in the 1990s: "I am proud to be Hawaiian. I learn hula, we sing Hawaiian songs, and I like to listen to Hawaiian music on the radio. I like to help people, and I like being one 'ohana and sharing things with others. I also like to eat Hawaiian food."[10]

THE ASIAN AMERICAN MOVEMENT

The Asian American movement of the 1960s evolved in response to the twentieth century's color line and the global transformations wrought by anticolonial, antiracist stirrings around midcentury. The movement followed a long history of resistance to migrant labor and dependency in the United States, but its immediate contexts were the U.S. war in Southeast Asia and the domestic freedom struggles that were, as Martin Luther King Jr. pointed out, intimately tied to imperialism and anticolonialism abroad. That recognition inspired the formation of a third world people in the United States in solidarity with the majority of the earth's peoples.

RACIAL FORMATION

Peoples of the third world shared a history of European colonization and were united in the decolonization struggle and the establishment of national self-determination and sovereignty. Similarly, within the United States, peoples of color shared a history of

united in
the struggle
for self
determination

exclusion and segregation not only with respect to land and labor, but also with respect to the U.S. nation-state and people. Additionally, they were united in the struggle for self-determination, which, as in the nations of the third world, led to unions on the bases of nation and race. National and racial chauvinisms, including cultural nationalism and black power, confounded colonialism, but they also spawned ideologies and institutions that established boundaries, policed diversity, diminished engagements across the color line, and impeded mobility.

The Asian American movement set out to create a pan-Asian subjectivity and sensibility. However, it was dominated by East Asians—Chinese and Japanese—followed by Filipinos and then Koreans. Calling themselves *Asian Americans* was a strategic essentialism. The earlier label of *Oriental* was a Eurocentric term, Asian Americans argued, that rendered Asia peripheral. Although *Asian American* was likewise fictive, its proponents nevertheless justified its use on the bases of a shared history and its necessity for political empowerment. As a racialized group, they observed, their numbers would be greater than as separate ethnicities, enhancing their political visibility and access to democracy.

The Asian American Political Alliance (AAPA), begun at the University of California at Berkeley in 1968, spread to college campuses in San Francisco and southern California. Besides bringing together Chinese, Japanese, Korean, and Filipino students, the AAPA joined with and supported other students of color. AAPA also took root in New York City and Minneapolis, and students at the University of Illinois formed the Asian American Alliance. The academic discipline of Asian American studies, so named since 1969, added to the term's visibility, and by the mid-1970s, the name *Asian American* and its panethnic embrace had been widely adopted. Yet the formation ignored and slighted certain Asian groups, including Asians not born in the United States and Asian *hapas* and multiracials.

Hawaiians and Pacific Islanders appear and disappear in Asian America, in a manner reminiscent of the marginalization of Pacific Islanders by Asians and the shifting affiliations of Hawaiians and Pacific Islanders, sometimes with Asians and at other times with Native Americans. From the 1970s onward, Pacific Islanders and Asians formed joint political, professional, educational, and community organizations, and in 1977 the federal government combined the two groups into an umbrella "Asian American and Pacific Islander" category, which was used in the 1980 and 1990 national censuses. After consultation with Hawaiian and Pacific Islander leaders, the Census Bureau assigned these peoples separate categories in the 2000 and 2010 censuses.

reminiscent
of the treatment
of pacific islanders,
sometimes with
Asians and
Native Americans,

With changes in immigration and demography, the political climate, and the coming of age of children born in the United States, the span of Asian America widened to encompass more Southeast Asians, such as Vietnamese, Laotians, and Cambodians; South Asians, including Indians, Pakistanis, Bangladeshis, and Sri Lankans; and in the twenty-first century, West and Central Asians. Despite its immense spread and diversity, its shifting racialized boundaries, and its disparate and often conflicting histories and cultures, the problematic and strategic racial formation of Asian and Pacific America continues to have merit.

THIRD WORLD WOMEN

As a racial formation, Asian America, like allied social movements among African Americans, American Indians, and Latinos, was largely inattentive to gender and sexuality. These issues entered the discourse mainly after women of color drew attention to their multiple oppressions. In 1968, Frances Beale presented a paper at a Student Nonviolent Coordinating Committee (SNCC) meeting on the impact of racism and sexism on the lives of African American women. She and others broke away from SNCC in 1969 to form the Black Women's Alliance, which renamed itself the Third World Women's Alliance when it reached out to American Indians, Asians, and Latinas. Its goal was to create a socialist society free from racism, economic exploitation, and sexism.

In 1977, the Combahee River Collective committed itself to eradicating racial, sexual, heteronormative, and class exploitation, which its members saw as interlocking systems of oppression. In 1989, the scholar Kimberlé Crenshaw proposed the concept of intersectionality, which she defined as the articulations of race with gender, sexuality, and class. Those theoretical insights derived from the Combahee River Collective's work with women of color in their everyday lives.

Asian women added to those intellectual advances. Both commonality and difference mattered. The unique legal status of Asians, excluded from citizenship until 1952, enabled their exploitation, segregation, and dependency. Asian women shared the multiple oppressions of race, gender, and sexuality particular to women of color.

In 1970, those interventions in the Asian racial formation coalesced in the first course on Asian women at the University of California at Berkeley. From that class emerged the journal *Asian Women* (1971). Both the class and the journal, the editorial collective recalled, stirred controversy, especially among Asian men, who derided them as "one of the women's group" and accused them of straying from the "real" work of the Asian American movement, which to their mind was racial, not women's, liberation. As the women recalled, the self-doubt provoked by the men's criticism of their efforts congealed into certainty and then resolve and political struggle.

The pages of *Asian Women* are remarkable, given the nationalisms, patriarchies, and heterosexual masculinities that characterized the times. The journal speaks to the intersection of race, gender, and sexuality, and it extended subjectivity to third world women, including Arab and Iranian women. Asian women thereby led the Asian American movement toward a more capacious understanding of the Asian subject.

The United States war in Southeast Asia directed the field to a transnational arena of struggle. As the black power advocate Stokely Carmichael characterized it, the war involved white people sending black people to wage war on yellow people to defend the land stolen from red people. Opposition to the war within the Asian American movement focused on the idea of Asians killing Asians to advance U.S. imperialism, and for many of the Asian and Pacific Islander soldiers who served in the war, the contradiction was a heavy burden. As the veteran Jose Velasquez recalled of shooting an enemy at point-blank range, "I saw his face. It was like looking at myself. I never thought of it before; it took me about 25 years for this thing to start coming back. It doesn't hit you right away."[11] Besides looking like the enemy, Asians and Pacific Islanders in the armed forces witnessed white racism directed at Asians, both foes and friends, and the sexual abuse of Asian women.

NATIONAL CULTURE

Like its Hawaiian counterpart, the Asian American movement strove to constitute a people, a task that could only be achieved through forging that people's history and culture. As the French philosopher Jean-Paul Sartre observed in the preface to Frantz Fanon's book *The Wretched of the Earth,* European colonialism manufactured "ex-natives" who were "branded" with "the principles of Western culture" and had their mouths stuffed with "high-sounding phrases, grand glutinous words that stuck to the teeth." Those "whitewashed" versions of their colonial masters, Sartre wrote, were "walking lies" who had nothing of their own to say; instead, they merely echoed.[12] Because that "colonial mentality" produces "cultural estrangement," Fanon noted, reconstituting national sovereignty requires the creation of a national culture. Fanon described that undertaking as "the whole body of efforts made by a people in the sphere of thought to describe, justify, and praise the action through which that people has created itself and keeps itself in existence." That rebirth, Fanon wrote, produces "a new humanity . . . a new humanism."[13]

Whereas the Hawaiian sovereignty movement was accompanied and bolstered by a revival of Hawaiian culture, including language, literature, music, and dance, the Asian American movement, like the reconstitution of African Americans, American Indians, and Latinos as peoples, involved searching for and creating a "national" culture. Some of the designers of that culture, such as the authors of the pioneering *Aiiieeeee! An Anthology of Asian-American Writers* (1975), limited the Asian American literary canon to Chinese, Japanese, and Filipino writers whose cultures and sensibilities were shaped in the United States. As *Aiiieeeee*'s editors wrote: "Our anthology is exclusively Asian-American. That means Filipino-, Chinese-, and Japanese-Americans, American born and raised, who got their China and Japan from the radio, off the silver screen, from television, out of comic books, from the pushers of white American culture that pictured the yellow man as something that when wounded, sad, or angry, or swearing, or wondering whined, shouted, or screamed 'aiiieeee!'. . . . It is fifty years of our whole voice."[14]

Formed in 1971, Third World Communications, a coalition of African Americans, American Indians, Asians, Latinos, and Pacific Islanders, staked a claim as united peoples, sharing "our involvement in writing, art, and our communities" and the "racism, poverty, lack of power and resources." They produced an anthology, *Time To Greez!*

We will fight and fight from this
generation to the next...

FIGURE 62
Cover of *Gidra* (March 1970), a
pioneering Asian American monthly
published by UCLA students beginning
in 1963.

Incantations from the Third World (1975), which, the book's editors wrote, "is a many-sided mirror of our lives, reflecting the colors and sounds, tastes, smells, touch of our homes, the rhythm of our inner music, the music of our food, the food of our lives."[15]

In Hawai'i in 1978, a group of writers who produced "local literatures" met at a gathering titled "Talk Story: Our Voices in Literature and Song; Hawaii's Ethnic American Writers' Conference." (In Hawai'i, *local* connotes nonwhite and working class.) The conference and the book that resulted, *Talk Story: An Anthology of Hawaii's Local Writers* (1978), adopted a literary "tradition" and reacted against "outsiders" who produced colonial and tourist representations of the islands and their peoples. Through "talk story," which is the oral tradition of exchanges and actions, the local project sought to break the silence and end the expropriation of Hawai'i's diverse cultures.

The boundaries of Pacific Islander and Asian American literature and art have continued to expand in the twenty-first century, together with the conceptions of Oceania, Asia, and America as contrived geographies and peoples. Pacific Islanders, Asians, and Americans stretch in multiple directions and across national borders, resembling the global transfers of capital, labor, and culture, even as the U.S. nation-state erects higher fences and expands its border patrols. National cultures that define Asian and Pacific America face deconstruction as quickly as they are built, and Pacific Islander and Asian subjectivities, the work and project of writers and artists, are constantly shifting, rendering them difficult to apprehend or describe.

ANTI-ASIAN VIOLENCE

Continuing episodes of anti-Asian violence remind its targets that they remain aliens within the nation-state. When Asians generally are the objects of venom, they can see themselves as a unified group. Mobilization thus crosses ethnic divides. Anti-Asian violence may involve not only race but also nation and at times gender and sexuality, revealing the multiple and intersecting aspects of the social formation.

Anti-Asian violence has occurred throughout Asian American history, as we have seen. The number of Asians in the United States grew rapidly after World War II, as a result of continuous U.S. wars in Asia and the influx of refugees from Southeast Asia in the 1970s and 1980s and from South and West Asia after 2001. These migrations, along with larger demographic changes that threaten white majority status in the United States, have triggered white nativism and reassertions of white power. During economic hard times in the 1970s and 1980s, Asia and Japan were regarded as the cause of the U.S. downturn, and a wave of violence against Asians, precipitated by whites, swept the land.

Violence was also directed against Southeast Asians. Vietnamese fishermen in Florida, California, and Texas became the targets for harassment, intimidation, vandalism, and physical attack. In Texas, along the Gulf Coast, Vietnamese shrimpers had their fishing lines cut, their boats sunk, and their houses firebombed. In 1981, Vietnamese fishermen in Texas filed suit against the Ku Klux Klan for violating their civil rights by burning crosses and wearing white robes and hoods, trying to intimidate and physically assault them.

From 1983 to 1985, Cambodian, Laotian, and Vietnamese refugees in and around Boston reported rock throwing, beatings, vandalized cars, arson, broken windows, and hate speech. A year later, the state's attorney general reported: "Racially motivated violence is a serious problem for Southeast Asian residents in our State. Often, these individuals cannot even walk along the public streets without being physically attacked and threatened because of their race or national origin."[16] Southeast Asian victims went to court to get injunctions and temporary restraining orders against whites, male and female, in response to harassment, beatings, and intimidation.

Whites were not the sole instigators of anti-Asian violence. Between 1978 and 1979, several thousand Hmong resettled in west Philadelphia, where African Americans predominated. Physical and verbal harassment and assaults, vandalism, and rock throwing were common, and by 1980 many Hmong left the city, mainly for Minnesota. Economic problems, language and cultural barriers, high insurance rates, a poor welfare system, and fear of racial violence in Philadelphia drove them away.

DETROIT, 1982

Vincent Chin, a resident of Detroit, was twenty-seven years old when he died from a beating he received a week before his wedding. Chin, a Chinese, was at a nightclub with friends the evening of June 19, 1982, when he got into an altercation with two white men, Detroit autoworkers who reportedly called him a "Chink" and "Nip," saying: "It's because of you motherfuckers that we're out of work." The 1980s were downturn years in the U.S. auto industry, igniting nationwide hostility to Japanese imports, especially cars. Outside the club, the pair hunted Chin and confronted him in front of a fast-food restaurant. While one held him, the other bludgeoned his head, chest, and knees with a baseball bat.

Chin, the only son of Lily and David Chin, was a draftsman whose father was a U.S. veteran of World War II and whose mother's great-grandfather was a railroad laborer in nineteenth-century America. Chin's assailants, arrested at the scene by the police, pleaded guilty to manslaughter and received minor sentences of three years' probation and fines of $3,000 and $780. "We must speak up. These men killed my son like an animal," Chin's indignant mother cried. "But they go free. This is wrong. We must tell the people, this is wrong."[17] "You go to jail for killing a dog," said a Chinese in disbelief, and another noted that Chin's life was worth less than the price of a used car.

That injustice outraged Detroit's Asian community, especially after the trial judge refused to revisit Chin's killers' sentence about a year after Chin's death. In 1983, they formed the organization American Citizens for Justice (ACJ) to secure justice in the Vincent Chin case. Although primarily a Chinese organization in Detroit, the ACJ received support from Canada and across the United States, with Japanese, Koreans, Filipinos, South Asians, and Vietnamese among its members. Donations to ACJ poured in not only from Asians but also from African Americans and whites. The white men who killed Chin, ACJ and its supporters held, by failing to distinguish among Asians, transformed all Asians into a generalized threat to the nation.

The ACJ pushed for an investigation into the case as a possible violation of Vincent Chin's civil rights, arguing that it was part of a trend of increasing hate crimes in the 1980s against Chinese, Japanese, Cambodians, South Asians, and Vietnamese. The final verdict in the Chin civil rights trial in 1987 was not guilty, but a civil suit against one of

FIGURE 63

Men from United Auto Workers Local 588 from the Ford Motors plant bash a 1975 Toyota Corolla with sledgehammers to protest Japanese car imports. March 3, 1981. AP/File.

Chin's killers resulted in a $1.5 million settlement. The defendant, however, refused to pay the agreed-on amount to Chin's mother.

While justice for Vincent Chin was not fully achieved, his death mobilized a pan-Asian movement and inspired the formation of several Asian and Pacific Islander legal centers to defend the civil rights of all peoples. Although the focus was on race, Vincent Chin's death also involved other elements of the social formation, including gender, sexuality, class, and nation. His encounter with the two working-class white men took place in a bar and strip club, a setting that valorized white heterosexual masculinity. According to stereotypes, Asian men—feminine and asexual—were especially suspect in that setting. In addition, Chin's killers subscribed to the common view of Asians as perpetual aliens and saw him as embodying the U.S. trade imbalance with Japan—a discourse involving nation.

NEW JERSEY, 1987

In early September 1987, a group calling itself the Dotbusters, referring to the *bindi* worn by Hindu women and girls on their foreheads, promised to rid Jersey City of South Asians. South Asians in New Jersey subsequently reported numerous incidents of harassment, from vandalism to assault. On September 27, 1987, Navroz Mody, an Indian, was beaten into a coma while his attackers, a group of some eleven youths, left his white friend unharmed; Mody later died. A few days after that assault, another Indian, Kaushal Saran, was beaten: he fell into a coma but he recovered. While many believed Mody's killing was racially motivated, the state refused to bring hate-crime charges against his killers. Instead, in April 1989, one of his assailants was convicted of assault and another of aggravated assault. No one was charged with murder.

STOCKTON, 1989

The most horrific instance of anti-Asian violence was the mass murder in Stockton, California, of Southeast Asian children who apparently disturbed Patrick Purdy's domestic tranquility. On January 17, 1989, Purdy, dressed in combat fatigues and armed with an AK-47 assault rifle, shot 105 rounds into a group of children at the Cleveland Elementary School. When the shooting stopped, four Cambodian children and one Vietnamese child lay dead—Sokhim An and Thuy Tran, age six; Ram Chun and Ocun Lim, age eight; and Raphanar Or, age nine—and thirty were wounded. Purdy then turned the gun on himself. Asians wanted the state not only to acknowledge the magnitude of the horror but also to treat this mass murder as a hate crime, which the governor refused to do. Lobbying prompted the attorney general to launch an inquiry, which concluded that Purdy held a particular animus against Southeast Asians for allegedly receiving benefits without having to work for them and that it was "highly probable" that Purdy chose his target school because it was attended by many Southeast Asian children.

NEW YORK CITY, 1990

Korean merchants in New York City were the focus of a boycott that lasted through 1990 and into 1991. Koreans in urban areas like Los Angeles, New York City, and Washington, DC, lived and worked at the edges of African and Mexican American communities and at times experienced conflicts with their neighbors. While Koreans bore the risks of operating small businesses such as liquor stores and fruit stands in these marginal, impoverished communities, some African Americans perceived exploitation and mistreatment by Korean proprietors. In 1984, after Koreans beat an African American for alleged shoplifting, the Concerned People of Harlem Committee picketed several Korean-owned stores.

Four years later, in Brooklyn, following an altercation between a Korean owner of Tropic Fruits and two black women customers, blacks boycotted the store. The action ended several months later when nearby Korean merchants agreed to transfer their accounts to local, black-owned banks, contribute to the community's economic development, hire black youths, and take cultural sensitivity training.

The Red Apple boycott of 1990 began when black activists, including Haitians and other Caribbean blacks, boycotted and picketed two Korean stores in Flatbush, Brooklyn, because Bong Ok Jang, a manager of the Family Red Apple store, allegedly beat Ghiselaine Felissaint, a Haitian woman customer. The protesters targeted the Red Apple and another Korean-owned store, Church Fruits, across the street. That boycott was much more influential in the city's racial politics than previous ones, and it involved black power and community controls. The alleged beating of Felissaint, the protesters contended, exemplified the wider powerlessness of black people and called for mobilization and redress. In their view, Korean merchants were complicit with the white power structure and systematic oppression of the black community.

Koreans rallied to support the embattled storeowners, Bong Jae Jang and Manho Park. Korean community leaders encouraged them not to sell their stores but to hold on. The Korean Produce Association and Korean American Small Business Service urged the mayor to intervene, and the Korean Association of New York organized the defense of the Korean storeowners by reframing the conflict, portraying it as involving not whites against blacks but blacks against Koreans, and by laying claim to the American dream. Koreans, including some in South Korea, donated money to the embattled storeowners, the stores' Korean landlords forgave their monthly rents, and fellow Korean store owners volunteered to work in shifts to keep the targeted stores open.

Not all African Americans supported the boycott, which the media portrayed as a case of angry blacks victimizing a model minority and as reverse discrimination, contrary to the spirit of the civil rights movement's call for a colorblind society. To some politicians, the issue pitted community stability against political interests, and businessmen saw the boycott as harmful to the city's business climate.

On September 18, 1990, between six and eight thousand Koreans, the largest assembly of Koreans in New York's history, gathered at City Hall for the Peace Rally for Racial Harmony. African Americans also participated. Besides speeches, the rally featured a display of patriotism and commitment to the civil rights movement in the singing of the national anthem and "We Shall Overcome."

The boycott and rally politicized many Koreans who might have preferred to avoid entanglement in U.S. politics. The Coalition of Korean American Voters was formed to mobilize voter registration, and Korean Americans for Social Concern, an organization of young professionals, demonstrated against police brutality and allied with progressive pan-Asian groups like the Committee against Anti-Asian Violence (CAAAV). Many of these Koreans saw racism as stifling both black and Korean freedoms, and they urged education and engagements across those racialized divides.

In January 1991, a jury acquitted Bong Ok Jang of assault charges against Felissaint, and in May the store owner, Bong Jae Jang, sold the store. The picketing subsided, and the Red Apple boycott came to a quiet end.

LOS ANGELES, 1992

Across the continent in Los Angeles, Korean storeowners again became the center of a firestorm. The 1992 Los Angeles uprising began on April 29 (a date rendered as *sai-i-gu* in Korean), the day that the police officers indicted for beating the African American motorist Rodney King were acquitted. It spread quickly from South Central Los Angeles to adjacent Koreatown, downtown Los Angeles, Hollywood, and even the city's middle-class neighborhoods on the west side. The uprising lasted for three days, leaving 58 people dead, some 2,400 injured, 16,000 arrested, and over $700 million in property damage. About one-third of the dead were Latinos. According to police reports, 45 percent of those arrested were Latinos, 41 percent African Americans, and 12 percent white. Mobs looted and burned more than 2,280 Korean businesses, causing losses of approximately $400 million, while 20 to 40 percent of the damage involved Latino-owned businesses.

The televised beating of Rodney King by three white and one Latino police officers and the equally brutal beating of a white truck driver, Reginald Denny, by African American youths during the riot led the media to portray it as a black-versus-white conflict. In fact, the multiracial cast of the uprising mirrored the changing demography of Los Angeles. Ignored by the media was a Japanese, Takao Hirata, born in a World War II U.S. concentration camp, who was almost beaten to death by a crowd yelling anti-Korean epithets at the same intersection where Denny was beaten.

Although the beating of Rodney King was the trigger for the violence, the riot was also fueled by a history of economic exploitation, political disenfranchisement, and poverty. It thus reflected some of the same issues as the 1965 Watts rebellion in Los Angeles. South Central Los Angeles, the main site of the unrest, had been largely an African American community in 1965, but by 1992 the population had shifted from roughly 80 percent African American to nearly 50 percent Latino. Between 1970 and 1990, the number of Mexicans in Los Angeles grew rapidly, through births and immigration almost equally. Central Americans added to the city's surging Latino population. In 1990, Los Angeles was home to about 302,000 Salvadorans, 159,000 Guatemalans, and 44,000 Nicaraguans. Unlike the Mexican economic migrants, most Central Americans were refugees fleeing from civil war and violence, and many were undocumented immigrants.

By the 1970s, Los Angeles was also home to the largest Korean community in the nation, with a cultural and business center called Koreatown. While a significant segment of the population of Koreatown was working class, a majority of the newer immigrants were highly educated and from the middle class. Most of them arrived seeking economic and educational opportunities, some to escape South Korea's repressive political situation. These urban immigrants arrived with education, motivation, and capital, and they invested in independent small businesses in marginal areas like South Central. The United States saw a 412 percent increase in the Korean population between 1970 and 1990, and the number of Koreans in Los Angeles leaped from 60,618 in 1980 to 145,431 in 1990.

Residential segregation in Los Angeles moved from a black/white divide to concentrations of white, African American, Latino, and Asian residents with pockets of poverty and wealth. The spread of the uprising mirrored those race and class distinctions, moving from impoverished areas to places of capital concentration. For some, looting was a way to alleviate poverty: one woman testified that the uprising allowed all six of her children to get shoes for the first time. The looters' concentration on Korean-owned businesses, however, revealed another type of motivation.

As early as 1984, the African American *Los Angeles Sentinel*'s executive editor sounded the alarm against "a bunch of foreigners, a bunch of folks who don't speak English, who can't vote, who come here with money" who have over the last five years "taken over" the African American community.[18] The editor went on to urge a boycott of Korean stores. The previous year, the Los Angeles Human Relations Commission helped form a Black-Korean Alliance, which held several gatherings to promote goodwill between the groups. But in May 1991, Soon Ja Du, a Korean storeowner, shot and killed an African American teenager, Latasha Harlins, in her store. Du's conviction of manslaughter, not murder, and her sentence of five years' probation and no jail time enraged many who sought justice for Harlins's death, including the *Korea Times,* a Korean American newspaper. Groups like the Brotherhood Crusade sought the removal of Korean stores from African American communities.

In Los Angeles, the relations among the city's communities of color and their relations with the dominant white minority were complex. Latinos formed the largest group among peoples of color. Asians were not a numerically significant obstacle to black empowerment, but one source of conflict was a perceived preference by Asians for Latino workers. Korean storeowners, positioned between white suppliers and nonwhite workers and consumers, faced pressures from both sides, even as Koreans, African Americans, and Latinos confronted common challenges as peoples of color.

Many Koreans never fully recovered economically from the devastation of 1992. Moreover, Koreans realized that, positioned by the media and political leaders between black and white, they were rendered invisible, despite the "model minority" label. In fact, as the uprising showed, models who are too upwardly mobile can be envied and despised by other minorities and hated by the majority. That understanding of their place within the U.S. social formation led many Koreans, especially the second generation, to recognize the need to move from a Korea-centered to a U.S.-centered subjectivity and to engage with the U.S. political and social order to find their voice and have it heard.

THE MODEL MINORITY

The contemporary image of Asians as a model minority, positioned between white and nonwhite, requires critical examination. Model minorities are those shaped in the image of the majority through resemblances with and assimilation into whiteness. The extent to which a minority group models itself on the majority group affects its purported success and social standing.

Although the stereotype's roots reach back to the 1950s or earlier, the casting of Asians as a model minority gained traction amid civil unrest in U.S. cities and during the Cold War. "At a time when Americans are awash in worry over the plight of racial minorities—

one such minority, the nation's 300,000 Chinese Americans, is winning wealth and respect by dint of its own hard work," declared the December 26, 1966, issue of *U.S. News & World Report.* "In any Chinatown from San Francisco to New York, you discover youngsters at grips with their studies. Crime and delinquency are found to be rather minor in scope. Still being taught in Chinatown is the old idea that people should depend on their own efforts—not a welfare check—in order to reach America's 'promised land'.... At a time when it is being proposed that hundreds of billions be spent to uplift Negroes and other minorities, the nation's 300,000 Chinese Americans are moving ahead on their own—with no help from anyone else."

The civil rights movement, the Watts rebellion in 1965, and the race riots the year before in Rochester, Philadelphia, and New York City were the immediate reasons for white Americans to "worry over the plight of racial minorities." The urban problems of crime, poverty, and unemployment invited studies of their causes and public-policy solutions like President Lyndon Johnson's War on Poverty. Following race riots in Detroit, Newark, and Baltimore in 1967, the Kerner Commission, led by Illinois governor Otto Kerner and charged by President Johnson to investigate the roots of the civil disturbances, famously concluded: "Our nation is moving toward two societies, one black, one white—separate and unequal." It went on to charge: "What white Americans have never fully understood—but what the Negro can never forget—is that white society is deeply implicated in the ghetto. White institutions created it, white institutions maintain it, and white society condones it."

For conservatives, the conditions in the urban ghetto and black reliance on government entitlement programs were attributable to the African American "culture of poverty," or behavior that produces poverty. That culture, they alleged, led to a dependency on welfare and other social programs that encouraged unemployment, women heads of households, sexual promiscuity, and children born out of wedlock. Liberals attributed the problems of the ghetto to a history of racism and segregation, and accordingly they saw civil rights legislation and government interventions as necessary to alleviate the plight of the black underclass. In that debate, the status of Asians as a model minority was invoked to affirm the "culture of poverty" thesis. African Americans were portrayed as the victims of their own inadequacies, whereas Asians were depicted as advancing without government handouts.

The model-minority discourse also attests to the power of white cultural norms and the prevailing social relations, including capitalism. Asian culture, according to the *U.S. News & World Report* account, possesses attributes, such as the work ethic, education, family values, and self-help, that are normally attributed to whites. Contrary to the nineteenth-century version of the Asian as unassimilable, this version portrays Asians as equal to whites, or even surpassing them, in income and educational attainment.

The success of a model minority, however, can imperil white dominance. This was the case when Japan's industries began to produce automobiles that outsold and outperformed U.S. models, leading to Japan-bashing, and when Korean small businesses were represented as staging a "foreign" takeover of African American communities. The flip side of the model minority stereotype is the yellow peril.

The two images flourished side by side in the 1980s with the rise of the political right and the Reagan revolution, named for President Ronald Reagan, which created the specter of a bloated government intruding into people's lives. This backlash against government intervention into social injustice dismantled many of the civil rights movement's achievements. The Reagan revolution began a trend toward greater inequality, in particular widening the gap between rich and poor, that has continued into the twenty-first century. The model-minority discourse was again invoked in support of those policies in national publications like *Newsweek, Time, Fortune,* and the *New York Times,* even as anti-Asian violence, which impaired Asian upward mobility, intensified and spread.

In the 1980s, as the Cold War pitted conservative governments in the United States, Great Britain, and other European nations against a weakening Soviet Union, success stories like those of Japan and the model minorities of the United States offered compelling narratives in support of the alleged superiority of U.S. capitalism and democracy. By 1989, communism had virtually collapsed in Poland, Hungary, and East Germany, and by the early 1990s, the Soviet Union's own communist regime fell. With the dissolution of the Soviet Union, the United States was left as the world's leading military power, able to pursue its global ambitions almost unilaterally.

The Cold War continued, nonetheless, in the U.S. confrontation with China. Notable was the case of the American scientist Wen Ho Lee, who was charged by his country with leaking nuclear secrets to China. The CIA and FBI were convinced that China had obtained classified information about a nuclear warhead developed at the Los Alamos National Laboratories, where Lee worked. Because Lee, a Taiwanese, had made several trips to China and met with Chinese scientists, he became a prime suspect. In March 1999 Lee was fired from his Los Alamos job, and in December he was arrested by the FBI, who charged him with violating the atomic energy and federal espionage acts.

Lee was held in solitary confinement for nine months, while the press, especially the *New York Times,* convicted and vilified him on the basis of reports from unidentified government sources. Lee, some in the press alleged, was the most dangerous traitor since Julius and Ethel Rosenberg, who were convicted of passing information about the atomic bomb to the Soviet Union and executed in 1953. Chinese and Asian American groups protested Lee's arrest as a case of racial profiling and anti-Chinese hysteria.

On September 13, 2000, the chief judge of the U.S. district court that had sentenced Lee to prison apologized to Lee for having been misled by the federal government and for the violation of his rights. "I believe you were terribly wronged by being held in custody . . . under demeaning, unnecessarily punitive conditions," the judge told Lee. "I am truly sorry that I was led by our executive branch of government to order your detention last December." That deception, the judge explained, embarrassed not only him: "They [the executive branch] have embarrassed our entire nation and each of us who is a citizen of it."[19] On September 26, the *New York Times* apologized in an editorial for its coverage of the Lee case, blaming itself for relying too heavily on government sources without checking their veracity. Both apologies were unusual for their candor. The case points not only to the power of the state over the lives of its subjects but also to the enduring power of the discourse of anti-Asianism, from the yellow peril in the late nineteenth century to the model minority of the twenty-first century. The portrait of Lee as both spy and scientist drew on both discourses.

THE WAR ON TERROR

President George W. Bush's National Security Strategy, announced in September 2002, made clear that the United States envisioned the establishment of a new world order. The so-called Bush Doctrine extended U.S. sovereignty from America (as was claimed by the nineteenth-century Monroe Doctrine) to the world. Despite its assertion that "the war on terrorism is not a clash of civilizations," the document espoused "a struggle of ideas," the bases for "civilizations," that divided the world between us and them, friends and foes, civilized nations and the "enemies of civilization." The hallmark of civilization, this doctrine declared, was adherence to the defining attributes of the United States: "freedom, democracy, and free enterprise."[20] Capitalism, cast as "free enterprise," was treated as a virtue on a par with freedom and democracy. In parallel with the demonization of Buddhism and paganism in the nineteenth century, Islam and fanaticism were represented as enemies and threats to Western civilization.

The Bush Doctrine was announced one year after the tragedy of September 11, 2001. On that day, hijackers crashed American Airlines Flight 11 and United Airlines Flight 175 into the Twin Towers of New York City's World Trade Center, symbols of international finance and capitalism, and aimed American Airlines Flight 77 at the Pentagon, the hub of U.S. military might, in Arlington, Virginia. A fourth hijacked airplane, United Airlines Flight 93, crashed in a field in Pennsylvania. Nearly three thousand people died in the attacks. What followed was a massive outpouring of grief from around the nation and world for the victims and compassion for their loved ones, and calls from U.S. leaders for tolerance and patience in locating the perpetrators. In 2004, Osama bin Laden of al-Qaeda claimed responsibility for the attacks.

In the days following September 11, the Bush administration focused on Iraq and its leader, Saddam Hussein, "radical" Islam, and al-Qaeda as continuing threats to the United States. In October 2001, the U.S. and its allies launched a war on Afghanistan, accusing the nation's Islamic rulers, the Taliban, of providing a haven for al-Qaeda. To combat the danger, Bush declared a "war on terror," a series of security measures with the declared purpose of identifying Islamist terrorists. The war was waged simultaneously abroad and at home by the state and citizens. Thousands of Arabs and West, Central, and South Asians in the United States reported instances of harassment and intimidation, including threatening gestures and speech, shootings, and the vandalizing of homes, businesses, and mosques. A Hindu temple was burned to the ground in Canada, and a white man drove his car into a mosque in Ohio. Whites attacked a South Asian and his white friend in San Francisco; and Waqar Hasan, a Pakistani, was killed in Dallas. As two men beat the Sikh American Surinder Singh Sidhu with metal poles in his Los Angeles store, they reportedly exulted: "We'll kill bin Laden today." Nervous air crews and passengers had dozens of Muslims and Sikhs, Arabs and Asians removed from flights, and hundreds of suspects were summarily arrested, questioned, and detained, often on flimsy pretexts.

Nationally, between September 11 and December 11, 2001, there were nine murders and 243 reports of bias crimes committed against Asians, according to a study released by the National Asian Pacific American Legal Consortium. New York and California led the way with forty-two incidents each. Normally, hate crimes against Asians averaged between four and five hundred a year. The racial and religious profiling continued in various guises, including discrimination in the workplace, housing, and education. The Equal Employment Opportunity Commission received so many allegations of discrimination against Muslims, Sikhs, Arabs, and South Asians that it created a special category called Code Z to track those complaints, and the Council on American-Islamic Relations received more than 1,500 reports of bias in workplaces and schools, airport profiling, and physical assaults.

Balbir Singh Sodhi, a Sikh, was fifty-two years old when he died, face up, among the flowers and shrubs outside his Chevron station in Mesa, Arizona. He was shot at least three times in the back by Frank Roque four days after the Twin Towers fell. When arrested and while being led away in handcuffs, Roque allegedly shouted: "I'm a patriot! I'm an American! Arrest me and let those terrorists run wild?"

Sodhi was a quiet, hard-working man inspired by his religion, his faith in the future, and the well-being of his children and family. He entered the United States to escape the bloody conflict between Sikh separatists and the Indian Army and to earn money to support his wife and five children in Punjab. He worked in Los Angeles and San Francisco. After one of his close friends, a Sikh and fellow taxicab driver in San Francisco, was killed, he moved to Phoenix, Arizona, to join his brothers. With their help, Sodhi opened the gas station and worked long hours to make ends meet.

After the September 11 attack, Sodhi and fellow Sikhs planned to wear buttons proclaiming themselves to be Sikhs from India and not Muslims from Afghanistan and to display the U.S. flag prominently. Hours before his murder, Sodhi donated seventy-five dollars to the Red Cross and checked in with his son, who was living in San Francisco. The last line of Sodhi's diary reads: "O God, you are my friend. Now the situation is this, that the task you are going to assign me, I am quite ready for it." Sodhi's ashes were taken from Arizona to join those of his ancestors on the banks of the Sutlej River near the holy temple of Anandpur Sahib.

The fight for justice for Balbir Singh Sodhi continued long after his passing. A jury convicted Roque of first-degree murder and sentenced him to death, dismissing his insanity plea. In 2006, however, the Arizona supreme court commuted the death sentence to life in prison without parole because of his mental illness and "mitigating factors." In 2011, the Arizona state legislature passed a bill to remove Sodhi's name from the state's memorial to the victims of September 11, 2001. After protests led by the Sikh community, Arizona's governor vetoed the bill.

That attempt by Arizona lawmakers to erase Sodhi's memory has a historical parallel in the American Legion's removal in 1944 of the names of Japanese who served in the U.S. military from a war memorial in Hood River, Oregon. After local and national protests, the American Legion restored the names the following year.

A CNN/*USA Today*/Gallup poll taken a few days after September 11, 2001, showed that 58 percent of Americans backed intensive security checks for Arabs, including those who were U.S. citizens; 49 percent favored special identification cards, and 32 percent supported "special surveillance" for them. In October 2001 Congress passed the U.S.A. Patriot Act to advance the Bush administration's "war on terror." The act authorized increased surveillance and expanded the ability of the government to conduct secret searches, gave the attorney general and secretary of state the power to designate domestic groups as terrorist organizations and deport any noncitizen who belongs to them, enabled investigations of U.S. citizens for intelligence purposes, and allowed for the indefinite detention of noncitizens deemed dangerous to the national security by the attorney general.

After about a year of those state initiatives, a national poll conducted in September 2002 showed that 62 percent of those surveyed said government efforts to thwart terrorism should not violate basic civil liberties, even as the attorney general pursued expanded use of wiretaps and e-mail monitoring, which the courts sanctioned in November 2002. Meanwhile, in preparation for its war on Iraq, the administration secretly investigated Iraqi Americans.

In 2002, the New York City–based Center for Constitutional Rights filed *Turkmen v. Ashcroft*, a class action suit on behalf of eight Muslim and Arab and South Asian noncitizens held in prisons in New York and New Jersey. Ibrahim Turkmen had been arrested after September 11, 2001 because he was in the United States on an expired tourist visa. He was held in jail for four months. The Immigration and Naturalization Service (INS) and the FBI arrested Turkmen, the other plaintiffs, and hundreds of others like them in a racial-profiling operation. They were presumed guilty and held in detention until proved innocent, contrary to the law. Although they were never charged with terrorism, the INS kept some of them in detention for up to nine months.

In 2006, the federal judge John Gleeson dismissed key elements of the petitioners' claims, ruling that under immigration law "the executive is free to single out nationals of a particular country." Although mass arrests of Arab Muslims and South Asians might be a "crude" method for uncovering terrorists, wrote the judge, it was not "so irrational or outrageous as to warrant judicial intrusion into an area in which courts have little experience and less expertise." Immigration law, Gleeson affirmed, bestows on the state the right to profile.

Judge Gleeson's ruling calls to mind the U.S. Supreme Court's deference to the military in its *Hirabayashi* and *Korematsu* rulings in 1943 and 1944, validating the Japanese internment. Indeed, in the appeal of Gleeson's ruling in 2007, Jay Hirabayashi, Karen Korematsu-Haigh, and Holly Yasui, descendants of Hirabayashi, Korematsu, and Yasui of the World War II court cases, filed a friend-of-the-court brief. The judge's sweeping language, the Japanese charged, resurrected the discredited legal theory that had placed their grandparents into U.S. concentration camps and overlooked the Civil Liberties Act of 1988, which acknowledged that act against Japanese as a fundamental injustice warranting an apology and the payment of reparations.

In November 2009, six of the eight *Turkmen* plaintiffs settled their claims for a total of $1.26 million from the U.S. government. In September 2010, the Center for Constitutional Rights added, in an amended complaint, six new plaintiffs: Muslims from Algeria, Egypt, Pakistan, and Turkey, a Hindu from India, and a Buddhist from Nepal. These people, the complaint charged, were kept in solitary confinement with the lights on all day; kept from communicating with attorneys, family members, or friends; subjected to physical and verbal abuse; forced to endure inhumane conditions of confinement; and hindered from observing their religious beliefs.

In another case, according to a February 28, 2006, *New York Times* report, the federal government agreed to pay $300,000 to settle a lawsuit brought by an Egyptian, Ehab Elmaghraby, who was held in detention in Brooklyn for months following the sweeps after September 11, 2001. Elmaghraby had charged the government with violating his and other Muslim detainees' constitutional rights on the grounds of their race, religion, and national origin.

The Justice Department began a special registration program that required the fingerprinting and photographing of all men over sixteen years of age on nonimmigrant visas from selected Muslim countries in Asia and Africa and from North Korea, the third member of the "axis of evil" identified by President Bush. By 2003, more than eighty-three thousand African, Arab, and Asian men had registered. The mass and sudden arrests and secrecy surrounding the proceedings spawned rumors and fears of more arrests, detentions, and eventual deportations. Indeed, in June 2002, the federal government tried to deport thirteen thousand of those men, none of whom had any proven terrorist ties. One was the Korean Hyung Joon Kim, whose deportation was upheld in April 2003 by the U.S. Supreme Court, based in part on the government's claim to broad powers to protect Americans from criminals.

Detained not on any evidence of wrongdoing but primarily on the basis of racial and religious criteria, America's twenty-first-century internees suffered cruel treatment, such as imprisonment in crowded and frigid cells, being hosed down with cold water, and being shackled and arbitrarily hustled to locations in the middle of the night. An INS spokesman said of the mass registrations and arrests: "We're doing what the American people want us to do. I don't think the American people would want known terrorists or wanted criminals running around the country attempting to harm the people."[21] But as the Justice Department's own Office of the Inspector General reported in 2003, the roundup of the more than seven hundred Muslim and Arab noncitizens after September 11 on the pretext of immigration violations was religious and racial profiling without any evidence that those people posed a danger. A second report detailed the physical, verbal, and psychological abuse inflicted on them and the inhuman conditions of their confinement.

The impact of government repression was dramatic in the Pakistani and South Asian communities of New York City and New Jersey. About two-thirds of those picked up and detained after September 11, 2001, in New York City were residents of Little Pakistan, and it is estimated that over fifteen thousand from Brooklyn and another thousand from New Jersey fled for Canada. A Shiite Muslim, thirty-eight-year-old Mukeem Butt, had been a civil servant in Pakistan, where he was beaten and shot at by thugs. He and his wife, Shagufta, entered the United States on visitors' visas in 2001, and he immediately applied for a work permit. Two years later, his papers were still being processed, but after September 11, he faced registration, detention, and deportation. In April 2003, he and his wife climbed into a van and, after a tearful farewell to friends and well-wishers, drove to Canada, where they were granted asylum.

The Pakistanis Anser Mehmood, his wife, Uzma Naheed, and their four children had lived in the United States for seven years when, on October 3, 2001, FBI and immigration agents raided their Bayonne, New Jersey, home and detained Mehmood for holding an expired visa. He spent months in solitary confinement and was deported to Pakistan in May 2002. Before September 11, Mehmood recalled, "My family did not have any problems with anyone and never felt any discrimination. I especially liked that people respected laws." Naheed added: "I felt so relaxed and enjoyed my time there [in the United States] because people treated each other like human beings." But after September 11, "Everything changed . . . , especially the way people looked at us. We lived in a white neighborhood, and our neighbors started looking at us suspiciously. The kids started feeling uncomfortable at school because the other kids called them 'Muslim terrorist.'"[22]

The United States "war on terror" was a campaign directed against immigrants, especially the undocumented, on the basis of racial and religious profiling. The state considered even those merely suspected of being illegal immigrants as enemies who sought to destabilize, impoverish, and harm the nation. "How do you defend your home if your front and back doors are unlocked?" asked Representative James A. Traficant Jr. (D-Ohio) when calling for military patrols to bolster the forces along the borders with Canada and Mexico about a month after the September 11 attacks. "What do we stand for if we can't secure our borders? How many more Americans will die?"[23]

In December 2005, the U.S. House passed HR 4437, which criminalized aid to undocumented migrants—whose numbers were estimated at 3.7 million, or about half of all immigrants since 2000—and the Senate debated its version of the bill in April 2006. Ultimately the bill failed, but a national poll conducted by *Time* magazine in

FIGURE 64

More than half a million people rallied in support of immigrant rights in Los Angeles on March 25, 2006, and about a month later, over a million marched in the Great American Strike to reinforce the claims "We are America" and "No one human is illegal!!" Los Angeles, May 1, 2006.

January 2006 found that 63 percent of respondents considered undocumented immigration a "very serious" to "extremely serious" problem. In the spring of 2006, supporters of immigrants' rights staged massive demonstrations that drew an estimated half a million in Los Angeles, one hundred thousand in Chicago, and tens of thousands in Atlanta, Denver, Phoenix, and New York City. In all, there were over 260 demonstrations in 163 cities, with millions of people marching in support of immigrant rights—the largest such movement in the world.

The criminalization of undocumented immigrants led to a boom in the private operation of prisons. The Corrections Corporation of America, one of the government contractors operating detention centers for immigrants, earned in excess of $300 million in 2005 from its detention centers and correctional facilities, each prisoner generating profits of about $50 daily. In January 2006 Halliburton, a U.S.-based international energy and building company, announced that it had received a $385 million contract from the Department of Homeland Security to build detention centers for "an emergency influx of immigrants into the United States, or to support the rapid development of new programs" in the event of a crisis.

Although immigrant detention began before September 11, the "war on terror" escalated the rates of detention and deportation. In 2001, the United States held approximately 95,000 people in immigration custody. By 2009, the total had grown to about 380,000. Violation of immigration laws is not a crime but a civil violation to be resolved through a hearings process. Since 1996, however, a process called expedited removal has allowed immigration officials to expel detainees from the United States without a hearing and, as a 2011 report found, without the benefit of accurate counsel. Those held in detention often failed to receive timely medical care and adequate food. Many were subjected to frequent sexual harassment and some to physical beatings, and they were routinely denied access to lawyers, relatives, and friends.

Guantanamo Bay, Cuba, is a relic of the U.S. imperial war with Spain in 1898, following which the United States gained control of the island. In 1903, after Cuba's independence, the United States obtained a perpetual lease of Guantanamo and its deep-water port for the U.S. Navy. In January 2002, as part of its "war on terror," the Bush administration established the Guantanamo Bay Detention and Interrogation Center. The Department of Justice ruled that those held there were outside U.S. legal jurisdiction and were not subject to the Geneva Conventions concerning the treatment of prisoners of war. In 2006, the U.S. Supreme Court decided against that interpretation, stating that the Geneva Conventions applied to those confined at Guantanamo, and since 2008, the United States has considered those sent to the detention and interrogation center to be "enemy combatants."

In 2003, an Asian Muslim chaplain, James Yee, who grew up in New Jersey and graduated from West Point, went to Guantanamo to minister to the Muslims at that base. "We say that the war on terror is not a war against Islam, but that's not how it felt most days at Guantanamo," Yee testified in his memoir.[24] Yee's predecessor, Chaplain Hamza al-Mubarak, had warned him: "This is not a friendly environment for Muslims, and I don't just mean for the prisoners." That anti-Muslim hostility, he confided, made it especially difficult to work there. "You need to watch your back," Mubarak advised.

Yee described his first visit to Guantanamo's cells, which were eight-by-six-foot cages inside a block with low tin roofs that trapped the heat. "It was steamy and moist with the odor of forty-eight men confined in close quarters. The sweat dripped from my forehead; the heat in the blocks was even more intense than it had been outside, and there was no air-conditioning or even fans." Contrary to Islamic custom, men had to expose themselves while using the toilet (installed at ground level on the cage floor), and the place attracted flies and mosquitoes.

When Yee served as the center's Muslim chaplain, there were about 660 prisoners. They came from Afghanistan, North Africa, Pakistan, Saudi Arabia, Turkey, and Yemen but also from Australia, Britain, France, and Russia. They also included Uighurs, a Muslim ethnic minority from northwestern China. Despite the inhumanity of their physical condition and treatment, all of the prisoners faithfully practiced their religion, praying five times a day and fasting during Ramadan. They spoke of torture, such as being forced to kneel on gravel in the hot sun for hours with their hands and ankles shackled until they fainted and were left there like animals on the ground. Guards taunted them for their religious beliefs and practices, taking every opportunity to disrupt and offend their devotions by actions such as stepping on the Koran.

On September 10, 2003, the FBI and the Naval Criminal Investigative Service arrested Yee on his return to the United States, cuffed his wrists and shackled his ankles, and charged him with failing to obey a lawful general order, among other charges. He was held in solitary confinement for six days, and on the third day was allowed outside to walk in his shackles under the hot Florida sun for an hour. He later found out that he was also being charged with associating with known terrorist sympathizers, promoting mutiny and sedition, aiding the enemy, and engaging in espionage and spying. By October, the charges were reduced to taking classified information to his housing quarters and transporting classified material outside its proper container—charges reminiscent of those made against the nuclear scientist Wen Ho Lee.

The press and media dragged Yee's name through the mud, calling him a traitor and a "Chinese Taliban," and legislators investigated whether Muslim "extremists" had infiltrated the U.S. military. After Yee had spent seventy-six days in solitary confinement, in November 2003, Yee's attorney reminded the government of the precedent of Wen Ho Lee, and a day later Yee gained his freedom, though he was subsequently charged with adultery and storing pornography on a government computer.

The Council on American Islamic Relations (the largest Muslim civil rights organization in the United States), the Chinese for Affirmative Action, and other groups supported Yee throughout his ordeal, and in March 2004, the military agreed to drop all charges against him except the adultery and pornography charge, which was handled not by a trial but administratively. A general found Yee guilty of conduct unbecoming an officer and a gentleman and issued a letter of reprimand that ended Yee's military career.

On March 24, 2004, the *New York Times* commented in an editorial titled "Military Injustice": "More than six months after Capt. James Yee, the former Muslim chaplain at Guantanamo, was arrested on suspicion of espionage, the military has dropped the charges. Military officials insist that the prosecution was halted only to keep sensitive information from becoming public. What they really are trying to hide from view, it seems clear, is not national security secrets, but the incompetence and mean-spiritedness of their prosecution." The pornography and adultery charges and his reprimand, the editorial added, appear to be "the military's feeble attempt to make Captain Yee look bad."

Other revelations of abuses at Guantanamo Bay came to light. On January 11, 2007, the *Los Angeles Times* published an article based on letters from Jumah al-Dossari, a Guantanamo prisoner since 2002 and a citizen of Bahrain, written, in his words, "from the darkness of the U.S. detention camp at Guantanamo in the hope that I can make our voices heard by the world." Dossari, detainee #261, described being arrested in Pakistan, blindfolded, shackled, drugged, and flown to Cuba. The United States described Dossari as a dangerous terrorist who was on his way to Afghanistan to join the Taliban to fight against U.S. forces.

FIGURE 65
Kneeling on gravel at Guantanamo, 2002. U.S. Navy photo.

At Guantanamo, he recounted, soldiers assaulted him, beat him unconscious, placed him in solitary confinement, threatened to kill him and his daughter back home, deprived him of sleep, forced him to listen to extremely loud music, and placed him in cold rooms for hours without food, drink, or toilet facilities. They wrapped him in an Israeli flag and told him to admit his membership in al-Qaeda and involvement in the September 11 attacks. "I would rather die than stay here forever," Dossari wrote, "and I have tried to commit suicide several times. The purpose of Guantanamo is to destroy people, and I have been destroyed. I am hopeless because our voices are not heard from the depths of the detention center." He urged: "If I die, please remember that there was a human being named Jumah at Guantanamo whose beliefs, dignity and humanity were abused."

The United States released Jumah al-Dossari to Saudi Arabia in July 2007. He admitted no ties with any terrorist group, and he was never charged with any crime. In an article published in the *Washington Post* on August 17, 2008, about a year after his release, Dossari confided: "I still have trouble sleeping sometimes." As of January 2015, there were still 122 men locked up at Guantanamo.

THIRD WORLD

The national movements for self-determination and antiracism constituted the solution to the "problem of the twentieth century." The third world liberation movements set out to upend some four hundred years of world history during which European imperialism had enmeshed the planet. The Hawaiian sovereignty and pan-Asian social movements within the United States were aspects of that global revolution and transformation. Third world women compellingly demonstrated that the century's problem was not the color line alone but a complex nexus of social relations involving gender, sexuality, class, and nation as well. That social formation framed realities of everyday life that required redress and remediation.

Even as third world peoples formed independent nations, people of color in the United States aspired to end oppression and create a new nation and people. Crucial to that regeneration were the post-1965 immigrations, unprecedented in numbers and ethnic, religious, and class diversity, which had sweeping demographic consequences for Asian America. Just as critical were groundings with the past like the strengthening of ties among Polynesian peoples and the common ground of struggles by indigenous peoples and peoples of color in the United States amid the Cold War, urban conflicts, and U.S. imperial ambitions.

The dream of a world free from oppression, imperialism and racism, and wars was articulated by Third World leaders at Bandung, Indonesia, in 1955. Convened by Indonesia's president, Ahmed Sukarno, the Bandung gathering of twenty-nine recently independent African and Asian nations called for human rights and self-determination, the equality of all races, economic and cultural cooperation, and the rule of justice and world peace. That spirit of unity evaporated as African and Asian nations competed for power and as peoples of color in the United States separated themselves into the races named by Europeans under the banner of self-determination. Those nationalisms united nation-states and races even as they excluded others.

Moreover, when African and Asian Americans and Latinos adopted nationalist agendas, they separated themselves from American Indians, Chamorros, Hawaiians, Samoans, and Tainos, who continued to live as colonized subjects within the nation-state. Insofar as nationalism devolved into claims for civil rights, it betrayed third world liberation and the international human rights freedom movement urged by Malcolm X in 1964 and Martin Luther King Jr. in 1967.

Third world subjectivity, unlike those nationalisms, is transnational and aspires to break down those borders of racial formation. In 1968, the students and community workers who formed the Asian American Political Alliance (AAPA) in Berkeley, California, endorsed the Third World Liberation Front and its strike for third world studies at San Francisco State College and the University of California at Berkeley. The AAPA participated in African American and Chicano (Mexican American) rallies and boycotts to establish solidarities with other peoples of color and sympathetic whites. In its newspaper, the AAPA expressed its belief in creating a society that is "just, humane, equal, and gives the people the right to control their own lives." It rejected racism and affirmed the right to self-determination and its support for "all oppressed peoples and their struggles for Liberation."[25]

A third world subjectivity and the objectives of the Third World Liberation Front constitute the guiding principles of this textbook and history: to heed the imperative to write oneself into history, to give voice to those silenced by those in power, and to empower individuals to free themselves and their communities from colonialism and its disciplines of racism, assimilation, and erasure—in effect, self-determination. The creation of a just, humane, and equal world, as the AAPA put it, is a continuing challenge and opportunity. Moreover, the cause is not a solitary effort but a collective one, in solidarity with all oppressed peoples and their struggles for liberation.

SUGGESTED READINGS

Kauanui, J. Kēhaulani. *Hawaiian Blood: Colonialism and the Politics of Sovereignty and Indigeneity*. Durham, NC: Duke University Press, 2008.

Kim, Claire Jean. *Bitter Fruit: The Politics of Black-Korean Conflict in New York City*. New Haven, CT: Yale University Press, 2000.

Maira, Sunaina Marr. *Missing: Youth, Citizenship, and Empire after 9/11*. Durham, NC: Duke University Press, 2009.

Manalansan, Martin F. IV. *Global Divas: Filipino Gay Men in the Diaspora*. Durham, NC: Duke University Press, 2003.

Rana, Junaid. *Terrifying Muslims: Race and Labor in the South Asian Diaspora*. Durham, NC: Duke University Press, 2011.

Shiekh, Irum. *Detained without Cause: Muslims' Stories of Detention and Deportation in America after 9/11*. New York: Palgrave Macmillan, 2011.

PRIMARY DOCUMENT

DOCUMENT 16

"Final Communique of the Asian African Conference," in *The Asian-African Conference, Bandung, Indonesia, April 1955*, by George McTurnan Kahin (Ithaca, NY: Cornell University Press, 1956), 76, 83–85.

The historic Bandung Conference of 1955 concluded with a stirring declaration and pledge. Richard Wright, the African American writer, hastened to Indonesia to witness the proceedings, and he described the scene: "Day in and day out these crowds would stand in this tropic sun, staring, listening, applauding; it was the first time in their downtrodden lives that they'd seen so many men of their color, race, and nationality arrayed in such aspects of power, their men keeping order, their Asia and their Africa in control of their destinies. . . . They were getting a new sense of themselves, getting used to new roles and new identities. Imperialism was dead here; and as long as they could maintain their unity, organize and conduct international conferences, there would be no return of imperialism" (Richard Wright, *The Color Curtain: A Report on the Bandung Conference* [New York: World Publishing, 1956], 133–34). Consider, when reading this statement from Bandung, the subsequent caricatures of the third world as "banana republics" led by witless dictators who ruled over semiliterate peasants. Also recall the 1950s Cold War and the tug between the first and second worlds for the submission of the third world, and the threat of a nuclear confrontation between the United States and the Soviet Union.

The Asian-African Conference, convened upon the invitation of the Prime Ministers of Burma, Ceylon, India, Indonesia and Pakistan, met in Bandung from the 18th to the 24th April, 1955. In addition to the sponsoring countries the following 24 countries participated in the conference:

1. Afghanistan
2. Cambodia
3. People's Republic of China
4. Egypt
5. Ethiopia
6. Gold Coast
7. Iran
8. Iraq
9. Japan
10. Jordan
11. Laos
12. Lebanon
13. Liberia
14. Libya
15. Nepal
16. Philippines
17. Saudi Arabia
18. Sudan
19. Syria
20. Thailand
21. Turkey
22. Democratic Republic of Vietnam
23. State of Vietnam
24. Yemen

The Asian-African Conference considered problems of common interest and concern to countries of Asia and Africa and discussed ways and means by which their people could achieve fuller economic, cultural and political cooperation. . . .

G. *Declaration on the Promotion of World Peace and Cooperation*

The Asian-African Conference gave anxious thought to the question of world peace and cooperation. It viewed with deep concern the present state of international tension with its danger of an atomic world war. The problem of peace is correlative with the problem of international security. In this connection, all States should cooperate, especially through the United Nations, in bringing about the reduction of armaments and the elimination of nuclear weapons under effective international control. In this way, international peace can be promoted and nuclear energy may be used exclusively for peaceful purposes. This would help answer the needs particularly of Asia and Africa, for what they urgently require are social progress and better standards of life in larger freedom. Freedom and peace are interdependent. The right of self-determination must be enjoyed by all peoples, and freedom and independence must be granted, with the least possible delay, to those who are still dependent peoples. Indeed, all nations should have the right freely to choose their own political and economic systems and their own way of life, in conformity with the purposes and principles of the Charter of the United Nations.

Free from mistrust and fear, and with confidence and goodwill towards each other, nations should practise tolerance and live together in peace with one another as good neighbors and develop friendly cooperation on the basis of the following principles:

1. Respect for fundamental human rights and for the purposes and principles of the Charter of the United Nations.
2. Respect for the sovereignty and territorial integrity of all nations.
3. Recognition of the equality of all races and of the equality of all nations large and small.
4. Abstention from intervention or interference in the internal affairs of another country.
5. Respect for the right of each nation to defend itself singly or collectively, in conformity with the Charter of the United Nations.
6. (a) Abstention from the use of arrangements of collective defence to serve the particular interests of any of the big powers.
   (b) Abstention by any country from exerting pressures on other countries.
7. Refraining from acts or threats of aggression or the use of force against the territorial integrity or political independence of any country.
8. Settlement of all international disputes by peaceful means, such as negotiation, conciliation, arbitration or judicial settlement as well as other peaceful means of the parties' own choice, in conformity with the Charter of the United Nations.
9. Promotion of mutual interests and cooperation.
10. Respect for justice and international obligations.

The Asian-African Conference declared its conviction that friendly cooperation in accordance with these principles would effectively contribute to the maintenance and promotion of international peace and security, while cooperation in the economic, social and cultural fields would help bring about the common prosperity and well-being of all. . . .
Bandung, 24th April, 1955

SIGNIFICANT EVENTS

1946   Filipino and Japanese sugar workers' strike in Hawai'i
1947   Army intelligence and governor target "communists" in Hawai'i
1948   West Coast longshoremen's strike
1949   dockworkers' strike in Hawai'i
1950   HUAC holds hearings in Hawai'i

1953   Reluctant 39 and Hawaii Seven convicted

1954   Democratic Party captures Hawai'i's legislature

1955   Asian-African Conference, Bandung

        Rosa Parks inspires a bus boycott in Montgomery, Alabama

1956   Dalip Singh Saund becomes first Asian elected to Congress

1959   Hawai'i statehood

1964   John Dominis Holt publishes *On Being Hawaiian*

        Merrie Monarch Festival

        riots in Rochester, Philadelphia, and New York City

        Civil Rights Act

        Patsy Takemoto Mink becomes first Asian woman elected to Congress

1965   Immigration Act

        Voting Rights Act

        Delano, CA grape strike and boycott by Filipinos and Mexicans

        Watts rebellion

        Malcolm X assassinated

1966   *U.S. News & World Report*'s "model minority" article

        United Farm Workers of Americaformed

1967   riots in Detroit, Newark, and Baltimore

        Kerner Commission report

1968   Third World Liberation Front strike at San Francisco State College

        Asian American Political Alliance formed in Berkeley, CA

        start of struggle over demolition of International Hotel, San Francisco

        American Indian Movement formed in Minneapolis

        Martin Luther King Jr. assassinated

        Robert Kennedy assassinated

1969   School of Ethnic Studies established at San Francisco State

        Third World Liberation Front strike at University of California, Berkeley

        Third World Women's Alliance

        founding of I Wor Kuen, a revolutionary Asian American group associated with the Black Panther Party and Young Lords Party

        American Indians occupy Alcatraz Island

        first of annual pilgrimages to Manzanar concentration camp

1970   struggle for Kalama Valley

1971   *Asian Women* published

        Roots: An Asian American Reader published

Amerasia Journal begins

1972 ALOHA founded

1973 Polynesian Voyaging Society founded

American Indian Movement occupies Wounded Knee, South Dakota

1974 'Ohana O Hawai'i

Lau v. Nichols affirms language rights in public education

1975 *Aiiieeeee!* published

Voting Rights Act (1965) amended to include language rights

1976 first landing on Kaho'olawe Island

Protect Kaho'olawe 'Ohana formed

Hōkūle'a voyages to Tahiti

1977 Combahee River Collective statement

1978 Constitutional Convention, Hawai'i

Office of Hawaiian Affairs founded

1979 Association for Asian American Studies founded

1980 second *Hōkūle'a* voyage to Tahiti

Refugee Act

Commission on Wartime Relocation and Internment of Civilians formed

1981 Vietnamese fishermen in Texas sue Ku Klux Klan

1982 Vincent Chin murdered in Detroit

Chol Soo Lee released from prison following two racially biased murder convictions

1983 American Citizens for Justice formed in response to murder of Vincent Chin

1986 Immigration Reform and Control Act

John Waihe'e becomes first Hawaiian governor of Hawai'i

1987 Constitutional Convention for a Hawaiian nation

Navroz Mody murdered in Jersey City, NJ

1988 Civil Liberties Act

1989 massacre of Southeast Asian children in Stockton, CA

Jim (Ming Hai) Loo murdered in Raleigh, North Carolina

Tiananmen Square demonstrations

1990 U.S. Navy stops bombing on Kaho'olawe Island

Hung Truong murdered in Houston

Red Apple boycott in Brooklyn

Peace Rally for Racial Harmony, New York City

1991	dissolution of Soviet Union
1992	Los Angeles uprising and *sai-i-gu*
1993	Apology Resolution for U.S. role in overthrow of Hawaiian kingdom
1994	California Proposition 187 denies rights and services to undocumented migrants
1996	Illegal Immigration Reform and Immigrant Responsibilities Act
	California Proposition 209, ending state affirmative action
1998	*Journal of Asian American Studies* begins
1999	Wen Ho Lee jailed
2000	Wen Ho Lee exonerated
2001	September 11 attacks on the World Trade Center and Pentagon
	U.S. "war on terror" begins
	U.S.A. Patriot Act
	Balbir Singh Sodhi and Waqar Hasan killed
2002	*Turkmen v. Ashcroft*
	Department of Homeland Security established
	Guantanamo Bay Detention and Interrogation Center opens
2003	James Yee jailed
2006	mass demonstrations in support of immigrant rights
	Ehren K. Watada refuses deployment to Iraq, claiming the war was illegal
2011	Arizona bill to remove Balbir Singh Sodhi's name from a memorial
2012	white supremacist kills six and wounds four at Sikh *gurdwara* in Oak Creek, Wisconsin
2014	*Hōkūleʻa* departs Hilo Bay on a "Care for our Earth" voyage

NOTES

INTRODUCTION

1. Quoted in Richard Drinnon, *Facing West: The Metaphysics of Indian-Hating and Empire-Building* (New York: New American Library, 1980), 232.

2. Ronald Takaki, *Strangers from a Different Shore: A History of Asian Americans* (Boston: Little, Brown, 1989), 80.

3. Daniel Lord Smail, *On Deep History and the Brain* (Berkeley: University of California Press, 2008).

4. Apparently the term *American exceptionalism* was coined in the 1920s by Joseph Stalin, who scolded a Communist Party official for claiming an apparent absence of class consciousness in the United States as unique in world history.

5. See, for example, Martin W. Lewis and Kären E. Wigen, *The Myth of Continents: A Critique of Metageography* (Berkeley: University of California Press, 1997), and Gary Y. Okihiro, *Island World: A History of Hawai'i and the United States* (Berkeley: University of California Press, 2008).

1. OCEAN WORLDS

1. A Hawaiian saying, as quoted in Davianna Pōmaika'i McGregor, *Nā Kua'āina: Living Hawaiian Culture* (Honolulu: University of Hawai'i Press, 2007), 27.

2. As cited in O. H. K. Spate, *The Spanish Lake* (Minneapolis: University of Minnesota Press, 1979), 1, 32, 33.

2. THE WORLD-SYSTEM

1. Quoted in Rhoads Murphey, *A History of Asia*, 2nd ed. (New York: HarperCollins, 1996), 222.
2. Gary Y. Okihiro, *Island World: A History of Hawai'i and the United States* (Berkeley: University of California Press, 2008), 143.
3. Lisa Yun, *The Coolie Speaks: Chinese Indentured Laborers and African Slaves of Cuba* (Philadelphia: Temple University Press, 2008), 80–82.
4. Samuel Eliot Morison, ed. and trans., *Journals and Other Documents on the Life and Voyages of Christopher Columbus* (New York: Heritage Press, 1963), 382.

3. THE UNITED STATES

1. Quoted in Gary B. Nash, Julie Roy Jeffrey, Peter J. Frederick, Allen F. Davis, and Alan M. Winkler, *The American People: Creating a Nation and Society*, 4th ed. (New York: Longman, 1998), 38–39.
2. Ibid., 70–71.
3. Quoted in Gavan Daws, *Shoal of Time: A History of the Hawaiian Islands* (Honolulu: University of Hawai'i Press, 1986), 106.

4. IMPERIAL REPUBLIC

1. Quoted in Gary Lawson and Guy Seidman, "The First 'Incorporation' Debate," in *The Louisiana Purchase and American Expansion, 1803–1898*, ed. Sanford Levinson and Bartholomew H. Sparrow (Lanham, MD: Rowman & Littlefield, 2005), 19.
2. John Jay, "Concerning the Dangers from Foreign Force and Influence," *Federalist Papers* (1787–88), No. 2, available online at www.gutenberg.org.
3. Alan Brinkley, *American History: A Survey*, 9th ed. (New York: McGraw-Hill, 1995), 352.
4. Theodore Roosevelt and Henry Cabot Lodge, *Addresses and Presidential Messages of Theodore Roosevelt, 1902–1904* (New York: G. P. Putnam's Sons, 1904).
5. Brinkley, *American History*, 420.
6. Robert Hunter, *Poverty* (New York: Macmillan, 1904), 261, 262–63, 268.
7. Josiah Strong, *Our Country: Its Possible Future and Its Present Crisis* (New York: Baker & Taylor, 1885), 159, 160, 161, 175.
8. "The White Man's Burden," in *Rudyard Kipling's Verse, 1885–1926* (Garden City, NY: Doubleday, Page, 1927), 373–74.
9. Elizabeth Mary Holt, *Colonizing Filipinas: Nineteenth-Century Representations of the Philippines in Western Historiography* (Manila: Ateneo de Manila University Press, 2002), 60.
10. Whitelaw Reid, *Problems of Expansion* (New York: Century, 1900), 13–14, 205, 208–9.
11. Melvin Holli, "A View of the American Campaign against 'Filipino Insurgents': 1900," *Philippine Studies* 17 (January 1969): 100.
12. Russell Roth, *Muddy Glory: America's 'Indian Wars' in the Philippines* (West Hanover, MA: Christopher, 1981), 24.

13. Paul A. Kramer, *The Blood of Government: Race, Empire, the United States and the Philippines* (Chapel Hill: University of North Carolina Press, 2006), 220.

14. From Samuel M. Kamakau, *Ruling Chiefs of Hawaii* (Honolulu, HI: Kamehameha Schools Press, 1992), 399–401.

15. Ibid.

16. Ronald Takaki, *Pau Hana: Plantation Life and Labor in Hawaii* (Honolulu: University of Hawaii Press, 1983), 5.

5. HAWAI'I

1. Cited in Rhoads Murphey, *A History of Asia*, 2nd ed. (New York: HarperCollins, 1996), 257.

2. Quoted in Robert J. Schwendinger, *Ocean of Bitter Dreams: Maritime Relations between China and the United States, 1850–1915* (Tucson, AZ: Westernlore, 1988), 32.

3. Waihee plantation rules cited in Edward D. Beechert, *Working in Hawaii: A Labor History* (Honolulu: University of Hawaii Press, 1985), 72–73.

4. Franklin S. Odo and Harry Minoru Urata, "Hole Hole Bushi: Songs of Hawaii's Japanese Immigrants," *Mana* (Hawai'i ed.) 6, no. 1 (1981): 72.

5. James H. Okahata, ed., *A History of Japanese in Hawaii* (Honolulu: United Japanese Society of Hawaii, 1971), 125–26.

6. Quoted in Kazuo Ito, *Issei: A History of Japanese Immigrants in North America*, trans. Shinichiro Nakamura and Jean S. Gerard (Seattle, WA: Japanese Community Service, 1973), 20–21.

7. From Franklin Odo, to whom I am grateful, personal communication.

8. From Franklin Odo.

9. "Baishiro Tamashiro," in *Uchinanchu: A History of Okinawans in Hawaii*, Ethnic Studies Oral History Project and United Okinawan Association of Hawaii (Honolulu: Ethnic Studies Program, University of Hawaii at Mānoa, 1981), 358, 360.

10. "Tsuru Yamauchi," in *Uchinanchu*, 489.

11. Wayne Patterson, *The Korean Frontier in America: Immigration to Hawaii, 1896–1910* (Honolulu: University of Hawaii Press, 1988), 16.

12. Ibid., 200–205.

13. Ibid., 199; Harold Hakwon Sunoo and Sonia Shinn Sunoo, "The Heritage of the First Korean Women Immigrants in the United States: 1903–1924," *Korean Christian Scholars Journal* 2 (Spring 1977): 152–58.

14. Quoted in Wayne Patterson, *The Ilse: First-Generation Korean Immigrants in Hawai'i, 1903–1973* (Honolulu: University of Hawai'i Press, 2000), 20, 21.

15. Ibid., 25.

16. As quoted in Gary Y. Okihiro, *Cane Fires: The Anti-Japanese Movement in Hawaii, 1865–1945* (Philadelphia: Temple University Press, 1991), 17.

17. "Eun-Ai Cho," in Daisy Chun Rhodes, *Passages to Paradise: Early Korean Immigrant Narratives from Hawai'i* (Los Angeles: Academia Koreana, 1998), 17.

18. Patterson, *Ilse*, 83, 92–93.

19. As told by Delores Quinto, "Life Story of a Filipino Immigrant," *Social Forces in Hawaii* 4 (May 1938): 71–78.

20. Ibid., 6–7.

21. Juan Kihano, "The Old Man of the Cane Fields," *The Filipinos in Hawaii: The First 75 Years* (Honolulu: Hawaii Filipino News Specialty, 1981), 38.

22. As quoted in Fred Cordova, *Filipinos: Forgotten Asian Americans* (Dubuque, IA: Kendall/ Hunt, 1983), 31–32.

23. Ibid., 32–33.

24. Robert N. Anderson, *Filipinos in Rural Hawaii* (Honolulu: University of Hawaii Press, 1984), 8.

25. Cordova, *Filipinos*, 33.

26. Ronald Takaki, *Pau Hana: Plantation Life and Labor in Hawaii, 1835–1920* (Honolulu: University of Hawaii Press, 1983), 23, 24.

27. Patterson, *Ilse*, 16.

6. CALIFORNIA

1. Assembly committee report cited in Charles J. McClain, *In Search of Equality: The Chinese Struggle against Discrimination in Nineteenth-Century America* (Berkeley: University of California Press, 1994), 10.

2. Marlon K. Hom, *Songs of Gold Mountain: Cantonese Rhymes from San Francisco Chinatown* (Berkeley: University of California Press, 1987), 46.

3. Ibid., 39.

4. Franklin Odo, ed., *The Columbia Documentary History of the Asian American Experience* (New York: Columbia University Press, 2002), 19–21.

5. Thomas W. Chinn, ed., *A History of the Chinese in California: A Syllabus* (San Francisco: Chinese Historical Society of America, 1969), 31.

6. Ibid., 45.

7. Wesley S. Griswold, *A Work of Giants: Building the First Transcontinental Railroad* (New York: McGraw-Hill, 1962), 16.

8. Yuji Ichioka, *The Issei: The World of the First Generation Japanese Immigrants, 1885–1924* (New York: Free Press, 1988), 25–26.

9. Steven Misawa, ed., *Beginnings: Japanese Americans in San Jose* (San Jose, CA: Japanese American Community Senior Service, 1981), 12.

10. Ichioka, *Issei*, 83.

11. Ibid., 99.

12. From a newspaper advertisement in Yo-jun Yun, "Early History of Korean Immigration to America," in *The Korean Diaspora: Historical and Sociological Studies of Korean Immigration and Assimilation in North America*, ed. Hyung-chan Kim (Santa Barbara, CA: ABC-Clio, 1977), 40.

13. Quoted in ibid., 42.

14. Ibid., 44.

15. Cited in Sun Bin Yim, "The Social Structure of Korean Communities in California, 1903–1920," in *Labor Immigration under Capitalism: Asian Workers in the United States*

Before World War II, ed. Lucie Cheng and Edna Bonacich (Berkeley: University of California Press, 1984), 519.

16. Ibid., 523–24.

17. Ibid., 541–42.

18. As told in Bong-youn Choy, *Koreans in America* (Chicago: Nelson-Hall, 1979), 106.

19. Cited in Yim, "Social Structure," 530.

20. Punjabi songs from Darshan Singh Tatla, *The Sikh Diaspora: The Search for Statehood* (Seattle: University of Washington Press, 1999, 45.

21. Kalyan Kumar Banerjee, "East Indian Immigration into America: Beginnings of Indian Revolutionary Activity," *Modern Review* 116, no. 5 (November 1964): 359.

22. As cited in Benito M. Vergara Jr., *Displaying Filipinos: Photography and Colonialism in Early Twentieth-Century Philippines* (Quezon City: University of the Philippines Press, 1995), 120.

23. Fred Cordova, *Filipinos: Forgotten Asian Americans* (Dubuque, IA: Kendall/Hunt, 1983), 85.

24. Ibid., 39.

25. Ibid., 46.

26. Ibid., 41.

27. This account is taken from "Alfonso Yasonia," in *Pinoy: The First Wave (1898–1941),* ed. Roberto V. Vallangca (San Francisco: Strawberry Hill Press, 1977), 75–80.

7. NORTHWEST, NORTHEAST, SOUTH, AND NORTH

1. Cited in M. V. Kamath, *The United States and India, 1776–1976* (Bombay: Times of India Press, 1976), 21.

2. Moon-Ho Jung, *Coolies and Cane: Race, Labor, and Sugar in the Age of Emancipation* (Baltimore: Johns Hopkins University Press, 2006), 78.

3. Contract reproduced in Lucy M. Cohen, *Chinese in the Post–Civil War South: A People without a History* (Baton Rouge: Louisiana State University Press, 1984), 55–56.

4. Quoted in Jung, *Coolies and Cane,* 155.

5. Ibid., 187.

6. Ibid., 218.

7. See, Alexander Saxton, *The Indispensable Enemy: Labor and the Anti-Chinese Movement in California* (Berkeley: University of California Press, 1971).

8. Cited in Anthony W. Lee, *A Shoemaker's Story: Being Chiefly about French Canadian Immigrants, Enterprising Photographers, Rascal Yankees, and Chinese Cobblers in a Nineteenth-Century Factory Town* (Princeton, NJ: Princeton University Press, 2008), 52.

9. Ibid., 256.

10. Andrew Gyory, *Closing the Gate: Race, Politics, and the Chinese Exclusion Act* (Chapel Hill: University of North Carolina Press, 1998), 54.

11. Robert Park, *Race and Culture* (Glencoe, IL: Free Press, 1950), 82.

12. Frank Füredi, *The Silent War: Imperialism and the Changing Perception of Race* (London: Pluto Press, 1998), 34, 50, 86–87.

1. Quoted in Gary Y. Okihiro, *Cane Fires: The Anti-Japanese Movement in Hawaii, 1865–1945* (Philadelphia: Temple University Press, 1991), 144.

2. Ibid., 103.

3. Ibid., 105.

4. Ibid., 105–6.

5. Ibid., 116.

6. Cited in Lawrence H. Fuchs, *Hawaii Pono: A Social History* (New York: Harcourt, Brace & World, 1961), 167.

7. Ibid., 169.

8. Quoted in Gavan Daws, *Shoal of Time: A History of the Hawaiian Islands* (Honolulu: University of Hawai'i Press, 1968), 296–97.

9. Ida Kanekoa Milles's story comes from "Getting Somewheres," in *Hanahana: An Oral History Anthology of Hawaii's Working People,* edited by Michi Kodama-Nishimoto, Warren S. Nishimoto, and Cynthia A. Oshiro (Honolulu: Ethnic Studies Oral History Project, University of Hawai'i, 1984), 3–15.

10. Quoted in Davianna Pōmaika'i McGregor, *Nā Kua'āna: Living Hawaiian Culture* (Honolulu: University of Hawai'i Press, 2007), 60–61.

11. Quoted in Clarence E. Glick, *Sojourners and Settlers: Chinese Migrants in Hawaii* (Honolulu: Hawaii Chinese History Center, 1980), 139, 140.

12. Cited in Tin-Yuke Char, ed., *The Sandalwood Mountains: Readings and Stories of the Early Chinese in Hawaii* (Honolulu: University of Hawai'i Press, 1975), 101–2.

13. Quoted in Glick, *Sojourners and Settlers,* 175.

14. Ibid., 222.

15. Ibid., 275.

16. Okihiro, *Cane Fires,* 46.

17. Ibid., 50.

18. Ibid., 50.

19. Ibid., 53.

20. Ibid., 56.

21. Ibid., 39, 186.

22. Ibid., 68.

23. Ibid., 78, 79.

24. From Masayo Umezawa Duus, *The Japanese Conspiracy: The Oahu Sugar Strike of 1920,* trans. Beth Cary (Berkeley: University of California Press, 1999), 94.

25. Okihiro, *Cane Fires,* 72.

26. Ibid., 76.

27. Ibid., 132.

28. Ibid., 144.

29. Ibid., 160.

30. Ibid., 135.

31. Quoted in Franklin Odo, ed., *The Columbia Documentary History of the Asian American Experience* (New York: Columbia University Press, 2002), 204–7.

32. Okihiro, *Cane Fires*, 154–55.

33. Ibid., 161–62.

34. As told in Wayne Patterson, *The Ilse: First-Generation Korean Immigrants in Hawai'i, 1903–1973* (Honolulu: University of Hawai'i Press, 2000), 58.

35. Ibid., 76.

36. Peter Hyun, *Man Sei! The Making of a Korean American* (Honolulu: University of Hawai'i Press, 1986), 1.

37. Margaret K. Pai, *The Dreams of Two Yi-min* (Honolulu: University of Hawai'i Press, 1989), 2.

38. Ibid., 36–37.

39. Nam-Young Chung, "Always a Patriot," in *Passages to Paradise: Early Korean Immigrant Narratives from Hawai'i*, ed. Daisy Chun Rhodes (Los Angeles: Academia Koreana, 1998), 36.

40. Sue Kim Shin, "Mother Love," in Rhodes, *Passages to Paradise*, 239–42.

41. Quoted in John E. Reinecke, *The Filipino Piecemeal Sugar Strike of 1924–25* (Honolulu: Social Science Research Institute, University of Hawai'i, 1996), 49.

42. Ibid., 76.

43. Ibid., 81–82.

44. Quoted in Edward D. Beechert, *Working in Hawaii: A Labor History* (Honolulu: University of Hawai'i Press, 1985), 260.

45. Fuchs, *Hawaii Pono*, 153.

46. Ibid., 152.

9. SAN FRANCISCO

1. Thomas W. Chinn, ed., *A History of the Chinese in California: A Syllabus* (San Francisco: Chinese Historical Society of America, 1969), 9.

2. Ira M. Condit, *The Chinaman As We See Him* (Chicago: Fleming H. Revell, 1900), 86.

3. Cited in Erika Lee and Judy Yung, *Angel Island: Immigrant Gateway to America* (New York: Oxford University Press, 2010), 10–11.

4. Victor G. Nee and Brett de Bary Nee, *Longtime Californ': A Documentary Study of an American Chinatown* (Boston: Houghton Mifflin, 1972), 63.

5. Quoted in Lee and Yung, *Angel Island*, 86–87.

6. Poems from Him Mark Lai, Genny Lim, and Judy Yung, *Island: Poetry and History of Chinese Immigrants on Angel Island, 1910–1940* (Seattle: University of Washington Press, 1991), 52–53, 58–59, 68–69.

7. Quoted in Yong Chen, *Chinese San Francisco, 1850–1943: A Trans-Pacific Community* (Stanford, CA: Stanford University Press, 2000), 153.

8. Ibid., 155.

9. Quoted in Victor Low, *The Unimpressible Race: A Century of Educational Struggle by the Chinese in San Francisco* (San Francisco: East/West Publishing, 1982), 62.

10. Ibid., 67.

11. Ibid., 199.

12. Quoted in Judy Yung, *Unbound Voices: A Documentary History of Chinese Women in San Francisco* (Berkeley: University of California Press, 1999), 395.

13. Chen, *Chinese San Francisco*, 198.

14. Quoted in Yuji Ichioka, *The Issei: The World of the First Generation Japanese Immigrants, 1885–1924* (New York: Free Press, 1988, 159.

15. Ibid., 104.

16. Ibid., 106.

17. Eileen Sunada Sarasohn, ed., *The Issei: Portrait of a Pioneer; An Oral History* (Palo Alto, CA: Pacific Books, 1983), 59–60.

18. Ibid., 100.

19. This account, "A Young American with a Japanese Face," appears in Louis Adamic, *From Many Lands* (New York: Harper & Brothers, 1939), 183–234.

20. Ibid., 194.

21. Ibid., 199.

22. Ibid., 203.

23. Ibid., 208.

24. Ibid., 213, 214.

25. Quoted in Gary Y. Okihiro and David Drummond, "The Concentration Camps and Japanese Economic Losses in California Agriculture, 1900–1942," in *Japanese Americans: From Relocation to Redress*, edited by Roger Daniels Harry H. L. Kitano, and Sandra C. Taylor (Salt Lake City: University of Utah Press, 1986),168.

26. As quoted in Jacobus tenBroek, Edward N. Barnhart, and Floyd W. Matson, *Prejudice, War and the Constitution: Causes and Consequences of the Evacuation of the Japanese Americans in World War II* (Berkeley: University of California Press, 1970), 46.

27. Cited in Timothy J. Lukes and Gary Y. Okihiro, *Japanese Legacy: Farming and Community Life in California's Santa Clara Valley* (Cupertino: California History Center, 1985), 58.

28. Ibid., 60.

29. Dora Yum Kim's account is from Soo-Young Chin, *Doing What Had to Be Done: The Life Narrative of Dora Yum Kim* (Philadelphia: Temple University Press, 1999).

30. Ibid., 17, 18.

31. Ibid., 51.

32. Ibid., 54.

33. Quoted in Ian Haney López, *White by Law: The Legal Construction of Race* (New York: New York University Press, 2006), 179–82.

34. Cited in Peggy Pascoe, *What Comes Naturally: Miscegenation Law and the Making of Race in America* (New York: Oxford University Press, 2009), 153.

35. Ibid., 158.

36. Ibid., 218.

10. SEATTLE, NEW YORK CITY, CHICAGO

1. Robert E. Park, "Racial Assimilation in Secondary Groups with Particular Reference to the Negro," *American Journal of Sociology* 19, no. 9 (1914): 610–11.

2. Jean Pfaelzer, *Driven Out: The Forgotten War against Chinese Americans* (Berkeley: University of California Press, 2007), 220.

3. Ibid., 222.

4. Kazuo Ito, *Issei: A History of Japanese Immigrants in North America*, trans. Shinichiro Nakamura and Jean S. Gerard (Seattle: Japanese Community Service, 1973), 96–97.

5. Ibid., 187.

6. Thomas H. Heuterman, *The Burning Horse: Japanese-American Experience in the Yakima Valley, 1920–1942* (Cheney: Eastern Washington University Press, 1995), 59.

7. Dorothy B. Fujita-Rony, *American Workers, Colonial Power: Philippine Seattle and the Transpacific West, 1919–1941* (Berkeley: University of California Press, 2003), 65.

8. Ibid., 146.

9. Quoted in Renqiu Yu, *To Save China, to Save Ourselves: The Chinese Hand Laundry Alliance of New York* (Philadelphia: Temple University Press, 1992), 10.

10. Lee, Chew, "The Life Story of a Chinaman," in *The Life Stories of Undistinguished Americans As Told by Themselves,* edited by Hamilton Holt (New York: James Pott, 1906), 292.

11. Ibid., 296.

12. Yu, *To Save China,* 35.1

13. Anonymous, "The Life of a Japanese Servant," in Holt, *Life Stories,* 259, 261, 269, 277, 280.

14. Quoted in Mitziko Sawada, *Tokyo Life, New York Dreams: Urban Japanese Visions of America, 1890–1924* (Berkeley: University of California Press, 1996), 27.

15. Haru Kishi's account is in ibid., 34–36.

16. Quoted in Vivek Bald, *Bengali Harlem and the Lost Histories of South Asian America* (Cambridge, MA: Harvard University Press, 2013), 104.

17. Ibid., 100.

18. Carl Becker, "Kansas," in *Essays in American History Dedicated to Frederick Jackson Turner* (New York: Peter Smith, 1951), 88, 107, 110.

19. As quoted in Paul C. P. Siu, *The Chinese Laundryman: A Study of Social Isolation,* ed. John Kuo Wei Tchen (New York: New York University Press, 1987), 17.

20. Quotes from Barbara M. Posadas, "The Hierarchy of Color and Psychological Adjustment in an Industrial Environment: Filipinos, the Pullman Company, and the Brotherhood of Sleeping Car Porters," *Labor History* 23, no. 3 (Summer 1982): 366, 368.

21. Ibid., 151.

22. Quoted in Paul G. Cressey, *The Taxi-Dance Hall: A Sociological Study in Commercialized Recreation and City Life* (Chicago: University of Chicago Press, 1932), 171–72.

23. Quoted in Evelyn Nakano Glenn, *Issei, Nisei, War Bride: Three Generations of Japanese American Women in Domestic Service* (Philadelphia: Temple University Press, 1986), 122.

11. WORLD WAR II

1. Quoted in Gerald Horne, *Race War: White Supremacy and the Japanese Attack on the British Empire* (New York: New York University Press, 2004), 77, 78.

2. Mahatir Mohamad, *A New Deal for Asia* (Tokyo: Tachibana Publishing, 1999), 15–17, 68.

3. Jawaharlal Nehru, *The Discovery of India* (London: Meridian Books, 1956), 443, 448.

4. Ibid., 488–89, 492, 495–96, 498–502, 584.

5. *Chicago Defender,* March 3, 1945.

6. Franklin D. Roosevelt, "Message to Congress," January 6, 1941.

7. Letter from Charles F. Wilson to Franklin D. Roosevelt, Tucson, Arizona, May 9, 1944, in Phillip McGuire, *Taps for a Jim Crow Army: Letters from Black Soldiers in World War II* (Santa Barbara, CA: ABC-Clio, 1983), 134–39.

8. Gary Y. Okihiro, *Cane Fires: The Anti-Japanese Movement in Hawaii, 1865–1945* (Philadelphia: Temple University Press, 1991), 173–74.

9. Ibid., 128.

10. Ibid., 174.

11. Ibid., 175.

12. Ibid., 183.

13. Ibid., 211–12.

14. Quoted and cited in John Armor and Peter Wright, *Manzanar* (New York: Times Books, 1988), 38, 43–44.

15. Okihiro, *Cane Fires,* 212–13.

16. Yoshiaki Fukuda, *My Six Years of Internment: An Issei's Struggle for Justice* (San Francisco: Konko Church of San Francisco, 1990), 7–8.

17. Tetsuden Kashima, "American Mistreatment of Internees during World War II: Enemy Alien Japanese," in *Japanese Americans: From Relocation to Redress,* ed. Roger Daniels, Sandra C. Taylor, and Harry H. L. Kitano (Seattle: University of Washington Press, 1991), 54.

18. Take Uchida, "An Issei Internee's Experiences," in Daniels, Taylor, and Kitano, *Japanese Americans,* 31.

19. Daisuke Kitagawa, *Issei and Nisei: The Internment Years* (New York: Seabury Press, 1967), 41.

20. Okihiro, *Cane Fires,* 217.

21. *Personal Justice Denied,* Report of the Commission on Wartime Relocation and Internment of Civilians (Washington, DC: Government Printing Office, 1982), 318–19.

22. Okihiro, *Cane Fires,* 228.

23. Roger Daniels, *Concentration Camps: North America, Japanese in the United States and Canada During World War II* (Malabar, FL: Robert E. Krieger, 1981), 65.

24. Linda Tamura, *The Hood River Issei: An Oral History of Japanese Settlers in Oregon's Hood River Valley* (Urbana: University of Illinois Press, 1993), 167–68.

25. John Tateishi, *And Justice for All: An Oral History of the Japanese American Detention Camps* (New York: Random House, 1984), 230–31.

26. Frank Seishi Emi, "Draft Resistance at the Heart Mountain Concentration Camp and the Fair Play Committee," in *Frontiers of Asian American Studies: Writing, Research, and Commentary,* ed. Gail M. Nomura, Russell Endo, Stephen H. Sumida, and Russell C. Leong (Pullman: Washington State University Press, 1989), 43–44.

27. Quoted in Eric L. Muller, *Free to Die for Their Country: The Story of the Japanese American Draft Resisters in World War II* (Chicago: University of Chicago Press, 2001), 112.

28. Chester Tanaka, *Go for Broke: A Pictorial History of the Japanese American 100th Infantry Battalion and the 442nd Regimental Combat Team* (Richmond, CA: Go for Broke, 1982), 14.

29. Tateishi, *And Justice for All*, 161.

30. Tanaka, *Go for Broke*, 167, 170–71.

31. Audrie Girdner and Anne Loftis, *Great Betrayal: The Evacuation of the Japanese-Americans during World War II* (London: Macmillan, 1969), 441–49.

32. Frank F. Chuman, *The Bamboo People: The Law and Japanese-Americans* (Del Mar, CA: Publishers, 1976), 327–29.

33. Edison Uno, "Therapeutic and Educational Benefits (a Commentary)," *Amerasia Journal* 2, no. 2 (Fall 1974): 111.

34. Cited in Judy Yung, *Unbound Feet: A Documentary History of Chinese Women in San Francisco* (Berkeley: University of California Press, 1999), 416.

35. Quoted in K. Scott Wong, *Americans First: Chinese Americans and the Second World War* (Cambridge, MA: Harvard University Press, 2005), 50–51.

36. Quoted in Judy Yung, *Unbound Feet: A Social History of Chinese Women in San Francisco* (Berkeley: University of California Press, 1995), 269.

37. Ibid., 252–53.

38. Wong, *Americans First*, 105.

39. Carina A. del Rosario, ed., *A Different Battle: Stories of Asian Pacific American Veterans* (Seattle: Wing Luke Asian Museum, 1999), 44.

40. Ibid., 63.

41. Quoted in Fred Cordova, *Filipinos: Forgotten Asian Americans* (Dubuque, IA: Kendall/Hunt, 1983), 220.

42. Ibid., 223.

12. MILITARIZED ZONES

1. Cited in Roland Kotani, *The Japanese in Hawaii: A Century of Struggle* (Honolulu: Hawaii Hochi, 1985), 68.

2. Ibid., 70–71.

3. Beth Bailey and David Farber, *The First Strange Place: The Alchemy of Race and Sex in World War II Hawaii* (New York: Free Press, 1992), 55.

4. Ibid., 104.

5. Jon Kamakawiwoʻole Osorio, "Memorializing Puʻuloa and Remembering Pearl Harbor," in *Militarized Currents: Toward a Decolonized Future in Asia and the Pacific*, ed. Setsu Shigematsu and Keith L. Camacho (Minneapolis: University of Minnesota Press, 2010), 5.

6. Cited in Stanley Karnow, *In Our Image: America's Empire in the Philippines* (New York: Ballantine Books, 1980), 323–24.

7. Ibid., 324.

8. Quoted in Bong-youn Choy, *Koreans in America* (Chicago: Nelson-Hall, 1979), 187.

9. Katsunori Yamazato, "The Birth of a University: The Background and Some Problems Concerning the Establishment of the University of the Ryukyus," *Okinawan Journal of American Studies* 1 (2004): 10.

10. As quoted in Wesley Iwao Ueunten, "Rising Up from a Sea of Discontent: The 1970 Koza Uprising in U.S.-Occupied Okinawa," in Shigematsu and Camacho, *Militarized Currents*, 115.

11. Ibid., 116–17.

12. Published in Carina A. del Rosario, *A Different Battle: Stories of Asian Pacific American Veterans* (Seattle: Wing Luke Asian Museum, 1999), 42–43.

13. Ibid., 40–41.

13. GLOBAL TRANSITS

1. Joanna C. Scott, *Indochina's Refugees: Oral Histories from Laos, Cambodia and Vietnam* (Jefferson, NC: McFarland, 1989), 97–105.

2. Ibid., 121–27.

3. Ibid., 161–72.

4. Sucheng Chan, ed., *Hmong Means Free: Life in Laos and America* (Philadelphia: Temple University Press, 1994), 161–72.

5. Ibid., 173–89.

6. Ibid., 190–205.

7. Ibid., 277–82.

8. As told in Robert S. McKelvey, *The Dust of Life: America's Children Abandoned in Vietnam* (Seattle: University of Washington Press, 199), 21–23.

9. Steven DeBonis, *Children of the Enemy: Oral Histories of Vietnamese Amerasians and Their Mothers* (Jefferson, NC: McFarland, 1995), 56–65.

10. Madhulika S. Khandelwal, *Becoming American, Being Indian: An Immigrant Community in New York City* (Ithaca, NY: Cornell University Press, 2002), 112.

14. REGENERATIONS

1. Quoted in Karen Umemoto, "'On Strike!' San Francisco State College Strike, 1968–69: The Role of Asian American Students," *Amerasia Journal* 15, no. 1 (1989): 20. On Third World women, see the journal *Asian Women* (1971).

2. Carter Goodwin Woodson, *The Mis-education of the Negro* (Washington, DC: Associated Publishers, 1933), 192.

3. As translated in Lawrence H. Fuchs, *Hawaii Pono: A Social History* (New York: Harcourt, Brace & World, 1961), 447.

4. Tom Coffman, *The Island Edge of America: A Political History of Hawai'i* (Honolulu: University of Hawai'i Press, 2003), 304.

5. Rodney Morales, ed., *Ho'i Ho'i Hou: A Tribute to George Helm and Kimo Mitchell* (Honolulu: Bamboo Ridge, 1984), 32.

6. Quoted in Ben Finney, *Sailing in the Wake of the Ancestors: Reviving Polynesian Voyaging* (Honolulu: Bishop Museum Press, 2003), 14.

7. Ibid., 15.

8. John Dominis Holt, *On Being Hawaiian* (Honolulu: Star-Bulletin, 1964), 7, 11.

9. Quoted in Margaret M. Lam, "Racial Myth and Family Tradition-Worship among the Part-Hawaiians," *Social Forces* 14, no. 3 (March 1936): 405–6.

10. *He Alo Ā He Alo: Face to Face, Hawaiian Voices on Sovereignty* (Honolulu: American Friends Service Committee—Hawai'i, 1993), 99.

11. Carina A. del Rosario, ed., *A Different Battle: Stories of Asian Pacific American Veterans* (Seattle: Wing Luke Asian Museum, 1999), 115.

12. Jean-Paul Sartre, preface to *The Wretched of the Earth,* by Frantz Fanon, trans. Constance Farrington (New York: Grove Weidenfeld, 1963), 7.

13. Fanon, *Wretched of the Earth,* 233, 246.

14. Frank Chin, Jeffery Paul Chan, Lawson Fusao Inada, and Shawn Hsu Wong, eds., *Aiiieeeee! An Anthology of Asian-American Writers* (Garden City, NY: Anchor Books, 1975), ix–x.

15. Third World Communications, *Time To Greez! Incantations from the Third World* (San Francisco: Glide Publications, 1975), v.

16. U.S. Commission on Civil Rights, *Recent Activities against Citizens and Residents of Asian Descent,* Clearinghouse Publication No. 88 (Washington, DC: U.S. Government Printing Office, 1986), 46.

17. Quoted in Helen Zia, *Asian American Dreams: The Emergence of an American People* (New York: Farrar, Straus and Giroux, 2000), 60–61, 65.

18. Edward T. Chang and Jeannette Diaz-Veizades, *Ethnic Peace in the American City: Building Community in Los Angeles and Beyond* (New York: New York University Press, 1999), 33.

19. Wen Ho Lee, *My Country versus Me* (New York: Hyperion, 2001), 2, 6.

20. *The National Security Strategy of the United States of America,* September 2002, iv–vi, 5, 6, 9–11, 31, available online at www.state.gov/documents/organization/63562.

21. Quoted in *Pacific Citizen,* January 17–February 6, 2003.

22. Irum Shiekh, *Detained without Cause: Muslims' Stories of Detention and Deportation in America After 9/11* (New York: Palgrave Macmillan, 2011), 95, 96–97.

23. Thomas Edsall, "Attacks Alter Politics, Shift Focus on Immigration Debate," *Washington Post,* October 15, 2001.

24. James Yee, *For God and Country: Faith and Patriotism under Fire* (New York: Public Affairs, 2005), passim.

25. *Asian American Political Alliance Newspaper* 1, no. 5 (Summer 1969).

INDEX

Page references followed by *fig* indicate an illustration or photograph; followed by *m* indicates a map.

of, 63–70; European expeditions and
imperial order discourse in early, 46–49;
examining the shaping of national
consciousness of citizens, 3; as a global
history, 386–403; offering a counter to the
traditional national, 3; oppression and
resistance as shaping the course of, 219;
theory as central to understanding, 10. *See
also* Asian American history; history;
United States
American India Company, 71
American Indians. *See* Native Americans
Americanization, 219. *See also* assimilation
American Missionary Association, 222
American Progress (Gast), 92*fig*
American Protective Association, 91
American Revolutionary War (1775–83), 4,
68–70
ancient Greece: Greek traders establishing
colonies along African coast, 42; myths
about the exotic Orient in, 29; Orientalism
beliefs during the, 17; racial taxonomies of,
13–15. *See also* Roman Empire
Angel Island (San Francisco Bay): Japanese
Americans removal (1941) to, 344;
Japanese women arriving at (1910), 277*fig*;
made into an immigration center, 269–71;
photograph (1917) of migrants in, 271*fig*
Anthony, Susan B., 88
anti-Asianism: against migrant laborers in
California, 124, 156, 158, 167, 170, 173, 176;
against migrant labor in the Northwest,
189, 191; Canada, 172, 173, 190, 192–93;
hi-imin (Japanese educated class) facing,
315; San Francisco as hub of, 276–77;
Seattle's Anti-Chinese League, 297–98. *See
also* racism; sexual violence/rape
anti-Asian violence: against Asians in Seattle's
Chinatown, 303–4; against Japanese
migrants in Northwest region, 300–302;
against New York City Chinese laundries,
307; Chinese expulsion from Tacoma
(1880s), 298–99; continued episodes of
anti-Asian, 420–26; September 11th attacks
and increase of, 429–31; Tacoma Chinese
expulsion (1880s), 298–99. *See also* race
riots; sexual violence/rape
Anti-Chinese League (Seattle), 297–98

Anti-imperialist Alliance, 310
Antonio (Virginia Colony enslaved African),
66–67
Aptheker, Herbert, 12
Aristotle, 14
Arkansas River Valley Immigration Company,
201–2
Armstrong, Richard, 222
Armstrong, Samuel, 222
Army Nurse Corps, 354
Arriola, Joseph, 179
Arthur, John, 299
Asia: Christian missionaries in, 118–19;
European search for routes to, 44–46;
European trade with, 17, 69; Islam in, 27,
27*fig*, 28; nineteenth-century turmoil,
118–20; as object of imperialism, 42, 44;
Orientalism and historic conflict between
Europe and, 16–18; transformation by
Islamic converts, 27; U.S. trade with,
70–72, 75, 101, 196, 198
Asian-African Conference (1955), 440–41
Asian American history: phases of, 9; standard
narrative of, 2, 8–10; terminology of, 8, 13.
s*See also* American history
Asian American movements (1960s): to create a
pan-Asian subjectivity of racial formation,
415–17; model minority stereotype,
426–29; national culture, 418–20; origins
of the, 415; racial formation and, 415–17;
third world women, 417–18
Asian American Political Alliance (AAPA), 416,
438, 439
Asian Americans: as "aliens ineligible to citizenship" until twentieth century, 7; Civil War
role of, 87–89, 90*fig*, 158, 201, 204, 316;
colonial America, 49–54, 88; Coney Island
Oriental curiosities (nineteenth century)
in, 308; domestic service occupation by,
323–24, 397; as elastic terminology, 8;
examining the historiography of, 2;
globalization and changing U.S. demography of, 399–401; increasing citizenship
rights following Civil War, 88; meaning
and fictive terminology of, 416; model
minority stereotype of, 426–29; naturalization rights granted in mid-twentieth
century to, 7–8, 73; primary document on

Chamorros *(continued)*
    migrant laborers in the Northeast, 197; social
    formations of the, 34; Spanish imperialism
    against, 37; World War II Japanese military
    and rape of, 372. *See also* Guam
Chandra, Ram, 176
Chang and Eng ("Siamese twins"), 308
Chang, Henry, 365–66
Cha'ng-ho Ahn's Chin'mok-hoe, 282, 283
Ch'en, I-hsi, 159
Cherokee Nation v. Georgia, 95
Cherokees' Trail of Tears, 344
Chiang Kai-shek, 309, 367
Chiang Kai-shek, Madame, 354–55
Chicago: "Chicago plan" for supervision
    taxi-dance halls, 323; Chinatown in,
    320–21*fig*; Chinese laundries in, 320–21;
    Chinese population living in, 319–21;
    discourse and material condition creating
    growth of, 319; Filipino Postal Club of
    Chicago of, 322; Filipinos population living
    in, 321–23; population growth (1860 to
    1900) in, 266; race riot (July 1919) and
    aftermath of, 295–96; taxi-dance halls in,
    323, 325–26
"Chicago plan" (taxi-dance halls supervision),
    323
Chicago school of sociology, 295–96
children: Cleveland Elementary School shooting
    (Stockton, 1989) of Asian, 423; fathered by
    occupying troops, 393–95; of indentured
    laborers and slaves, 64, 67; Operation
    Babylift (1975) relocating, 394; transna-
    tional adoptions of, 372
China: beating of Jinyong Tan, a diplomat from,
    272; Chinese American boycott and
    protests of Japan's 1915 Twenty-One
    Demands of, 275; First Opium War
    (1839–1842), 52, 118, 120, 154, 199;
    Guomindang (KMT) government
    overthrown by Mao Zedong's communist
    forces (1949), 367–68; Japanese invasion
    (1937) of, 311; Ming Dynasty Zhenghe
    expeditions, 29–30; nationalism movement
    in, 237–38, 272–73; nineteenth-century
    turmoil, 118, 154; opium trade, 199; as
    prime source for migrant labor (nineteenth
    century), 52–53; Six Companies represent-

ing Manchu government in the U.S., 272,
    276; Society for Aid to the Korean
    Volunteer Corps in, 358; U.S. confrontation
    over Wen Ho Lee (1999–2000) with,
    428–29; U.S. trade with, 71, 75, 101, 102,
    188; World War II Japanese atrocities
    against, 335; Zhenghe expeditions, 29–30.
    See also Taiwan
Chinatown (Boston), 272
Chinatown (Chicago), 320–21*fig*
Chinatown (Hawai'i), 234–35, 366–67
Chinatown (New York City), 307–12, 315
Chinatown (San Francisco), 267, 273–75, 284,
    354
Chinatown (Seattle), 303–4
Chin civil rights trial (1987), 421–22
Chinese Alien Wives of American Citizens Act
    (1946), 355
Chinese American Bank, 232
Chinese Americans: boycott and protests of
    Japan's 1915 Twenty-One Demands of
    China by, 275; Civil War role of, 89;
    colonial period, 49, 50; early nineteenth
    century history of, 9, 85; *gongsi fang*
    (Chinese mutual-aid societies) [New York
    City] of, 309; Hawaiian dependency and,
    229–38; Hawaiian rice plantations
    established by, 229–33; historic exception-
    alism of, 9–10; history of citizenship rights
    of, 8, 73, 157, 202, 206–7; immigration
    exclusion of, 7, 91; interracial marriages in
    Chicago (1900–40), 321; Irish Americans
    and, 84–85; living in Chicago, 319–21;
    living in New York, 306–12; living in San
    Francisco, 266–75; living in Seattle,
    297–300; Madame Chiang Kai-shek's
    American tour and boosting the morale of,
    354–55; population in Hawai'i (1990–
    1940), 231*t*; population in New York City
    and New Jersey (1880), 307; population in
    New York City and New Jersey (1900–
    1940), 308; population in the Northwest
    (1880s), 299; repeal of Chinese exclusion
    laws (1943) allowing petitions for
    citizenship by, 355; serving in the World
    War II military, 354; the "shed" in San
    Francisco where migrants were held,
    268–69; in standard Asian American

histories, 9; Tacoma Chinese expulsion (1880s) of, 298–99; woman and child (1914–15), 233*fig*; World War II and jobs taken by, 353–54

Chinese Consolidated Benevolent Association (CCBA), 309–10, 311, 312

Chinese Exclusion Act (1882), 7, 91, 123, 124, 131–32, 133, 150, 162, 200, 299

Chinese Hand Laundry Alliance (CHLA), 310, 316

Chinese Immigration (Coolidge), 9

Chinese laundries (Chicago), 320–21

Chinese laundries (New Jersey), 306–7

Chinese laundries (New York City), 307, 310–12

Chinese laundries (San Francisco), 271–72

Chinese migrant labor: in California, 151, 151*fig*, 152, 154–62, 156*fig*; early history of, 50, 52–54; exclusion laws impacting, 150; in Hawai'i, 120–25, 121*fig*, 123*fig*, 124*fig*, 229–38; imported to work in Passaic Steam Laundry (New Jersey), 306–7; kidnapping as common means of obtaining indentured, 122; in Mexico (seventeenth century), 49; newly arrived coolies in Trinidad (1897), 52*fig*; in the Northeast, 199, 204–5; in the Northwest, 190*fig*; Polly Bemis photograph of laborer, 190*fig*; Radical Reconstruction (1867) and recruitment of, 201–3; slavery of, 204; in the South, 200, 201–3; violence against workers (1885) in the Northeast region, 297–98

Chinese Museum (1850) [New York City], 308

Chinese Sunday School (New York City), 315

Chinese Unemployed Council–Greater New York, 310

Chinese Vanguard (newspaper), 310

Chinese Women's Patriotic Association (1930s and 1940s), 312

Chin'mok-hoe (Friendship Society), 170

Chinn, Ron, 378

Chin, Vincent, 421–22

Cho, Eun-Ai, 138

Choi, Yong-man, 282–83

Chou Nou Tcha, 392

Choy, Rudy, 412

Christianity: citizenship rights linked to whiteness and, 68; colonialism as opening lands for capitalism, labor exploitation, and, 115; Philippine-American War (1899–1902) framed as war between Islam and, 99. *See also* Catholic Church; religion

Christian missionaries: in Asian countries, 118–19; in Hawai'i, 102, 103, 196, 248–49; Hawaiian migrant labor in the Northeast and, 193, 194–96; Hawai'i dependency role of, 221, 223; Hawai'i Methodist Mission, 248–49; Korean migrant workers in Hawai'i taught by, 133–35; in Korea sent by the Catholic Church, 118–19; Northwest region, 185, 189

Christian mission schools: designed to create dependency, 221–23; Foreign Mission School (Connecticut), 221; Hampton Normal and Agricultural Institute (Virginia), 222; Hilo Boarding School, 222; Iolani (Hawai'i), 237

Chuman, Frank, 348–49

Chung Wah Wui Goon (Chinese Union, later United Chinese Society), 237

Churchill, Winston, 334, 336

"citizen race" concept: description and implications of, 3, 4–5, 72; Fifteenth Amendment (1870) as revolutionary break with, 5

citizens: "citizen race" concept of, 3, 4–5, 72; danger of concerning common race, religion, and culture as defining identity of, 3; examining the shaping of national consciousness of, 3; Virginia Colony law equating *Christian* to *white*, 68

Citizens Committee to Repeal Chinese Exclusion (1943), 355

citizenship: African Americans and, 5, 72–73, 88, 108, 202; case of Anthony Johnson, freed slave in Virginia Colony denial of, 4–5, 66–67; Chinese Americans and, 8, 73, 157, 202, 206–7; "citizen race" concept of, 3, 4–5, 72; colonial America, 68; dependency and, 211–12; early Republic, 5, 72–73, 79–81; Filipino Americans, 2, 95; Hawaiian Americans, 189–90; Hawai'i dependency and issue of, 223; Korean Americans, 8, 136; Mexican Americans, 5, 7; national histories of peoples of color and, 6–8; Native Americans, 72–73, 84, 95, 108;

4–5, 66–68; English settlement of, 63–64; extractive system during, 63–64, 68; indentured labor during, 50, 51*fig*, 52; Native Americans, 3, 64–66; primary documents on, 76–81; slave trade during, 50, 64; social formations of, 66–68; suggested readings on, 76; timeline of significant events, 81–82; white nation and, 3, 4–5; working-class resistance in, 67–68. *See also* New Spain; United States (early Republic)

colonialism: education designed to create dependency during, 221–23; European empires as built on, 333–34; finding the Americas and start of European, 46–48; imperial order discourse driving trade and expansion of, 48–49; Korean American impacted by Japanese, 250–53; opening lands for capitalism, Christianity, and labor exploitation, 115; post-World War II decolonization movements to dismantle, 6, 336; world-systems theory as shaping, 11–12, 43, 46–49, 54, 115, 207. *See also* British colonialism; decolonization movements; imperialism; Spanish colonialism

color line: the Pearl Harbor attack (1941) framed as victory for the, 334–35, 340, 341, 344–45, 353; as the "problem of the twentieth century," 219. *See also* race; skin color

Columbia (ship), 75, 188, 193, 305

Columbus, Christopher, 18, 46, 47, 54–60

Combahee River Collective (1977), 417

"comfort women" (World War II), 335

commerce. *See* trade

Committee against Anti-Asian violence (CAAAV), 424

communism: Communist Party, U.S.A. (CP-USA) [1930s] in Hawai'i, 406–7; House Un-American Activities Committee (HUAC) investigation of sympathizers of, 352, 368, 406–7; Mao Zedong's government in China, 367–68; Vietnam War framed as fight against, 376–81. *See also* Cold War

Communist Party, U.S.A. (CP-USA) [1930s], 406–7

Compromise of 1850, 86

"Concerning the Dangers from Foreign Force and Influence" (Jay), 3

Condit, Ira, 268–69

Coney Island Oriental curiosities (nineteenth century), 308

Conference of New Americans (Hawai'i), 245–46

Congress of Industrial Organization (CIO), 257

continent myth, 20, 25

Convention of 1886, 127

Cook, James, 37, 74, 101

Coolidge, Mary Roberts, 9

coolies. *See* Chinese migrant labor

Coon, Ah, 206

Corrections Corporation of America, 434

Cortés, Hernán, 62

cotton agriculture, 85

Council on American Islamic Relations, 436

Coxe, John (Naukane), 186

CP-USA (U.S. communist Party), 310

Crawford, David, 221

Crenshaw, Kimberlé, 417

Crispin labor strike (1870), 204–5

Crispins, 204–5

crops. *See* agriculture

Crusades, 17

Cruz, John, 323

Cuba, 94, 99

cultural nationalism: description of, 1; historiography of, 1–2; national histories of, 6–8; racial formation and, 415–16

Cummins, John, 54–60

da Gama, Vasco, 45

Dana, Richard Henry, Jr., 154

"dancing schools" (New York City, 1920s), 315

Dangaran, Alfonso Perales, 179

Darrow, Clarence, 365

Darwin, Charles, 25

Das, Taraknath, 174–75, 176, 318

Davies, Theophilus, 142

Davis, Sylvester, 290

Davis, William, 152

Dawes Act (1887), 4, 108, 301

Dayal, Har, 175, 176

Debs, Eugene V., 208

decolonization movements: as changing the course of four centuries of imperialism, 334; post-World War II African and Asian, 6, 336; South Asian American Ghadar movement supporting India's independence, 175, 176, 284–85, 318–19; World War II as fight for the, 333. *See also* colonialism; national liberation movements; self-determination

deep history, 18–19

Defense Of India Act (Great Britain), 336

del Rosario, Gene, 356

democracy: Roosevelt's "four freedoms" speech (1941) on, 338–39; world War II martial law suspending, 366

democracy "four freedoms" speech (Roosevelt, 1941), 338–39

Democratic Party (Hawai'i), 407–8

De Orbe Novo (Martir de Anghiera), 47

dependency: Asian American history phase of, 9, 211–12; assimilation relationship to, 12, 211; of Chamorros people, 372; education designed to create, 221–23, 405; as pedagogy of powerlessness, 221; segregation as tool for creating, 12, 323–24; social formation role of, 11; white supremacy for maintaining nonwhite, 300. *See also* assimilation; Hawaiian dependency; oppression; social formation

Deshler, David, 133, 134

Detroit anti-Asian violence (1982), 421–22*fig*

Dewey, George, 94, 95

DeWitt, John, 345–46

Dias, Bartolomeu, 45

Dillingham Commission, 209

Dimas Alang, 304

Dionisio, Juan, 143

discourses: of Asian decadence and European superiority, 23; case against Wen Ho Lee, 428–29; comparing European and Orientalism, 16–18; driving Chicago growth and development, 319; eugenics, 208–9, 212–14; imperial order, 46–49; material conditions advanced through, 10; and migrant labor, 208–10; model minority, 426–29; Oceania's decolonizing, 20; shared ideology and language enabling, 10; social formation through, 10–11, 11–12;

subjectivity as understanding of, 12–13; U.S. imperialism race relations, 210; World War II as "good war," 336–37

discrimination: changing demographics of Los Angeles housing segregation (1980s) and, 425–26; Fair Employment Practices Commission (1941) to investigate job, 337; *hi-imin* (Japanese educated class) and housing, 315; "Jim Crow" laws legalizing, 99, 266. *See also* racial segregation

disease: bubonic plague scare in Honolulu's Chinatown (1900), 235; English America and Indian nations decimated by, 65–66; Spanish conquest bringing, 47, 62, 63

dispossession: Hawaiian social movement to restore land, 410–11; Native American and Hawaiians' shared histories of conquest and, 414

Doi, Shig, 351

Dole, Sanford, 106, 130, 223–24

dong-hoe (Korean village council), 248

Doric (ship), 145

Dorming, John, 319–20

al-Dossari, Jumah, 436–37

Dotbusters (1987), 422–23

Douglas, James, 152

draft resisters (World War II), 349–50

Dred Scott v. Sandford (1857), 3, 4, 5, 72–73, 299

Du Bois, W. E. B., 209, 219, 333–34, 359

Dudley, Delia, 315

Dumlao, Flipe, 303

Dumont d'Urville, Jules, 30–31

Dunn, James, 71, 198

Dunyungan, Virgil, 305

Ebat, Becky, 142

education: *Brown v. Board of Education* (1954) ending racial segregation in, 5, 265, 324, 380; as crucial field of engagement in the civil rights movement, 405; designed to create dependency, 221–23, 405; Foreign Mission School, 193, 194–95, 199, 221; Hawaiian-language immersion schools, 415; Hawai'i's two-track school system creating racially segregated, 246; *Independent School District v. Salvatierra* (1930) upholding racial segregation in, 6; regeneration through, 405; *School Begins*

poster (1899), 100*fig*; Third World
  Liberation Front (TWLF) focus on, 405
Eisenhower, Dwight, 368
Elk v. Wilkins, 108
Elmaghraby, Ehab, 432
Emancipation Proclamation, 243
Empress of China (ship), 70–71, 193
Eng, Dorothy, 353
England. *See* Great Britain
The Enlightenment, 15, 18, 210
enslaved Africans. *See* slavery
equality: decolonization movements for, 6, 175,
  176, 284–85, 318–19, 333, 334, 336;
  education as a crucial field of engagement
  in, 405; social movements for justice and,
  331, 405–44; struggle for self-determination and, 223–29, 231, 333, 437–39
essentializing process of taxonomies, 13
eugenics discourse: origins and spread (late
  nineteenth century) of, 208–9; primary
  document on, 212–14
Europe: the Enlightenment era of, 15, 18, 210;
  expeditions seeking trade routes and
  finding America, 46–48; Orientalism and
  historic conflict between Asia and, 16–18;
  post-World War II Marshall Plan to rebuild,
  368; search for Asian trade routes by, 17,
  44–46, 69. *See also* imperialism
European superiority discourse, 23
exclusion laws. *See* immigration laws
Executive Order 9066 (authorizing Japanese
  removal), 343
extractive system, 43, 48–49, 63–64, 68

Fabie, Ramon, 48
Fagel, Antonio, 257
Fair Employment Practices Commission (1941)
  [U.S.], 337
Fair Play Committee (Heart Mountain
  concentration camp), 349–50
Fanon, Frantz, 418
F. A. Rozier & Company, 306
Fayerweather, Julia, 120
FBI (Federal Bureau of Investigation): case
  against Wen Ho Lee (1999–2000) made by
  the, 428–29; continuing investigation into
  Pearl Harbor attack by the, 344–45;
  reporting on the removal of Japanese

Americans (1941), 342. *See also* Bureau of
  Investigation (later the FBI)
Federal Women's Penitentiary (Texas), 342
Federation of Japanese Labor (Hawai'i), 244
Feng, Xiawei, 272
Ferdinand II (king of Aragon), 45
Ferrara, Teresa, 309
Fifteenth Amendment (1870), 5, 88, 206, 239
Filipino Americans: Cannery Workers' and
  Farm Laborers' Union (CWFLU) organized
  in Seattle by, 304–5; citizenship status of, 2,
  8, 95; Civil War and, 89; confronting
  racism and segregation by claiming their
  rights, 304–5; domestic service work by,
  397; Filipino Repatriation Act (1935) on
  removal from U.S. of, 6, 150, 181; First
  Filipino Infantry Regiment (1942) of, 356;
  globalization impact on, 396–97; Hawaiian
  dependency and, 253–59; Indipinos born of
  First Nations women and, 357; interracial
  marriages in Chicago (1900–40), 321;
  living in Chicago, 321–23; living in San
  Francisco, 288–91; living in Seattle, 302–5;
  Los Angeles zoot-suit riots (1943) attacks
  on, 337–38; nationalism of, 256–57, 304;
  naturalization (1946) process opened to,
  355; pan-Filipino subjectivity rooted in
  religion and nationalism of, 256–57;
  population in Hawai'i (1990–1940), 231*t*;
  Pullman Company employment of, 322–23;
  Roldan (1933) decision allowing marriage
  between races and, 288–90; sponsored
  pensionados enrolled in school, 303;
  taxi-dance halls patronized by, 323, 325–26;
  working as scouts during the Indian wars,
  99; World War II and, 356–57; Yakama
  Indian Agency refusal to lease land to, 302,
  305. *See also* Philippines
Filipino Farmers' Marketing Co-operation, 305
Filipino Federation of America, 256
Filipino Labor Union, 242, 254
Filipino migrant labor: in California, 177–81;
  exclusion laws impact on, 150–51; in
  Hawai'i, 139–44, 141*fig*, 143*fig*, 224, 242–43,
  396–97; recruitment of *sakadas* for, 396
Filipino Postal Club of Chicago, 322
Filipino Repatriation Act (1935), 6, 150, 181
Fillmore, Millard, 86

Finney, Ben, 412

First Opium War (1839–1842), 52, 118, 120, 154, 199. *See also* opium

First World War. *See* World War I

fishing industry (California), 160–61

Fong, Hoy Kun, 269–70

food crops. *See* agricultural production

foreign-adoption program (1955), 372

Foreign Mission School (Connecticut), 193, 194–95, 199, 221

Forrest, Nathan Bedford, 201

Fortescue, Grace, 365–66

Foucault, Michel, 12

442nd Regimental Combat Team (World War II), 350–51

"four freedoms" of democracy speech (Roosevelt, 1941), 338–39

Fourteenth Amendment (1868), 5, 7, 73, 88, 99, 108, 207, 269, 273, 281, 299

Fourth Crusade, 17

France colonization, in the Americas, 46

Frear, Walter, 132, 241

French Canadian migrant labor, 204, 207

Friends of Freedom for India conference (1920) [New York City], 318, 319

frontier, 91

frontier hypothesis, 25

Fujimoto, Eileen, 407

Fukuda, Yoshiaki, 342

fur trade, 75, 188, 199

Gaelic (ship), 134

Galton, Francis, 208

Gast, John, 92*fig*

Geary Act (1892), 324

gender: and citizenship rights, 73; and myth of continents, 26; and U.S. imperialism, 92–93. *See also* racial/gender power formations

Geneva Conference (1954), 377

Genghis Khan, 17

Genkai Maru (ship), 134

Gentleman's Agreement (1908) [Japan and U.S.], 132, 139, 167, 210, 275, 313

geographical determinism, 13, 14, 15

Germany: immigration from, 84; Nazi, 333–36

Geronimo (Apache chief), 97

Ghadar movement (South Asian Americans), 175, 176, 284–85, 318–19

Ghadr (Mutiny) [Ghadar Party newspaper], 318–19

Ghadr di Ganj (Echoes of Mutiny) [South Asian American newspaper], 319

Gho, "Jack," 297

Ghose, Sailendranath, 318

G.I. Bill of Rights (1944), 357

Gidra magazine (1970 cover), 419*fig*

Gillespie, Charles, 266, 267

ginseng, 70

Gleeson, John, 431–32

globalization: American history as a global history of, 386–87; changing Asian demography in the U.S. due to, 399–401; Flipinos workers and, 396–97; global workers and capitalism, 395–96; primary document on, 402–3; South Asian workers and, 397–99; suggested readings on, 401–2; war refugees entering the U.S., 387–95

Goa, 45

Gobaleza, Dominador, 356

gold: California Gold Rush, 86, 103–4, 153, 154, 156, 157, 265; Spanish conquest and expeditions for, 47, 55, 62–63

Gompers, Samuel, 166, 208, 257

Gong Lum v. Rice (1927), 324

gongsi fang (Chinese mutual-aid societies) [New York City], 309

gospel of wealth, 207–8

Goto, Katsu, 131, 131*fig*

Gramsci, Antonio, 8, 12

Grant, Madison, 209, 212–14

Great American Strike (2006), 434*fig*

Great Britain: Atlantic Charter (1941) defining Allied goals for postwar world, 336; Defense Of India Act used for suppression by, 336; immigration from, 84; Northwest region claimed by both the U.S. and, 185; Treaty of Paris (1783) granting U.S. independence from, 70; U.S. westward expansion and, 85–86; War of 1812 between U.S. and, 186–87, 193–94, 196. *See also* British colonialism

Great Depression: African Americans during the, 211; Chinese entrepreneurs in San Francisco during the, 274–75; Chinese women seeking employment during the, 308; exclusion laws during the, 6, 150;

sovereignty, 414–15; *Hawai'iloa* voyage driven by, 413–14; *Hōkūle'a* voyage driven by, 412–13*fig*; Kaho'olawe Island protest of the, 410–11*fig*; Kalama Valley protest (1970) of the, 248–49, 408–9; Merrie Monarch Festival (1964) revival of hula, 415; to restore sovereignty, 408–15. *See also* Hawaiian social movements

Hawaiian-native migrant laborers: in California, 152–54; in the Northeast, 193–98; in the Northwest, 185–90; sailors, 50, 51*fig*, 152. *See also* Hawai'i agriculture; Hawaiian migrant labor

Hawaiian Pineapple Company, 232

Hawaiians: ancestral genealogies of, 38–39; Civil War and, 88–89; colonial period, 50, 51*fig*; creation story of, 35, 39–41; *kapu* system or rules of conduct and elites among, 36; Organic Act (1900) granting citizenship to, 7, 223, 225; racial formation of, 416; serving on foreign ships (1845 to 1847), 50; serving under the Confederate flag during Civil War, 89; U.S. Census difference categories for Pacific Islanders and (2000, 2010), 416. *See also* Hawaiian migrant labor; indigenous peoples

Hawaiian social movements: Aboriginal Lands of Hawaiian Ancestry (ALOLHA), 410; Democratic Party role in, 407–8; issue of land as central to, 410–11; Kaho'olawe Nine protest, 410–11*fig*; protest to save Kalama Valley (1970), 408–9; to remedy labor exploitation, 406–7. *See also* Hawaiian movement

Hawaiian Sugar Planters' Association (HSPA), 224, 239, 240–45, 249, 255

Hawaii Laborers' Association, 244

Hawai'iloa voyage (1993), 413–14

Hawai'i Methodist Mission, 248–49

Hawai'i Republic, 106–8, 223–24

"Hawaii Seven," 407

Hawaii Shimpo (Japanese newspaper in Hawai'i), 239, 240

Hawaii Suisan Kaisha, 232

Hay, John, 94, 101

Haymarket affair (1886), 91

Heard, Augustine, 71–72

Heart Mountain concentration camp (World War II), 349

The Heathen Chinese and the Sunday School Teachers (1904 film), 307

hegemony, 12

Helm, George, 410, 411

Henry the Navigator (Prince of Portugal), 45

Hervey, James, 306

hierarchies: racial taxonomy, 15–16, 16*fig*; social formation role of, 10–11

Higher Wages Association (Hawai'i), 239

High Wages Movement (Hawai'i), 254

hi-imin (Japanese educated class): anti-Asian and housing discrimination against the, 315; Gentleman's Agreement (1908) limiting immigration to, 132, 139, 167, 210, 275, 313; Japan Society (1907) founded by the, 313–14. *See also* Japanese Americans

Hillebrand, William, 122

Hilo Boarding School (Hawai'i), 222

Him Mao, 389–91

Hinduism, 27

Hindustani Association of America, 175

Hindustani Welfare and Reform Society of America, 173

Hing Chung Wu (or Save China Society) [Hawai'i], 237

Hippocrates, 14–15

Hip Yee Tong, 161

Hirabayashi, Gordon, 347

Hiroshima bombing (1945), 367

Hiroshima Kaigai Tokō Company, 163–64

historical formation, 13

historiographies: as chronicle of the formation of the white nation, 1, 2–6; and cultural nationalism, 1–2, 6–8; defined as "history as written," 1; standard histories of Asians and Pacific Islanders, 2

history: distinction between identity and subjectivity in, 12–13; as the expressions of ordinary people, 12; informed by theory and politics, 12; parallel national histories of U.S. and peoples of color, 6–8; as a representation and a counter-representation, 1; role of agency in, 12. *See also* American history

Hmong refugees, 391–93, 421

Ho Chi Minh, 377

Ho Chi Minh City (Vietnam), 379, 394
Ho, Hui, 168
Hōkūleʻa (Star of Gladness) voyage [1975],
    412–13*fig*
hole hole bushi, 128
Holt, Bertha, 372
Holt, Harry, 372
Holt, John Dominis, 414–15
Holt's Adoption Agency (renamed Holt
    International Children's Services), 372
Home Rule Party (Hawaiʻi), 223
Homo sapiens, 15
Hong, Chi Pum, 135
Hong Kong, 52
Hong Kyongnae, 119
Hong Xiuquan, 118
Honolulu Star-Bulletin (newspaper), 255
Hooper, William, 104, 120
Hopu, Thomas, 153, 193–94, 196
Hoshi, Hajime, 315
H. O. Sloane Company (Chicago), 320
House Un-American Activities Committee
    (HUAC), 352, 368, 406–7
housing discrimination: changing dynamics of
    Los Angeles segregation (1980s) and,
    425–26; *hi-imin* (Japanese educated class)
    and, 315; "Jim Crow" laws legalizing, 99,
    266, 342
HR 384 (1945), 351
HR 4437 (2005), 433–34
HSPA (Hawaiian Sugar Planters' Association),
    224
humors, 14, 15
Hundred Years' War (1337–1453), 44
Hung Sa Dan (Los Angeles, 1916), 283*fig*
Hunter, Robert, 91
Hussein, Saddam, 429
Huston, John, 85
Hyon, Sun, 248–49
Hyun, Peter, 250

Iaukea, Curtis, 126, 243, 244
Ida, Horace, 365–66
identity: danger of using common culture for
    defining citizen, 3; definition of, 12;
    distinction between subjectivity and, 12–13;
    fictive distinction between white and
    nonwhite, 209; and migrant labor in

Hawaiʻi, 121, 128, 137; national histories
    shaping peoples of colors,' 6–8
ideologies: capitalism justifying conquest for
    privatized property rights, 223; discourse
    through shared language and, 10; fictive
    distinction between white and nonwhite,
    209; historical formation of, 13; Nazi
    Germany's Aryan supremacy, 333; white
    supremacy, 206, 208–9, 212–14, 299–300
Ignacio, Amos, 406
imin (Japanese migrants of laboring class), 313
immigrants: Great American Strike (2006)
    support of civil rights of, 434*fig*; U.S.
    Justice Department's registration program
    for, 432–33; war on terror criminalization
    of undocumented, 434–35
immigration: eugenics discourse on, 208–9,
    212–14; Gentlemen's Agreement (1908)
    ending Japanese migrant labor, 132, 139,
    167, 210, 275, 313; material conditions of,
    207, 208; racialization of, 203; standard
    Asian American histories on, 8–9;
    whiteness and, 209, 210. *See also* migrant
    labor
Immigration Act (1965), 386, 395, 399
Immigration Act (Barred Zone Act) (1917), 177
immigration laws: Amerasian Homecoming
    Act (1987), 394; Amerasian Immigration
    Act (1982), 372, 394; Cable Act (1922), 324;
    Canadian, 192–93; Chinese Exclusion Act
    (1882), 7, 91, 123, 124, 131–32, 133, 150, 162,
    200, 299; eugenics discourse driving,
    208–9, 212–14; exclusion laws during the
    Great Depression, 6, 150; Geary Act (1892),
    324; Gentlemen's Agreement (1908), 132,
    139, 167, 210, 275, 313; Hawaiian kingdom,
    123–24; Immigration Act (1965), 386, 395,
    399; Immigration Act (Barred Zone Act)
    (1917), 177; Immigration Reform Act
    (1965), 380; Indochina Migration and
    Refugee Assistance Act (1975), 387;
    Johnson-Reed Act (1924), 209, 301, 355,
    380; McCarran-Walter Act (1952), 357, 380;
    migrant labor in California impacted by,
    167, 177, 181; migrant labor in Hawaiʻi
    impacted by, 131–32, 139–40, 144;
    Naturalization Act (1790), 5, 7, 72–73, 206,
    285; Page Act (1875), 162, 200; pattern of,

interracial marriage *(continued)*
321; HR 384 (1945) "repatriation" of
native-born women married to aliens, 351;
In re Camille (1880) decision on, 6; migrant
labor in California and issue of, 173;
migrant labor in the Northeast and issue
of, 198; migrant labor in the Northwest and
issue of, 185, 189; in New York City, 308–9;
Pérez v. Sharp (1948) challenging, 290;
post-World War between U.S. soldiers and
Japanese women, 351–52; of Punjabi men
and Mexican women, 285, 288; recorded at
Japan's New York City consulate, 315;
Roldan (1933) decision allowing Filipino
and white, 288–90; South Asian Americans with African Americans or Latinas,
316–17. *See also* marriage; miscegenation
laws; white women

Iolani (Hawaiian mission school), 237

Iraq War, 333, 429

Irish Americans, 84–85

Irwin, Robert Walker, 126

Isaac Todd (ship), 186–87

Isabella (queen of Castile), 45

Islam: connecting commerce between Muslim
Arabs and Indian traders, 27; Philippine-
American War (1899–1902) framed as war
between Christianity and, 99; rule of
Iberia, 45; Taj Mahal example of Islamic
architecture, 27*fig*. *See also* Muslims

island hopping, 26, 313

islands: myth of continents and, 25, 26; ocean
worlds and, 25–26

Isobe, Hosen (Buddhist bishop), 244

Itashiki, Mary Ann, 346*fig*

Ito, Okei, 163

Ito, Yuriko, 302

Iyuptula, Yako, 305

Jackson, Andrew, 344

Jamaica, 52*fig*

Jamestown (1607), 64

Japan: annexation of Korea (1905) by, 247;
Asian "mental servitude" broken by
victories of, 335–36; brutality against Korea
by, 250–51; Gentleman's Agreement (1908)
between the U.S. and, 132, 139, 167, 210,
313; Hiroshima and Nagasaki bombings

(1945) of, 367; how Korean Americans
were impacted by colonialism of Korea by,
250–53; imperialism, 118, 119, 133, 138–39,
169, 170; invasion of China (1937) by, 311;
marriages between U.S. soldiers and
Japanese women, 351–52; Meiji restoration
of, 275; nineteenth-century turmoil, 118;
occupation of Okinawa Island (or the
Ryukyus) by, 129–30, 374; Pearl Harbor
attack (1941) on the U.S. by, 334–35, 340,
341, 344–45, 353; Twenty-One Demands
(1915) made by, 275; U.S. "Great White
Fleet" (1908) visit to, 210; U.S. imperialism
and, 86–87; U.S. military occupation of,
351–52; World War II atrocities by, 335–36;
World War invasion of Philippines by, 356.
See also World War II

Japanese American Citizens League (JACL),
276, 316

Japanese American Commercial Weekly (New
York City), 315

Japanese-American concentration camps (World
War II): Civil Liberties Act (1988) passed as
formal apology and financial redress for,
352–53; court decisions validating the,
432; Fair Play Committee (Heart Mountain
concentration camp) fighting for civil
rights, 349–50; last one closing on March
1946, 351; Manzanar children's village
(1942) in, 349*fig*; termination policy
of, 4

Japanese American Courier (New York City
newspaper), 316

Japanese-American removal (World War II): on
Bainbridge Island, 346–47; Civil Liberties
Act (1988) passed as formal apology and
financial redress for, 352–53; court
decisions validating the, 432; Executive
Order 9066 authorizing, 343; Honouliuli
detention camp, 345*fig*; Japanese American
resistance to, 347; Sand Island (Hawai'i)
detention station, 343–44, 345; strip
searches and intimidation during the, 343;
War Relocation Authority (WRA) over the
ten concentration camps following, 4, 344,
348–51; Wartime Civil Control Administration (WCCA) authority over the, 347. *See
also* World War II

Japanese Americans: accused of having loyalty to Japanese government, 242–43, 246–47; children pledging allegiance to the flag (1942), 346*fig*; expansion of land ownership by (1909–1919), 280; *imin* (Japanese migrants of laboring class) among, 313; Japanese women arriving at Angel Island (1910), 277*fig*; land exploitation of (early twentieth century), 281–82; living in New York, 312–16; living in San Francisco, 275–81; living in Seattle, 300–302; migrant labor in California, 131, 139, 151*fig*, 152, 162–67, 165*fig*; migrant labor in Hawai'i by, 124, 125–33, 128*fig*, 129*fig*, 133, 135, 137, 238–47; naturalization (1952) process opened to, 355; New York City sex workers (late nineteenth century), 315; 1920 law prohibiting transfer or lease of land to Japanese nationals among, 280–81; Northwest region violence against, 300–302; picture brides (1909–21), 132, 138, 171, 314–15, 324; population in Hawai'i (1990–1940), 231*t*; public distrust (1920s and 1930s) of, 339–41; Public Law 405 (1944) allowing citizenship renunciation by, 351; removal to concentration camps during World War II, 4, 341–53; serving in the World War II military, 350–51; U.S. Census count of California population (1900–40), 275, 276*fig*; working on the railroad (1910), 300; working on the Yakama Indian Reservation (1905), 300–301; World War II and, 353–55. *See also hi-imin* (Japanese educated class); nisei (second-generation Japanese)

Japanese and Korean Exclusion League (renamed Asiatic Exclusion League), 276–77

Japanese Association, 276

Japanese Exclusion League, 281

Japanese-Mexican Labor Association (JMLA), 166–67

Japanese Mutual Aid Society of New York (1907), 315–16

Japanese picture brides (1909–21), 132, 138, 171, 314–15, 324

Japanese Reform Association (Hawai'i), 128

Japanese Workers' Association (New York City), 277, 316

Japan Society (1907), 313–14

Japantown (or Nihonmachi) [San Francisco], 276

Jay, John, 3, 84

Jefferson, Thomas, 75, 83, 186

Jesuits, 37

"Jim Crow" laws, 99, 266, 342

Jinyong Tan, 272

JMLA (Japanese-Mexican Labor Association), 166–67

Johnson, Albert, 209, 301

Johnson, Anthony (Antonio, freed slave), 4–5, 66–67

Johnson, Charles, 295

Johnson, Lyndon, 377, 380, 427

Johnson-Reed Act (1924), 209, 301, 355, 380

Jones Act (1917), 108

Jones, George, 133–34

A Journal of Captain Cook's Last Voyage (Ledyard), 75

The Journals of Lewis and Clark (Bergon), 78–79

The Journals of the Expedition Under the Command of Capts. Lewis and Clark (Biddle), 76–78

Judaism, 63

Julles, "Charley," 297

Jung, Moon-Ho, 200, 204

justice: Civil Liberties Act (1988) passed as formal apology and financial redress, 352–53; demands for an apology from the U.S. government for overthrow of Hawaiian kingdom, 414; Fair Play Committee (Heart Mountain concentration camp) fighting for, 349–50; social movements for equality and, 223–29, 231, 331, 333, 437–39

Juvenile Protective Association's "Chicago plan" for taxi-dance halls, 323

Kahahawai, Joseph, Jr., 365–66

Kaho'olawe Island protest, 410–11*fig*

the Kaho'olawe Nine, 410

kahuna, 36

Ka'iana, 50, 186

Kai'iana, Ionae ke'a'ala O, 153

Kakazu, Hashiji, 146–48

Kakua, Peter, 185–86, 189

Native Americans: agriculture, 47; Alcatraz Island occupation (1969) by, 410; assimilation of, 4; British colonialism and, 64–66; Cherokees' Trail of Tears, 344; citizenship rights, 72–73, 84, 95, 108; as colonized subjects, 8; cultural nationalism of, 7; Dawes Act (1887) designed to promote assimilation of, 4, 108, 301; decimated by diseases, 65–66; examining the cultural nationalism of, 1; forced expulsion (nineteenth century) of, 344; granted citizenship (1924, amended 1940), 4, 73; Hawaiian migrant labor in California and, 153–54; Hawaiian migrant labor in the Northwest and, 185; histories of conquest and dispossession shared by Hawaiians and, 414; legal recognition of tribal memberships and loyalties of, 7; Orientalism and, 18; Proclamation of 1763 (English America) establishing segregation of, 66; removal policies, 153; resistance to British colonialism, 64–66; resistance to Spanish imperialism, 63; solidarity with Pacific Islanders, 2, 8; and Spanish imperialism, 46–47, 54–60; sweet potato as evidence of trade between South Pacific and, 33, 35; as symbols in American Revolution, 69; termination policy (1950s) on treatment of, 4; U.S. imperialism in the Philippines and, 95; U.S. westward expansion and, 4, 70, 75, 83, 84, 97, 97fig, 188; white nation and, 3, 4; Yakama Indian peoples, 300–301, 305. *See also* Pacific Islanders

Native American studies, 6

nativism, 91. *See also* anti-Asianism

Naturalization Act (1790), 5, 7, 72–73, 206, 285

Naukana, William, 189

Naukane (John Coxe), 186

navigation, 33

Nazi Germany: Aryan supremacy ideology of, 333; race war conducted by, 334–36. *See also* World War II

Negoro, Motoyuki, 238–39

The Negro in Chicago report (1919), 295–96

New Chinese Laundry (1903 film), 307

New Jersey anti-Asian violence (1987), 422–23

New Orleans, 199–200

New Spain, 46–48, 62–63, 75. *See also* Spanish-American War

new woman, 92–93

New York City: anti-Asian violence (1990) in, 423–24; Asian and Pacific Islander migrants to, 305; Chinatown in, 307–12, 315; Chinese laundry workers in, 307, 310–12; Chinese Museum (1850) opened in, 308; Chinese population living in, 306–12; Coney Island Oriental curiosities (nineteenth century) in, 308; "dancing schools" (1920s) in, 315; Friends of Freedom for India conference (1920) held in, 318, 319; *gongsi fang* (Chinese mutual-aid societies) in, 309; Harlem race riot (1943) in, 338; *hi-imin* (Japanese educated class) living in, 313–14, 315; interracial marriages taking place in, 308–9; Japanese Mutual Aid Society of New York (1907) helping Japanese needy in, 315–16; Japanese population according to U.S. Census (1920–1940) living in, 312; Japanese population living in, 312–16; Japanese Workers' Association founded in, 277; Nancy Campbell's Chinese Sunday School in, 315; Peace Rally for Racial Harmony (1990) in, 424; population growth (1860 to 1900) in, 266; South Asians living in, 316–19. *See also* Northeast region

New York Times, 428, 432, 436

New York Times (1856), 306

Ng, Gladys, 354

Ngo Dinh Diem, 377

Niagara movement, 98

Nichi Bei Times (Japanese newspaper), 278

Nihonmachi (or Japantown) [San Francisco], 276

Nippon Club (New York City), 313

Nippu Jiji (Japanese newspaper in Hawai'i), 238, 240

nisei (second-generation Japanese): anonymous storyteller on story of a, 278–80; classified as "enemy aliens" by World War II draft boards, 339; Conference of New Americans focus on, 245–46; 442nd Regimental Combat Team (World War II) made up of, 350–51; mistaken military belief that dogs

dependency in Hawai'i, 260–63; globalization, 402–3; migrant labor, 146–48, 212–14; ocean worlds, 38–41; social movements, 439–41; U.S. imperialism, 109–10; world-system, 54–60; World War II, 359–61

Proclamation of 1763 (English America), 66

property ownership: Alien Land Law (1913) [California] on, 280, 281; Alien Land Law (1920) [California] on, 280–81; Alien Land Law (1937) [Washington] on, 305; Dawes Act (1887) designed to promote Native American assimilation by offering, 4, 108, 301; *Dred Scott v. Sandford* (1857) making African Americans subject to, 3, 4, 5, 72–73, 299; expansion of Japanese American (1909–1919), 280; exploitation of Japanese Americans (early twentieth century), 281; Hawaiian dependency and issue of, 223–29; Hawaiian movement regarding dispossession of lands, 410–11*fig*; 1920 Alien Land Law prohibiting transfer or lease of land to Japanese nationals, 280–81

property rights: California Alien Land Law (1913) denying "aliens," 280, 285; California Alien Land Law (1920) prohibiting transfer or lease to Japanese nationals, 280–81; capitalism justifying the idea of conquest for privatized, 223

Prosser, Gabriel, 195

prostitutes. *See* sex workers

Protect Kaho'olawe Association, 410

Protect Kaho'olawe 'Ohana, 410

proto-Austronesians (Guam), 33–34

Provisional Battalion (later 100th Infantry Battalion) [World War II], 350–51

Public Law 405 (1944), 351

Pueblo Indian Revolt (1680), 63

Puerto Rico, 7, 95, 99, 108

Pukui, Mary Kawena, 412

Pullman Company, 322

Pullman strike (1894), 208

Punjabis: intermarriage between Mexican women and, 285, 288; South Asian migrants primarily made up of, 285; *U.S. v. Bhagat Singh Thind* ruling on "whiteness" of, 285–88

Purdy, Patrick, 423

Pyun, Ekpo, 135

Quinsaat, Jesse, 289*fig*

race: and Bacon's Rebellion (1676), 67–68; citizenship defined by, 3, 4–5, 66–67, 72–73; cultural nationalism role in the social formation of, 415–16; eugenics discourse on, 208–9, 212–14; *In re Najour* (1909) denying skin color as determinant of, 285–86; one-drop rule determining, 5–6, 67; *Takao Ozawa v. U.S.* (1908) denying skin color as determinant of, 286; *U.S. v. Bhagat Singh Thind* (1920) decision vacating the notion of a Caucasian race, 285–88; World War II Nazi project of producing a master, 334–36. *See also* color line; racial taxonomies

race relations: colonization giving way to neocolonialism and assimilation, 219; discourse of, 209–10; emerging as a field of study, 209–10; "Oriental problem" of, 219; Park's Pacific Coast Survey of Race Relations (1924–26) on, 296

race riots: anti-Chinese violence (1885) in Seattle, 297–98; in Chicago (July 1919), 295–96; following the death of Martin Luther King, Jr. (1968), 380–81; Harlem race riot (1943), 338; Kerner Commission (1967) to study causes of, 427; Los Angeles zoot-suit riots (1943), 337–38*fig*; *The Negro in Chicago* report (1919) on causes of, 295–96; Red Summer (1919), 211; Rodney King decision sparking (1992), 425; throughout the U.S. during World War II, 338; Watts rebellion (1965), 427. *See also* anti-Asian violence

racial formation, 415–17

racial/gender power formations: colonial America, 3, 4–5, 67, 68; early Republic, 73, 79–81; eugenics discourse used for, 208–9, 212–14

racialization: Anthony Johnson, freed slave in Virginia Colony case of, 4–5, 66–67; *Dred Scott v. Sandford* (1857) affirming, 3, 4, 5, 72–73; eugenics discourse as, 208–9, 212–14; migrant labor, 196, 197–98, 200,

racialization *(continued)*
203, 207; *The People v. George W. Hall*
(1854) affirming, 7, 73, 79–81, 157; U.S.
Census race categories as form of, 6. *See also* "aliens ineligible to citizenship"

racial profiling: CNN/*USA Today*/Gallup poll
(2001) on, 431; Juvenile Protective
Association's "Chicago plan" as form of,
323; U.S.A Patriot Act (2001) allowing, 353,
431–32; as war on terror civil rights
violation, 432–33

racial segregation: *Brown v. Board of Education*
(1954) ending educational, 5, 265, 324, 380;
changing dynamics of Los Angeles
(1980s), 425–26; in English America's
Proclamation of 1763 establishing, 66;
Filipino's confrontation of racism and,
304–5; Gentlemen's Agreement (1908)
between Japan and the U.S. applied to the
issue of school, 210; *Gong Lum v. Rice*
challenge to, 324; Hawai'i's two-track
school system creating, 246; *hi-imin*
(Japanese educated class) facing housing,
315; *Independent School District v. Salvatierra*
(1930) upholding educational, 6; "Jim
Crow" laws of, 99, 266, 342; as key
instrument for maintaining white
supremacy, 300; *Méndez v. Westminster
School District of Orange County* (1946–47)
challenge to, 342; *Plessy v. Ferguson* (1896)
upholding, 5, 98–99, 203, 265, 273, 324;
protest in San Francisco (1885) over school,
273; as tool to create dependency, 12,
323–24; widespread national impact of,
323–24; World War I military service, 211;
World War II military service, 339. *See also*
discrimination; peoples of color; racism

racial taxonomies: biological determinism of,
13–14–16*fig*; Blumenbach's racial geometry,
15–16*fig*; essentializing process of, 13;
geographical determinism notion of, 13, 14;
imperialism role in, 13, 15, 48, 49; Linnaeus'
Systema naturae and *Homo sapiens*, 15;
Orientalism, 16–18; Pacific Islanders, 30–31;
of peoples into racial groups, 13–14. *See also*
peoples of color; race

racism: dream of a world free from, 438;
eugenics discourse on, 208–9, 212–14;

Filipino's confrontation of segregation and,
304–5; migrant labor in California and, 153;
migrant labor in the Northwest and, 191;
school segregation form of, 5, 6, 246, 265,
273, 324, 380. *See also* anti-Asianism; civil
rights movement (1960s); racial segregation

Radical Reconstruction (1867), 201–3

railroads, 156, 158–60, 164, 172, 173

Railway and Navigation Company, 300

Ram, Kanshi, 175, 176

Randolph, A. Philip, 322, 323, 337

Rapa Nui (Easter Island), 52

rape. *See* sexual violence/rape

Raphael Weil Public School (San Francisco,
1942), 346*fig*

Reagan, Ronald, 428

Reciprocity, Treaty of (1875), 105, 203

Reconquista, 45

Reconstruction, 201, 203

Red Apple boycott (New York City, 1990),
423–24

Red Cross, 358, 430

Red Summer (1919), 211

Refugee Act (1980), 388–89

regeneration: Asian American movements as,
415–20; Hawai'i's history of, 406–15;
revolutionary spirit sign of, 405; role of
education in, 405

Reid, Whitelaw, 95

religion: Buddhism, 27, 246; danger of defining
citizen identity in terms of common, 3;
Islam, 27*fig*, 45, 99; Zoroastrians, 27. *See
also* Christianity

religious freedom, 84

repatriation schemes, 115

Republican Party (Hawai'i), 224

Republic of Korea. *See* South Korea

resistance: colonial America, 67–68; Hawai'i,
105, 120–22, 123, 223; by Japanese
Americans to the World War II removal
order, 347; migrant labor in California, 159,
166–67, 174–75; migrant labor in Hawai'i,
120–22, 123, 126, 127, 128, 132–33, 135,
137–38, 139–40; migrant labor in the
Northeast, 205–6; migrant labor in the
Northwest, 192; migrant labor in the South,
202, 203; Native Americans, 63, 64–65;

oppression as inspiring, 12; Orientalism
and, 18. *See also* subjectivity

Revolutionary War (1775–83), 4, 68–70

Rhee, Syngman, 250, 359, 370–71

Rice, Louisa, 410

*The Rising Tide of Color Against White World-
Supremacy* (Stoddard), 209, 212–14

Ritte, Walter, Jr., 410

Robert Bowne (ship), 120–22

Rockefeller, John D., 319

Rodriguez, Antonio, 49

Rogers, Marjorie, 288–89

Rojo, Trinidad, 303

Roldan, Salvador, 288–89

Rolfe, John, 64, 65

Roman Empire: Orientalism beliefs of the, 17;
trade from India reaching, 42. *See also*
ancient Greece

Roosevelt, Franklin D., 247, 291, 337, 338–39,
340, 343, 354, 355, 369

Roosevelt, Theodore, 4, 85, 94*fig*–95, 99, 132,
167, 210, 275, 364

Root, Gladys Towles, 289

Roque, Frank, 430–31

Ross, Peggy Ha', 410

Rough Riders, 94*fig*, 95

Roxas, Manuel, 369

Ruiz, Magdalena Domingo, 357

Russia, 138, 189

Russo-Japanese War (1904–1904), 138, 210

Said, Edward W., 16

St. John de Crèvecoeur, J. Hector, 84

St. Louis Exposition (1904), 177–78

Saito, Miki, 128

Samoa: early history and inhabitants of, 34–35;
U.S. imperialism, 101, 108

Samoans: early history of, 34–35; and imperialism, 37; as indigenous peoples, 8

Samonte, Cypriano, 322

Sampson, Calvin, 204, 205–6, 222, 306

Sand Island (Hawai'i), 343–44, 345

San Francisco: Alcatraz Island occupation
(1969) by American Indians in, 410; Angel
Island made into an immigration station,
269–71*fig*; Angel Island used during World
War II removal of Japanese, 344; Chinatown in, 267, 273–75, 284, 354; Chinese

Americans living in, 266–75; Chinese
Americans working in shipyards (1942–
43), 353; Chinese entrepreneurs during the
Great Depression, 274–75; Chinese
laundries and businesses in, 271–72; cigar
making industry during Civil War in, 268;
Filipino Americans living in, 288–91; as
hub of anti-Japanese and anti-Asian
agitation, 276–77; Japanese Americans
living in, 275–81; Korean Americans living
in, 282–84; League of Labor demanding
workers' rights, 273; National Dollar Stores
strike, 274; Nihonmachi (or Japantown) in,
276; primary documents on Asian
Americans in, 291–92; protest (1885) over
school segregation in, 273; the "shed"
where Chinese migrants were held,
268–69; Six Companies representing
Manchu government in the U.S. located in,
272, 276; South Asians living in, 284–88;
suggested readings on Asian Americans in,
291; Takahashi Clinic of Midwifery for
Japanese women in, 278; timeline of
significant events of Asian Americans in,
292–94. *See also* California

San Francisco Chronicle (newspaper), 276–77,
282

San Francisco earthquake (1906), 269

San Francisco State College, 438

Santos, Jose Abad, 322

Saran, Kaushal, 423

Saxton, Alexander, 204

Schnell, John, 162

School Begins poster (1899), 100*fig*

schools: Cleveland Elementary School shooting
(Stockton, 1989), 423; Hawaiian-language
immersion schools, 415

school segregation: *Brown v. Board of Education*
(1954) ending, 5, 265, 324, 380; Gentlemen's Agreement (1908) between Japan
and the U.S. applied to issue of, 210; *Gong
Lum v. Rice* challenge to, 324; Hawai'i's
two-track school system creating, 246;
Independent School District v. Salvatierra
(1930) upholding, 6; *Méndez v. Westminster
School District of Orange County* (1946–47)
challenge to, 324; protest in San Francisco
(1885) over, 273. *See also* African Americans

South Asian Americans *(continued)*
U.S. Civil with the Union army, 316; *U.S. v. Bhagat Singh Thind* (1920) challenging racial category of, 285–88. *See also* Sikhs
South Asian migrant labor, 50, 52, 53; "asiatic" or "lascar" contracts made with, 316; in California, 171–77, 174*fig*; in Canada, 172, 173, 174, 290–91; in the Northeast, 198; in the Northwest, 290–93; in the South, 199–200
Southeast Asian religions, 28
Southeast Asians: Amerasian children of, 372, 393–95; Cold War displacements of, 389; population (2010) in the U.S., 386–87; violence directed against, 420–21. *See also* war refugees
South Korea: children born of U.S. servicemen and Korean mothers, 371–72; international adoptions (1953–2004) from, 372; Korean War (1950–53) between North Korea and, 369–71; sex workers (1960s) in, 371; student uprising (1960) in, 371; Syngman Rhee heading government of, 359, 370–71; thirty-eighth parallel line dividing northern and, 359; transnational adoptions from, 372. *See also* Korea
South region: Asian immigrants coming through New Orleans, 199–200; connections between slavery and migrant workers in nineteenth century, 200–202; Ku Klux Klan violence in the, 206; Radical Reconstruction (1867) and recruitment of Chinese migrants to, 201–3. *See also* United States
Southwest region, 210–11
sovereignty: Bush Doctrine extending U.S., 429; Hawaiian kingdom's loss of, 101–7, 223–29; the Hawaiian movement to restore sovereignty to Hawai'i, 408–15; U.S. recognition of Native American tribal, 7. *See also* imperialism
Soviet Union: collapse (1991) of the, 379, 428; competing ideologies of the U.S. and, 368; Sputnik race between U.S. and, 380. *See also* Cold War
Spanish-American War (1898), 37, 85, 93–95, 94*fig*
Spanish Armada (1588), 63

Spanish colonialism: imperial order discourse driving, 48–49; Manila-Acapulco galleon trade during, 47–48, 49, 63, 88; migrant labor in California under, 177; in the ocean worlds, 36–37; Pueblo Indian Revolt (1680) against, 63; seeking Asian trade routes, 44–45. *See also* colonialism
Spencer, Anna Garlin, 93
Spencer, Herbert, 208
spice trade, 44
Spivak, Gayatri, 8
Sputnik satellites (1957), 380
S.S. Marine Jumper (troop ship), 357
Stalin, Joseph, 445n4
Stanton, Elizabeth Cady, 88
Steadman, Alva, 365
Stevens, Durham, 282
Stevens, John, 101, 106
Stevens, Thaddeus, 159
Stewart, William, 206
Stimson, Henry L., 349
Stirling, Yates, Jr., 247
Stockton anti-Asian violence (1989), 423
Stoddard, Lothrop, 209, 212–14
strategic essentialism, 8
Strong, Josiah, 92
Student Nonviolence Coordinating Committee (SNCC), 417
Sturgis, William, 188
subjectivity: Asian American movement (1960s) to create a pan-Asian racial formation, 415–17; distinction between identity and, 12–13; migrant labor in California and, 173, 174*fig*; third world, 439. *See also* resistance
suffragist movement, 88, 109–10
sugar production: Chinese migrant workers during Reconstruction era, 201; Chinese slave labor working on, 53–54; Civil War crippling of the South's, 104, 105; great strike of 1909 by Japanese laborers in Hawai'i, 238, 239–40; women cane workers of various ethnicities, 226*fig*
suggested readings: Asian Americans living in urban centers, 291–92, 324–25; colonial America/early Republic, 76; dependency in Hawai'i, 260; globalization, 401–2; migrant labor, 146, 181–82, 212; migrant

labor in California, 181–82; migrant labor in Hawai'i, 146; ocean worlds, 37–38; social movements, 439; U.S. imperialism, 108–9; world-system, 54; World War II, 359

Sukarno, Ahmed, 438

Sumitomo Bank, 315

Sumner, Charles, 206

Sun Yat-sen, 237–38, 309

Sutter, John, 86, 152, 154

Swahili, 29

sweet potato agriculture, 33, 35

Systema naturae (Linnaeus), 15

Tacoma: Chinese expulsion from (1880s), 298–99; Japanese population (1910) in, 300

Taft, William Howard, 99

Tagalog language (Filipino workers), 304

Tahiti, 36

Taiping Rebellion (1850), 118

Taisho, Genichi, 167

Taiwan: Guomindang (KMT) government flees China for, 367; U.S. recognition of, 367. *See also* China

Taj Mahal, 27*fig*

Takagaki, T., 315

Takahashi Clinic of Midwifery (San Francisco), 278

Takahashi, Kamechiyo, 278

Takaki, Ronald, 9, 145

Takamine, Jokichi, 313–14

Takami, Toyohiko Campbell, 313

Takao Ozawa v. U.S. (1908), 286

Takata, Yasuo, 350

Talk Story: An Anthology of Hawaii's Local Writers (1978), 419

"Talk Story: Our Voices in Literature and Song: Hawaii's Ethnic American Writers' Conference" (1978), 419–20

Tamashiro, Baishiro, 129–30

Tanaka, Tadashichi, 164

Taney, Roger, 3, 4, 5, 72–73

Taosug Muslims massacre (1906) [Philippines], 99, 100*fig*

Tape, Joseph, 273

Tape, Mamie, 273

Tape, Mary, 273

taxi-dance halls, 323, 325–26

taxonomies. *See* racial taxonomies

Tchue Vue, 392

Tea Act (1773) [Great Britain], 69

tea trade: *Empress of China* (1784) role in, 70–71; Tea Act (1773) [Great Britain] promoting, 69

technologies (Pacific Islanders), 26, 31, 32

Temple, Lewis, 196

termination policy, 4

Tet offensive (Viet Minh, 1968), 378

Texas, 86

theory/theories: as central to understanding American history, 10; to explain and assign significance to past history, 10; social Darwinism, 92, 208; social formation, 10–12; world-systems, 11–12, 43, 46–49, 54, 115, 207

Thetis (ship), 120

Thind, Bhagat Singh: photograph (1918) of, 286*fig*; *U.S. v. Bhagat Singh Thind* (1920) decision on race of, 285–88

third world: liberation movements of the, 437–39; subjectivity of, 439; women of the, 417–18

Third World Communications (1971), 418–19

Third World Liberation Front (TWLF), 405, 438, 439

Third World Women's Alliance, 417

Thirteenth Amendment (1865), 5, 88

Thompson, Myron, 409, 412

Thompson, Nainoa, 412, 413

Thurston, Samuel, 189

Tiger Brigade (all-Korean unit of the militia), 358

timelines. *See* significant events timelines

Times (London newspaper), 334

Time To Greez! Incantations from the Third World (Third World Communications), 418–19

Tinker, Hugh, 50

tobacco agriculture, 64, 75

Tokugawa shogunate (Japan), 118, 162

Tommy, John, 89

Tordesillas, Treaty of (1494), 46

tourist industry (Hawai'i), 397

Toy, Ah, 161

trade: Asia and newly formed U.S., 71–72; Hawai'i and California, 154; mercantile capitalism, 42, 84, 85, 102; spice, 44; tea (colonial America), 69, 70–71

indentured labor during, 71; primary documents on, 76–81; slavery in the, 71, 75; suggested readings on, 76; timeline of significant events on, 81–82; trade with Asia by the, 70–72, 75; westward expansion during the, 70, 75, 76–79, 83, 184. *See also* colonial America

University of California, Berkeley, 284, 416, 417, 438

University of Chicago, 295–96, 322

University of Kansas, 319

University of Washington, 303

Uno, Edison, 352

U.S.A. Patriot Act (2001), 353, 431–32

U.S. Cadet Nursing Corps, 350

U.S. Census: Asians as fastest-growing group since 2000, 386–87; Chinese population in New York City and New Jersey (1880), 307; Chinese population in New York City and New Jersey (1900–1940), 308; Chinese population in the Northwest (1880s), 299; counting California Japanese Americans (1900–40), 275, 276*fig*; declaring that the nation has been fully settled (1890), 91; Filipino population (1940) living in Chicago, 323; Hawaiian and Pacific Islanders assigned different categories (2000, 2010), 416; Japanese population in New York city (1920–1940), 312; listing Chinese and other "washermen" in Honolulu (between 1884 and 1950), 234; lower median age of migrant population (2000), 395; *Mexicans* race category distinguished from white (1930) in the, 6; racialization of the race categories used in the, 6; South and Southeast Asians (2010), 386–87

U.S. Civil War: African American U.S. Colored Troops (USCT) during the, 88–89; Asians and Pacific Islanders in the, 87–89; boom of migrant labor in the Northeast region during and after the, 204–7; cigar making in San Francisco during the, 268; Felix C. Balderry in Union Army uniform, 90*fig*; Hawaiians serving under the Confederate flag during, 89; Hawaiian sugar production increased during, 104, 122; manufacturing boom in the North during, 204;

material conditions of, 207; migrant labor and the, 158, 201, 204; South Asians serving in the Union army during, 316; South's sugar industry crippled by the, 104; transcontinental railroad growth during, 158. *See also* wars

U.S. Communist Party (CP-USA), 310

U.S. Constitution: Article 1 specifying race and taxation criteria for citizenship, 72; Fifteenth Amendment (1870), 5, 88, 206, 239; Fourteenth Amendment (1868), 5, 7, 73, 88, 99, 108, 207, 269, 273, 281, 299; peoples of color as not part of the "We, the people" in the, 3; Thirteenth Amendment (1865), 5, 88; white nation and, 3, 5

USCT (African American U.S. Colored Troops), 88–89

U.S. imperialism: African Americans and, 98–99; Bud Dajo massacre photograph, 100*fig*; citizenship rights and, 107–8; early Republic, 73–75; gender and, 92–93; impact of the Civil War on, 87–89; Japan and, 86–87, 162; late-nineteenth-century immigration driving, 90–91; manifest destiny doctrine driving, 85, 89, 331; Mexico and, 85, 86; Native American and, 4, 63, 96–99; naval power role in, 91–92; ocean worlds and, 37; Oregon Territory, 85–86; Pacific Islanders and, 73–75; primary documents on, 109–10; race relations discourse on, 210; St. Louis Exposition on, 177–78; social Darwinism rationale for, 92; Spanish-American War, 37, 85, 93–95; suggested readings on, 108–9; timeline of significant events, 110–11; United States as an "imperial republic," 83–85, 107–8; westward expansion as, 83, 85–86, 92*fig*, 184. *See also* imperialism; militarized zones; United States

U.S. imperialism (Hawai'i): annexation of Hawai' as, 107, 108, 131, 223; Gold Rush and, 103–4; Hawaiian social formations and role of, 101; land division and, 103; resistance to, 105–6; role of Christian missionaries in, 102, 103, 196, 248–49; trade and, 101–2; Treaty of Reciprocity (1875), 105, 203

significant events, 60–61; United States as materializing from European Enlightenment and modern, 18

world-system theory, 11–12, 43, 46–49, 54, 115, 207

World Trade Center attack (September 11, 2001), 353, 429

World War I: the color line during, 333–34; as fight over material conditions, 333; impact on agricultural demand and prices by, 241–42; manifest destiny role in, 85, 89, 331; migrant labor in California during, 169; racial segregation of African Americans soldiers during, 211; Treaty of Versailles (1918–19) ending the, 334. *See also* wars

World War II: Asian "mental servitude" broken during, 335–36; Bataan Death March during, 356; Chinese Americans during, 353–55; the domestic front during, 336–39; draft resisters during, 349–50; as fight over material conditions, 333; Filipinos during, 356–57; "good war" discourse of, 336–37; Hiroshima and Nagasaki bombings (1945) at the end of, 367; Japanese Americans during, 4, 339–53; Japanese atrocities during, 335–36; Korean Americans and, 357–59; Los Angeles zoot-suit riots (1943) by sailors during, 337–38*fig*; Marshall Plan to rebuild Europe after, 368; Miles Cary's work with interned Japanese students, 246; nisei (second-generation Japanese) serving in the military during, 350–51; nisei classified as "enemy aliens" by draft boards during, 339; Pearl Harbor attack (1941) during, 334–35, 340, 341, 344, 345, 353; primary document on, 359–61; prominent role of race during, 334–36; race war conducted by Nazi Germany during, 334–36; suggested readings on, 359; timeline of significant events during,

361–63; U.S. Joint Defense Plan, Hawaiian Theater during, 340–41; war refugees due to, 388. *See also* Japan; Japanese-American removal (World War II); Nazi Germany; wars

Wounded Knee massacre (1890), 4, 97*fig*

The Wretched of the Earth (Fanon), 418

Wright, George, 254, 255

Wu Lan, 195

Wyches, Edward, 201

Wyllie, Robert, 125

Yakama Indian Agency, 302

Yakama Indian peoples, 300–301

Yakama Indian Reservation, 300–301, 305

Yakima Valley (Washington), 300–302

Yale, Elihu, 198

Yamada, Kakichi, 166

Yamada, Waka, 166

Yamane, Tsuta, 343

Yamauchi, Tsuru, 130

Yasonia, Alfonso, 180–81

Yasui, Minoru, 347

Yee Ho, 230–31

Yee, James, 435–36

Yokoi, Daihei, 163

Yokoi, Saheita, 163

Youg-sook Chin, 371

Young, Ah In, 231–32

Young Men's Buddhist Association (YMBA), 242

Youngnam Puin Hoe (Hawai'i), 251

Yuan Guan, 53–54

Yuen, Bow, 232

Yum, Man Suk, 283

Yun, Ch'i-ho, 146

Zer Lo, 391

Zhenghe expeditions (Ming Dynasty), 29–30

zoot-suit riots (Los Angeles 1943), 337–38*fig*

Zoroastrians, 27